Culinaria China
Cuisine. Country. Culture.

Culinaria
China

Cuisine. Country. Culture.

Katrin Schlotter
Elke Spielmanns-Rome
Text

Gregor M. Schmid
Lisa Franz
Photography

h.f.ullmann

Abbreviations and quantities

1 oz	=	1 ounce = 28 g
1 lb	=	1 pound = 16 ounces
1 cup	=	8 ounces* (see below)
1 cup	=	8 fluid ounces = 250 milliliters (liquids) / 2 cups = 1 pint (liquids)
1 g	=	1 gram = $^1/_{1000}$ kilogram
1 kg	=	1 kilogram = 1000 grams
1 l	=	1 liter = 1000 milliliters (ml)
$^1/_8$ l	=	125 milliliters = approx. 8 tablespoons
1 tbsp	=	1 level tablespoon = 15–20 g dry ingredients (depending on density)
	=	15 milliliters (liquids)
1 tsp	=	l level teaspoon
	=	3–5 g dry ingredients (depending on density)
	=	5 ml (liquids)
1 cup	=	250 milliliters (liquids) and the corresponding volume in dry ingredients

*Where measurements of dry ingredients are given in spoons, this always refers to the raw state of the ingredient as described in the wording after the measurement, e.g. 1 tbsp chopped onions BUT: 1 onion, peeled and chopped.
It is advisable not to serve any dishes that contain raw eggs to very young children, pregnant women, elderly people or anyone weakened by serious illness. If in any doubt consult your doctor. Be sure that all the eggs you use are as fresh as possible.

Quantities in recipes

Recipes serve four people, unless otherwise stated. It should be borne in mind, however, that if the portions seem rather less than generous in some cases, it is because these are not Western-style dishes and the recipes take into account the fact that a Chinese meal often consists of small amounts of several different dishes which are served with rice.

Romanization of Chinese terms

This book uses the Pinyin system for converting Chinese names and terms into the Latin alphabet. This romanization system was officially approved by the People's Republic of China in 1957 and adopted as the international standard in 1982. The only exceptions are a few geographical and proper names, which have been rendered in normal English script.

© 2009 Tandem Verlag GmbH
h.f.ullmann is an imprint of Tandem Verlag GmbH
Original title: *Culinaria China. Küche. Land. Menschen.*
ISBN 978-3-8331-4994-8

Original concept: Bernd Klaube, Katrin Schlotter, Elke Spielmanns-Rome
Layout: Hubert Hepfinger, Freising
Studio photography & food styling: TLC Fotostudio GmbH
Editor, photo stories & glossary: Kirsten E. Lehmann, Cologne
Local research & editorial assistance: Yuan Huo, Beijing
Recipes: Yuan Huo, with the assistance of Bernd Klaube
Translation from Chinese: Martin Dlugosch
Recipe editor: Kathrin Jurgenowski
Photo selection and captions: Christoph Eiden
Photo research: Malgorzata Meys, Felicitas Pohl, Almut Tscheuschner, Anne Williams
Maps: Umberto d'Orsini, Freising (regional maps), Kartographie Huber, Munich (national map)
Calligraphy: Baruch Genico, Freising
Index: Regine Ermert, Kathrin Jurgenowski
Cover photography: © Tandem Verlag GmbH/TLC Fotostudio GmbH
Project management & coordination: Swetlana Dadaschewa
Production: Sabine Vogt
Overall responsibility for production: h.f.ullmann publishing, Potsdam, Germany

For this English edition © 2010 Tandem Verlag GmbH
h.f.ullmann is an imprint of Tandem Verlag GmbH
Translated by Maisie Fitzpatrick, Susan Ghanouni, David Hefford, and Rae Walter in association with
First Edition Translations Ltd, Cambridge, UK
Edited by Lin Thomas in association with First Edition Translations Ltd, Cambridge, UK
Typeset by The Write Idea in association with First Edition Translations Ltd, Cambridge, UK
Project management by Sheila Waller in association with First Edition Translations Ltd, Cambridge, UK

Printed in China

ISBN 978-3-8331-4995-5

10 9 8 7 6 5 4 3 2 1
X XI VIII VII VI V IV III II I

If you would like to be informed about forthcoming h.f.ullmann titles, you can request our newsletter by visiting our website (**www.ullmann-publishing.com**) or by emailing us at: newsletter@ullmann-publishing.com
h.f.ullmann, Birkenstraße 10, 14469 Potsdam, Germany

Contents

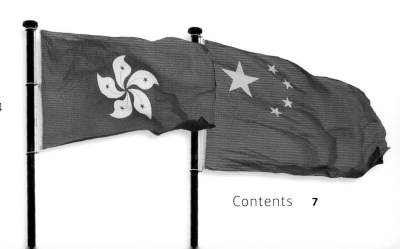

Foreword

Can the entire spectrum of China's culinary arts be condensed into one book? Is such a concept possible? It is indeed an ambitious undertaking to attempt to encompass such a long history of culinary tradition, so many different types of regional cuisine, and such a variety of ingredients and spices, cooking methods, and styles of presentation in a single volume. Yet this is precisely why the prospect of studying the tempting delicacies of Chinese cuisine is such an attractive one. Whether it be dumplings stuffed with delicious fillings, juicy shellfish, romantic wild mushrooms or sumptuous feasts offering abalones, sharks' fins or swallows' nests, there is always something new to discover, unusual dishes to sample, and countless opportunities for surprise. In the words of a Chinese celebrity chef: "One lifetime is probably not long enough to sample the whole of Chinese cuisine. Despite my many years in China I still keep coming across traditional dishes which are new to me."

Chinese regional cuisine boasts a veritable plethora of specialties—it is a banquet offering far more dishes than even the most enthusiastic gourmet can sample. That is why—as befits a good host—we have selected the most delicious and most unusual culinary delights for inclusion in Culinaria China. In addition to the classic dishes typical of the coastal provinces and Peking-style cuisine, this book quite deliberately highlights some examples of regional cuisine which are less well known in the West. China's culinary repertoire ranges from the devilishly hot specialties of Sichuan and Hunan to the traditional recipes found among the national minorities in the southwest of the country. Exciting discoveries

may likewise be made among the traditional local dishes found in the northern provinces of Xinjiang and Gansu as well as in Heilongjiang and Inner Mongolia, including unusual recipes such as snow mussels or Horhog, a traditional lamb dish. With this goal in mind, writers and photographers set forth to take a peek inside kitchens far away from the main tourist routes with the aim of bringing back recipes which are still relatively unknown in Europe.

The important principle to remember with all these dishes is that it is not simply a case of meticulously following a recipe aided by a set of kitchen scales and measuring jugs but of delicately bringing out the flavor of each individual ingredient, creating a perfect combination of different aromas and achieving the best possible result with only a minimum of equipment.

The background information and explanatory notes to the recipes together with descriptions of everyday life in China are intended to help the reader not only to sample Chinese cuisine but also to develop an understanding of it: in other words, to undertake a little mental journey between the preparation and consumption of the food in order to appreciate the spirit behind all Chinese culinary traditions. Cooking in China is never simply a matter of satisfying the appetite: it is about harmony and well-being, about enjoyment and conviviality. Perhaps this is why people in China do not wish each other "Bon Appétit"—a healthy appetite—before a meal but say "Eat slowly" or "*Man man chi*!"

Katrin Schlotter

慢慢吃

Culinary basics

The best way to discover the Chinese soul is not by studying history books and archaeological information but simply by understanding its cuisine. The most efficient way to experience the essence of China is to embark on an orgy of eating, sampling the choicest and best of the country's food, for the saying "you are what you eat" is doubly true in China. According to traditional Chinese medicine (TCM), each ingredient and every method of preparation has a specific influence on a person's "Qi," the vital energy that sustains living beings. Qi is nurtured by breathing and eating and a person will remain in good health as long as the body's Qi maintains a balanced flow along the meridians—a series of invisible channels in the body. At the same time, it is also important to maintain the equilibrium of "Yin" and "Yang," the two fundamental principles that are the foundation of the universe. Everything on earth is aligned with one or the other. Yin is associated with the feminine and represents the dark and moist: cucumbers and sugar, for instance, fall into this category. Yang, by contrast, symbolizes things that are hard, light, and masculine and encompasses items such as nuts, salt, and coffee.

Consequently, any meal can either promote or disrupt the flow of energy through the body, thereby affecting every organ. Eating a bar of chocolate or a sandwich between meals is something which would hardly ever occur to a health-conscious Chinese person.

Even a shopping trip to the market requires a good deal of careful forethought of a kind that Western visitors would find it difficult to comprehend. Are, for instance, any of the expected dinner guests suffering from any allergies or illness? Does grandfather need something to boost his energy? And how best to help the daughter of the family get over her cold? Each ingredient is attributed with specific, beneficial "side effects." Nowadays, there are even restaurants in which traditional doctors, on the basis of an on-the-spot diagnosis, prescribe the dish which is most suitable for the individual diner. It is small wonder, therefore, that many Chinese people are self-appointed experts on culinary matters and hardly surprising that particularly good dishes—or perhaps ones which it is only possible to serve up fresh in a specific region—attract a great deal of attention.

No single "Chinese" cuisine

The variety of Chinese regional dishes is often confusing to the European visitor. Accustomed to the more or less standard menu to be found in Chinese restaurants in the West, he or she will encounter in China itself a wealth of culinary surprises which could not be more diverse.

This is partly due to geographical reasons: China does, after all, comprise an area of over 3.6 million square miles (9.5 million sq km) and spans four climatic zones, ranging from the cold regions bordering on Siberia to the tropical island of Hainan, and from the high mountains of the Himalayas to the steppes of Central Asia and the Gobi desert. It is little wonder, therefore, that local culinary traditions vary considerably. Generally speaking, however, Chinese food can be divided into four main culinary regions:

Hearty dishes of the North

Northern China can become very cold—temperatures sometimes fall to below minus 13 °F (-25 °C), so when the icy winds from the steppes blow through Beijing, Shandong or Manchuria, meals need to be warming and nourishing! Consequently, northern China is famous for its good, solid dishes, which include generous amounts of garlic, onions, black bean paste, and cabbage. What many Europeans find surprising is that rice does not figure as one of this region's staple foods. Thanks to the influence of the nomadic people of the steppes, wheat—in the form of flat cakes, steamed and boiled noodles, dumplings, and pancakes—is more common here than anywhere else in China. Despite its hearty, solid characteristics, Peking-style cooking is one of China's best-known types of cuisine. This is largely thanks to the influence of Imperial Palace chefs, who in times past produced sophisticated dishes which were also very popular among the upper classes.

Mild dishes of the East

In eastern China, the cuisine is generally fresh and mild in flavor. Subtle seasoning is preferred in the provinces of Jiangsu, Anhui, Shanghai, and Zhejiang; chili or other hot seasonings are seldom used in the cooking recipes here. Instead, the area around the Yangtse delta has developed a reputation for its duck-based dishes and delicious fish and seafood. "Dazha crab" and "red-braised" Hongshao dishes, which derive their color from a stock made of rice wine, sugar, and soy sauce, are famous throughout China. Food from this part of the country is also visually easy to recognize as people here place special emphasis upon garnishing the food in a distinctive manner.

Above: In China, eating is considered a social occasion, ideally enjoyed with a large group of people—as shown here in Beijing's lavish, traditional Fangshan restaurant.

The creative South

The cuisine found in the southern part of the country is regarded by the Chinese themselves as being particularly imaginative and delectable—yet it is this particular style of cooking which, more than any other, fills the visitor with dread. It is here that the cooking-pot might contain the type of ingredients which Westerners prefer not to find on their plates. To the Western mind, dogs, cats, and rats are something of an acquired taste as far as meat is concerned. It is worth pointing out, however, that Cantonese people only eat such dishes on special occasions for—like other exotic delicacies, for example, snake, turtle, sea cucumber or sharks' fins—these ingredients are extremely expensive. However, if the European visitor is able to overcome his preconceptions, he can anticipate discovering an extremely fresh and

creative style of cooking which, thanks to the subtropical lushness of local vegetation, includes many types of vegetables and fruit as well as some exquisite sauces.

The hot and spicy West

Although the food typical of the Sichuan and Hunan provinces is regarded—with every justification—as being particularly fiery, it is mainly Sichuan dishes that are found on menus throughout China. Distinctively named dishes such as "pockmarked Ma's tofu" and "stinking tofu" get their hot flavor not only from chiles but also from Sichuan pepper. Vinegar, sesame, oil, and bamboo shoots are likewise essential ingredients, which a Sichuan or Hunan chef would never be without. Only Yunnan in southwest China differs somewhat in this respect as a result of southeast Asian influences. Its cuisine in this area is simply too mild to be taken seriously by people in Hunan or Sichuan.

In addition to splitting the country into four main culinary regions, Chinese gourmets frequently refer also to the "eight great culinary traditions" of China, namely Sichuan, Hunan, Guangdong, Shandong, Jiangsu, Anhui, Fujian, and Zhejiang. Mention should also be made of the cuisine found in the Muslim province of Xinjiang, which is characterized by strong Oriental influences, the Manchurian dishes of northeast China, and the culinary traditions of Beijing which reflect the influence of the Imperial Palace kitchens.

Culinary pleasures

Despite the many regional differences in Chinese cooking, mealtimes in China have one striking feature in common: they are a time to have fun! The evening meal taken with family or friends is the highpoint of the day and the larger the group, the better. Noisy discussions and merry laughter are as much a part of the occasion as sauce stains and contented burping at the end of the meal. And to make sure that everyone can also see exactly what the cook has prepared, the meal is consumed under stark neon lights. This is also true in most restaurants, which are furnished along rather Spartan lines in laminate and plastic. It is only in the past few decades that luxury restaurants have begun to spring up, particularly in the big cities, where they compete with each other in terms of elaborate design and atmosphere.

Even so, the convivial get-togethers around the table are nonetheless subject to certain rules of behavior. The cook must offer at least one dish more—not including starters—than the number of guests at the table in order to avoid the host appearing stingy. Furthermore, the appearance of the fish course is the signal for the guests to prepare to make their farewells. There is now only the soup to follow before it is time to start making tracks for home. Indeed, hardly has the last person leant back satiated than the guests begin getting up to leave. The reason for this is that anyone remaining seated is signaling that he or she is still hungry. The fact that this never happens is, of course, a matter of honor and is less a question of Qi than of hospitality: no Chinese host would ever run the risk serving too little!

Chinese culinary culture

Hunters, fishermen, and collectors began settling in China and cultivating the soil at a very early stage of its history, thereby fulfilling the basic prerequisite for the development of culinary traditions. In the Chang delta (Yangtse), there is evidence of rice cultivation dating back to 8000 B.C. The production of rice wine began shortly thereafter and from the Neolithic period onward pigs, dogs, and poultry formed part of the staple diet. Apart from these few clues, there is little clear evidence available to throw light on early Chinese culinary traditions as they developed over several thousands of years.

One thing we now know for certain, however, is that the dispute between Italy and China as to who first invented the noodle has finally been resolved in China's favor. In 1985, excavations at an archaeological site in Lajia, northwest China, unearthed some 4,000-year-old millet noodles. These long, thin noodles measured about 20 inches (50 cm) in length and were similar to Lamian noodles, which are still hand-pulled to this day.

A clearer insight into Chinese culinary traditions can be gleaned from the Zhou dynasty (1066–221 B.C.): foxtail and broomcorn millet, rice, barley, and wheat constituted the main basic foodstuffs. These were supplemented in times of plenty with strips of vegetables, fish or meat and prepared in a three-legged bronze pot. Even in those days, food was eaten with the aid of long chopsticks made of wood, bamboo or animal bone. While ordinary folk filled their stomachs with grain-based dishes, however, the country's rulers were feasting on sumptuous delicacies. Imperial culinary skills under the Zhou dynasty were already extremely sophisticated. Thousands of chefs dedicated themselves to the creation of exquisite dishes for court banquets, each one meticulously prepared according to medical and seasonal considerations.

It was common knowledge even then that a balanced combination of fresh ingredients and careful preparation was a recipe not only for epicurean enjoyment but also for good health and a long life. Even today dietary traditions are still dictated by Confucian, Taoist, and Buddhist influences. While Confucianism concentrates mainly upon achieving harmony between the different ingredients, Taoism is more concerned with their healing and life-extending properties. Buddhism, on the other hand, teaches respect for life, thereby prohibiting, or at the very least restricting, the consumption of meat.

Articles found at the tombs of Mawangdui in the Hunan province, which date from 163 B.C., illustrate just how well the Han princes (202 B.C.–220 A.D.) dined: sparrows' eggs, wine or lotus soup and even recipe collections to amuse the prince's deceased spouse after her death. The corpse was even embalmed with her stomach left intact. In the world of the living, ordinary folks' food consisted mainly of grain and soya, dried meat or fermented fish. A large number of different methods for conserving or cooking food, such as deep-frying, steaming, braising, were already common at this time. Stews were accompanied by a type of steamed bun, known as *mantou*.

The annexation of large parts of present-day southern China by the Han rulers led to culinary traditions developing in different ways: while people in northern China were sustained largely by millet, wheat, and meat, the conquered southern regions relied more on rice, vegetables, fruit, and fish for their food. New ingredients and fresh ideas were absorbed into established cooking traditions as a result of trade within the Empire and with other countries, initially along the Silk Road and—from the 6th century onward—along the Grand Canal, a waterway which was used for shipping large

Above: Freshness is the order of the day, a principle also upheld by market stallholders, who check and sort their goods on a constant basis.

Right: Hong Kong restaurants—like the Aqua shown here—are not the only ones to cause a sensation: there are many excellent gourmet temples to be found in other major Chinese cities.

Above right: China's varied cuisine is diversified even further thanks to the influence of a total of 55 national minorities.

quantities of rice, silk, tea, and other goods from the fertile south to the north of the country. During the heyday of the Tang (618–907) and Song (960–1279) dynasties, China came to enjoy considerable affluence, a state of affairs which was reflected in its cuisine. Be it fish, chicken, pork, bear's claws or camel's hump—it was no longer only the palace chefs who had the choice of virtually every ingredient and spice available at the time, some of which are still used to this day. Traders, government officials, artists, and men of letters were likewise able to enjoy having their palates tickled in various hostelries, at least while they were not busy producing culinary works of their own or books on tea, an increasingly popular commodity, or on medicinal plants. As a frequent subject for drawings, songs, poems, and

Above right: Fish and seafood are two important specialties of Chinese cuisine.

Left: The tradition of the tea-house is currently undergoing a revival...

Above: ...despite the undeniable trend in China toward fast food.

Right: A fast food dish typical of the north: steamed dumplings.

Chinese culinary culture   **13**

anthologies, food was regarded as an altogether civilized area for artistic expression.

As culture blossomed, Buddhist influences began to play an important role—so much so that a vegetarian cuisine developed in China, which included tofu as an alternative to meat. A desire for purity, youth, and power also encouraged diet specialists to engage in research into different remedies. Other culinary innovations were introduced as a result of frequent contact with foreigners: dates, figs, and pistachios found their way into China (from Persia, for instance, now present-day Iran) while sugar cane was introduced from India, unleashing a fashion for sweet dishes. Improved cultivation methods, combined with the import of Champa rice, a robust variety originating from Vietnam, insured abundant harvests, producing large surpluses that could be used for trade. By 1270, Hangzhou, at that time China's capital city, had a population of over one million inhabitants and its innumerable restaurants, kitchens, and night markets already offered a wide variety of food based on different types of regional cuisine from all over China.

Under the Mongolian Yuan dynasty (1271–1368), the seat of government was moved to Beijing. Although trade flourished under these nomadic conquerors, their rustic style of cooking, based on traditional dishes such as fiery stews, whole cooked lamb, and fermented mare's milk, contributed very little to the development of sophisticated Chinese cuisine.

The return of Chinese rulers to the throne under the Ming dynasty (1368–1644) marked the beginning of a new era in culinary history, which continued until the time of the Qing dynasty (1644–1912). Thanks to contact with foreign markets and improved methods of cultivation, various new vegetables were introduced into Chinese cuisine from the 16th century onward: corn, tomatoes, peanuts, chiles, potatoes, and yams all contributed to revolutionize cooking. On the one hand, cooks in southwestern China were now able to add another powerful spice, chili, to their formidable collection and, on the other, the new range of staple foodstuffs made it possible to alleviate the shortage of food in some areas. The Qing dynasty (under the foreign rule of the Manchurians, who were known to appreciate Chinese food culture) is noted for having introduced wild game dishes to what was already a sophisticated culinary repertoire. The high value which the society's elite placed on the culinary arts and the extent to which these symbolized luxury, affluence, art, and culture are clearly illustrated to this day by historical recipe collections and in literary works, such as the *Dream of the Red Chamber*.

It was not always a time of plenty, however: wars broke out and natural disasters occurred at frequent intervals. If the Chang river broke its banks, for example, or marauding armies invaded the country, the food supplies would often collapse and hunger and necessity would force the population to resort to scavenging for grasshoppers, scorpions or roots.

Top: Elaborately elegant restaurants such as the Cloud No. 9 bar in Shanghai's Grand Hyatt hotel are popular with devotees of themed interior design.

Above and right: Whether in a large restaurant...

Above and far right: ...or at home, the food is always native Chinese.

Below right: All parts of the animal are used in Chinese cuisine.

Below and far right: Mealtimes—even private occasions at home—are the high point of the day.

Gastronomy suffered a dramatic setback as a consequence of the founding of the People's Republic (PR) of China. Elegant dishes, lavish banquets, and autumn moonlight feasting on crabs and moon cakes were replaced by canteen food for the masses. Agriculture was collectivized, food was rationed, and people's communes with unrealistic production goals were established. The result was a shortage of food that in 1961/62 cost the lives of around 30 million people. The Cultural Revolution (1966–1976) also achieved one other thing: anything associated with ancient traditions or betraying a Western influence was classed as "decadent" or "bourgeois" and as such had to be eliminated. Culinary traditions also fell into this category. Many chefs fled to Hong Kong or Taiwan and in doing so saved countless traditional recipes. It was not until the decollectivization of agriculture and the reform and openness policies of the mid-1980s that the art of cooking experienced a revival in the People's Republic of China. Initially, markets and snack-bars gained a foothold on the streets, followed shortly after by restaurants offering delicacies from every province and from all over the world. People's enthusiasm for new culinary delights in China is now evident on every street corner, in every night market and in many of the restaurants. Chinese people dine out even more frequently than Europeans, celebrating and enjoying themselves. Little wonder then that new restaurants are opening up every day. Be it royal banquets or regional specialties, organic food or fast food, elaborate fusion cuisine or French haute cuisine, in virtually no other country is it possible to find a cuisine as varied and experimental while also—despite all its internationality—remaining so comfortably rooted in its native land.   KATRIN SCHLOTTER

Above left: The night markets provide plenty of opportunities for a quick snack.

Below left: Traditional recipe: "Beggar's chicken" can be found in every cookery book yet it tastes best when bought from a roadside snack bar.

Right: Popular all round the clock: *Jiaozi*, stuffed Chinese dumplings.

Cooking equipment in Chinese kitchens

The basic equipment found in a Chinese kitchen consists of a variety of utensils, some of them typically Chinese, which are used in the preparation of classic Chinese dishes.

A large, sharp **kitchen knife** and a **wooden chopping block** are essential for cutting up meat and chopping vegetables or other ingredients. Cutting techniques vary depending on the dish and the consistency of the ingredient (see p. 18).

Another familiar utensil in a Chinese kitchen is a **sieve**—used for sifting flour, for example—likewise a **food processor** (for grinding nuts and so on). A **whisk** and an electric **handheld mixer** for mixing and blending ingredients are also indispensible pieces of kitchen equipment.

The preparation of dumpling-type dishes, such as *jiaozi* (from Heilongjiang province) or *xiaolongbao* (from Shanghai) involves the use of a **wooden rolling pin**: usually a simple length of rolled wood 8 inches (20 cm) long and around 1 inch (3 cm) in diameter. To make *jiaozi*, the dough is shaped into a roll about 1 inch (3 cm) across, then cut into ½-inch-thick (1 cm) slices. The individual rounds of dough are then rolled out until they are wafer-thin and measure around 3 inches (8 cm) in diameter. Alternatively, a standard Western-style rolling-pin may be used although this is not quite as well-suited to the task. The Chinese version may be purchased in Chinese stores and is easier to handle. The pressure is also transferred more directly than in the case of a Western-style rolling-pin. If the process of making and rolling out the dough

is considered too time-consuming, ready-made frozen dough slices can be purchased in Chinese food stores. Place the disc of dough in the palm of the hand, carefully dampen the edges with water, and then, using the other hand, transfer the filling to the center of the circle of dough with the aid of **chopsticks** (Chinese: *kuaizi*) before folding the edges together using both hands. Anyone unskilled in the use of chopsticks can use a teaspoon.

It was purely reasons of economy that produced the rounded base of the Chinese cooking-pot *guo*-known throughout the world by its Cantonese name of **wok**: in the old days, people used to cook over an open fire and this design allowed the heat to collect at a single point and be distributed evenly around the rounded base. Nowadays, following the advent of the electric hob, woks have largely relinquished their original energy-saving function and are now obtainable with a flat bottom. Trivets, designed to accommodate round-bottomed woks, are available for use on gas hobs. The wok's high sides and conical shape give it one further advantage: the ingredients are easier to turn and stir. If you do not possess a wok, you can always use an ordinary skillet. Traditional woks are made of iron and should be oiled after each use to prevent rusting. A more practical alternative nowadays—and one which is also widespread and popular in China itself—is the aluminum wok which has a non-stick coating.

Clay pots (*shaguo*) are used in China for stews and other dishes which require longer cooking. These are also good for keeping food hot as the clay does not affect the flavor.

In Chinese kitchens, steamed dishes—for example *xiaolongbao*, a kind of dumpling, and *baozi*, a type of steamed bun—are traditionally cooked in **bamboo baskets** or **steamers** which usually have a diameter of around 8 inches (20 cm) and are designed to fit inside a wok. Water is first added to the wok and brought to a boil. It is important to make sure that the water level is lower than the base of the basket as it rests on the sloping sides of the wok; in other words, the basket should not be sitting in water. The bamboo baskets containing the dumplings are covered with a lid and placed in the wok. A Chinese housewife will usually have one or two baskets in use, which can, if necessary, be stacked one on top of the other. Only the top one is then covered with a lid. If you do not possess a wok, you could try the following arrangement: using a high-sided pan, place a bowl upside down in the pan and add just enough water to leave the base of the bowl above water. Once the water is boiling, place a deep plate containing the food to be steamed onto the upturned bowl and cover the pan with a lid. Nowadays, **electric steamers** are becoming increasingly popular kitchen gadgets. Not only are they simple to use but also have the distinct advantage over traditional steaming methods in that there is no need for a hob.

A **pressure cooker** is another alternative to a steamer. As in the West, these are used in China as a fast and efficient way of cooking vegetables, etc. It is very important, however, to pay particular attention to the difference in cooking times between the two devices.

Almost every modern Chinese household will have an **electric rice-cooker**, another appliance which also removes the need for a hob. Most Chinese stores in the West stock these useful gadgets. Allowing one-and-a-half cups of water to each cup of rice, place the ingredients in the rice cooker and switch on. That done, you can now confidently devote yourself to the preparation of the remaining dishes as the cooker automatically switches to keeping the rice warm once it is cooked.

In Sichuan, another essential piece of standard kitchen equipment is the **hotpot** (*huoguo*). Its method of use is described in the chapter on Sichuan (see p. 388).

Left: Even a simple gas-heated hotplate is enough to conjure up delicious dishes.

Facing page, center left: Ideally, cooking with a wok with its traditional rounded base should be done over a specially designed gas ring.

Facing page, below and right: Griddles are ideal for making Chinese pancakes.

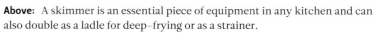

Above: A skimmer is an essential piece of equipment in any kitchen and can also double as a ladle for deep-frying or as a strainer.

Left: Fast cookers are standard equipment in most commercial kitchens.

Below: Pressure-cookers work in the same way with a build-up of pressure causing the food to cook faster.

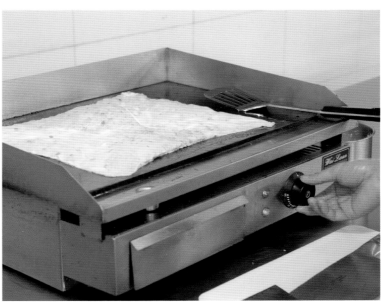

Cutting techniques

China has a long tradition of energy-saving cooking methods. Limited supplies of firewood made it logical from the outset to cut ingredients up into small pieces, which would cook quickly. What originally began as a simple process of chopping up ingredients has evolved over the course of thousands of years into a veritable art form, involving cutting techniques that vary considerably depending on the consistency of the ingredient and on the requirements of the dish in question.

The Chinese use an all-purpose chopping knife that not only performs a variety of chopping tasks but also can be used for creating artistic garnishes and for crushing purposes. Although a Chinese kitchen knife resembles a cleaver in shape, it is constructed differently, being both lighter in weight and possessing a fine, very sharp blade that should never, therefore, be used to chop bones. The knife is held in the hand used to write with, known in China—unsurprisingly—as one's chopstick hand. The handle is grasped in such a way that the thumb rests on one side of the broad blade and the forefinger on the other. By securing the blade firmly between the curved thumb and forefinger, good control may be exercised over the knife. The other hand is used to hold the food in place, taking care to keep the fingertips curved slightly away from the blade to avoid injury. And finally, one should always bear in mind the advice of experienced chefs that the only safe knife is a sharp knife! The individual techniques are as follows:

1 Cutting vertically from above

This technique is suitable for crunchy vegetables like Chinese cabbage, white radish, zucchini, bamboo sprouts: The knife is brought down vertically from top to bottom, rolling it down along the curved knuckles of the free hand and cutting the vegetable with the front of the blade. This technique can be used to produce slices (**1 a**), batons (**1 b**) and segments (**1 c**) as well as cubes.

2 Cutting vertically away from the body

This technique is used to cut smaller vegetables like water chestnuts and scallions into fine strips. The knife is drawn down through the ingredient while angled slightly away from the body. The vegetable is sliced along the curved knuckles of the other hand using the rear end of the blade.

3 a, 3 b Cutting vertically and drawing the knife towards the body

This technique is used to slice tougher ingredients, such as meat. The point of the knife is pressed down into the meat and drawn toward the body. Slices, batons, and cubes can also be cut by this method.

4 Cutting horizontally with the knife angled away from the body

This technique is used to cut crunchy vegetables, such as carrots, into fine strips or slices. Place the vegetable at the edge of the chopping board nearest to the body, pressing it down with your free hand. Now run the knife through the vegetable horizontally from right to left (or from your cutting hand to the other hand).

5 Cutting horizontally with the point of the knife and drawing the knife toward you

This method is used to cut meat into thin strips. The meat is laid on the edge of the chopping board nearest to the body and pressed down flat with the free hand. Using the point of the knife, cut through the meat from right to left (or from your cutting hand to your free hand).

6 Cutting/peeling and rolling

This type of cutting technique allows the peeling or fine slicing of elongated types of vegetable, such as cucumbers, white radishes, carrots, or zucchini, which are intended to be cooked quickly or eaten raw. The knife is held flat—parallel to the board—with the sharp edge of the blade pointing toward the body and drawn forward and back along the vegetable while the fingers of the hand gradually roll the vegetable round during the cutting process.

7 Fine chopping

The ingredients are first prepared by being cut into thin strips, cubed, then coarsely chopped. Using the free hand, repeatedly press the upper side of the knife onto the board using short, sharp movements until the vegetable is finely chopped. The knife should be moved back and forth during this process, keeping the tip of the knife firmly in contact all the while with a point on the chopping board. Push the chopped mass together occasionally and resume chopping. The process is continued until the vegetable is finely and evenly chopped all over.

8 Crushing

Ginger and garlic can also be chopped using a knife. Lay the item on the chopping board and press the blade down flat, keeping the sharp edge of the knife away from you. With the ball of the other hand, press down firmly onto the upper surface of the knife.

9 Making incisions

When preparing squid or similar ingredients, lengthwise incisions must be made in the flesh before it is cut into pieces. The cutting method used in this case is drawing the tip of the knife vertically towards you (see 3a, 3b). The incisions should not be too deep so that the flesh is not completely cut in two and the ingredient can be pulled apart like a fan.

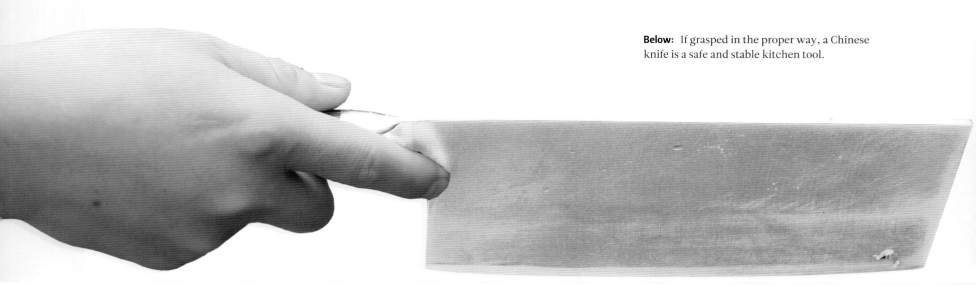

Below: If grasped in the proper way, a Chinese knife is a safe and stable kitchen tool.

1 a

1 b

1 c

2

3 a

3 b

4

5

6

7

8

9

Marinating and coating food

Although marinating was originally developed as a means of extending the life of a particular food item, especially meat, by preserving it in an acid-based liquid, this culinary technique is now more concerned with intensifying flavor and tenderizing the ingredient. Meat from older animals, in particular, is prepared for cooking or roasting in this way, for the acid breaks down the connective tissues in the muscle and makes the meat softer and more tender. The fact that marinating dissolves the structure of the ingredient also reduces cooking times, which in turn means that dishes can be cooked in a much gentler and more energy-saving manner—a factor which has been a key consideration in Chinese kitchens since time immemorial because of limited firewood supplies. Meat is usually chopped into small pieces before being placed in the marinade whereas fish is generally marinated whole. The following section looks at various methods of marinating and examines some of the ingredients that can be used in marinades; followed by a section devoted to the various coatings that can be used to cover food. The chapter on Hunan devotes a double page to the subject of marinating (see p. 352).

Marinating ingredients involves placing them in an acid solution for several hours or even days. It is essential to bear in mind that metal containers should not be used for marinating food as the acid may react with the metal. An ordinary bowl made of glass or glazed porcelain is the ideal container for this purpose, preferably one with an airtight lid to make sure that the marinade is absorbed more effectively. A wooden spoon is useful for giving the marinade an occasional stir.

In China, the most common ingredients used for marinating include vinegar, lemon, and lime juice. (Vinegar, in particular, prevents the growth of bacteria.) Rice wine is also frequently used and the addition of this, or other alcoholic liquids, serves to intensify and accelerate the effect of the marinade on the food. Mild rice vinegar, made from fermented rice, is a particularly popular marinade ingredient. However, since it loses its aroma very quickly, it should only be purchased in small quantities.

Shaoxing rice wine from Zhejiang province is one of the best of its kind. It is made from top quality ingredients and is not released for sale until it is three years old. A delicious dish made with this kind of marinade is Drunken chicken in rice wine.

Soy sauce is another classic ingredient in Chinese marinades. People make a distinction in China between light and dark soy sauce—light soy sauce is thinner and has a fairly salty taste whereas dark soy sauce is thicker and has a more intense but slightly less salty flavor. The difference in color is due to brown sugar being added to the darker sauce. Both types of sauce are ideal for marinating purposes, although the darker version produces marinated food which is visually more attractive. The respective recipe instructions should always be followed very carefully, however. Both versions are cheap to buy but some may be produced chemically. It is best to check the label before purchasing if you want to make sure you are getting a natural product. If necessary, you can resort to Japanese soy sauce, which is subject to product purity regulations and is produced by natural methods.

Ginger, scallions, and Sichuan pepper are the typical seasonings, which go into almost every marinade in China. Salt, on the other hand, should be avoided since it draws water from the food, making it more difficult for the marinade to be absorbed, apart from which soy sauce is already very salty. In order to achieve a perfect result during cooking, Chinese cooks also add a small amount of cornstarch dissolved in a little water to the marinade. This helps keep the meat juicy and tender when cooked.

Fish and meat are not the only ingredients to be marinated in Chinese cuisine—vegetables, mushrooms, and tofu are equally popular. An excellent tofu marinade consists of soy sauce, lime or lemon juice, and rice wine, seasoned with pepper, cilantro, garlic, scallions, and ginger. Those who like their food a little hotter may also wish to add a little chili.

Covering food with various **coatings** is another popular method of food preparation in China. The simplest method is to dip the food in cornstarch *gouqian*. The starch (corn or potato starch) is first dissolved in water and the ingredients then tossed in the mixture. This seals in the liquid, keeping the meat, fish, vegetables, mushrooms or tofu juicy.

Another popular method is to coat the ingredients with a mixture of egg and cornstarch *guahu*: the batter-type coating is made by combining water, cornstarch, and eggs. The ingredients are then dipped in the mixture one by one before being fried in oil. This procedure leaves them tender on the inside and crisp on the outside. The coating is sometimes made with egg whites rather than whole eggs. In this way, not only does the consistency of the coated ingredients remain unchanged but the shape is also retained. This method (known as *shangjiang*) is used, for example, in the preparation of a Zhejiang specialty consisting of a fillet of freshwater fish, prepared with ham, green bell peppers, and bamboo shoots.

1 The batter-type coating is made from cornstarch or potato starch mixed with water.

2 Pieces of food—in this case, famous Jinhua ham from Zhejiang—are then tossed in the mixture.

Left: Vinegar is the key ingredient in a marinade; on the right is rice vinegar, which is available in any Oriental store.

Left: There is a long tradition of pickled vegetables in China. They are mainly used in southern Chinese cuisine.

1 Ingredients for the batter-style coating: eggs, cornstarch, and water.

2 Water chestnuts are tossed in the mixture, ideally using *kuaizi* (chopsticks).

3 They are then lowered into hot oil on a skimmer.

4 After a few minutes, the batter-coated water chestnuts are removed from the oil and left to drain before the next stage of cooking.

5 Finally, the fried water chestnuts can be stir-fried for a few minutes in a wok—in soy sauce, for example.

Cooking methods

In Chinese cuisine, the all-round success of a dish depends not only on the selection and skilled combination of suitable ingredients but also, and more importantly, on the art of preparation. The repertoire of a Chinese master chef includes around 60 different methods of preparation, the most important of which are outlined below. They can be divided into four main categories of cooking methods: involving the use of water, heat, steam, or oil. The type of cooking method selected depends on the nature of the ingredients and the demands of the dish. A classic menu in China normally consists of numerous dishes, all prepared in quite different ways. If a chef succeeds in serving all of them simultaneously, he can be assured of his guests' admiration.

In addition to rice and dumpling-type dishes, some of the most important foods that lend themselves to **cooking in water** include meat and vegetables. Blanching is likewise covered by this cooking method. In China, rice is normally prepared in a rice cooker (see p. 16). Anyone who prefers not to buy this extremely practical piece of equipment should bear in mind the following: **rice** (ideally, scented or jasmine rice) should be washed in cold water before cooking. The washed rice—reckon on approximately half a cup per person—is placed in a pan and covered with twice the amount of cold, unsalted water. Cover with the pan lid but in such a way as to leave a gap. Once the rice begins to boil, close the lid properly and reduce the heat to medium or low. The rice should be ready in approximately 20 minutes.

Freshly made **noodles** (for example, *Lanzhou lamian* from Gansu) are dropped into a pan of rapidly boiling salted water, then brought up to a boil again. After a few minutes, when the noodles begin to float to the surface, they are ready and can be removed from the pan to await further developments. The same applies to *jiaozi*, **dumplings**: these are placed in rapidly boiling water and left until they float to the surface. A cup of cold water is added at this point and they are left once more until they float to the surface. This procedure is repeated twice more. After the third time of being brought to a boil, the dumplings can be removed from the pan. An even more delicious version, known as "pot stickers" *(guotie)*, are made by first frying them in a skillet in a little oil before adding a finger's depth of water. Cover with a lid and leave the "pot stickers" to cook for about five minutes.

When cooking meat, vegetables, or tofu in water or for **blanching** purposes—for example, in the case of asparagus and mushrooms (see the chapter on Yunnan) or Xiamen squid (see the Fujian chapter)—a wok is the required cooking utensil. The quantity of water used and the cooking times vary depending on the recipe being prepared.

Liu (shaking the skillet) is another popular cooking method in Chinese kitchens, whereby the ingredients are cooked in a hot stock, for example, while being constantly stirred and shaken.

There are two ways of **cooking by fire**: on the one hand, the food may be grilled over an open fire *cha shao*—for example, the delicious kebabs produced in the snack bars of Hui (see chapter on Gansu)—or it can be roasted, like Peking duck *kaoya*, a Chinese classic, in a closed oven *kao*.

Steaming is a very popular method of cooking in China: gentle steaming *(zheng)* not only intensifies the flavor of the individual ingredients but also heats the food evenly. Fish, especially, is cooked by steaming—for instance, steamed sea fish (see chapter on Shandong)—as well as dumpling-style dishes like *baozi* and *mantou*. Steaming is also ideal for warming food up as it provides a gentle form of heat and prevents the food from drying out.

Chao—or stir-frying—is the best-known method of **cooking with oil**. The ingredients are cut into small pieces, placed in a skillet and cooked in a little oil over high heat while being stirred constantly. It is important that the food is cut into equal-sized pieces and kept constantly in motion to prevent sticking. Meat and vegetables are best fried separately so that each preserves its individual flavor.

Bao—fast-frying—means that the ingredients are fried in very hot oil. This seals the pores and retains both the aroma and tender consistency of the food.

Zha—cooking or deep-frying in hot oil—is another method of cooking in oil whereby the ingredients are immersed in hot oil until cooked. This can be done either by slower cooking in moderately hot oil (which will result in paler colored food) or by cooking in very hot oil until the food is crisp.

Shao is the Chinese name for braising food in stock. *lu*, on the other hand, is the term for braising food in soy sauce. Both methods require that the food is first brought to a boil before being reduced to a low heat and cooked until the liquid is reduced.

ELKE SPIELMANNS-ROME

Kao

Peking duck, a classic Chinese dish, can be cooked in two ways: either in an open or in a closed oven, as shown here.

In former times, these ovens were fired by straw; nowadays, they are mostly heated by gas.

The duck emerging from the oven is beautifully and evenly roasted.

Liu

Stir-frying involves the ingredients being cooked in a hot stock while being kept constantly in motion. The chef must keep stirring...

...and shaking; stirring and shaking repeatedly.

Chao

Stir-frying is one of the most familiar methods of Chinese cooking. All the ingredients in the wok should be cut to the same size.

Three things should be kept constant during this cooking process: not too much oil, a high heat, and constant stirring.

A wok is not absolutely vital for stir-frying. Food can also be cooked by this method using a normal skillet.

Bao

This type of cooking relies on the oil being as hot as possible. Be careful if cooking over an open fire, —it is a technique that requires experience!

Food should be carefully patted dry and ideally lightly dusted with flour before being slipped into the hot oil.

It is then covered immediately with hot oil to seal the surface. It will be cooked in just a few minutes.

Steaming

Steaming is a particularly gentle method of cooking. Traditional bamboo baskets are used in China but metal steamers are just as good.

It is important to keep the lid closed during the cooking process to make sure that the steam circulates.

Steaming is better for preserving the food's nutrients and flavor; it is also a low-calorie cooking method.

Oven roasting

This is not a typically Chinese method of cooking. Many private homes do not even possess an oven.

The correct temperature is critical. The food can be covered in aluminum foil to prevent it burning on the outside before it is cooked on the inside.

Zha

The food being fried needs plenty of room in the wok or, if you are using one, the frying-basket so it can be turned easily.

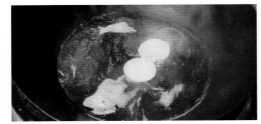

The temperature of the oil should be adjusted depending on what type of food is being cooked. A simple rule of thumb is: the hotter, the crisper.

Shao

Braising in Chinese cuisine is similar to the European method. First bring the liquid—traditionally stock or soy sauce is used in China—to a boil...

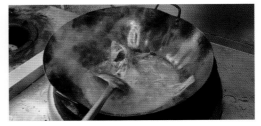

...then allow the food to simmer over low heat for a long time.

Beijing

北京

Katrin Schlotter
Elke Spielmanns-Rome

Beijing is regarded as the center of China—both in political as well as cultural terms. Situated on the lowland plains of northern China, this former imperial city and present-day capital of the People's Republic has not only influenced the country's history for around a thousand years but will continue to determine China's future development.

Although no one was really prepared to admit it, apart from the Imperial Palace and a few other impressive buildings, Beijing—in contrast to the vibrant city of Shanghai—was, for many years, a rather gray, cold, and bureaucratic place to live. All this changed when China was selected to host the 2008 Olympic Games. The city planners made huge efforts to improve not only the quality of life in Beijing but also the quality of the city's air. Numerous industrial plants were moved to the outskirts while the city center was renovated and enhanced with green areas. The city's international airport was enlarged to accommodate one of the world's largest air terminals, and new roads and subway lines were built, as well as around 20 impressive sports arenas. In short, scarcely a building was left untouched across the whole 6,564 square miles (17,000 sq km) of Beijing's administration area. As a result, the metropolis now has a modern yet traditional appearance that is entirely in keeping with its capital city status.

Beijing is governed as a municipality under the direct administration of the central government and enjoys the status of a province. From Beijing, the government directs the fate of a country that is home to the world's largest population. More than 1.3 billion people live in an area covering around 3.7 million square miles (9.6 million sq km). Administratively speaking, the People's Republic can be divided into 23 provinces (including Taiwan, which as far as the People's Republic is concerned, is still part of Chinese territory); five autonomous regions; four cities under direct government administration as well as the special administrative zones of Hong Kong and Macau.

Since the People's Republic was established in 1949, its policies have been determined solely by the Chinese Communist Party (CPC) and the National People's Congress (NPC), which is nominally the most important state body. Whether the issue concerns a planned or private economy, a one-child-only policy or a one-China policy, all such fundamental policy decisions are the preserve of party organs and state bodies in Beijing where the top CPC bodies and highest administrative, justice, and military departments have their headquarters. The country's intelligentsia is also concentrated in Beijing—at the Academy of

Top: The architecture of the so-called Bird's Nest national stadium, built for the 2008 Olympics, resembles a giant bird's nest made of steel twigs.

Above: Even in a huge metropolis like Beijing, oases of peace and quiet still exist away from the bustle of the city.

Facing page: Although the ancient city walls of Beijing have crumbled over the centuries, most of the imposing city gates have remained intact and been carefully restored.

Beijing (Peking)

Above: The world-famous Chinese lanterns are an integral part of Beijing's street markets.

Below: Even the youngest generation of Beijing residents has discovered the joys of modern technology.

Chinese Sciences, for example, or at the famous Peking University (founded in 1898) and Qinghua University (founded in 1911), or at other notable universities and research institutes. Because of the proximity of the government, many national and international firms, organizations, and embassies have likewise established themselves in Beijing, a city which is visited each year by around 4 million tourists, who also serve as proof that all roads lead to Beijing.

It is little wonder, therefore, that Beijing's economy is thriving: with a growth rate of 12.3 percent in 2007, the gross domestic product (GDP) was approximately 118 billion US dollars. The per-capita income of over 7,000 dollars is one of the highest in the country. The service sector, which encompasses commercial and financial institutions and IT firms, produces more than 70 percent of the GDP, but industry, especially in the fields of electronics, automobiles, and textiles, also contributes substantially to Beijing's wealth.

Generations of Beijing's 16 million inhabitants have felt great pride in their home city, which for around 800 years was the capital of the Chinese empire. Anyone with ambitions to achieve great things for himself

or his homeland was obliged to approach the government in Beijing. That is how it was in the old days and it remains the same to this day. It is hardly surprising that Beijing residents often regard their city as the hub of the universe, an attitude which others sometimes consider a strident and arrogant big-city mentality. This may be partly to do with the harsh dialect, which, though classed as High Chinese, includes added "R"-sounds at the ends of words that can sound like a growl. Or it may also be due to the fact that Beijing, since time immemorial, has always attracted external influences—sometimes more than it would have liked. As a result, the city's inhabitants barricaded themselves behind walls so as to protect their individuality—either behind the Great Wall to the north of the city or, depending on their social status, behind the purple walls of the Imperial Palace, the gray walls of the Hutong (court) district or, as they do today, behind the polished marble façades of the guarded residential apartments.

Beijing—capital city of many dynasties

Beijing has been the capital city of China almost without interruption for the past 800 years. Built on the fringes of the lowland plains of northern China, the city's development reflects the rise and fall of ruling dynasties that had their seat of power in Beijing. Changes of dynasty also resulted in changes to the name of the city, which first became known as Beijing ("northern capital") during the 15th century. Nor have the city's other names been forgotten: they are still kept alive throughout the city as part of restaurant or hotel names and are a reminder of Beijing's long history.

With the exception of the Ming dynasty, China's rulers were by no means all Han Chinese. On the contrary, the country was governed for many centuries by foreign tribes from the north: Beijing first became an important center under the eastern Mongolian people of Khitan. However, its 32-feet (10-m) high city walls did not afford protection against the Jurchen, who occupied the city in the early 12th century. They increased its fortifications and made it capital of their Jin dynasty (1115–1234), naming it Zhongdu ("middle capital").

In the early 13th century, the city was attacked yet again, this time by the Mongolian hordes of Genghis Khan (1206–1227), and not long after its capture all of China was overrun by the Mongols. The Mongol-led Yuan dynasty (1271–1368) made Beijing its capital, developing it into a prosperous city and renaming it Dadu ("large capital", or in Mongolian, *khanbaliq*, city of the Khan), a city which impressed Marco Polo (1254–1324) more than any other.

The city was renamed Beijing in the early 15th century when the Ming dynasty (1368–1644) under the Han Chinese adopted it as their capital. It was they who created the grid-like pattern of streets running directly from east to west and north to south and which still largely survives to this day.

Beijing's huge historic buildings and structures, such as the Imperial Palace, the Temple of Heaven and the Great Wall to the north of the city, date back to this period. The city's equally impressive city walls were torn down by the Communist leaders in the early 1950s in order to make way for a second ring road and a subway train line.

In 1644, a band of peasant rebels stormed the city, bringing the Ming dynasty to an end. The last Ming emperor hanged himself from a tree north of the Imperial Palace. He turned out to be the last Han Chinese emperor and soon afterward the peasants themselves were overthrown by Manchurian armies from northeast China, who founded the Qing dynasty (1644–1912) in Beijing, an empire which was to last nearly 300 years.

In the 19th century, the main threats to China's sovereignty were coming increasingly from the West. Beijing was plundered in 1860 by both the British and the French during the Second Opium War. They destroyed the Imperial Summer Palace, which had been built by Western architects in the northwest of the city. Then, in

Below left: The real masterpieces of Chinese architecture are the palaces and pavilions in the Forbidden City.

Below: The bicycle is the most popular and quickest mode of transport in Beijing today.

Bottom: A boat trip on Lake Houhai in the center of Beijing is a must for every visitor to Beijing.

1900, the Boxer Rebellion against foreign powers was quashed by an allied task force and Beijing was plundered yet again.

Soon after China was proclaimed a People's Republic in 1911, large areas of the country fell into the hands of local military leaders (so-called "warlords," who waged war with each other) or became nationalist- or Communist-controlled regions. In the late 1920s, when the Nationalists led by Chiang Kai-shek (1887–1975) moved their capital to Nanjing, Beijing's name was changed to Beiping ("northern peace"). The ensuing political confusion and power vacuum served to benefit the Japanese in their attempts to occupy the country. It was not long before large parts of China were occupied and in 1937 Beijing fell into the hands of the Japanese.

Left: The Temple of Heaven (Tiantan), one of Beijing's main landmarks, is where the Ming and Qing emperors prayed for a good harvest.

Below: Chinese tourists share the same reputation as the Japanese—they take snapshots of everything they see.

Beijing—city of the "Great Chairman"

When Mao Zedong (1893–1976) proclaimed China a People's Republic from the rostrum of the Tiananmen Gate to the south of the Imperial Palace, Beijing resumed its role as China's capital city—as well as a showcase for its new rulers. The "Great Chairman" took up residence in the Imperial Palace complex.

For almost 40 years, China had been suffering the rigors of war and unrest and by the time of the Communist takeover, the country had been bled dry. By the early 1950s, however, agrarian reform—which included confiscating the property of large landowners and redistributing it among the peasants—as well as the nationalization of factories were contributing greatly to a rapid economic recovery.

From his base in Beijing, Mao directed various campaigns and movements, all with the aim of strengthening the power of the Party and its Great Chairman: the "Hundred Flowers Campaign" in 1957, for example, encouraged intellectuals to criticize the government and Party. In 1958, they were then persecuted as "right-wing deviants." Simultaneously, China's "Great Leap Forward" policy was designed to help China catch up with Western industrial nations. Instead, however, it led to mismanagement of the economy, which was further aggravated by natural disasters and poor harvests. Famines cost the lives of 20 to 30 million people, mainly in rural areas. The residents of Beijing, on the other hand, benefited from the preferential treatment reserved for the country's capital city. In the wake of these problems, Mao was obliged to hand over the office of State President to Liu Shaoqi and watch his own influence within the Party dwindle. Aided by his wife, he launched the "Great Proletarian Cultural Revolution" in a bid to reimpose his authority. On August 18, 1966, he received around a million high school and university students, known as the "Red Guard," in the Square of Heavenly Peace (Tiananmen Square) where he proclaimed the start of the Cultural Revolution. In the ensuing power struggles, Mao instigated the persecution not only of intellectuals and people with bourgeois backgrounds from all over the country but also of personal opponents and rivals. The political power struggles and chaos that dominated the first few years of the Cultural Revolution brought normal life to a standstill. The so-called Gang of Four, which included Mao's wife and was the power behind the Red Guard, was overthrown soon after Mao's death in 1976.

Above: The mummified body of Mao Zedong now lies in the Mao Mausoleum. This is an unusual photo, as there are normally long queues of visitors outside the building.

Beijing—center of reform and openness policy

The introduction of the reform and openness policy under Deng Xiaoping (1904–1997) after 1978 led to the modernization of agriculture, industry, technology, and the military. Special economic zones in the coastal areas of eastern China acted as the advance guard of economic development. Following Deng's legendary journey to southern China in 1992, the country began to experience an economic boom that resulted in remarkable growth rates.

Although this economic upturn has meant a better life for many Chinese people, it has also generated some fresh problems, including unemployment, migration from the countryside to the towns, environmental problems, and corruption. It was these concerns which united and brought students and workers to the Square of Heavenly Peace in 1989. The savage way in which Deng Xiaoping, supported by a few conservative party leaders, put down the demonstrations left the country paralyzed for years afterward.

The course of economic and political development pursued by China since the 1990s was undoubtedly reinforced still further by its hosting of the 2008 Olympic Games. Even so, any radical political reforms still appear to be a thing of the distant future. It will be some time yet before China becomes anything other than a one-party state where—in a difficult situation—the Party's word counts for more than anything else.

The Olympic Games served to modernize Beijing's appearance—green areas were created in the city center, industrial plants were transferred to the suburbs and the airport was expanded. At the same time, however, the old streets, residential areas, and historic sites were decimated. Some such sites were protected by conservation order—one of these is a branch of the renowned Tong Ren Tang pharmaceutical company and the country's biggest supplier of traditional Chinese herbal medicines. This company's origins date back to the early Qing dynasty (1644–1912). The ancient pharmacy is situated in the middle of a delightful residential Old-Peking-style courtyard. Examinations are available by a TCM doctor who will prescribe a herbal remedy. The recipes have been tried and tested and handed down through the generations—many of them have survived several dynasties.

Above left: Mao is no longer omnipresent, but his portrait above the main entrance to the Forbidden City remains sacrosanct.

Above: A changing city. Many of the traditional districts have been obliged to give way to a more modern style of architecture.

Right: This pharmacy belongs to the Beijing Tong Ren Tang company, founded in 1669 and one of the oldest producers of traditional Chinese medicine (TCM) preparations.

Below: Historical instruments are not just ornamental items—they are still used today in Chinese pharmacies.

A stroll through the Forbidden City

The Imperial Palace in the heart of Beijing was the residence and seat of government of Chinese emperors of the Ming (1368–1644) and Qing (1644–1912) dynasties for 500 years. It was also the home of China's last emperor, Pu Yi, who ruled from 1908 to 1911/12.

The Palace Museum with its valuable collection of Chinese art now attracts large numbers of visitors every day but it was once the exclusive preserve of members of the imperial court and of high-ranking legations. Ordinary citizens were prohibited from even entering the 178-acre (72-ha) site of the Imperial Palace—the "Forbidden City."

It was Yongle, the third emperor of the Han Chinese Ming dynasty (1402–1424), who ordered the building of the palace at the beginning of the 15th century, a task which took about 17 years. It was constructed from marble, granite, clay tiles, and hardwood and furnished with around 9,900 rooms; 200,000 master builders, artisans, and laborers are said to have been involved in the building work. A ramp carved from a 200-ton block of white marble and used for transporting the emperor in his ceremonial litter into the "Hall of Preserving Harmony" is decorated with carvings of writhing dragons before a background of waves and clouds, symbolizing the masculine force of yang. The yellow glazed roof tiles, permitted only on imperial buildings, were fired in factories in southern Beijing. The expensive wood needed for this came from the southern provinces.

China has, since time immemorial, regarded itself as being at the center of the world. The Imperial Palace was, in turn, built at the heart of this center and the emperor's task was to mediate between heaven and earth and preserve harmony on earth. The architecture of the Imperial Palace reflects this universal order. It was built on the central north–south axis that runs through Beijing. At points north and south along this axis are two gates, through which only the emperor was allowed to pass, and between these are situated the main halls. On either side are further buildings and palaces, likewise laid out symmetrically along an east–west axis. Architectural details are characterized by strict hierarchy and order yet at the same time a perfect sense of harmony radiates from this unique masterpiece of world art.

The main halls are dedicated to harmony—harmony between heaven and earth, and peace on earth: the largest building, the Hall of Supreme Harmony with its gold-encrusted dragon's throne was used for important court ceremonies such as imperial coronations, the emperor's birthday celebrations and the appointment of military leaders. The Hall of Central Harmony served as a place for the emperor to rehearse and prepare for different ceremonies. The Hall of Preserving Harmony was originally used for banquets but was where the final stage of exams in the appointment of imperial bureaucrats was held.

The red-painted halls, built on marble bases and featuring ornamental pillars are connected by broad, gray-paved courtyards. The largest of these courtyards could accommodate up to 100,000 people at imperial audiences.

Farther north is a gate, which separates the sumptuous ceremonial halls from the so-called Inner Chambers. This was where the imperial family lived and included six smaller palace complexes to the east and west, providing living quarters for the emperor's less important wives and concubines. The courtyards farthest away from the main axis—and consequently away from the main tourist track—conceal some true gems: idyllic spots and corners that entice the visitor to sit a while in the shade of the trees. A theater and a Lamaist temple can also be found among the adjacent buildings.

These inner chambers, in particular, are rich in history; there are, for example, many anecdotes surrounding Cixi, the power-hungry, intriguing dowager empress (who ruled de facto 1898–1908), the concubine of Emperor Xianfeng (who ruled 1850–1861) and mother of the future Emperor Tongzhi (who ruled 1861–1875).

The Imperial Gardens, situated in the northern part of the palace complex, provide a contrast to the severity of the palace walls, although their layout likewise follows a strict pattern.

Right: Every hall in the Forbidden City had a specific ceremonial function and was used either for coronations, birthday celebrations, weddings, civil servant examinations or court ceremonies.

Below: Ordinary people were prohibited from entering the palace complex until 1911. Nowadays, the Forbidden City is a tourist attraction for Chinese and foreign visitors alike.

The grounds are criss-crossed with narrow, mosaic-patterned paths winding around ancient firs and cypresses. In springtime, the gardens are a riot of peonies in full bloom. Situated in the center of the gardens is the Hall of Imperial Peace, a temple dedicated to Taoist divinities, and these gardens remain a place of peace to this day.

The works of art on display in many of the buildings are all part of the imperial collection: the Palace Museum also has a large collection of valuable scrolls and calligraphies. For preservation reasons, many of these can only be displayed for brief periods at a time—mainly in autumn when humidity is low. The bulk of the collection was transferred to Taibei (Tai-wan) by nationalists before the Communist takeover of power.

Soak the meat for two hours, pat dry with paper towels and cut into cubes. Slice the leek diagonally into pieces.

Place the meat in a bowl, add the salt, vinegar, sesame seeds, garlic, ginger, soy sauce, chili powder, rice wine, and sesame oil, and mix together. Leave all the ingredients to marinate for 20 minutes.

Meanwhile, soak the mushrooms until soft, remove from the water, pat dry and cut into long, thin strips. Heat the soybean oil in a wok until it begins to smoke, then add the meat and stir-fry until it is nearly cooked. Add the mushrooms and leeks and cook until the leeks are soft.

Above: The grid-like layout of the Forbidden City along a north-south axis is best appreciated from an elevated viewpoint.

Below: Wealth, power, and influence—red, sometimes combined with gold, has always been an outward symbol of the authority which sprang from here.

Beef with leeks

1 ¾ lb (750 g) beef
4 ½ oz (125 g) leeks
1 tsp salt
2 tsp vinegar
6 tbsp sesame seeds
1 garlic clove, finely chopped
1 slice of ginger, finely chopped
2 tbsp soy sauce
½ tsp chili powder
2 tbsp rice wine
2–3 tbsp sesame oil
6 dried shiitake
   mushrooms
3 ½ tbsp soybean oil

A stroll through the Forbidden City **35**

Dining like the Emperor of China

Meals at the court of the Qing emperors were the joint responsibility of the imperial kitchens and the Office for Special Dishes within the Ministry of Rites. The latter employed more than 150 officials. The imperial kitchens were tightly organized and subject to a very finely tuned

division of labor. Chefs of the so-called Internal Kitchen were responsible for the preparation of the imperial family's meals while External Kitchen cooks were in charge of the food for banquets. Meat was the specific responsibility of a meat official, while the peeling and preparation of fruit and vegetables was the domain of fruit and vegetable cooks. Assistant cooks kept the fires and ovens going and were responsible for fetching water and looking after the kitchen equipment. So-called ice masters were employed to produce and store blocks of ice used to keep food and drinks cool.

The emperor was served an elaborate choice of dishes at every meal, even though he was only likely to taste a few—and then only after they had first been sampled by one of the eunuchs in order to frustrate anyone trying to poison the ruler. After the meal, the untouched food was

shared among the concubines, members of the imperial house and high-ranking officials.

Imperial Palace meals were a combination of the very best of all China's regional cuisines. This was largely thanks to Emperor Kangxi of the Qing dynasty, a clever ruler and a man of many different interests, who reigned from 1662 to 1722. Not only did he favor the local Manchurian dishes but he also appreciated the cuisine typical of the Han Chinese and other ethnic groups. At his request the Imperial Court was supplied with specialties from all parts of the country. To mark his 66th birthday, he ordered a *Manhan Quanxi*—an Imperial banquet combining Manchu and Han—consisting of Manchurian specialties (such as bear's claws) and other exotic delicacies of Chinese cuisine, including sharks' fins and birds' nests. The feast comprised more than a hundred different dishes and to this day the Manchu Han banquet remains symbolic of the culinary diversity typical of China. The dishes would certainly have included a cold beef platter with pepper from Sichuan as well as fish in tomato sauce; tomatoes had found their way into Chinese cuisine along the Silk Road.

Anyone wishing to dine like the emperor of China should visit the traditional Fangshan restaurant in Beijing—a restaurant with the reputation for imitating imperial cuisine. The

Above left: An experience in itself: enjoying a meal fit for a king in the famous Fangshan restaurant in Beihai Park. Over 800 dishes, including Peking duck, swallows' nests and camels' hooves, are on the menu, prepared according to traditional Imperial Palace recipes.

Left: A special banquet would not be complete without staff in period costume. The number of dishes being served determines the number of staff that is required.

food served here is typical of what would have been cooked for the Qing rulers and is served by staff wearing traditional costume. After the downfall of the last Chinese dynasty, the restaurant was opened in 1925 by five former imperial chefs and is situated in the Tea House of Beihai Park, once the pleasure grounds of the Imperial Palace. For the first time in history, ordinary people were able to sample dishes that had been prepared for centuries from closely guarded secret recipes originating from the Imperial Palace kitchens. The Fangshan restaurant is said to have been Mao's favorite restaurant after 1949.

China's growing prosperity has also led to a revival of people's interest in their country's historic cultural heritage. Imperial cuisine is enjoying increasing popularity among Beijing's new middle classes, for example. In addition to the Fangshan, various other establishments have sprung up which pride themselves on producing original recipes originating from the Imperial Palace. These include the Tingliguan restaurant situated in the summer palace, which boasts over 300 dishes from the Ming (1368–1644) and Qing (1644–1912) dynasties on its menu as well as the recently opened Gugong Yushan restaurant in the Forbidden City. The chief chef here was once Mao's chef and subsequently attended to the culinary well-being of the reformist politician Deng Xiaoping.

Cold beef

2 ¼ lb (1 kg) rump steak
1 tbsp Sichuan pepper
5 star anise
1 cinnamon stick
2 tsp fennel seeds
1 piece of licorice
2 tsp grated mandarin orange peel
few lilac blossoms
1 piece of ginger (2 ½ inch / 6 cm long), cut into strips
1 piece of leek (2 ½ inch / 6 cm long), cut into strips
2 tbsp soy sauce
1 tbsp sugar

Rinse the beef and cut into pieces 4 inches (10 cm) wide. Bring some water to a boil in a pan, add the beef and cook for two minutes. Remove the meat and place in cold water.
Place the Sichuan pepper, star anise, cinnamon stick, fennel seeds, licorice, mandarin orange peel and lilac blossoms in a small muslin bag and tie it closed.
Bring 2 quarts (2 liters) of water to a boil and add the muslin bag together with the ginger, leek, soy sauce, and sugar and bring the water back to

a boil. Add the meat and cook over a high heat for 15 minutes before reducing the heat and simmering for 2–3 hours over a low heat until the meat can be pulled apart with chopsticks. Remove the beef from the pan and allow it to cool slowly. Then cut into thin slices and arrange on a serving plate.

Fish in tomato sauce

Ginger sauce:
1 piece of ginger (1 ½ inch / 4 cm long), finely chopped
½ tbsp vinegar
½ tsp salt
1 tbsp sesame oil

1 freshwater fish (approx. 2 ¾ lb / 1.25 kg)
1 tbsp rice wine
1 tsp salt
1 tsp cornstarch
4 tbsp tomato sauce (or canned crushed tomatoes)
1 tbsp sugar
3 ½ tbsp rice vinegar
1 tsp dry cornstarch
½ tbsp cornstarch, mixed with 1 tbsp water
1 ½ quarts (1.5 liters) vegetable oil, for frying
1 thick slice of ginger, finely chopped
1 garlic clove, crushed
1 tbsp sesame oil

To make the ginger sauce, thoroughly mix the ingredients together.
Carefully wash the fish, both inside and out. Separate the flesh from the spine and lift it off the bones to produce two fillets. Using a sharp knife, make cross-shaped incisions both in the outer skin and in the flesh on the inside, then cut it into sections 1 ½ inches (4 cm) wide. Combine the rice wine, salt and ginger sauce in a bowl and leave the fish to marinate in the liquid for 10 minutes. Remove the fish segments and dust with the teaspoon of cornstarch.
Mix together the sugar, tomato sauce, and rice vinegar with the cornstarch and water mixture. Heat the oil in the wok to 340 °F (170 °C), tap off any excess cornstarch from the fish before frying it in the oil until golden yellow. Remove the fish from the oil, reheat the oil to 340 °F (170 °C), replace the fish in the oil and repeat the frying process. Remove the fish from the oil and drain, before arranging on a plate. Leaving ¼ cup (60 ml) of oil in the wok, stir-fry the chopped ginger and garlic until they begin to release their aromas. Add the tomato sauce mixture and stir the ingredients together. Finally, add the sesame oil and pour the sauce over the fried fillet of fish before serving.

Top: Dining in golden surroundings; yellow and gold have always been the traditional colors of the imperial court.

Above: Each evening, restaurants on either side of the street beckon invitingly to diners. The chef on his way to work in this photo has this traditional street to himself.

Beijing's cuisine—from sophisticated to rustic

Bears' claws, swallows' nests, sea cucumbers...for generations the best ingredients and recipes have reached Beijing, the seat of government, from all over China. Nowadays, in addition to local and regional delicacies, virtually every specialty in the world has been added to the varied array of culinary treats on offer—and they are certainly no longer the exclusive preserve of the emperor and his staff. With almost 50 Five-Star hotels and thousands of restaurants, fast food chains and snack bars, Beijing boasts an unlimited choice of culinary diversity. Be it *jiaozi* dumplings, hotpot, or mutton kebabs among the residential areas, Peking duck in the Da Dong restaurant, the excellent Sichuan cuisine served in the Chuan Jing Ban Canting restaurant or the fusion cuisine available in the amazing atmosphere of Tiandi yijia, the Courtyard or the Whampoa Club, one week is simply nowhere near long enough to gain even a rough idea of Beijing's impressive gastronomic opportunities.

In terms of haute cuisine, Beijing easily rivals other major Chinese cities like Shanghai or Hong Kong. In the days of the emperor, it was mainly chefs from Shandong province who were drawn to the imperial court—nowadays, however, China's capital city is a magnet for top chefs from all over the world who want to demonstrate their culinary skills. The luxury restaurants offer international or modern Chinese cuisine, frequently posing a challenge to the conservative tastes of the native population.

The Courtyard restaurant, for example—often described in international epicurean magazines as one of Beijing's best restaurants—includes items such as foie gras with Maotai spirit, Sauternes wine and pineapple chutney on its menu. The main course includes surprising dishes such as broiled portobello mushrooms on saffron and coconut risotto with onion confit, or rack of lamb with a cashew nut crust served with Xinjiang vegetable gratin and minted yogurt. The desserts to follow feature a

tart that combines the ingredients of jasmine tea, chocolate, and Grenache wine.

The menu served at the Tiandi yijia restaurant with its breathtaking atmosphere is just as delicious and equally impressive but geared more to Chinese specialties, such as sharks' fins and abalone. Yellow paper parasols float beneath a glass ceiling, a plinth surrounded by water stands in the center of the restaurant, statues placed in the corners are supposed to bestow good fortune on the diners and the bare concrete walls are decorated with ancient works of art. Guests sit at elegantly set tables on rough granite floors—a contrast that works well. "Hotpot" is served here alongside dishes from Guangdong and Shandong. Hotpot, a fiery hot dish that has been around for well over a thousand years, is one of the three classics of Peking cuisine, along with Peking duck and *jiaozi* dumplings. It was traditionally made in Mongolian fashion with mutton cut into fine strips and cooked in hot stock. Nowadays, fish,

Far left: China's open-door policy has also had a knock-on effect in terms of food: there are now fast-food restaurants on almost every street in major Chinese cities.

Left: The advantage of an international brand name: "McDonald's" remains "McDonald's"—or rather "Maidanglao"—even in Chinese.

Below left: The entrance foyer of a restaurant...

Below right: ...leads directly to a display of the exclusively traditional Peking-style food on offer.

meat, vegetables or mushrooms are dunked fondue-style into the hot stew, which can vary in flavor from devilishly spicy to mild. Hotpots are usually divided into several segments so that the guest can select not only his own choice of ingredients for dunking but also his preferred type of sauce. The most authentic way to sample this popular Peking dish is in a steaming, neon-lit hotpot restaurant, which is packed full of noisy diners—ideally on a bitter cold winter's evening.

And there are more than enough of such evenings. Thanks to China's predominantly continental climate, Beijing experiences ice-cold, dry, winter months, followed by winds and sandstorms from the steppes of Mongolia. A very brief spring is followed by hot and humid summer months, which turn into a golden autumn (the best months to travel are September and October) before the "ice age" returns to the city. Local Peking-style cuisine is a great comfort at this time of year, providing sumptuous, spicy, or salty dishes to give warmth to the soul.

The intensely cold winter months bring out the traditional character of Peking cuisine. Thanks to the harsh climate, the main cultivated crop is wheat and as a consequence, numerous variations of dough-based dishes—from dumplings to hand-pulled noodles—as well as tofu are staple items of the basic diet, which also includes soya, cabbage, leeks, cucumbers, celery, white radish, and preserved vegetables as well as hearty types of meat, such as mutton or beef. Many dishes in Beijing are either braised, fried, or broiled with generous amounts of ginger, garlic, and scallions while bean pastes, dark soy sauce, sesame oil or chili oil and occasionally cilantro and vinegar provide the strong flavors.

The compatible way in which all these different regional ingredients have been married together over the course of generations to create true delicacies is illustrated by dishes such as sweet-and-sour soup, noodles and black bean sauce, pork spare ribs, *jiaozi* dumplings and—that perfect culinary masterpiece—Peking duck.

Hot and sour soup

2 tbsp tofu
3 oz (100 g) Shiitake mushrooms
1 tbsp sea cucumber (soaked in water)
1 tbsp squid (soaked in water)
3 ¼ cups (750 ml) chicken stock (made with chicken meat, leek, ginger, rice wine, salt and pepper)
1 tbsp lean pork fillet, boiled and cut into strips
1 tsp salt
1 tsp sugar
2 tsp soy sauce
1 tbsp cornstarch, dissolved in 2 tbsp water
1 egg, lightly beaten
½ tsp white pepper
1 tsp rice vinegar
1 tbsp scallions, coarsely chopped

Cut the tofu, shiitake mushrooms, sea cucumber, and squid into thin strips. Pour the chicken stock in the wok and add the strips of pork along with the salt, sugar, and soy sauce and bring to a boil over a high heat. Thicken with the cornstarch and water mixture. Reduce the heat and stir in the lightly beaten egg. Add the pepper, vinegar, and scallions. As soon as the egg begins to solidify, bring the mixture back to a boil over a high heat. As soon as the strips of pork fillet begin floating to the surface, remove the wok from the hob and serve.

Caramelized pork rib chops and potatoes

generous 1 lb (500 g) pork rib chops
generous 1 lb (500 g) potatoes
1 piece of ginger (1 inch / 3 cm long)
1 piece of leek, (1 inch / 3 cm long)
4 tbsp vegetable oil
2 tbsp sugar
1 tsp Sichuan pepper
1 tsp Shaoxing rice wine
2 tsp salt
freshly chopped cilantro leaves to garnish

Chop the rib chops into 2-inch (5-cm) pieces. Peel and cut the potatoes into cubes.
Slice the ginger and chop up the leek. Pour water into a wok and bring to a boil. Blanch the pork rib chops in the boiling water before removing and rinsing under running water.
Add the oil to the wok. Before it gets hot, add the sugar and caramelize, stirring all the time. As soon as bubbles begin to appear in the sugar, add the chops and stir-fry in the caramelized sugar until the meat is completely coated with caramel. Remove the wok from the hob and add just enough water to cover the chops.
Return the wok to the hob. Add the leek, ginger, Sichuan pepper, rice wine, and salt. Cover with a lid and simmer for 30 minutes over a moderate heat. Add the potatoes and cook for an additional 30 minutes. Remove the leek and ginger. Tip the contents of the wok onto a plate, sprinkle with the chopped cilantro, and serve immediately.
Tip: The optimum temperature for caramelizing sugar is between 355 °F/180 °C and 375 °F/190 °C. If the heat is too high, the sugar will develop a bitter flavor, or become burnt.

Right: Large, spacious restaurants are very popular in China. Although the quality and standard of service are usually good, the atmosphere is unlikely to be very intimate.

Peking duck—an explosion of flavors

What would Beijing be without "Beijing kaoya," otherwise known as Peking duck? By no means a culinary wasteland, certainly, yet there would definitely be something missing in the shape of a national dish, which represents 300 years of old Peking-style culinary traditions and therefore a juicy morsel of Beijing's cultural identity: crisp on the outside and delicate on the inside.

Many restaurants specialize in Peking duck. These include the Quanqude, the Bianyifang, the Liqun, the Beijing Dadong, the Jiuhuashan, the Xiao Wan Fu, and the Made in China restaurant, which have menus specializing (almost) exclusively in dishes based on Beijing's most popular feathered friend: the famous Peking duck. White-feathered ducks, weighing 5–6 lb (2.5 kg), are bred and fattened exclusively for use in this traditional Beijing dish. They are roasted in a particular way—sometimes in closed ovens, sometimes over an open fire of hardwood from fruit trees. Given the level of expertise required, no one in Beijing would ever think of preparing Peking duck themselves.

A Peking duck dinner is a ceremonial occasion—at least in all good restaurants. The tables groan under the weight of small plates filled with scallions, cucumbers, radishes, not to mention little bowls of sauces, including hoisin, bean or plum sauce, sugar or garlic paste for the skin, and baskets full of sesame seed rolls and warm, wafer-thin pancake wraps. Under the attentive gaze of the diners, the chef wheels the serving trolley, bearing the reddish-brown glazed duck, toward the table, where he expertly carves his aromatic masterpiece into about a hundred thin slices, beginning with the crisp skin and its underlying layer of delicately juicy fat—the yardstick of a perfectly cooked Peking duck—and finishing with the succulent meat. In a feast of self-indulgence, the diners wrap a little skin and duck meat—or perhaps just skin on its own to start with—in a pancake garnished with sauce and top it with a small amount of scallions, cucumber or radish. The result is a veritable feast for the palate, an explosion of flavors par excellence: silky smooth pancakes with sweet, thick sauce, sharp scallions and fresh, juicy cucumbers combined with aromatic, crisp skin and tender duck meat. Anyone who is still not satisfied by this culinary showpiece can easily expand his epicurean horizons by embarking on a feast of duck, featuring hundreds of other dishes, such as baby duck and duck feet, or specialties like duck stomach or duck tongue. The finale is the soup, which will meanwhile have absorbed the full flavor of the leftover duck. Little wonder that Peking duck is a dish that has come to symbolize Chinese culinary expertise.

Once a dish reserved exclusively for the emperor, the recipe for Peking duck has remained a secret guarded by Chinese cooks since the days of the Yuan dynasty (1271–1368). It was not until the Bianyifang and Quan Ju De restaurants began firing their duck ovens in the mid-16th and –19th century, respectively, that the upper classes (and in time even "ordinary" citizens) were able to taste this delicious delicacy. Since then, the debate among bon viveurs as to which is the best Peking duck restaurant has been endless.

According to the original recipe, which is over 300 years old, a hundred pages long and allegedly still used to this day, breeding this special species of duck requires as much skill as preparing the dish itself. The ducks are restricted in movement as much as possible and fattened up for 65 days until they are plump. When the ducks are killed, the head and neck are left on the body since the brain and skin around the head are considered a particular delicacy. They are then plucked and cleaned out through an incision underneath the wing, which is then resealed. Why such a complicated procedure? So that the fatty layer of skin, which will later turn beautifully crisp, can be separated from the flesh by massage or by pumping air into the bird. The duck is then dipped in boiling water and may be left to dry for several hours, after which it is glazed with a marinade of malt, honey, cornstarch, and vinegar and hung up to dry again. Finally, it is hung up to cook—in some cases, its cavity filled with stock—for about one hour in a specially designed, hot oven, where it is transformed into crisp, tender Peking duck.

Peking duck

1 duck, plucked and innards removed
  (4 ½ lb / 2 kg)
2 tbsp brown sugar

Pancakes:
2 ½ cups (300 g) all-purpose flour
sesame oil
vegetable oil, for frying

For serving:
scallions, freshly cut into matchsticks
cucumber, freshly cut into matchsticks
black bean sauce (hoisin sauce)

Pour some water into a large saucepan and bring to a boil. Place the duck in the pan and boil for five minutes. Remove the duck and pat dry. Dissolve the sugar in a generous ¾ cup (200 ml) of water,

Bing pancakes, something a bit different

Whether wafer-thin as a wrap for scallions, cucumber, and black bean sauce and served as an accompaniment to Peking duck, or up to 1-inch thick (2–3 cm) and the size of a breakfast plate, there are many different versions of Chinese pancakes. Whether served at the dinner table or eaten as finger food, their only resemblance to European-style pancakes is their shape since the batter, unlike in the West, consists simply of flour, water, and maybe, depending on the region, a light coating of sesame oil. They have a unique flavor nonetheless; sprinkled with sesame seeds or garnished with scallions and served as a snack or accompaniment to another dish, they are an integral part of Chinese cuisine.

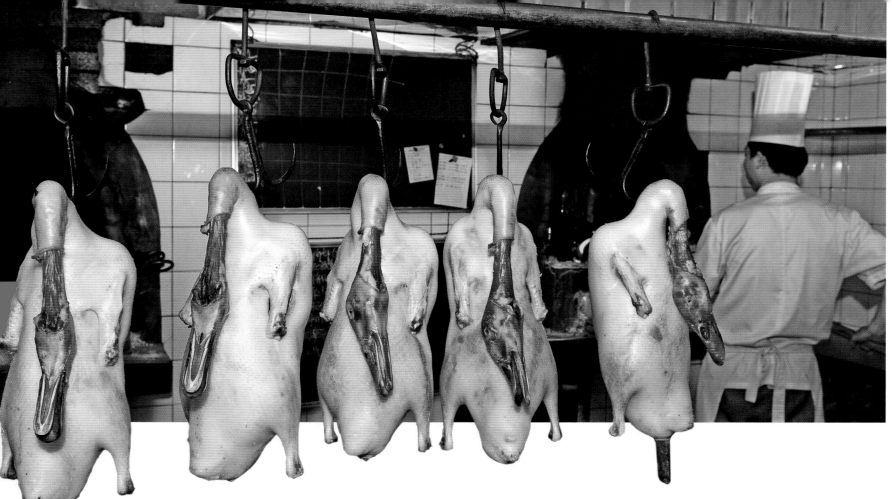

stirring well. Brush the duck with the
sugar water and hang up to dry for one hour.
Brush the bird once more with the sugar water
and hang up to dry for 7–8 hours.
Preheat the oven to 400 °F/200 °C. Cook the duck
for 50 minutes, then remove it from the oven,
turn it over and cook for another 50 minutes,
reducing the temperature slightly if necessary.
To make the pancakes, add the flour to ²/₃ cup/
150 ml of lukewarm water in a bowl and knead
the mixture together until the dough no longer
sticks to your hand and develops a smooth consistency. Cover the bowl with a damp cloth and
leave to rest for 15 minutes. Dust the work surface
with a little flour, then shape the dough into a roll
about 1 inch (2–3 cm) in diameter and divide into
15 pieces. Using a rolling pin, roll out each piece
into thin rounds. Brush with sesame oil and fry
the pancakes in a skillet over a moderate heat for
two minutes each side. When ready to serve,
each diner takes a pancake, smears a little sauce
along the center, adds a small portion of duck
meat (already sliced into fine strips), some scallions and cucumber, and then wraps up the pancake and—enjoys! The duck's head, the skin and
brain of which are considered delicacies, is cut in
half lengthwise and offered to the guest of honor.

Facing page, far left: A Peking duck dinner is
always a major social event.

Facing page, left: The Quan Ju De is the traditional
restaurant for Peking duck.

Top: The head and neck are left on the body when
the duck is killed.

Above (from left to right): The
restaurant chef wheels in the
duck on a serving trolley…

…expertly carving it in front of
the diners…

…and finally cutting it into slices.

Dining etiquette in China

Slurping, sucking, burping, smoking—these are almost always regarded as acceptable behavior at dinner tables throughout China. Even so, it would be wrong to assume that rules of etiquette do not exist. That being so, it is far more important for Western visitors to be aware of any cultural differences—between China and Europe, for example—than to learn the correct way of handling chopsticks and bowls. However banal it may sound, eating is a favorite occupation among the Chinese. Regardless of whether it is a family meal, a dinner party, or a meal in a restaurant, such times are considered both a special occasion and a social event at which guests are expected to enjoy themselves. The table should be weighed down with food—no matter what time of day or night. Mealtimes are an opportunity for eating, talking, smoking, drinking, and placing bets—often all at the same time and in the company of as many other people as possible. Relatives, friends, colleagues, and neighbors are all welcomed into the group and the idea of eating alone, especially in public, is simply inconceivable to most Chinese, as is the notion of ordering a dish for oneself alone, or sharing the check. In China, you are expected to share the table, share the food, and share the pleasure. A Chinese host would be very reluctant to relinquish the honor of hosting a meal and the reason for this generosity is usually a little more complicated than simple pleasure and conviviality. In China, if you have a large number of friends and can afford to invite them to dinner, you will, in return, be rewarded with respect—or gain "face" *mianzi*, as the Chinese put it. High social standing plays an important role, not just in private, but also in the world of business. Arriving with guests at a famous restaurant and ordering the most expensive delicacies, will not only boost one's social status but also will promote good relations— *guanxi*—with friends and business partners. Virtually nothing functions in China without *guanxi*. In return for the invitation, it is the guest's duty to give his host "face," in other words, to show him just how much his company, his invitation, and the meal is appreciated. Punctual arrival, small gifts, words of praise and gratitude, as well as toasts, are all an indication of good manners—as are pleasant topics of conversation. Becoming involved in controversial debates concerning politics or business deals during a meal is regarded

by the Chinese as impolite—the intention is, after all, for everyone to enjoy the food and have a good time. The festive meal in the restaurant usually begins with a selection of nuts or pickled vegetables, followed by cold or warm appetizers and then the main courses, the number of which must exceed the number of guests. As if this were not lavish enough, there is often soup or rice to follow. All the dishes are placed on a revolving tray (a Lazy Susan) in the center of the table where they are available to everyone. At the invitation of the host, the guests—using a serving spoon or serving chopsticks but never one's personal set of chopsticks—each transfer a small amount of food from one of the dishes into their own bowl, which normally rests on a plate. (The smaller bowl is intended for tea and the flat one for dips). Even if a Western guest accidentally dropped his dumpling into his neighbor's lap or inadvertently dunked it in the tea bowl instead of his dipping bowl, no one would regard this as an unforgivable social blunder. Keeping hold of the revolving tray, on the other hand—so as to keep the best dish close to hand, for example, and be able to pick out the choicest morsel or even return a piece of food after selecting it—would be considered very inappropriate behavior. The best approach is just to sit and wait since Chinese table manners dictate that the guest should be served as a priority at all times. Choice morsels of food may land in a guest's bowl as if by magic—maybe much to the guest's chagrin in some cases. Westerners can find it difficult to swallow some of the dishes, such as fish eyes or duck stomachs, which are regarded as delicacies by the Chinese. Be that as it may: they just have to be coped with and then praised into the bargain. And who knows what the next morsel will be? Given the almost endless diversity of delicacies, there is bound to be something to suit every taste.

Top right: A circular affair: the dishes are served on a revolving tray so that each guest can view and sample the wide variety of food.

Below left: When arranging a meal, especially for business partners, it is important to consider not only the quality of food but also the ambience of the restaurant.

"Ganbei!" is the equivalent of "Cheers!" or "Good health!" in English.

The Chinese greet each other by shaking hands although the handshake may not be quite as firm as in Western countries.

The host will often place food onto his guest's plate.

Chinese dining etiquette made easy

Praise, praise and yet more praise: praise the restaurant, the table decorations, the aromas emanating from the kitchen...

Let others, especially older members of the party, go first—in every respect.

Observe what the other guests do and, if in doubt, ask.

Avoid controversial subjects: the meal in itself should provide adequate food for conversation.

Ignore any sounds of burping, slurping or lip-smacking made by your table companions. However, do not, under any circumstances, blow your nose while sitting at the table.

Always urge others to serve themselves first.

Exercise restraint: only accept something when it is offered a second time, and always express thanks at every opportunity.

Only take a small amount and only from one dish at a time as there will be a vast amount of food to get through.

Practice using chopsticks before your visit to China but if you still feel too awkward, it is perfectly acceptable to ask for cutlery.

Keep your chopsticks for your own personal use; serving spoons are used for everything else.

Only use your chopsticks when you are eating; lay them down while you are talking or drinking. Do not poke them into the rice, fiddle with them, or use them to point at other people.

You should only dip your piece of food into the separate sauce bowl once. Do not pour sauce over the food in your eating bowl.

Do not leave any bones in your eating bowl. Instead, place them on the plate underneath or on the table next to your plate.

Return any toasts, remembering to hold your glass a little lower than the other person's.

Sample everything, but never take the last piece of food from the plate.

Always leave a small amount on your plate.

Always extend a reciprocal invitation—even if you know that such an opportunity is unlikely to arise.

Conversation around the table should be limited to pleasant topics. Politics or business matters are taboo subjects on these occasions.

The meal is generally accompanied by green tea or jasmine tea.

A waiter is on hand in the restaurant to top up the drinks.

A mark of respect: when clinking glasses, the guest keeps his or her glass lower than that of the host.

Dumplings—delicious inside and out

Whether boiled, steamed, baked or fried, the sheer diversity of flour-based foods—ranging from filling steamed noodles to filled ravioli-style dumplings—is quite simply enormous. These somewhat salty snacks, which are hugely popular throughout the whole of China, are extremely delicious—both inside and out. Here is a selection:

White and soft, or crisp and golden: steamed noodles and *youtiao*

It is amazing what can be created from a simple combination of water, yeast, and flour—*mantou*, or Chinese-style steamed buns, for example. In Beijing especially, these are regarded as an essential part of any meal, but are especially popular as a breakfast dish. On almost every street corner you will find a stall or small restaurant selling mountains of soft, warm steamed buns to get the day off to a good start. Virtually no one bothers to make these buns themselves as they can be bought almost anywhere and are often sold precooked and deep-frozen ready for heating up in the microwave. Unfilled, these nutritious snacks are known as *mantou*, while the filled version is called

baozi. The latter are available with a variety of fillings including a sweet, yellow bean paste, black sesame paste, or a salty filling made from broiled pork and/or vegetables. If something a bit more substantial is required for breakfast, golden-brown *youtiao*— lightly salted, deep-fried strips of dough about 8 inches (20 cm) long—are a popular alternative. This power-packed snack is often accompanied by warm, sweetened soya milk and is regarded as a typical Beijing breakfast for eating on the move.

Chinese-style dumplings

No less popular but rather more sophisticated are *jiaozi*, known in the West as "Chinese ravioli," a dish that has remained largely unknown in the West unlike *dim sum* a culinary art based on a variety of dumpling-type dishes that originated in southern China. Dim sum became known throughout the world many years ago thanks to the large number of Cantonese who emigrated to the western hemisphere. They are prepared from and filled with different ingredients, which vary depending on the region, season, and upon individual family traditions. Sometimes the

outer casing is made from wheat flour, and sometimes from corn or rice flour. *Jiaozi* may be filled with finely chopped meat, fish, seafood, or vegetables and may be round or semicircular in shape. But one thing that all versions of *jiaozi* have in common is that these skillfully produced, mostly handmade ravioli-type dumplings can leave many other celebrated Chinese delicacies tasting positively bland.

One of the classic versions of *jiaozi* is *shuijiao*, or steamed dumplings, which consist of a thin outer skin encasing a mixture of finely chopped pork, cabbage, ginger and scallions. Chopped duck, lamb, shrimp or pork mixed with finely chopped mushrooms make another tasty alternative, which may be seasoned with a little soy sauce and pepper, or, in some regions, with rice wine and sesame oil. Whether eaten for breakfast, as a midday snack in a fast-food eatery or as an appetizer in a restaurant, *shuijiao* is a round-the-clock favorite, especially in northern China. They also assume special significance when eaten as part of a family meal—particularly on the eve of the celebrations to mark the Chinese New Year as they are considered a symbol of togetherness and good fortune.

Above: *Jiaozi* dumplings (made with wheat, corn or rice flour) with various fillings.

1 Preparing the dough, which is usually a simple mixture of flour and water, is a relatively easy task. The dough is then rolled out wafer-thin.

2 Chopsticks are perfect for transferring small amounts of filling onto the rounds of dough. Alternatively, you can use a teaspoon.

3 It is important not to overdo the amount of filling otherwise the dough "envelope" might burst open during cooking.

4 Finally, the edges of the round of dough are moistened with a little water, folded in half and crimped together.

5 *Jiaozi* are traditionally semicircular in shape—by no means an easy task for a beginner.

6 If you are invited to a *jiaozi* meal, be prepared to help with the preparation and cooking.

7 The art of preparing *jiaozi* is not just a matter of preparing the right filling; it is equally important to make sure that the ravioli-style dumplings neither fall apart nor stick together while they are being boiled (in private homes they are not only steamed, but also boiled.)

The dough—a mixture of flour and water—is easy to make, or can be bought ready-made from the frozen food section of a Chinese supermarket and rolled out into circular discs. A teaspoon of filling is placed in the center of one of the wafer-thin rounds of dough, then the edges are moistened with water and folded together. If one reckons on 20 to 30 *jiaozi* per person, the process is fairly labor-intensive but in China even the preparations are seen as part of the social occasion, with all the guests lending a helping hand. Next, the now half-moon-shaped *shuijiao* are placed in a bamboo steamer (or alternatively in a saucepan with a steamer shelf) and steamed over boiling water for a few minutes (to reduce the risk of them falling apart). They are then ready to serve. An experienced eater will use chopsticks to dunk them into a dip consisting of dark rice vinegar and soy sauce, seasoned and flavored—depending on region and family tradition—with garlic, chili or sesame oil.

Shuijiao taste even more delicious when fried. There are two versions of these pan-fried dumplings, or *guotie*, as they are known: either the cooked dumpling is fried quickly on one side or, the uncooked dumpling is added to a skillet containing hot oil, fried briefly, before being covered with a lid and steamed to finish. The result is a soft and fluffy dumpling on the outside, a succulent filling in the center and a crunchy, golden-brown crust underneath. Dipped in Zhenjiang rice vinegar and soy sauce—truly delicious! Farther south, the Chinese live rather more extravagantly: here, the outer wrap often consists of a mixture of wheat and corn flour, water, and eggs. The southern Chinese equivalent of *shuijiao* are known as *wantan* and are stuffed with a wide variety of different fillings, ranging from marinated vegetables and cilantro, to crabs, fish, chicken, or even sea cucumber. Somewhat smaller in size and a different shape, they may be added to soups, or can be fried or steamed in bamboo baskets. *Shaomai*, open-topped dumplings, are likewise cooked by steaming. Depending on the season and region, the transparent-looking wrapper contains a delicious filling, usually consisting of shrimps or crab meat, topped with a decorative garnish. These miniature works of art—like *shuijiao*, *guotie*, or *wantan*—are often included among the wide variety of dishes of dim sum cuisine, a feast of numerous light dishes which—as its Chinese name suggests—"touch the heart!"

Vegetarian *Jiaozi*

Dough:
2 ²/₃ cups (300 g) all-purpose flour
¹/₂ cup (120 ml) water
Filling:
2 ¹/₄ lb (1 kg) Chinese cabbage
5 oz (150 g) shiitake mushrooms, (softened in water)
3 ¹/₂ oz (100 g) dried tofu
4 eggs
1 tsp Sichuan pepper
7 tbsp finely chopped scallions
pinch of salt
1 tbsp sugar
1 tbsp sesame oil
¹/₂ cup (125 ml) vegetable oil

Wash and finely chop the cabbage, sprinkle generously with salt and leave to stand for a while before pressing out the water. Cut the shiitake mushrooms and tofu into small cubes, lightly beat the eggs in a bowl.
Heat the wok, add the Sichuan pepper and stir it around until it begins to release its aroma. Next, grind the pepper into a fine powder using a pestle and mortar. Heat 5 tablespoons oil in the wok and fry the beaten eggs until cooked. Remove the eggs and chop into small pieces. Place the cabbage, chopped egg, shiitake mushrooms, and tofu in a bowl and well. Add the scallions, a pinch of salt, Sichuan pepper, sugar, sesame oil, and 6 tablespoons vegetable oil. Mix the ingredients together. Prepare the dough and roll out very thinly. Make the *jiaozi* according to the instructions on page 44.

Youtiao (Deep-fried bread sticks)

1 ¹/₂ tbsp alum powder (potassium aluminum sulphate has been used for centuries in China to make *youtiao*)
1 ¹/₂ tsp salt
1 tbsp baking soda
1 ¹/₄ cups (300 ml) warm (86 °F / 30 °C) water
4 ¹/₃ cups (500 g) all-purpose flour
4 cups (l liter) cooking oil

Above right: Fried *Youtaio*, bread sticks

Right: *Jiaozi* with ground beef

Below: Vegetarian *jiaozi*

Mix the alum powder, salt, and baking soda together in a bowl. Add the water very gradually and mix thoroughly until all the ingredients are completely dissolved. Put the flour in another bowl and gradually add the liquid, kneading and folding the mixture into a dough. Once the dough is smooth and no longer sticks to the hands, cover and leave for 30 minutes before kneading it again. Repeat this procedure three times until the dough is smooth and shiny and possesses the correct degree of elasticity. Divide the dough into 2 rolls, brush plastic wrap with oil, wrap each roll, and leave to stand for 4–8 hours.
Unwrap and transfer the dough to a lightly oiled surface. Flatten each roll a little and then gently and gradually stretch and shape them into lengths which are about 4 inches (10 cm) wide and ¹/₃ inch (1 cm) thick. Cut these into 1-inch (3-cm) wide strips. Taking two strips at a time, place one on top of the other and press down from top to bottom with a chopstick to make a groove, then, holding the ends in both hands, stretch out to a length of about 9–10 inches (25 cm). Heat the oil in the wok to 355–390 °F (180–200 °C) and fry the *youtiao*, turning frequently. As soon as they are golden-brown in color, remove from the oil and serve hot.

Below: A portion of *shuijiao*, steamed in a bamboo basket placed over a small amount of boiling water in a saucepan.

Beijing's hutongs—little worlds of their own

The far-off rumblings of the big city and the sound of horns blaring reach the ear as if muffled by a wad of cotton wool; now and then, the sound of a bicycle bell is heard as a street trader peddles his goods, and housewives and pensioners stand together, gossiping... For the rest, all is otherwise quiet in Beijing's 500 or so surviving "hutongs"—the ancient alleys or lanes connecting Beijing's historic residential areas; it is like being in a completely different, secluded world.

The alleys, which are often not even wide enough to admit a medium-sized car, are lined on either side by high, gray-painted, walls, punctuated by red entrance gates. These may be either simple in design or, depending on the social status of the former owner, feature stone carvings and be guarded by statues of lions. Behind these walls are residential courtyards, or "siheyuan." The houses are built around four sides of a quadrangle with a courtyard garden in the center. The main house is situated at the northern end of the courtyard with the entrance facing south so that the inner courtyard benefits from maximum sunshine while resisting the icy winds. For this reason, the alleyways and lanes, which link the siheyuans, mostly run from east to west.

The layout of the hutongs dates back to the 13th century when the Mongols built their great capital known as "Dadu"—albeit to a Chinese design. At the center stood the Imperial Palace, encircled by residential areas, built to a design based on the shape of a chessboard, as is evident to this day. Later dynasties also adopted this system. The higher a citizen's social standing, the closer to the Imperial Palace he was permitted to live, while to the east and west of the palace lived the emperor's relatives and high-ranking officials. The former splendor of the siheyuans can still be seen today in the hutong neighborhoods around Houhai Lake, where up to four generations of one family would once have lived under the curved, overhanging roofs of the many main buildings and large number of less significant properties. Farther away from the Imperial Palace—to the north and south—lived the workers and merchants, many of whom often congregated together in guilds. The residents of Zhonggu hutong, for instance, made bells and drums, while Dashizuo hutong's inhabitants were mainly palace stone masons and the Zhiranju hutong was a district where silk was produced for the imperial family's clothes. Some hutongs bear the name of an individual family, while others are named after temples or even a particular shape. The most ancient and most beautiful hutongs, or at least among those that have survived, are grouped around the Forbidden City in a square grid pattern. Around 6,000 hutongs are said to have sprung up during the Yuan (1271–1368), Ming (1368–1644), and Qing dynasties (1644–1912). Only comparatively few of these have survived China's turbulent history to the present day.

After the founding of the People's Republic (1949) and the nationalization of private property, the residential areas became seriously overcrowded. Several households were obliged to share the space originally designed for a single family. Inner courtyards underwent crude conversions to create more living space. A large family inhabited what might once have been a music room; the kitchen, which once would have occupied a separate wing, was now likely to have been relegated—as a communal kitchen—to the farthest corner of the former courtyard area. The lack of sufficient living space, of adequate electricity and water supplies, not to mention of sanitary facilities, meant that life was lived out in the alleys, where neighbors would meet while shopping, or drink tea together, play chess, or eat *jiaozi*.

And it has remained so to this day—only with greater comfort. Many of the hutongs have been renovated to include sanitation, air conditioning, and even high-speed Internet connections. However, despite the undeniable advantages of hutong living—most importantly, the sense of closeness and community spirit—life here does have certain drawbacks. The most serious of these is the lack of space or privacy, as well as being under the constant scrutiny of one's neighbors, but even these can always be surmounted with sufficient funds.

Left: Community supervision or romantic tradition? In Beijing's hutongs, a sense of mutual involvement and consideration are essential requirements for successful neighborhood coexistence.

Below: Bicycles are twice as quick as automobiles in places the latter find difficult to negotiate.

Dumplings stuffed with ground pork

Dough:
1 envelope dried yeast
4 cups (500 g) all-purpose flour
sesame oil for brushing
1 tsp salt
2 ½ tbsp sesame seeds

For the filling:
sesame oil
2 ¼ cups (500 g) ground pork
2 tsp finely chopped leek
1 tsp finely chopped ginger
2 oz (50 g) bamboo shoots, finely chopped
1 tbsp rice wine
½ tsp salt
2 tsp sugar
1 ½ tbsp soy sauce

Stir the dried yeast into ¾ cup (200 ml) luke-warm water. Add 3 cups (450 g) of the flour and knead the dough until it is smooth and no longer sticky. Cover with a damp cloth and set aside for 30 minutes.

To make the filling, heat sufficient sesame oil in the wok to fry the ground pork. Add the ginger and leek and stir-fry, then add the bamboo shoots and stir until cooked. Add the rice wine, salt, sugar, soy sauce and mix together. Add a little sesame oil, to taste, stir once more before removing the mixture from the wok and set aside. Place the dough on a surface dusted with ⅓ cup (50 g) of flour and knead. Roll it out into a large, thin pancake of dough. Brush with a little sesame oil, sprinkle with salt and shape it into a roll. Cut the roll into 5–7 segments. Knead each portion one more time and shape into small pancake shapes, sprinkle each with sesame seeds and fold up to make a "pocket."
Pour sufficient sesame oil into a skillet to fry the dumplings over a low heat for two minutes until golden-brown. Turn over and fry for two more minutes.
Before serving, cut open the dumplings (without cutting them all the way through) and, using a spoon, remove a little of the dough. Spoon a small amount of filling into the resulting hollow.

Above left: Collecting paper and cardboard is not just about protecting the environment but also earns the collector a little money.

Above: Anyone who suffers from claustrophobia may be well advised to avoid Beijing's hutongs, especially in the evening.

Below: Hutong residents enjoy getting together on many different levels.

Bottom: Hutong residents set off for work early in the morning—mainly on their bikes.

Beijing specialties

Celery and pork

11 oz (300 g) celery hearts
3 ½ oz (100 g) pork
1 piece of ginger (1 inch / 3 cm long)
1 piece of leek (1 inch / 3 cm long)
1 tsp cornstarch
1 tsp salt
4 tbsp vegetable oil
1 tbsp soy sauce

Cut the celery and pork into strips, 1 ½ inch (4 cm) long.
Slice the ginger into thin strips and the leek into small pieces.
Mix the pork with the cornstarch and salt.
Heat the oil in the wok over a medium heat, add the ginger and leek and stir until they both begin to release their aroma. Add the meat, then stir in the soy sauce. Finally, add the celery to the wok and stir-fry.

Pancakes stuffed with wild garlic

1 ²/₃ cups (250 g) all-purpose flour
1 bunch of wild garlic (or garlic chives)
4 shrimp, deveined
1 tsp salt
2 tbsp vegetable oil
1 tbsp sesame oil
½ tsp pepper
vegetable oil, for frying and brushing

Mix 1 ¹/₃ cups (200 g) flour with 7 tablespoons (100 ml) lukewarm water and knead the mixture into a smooth, nonsticky dough. Wash and finely chop the garlic chives and place in a bowl. Finely chop the shrimp, add to the chives along with the salt, vegetable oil, sesame oil, and pepper and mix thoroughly. Place the dough on a surface lightly dusted with the remaining flour and knead well. Roll out into a large, thin pancake of dough and brush with a little vegetable oil. Roll up the pancake and divide this into five segments. Using a small rolling pin, roll out each piece into a small disc. Place a small amount of the garlic chives/shrimp mixture in the center of each round and fold in half, pressing the edges of the semicircle firmly together.
Pour a little vegetable oil into a skillet. Fry the pancake pockets over a medium heat for 3–4 minutes until golden-brown. Turn over and fry for a further 3–4 minutes.

Sweet steamed corn bread

1 ¹/₃ cups (300 g) sugar
2 cups (500 ml) water
3 cups (450 g) all-purpose flour
¹/₃ cup (50 g) cornmeal
1 envelope dried yeast
1 egg

Stir the sugar in the water until it dissolves. Add the flour, cornmeal, dried yeast, and the egg and mix all the ingredients together thoroughly until they form a dough. Leave to stand for 10 minutes. Line a heatproof bowl with baking parchment and place the dough in the bowl. The dough should fill two-thirds of the bowl. Place the bowl in a steamer containing boiling water and steam over a high heat for 15 minutes.

Fried tofu with red chile

1 ³/₄ lb (750 g) chunks of tofu, fried
1 tbsp soy sauce
1 tbsp rice wine
1 tbsp cornstarch, mixed with 2 tbsp water
5 g red chile
5 garlic cloves
½ tsp Sichuan pepper
1 tbsp vinegar
1–2 tbsp sesame oil
3 ½ tbsp chicken stock
1 ¼ quarts (1.25 liters) peanut oil, for frying
1 tsp salt

Cut the tofu into ³/₄-inch (2-cm) cubes and combine with half the soy sauce, the rice wine, and the cornstarch/water mixture. Thinly slice the garlic and crush the Sichuan pepper using the tip of a knife.

In a bowl, combine the remaining soy sauce with the vinegar, sesame oil and chicken stock, stirring well.

Heat the oil in a wok until it begins to smoke, slide in the chunks of previously fried tofu, fry for half a minute, then remove from the oil. Leave about 4 tablespoons oil in the wok.

Heat the remaining oil in the wok until it begins to smoke. Add the red chile, sliced garlic, Sichuan pepper, and salt and stir-fry the ingredients. Return the fried tofu to the wok, pour in the sauce and stir thoroughly before dishing out onto a serving platter.

Pork with green garlic shoots

7 oz (200 g) green garlic shoots
3 ½ oz (100 g) pork
1 piece of leek (1 inch / 3 cm long)
1 ½ tsp cornstarch
1 tsp salt
3 ½ tbsp vegetable oil
2 tsp rice wine
1 tbsp soy sauce
1 tbsp sesame oil

Rinse the garlic shoots and cut into 1-inch (3-cm) lengths. Cut the pork into 1-inch (3-cm) strips. Chop the leek.

Bring water to a boil in a saucepan. Blanch the garlic shoots quickly and drain. Toss the strips of pork in the cornstarch and salt.

Heat the oil in the wok over a moderate heat, stir-fry the chopped leek, until it begins to

release its aroma, then add the meat and stir-fry. Add the rice wine and soy sauce, and stir in the garlic shoots. Finally, drizzle over the sesame oil and tip onto a dish to serve.

From left to right:
Celery and pork; pancakes stuffed with wild garlic; sweet steamed corn bread (served here in individual bowls); pork with green garlic shoots.

Peking opera and tea houses

Beijing music theaters offer traditional Chinese performances. Their program consists mainly of different regional schools of opera, acrobatics—performed without the benefit of technical aids—clapper ballads, an ancient form of storytelling, as well as a Beijing stage performance known as "Cross Talk," which is an ironic and comic dialogue between two actors talking back and forth.

The major stages are equipped with all the latest, sophisticated devices of modern stage technology. Smaller theaters were staging Chinese operas 200 years ago but nowadays their ancient décor has been given a facelift with bright, new paint.

Not long ago, the Mei Lanfang Theater opened a new opera stage and the new Beijing middle classes seem quite happy to pay its comparatively high admission charges.

Tea houses have always been a focus for the performing arts. It was here that people met to discuss business, exchange news, play mah jong—and listen to professional storytellers. Many of the ancient tea houses were casualties of the revolutionary doctrines of Mao or disappeared as part of modernization programs introduced during the era of reform and openness policy (1978).

However, tea houses are now springing up again and reviving the old traditions. One such establishment is Lao She's Tea House, named after one of the greatest Chinese writers and dramatists of the 20th century (Lao She, 1898–1966). His most famous play, entitled *Tea House*, spans the five decades from the last days of imperial China to the birth of new Communist China, and mirrors the course of history through the lives of characters who visit a

Right: Lao She's Tea House, named after one of China's most famous writers.

Below: Real treasures, in the shape of antique teapots, can sometimes be found at Beijing's flea markets.

Top: One of the successes of the Communist revolution was to provide people with the opportunity to drink tea cheaply for the first time.

Above: "A tea house as big as the one built on stage no longer exists in cities any more. Decades ago, every town would have had at least one tea house which not only served tea but also sold cheap cakes and simple food" (from Lao She's *Tea House*).

Right: Whether the purpose of your visit is to talk business or relax in cultured surroundings, a tea house provides the perfect atmosphere for every conceivable occasion.

Beijing tea house. Lao She was one of the first victims of the cultural revolution—branded as a "reactionary force in the cultural sphere," he was terrorized and abused on numerous occasions. The Lao She Tea House occupies one floor of a building not far from Tiananmen Square in a part of Beijing, which is not particularly picturesque. It offers a varied program of entertainment including acrobatics, various acts, and folklore shows.

Peking opera, the most notable of China's numerous regional forms of opera, also stages performances here. However, anyone expecting to see the type of opera performed in European theaters should prepare themselves for a surprise, for Chinese opera conforms to conventions of its own: the orchestra is small, the stage sets are characteristically sparse, and props are scarce. What is expressed in word

and song in Western opera is merely hinted at in Peking opera while gestures and mime, on the other hand, play a key role. A few steps can represent a long journey, and a small hand movement can be packed with symbolism. You will wait in vain for a ballet interlude in Peking opera; instead the audience will be captivated by a dazzling acrobatic display.

The individual roles in Peking opera form part of a set piece consisting of a few main roles with various supporting roles. These include the main male role, the female role (played by men until well into this century), the gallant warrior, the villain, and the clown, often in the guise of a court jester. The costumes and colors used for the elaborate face makeup clearly distinguish each character. Red, for example, symbolizes warm-heartedness and loyalty, white stands for cunning and hypocrisy, while black represents sincerity and justice.

At the heart of Peking opera, however, is song, either set to orchestral accompaniment or expressed as a kind of singsong. The characters themselves determine the pitch: the young

men often sing in falsetto while the female characters sing in a high-pitched and, to the unfamiliar ear, shrill, nasal singing style. The musicians, a small ensemble of wind, string, plucked instruments, and percussion, do not follow a conductor, as they do in the West, but are guided by the drum, which dictates the rhythm.

Whatever the artistic entertainment being performed in the tea house, one thing is absolutely indispensible and that is tea, numerous varieties of which are available. Professional hot-water pourers circulate, their job being to pour water onto the tea. They use a kettle with an extremely long, narrow spout, pouring the boiling water in a high arc, which is carefully aimed to land in the cup and make the fine green tea leaves dance. Small delicacies of Peking cuisine are served as an accompaniment to the tea—a selection of sweet nibbles, for example, consisting of white peas, corn kernels, or almond pudding. In this way, Lao She's Tea House provides a taste of the cultural and culinary delicacies to be found in traditional Beijing culture.

Left: Tea is the obligatory companion to all manner of Chinese specialties, from tiny sweet cakes and pistachio nuts to filling little snacks.

Left: To Western ears, the singing style of the Peking opera performers is an acquired taste.

Top right: Drama, pantomime, dance, and acrobatics are all integral parts of every opera.

Above: The background, costumes, and masks for the individual opera roles—usually characters from ancient myths and legends—are all suitably lavish.

Nightlife in Houhai

People visiting China in the 1980s were still discovering that the opportunities for evening entertainment in Beijing were limited to the Peking Opera, Peking duck dinners and a futile attempt to find a bar outside their hotel that was still open after 9 p.m. Nowadays, tourists find themselves hard-pressed to make a decision from the wide choice of available restaurants, bars, and night clubs—unless of course they spend the evening in Houhai, a trendy entertainment district clustered around three lakes to the north of the Forbidden City. As early evening falls upon the lake, willow trees sway in the breeze, neon lights and red lanterns cast their reflections in the water, bathing the lakeside promenade in a soft glow, and the air is stirred by the quiet hum of conversation. The lakeshores are lined with cafés, bars, and restaurants, many of them with views over the water. The terraces are furnished with colorful sofas and soft blankets, awaiting customers from the affluent Chinese middle classes, "expatriates," or tourists.

Houhai is the "in" place to be, which is small wonder given that the opportunities for relaxation and entertainment, for luxury or a taste of bohemian atmosphere are no more than a stone's throw apart. Bordering the shores of the three lakes of Houhai, Xihai and Qianhai, also known as Shichahai, is a hutong district, which experienced a revival in the mid-1990s. Its renaissance was said to have been sparked by Bai Feng, a former cellist from Shanxi province, who started out by opening the No Name Bar in an old hutong ruin, followed by the Nuage, a Vietnamese restaurant with a roof terrace and night club, on Lake Qianhai. Other entrepreneurs followed suit, opening boutiques, galleries, and hundreds more restaurants, most of which are run by their owners. Hidden behind high walls along the lakeshore are former aristocratic and patrician houses with their large

gardens—the most expensive property in Beijing. Now tastefully renovated, they offer a glimpse of the splendors of imperial China.

By the time of the Yuan dynasty (1271–1368), the lakeshore area, now artistically landscaped, was already in use as a port and commercial district. The 1,118-mile (1800-km) Imperial Canal served as a main artery for transporting trade goods from all over China to Shichahai where they were unloaded, processed and brought to the nearby Imperial Palace. As time went by, it became a popular district with distant relatives of the imperial family, ministers, wealthy scholars, and artists who began building themselves houses with magnificent gardens. The 40 or so historic sites scattered around the lakes are best explored by bicycle rickshaw. An outstanding example of a residence dating from the Qing dynasty is the 15-acre (6 ha) property which belonged to Prince Gong (1833–1898), a half-brother of Qing Emperor Qianfeng (1831–1861), who campaigned for an open-door policy toward the West.

Surrounded by the aroma of food emanating from the nearby restaurants, it is difficult to choose between Beggar's chicken at the Kong Yiji, a restaurant serving specialties from Zhejiang province, or a meal of Pipa shrimp eaten on board a lake cruiser during a peaceful evening boat ride, or perhaps even deer penis at the Guo Li Zhuang, a restaurant specializing in dishes which supposedly increase male potency. On the other hand, a civilized glass of French wine in La Baie des Anges restaurant accompanied by a salad and a cheese platter might be preferable. Houhai also offers many types of musical entertainment, including rock music in the Houhai Zoo, house music in Houhai Paradise, jazz music in the East Shore Live Jazz bar, or even reggae in the Upsetter's Bar. The sound of music echoes across Lake Houhai until late into the night.

Pipa shrimp

¾ lb (350 g) shrimp
1 tsp rice wine
1 egg white
2 tbsp cornstarch
1 ¼ quarts (1.25 liters) oil
1 piece cucumber
1 small carrot
salt, pepper

Using a knife, make several incisions along the back of each shrimp, without actually cutting right through, and remove the black vein. Pull the shrimp gently apart so that it opens out like a fan. Season with salt and pepper, then sprinkle with rice wine.
Combine the egg white and cornstarch. Lay the shrimp flat on a plate and brush each one with the egg-white mixture.
Heat the oil in a wok. To check it is the right temperature, dip a wooden chopstick in the oil—the oil is hot enough when bubbles stop rising up the chopstick. Slide the shrimp carefully into the oil and fry for about 1 minute. Remove and allow to drain. Reheat the oil and fry the shrimp a second time until they are golden-yellow. Remove the shrimp, drain, and place on a serving platter.
Peel the cucumber and carrot, then slice into matchsticks. Arrange in the center of the shrimp to serve.

Muxu pork

1 oz (25 g) Mu Err (cloud ear) mushrooms
1 oz (25 g) tiger lily buds (also known as
  "golden needles" and available dried in
  Chinese stores)
7 oz (200 g) pork tenderloin, cut into strips
3 tsp soy sauce
4 eggs
1 tsp cornstarch
1/3 cup (85 ml) vegetable oil
6 thin slices of ginger
1 tsp rice wine
1/2 tsp Sichuan pepper
3 garlic cloves
1 small cucumber

Soak the dried Mu Err mushrooms and tiger lily
buds in water until soft. Cut the cucumber in half
lengthwise and cut into slices.

Mix 1 teaspoon of the soy sauce with half a lightly
beaten egg and the cornstarch and stir in the
strips of pork. Add two tablespoons of the oil to
the wok, add the pork strips and fry lightly,
removing them before they are completely
cooked. Set aside.

Lightly beat the remaining half an egg with the
remaining 3 eggs and season with salt. Heat 1 1/2
tablespoons oil in the wok, add the beaten eggs
and fry. Using a spatula, divide up the egg into
small pieces and transfer to a bowl.

Add 3 tablespoons oil to the wok and heat, then
add the ginger slices, rice wine, remaining soy
sauce, Sichuan pepper, and the garlic and fry
quickly. Add the tiger lily buds, and stir-fry until
semicooked. Add the mushrooms and fry lightly,
then add the cucumber and fry briefly. Finally,
stir in the pork and pieces of egg and cook over a
low heat until the pork is cooked through.

Above and left: Chilling out in Beijing's nightlife
district—in summer it is pleasant to sit outside
and enjoy the lake view.

Below left: The lakeshore is particularly inviting in
the evening and a good time for a pleasant stroll.

Supermarkets—an abundance of fresh produce

In the 1980s, there was still no sign of supermarkets in Beijing. Shopkeepers in stuffy little shops with half-empty shelves responded to customers' requests for fruit or foreign products with a brusque "*mei you*," meaning: "there isn't any!" In those days, fresh fruit and vegetables were traded on the street by peasants from rural districts outside Beijing. However, it was a very different city that greeted the 2008 Olympic Games: the peasants had disappeared from the streets and numerous well-stocked supermarkets had opened their doors. In addition to a large number of Chinese chains, the US firm Wal Mart (pronounced Wo-er-ma by the Chinese), two French chains, Auchan (known as "Ou-shang" in Chinese and meaning "European value") and Carrefour (or "Jia-le-fu," meaning "Family Joy and Happiness"), and various other European firms, some of which have several branches, all have outlets in Beijing. These supermarkets also offer a wide choice of imported goods, for sale at Western prices, naturally.

The most common supermarket in Beijing, however, is Wu Mart, a Chinese chain that has numerous branches throughout the city. It opened in 1994 with one store in Beijing. The company, which has been represented on the Hong Kong stock market since 2003, now has over 500 branches, one of which is situated on the fourth ring, around 20 minutes by car from the city center. It is open daily from 9 a.m. until 10 p.m. and is busy at all times. It is located in the middle of an area inhabited by 300,000 people, many of whom visit the grocery department on a daily basis. A daily shopping trip, is after all, an essential ritual for the Beijing housewife. Chinese cuisine has always placed great store on fresh ingredients, ideally purchased just before they are used in cooking. The fresh-produce counters are consequently always packed with customers, especially at the weekend. As well as a seasonal range of fruit and vegetables, there is invariably a wide selection of fresh meat, fish, and seafood. The fish are kept in large tubs of water and killed in front of the customer—the only way to guarantee Chinese standards of freshness.

At first glance, the long aisles of well-stocked shelves in any Wu Mart branch scarcely differ from those of Western supermarkets although a different emphasis is sometimes placed on particular products. A Wu Mart store, for example, will stock not just two or three varieties of soy sauce, but dozens of different brands. The same is true of vinegar and rice wine, which are also key ingredients in sauces and which are therefore essential store-cupboard items in every Chinese kitchen. Various kinds of rice can be bought in prepacked 22 lb (10 kilo) bags or are sold by weight in plastic sacks and between the shelves are stands promoting an ever-changing selection of special offers.

Special promotions are regular events, selling traditional delicacies to coincide with specific festivals: from mid-September to early October, for example, moon cakes are offered between friends and at family gatherings during celebrations to mark the lunar festival. Wu Mart sells these traditional, round pastries, measuring about 4 inches (10 cm) across, with a variety of different fillings. Moon cakes also compete with each other in terms of elaborate packaging and are by no means a cheap treat, but if you skimp on this gift you run the risk of losing "face."

The scene at the check-outs, however, is exactly the same as you would find in any European supermarket: all the items are barcoded and scanned at the tills, with long lines forming during busy periods.

Below left: An inconceivable prospect during the 1980s: Western-style shopping malls.

Below: The range of goods also includes many non-Chinese brands.

Bottom right: The political slogans, which once filled the market halls, have now been replaced by advertisements.

Facing page: Chinese consumers view the goods as critically as their Western counterparts.

Right: Ten years ago there were numerous gaps in the shelves, but nowadays consumers confront a seemingly endless choice of products. Fruit and vegetables are always sold fresh in supermarkets. The same applies to fish, which are kept in large tubs and are killed and gutted in front of the customer.

Supermarkets—an abundance of fresh produce **57**

Sundays in Beijing

Beijing's residents like to spend their Sundays surrounded by their families. Wang Pei, a young mother, who is studying for her doctorate, is no exception. Until recently, she worked at the Center for International Economic Ethics (an NGO: nongovernment organization), but since the birth of her daughter she has been devoting her time to her baby and concentrating on her doctorate, as well as doing some occasional teaching. She is looking forward to Sunday and a visit from her parents. Wang Pei's family is from the (relatively new) Chinese middle classes: her father is a senior local government official, her mother has recently retired. Wang Pei's husband also works for Beijing's municipal administration. The two of them can afford the services of a babysitter, who also helps with the housework from time to time.

Get-togethers with family and friends—which in China include joint preparation of the meal—are the highlight of everyone's day off work. Not every member of the family is able to participate, however: Wang Pei's husband is leaving straight after breakfast for a two-day business trip and her father also has tasks to perform for work this Sunday so must wait until evening before he can see his daughter and granddaughter. Wang Pei is planning to prepare one of his favorite dishes for the evening meal: Pancakes stuffed with wild garlic (see recipe on p. 48).

Wang Pei's mother invites her daughter and
son-in-law to breakfast in a restaurant.

Afterward, mother and daughter go shopping in a
supermarket for fresh celery...

...a prepacked portion of tofu—which, served with
bean sauce, makes an excellent accompaniment...

...and other fresh vegetables. Wang Pei searches
for one ingredient in particular: fresh wild garlic!

Back at home, the two of them begin preparing
lunch in Wang Pei's spacious kitchen.

Eggs are beaten in the wok, fried for a few minutes, before being mixed with leeks and tomatoes.

Meanwhile, Wang Pei's mother lays the table—
setting out dishes of pumpkin, celery, and pork.

Later, Wang Pei and her mother begin preparations for the wild garlic stuffed pancakes.

Eventually, the family sits down to enjoy today's meal along with the babysitter. Wang Pei's baby daughter is keen to try a bit of everything—but will only allow grandmother to feed her!

While one of them divides the dough into pieces and rolls them out into rounds…

…the other chops the wild garlic for the filling and mixes it with shrimp.

Wang Pei's mother insists upon filling the pancake wraps her special way. She positions…

…the filling accurately, pulls up the sides of the circular wrap and seals the dumplings firmly.

She then gently molds them into a rounded shape, before sliding them into the wok.

The dumplings should not disintegrate or burn on the bottom.

In the evening, Wang Pei's father, mother, and baby daughter enjoy their dinner together. It is a pity Wang Pei's husband cannot join them today—but hopefully next Sunday!

Left: As dusk begins to fall, Beijing residents set out for a stroll around the city's night markets where all aspects of life, including cooking and eating, are conducted exclusively out on the street.

Facing page: Not for the faint-hearted—the food stalls, in particular, offer an array of dishes containing unusual and often bizarre ingredients, which those of a delicate disposition are likely to find a little disturbing.

Snacks at Beijing's night markets

Be it roasted grasshoppers, grilled starfish, or sea-horses—it is actually the southern Chinese who have a reputation for eating anything with four legs, except the table, but Beijing, too, is a place where you will find some curious ingredients on skewers.

And where? At a night market, a well-known Chinese "institution" and feast for the senses. Nowhere else could you sample such a diverse and, above all, entertaining choice of regional delicacies as cheaply as the snacks on sale here at the food stalls at the city's night markets. Beijing has, for generations, been attracting regional delicacies from all over China. Manchurians and Mongols introduced grilled mutton kebabs to the city from the distant steppes of northern China, the cooks of Shandong introduced popular pancake wraps and snacks fit for an emperor, while specialties from western and southern China include spicy tofu cubes and fried dishes. All these, not to mention some other, extremely interesting specialties, are offered for sale every evening at Beijing's many night markets to visitors and residents alike.

Just a stone's throw away from Wangfujing, Beijing's glittering shopping mile, are two well-known night markets. Situated in a narrow alley at the southern end is Snack Street (Xiaochi jie) and at the northern end is Beijing's most famous night market, the considerably larger Donghuamen market.

Far left: Tasty chicken feet are a very popular snack at the night markets among visitors and residents alike.

Above left: Anyone who finds a starfish tough is tackling it the wrong way: break off one of the arms, split it down the middle—and suck out the contents.

Below left: When widening one's culinary horizon, it is sometimes best not to ask what the food is—but to just try it.

When wandering along Snack Street, one cannot help but notice the unusual aroma of some of the dishes on sale. There are glowing skewers, woks spitting sparks, steaming bamboo baskets...and all the ingredients are at the ready. One only needs to point at something and the chef will set to work, right there in front of the customer. Payment is also transacted by simple hand gestures: it really could not be any easier for tourists to make themselves understood. Yet even when the meat on the skewer looks reasonably identifiable, there is still an element of risk involved: Is it beef or might it be dog? If you do not speak Chinese, you may have to clarify this burning question by mooing or barking—to the great amusement of Chinese bystanders.

On this particular evening, something special is causing excitement, something more than just the usual vast array of different skewers, noodles or fried tofu dishes. A crowd of around 20 people, hardly any of them tourists, are thronging eagerly around one particular food stall, holding their digital cameras aloft. The counter is packed with starfish, sea horses, frogs, beetles, grasshoppers, and even scorpions, all neatly arranged on individual skewers. Other trays contain silk worms and millipedes wrapped around bamboo skewers (at least none of them is wriggling!)

What tourists regard as a daunting culinary adventure, the Chinese take in their stride as the most normal thing in the world—exotic ingredients are often regarded as useful for increasing potency but most of the time it is merely an entertaining test of courage. Mealtimes are, after all, supposed to be colorful, noisy, and fun occasions, and, ideally, practical and cheap. Beijing's night market functions simultaneously as a cinema, an extended living-room, snack-bar, and a social meeting-place. It is a place where, regardless of the generally limited living conditions and financial situation of most Chinese, people can satisfy their hunger and enjoy their leisure time.

The larger Donghuamen night market consists of (what seems like hundreds) of aisles of smart food stalls, all lined up side by side. The market is a popular attraction, especially for tourists. A typical selection of foods ranges from crabs, chicken, and lamb, to meatballs, handmade noodles, and exotic curiosities such as boiled sheep's head—a traditional midnight snack, eaten cold and served in slices sprinkled with coarse salt. There is also much to tempt visitors who have a sweet tooth, including sweet little rice cakes, soy milk or natural yogurt. Further specialties are the deliciously attractive skewers of candied fruit, which are almost too pretty to eat. Beneath their shiny sugar coating, slices of haw fruit, orange, apple, and pear glitter in the bright lights of the night market.

Right: Kebabs are made of virtually anything that can be skewered—the snacks here represent a real test of nerve.

Snacks at Beijing's night markets   **61**

Life in Beijing's parks

Beijing sometimes gives the impression of being a "closed" city. A stroll through its alleys, or *hutongs*, takes the visitor past gray, windowless façades, brightened only occasionally by red or brown gateways. However, there is a marked contrast between the interior and exterior architecture of these aristocratic houses, which reflects, to some extent, an aspect of Chinese thinking. For the most part, the everyday life of the Chinese is played out behind these gray walls.

The opposite is true of the public parks which are used both for recreation and as a place to exercise, thereby maintaining the nation's health. To an observer, the parks represent a kind of showcase of Chinese life and a mirror of social development.

The parks open at the crack of dawn as many of their clientele are early risers, usually elderly folk, who like to keep fit and know how to make the most of their low-priced season ticket for senior citizens. By 6 a.m. there will already be groups of women with fans and brightly colored bands dancing in the park's broad plazas. The rhythmic beat of aerobic music echoing from cassette players competes with waltz music as mature ballroom aficionados, a combination of mixed couples as well as women partnering each other, progress around the square—some wearing dancing shoes, some wearing trainers, depending on taste. Social dancing as a form of early morning gymnastics is yet another Chinese invention.

Elsewhere, gray-haired gentlemen keep themselves supple by practicing shadow boxing—totally unperturbed by the loud music going on around them. Health insurance organizations were quick to recognize the importance of parks in terms of people's health and provide them with Chinese-style exercise equipment. Badminton and juggling are practiced along the broad pathways while kite-flying is a popular sport among young and old alike. However, some park authorities have even banned people from flying kites because so many are lost as a result of snapped strings that the tops of the trees are in danger of disappearing under the large number of crashed kites.

Meanwhile, areas surrounded by trees—especially ancient fir trees where the Qi is supposed to be particularly favorable—are popular spots for practicing Qigong, an exercise in meditation, concentration, and movement, which is part of traditional Chinese medicine (TCM). It comprises a wide variety of movements, all of which demand a high degree of concentration, and occasionally involves shouting. If piercing cries are heard echoing through the park in the early morning, it is unlikely to signify that a crime is being committed—it is probably an exercise being carried out to regulate one's Qi, or vital energy. The sounds produced by amateur singers and musicians who congregate here to perform music together are likely to be rather gentler on the ear. Almost every Chinese park also has a designated place where people can display their skills at singing opera arias, accompanied by a Chinese two-string fiddle and cymbals, or where entire choirs belt out patriotic folksongs.

Yet above all these other noises there is the sound of birdsong from birds in bamboo cages hanging from tree branches. Their proud owners—usually elderly men—have brought the songbirds here in their covered cages early in the morning. Finding themselves among others of their own kind clearly inspires these songsters to ever greater heights and their tuneful rivalry even manages to drown out the sound of rush-hour traffic on the nearby orbital highway. It also compensates a little for the fact that wild birds are a thing of the past in public parks (partly as a result of serious pollution).

The parks are also a microcosm of Chinese society because it is in these green lungs of the

Below left: A common early morning scene in a public park—Beijing residents practicing Qigong.

Below: All the exercises are designed to keep people fit—be it classical Taijiquan...

Bottom: ...or exercises involving different pieces of equipment.

city that you will meet the whole cross-section of society—a grandfather and his grandson, the latter wearing a pioneer's red neckerchief, doing homework together at a small stone table; giggling schoolchildren enjoying a picnic; gray-haired intellectuals reading books or newspapers, or a mature couple meeting for a tryst. In recent times, these regular visitors have also been joined by itinerant workers and the unemployed. Apart from these relative newcomers, people are otherwise using these recreation facilities far less frequently than they did in the past—perhaps because growing prosperity means they are now too busy. The young couples, who used to shyly hold hands on the park benches, have likewise become an infrequent sight—nowadays they prefer to meet in bars and cafés.

Top: In addition to movement and gymnastics, most of the exercises also involve meditation techniques.

Above: Public parks are a popular meeting-place for young people.

Left: Instrumentalists will undoubt-edly find a few fellow musicians.

Below left: And if you want to sing, you can be sure of finding a suitable accompanist in one of Beijing's many parks.

Right: The erhu—a key instru-ment in Peking opera—is also a favorite among amateur musicians.

A visit to the university refectory

The large canteen is located in this block and occupies three floors.

Around 6–7,000 students, lecturers, and employees congregate here at every meal.

The University of International Business and Economics is situated in the northeast of Beijing—about 20 minutes from the city center. It is attended by about 11,000 students from all over China. Two canteens provide the students, teaching staff, and other university employees with hot meals three times a day. Breakfast is served between 6.30 a.m. and 8 a.m. A Western-style breakfast, which is very popular among the students, is also available and consists of bread, buns, and instant coffee. Lunch is available between 11.20 a.m. and 1 p.m. and the evening meal is served between 5 p.m. and 7 p.m. Since student dormitories are not equipped with cooking facilities, students eat in the canteen on a regular basis and the dining halls are correspondingly large. Meals are paid for with a chip card, which students can also use in the university's own supermarket, Internet rooms, and for the showers.

In addition to a wide range of typical Chinese dishes, there is always a large quantity of rice available as well as various types of steamed buns. The canteen also offers a selection of ethnic specialties as there are students here from every Chinese province, including members of ethnic minorities, such as the Uigur or Hui minority groups. Hand-pulled noodles *(lanzhou)*, for example, are a specialty of Chinese Muslims.

The chef prepares the work surface before starting to prepare today's specialty—*lanzhou lamian*.

The dough (see recipe on p. 402) is first pulled into flat lengths.

A slicing comb is pulled through the lengths of dough to produce strands of noodles.

These are increased by pulling them apart and joining them together again...

...then again to the desired length and thickness. Just watching is enough to whet the appetite!

The chef skillfully slides the strands of noodles into boiling water.

After a few minutes' cooking, they are ready to be scooped out of the water.

A varied choice: lotus flower with shiitake mushrooms, garlic shoots, and white cabbage with chili.

If a dish proves particularly popular, fresh supplies are brought in.

Students pay between 5 and 10 RMB (between about 75 cents and $1.50).

Individual wok dishes, usually different types of vegetables on rice with meat or eggs, stay hot longer.

The kitchen staff will happily recommend something if a person cannot make up his or her mind.

Low-maintenance tables, accommodating four or eight people, are arranged in long rows.

Early birds can reserve window seats for friends and colleagues.

The dining hall may not differ much from those found in Western universities, but the students and the range of dishes on offer leave no doubt as to this being Beijing University's refectory.

The Summer Palace—imperial summer retreat

Chinese culture would be unimaginable without its gardens. There are even references dating back to pre-Christian centuries, which describe extensive park areas in China. Southern China is noted for its artistic landscaping and delicate design of the elegant small gardens that once belonged to scholarly officials. Beijing, on the other hand, is famous for the grandeur and extensive splendor of its imperial gardens. Common to both garden styles is the presence of water and stone, or rocky outcrops, which, in the Chinese philosophy of opposite (yet simultaneously mutually complementary) forces represent the female yin and male yang.

The largest of the imperial gardens is known as Yiheyuan, or the Summer Palace, and is situated to the northwest of the capital at the foot of the western mountains. The first landscaping work began in the 12th century when one of the Yin emperors (1115–1234) built a summer residence here. The gardens were expanded under the Mongolian Yuan dynasty (1271–1368) and pavilions and a palace added under the Ming rulers. The complex was extended to its present size of 867 acres (290 ha) during the second half of the 18th century when Emperor Qianlong (1735–1796) had the Garden of Pure Water built to commemorate his mother's 60th birthday. The extensive park with its temples, pavilions, garden corridors, and lakes served the imperial family as a summer residence—a place to escape from the heat of the city. Since the country still had to be governed even

during the hot summer months, however, the palace complex was not only generously furnished with private residential quarters, but it was also equipped with audience chambers for receiving envoys and delegates.

The Summer Palace, like the smaller imperial gardens in the western hills, was destroyed by French and English forces during the Second Opium War in 1860. Only a handful of buildings survived unscathed. Thirty years later, the imperial family had the palace complex rebuilt from public funds, but the Garden of Harmonious Unity, as it had been renamed, was ransacked once more in 1900 by vengeful allied forces in the wake of the Boxer Rebellion. The Dowager Empress Cixi, who ruled de facto from 1898–1908, ordered the complex rebuilt yet again but after her death the Summer Palace was closed and remained so until it was opened to the public in 1924. Many of the buildings had become dilapidated, however, and the gardens overgrown. It was not until after 1949 that renovation work was restarted.

The largest feature of the gardens is the entirely man-made Kunming Lake, which, with its series of dikes and bridges, is largely an imitation of West Lake in Hangzhou (Zhejiang province). It lies at the foot of Longevity Hill like a large mirror and between these two landmarks are situated—in complete harmony with the principles of feng shui (Chinese geomantics)—the imperial apartments, halls, and pavilions. In total, the Summer Palace is said to have 3,000 rooms, including the apartments

belonging to the Dowager Empress Cixi and those of reform-minded Emperor Guangxu (ruled 1875–1908), who was in practice no more than a prisoner of the conservative empress. A theater was provided for the imperial court's entertainment and consisted of three levels connected by trapdoors. Further diversion was provided by a specially created commercial district with small shops—the luxury of shopping in ordinary stores was a novelty to the emperor and his family. Spiritual needs were catered for by various temples—the Temple of the Sea of Wisdom, situated high on Longevity Hill and decorated with yellow and green glazed tiles, houses a gold statue of Buddha. From here, there are wonderful views over the lake.

Running along the northern shore of the lake is the Long Corridor, the ceiling of which is decorated with colorful paintings of figures from classical Chinese literature, landscapes, floral designs, and symbols. The corridor is so long (more than 2,296 feet/700 m) that, according to popular myth, a couple who were exchanging their first words of love as they entered one end of the corridor, would be able to set a date for their wedding by the time they emerged at the other end. Given the large numbers of tourists walking the narrow corridor today, however, the chances of overhearing declarations of everlasting devotion are fairly remote.

The Long Corridor leads to the Marble Boat, which is anchored in Kunming Lake and is intended as an illustration of the extravagant lifestyle of the imperial court. Only the base of this immovable fixture is made of marble: the superstructure, which dates from the Qing dynasty (1644–1912), was designed to look like marble but is actually made of wood.

More maneuverable than the famous Marble Boat are the excursion boats with dragon heads at the prow, which bring visitors to a small island, the site of the Dragon King Temple, where the emperor would come to pray for rain during periods of drought. The island can also be reached by an elegant white marble bridge, which has 17 arches and is decorated with 500 small lions, no two of which are alike.

The Summer Palace takes on a truly magical appearance in the evening when the sun is setting behind the western hills and the gardeners are cycling leisurely homeward along the opposite, western shore of the lake.

Left: Harmony is the basic precept and ultimate goal of Chinese garden design. The relationship between water, wood, stone, and other materials should always be in perfect proportion and harmony with each other.

Steamed duck

1 plump duck (approx. 5 ½ lbs / 2.5 kg),
   dressed
2 quarts (2 liters) duck stock
1 oz (25 g) ham
3–4 shiitake mushrooms, soaked in water
   and sliced
2 tsp salt
2 tbsp Shaoxing rice wine
1 scallion, cut in half
1 piece of ginger (2 ½ inch / 6 cm long),
   cut into thick slices

Rinse the duck and place in a saucepan of cold water. Bring to a boil, remove from the pan and rinse once more and pat dry inside and out. Place the duck in a large wok, add the duck stock, ham, sliced shiitake mushrooms, salt, rice wine, scallion, and ginger and braise over a low heat for 4–5 hours. Remove the scallion and ginger before serving the duck. This was one of Dowager Empress Cixi's favorite dishes. The palace chefs in the Forbidden City would steam the duck for three days until the water had completely evaporated and the flesh was crisp and the bones very soft. Needless to say, the empress only ate a few morsels of the deliciously crispy skin.

Right: Dowager Empress Cixi's boat: only the base is made of marble.

Far right: Knowledgeable guides explain the background of the Summer Palace's individual halls and pavilions to tourists.

The Great Wall

The concept of interior and exterior space, of belonging and not belonging, is one of the cornerstones of Chinese philosophy. Accordingly, a husband's family is regarded as immediate family while a wife's relatives are viewed merely as members of the extended family circle. The family's main preoccupation concerns what happens within the four walls of the home—what goes on outside is essentially of little concern. When construction is about to begin on a plot of land, the first step is to build a wall around the boundary of the property with "No Entry" signs. The same attitude is also reflected in Chinese politics: noninterference in the country's internal affairs, warns Beijing repeatedly. This is due in no small part to what the Chinese perceive as an ignominious period of their history when Western powers not only actively interfered in the country's affairs but even attempted to divide up the Chinese empire among themselves. Such events inevitably remain very much at the forefront of Chinese awareness in the current debates between China and the rest of the world concerning Tibet and human rights issues.

The most visible example of this philosophy of interior and exterior space is undoubtedly the Great Wall, located about 60 miles (100 km) north of Beijing, which runs from east to west for 3,900 miles (6300 km) through mountainous terrain. The Great Wall is part of a defense system, which was developed over the centuries to protect China from the "barbarian" horsemen of the north. The Chinese call it the "Ten Thousand Li Long Wall" (1 Li is roughly one third of a mile/500 m) but the name is purely descriptive and simply signifies a very long distance, in much the same way that people might say "May the emperor live ten thousand years."

Even a wall has to "grow"—and that takes time. The Great Wall was first begun 2,200 years ago in the early days of the Qin dynasty (221–206 B.C.) when Emperor Qin Shi Huangdi—famous for the Terracotta Warriors which he created to guard his mausoleum—succeeded in subduing several warring kingdoms and subsequently established China's first central government. Within a few years he had combined existing walls along the frontiers of various states to form an unbroken wall stretching 3,100 miles (5000 km). The two parallel outer walls were constructed of stone and the section in between filled with an estimated 235 million cubic yards (180 million cubic meters) of earth. Altogether 300,000 soldiers and 500,000 forced laborers were involved in its construction, many of whom died from the great hardships they suffered. Their bodies were used to help fill in the middle

section between the two walls. Eventually, 12 years after the Wall was begun, the population rebelled in protest and the Qin dynasty was overthrown.

There are numerous legends surrounding the victims who sacrificed their lives to the building of the Great Wall, one of which is the story of Meng Jiangnü, a young woman whose husband was conscripted to work on the Wall the very day after their marriage. As winter set in, she set off to bring him warm clothing but when, after a long and arduous journey, she finally reached the easternmost end of the Wall, she discovered that her husband had died from the rigors of hard labor and been buried beneath the Great Wall. The widow's heartrending cries of grief caused the Wall to collapse, delivering forth her husband's body, which Meng Jiangnü identified from a piece of jade hairpin which she had given her husband as a pledge of her love. After giving her husband's body a decent burial, she took her own life by drowning herself in the sea. The place now attracts a large number of visitors trying to locate Meng Jiangnü's grave among the rock formations along the coast. The original Wall was situated farther north of the present–day structure and only a few sections of it survive. The Great Wall was further extended during the Han dynasty (206 B.C.–A.D. 220) to a length of more than 6,200 miles (10,000 km).

Watchtowers and beacon towers were also constructed at regular intervals so that guards could spot approaching enemies from afar and quickly send warnings along the Wall from tower to tower. Remains of the Wall, consisting of a tamped clay and straw mixture can still be found, for example in the middle of the desert in the Western province of Gansu.

The Ming emperors fortified this monumental structure even further during their rule from the 14th to the 17th century. The section of the Great Wall, which it is possible to visit from Beijing dates from this period. It is around 33 feet (10 m) high as well as wide. Stones and bricks were used for the outer walls and the section in between was filled with rubble and chopped wood. The passes, particularly those at the western end of the Wall (in Gansu province) and at the eastern end (Hebei province) were developed into fortresses. Impressive evidence, including a decorated platform of white marble, has been found indicating the presence of a grand fortress near Beijing.

The Great Wall, like various other walls, did not ultimately achieve its intended objective of preventing the northern barbarians from attacking China. Only very rarely did it withstand invasion assaults. Today, the Great Wall snakes its way like the tail of a kite along the crest of mountains, which are now covered with trees again following re-forestation programs. In some places, it nestles comfortably in the landscape, elsewhere, it plummets down to lower ground from breathtaking heights. Several sections are easily reached from Beijing. Unfortunately, however, the more accessible—and consequently the best restored—parts of the Wall also attract the most tourists with all their attendant paraphernalia. Each day, convoys of tourist buses climb the road up to the 3,280-feet (1000-m) high section of the Wall at Badaling, 50 miles (80 km) northwest of Beijing, passing en route the words of Chairman Mao Zedong: "He who has not climbed the Great Wall is not a true man." Nowadays, the steep climb can be avoided by taking a chairlift and a toboggan slide can facilitate the descent.

The more remote sections of the Great Wall—which were added to the list of UNESCO World Heritage Sites in 1987—are still awaiting renovation. In the meantime, it is nature that is at work here, gradually repossessing the terrain. Self-seeded birch trees and firs are now growing along the Wall, loosening the ground where, centuries ago, five horses could ride abreast. Farmers have removed stones for their own houses and, in doing so, may have—without realizing it—afforded their ancestors, who perished during the Wall's construction, a certain amount of satisfaction.

Left: There are only a few sections of the Great Wall that are as well preserved as here in Badaling. However, the claim that its long length makes it discernable from the moon with the naked eye remains debatable.

Shandong 山东

Elke Spielmanns–Rome

Confucius came from Shandong — to be more precise, from the historic state of Lu, which was in the area now covered by Shandong. The province, which lies on the east coast of China, not far from Beijing, still proudly flaunts the characters that spell out lu even today; all vehicles registered in Shandong have them on their number plates. Shandong was the birthplace not only of some outstanding thinkers, artists, and strategists, but also of some excellent cooks, and of one of the eight great culinary traditions of China. Moreover, this part of China is blessed with a very impressive landscape. In the center of an extensive mountainous region is Taishan, the most famous of China's five holy mountains, while to the north lies the estuary of the Huang (Yellow River). Chinese high culture had its beginnings along the lower courses of this river and in the loessical region which borders the river to the west.

Between the Huang and Taishan lies the city of Jinan, the provincial capital since the time of the Ming dynasty (1368–1644), which has about 3 million inhabitants. Another 3 million people live in the surrounding countryside. The Longshan culture flourished not far from here between 4000 and 2000 B.C., one of the most important Neolithic cultures of China. They already knew how to shape pots, and produced fine, thin-walled ceramic objects with graceful, complicated shapes, which were copied in the great bronze vessels which were cast later—for example, for use in sacred rites.

Jinan was already an important center for trade at a very early date. But the city is better known for its springs. It is said that there were over a hundred at one time. Most of them have dried up now—the persistent dry conditions in the north of China have caused the water table to fall considerably. Only a sparse amount of water flows from the few remaining springs. The local tourist offices pipe in water to make them look more attractive. Close by one of the springs is a memorial hall commemorating the most famous poetess of the Song era, Li Qingzhao (1084–1151). Her odes of natural elegance celebrate life and beauty. The dramatic turning point of her own existence came when she was forced to flee for her life. But the experience of flight and the threat of death inspired her finest poetry.

Top: There are said to be 90 springs in Jinan, the provincial capital of Shandong. One of them feeds the lakes and ponds in the popular Baotu Park in the middle of the town center.

Above: Lu Cai, Shandong's cuisine, is one of the eight great culinary traditions of China. You can see this (and taste it!) even at the popular little fast-food outlets.

Facing page: Stone lions on guard before the gate: Anyone who dares to go past them enters the narrow streets of Jinan's old town.

Jinan

Shandong **73**

Top: Jinan is a favorite destination for both Chinese and foreign tourists.

Above: During the Spring festival, the whole city is decorated with red Chinese lanterns.

Above right: View of a pedestrianized area decorated for the festival.

Below: Entrances, bridges, and streets in the old city of Jinan are guarded—not only by lions but also by other fabulous stone beasts.

During the Qing era (1644–1912) there were several academies in Jinan, in which pupils took the entrance examinations for the imperial civil service. The examinations tested their knowledge of the classical texts written by Confucius (551–479 B.C.). China's great teacher came from the Qufu area, which was not far from the capital of the state of Lu that flourished at the time. It is believed that Confucius was born into a poverty-stricken but well-educated family, and earned his living as a very low-ranking civil servant. Later he became an adviser to several aristocrat families in turn, but never really achieved due recognition. And yet soon after his death he was elevated to high fame. His former home was converted into a temple. His descendants were ennobled and moved into a residence near the temple. Today, Confucius is once again being venerated as a saint. The Confucian temple in the center of Qufu is a magnet for pilgrims from all over China. Many purchase little red wooden plaques from vendors in the temple precincts, and have their names engraved on them. Before their plaques are hung up in the temple, the pilgrims pray for success in their examinations, for a successful career, for good fortune, long life—and wealth.

But the Confucius Forest in north Qufu has more atmosphere than the temple or the residence. At 495 acres (200 ha), it is reputed to be the largest park and the best-kept cemetery in China. It is one of the most impressive places in the province, so it is no surprise that it became a cult center for Chinese rulers at a very early time. Ancient pines and cypresses cast their shade over the tombs of Confucius (Master Kong) and his descendants, of whom there have now been more than 70 generations. This peaceful place resembles an enchanted forest. The tombs are embedded in nature. High grass is growing over the imposing gray marble gravestones (most of them are weathered, only a few of them are new), with small temples, pavilions, and sculptures scattered among them. A Path of the Soul leads to the tomb of Confucius—it is flanked by statues of animals and guardians, arranged in pairs facing one another. The tomb itself consists of a simple mound of earth, overgrown with grass and surrounded by a wall. An atmosphere of repose and simplicity covers the entire forest of tombs, which completely envelops visitors and invites them to wander through the surrounding light and shade, and to speculate idly on whether this is really Confucius's last resting place...

Above: Its position on the coast lends Qingdao a very special charm, which was formerly also appreciated by many Germans from the colony of Tsingtau.

Below: While the sandy beach in Qingdao invites you in for a swim, only a few miles away to the east the foothills of the Laoshan range run right down to the sea.

The German colony of Tsingtau

All the year round, the Huang brings alluvial loess down from the interior of the country and fertilizes the plains. But simultaneously the river has time and again been the cause of devastating natural catastrophes. It has changed its course, broken through dikes and flooded the country-side. The entire lowland plain of the province was flooded in 1899.

But Shandong has suffered from more than just floods and periods of drought. Europeans settled here at the end of the 19th century. This is still testified to nowadays by buildings in the Western style erected in Jinan, in the coastal towns of Yantai and Weihai, and in particular in Qingdao. In 1898, Kaiser Wilhelm II forced through a 99-year lease covering the Bay of Jiaozhou in the south of the peninsula and Qingdao (still a small fishing village at that time). The murder of two German missionaries had given him the opportunity to do this. Tsingtau—the German colony on Chinese soil—was constructed as a copybook German town. It was put under the authority of the Imperial German Navy, since it was intended to serve as a naval supply base. The Germans built a rail link to Jinan and established the famous Germania brewery. Today its successor company is still said to use the water from mineral springs in the nearby Laoshan range of mountains. At the start of World War I, Qingdao fell to the Japanese, and then in 1922 it reverted to Chinese possession. But at the beginning of the Sino-Japanese War (1937–1945), when Japan occupied large areas of China, the Japanese returned. They remained until their defeat in 1945.

The foreign occupation was seen as a humiliation by China—the work of Western missionaries and the construction of railroads through the province angered the Chinese. It was believed that the gods were offended and that geomantic harmony (good feng shui) was harmed by the rail tracks. At the end of the 19th century, this brought the Society of Righteous Harmony Fists (the Boxers) into the equation. The Boxers' secret society had its origins in northwestern Shandong. They rapidly expanded their influence out from their hometown toward the northwest, destroying churches, attacking foreign settlements, and pursuing Chinese converts to Christianity. In Beijing, the embassy quarter was besieged by rebels for weeks, until they were defeated by Allied troops. China was compelled to agree to pay considerable sums as compensation in the Boxer Protocol of 1901.

Taishan the sublime

The period of domination by foreigners must have been experienced with particular intensity in locations that were of importance for the Chinese creation myth and for the idea of heavenly authority being conferred on the emperor. Taishan, the "sublime mountain" rises to a height of more than 4,920 feet (1500 m) in the center of the mountainous area in northeast Shandong, and is also the origin of the province's name (Shandong means East of Taishan Mountain). The mountain is associated with one of the central figures in the Chinese creation legend, Pan Gu. He brought chaos to an end when the world began, and divided the heavens from the earth with his body. After keeping Heaven and Earth apart for many thousands of years, he died. His left eye became the Sun, his right eye the Moon. His limbs and stomach became four holy mountains, but his head became Taishan, which is more sublime than all other mountains. It is located at the eastern edge of China, in the land where the sun rises. For thousands of years, Chinese emperors (there are said to have been 72 of them) have ascended it, in order to be nearer to Heaven and to request from it the "mandate of Heaven," the mastery of the world. Even Mao Zedong ascended Taishan in an attempt to join the ranks of Chinese autocrats.

Facing page: There are countless idyllic piazzas in the parks of the province's towns and cities.

Above: There is water everywhere in Shandong. Suitably large and attractive stretches of water can be found in the municipal parks.

Below: According to the rules of feng shui, water also plays a role in Chinese garden structure architecture as a central element in the creation of harmony.

The cradle of the imperial cuisine

Shandong can thank its long coastline, which runs around the big peninsula projecting eastward into the Yellow Sea, for its position as the largest producer of seafood in China. In spite of recurrent droughts and floods, Shandong is also one of the most important provinces of China from the agricultural point of view. The main crops cultivated are soybeans, millet, wheat, and sorghum millet—*gaoliang*. Sweet potatoes and corn also flourish in the fertile soil. Moreover, the mountain areas provide a wide selection of mushrooms and game. And much of the produce of the local farming and fishing industries is exported to neighboring Asian countries through the province's ports. The land where the emperors once ascended to Heaven has become a gateway to the world.

Over 3,000 years ago, the states of Qi and Lu, with their highly developed economies and cultures, occupied the territory of the present-day province of Shandong. Blessed with an abundant supply of fish and with the salt from the surrounding sea, together with the agricultural produce from the fertile arable land along the Huang (especially corn, cabbage, and root vegetables), this area very early became a culinary center, and the Shandong cuisine developed from this over many centuries. It is considered as being one of the eight great regional culinary traditions of China, and it put its stamp on the imperial cuisine of the Ming dynasty (1368–1644) and the Qing period which followed it (1644–1912). For Shandong was not just considered as being a larder and a supplier of foodstuffs for the imperial court. More and more, the imperial household in Beijing recruited its chefs from Shandong, who then refined the hearty Peking cuisine. The Shandong and Peking cuisines are considered to be the most famous culinary traditions of the north (it is assumed that the Shandong cuisine is the older and more prominent of the two). Both of them influenced the cuisine of other parts of northern China.

It was in Shandong that techniques for preparing food were perfected which are nowadays practiced all over China. The most important of these are spicy frying (*bao*), spicy frying with starch flour (*liu*) and searing (*pa*). The province's cuisine is distinguished by sparing but refined seasoning of the ingredients. So their high quality, their aroma, their consistency, and their freshness are always the central focus point. The typical, mildly spiced Shandong taste is created, above all, by the addition of shallots and garlic—and a freshly tapped Tsingtao beer goes very well with it!

A distinction is also made within the province's cuisine between the Jiaodong and Jinan as well as the Confucian culinary traditions. Sea cucumbers, abalone, shrimp, mussels, and crabs are harvested on the Jiaodong peninsula, and so the Jiaodong cuisine is famous for its seafood specialties. The standard dishes from the cities of Qingdao, Fushan, and Yantai thus include steamed saltwater fish, green beans with shrimp, and "thousand-year-old eggs" (see p. 361)—and also Venus mussels, clams, fried squid, and shrimp with Sichuan pepper and ginger. Another Jiandong specialty has even become internationally known, though nowadays it is eaten only on very special occasions—shark-fin soup. But the consumption of such rare delicacies has tended to fall into decline in China recently on grounds of species protection.

In the capital, Jinan, the delicacies most often converted into tasty dishes are those from the interior. These include freshwater fish from the Huang, as well as poultry, meat, and giblets. Included among the general favorites are sweet and sour carp, which is a special treat, and Jinan-style roast duck.

By contrast, Confucian cuisine is considered to be very simple and hearty. Pork with bell pepper—spicily fried with cornstarch —is a typical dish, rapidly prepared, with no aromatic "flourish," and yet very tasty.

As Shandong lies north of the so-called rice equator, the basic foodstuffs here, in addition to wheat, also include millet, sweet potatoes, and corn. In Shandong, *jiaozi* and *baozi* (various types of dumplings) which are popular all over the north, are dunked in a sauce composed of vinegar, soy sauce, and chopped garlic. Leek and garlic are also often eaten raw. This strengthens the body's natural defenses.

Right: Taking a short break before the first customers arrive.

Far right, top: The banner sings the praises of delicious Laiyang pears and Fushi apples.

Far right, bottom: This vendor at the motorized rickshaw stand hopes to attract the man to buy his fresh fruit as well.

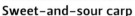

Sweet-and-sour carp

1 carp (about 1 ¾ lb / 750 g)

Marinade:
3 tsp rice wine
½ tsp freshly ground white pepper
½ tsp salt

1 ¼ cups (300 ml) clear stock
2 tsp soy sauce
2 tsp Shaoxing rice wine
½ cup (125 ml) rice vinegar
¾ cup + 2 tbsp (200 g) sugar
½ tsp salt
2 tbsp cornstarch, mixed with 4 tbsp water
6 cups (1.5 liter) peanut oil
1 tbsp chopped scallions
1 tsp chopped ginger
1 tsp finely chopped garlic

Descale the carp and remove the gills. Slit the fish lengthwise and clean interior. Slice across the body on both sides leaving a 1-inch (3-cm) space between the cuts. Carefully pull on the tail so that the slits expand. Mix the rice wine, the freshly ground white pepper and the salt into a marinade, and pour over the slits. Cover and leave to marinate for a short time.
In a pan, stir together the stock, soy sauce, Shaoxing rice wine, half the vinegar, the sugar, and salt over low heat. Add the cornstarch mixture and stir until it thickens into a sauce. Set aside. Pour up to 3 tablespoons of the peanut oil into a wok over high heat. Deep fry the

fish briefly, turn down the heat and cook the fish to golden yellow over medium heat. Remove the fish from the wok and rest it for a few minutes. Then return it to the hot oil and bake it to a crispy light brown.
Meanwhile, heat a second wok over high heat. Pour in 3 tablespoons of peanut oil, add the finely chopped scallions, ginger, and garlic, and fry until everything gives off an aroma. Add the prepared sauce and bring to a boil. Add the remaining vinegar and bring to a boil. Pour 3 ½ tablespoons of hot oil over the fish, then place it on a plate, pour over the hot sauce, and serve.

Top left: Most of Shandong's farmland is considered as fertile. Among the most important crops grown in the province are wheat, corn, sorghum, millet, sweet potatoes, and beans.

Top right: At harvest-time, street vendors are an everyday sight.

Above: Those who cannot bring their fruit into town sell it directly on the spot.

Pure luxury—wine-drinking in China

Grapes have been cultivated in China for more than 2,000 years. For a long time this did not lead to any significant production of wine. While high-quality tea and "choice" spirits, or rice wine had been generally prized all over the Middle Kingdom since time immemorial, wine produced from grapes was in no way part of the staple fare of the Chinese. It was not until the 19th century that wine cellars first made their appearance, and even then they were mainly set up to meet the requirements of the Europeans living in China.

When the country opened up economically in the 1980s, once again it was Europeans who invested in Chinese wine production and exported know-how to China, along with entire production installations and cellar equipment. This time the aim was to convert the Chinese into wine-drinkers.
Due to the high prices, only a small percentage of the Chinese population can afford the luxury of a bottle of wine. Yet, thanks to clever marketing, wine has recently developed into a status symbol in China. You can give an attractively packaged bottle of Riesling as a present, to show that you have money and class. Wine is still not regarded as an everyday food and drink item. At a banquet, people cautiously sip at decidedly expensive vintages, or they mix what is often considered a "sour" drink with lemonade or the like.

So even today the consumption of wine in China is still rather modest. On average, a Chinese consumer drinks just over half a US pint (0.3 liter) a year—as a comparison, the per capita consumption in Germany is a good 42 US pints (20 liters), and in France it even reaches 70 US pints (33 liters). Only a small part of the domestic requirement (about 10 percent) is imported—mainly from Chile, Australia, France, and Spain.

China has about 642,500 acres (260,000 ha) of vines—which still means it ranks fifth in the world. About a third of this cultivated area is in the north-western province of Xinjiang, a fifth in Shandong, and other areas lie in Hebei, Jilin, and Liaoning, and around the city of Tianjin. In Xinjiang, where there is a strong Muslim influence, a large part of the crop is reserved for the production of dessert grapes and raisins. So as regards wine production, China ranks only sixth in the world (following Spain, France, Italy, the United States, and Argentina). White grape varieties such as Chardonnay, Chenin Blanc, Riesling, Gewürztraminer, Müller-Thurgau, and Sauvignon Blanc flourish in China, as do red varieties (which form the bulk of the crop—70 percent) such as Cabernet Sauvignon, Blaufränkisch, Merlot, Carignan, Malbec, Gamay, and Pinot Noir.

Almost half of China's wine is produced in Shandong. Not the least important reason for this is that the local climate favors wine production and wineries extend over the peninsula between the Gulf of Bohai and the Yellow Sea. This is also where the city of Yantai can be found, which is commonly depicted as China's "Wine City." The oldest winery in China, the Changyu Pioneer Wine Company, was established in 1892. The Chinese founder was advised regarding his property (according to several sources) by the Austrian consul, Baron Max von Babo, a recognized expert on wines. The historic wine cellar is situated not far from the Yellow Sea, 23 feet (7 m) below ground level, and thus 3 feet (1 m) below sea level. Today it forms part of the Changyu Museum of Viticulture. The Changyu Pioneer Wine Company, which is 51 percent owned by the state, has a total of 13 production sites. It not only produces high-quality wines (the most expensive being a Chardonnay at a price that converts into about US $20 or 30 euros a bottle) but also, and predominantly, fine brandies.

In 2007, the first China Yantai International Wine Festival took place in Yantai. The Organization of International Viticulture (OIV) played a part in this. Since 2008, wine exhibitions have also been held in Shanghai and Hong Kong. In April 2008, the alcohol tax imposed on beverages with an alcoholic content of less than 30 percent was abolished in the Special Administrative Area. This reduces the price, and so increases the sales opportunity for wine—whether as an enjoyable beverage or as a prestigious gift. Another Eldorado for wine in China is nearby Macau. Thanks to the import of Portuguese wine (which pays no Customs duty), you can still always get a nice drop of wine from back home in Europe—and at an unbeatably low price.

Left: Entrance gate to the state-owned Changyu Castle winery.

Top left: Viticulture—and thus grape cultivation—is orientated toward European and American autotypes, whether it is the goblet system...

Bottom left: ... or rows of vines.

Top right: No trace remains of the casks which the Austrian consul, Baron von Babo, brought with him to Yantai. In Changyu Chateau, the wine matures in new barrels.

Bottom right: Wine, which was originally not a traditional drink in China, is still classed as a luxury product, but here too wine consumption is rising in step with the standard of living.

Once German, now international—Qingdao

When the international beer festival is declared open in Qingdao during the second weekend in August with "Good health to Qingdao and to the whole world," a visitor from Germany might well ask whether these green fields are actually in Munich, or have really been transferred to this part of the north China coast. Every year since 1991, the beer festival has turned the city on the Yellow Sea into a beer garden for two weeks. Dozens of brands of "liquid bread" from all over the world quench your thirst, drinking contests make sure everyone's happy, new special beer creations tickle the palate, German brass bands and Chinese rock music get everyone in a party mood. Qingdao (the "Green Island"), with its docks and its beaches, and with 2.5 million inhabitants in the urban areas alone, is gearing up to give the Munich *Oktoberfest* a run for its money.

Beer's been a part of life in Qingdao since 1903. People do not just drink it here, they brew it here in the Germania brewery, in accordance with the German purity law. Some parts of the equipment set up here by the Germania machinery manufacturing company from Leipzig are still here. Nowadays, Tsingtao beer is Qingdao's top export. There's no self-respecting restaurant in China, and no Chinese restaurant abroad, which does not sell quite a few more or less well-chilled bottles of this brand. In the late 19th century, Kaiser Wilhelm II sent the German navy on an expedition to the China coast. Their orders were to find a suitable site for a German naval base on the Yellow Sea, for this was the era in which the European powers were carving out spheres of influence for themselves in China. Treaty ports were opened, concessions were extracted; Western fleets lay off the east coast of China; river gunboats patrolled the waterways of the interior. The German navy decided that the Bay of Jiaozhou on the south coast of Shandong was particularly suitable. The killing of two German missionaries at the end of 1897 gave the German empire an excuse to implement the plan it had already been maturing for some time. When German troops went ashore and presented the Chinese with an ultimatum, they withdrew without resistance. By the 1898 Treaty of Kiautschou, Germany leased the region for 99 years, and was granted the right to build railroads throughout Shandong and to extract coal from the leased area.

Until now, Qingdao had been little more than a fishing village that contained a military support base. The first thing to do was to create an infrastructure and transportation links with the hinterland and with overseas countries. A city now arose which could bear comparison with any city in Germany—water supplies and sewers, medical facilities, and residential accommodation, all constructed to the newest standards. A railway link was constructed to the provincial capital, Jinan, and by 1912, when the line was connected to the international rail network, the journey from Qingdao to Berlin took only two weeks!

Top left: Reminders of the colonial era are still to be seen in the layout of the city of Qingdao.

Top right: Structures like the German church demonstrate how strong was the influence exerted by the colonial power, even with regard to architecture.

Left: The bigger the advertisement, the more famous the brand—even in China: gigantic beer cans at the entrance to the Tsingtao brewery.

The building project for the trading center and garrison town envisaged several different areas. A European quarter with public buildings, a villa suburb in which foreigners would live, a traders' and storekeepers' quarter for the Chinese part of the population, and a port area. Chinese settlements had to be swept away for the new buildings. Their inhabitants were transferred to workers' neighborhoods in which Western town planning was successfully combined with Chinese styles of construction. This was also where the workers lived who had come from other regions of the country and who were also part of the workforce building the town. Certainly, not everyone was grateful for being uprooted and forced to move—just as today, a hundred years later, modernization schemes in the big Chinese cities have long been greeted with somewhat negative reactions.

Qingdao was turned into a seaside resort, and attracted many foreign visitors in the summer. When the ruling house was driven from power in the revolution of 1911, many Chinese families who had previously been very influential fled to the foreign settlements, including Qingdao. They purchased land, on which they built European-style villas (in accordance with the building regulations). "Tsingtao Colony," as Qingdao was known at the time, was to last for only 15 years. When Japan entered World War I, the German colony was besieged and finally overrun. In 1922, Qingdao was returned to Chinese rule, until it once more fell into Japanese hands during the Sino-Japanese War (1938–1945).

Today, Qingdao is conscious of its special heritage, and knows how to make use of it, both culturally and commercially. The state-owned public buildings that remain in existence are being carefully restored. Official receptions take place in the imposing Governor's residence on the hill in the historic center of the city (even, now and then, those hosted by the German ambassador). There is an air of slightly decadent charm about the quarter where the European villas stand. Something is carried on the wind from a long-forgotten time, in which the mighty land of China was not the master of its own destiny.

Top left: The beer museum uses historical exhibits to tell the story of how beer was brewed in Qingdao.

Left: No counterfeiting here! At the beer festival, foreign producers naturally want to show off their beers too.

Bottom left and far right: Once a year, it is just like the *Oktoberfest* in Munich here— "One, two, down the hatch!" in Chinese.

Bottom center: Chinese beer gardens can be cosy too.

Above: Chinese designers are just as innovative in designing beer bottle labels as in designing cigarette packets.

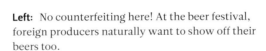

Confucianism—the state philosophy

Like many personalities from world history, Confucius was recognized only after his death. His teachings concerning a better order in the world and the cultivation of the individual's own personality were not elevated into an ideology in China during his lifetime. As the state philosophy, it determined policy and moral positions during the Chinese imperial period. Confucianism (adjusted to the prevailing circumstances) also made its mark on the spiritual and political systems of Japan and Korea.

Kong Qiu (551–479 B.C.), was referred to by his pupils as Kongzi or "Master Kong" (Kong Fuzi)—17th-century Jesuit missionaries latinized this name to "Confucius." He lived in a time of profound political and social upheaval. During the Eastern Zhu Period (770–256 B.C.), the empire broke up into warring successor states. Nevertheless this age, in which law and order had for the most part vanished, was a time of spiritual blossoming, which has passed into history as "the age of a hundred schools." Numerous schools of philosophy sprang up, wise men wandered the countryside and hired out their services to princes as advisers. The central theme of their teaching was the reestablishment of order and the creation of an ideal state. Confucius founded one of these schools of philosophy.

Confucius is said to have been a native of the state of Lu (which roughly approximated to the present province of Shandong). Initially, he occupied numerous government posts, and he ended up going from court to court as an adviser to princes. But this in no way made him a well-known figure. His pupils recorded their discussions with him and collected his sayings. Long after his death, these formed the basis of the "Sayings of Confucius" (Lunyu), consisting of about 500 records of discussions and sayings of the master.

Confucius' teachings were developed further by his pupils, and later scholars wrote commentaries on them. The Han dynasty (208 B.C.–220 A.D.) elevated Confucianism to the status of an official doctrine, which remained its position through almost the whole of the imperial epoch—even educational syllabi were marked by Confucianism. Candidates who wished to enter the civil service or were seeking promotion had to immerse themselves in Confucian teachings, and their knowledge was tested repeatedly in examinations. Thus Confucianism became the ideology which upheld the state.

The Confucian system of values is orientated around Chinese antiquity. Its originator preached a return to the order and prosperity of the Western Zhu Period (11th century B.C.–771 B.C.) and to the rituals practiced then. As his maxim states, "Pass on what you have and do not create anything new. Be worthy of trust and honor the old ways." In the course of history, Confucianism has undergone various changes of emphasis, but without any alteration in its universal central core. This also refers to a hierarchically structured social order, with the emphasis on relationships within society, as against relationships with the outside world, and in the context of human pliability. As the state-approved doctrine, Confucianism helped the Chinese empire to shore up its legitimacy. It supported the hierarchical structure of society and the power of the rulers. However, at the same time it also foresaw the limitation of the ruler's power. It was subordinate to the welfare of society as a whole.

In an ideal Confucian society, every individual has a part to play, which stems from his or her social position, and this role has to be fulfilled responsibly and obediently. In this system, rulers and subjects, fathers and sons, husbands and wives, older and younger brothers, and older and younger friends are all given their relationships to one another. Moral conduct already has its basis in the nuclear form of society, the family. This ranking system can still be observed, even in the complicated networks of relationships in modern China. Even today, the way in which Chinese children are brought up lays the greatest emphasis on filial piety—obedience in everyday matters, care of the older generation, and veneration of the ancestors.

In the Confucian hierarchy, the ruler has to be virtuous, and to set an example to his subjects of morality and truthfulness. He should behave justly and resist any temptation to arbitrary use of power. Anyone who achieves perfection in virtuous and moral conduct and behaves morally to others is a "noble" (junzi). The concept was originally restricted to meaning "a son of a prince." Confucius freed it from its restrictions to a specific position in society and at the same time made it into a sociological concept. Now anyone could be a "noble," irrespective of his or her origins. Only education, conduct, and morality counted. Humane conduct and love of humanity became one of the essential characteristics that distinguished the nobles. "I will not do unto others what they should not do unto me."

The "Sayings of Confucius" have been interpreted, praised and criticized in many ways in the course of history by scholars with their own systems of thought. And still today, in spite of all the upheavals of the last century, Chinese society is distinguished by Confucian traits, as shown, for instance, by the seniority principle which everyone respects (the old take precedence). And many of the master's utterances are still relevant today—and are always quoted with approval in speeches, at banquets, and on other public occasions in China. For instance, Confucius said " To learn how to do something and then keep practicing

Far left: The simple monumental pillar erected in honor of Confucius.

Top left: The entire estate in Qufu—reputed to be the place where Confucius was born and died—comprises nine courtyards, around which are grouped almost 500 buildings.

Bottom left: Destroyed by the Communists in 1947, the estate has recently been conscientiously renovated and refurbished.

Facing page: No single work by Confucius has been handed down in written form, and there is certainly no authentic portrait of him. So even this sculpture is essentially based on the sculptor's imagination.

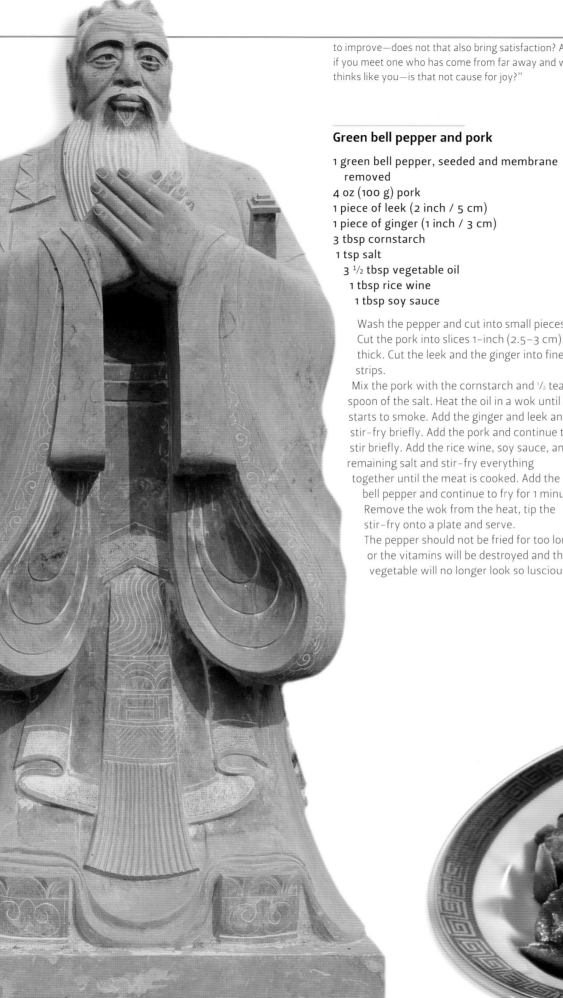

to improve—does not that also bring satisfaction? And if you meet one who has come from far away and who thinks like you—is that not cause for joy?"

Green bell pepper and pork

1 green bell pepper, seeded and membrane removed
4 oz (100 g) pork
1 piece of leek (2 inch / 5 cm)
1 piece of ginger (1 inch / 3 cm)
3 tbsp cornstarch
1 tsp salt
3 ½ tbsp vegetable oil
1 tbsp rice wine
1 tbsp soy sauce

Wash the pepper and cut into small pieces. Cut the pork into slices 1-inch (2.5–3 cm) thick. Cut the leek and the ginger into fine strips.

Mix the pork with the cornstarch and ½ teaspoon of the salt. Heat the oil in a wok until it starts to smoke. Add the ginger and leek and stir-fry briefly. Add the pork and continue to stir briefly. Add the rice wine, soy sauce, and remaining salt and stir-fry everything together until the meat is cooked. Add the bell pepper and continue to fry for 1 minute. Remove the wok from the heat, tip the stir-fry onto a plate and serve.

The pepper should not be fried for too long or the vitamins will be destroyed and the vegetable will no longer look so luscious.

Top: Whether the visitors to these halls find Confucian inspiration or cheap liquor is up to them.

Above: Visitors to the temple of Confucius leave small red plaques behind with their names, their wishes, their impressions or their prayers.

Confucian canon—the five classics

In the year 136 B.C., Wudi, an emperor of the Han dynasty, declared Confucianism to be the state philosophy. Henceforward everyone who wished to enter the civil service would have to study the so-called five classics (*Wu Jing*). These comprised the **Book of Changes** (*Yi Jing*), the **Book of Songs** (*Shi Jing*), the **Book of History** (*Shang Shu*), the **Book of Rites** (*Li Ji*), and the **Annals of Spring and Autumn** (*Chun Qiu*). They are standard works which were edited partly by Confucius himself and partly by his pupils, and which have been elevated to become the norm for society, for the law, and for governance, but also for education, literature, and religion.

A Sunday in Qingdao

In China, Sunday is a family day whenever possible. Substantial meals are then the first item on the program, together with a shared visit to the market. And that's a special pleasure in Qingdao. After all, the city's numerous markets are famous for offering extremely fresh produce—with the sheer endless variety of fresh-caught fish and seafood being top of the list. They are among the specialties of the great port. Chinese husbands are usually just as good at cooking as their wives. Indeed, as in many families the husband and wife both go out to work and they frequently work different hours, whoever arrives home first is usually the one who does the cooking on working days.

Here the civil servant Chen Yanliang (42) is at home with his wife Ji Yujun (40), who works in a bookshop. They live in an apartment measuring 970 square feet (90 sq m), into which they moved a few years ago with their pride and joy, their son, Chen Daxu (16). It is in the northern part of Qingdao, about 20 minutes from the center by automobile. Qingdao city and the surrounding districts have well over 7 million inhabitants. Sunday begins with an extended family breakfast—exceptionally, not until about 9 a.m. Chen Daxu reports on his schoolwork. Chen Yanliang and Ji Yujun talk about the previous week and plan their joint trip to the market.

Deep-fried pastry sticks are the son's favorite dish; Chen Yanliang likes marinated vegetables.

Chinese breakfast: steamed corn, tea eggs, pastry sticks, and marinated vegetables.

They stroll past all the market stalls and cast a glance at what's on offer.

The market is a shared pleasure, which the couple can not enjoy except on Sundays.

The question of who will look for fish and who will look for vegetables is a new problem every time.

First stop, the fish stall. They are famous far beyond Qingdao.

The fish are guaranteed to be fresh—caught here. You can see that many are still wriggling around.

Sharks' heads are a treasured specialty. In Qingdao, people like to use them to make soup. But today Ji Yujun and Chen Yanliang ignore the shark showing its teeth.

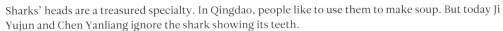

Instead they search through all the vast produce to find a well-proportioned fish for steaming.

In Qingdao you can find both marine and fresh-water eels, which are caught in the rice paddies.

Looking at the fresh zucchini, Chen Yanliang is thinking about suitable vegetables.

The choice available from the vegetable sellers of Qingdao is just as wide as that from the fish stalls—various types of cabbage, leek, cucumbers, celery, ...

... and here we have apples, lemons, melons, papayas, pomelos, and so on. Ji Yujun and Chen Yanliang are spoilt for choice with regard to fruit as well.

At home Ji Yujun carefully washes the fish, mussels, and shrimp.

Meanwhile Chen Yanliang cuts up the vegetables, together with the ginger, chiles, and leek.

Ji Yujun tests the fish on steamed yeast bread. There's Tsingtao beer to go with it.

Everything depends on good timing now. While the last cucumbers are being chopped up...

... the young garlic shoots are already sizzling in the wok.

Meanwhile the fish is being steamed on a second gas ring.

Nearby, the soy sauce for the table is prepared with ginger—everyone has a little bowlful.

The family enjoy their lunch. Chen Daxu is hungry—he's just come home from sport.

Chinese people like to eat lots of different things at all their meals—here we see mussels, garlic shoots, sugar tomatoes, fish, shrimp, and *mantou*—the dumpling-shaped yeast bread popular everywhere.

The family spends this Sunday afternoon at home—apart from a stroll through the green parts of the residential area. Chen Daxu tags along as well, and then spends the rest of the afternoon doing his homework, for there's an examination to come at the end of the school year. Then Ji Yujun and Chen Yanliang join forces in the kitchen again. While they're preparing the evening meal, they talk about their work, about both sets of parents, and about their son's approaching school-leaving examination. Today's meal is comparatively simple and inexpensive—but there are just as many dishes available nevertheless. Apart from rice soup, Chen Yanliang prepares pork with green bell peppers. For this, small pieces of meat are turned over in a mixture of salt and cornstarch and then fried with some spices. But first strips of ginger and leek are put into the heated wok. That gives the meat the special flavors! He also wants to make a garlic sauce for the cucumbers. These were originally supposed to be for lunch, but everyone forgot about them. Since Ji Yujun found some precooked diced beef in the supermarket as well as the *mantou* on her way home from the market, there's another dish for the evening meal, which now needs only to be briefly heated up.

When the aroma of leek and ginger starts to come from the wok, it is time to add the meat.

Ji Yujun cuts up the cucumbers for Chen Yanliang's soy sauce with garlic, vinegar, and salt.

Dried shrimp are ground in the mortar. This gives the sauce and cucumbers some "bite."

When it gets dark, Ji Yujun, Chen Yanliang, and Chen Daxu tuck in once more.

In China, people enjoy rice soup (congee) in the evening—but they do not miss out on sticky rice.

Later, the parents have tea and fruit and watch television. The young lad prefers his computer.

Here again, the evening meal in Qingdao at a glance: rice and rice soup, pork with green bell peppers, little pieces of braised beef and cucumbers in garlic sauce.

Universal harmony—Taoism

Taoism is the only religion which originated in China, and so it has a special place among the five religious systems officially recognized in the People's Republic—Buddhism, Taoism, Islam, Catholicism, and Protestantism. It is just as important as Confucianism in relation to the Chinese way of looking at the world and the Chinese system of values. Nowadays, a distinction is made between religious Taoism and philosophical Taoism—even though no clear borders can be drawn between the two. Both are based on the same writings from antiquity, but religious Taoism incorporated into itself some concepts from popular beliefs, Buddhism and Confucianism, and thus was always developing further.

The scholar Laotse ("Honored old master") is considered to have been the founder of Taoism. He is believed to have lived in China in the 6th century B.C. Legend has it that he fled into the west from the turmoils of war on an ox. In this way, he reached a frontier post. Since Laotse had no money, he wrote down his teachings in a single night in 5,000 characters and handed them over to the border guards as a toll. This is how the Taodejing was born—the "Guide to the Path and to its Virtue" (also referred to as "Laotse" for short), which formed the basis for both religious and philosophical Taoism. Current research now tends to think that this work dates from no earlier than the 4th century B.C., and was compiled by several scholars working together.

Philosophical Taoism

At the center of Taoism stands the Tao (frequently translated as "the path" or "the insight"). The guiding principle of the universe is considered to be the creation principle of all things, and is simultaneously present within them as the eternal and convertible changes of Nature. From this great unity, the forces of yin and yang go forth, the interaction of which determines all the processes of the universe. Yin represents the female, the passive, the Moon and darkness; Yang represents the male, the active, the Sun and light. Only when both are in equilibrium does harmony ensue. In their turn, yin and yang bring forth the three treasures, of which every being and everything are composed: essence (*jing*), spiritual energy (*shen*), and the life force (*qi*). Thus, according to Taoist beliefs, all living creatures and things in Nature are of equal value—in spite of all their different forms and shapes. The highest ideal of Taoism is the harmony of the universe. In order to promote this, each human being should live in harmony with the laws of Nature, the Tao.

This condition is attained if people embrace "non-interference" (*wuwei*), which means acting unconsciously of either Nature or the natural circumstances. Moreover, one should remain moderate in all things and not take any action to excess, as otherwise yin and yang will be brought out of harmony. This high regard for Nature and the emphasis on harmony within society still form the central constituents of Chinese culture.

Religious Taoism

Taoism's complex philosophical system of thought is believed to have flourished initially in the studies of the upper class. Indeed, it seemed to the simple folk that it had little relevance to their daily lives. Yet even the very first emperor of China, Qin Shi Huangdi (ruled 221–210 B.C.) was fascinated by the idea of becoming one with the eternal Tao and thus achieving immortality. He enlisted shamans and alchemists to manufacture elixirs and develop methods that could be used to conserve the life force, the qi, for ever. In the course of these researches, physical exercise and breathing exercises were developed—such as tai chi (shadow boxing), qigong, and also meditation and acupuncture. Many practices that are nowadays considered as part of traditional Chinese medicine (TCM), which also include a balanced diet and various sexual practices, stemmed from Taoist thought and from the idea that in a healthy body yin and yang are in harmony.

The mixture of philosophy and popular superstition led to institutionalization, with the founding of the "Sect of Heavenly Masters" in the late Han dynasty age (206 B.C.–220 A.D.). The basis of the faith was Laotse's teaching, the taodejing, and the veneration of Laotse and other Taoist scholars—for example, Zhuangzi (c. 350 B.C.) as saints. Five mountains were especially significant, being the home of the immortals and the region where the borders of life and death could be found. Even today, they are venerated as holy places—Taishan in Shandong province, Huashan in Shaanxi, Songshan in Henan, together with North Hengshan and South Hengshan in Hunan province. They are all characterized by forested slopes, which are otherwise rare in China. For Taoists, ascending the 6,600 steps to the summit of Taishan is still considered today to be a sacred duty and a spiritual act—like the journey to Mecca in the Muslim faith.

With the spread of Buddhism in China from the 7th century onward, the pantheon of Taoist saints was extended to include numerous deities which are not only active in the wide universe but also inhabit specific parts of the human body, and with which people must be on good terms. At the same time, the idea became current that on his journey west Laotse had reached India and that there he had been reincarnated as the Buddha. Thus there were also Taoists who translated some Buddhist sutras into Chinese for the first time, at the beginning of the 2nd century.

In the centuries which followed, various Taoist sects and communities grew up, each of which had a few monasteries. Only two of these are still of great importance today. The Zhenyi sect (Straightness and Unity) in south China emphasizes pious thinking and a retreat into solitude as the path to knowledge of the Tao. By contrast, the Quanzhen sect (Protection of the Truthful Ones), which has its headquarters located in the north, is distinguished by formal ordination

Top left: In general, Taoists can make sacrifices to their gods even at home, but special prayers are commonly emphasized by lighting joss sticks in a temple.

Bottom far left: The main feature of Taoism's holy places is the presence of large-scale temple buildings.

Left: Today there are over 1,500 Taoist temples and places of worship in China.

procedures and the strict cultivation of the spirit in communal monastic life. The first temple of the Quanzhen sect, the Baiyunguan (Temple of the White Cloud) in Beijing is today considered as being the center of Taoism in China, and is the headquarters of the Chinese Society of Taoists. The Tang emperor Xuan-zong (712–756) was the first to permit a temple to be erected in honor of Laotse, and presented a statue to it of the highly respected master, which can still be seen today.

Left: Taishan is one of the five holy mountains of Taoism.

Below: One must climb 6,293 steps, in a walk of over 5 ¹/₂ miles (9 km), to reach the top of Mount Taishan. Those who are short of breath—and agnostics—take the cable car instead.

Bottom: Laoshan, which is located east of Qingdao and is more a range of mountains than a single peak, is also a sacred site of Taoism.

Fish and seafood

Fish is a very popular food in China. Fish symbolize abundance, and so they form an essential ingredient of the New Year festivities and other celebrations. According to the teaching relating to yin and yang, they are considered to be a warming yang dish, which has a stimulating and vitalizing effect.

Dishes containing saltwater fish and seafood are found mainly in the repertory of the coastal regions of China. In Fujian province, Xiamen octopus and steamed abalone are very popular—abalone have been cultivated on a large scale in China since the mid-1980s.

But there are numerous fish dishes to be found, not only on the Chinese coasts but also in the provinces of the interior. And the essential point is the same everywhere—the fish must be fresh. So in China the lively fish swimming in the big tub in the market, in the water basin in the supermarket or in the aquarium at the restaurant is picked out as a delicacy only a short time before being prepared for the table. The most popular freshwater fish are carp, trout, and perch. Steamed river carp is a specialty in Shandong province and was a favorite dish as far back as the Tang period (618–907).

Shrimp with ginger

9 oz (250 g) shrimp
½ tsp salt
1 tsp Sichuan pepper

Sauce:
1 piece of ginger (1 inch / 3 cm)
2 tsp rice vinegar

Boil just enough water in a pan to cover the shrimp. Add the salt and pepper to the boiling water, then the shrimp and briefly cook until they turn pink. Finely chop the ginger and stir in with the vinegar. Drain the shrimp, put in a dish and pour over the sauce.

Venus mussels

generous 1 lb (500 g) Venus mussels (or preferred choice)
1 piece of ginger (1 inch / 3 cm)
3 tbsp vegetable oil
2 tbsp rice wine
1 tbsp soy sauce
1 tsp salt
1 tbsp sugar

Thoroughly scrub the mussels, pat dry, and discard any that do not open when firmly tapped. Cut the ginger into strips.
Heat the oil in a wok, add the ginger and stir-fry for 30 seconds, then add the mussels. Stir-fry at high heat until they open. Add the rice wine, soy sauce, salt, and sugar, and cook for 3–5 minutes over low heat. Discard any mussels that have not opened during cooking. Tip out into a dish, pour over the cooking juices and serve.

Steamed saltwater fish

1 piece of ginger (2 inch / 5 cm)
1 piece of leek (4 inch / 10 cm)
1 whole fish (about 1 ¼ lb / 500 g)
1 tsp salt
2 tbsp peanut oil
¾ oz (20 g) dried chiles, or to taste

Cut the ginger and leek into 1-inch (3-cm) strips. Clean fish thoroughly inside and out, remove the gills and tail. Make several cuts in both sides and rub in the salt.
Bring 1 scant cup (200 ml) water to a boil in a wok. Put the fish into a steamer and place over the boiling water. Alternatively, put the fish into a dish and place in a waterbath (bain marie) on an inverted rice bowl. Cover the wok with a lid and steam the fish for 10 minutes on high heat. Remove the fish and dry the wok. Heat the oil in the wok, and stir-fry the ginger, leek, and chiles together. Arrange the fish on a serving plate and pour over the sauce.

Top right: Whereas in Europe eating oysters is still associated with a certain degree of luxury, in China they are considered an absolutely normal delicatessen product.

Center right: Most mussel dishes in Chinese cuisine are basically less expensive to prepare than, for example, meat dishes.

Right: The precondition for real success though, is to have fine examples like these.

Poetic names for countless courses

Hardly anything plays such a big part in Chinese life as food—because people always have to eat, whatever their social position, whatever the time of day or night. Since the period of greater openness and reform in the mid-1980s at the latest, fast-food stalls and restaurants have sprung up like mushrooms popping out of the soil in the People's Republic, and there has been a return to a food culture which knew how to value diversity and flexibility. In Mao's China, both had been markedly reduced (for the ordinary people). Lunch was at noon and the evening meal was eaten between five and six o'clock. If you were late, there was nothing left for you.

Nowadays, the Chinese prefer to eat among a large circle of friends—the style is free and easy, expansive and, if possible, all at one table, which is almost bending under the dishes heaped upon it. Then everyone gets merry and there's a lot of noise for a while—and that's good, for the company is bound to be lively if things are going well.

The Chinese banquet has far more rules governing it. It is usually held to mark some significant occasion—such as the signing of a contract, a visit by a distinguished guest, the establishment of a company, a wedding, or else to celebrate new social relationships. However, except for formal business meals, people avoid talking shop. The festive spirit goes against that. Instead, people concentrate on ordinary and inconsequential subjects, such as Chinese history and culture, legends, local peculiarities and, naturally, the favorite topic—eating and drinking. That's why people keep inventing new descriptions for the dishes that crop up during a banquet.

There can be perhaps eight or ten people at a small banquet—as many as can fit round a restaurant table. At big banquets—for an occasion such as a marriage or the establishment of a company—hundreds of guests may sometimes be invited, and they are seated around several different tables. The big hotels in China are equipped to cater for a thousand or more guests at the same time.

At a classic banquet, the round table is graced by a luxurious flower arrangement. A glance at the menu is sufficient to convince yourself that you will not be going home hungry. A simply endless succession of courses is listed—there have to be at least eight or ten. The more courses there are and the more the host has spent on the meal, the pleasanter it is! The dishes often have poetic names and sometimes they only make a veiled allusion to their ingredients. Even experienced gourmets can not always work out what the grandiloquent descriptions mean. So there's only one thing for it—just wait until the delicacies appear.

The waitresses announce the arrival of the individual creations as they bring them in, but often not in a loud voice, just in a brief whisper. In the end, hardly any of the guests are listening. Each course has already been doled out into portions, and the guest of honor, sitting on the right of the host, is served first. Then the sequence goes around the table, and the host is served last. Only when the host picks up his chopsticks to start eating do the guests begin. The result of this is, quite frequently, that the delicacies do not melt on the tongues of the honored guests until they have become quite cold. At a big banquet with guests on several tables, this ritual applies only to the main table. The guests seated at the subsidiary tables are unaffected by this rule, and can all begin eating without waiting.

Bottom left: In contrast to the festive banquet, the food eaten, for example, at a birthday party, is far less controlled by rules.

Below: People usually drink tea. If alcohol is on offer, beer is normally preferred to wine (if only for reasons of cost).

Bottom right: Birthday cakes are on Western lines—and a deliberate contrast to the otherwise typically Chinese dishes on the table.

The art of carving also comes into play at the banquet. The individual courses are served in pleasant little portions and imaginatively decorated, for it is not the quantities but the variety and the appearance that are important. If the next course arrives while a guest is still busy with the previous one, the waitress puts the new plate down next to the previous one. And this can go on until the guest is surrounded by a number of colorful dishes (which have now gone cold). How guests deal with these culinary rules is left up to them. Thus at a banquet you are spared the embarrassment of continuously being offered second helpings by your host, or having them placed in front of you. This may not apply if you are served highly alcoholic beverages—but first we should mention a less awkward aspect of drinking. Traditionally, the standard green tea which is available everywhere is served at a banquet. Nowadays, young Chinese also opt for soft drinks or beer as a liquid accompaniment to a banquet. But the two are in no way mutually exclusive. It is perfectly normal for tea and alcoholic drinks to share the same table.

The tables often already have shot glasses on them. The Chinese feel more at home with highly alcoholic beverages made from grain than they do with wine. Expensive spirits flowed in rivers at banquets at one time—even at official gatherings paid for from the public purse. Recently good brands have become a cost factor, as a bottle of high-class spirits can cost as much as an imported malt whisky. On the other hand, knockoffs are considerably cheaper.

At a formal dinner, the host must propose the toasts— and not just to the guest of honor on his table. He turns his attention to all the other tables, so that in the course of the banquet he will reciprocally drink the health of each individual guest. He is accompanied by a protocol aide, who introduces the most important guests to him, and by a waitress who makes sure that the glasses are always full. These progresses through the crowd are a real challenge to the host's capacity to hold his drink—and in most cases he comes through with flying colors.

In the 1990s, a government directive imposed a ban on costly consumption of spirits and on banquets lasting more than 90 minutes. Since then, toasts are often drunk only in beer or wine. Anyone who passes by a banqueting hall in the provinces, and whose nostrils pick up the scent of highly alcoholic beverages, will see people clinking glasses in the dimly lit room full of chairs, which have been pushed back from the table for a long time, and will remember that this is a big country, and the emperor is far away. The banquet is over, the company has broken up long ago, but the good times are far from over.

Green beans potpourri

9 oz (250 g) green beans
1 thousand-year-old egg, optional (see p. 361)
1 egg
½ tsp salt
3 tbsp vegetable oil
2 garlic shoots, finely chopped
1 cup (50 g) fresh shrimp

Wash and trim the beans and cut into pieces ⅓ inch (1 cm). Dice the thousand-year-old egg, if using, and whisk the fresh egg in a bowl with the salt.
Heat 1 tablespoon oil in a wok, add the fresh egg and stir-fry. When the egg is cooked, but not yet dry, transfer to a plate. Heat the remaining oil in a wok, add the garlic and stir until it gives off an aroma. Add the shrimp and stir together until they turn pink. Add the beans, plus ½ a tea-bowl of water, and simmer until the beans are cooked. Mix in the stir-fried egg and thousand-year-old egg, if using.

Wok-fried squid

11 oz (300 g) squid
3 ½ tbsp vegetable oil
2 tbsp chopped onion
1 garlic clove
1 tsp black pepper
1 tbsp sa-cha sauce
1 tbsp hoisin sauce

Garnish:
1 tbsp chopped leek leaf
1 tbsp sesame seeds

Clean the squid and cut into pieces about 1 inch (3 cm) wide. Boil water in a saucepan and cook the squid for 2 minutes. Take it out and leave to drain on paper towels.
Heat the oil in a wok, and stir-fry the onions and garlic until they give off an aroma. Mix in the black pepper, sa-cha sauce, and hoisin sauce. Add the squid and heat through. Mix everything together and season. Serve garnished with the chopped leek leaf and sesame seeds.

Below: In China, it is taken for granted that men are also involved in preparing food—and has been for far longer than in the West.

江苏

Jiangsu

Katrin Schlotter

The coastal province of Jiangsu was known to the ancient Chinese world as "the land of fish and rice." Lying between Shanghai, Zhejiang, Anhui, and Shandong and covering approximately 40,000 square miles (103,000 sq km), it is one of the country's most affluent regions. The province's scenery is like a picture postcard; thanks to its subtropical climate, which bestows warm summers and wet winters, even the villages are wonderfully green all year round, unlike in the north of China. Countless canals, lakes, and pools full of lotus blossoms lie between rice and vegetable plantations, and the hills and mountains of the northern and southeast areas offer great hiking.

The province, which is home to more than 75 million people, has always been a key region. A spate of reforms was already well underway in Nanjing by the time that policies of greater openness were implemented in Shanghai. While Shanghai was still subject to socialist frugality, in the provincial capital department store shelves were creaking under the weight of merchandise, international joint-ventures were being launched, and foreign specialties were on offer in the shops. The very first nightclubs enticed party-goers to sample their delights into the small hours. As for infrastructure, in the 1990s Nanjing was in pole position. When China's first express line was constructed to run out of Shanghai, the railroad went not to Beijing, but to Nanjing. Along the way, it made the minor towns (by Chinese standards) of Suzhou and Wuxi more accessible from other parts of the country.

Jiangsu Province remains a model for China and the rest of Asia, and is one of the most popular international destinations. This goes for foreign investment, too: Suzhou, Nanjing, and many other towns in the province have transformed themselves into technological and commercial powerhouses, and thousands of international companies and branch offices have relocated here in order to benefit from the area's good infrastructure and the high level of education.

Yet Jiangsu has even more to offer than electronic, automobile, chemical, and IT industry on a country-wide and international level; like Zhejiang, the province is a center of silk production, and its capacity as an important food producer also contributes to its prosperity. The province's wealth has spread to everywhere apart from its northernmost reaches. Jiangsu's migrant workers invariably come from this area. Their richer countrymen are loath to leave their province—and who can blame them?

Top: Home to both heavy industry and park-like landscapes, Jiangsu has become an affluent model province.

Above: Suzhou's setting on the Grand Canal is the city's iconic image. It makes perfect sense that the "Venice of the East" has agreed to a twinning arrangement with the Italian "La Serenissima."

Facing page: Great waterways like the Yangtze (or Chang Jiang) are the backbone of the province's infrastructure.

Nanjing—China's "Southern Capital"

Mention Nanjing in a conversation with a Chinese person, and they're sure to pipe up, "Yes, one of the three ovens!" They are referring to Chongqing, Wuhan, and Nanjing itself, all cities on the Yangtze that suffer from extreme heat in the summer. In July and August, the mercury here soars far above 104 °F (40 °C). Unsurprisingly, life takes a much slower pace than in Shanghai, only 250 miles (400 km) away.

In spite of the difficult climate—or perhaps because of it—Nanjing is one of the most beautiful cities in China. Even following modernization, the streets are still lined with thousands of sycamores, which were originally planted to protect pedestrians from the glaring sunshine, and countless parks and lakes offer a place to relax and catch your breath right in the middle of the town.

The quality of life in Nanjing is not the only reason why it is one of China's most popular cities. It was founded back in the 4th century B.C. as Jinling, and soon began to profit from its favorable setting in the fertile Yangtze Delta, growing to become the trade hub of the region. This was reinforced by its role as capital of the province; its name literally means "southern capital." If the nomadic peoples on the northern border of China ever grew stronger or even conquered parts of China, the imperial court would withdraw to the safety of Nanjing.

In more recent times, however, the fate of the city was not an entirely happy one. In 1850 Hong Xiuquan (1813–1864), the leader of the Taiping Rebels and self-proclaimed brother of Jesus Christ, chose Nanjing as the capital of his "Heavenly Kingdom." Using a mixture of Christian promises of salvation and quasicommunist ideology he managed to control all of southern China from his base at Nanjing.

The Qing emperor's troops only succeeded in defeating the movement with foreign help in 1864, and 100,000 people were killed in Nanjing alone during the struggle. The dynasty ceased to exist in 1911, and Nanjing became the capital of the new Republic. Sun Yat-sen (1855–1925), the founder of the Republic, was buried on a picturesque hillside located just outside the city.

Nanjing won new notoriety during World War II. In 1937 the Japanese army conquered the city and massacred around 300,000 people over the course of three days—a third of the city's population! Nevertheless, it did not take long for Nanjing to regain its former standing. By the end of the 1960s the city had become a symbol of Chinese self-sufficiency; in spite of Soviet-Chinese disagreements, Chinese engineers single-handedly completed a jointly planned, two-tier bridge over the Yangtze. From then on the structure was proudly presented to every group of visitors from abroad.

Today the city, with a population of 6 million, is not only the provincial capital, but also China's largest domestic harbor and one of the country's most important cities for education. Even back in the imperial age, the top public examination authorities in southern China were based in Nanjing, and today numerous universities, academies, and technical schools cater to a large student population, while Nanjing University is one of the country's top five colleges. As a result, Nanjing developed a buzzing nightlife long before Shanghai. Among the restaurants and bars there is also an array of beer gardens; for unlike their compatriots elsewhere in China, the city's residents take pleasure in sitting outside.

Later in the evening, visitors from all over the south of the city flock to the area around the

Below left: The foundations of Nanjing are said to have been laid as early as 495 B.C.—today skyscrapers also loom over traditional Chinese architecture on the city's misty skyline.

Below: Wide avenues are typical of the pedestrian zones in the provincial capital.

Bottom: Today the city's nightlife is concentrated in the area around the Confucius temple, where prostitution had once thrived before the Communist takeover.

Confucius temple on the Qinhuai river. A veritable amusement quarter has sprung up around the temple complex. Where once "ladies of the night" furtively enticed their clients onto boats, today both roadside stalls and specialty restaurants provide the temptation—demonstrating that Nanjing is not only a place of historical interest, but also a heavyweight on the gastronomic scene.

Left: At first glance, Nanjing's skyline does not look markedly different from other Chinese megacities.

Bottom left: Yet the city's charm can be uncovered in many places.

Below: Pedestrianized zones are guarded by mythical creatures!

Bottom: The old city wall is an eloquent testament to the past.

Nanjing salted duck

1 duck 4 ½ lb (2 kg)
1 ½ tbsp salt
2 tsp Sichuan pepper
1 tsp five-spice powder
1 ½ tbsp rice vinegar
1 small scallion
1 piece of ginger (1 ½ inch / 4 cm), chopped
1 star anise

Rub the duck inside and out with the salt, Sichuan pepper and five-spice powder and leave to stand for 2 hours.
Steep the duck in salted water for another hour, then remove and rinse well. Fill a wok with water and add the duck, along with the vinegar, the white bit of the scallion, the ginger, and the star anise, and bring to a boil over high heat. Leave to simmer, uncovered, for 20 minutes.
Turn over the duck and leave to simmer for another 20 minutes, until the meat is tender.
Then take it out, leave to cool, slice, and serve. What makes this dish so special is the oily sheen of the duck's skin, and the succulence, flavor, and exceptional tenderness of the meat.

A subtle sensation—Jiangsu cuisine

As the principal city, bread-basket, and the main commercial hub on the lower reaches of the Yangtze river, over the years Jiangsu's cuisine has become one of the eight great cooking traditions in China. The area between the mighty rivers Huaihe and Yangtze is the core region of Jiangsu cuisine, and the origin of the name "Huaiyang" cuisine.

At first glance it doesn't seem much to write home about. The Jiangsuese treat spices in the same way that they treat their money: they have it, but they don't flash it around. Extreme flavors are anathema to Jiangsu cuisine. Everything must work together in harmony: no spice should take center-stage or muscle its way to the fore; no ingredient should overwhelm the others. Chiles, garlic, onions or cilantro— all are used in moderation, and ultimately the unique taste of the combination of ingredients should take precedence. Chefs simply bring out the flavor with some salt and sugar, and let it develop by stewing or braising it, or preparing it in a stock. One glug of good soy sauce, or the famous dark, sweet Zhenjiang vinegar (see p. 114), should round off the taste.

The mild climate and fertile marshy land have given Jiangsu cuisine a very rich palette of ingredients. Not only does Jiangsu lie on the coast, but it is also the Chinese province most abundant with water. The flat landscape is scored by canals and rivers, forming pools full of lotus flowers or accumulating in great lakes. It is hardly surprising that Jiangsu is one of the foremost fish-farming areas in China. Around 140 species of fish cavort in the waters of the province, including mandarin fish, carp, grass carp, eel, cutlassfish, drums, and butterfishes. Ducks and geese, along with tortoises, frogs, crabs, and crayfish, feel at home in the wetlands and marshy areas until, at last, well-nourished, they end up in Jiangsu's kitchens. Lake Yangcheng's fame as the home of the large, succulent Dazha crab (see p. 110) has spread far and wide.

So long as dams and canals continue to regulate the powerful waters, agriculture also benefits from the marshy land. Rice and wheat flourish here, along with corn, millet, and soybeans. Peanuts, sesame, bamboo tea, and wild herbs grow in abundance, as do mulberry and fruit trees laden with apples, pears, loquats, and peaches.

From the cornucopia of local ingredients provided by the region's soil and water, Jiangsu's chefs have created scores of specialties, some with rather startling names, such as "lionhead meatballs" or "squirrel fish." Contrary to what you might expect, the former refers to balls of crabmeat or pork wrapped in green cabbage, like a lion's mane, while the latter is a type of fish whose head resembles a squirrel. Jiangsu pancakes, which contain scallions or thin strips of tofu with bamboo, mushrooms, chicken or crabmeat, seasoned with sesame oil and coriander, have also put it on the map. However, all these delicious dishes pale in comparison with the famous duck dishes from Nanjing. Whether as a soup, steamed, roasted, dried or delicately flavored with cinnamon flowers, duck is considered a real treat well beyond the borders of Jiangsu.

Royal soup with green vegetables

generous l lb (500 g) fresh spinach
2 eggs
1 tbsp cooking oil
1 piece of leek (¾ inch / 2 cm), finely chopped
1 tsp salt
1 tbsp sesame oil
1 tsp light soy sauce

Wash the spinach and pat dry. Whisk the eggs in a bowl.
Heat the wok, add the oil and, when warm, sauté the leek in the oil. Add 1 quart (1 liter) water and bring to a boil. Add the spinach and cook briefly. Add the eggs, along with the salt, and drizzle the sesame oil and the soy sauce over the top. Pour the mixture into bowls and serve.

Left: The standard of living is relatively high in Nanjing, and the city's restaurants are always busy.

Bottom left: With the sparkling new world as a backdrop, an occasional snack tastes twice as good.

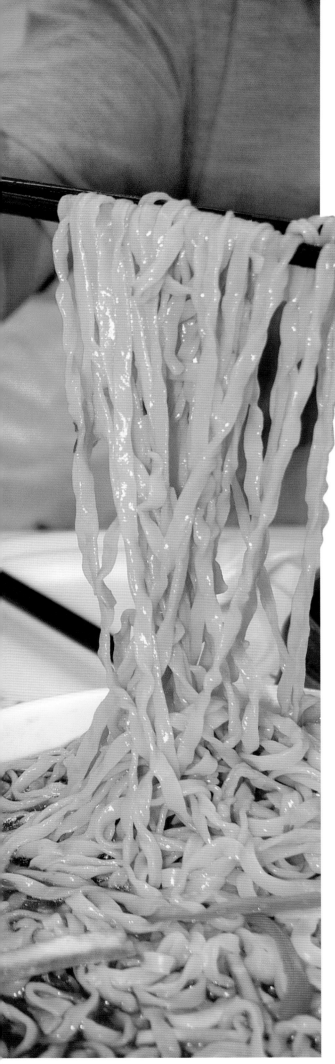

Bok choy with shiitake mushrooms

14 oz (400 g) bok choy
$1/3$ cup (75 ml) peanut oil
3 $1/2$ tbsp chicken stock
1 tsp salt
$1/2$ tsp sugar
5 $1/2$ oz (150 g) fresh shiitake mushrooms
2 tsp Shaoxing rice wine
    1 tsp cornstarch mixed with 2 tsp water
    2 tsp chicken dripping or schmaltz

Wash the bok choy, and score the stalks across.

Heat 3 $1/2$ tablespoons oil in a wok, add the bok choy and sauté until they turn light green, then remove from the wok, and pour off the oil until there is only about 1–2 tablespoons left.

Add half of the chicken stock, half the salt, and the sugar. Stir-fry everything until it gives off a good aroma, then remove from the wok and arrange on a plate.

Put 1 $1/2$ tablespoons fresh oil in the wok, add the remaining chicken stock, the shiitake mushrooms, the rice wine, the remaining salt and sugar, and sauté, then bind together with the cornstarch–water mixture. Trickle the chicken dripping through the mixture, pour the sauce from the wok over the bok choy, and serve immediately.

Lionhead meatballs

9 oz (250 g) pork belly
40 g shepherd's purse
few leaves of bok choy
$1/2$ tsp salt
$1/4$ tsp ground white pepper
1 tsp Shaoxing rice wine
1 tbsp egg white
$1/2$ tsp cornstarch
1 tsp minced ginger
3 oz (80 g) crab roe
9 oz (250 g) spare ribs
1 tbsp chopped scallions

Chop the pork belly meat into pieces with a kitchen cleaver and put through a meat grinder. Discard the outer leaves of the shepherd's purse and chop finely. Wash the bok choy leaves and pat dry.

Mix the ground pork with salt, white pepper, and rice wine. Stir the egg white thoroughly, then add the cornstarch, minced ginger and shepherd's purse, and mix into the meat. Season the crab roe to taste, and stir into the mixture. Form the mixture into four round meatballs, cover, and set aside. Heat the wok. Place the spare ribs and scallions in the wok, add a little water and bring to a boil. Skim off any foam that rises to the top. Place the meatballs in the wok, skim off any remaining foam, and simmer gently for 2 hours over low heat.

Remove the spare ribs. Add the bok choy and serve the meatballs from the pot.

Left: What noodles were made for— loading up your chopsticks.

Right: Bok choy with shiitake mushrooms (background) and lionhead meatballs (foreground).

All over the place—Chinese vegetables

The importance of vegetables for the Chinese is evident in their language. The character *cai* means both "vegetable" and "dish." After rice or noodles, vegetables are the second-most important foodstuff, and are served according to the season and region, dried or marinated in the kitchen and then served lightly steamed, fresh and crisp, stir-fried or deep-fried.

Of more than a hundred types of vegetable native to China, 60 grow in this region. Archaeological discoveries show that many typically Chinese vegetables, such as cabbage, soybeans, bamboo shoots, taro, lotus root, melon, pumpkin, and water chestnuts, were used as early as the Han dynasty (202 B.C.–A.D. 220). A wander through any Chinese market reveals the country's rich and bizarre array of vegetables, many of which can also be found in Asian supermarkets worldwide. Here is just a small selection of what is on offer:

Bitter melon (*Mormodica*), also called bitter cucumber, is a gourd vegetable that has been popular as a food and medicinal substance all over Asia for centuries. It looks like a light green cucumber with warts, and contains a sticky red pulp. After being blanched or steeped (to remove the bitterness), it can be cooked—stuffed with flaked fish, ginger, coriander, and soy sauce, and then roasted, or chopped and used to make Thousand-year-old eggs (see p. 361).

Similar to a mango or pear, **chayote** (*Sechium edele*)—also a gourd, but with only one core—is light green in the middle and tastes vaguely like a cucumber or cabbage. Both the roots and the young leaves are edible, however, and can be added to soup or cooked in the same way as spinach. The chayote fruit is normally cooked, but can be grilled, fried, or served raw as a side dish in Chinese cuisine.

The stalks of Chinese **celery** (*Apium graveolens var. dulce*) are darker than the European variety and have a more distinctive taste. This makes them popular in salads, particularly the young stalks; the stringy strands should be removed from the more mature stalks beforehand. But celery also makes an appearance on the lunch menu almost everywhere in China as a wok vegetable—perhaps together with strips of chicken breast in a stock of sesame oil, soy sauce, and rice wine.

Okra (*Abelmoschus esculentus*) is one of the longest-established vegetables, with six- to eight-pointed capsule fruits (pods) that can grow up to 8 inches (20 cm) long. The low-calorie okra pods, which taste a little like green beans, are light to dark green, and ooze a viscous substance when cooked, which is ideal for thickening sauces. Anyone who dislikes this viscous substance can soak the okra pods in cold lemon-infused water for 1–2 hours before preparation, or blanch them rapidly (having removed the stalks and topped and tailed them) and then plunge them into cold water.

Left: The best possible use of the land: vegetable cultivation on the Grand Canal.

Below left: The hustle and bustle of the night markets always makes for an adventure.

Right: The market economy works brilliantly here.

Below right: Very few cooks buy prepacked goods in China.

The ability of the **lotus** (*Nelumbo*) to repel dirt has made it a symbol for purity and enlightenment in Buddhist cuisine. In China it represents love, marital harmony, and loyalty (the words sound the same). In Chinese cuisine all parts are used: the leaves (to wrap sticky rice, for instance); the seeds served candied, dried or fresh, and used for their healing properties in Buddhist cuisine (eight treasure dishes); but above all the lotus roots, fresh or pickled as a side dish or a salad, or dried in stews.

Daikon or *Chinese radish* (*Raphanus sativus* var. *longipinnatus*) is a mild-flavored, very large radish with firm and juicy flesh. It is a vital ingredient in Japanese cuisine, but can be found all over China, where it is eaten raw or pickled, for example in the traditional Mooli cake at New Year, as a garnish or in soup, as a sauce, or in salads.

The underground storage roots of the **sweet potato** (*Pomoea batatas*) are eaten in the first instance, but the leaves may also be used. The People's Republic of China is the biggest producer of this, the most important edible root or tuber after potatoes and manioc (135 million US tons/124 million tonnes in 2007). Its sweet taste comes from its high sugar content. Apart from water, carbohydrates, protein, and starch, the tuber also has a number of other nutrients, including vitamins such as potassium, calcium, and zinc. In China the sweet potato may be boiled, baked, deep-fried or roasted. It can also be baked, unpeeled, inside the oven.

For more than 2,000 years, **taro corms** (*Colocasia esculenta*) have been cultivated principally in the humid, tropical climate zones of America, Africa, and Southeast Asia. Like potatoes, taro corms are important for providing starch for people in manufacturing countries like China. They are skinned and then repeatedly cooked in salted water so that they lose their viscous substance (poisonous calcium oxalate), which must be removed by pouring it away with the cooking water at least once. Taro corms can also be baked, broiled or deep-fried.

Water spinach (*Ipomoea aquatica*) has long, tapering, dark green leaves and tall stalks, and is widespread in Asia. It is particularly prized in Thai and Chinese cuisine—in China primarily as a summer vegetable, often accompanied by shrimp paste.

Winter melon (*Benincasa hispida*), also called Chinese winter melon, has a protective layer (cuticle) which prevents water loss from the inner tissue. In other respects this large, dark green gourd bears some resemblance to a watermelon, although its flesh is white to light green, crunchy and juicy. Winter melons are grown all over Southeast Asia, especially in the Philippines and China. Here both ripe and unripe fruit are eaten, whether raw, canned or added to soup. On festive occasions the hollowed-out shell is decorated with carvings and used as a soup tureen.

Yam (*Dioscorea*) can be found in tropical climate zones in every continent; the longish tubers, which grow underground, have dark brown to black skin, can grow up to 6 ½ feet (2 m) in length, and taste sweet, similar to sweet chestnuts and potatoes. The root, which is rich in A provitamins like potassium, is also an important source of starch in China. Eaten raw, however, yam roots are toxic.

Sugarsnap peas (*Pisum sativum* macrocarpon), also called mange tout or snow peas, are one of the world's most popular varieties of peas, and are predominantly grown in India and China (followed by the US, France, and the UK). The succulent and sweet pods are eaten along with the undeveloped peas inside the young pods. Sugarsnap peas are a wonderful and versatile wok vegetable, for example with beef and noodles, in a stock made of oyster- and soy sauce, rice wine, meat broth, ginger, and scallions, or together with abalone and mushrooms.

KIRSTEN E. LEHMANN

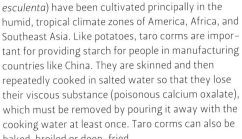

Left: Chiles are used very sparingly in Jiangsu cuisine.

Below left: Eggplants feature among the summer vegetables used in Chinese and Jiangsu cuisine.

Below: It's a no-go without scallions.

Right: The markets are a veritable El Dorado for vegetable lovers.

Below right: A rare sight: prepackaged Chinese cabbage.

Left: Romantic, idyllic, yet vast: at over 850 square miles (2201 sq km), Lake Tai, Wuxi, is China's third largest freshwater lake.

Below: Jiangsu's cities were the first to benefit from China's opening-up policies, but the march of modernization has stifled many things that were worthy of preservation.

Between Suzhou and Lake Tai

The city of Suzhou is associated with the finest things that China has to offer: the most beguiling women are said to live here (a reputation that proceeds more from their charming accent, rather than their beauty), the loveliest gardens, the most romantic streets and, last but not least, the most picturesque canals. All these clichés have survived in spite of radical modernization.

Even though the city is relatively small, with approximately one million inhabitants in the downtown, it has proved one of the beneficiaries of reformist politics. International firms were positively encouraged to relocate here so as to profit from the proximity to Shanghai; thanks to the latest thing in motorways, the megacity—traffic permitting—is only half an hour away. Foreigners particularly appreciate its small-town flair on Shanghai's doorstep.

Yet Suzhou took its place among China's most important cities long before the period of reforms. As early as the 5th century B.C. it flourished for a short time as the capital of the Wu Kingdom, one of the many principalities fighting for supremacy in China's "Warring States Period." Its heyday really began, however, with the Sui dynasty (581–618); its location at the southern end of the Grand Canal, built in the 7th century, allowed the local merchants to amass real treasures. Suzhou became synonymous with a pleasant, sophisticated lifestyle. The small, luxurious city soon became the ideal retreat for wealthy officials and artists, who kept second residences in Suzhou, and tried to outdo one another with the design of their gardens. These private gardens were places of contemplation, for receiving guests, holding concerts, or drinking tea, especially Bi Luo

Chun, a green tea from the slopes of nearby Dongting mountain.

Today many notable gardens remain; over a hundred adorn the city, and seven of them are designated UNESCO World Heritage sites. All of them are bizarre, dark limestone crags centered round a pond. These rocks have always come from Lake Tai, and are prized by garden-lovers for their beauty, with no expense spared. Lake Tai's fame grew with the evening soap opera "The People of Tai" (one of the most popular series ever to be filmed in China). In fact, China's third-largest lake covers 870 square miles (2,253 sq km), but has an average depth of only 6 ½ feet (2 m). This means that in summer it warms up quickly, to 93 °F (34 °C) — an ideal habitat for algae! In May 2007 the lake was disturbed by a blue-green algae bloom, and 2 million people were cut off from drinking

Silk: From Cocoon to Cloth

Silk comes from the spinning thread of the silkworm caterpillar (*Bombyx mori*), which it uses to make its cocoon, developing into a pupa, before emerging as a butterfly. During pupation, the caterpillar feeds solely on mulberry leaves; 485 lb (220 kg) of mulberry leaves must be eaten in order to produce 2 ¼ lb (1 kg) of raw silk. After a growth phase of around six weeks, the ¾–1 ½ inch-long (3–4 cm) pupa is killed by hot steam and the cocoon is swirled in boiling water until the end of the spinning thread works itself free. Up to ten threads, stuck together by sericin, an agent unique to the silk, combine to produce a relatively

thick thread, which is twisted again with other threads until it becomes sufficiently strong for further processing. The type of silk produced by this method depends on the frequency and intensity of the thread-twisting. Crêpe silk, for example, has a creased appearance because it contains threads that have been twisted in different directions. Suzhou is the center of the silk industry and is famous throughout China and abroad for its satin and brocade, as well as embroidered silk.

Left: Healthy minds in healthy bodies—groups of people practicing Tai Chi are an everyday sight in Chinese parks and public squares.

Below: Suzhou's narrow streets are best negotiated on two wheels.

Bottom: A spur-of-the-moment sale is quickly accomplished if the buyer is on a bicycle.

water for ten days. To prevent such a catastrophe from recurring in the future, hundreds of industrial plants were closed, and the Chinese government aims to spend approximately 20 million yuan (about 3 million US dollars) by 2012 on improving the water quality. Visitors will find peaceful views, and fish and crabs from Lake Tai take pride of place on menus all over the region.

The roughly 2 million inhabitants of the city of Wuxi, on the northern shore of the lake, also have reason to be glad. Wuxi's place among the most wealthy cities in Jiangsu can be attributed not only to its fantastic transportation connections with Shanghai and Nanjing, but also to the municipal council's economic foresight back in the 1990s, when it succeeded in attracting many foreign investors.

Indeed, the region can look back on a long history of economic innovation. As early as the 3rd century B.C., silk production spread from here to the whole of China. Many other countries now also produce silk, but almost 60 percent of silk produced worldwide comes from the Middle Kingdom. Indeed, today 10 million Chinese women farmers (silkworm breeding is traditionally a female role) cultivate silkworm larvae, and the cocoons are processed in more than 600 spinning mills across the country.

Deep-fried spinach

5 ½ oz (150 g) fresh leaf spinach
2–3 tbsp dried shrimp
1 ¾ oz (50 g) fatty pork
several pieces of winter bamboo shoots
several fresh shiitake mushrooms
1–2 tsp salt
1 tbsp Shaoxing rice wine
½ tsp onion juice
1 ¾ oz (50 g) tofu skin
½ cup (120 g) egg white
1 tsp all-purpose flour
½ tsp cornstarch
2 ½ oz (75 g) peanut oil

Wash the spinach, then blanch briefly in the water clinging to the leaves, squeeze out as much as possible, and chop into small pieces. Chop the dried shrimp, and dice the fatty pork, several bamboo shoots and shiitake mushrooms to taste. Place the spinach in a bowl and add the salt, rice wine, and onion juice, and mix everything to form stuffing.

Cut the tofu skin into round slices. Divide the spinach stuffing between the slices of tofu skin. Beat the egg white until it forms stiff peaks, then add the flour and cornstarch, and blend in. Put the peanut oil in a wok and heat over medium temperature. Dip the slices of tofu, with their spinach topping, into the egg white and then carefully place them in the wok. When the pieces bob to the surface, turn them over with a chopstick, then remove from the wok and allow to drain on paper towels. Leave the oil in the wok and heat once again to medium temperature. Add the drained tofu slices a

second time and deep-fry until they appear golden, then remove, allow the excess oil to drip off, and serve on a plate.

There are various ways of making onion juice, e.g. from 2 ½ oz (75 g) shallots, ½ cup (125 ml) sesame oil, 3 tablespoons peanut oil, 1 tablespoon ground white pepper, 2 tablespoons salt and 2 cups (500 ml) of boiled water.

Chinese gardens—a cosmos in miniature

Although they look almost as though they are untouched by human hands, in Chinese gardens nothing has been left to the whim of nature. Here there is one sole purpose: to amuse the visitor and offer a beautiful prospect. The Chinese garden is intended to depict the universe in miniature form, and all its elements (the so-called "seven things"— earth, sky, stone, water, buildings, paths, and plants) combine in utter harmony, allowing the life energy, the *qi*, to flow unhindered.

As is so often the case in China, the design of the gardens is based on the two cosmic principles of yin and yang. Everything in the universe is attributed to these forces, and so are the main components of landscaping: rocks and water. In Chinese feng shui, the rocks represent the "bones" of the earth, and stand for the masculine yang principle, while water symbolizes the "veins" and represents the female yin force. The Chinese word *shanshui*, meaning landscape, derives from this; it is made up of the words *shan* (mountain) and *shui* (water). As in painting, the individual elements of the design play a minor part; instead, the interplay of the different components, and thus the overall appearance of the garden, must enchant the viewer.

The Chinese garden, as a place of edification and contemplation, inspires the visitor and allows him to relax. Evoking this feeling of relaxation is the landscape gardener's aim, and he is adept at steering the visitor toward it. Serpentine walkways, miniature ponds, little bridges, and the subtle fragmentation of the gardens by stone walls allow the life energy to flow freely, while also giving a sense of space. Cleverly placed "windows" lead the visitor's gaze; at any given time he only has a partial view, and the same elements are presented to him time and time again from different perspectives. The outside world is also integrated into the picture; trees that are far outside the garden walls are brought into the composition, giving the illusion of a rambling park. Chinese landscape architects are such masters of their art that even those who are aware of all this fall under their spell. Anyone who has strolled through Shanghai's Yu garden for hours on end will be astounded when he sees the area that it covers on a map: only five acres!

Even the arrangement of the plants is an art in its own right. Every flower and shrub has a meaning. Bamboo stands for perseverance and flexibility, while the hibiscus represents fame and riches. Yet others, such as pine trees or cypresses, symbolize longevity because they are long-living plants. The composition of the plants and flowers is also chosen in such a way that there is a harmonious vista of flowers at any time of year.

The Chinese gardens of today have a considerable heritage. The earliest gardens existed as early as the Zhou dynasty (1066–221 B.C.), and landscaped gardens full of nooks and crannies really came into fashion in the Tang dynasty (618–907). This golden age, which blossomed due to the thriving economy, first saw the construction of countless private gardens. Officials, wealthy literati, and artists built them as retreats, as havens of peace and inspiration. The private gardens of Suzhou, in particular,

Above left: Chinese gardens aim to enchant rather than impress.

Below left: The first bonsai gardens existed in China back in the early Han dynasty (206 B.C.–A.D. 220).

Right: The harmonious overall view of water and plants makes up the charm of a Chinese garden. A city like Suzhou, criss-crossed by canals, is simply made for the creation of private gardens.

are full of allusions to classical Chinese culture which the Western visitor may have difficulty in grasping. Often the gardens are inspired by literary works, or modeled on scenes from famous paintings. The "Garden of the Master of the Net" recalls the "Saga of the Peach Blossom Spring" by the poet Tao Yuanming (365–427). In this work a penniless fisherman discovers a paradise where people live their lives unencumbered by humdrum cares. Today, China's gardens still succeed in bringing this beautiful idea to life.

Top: The art of *Penjing* (the Chinese version of bonsai) led to the development of regional schools and styles.

Above left: "Seeing the big picture in the small one," as the saying goes. In landscape gardening this means creating trees and whole scenes in miniature.

Middle left: Gardens should blend in harmoniously with other architecture.

Left: Walkways, pavilions, and places to sit afford the visitor peace and relaxation, allowing the overall scene to work its magic.

Chinese gardens—a cosmos in miniature   **109**

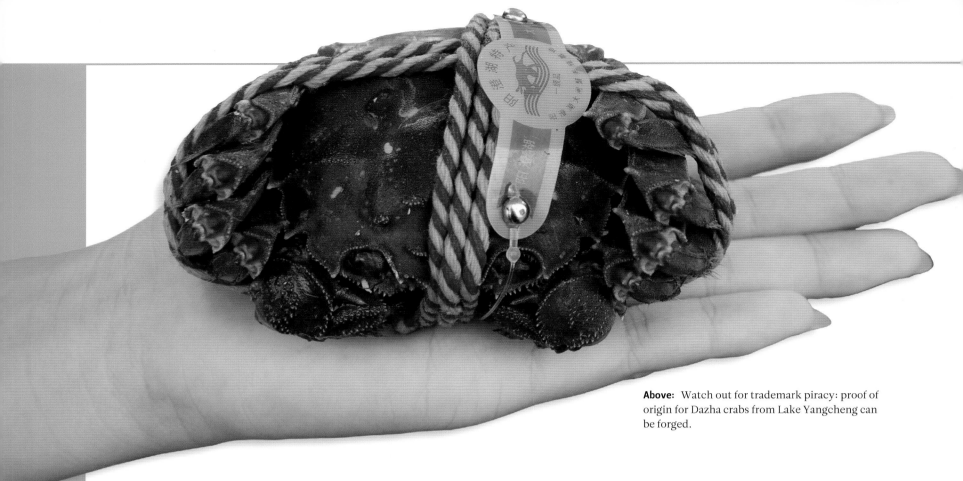

Above: Watch out for trademark piracy: proof of origin for Dazha crabs from Lake Yangcheng can be forged.

Dazha crabs from Lake Yangcheng

When the golden chrysanthemum blooms, the osmanthus trees start to exude their sweet fragrance, and cold winds drive away the summer heat, the great moment has arrived: the beginning of the Dazha crab season. Between October and December there is intense activity all over Jiangsu's lakes, especially Lake Yangcheng, near Suzhou, which is home to the original and best Dazha crabs.

The crabs, which weigh approximately 7 oz (200 g) and have shells the size of rice bowls, are known in the United States as Chinese mitten crabs (*Eriocheir sinensis*). They tickle the palates of gourmets year after year, not only in Jiangsu, but all over China. Gastronomes recognize the original Dazha crab by its powerful pincers with yellowish tips, its dark green, iridescent shell, hairy legs, and white underside, and, above all, by its formidable size, firm meat, and unique slightly sweet taste. This exceptional flavor is due to the clear, nutrient- and mineral-rich water and the ferrous, muddy bottom of Lake Yangcheng. In the fall hordes of gastronomes descend on Jiangsu Province, as they all insist on obtaining the coveted crab at the source, or, better still, sampling it in one of the many restaurants devoted to this specialty.

Whether it is steamed, roasted, deep-fried, or cooked in a hotpot, and whether the recipe calls for leg meat, pincers, roe, or sperm, there are myriad methods of preparation. Traditionally the Dazha crabs are steamed for about 15 minutes (according to size), whereupon they turn bright red, and are then served whole, accompanied by dark Zhenjiang vinegar spiced up with some sugar and chopped ginger. Many restaurants dismember the crabs for the patrons or offer dishes made with particular parts of the crab, such as pincer meat with asparagus tips, or crab roe with tofu. A sumptuous crab banquet can run to 12 courses, and rice wine flows freely.

Left: As the year starts to draw to a close, the crab fishing season at Lake Yangcheng is only just beginning.

If, in days gone by, the poets praised the Dazha crab's juicy meat and roe to the skies as sweet and succulent, extolling its white jade and golden yellow sheen, today it is the market strategists who have unleashed a "Dazha boom" in Shanghai, Hong Kong, and Beijing—a demand that Lake Yangcheng is now barely able to satisfy. Since vast numbers of supposedly authentic Dazha crabs have suddenly flooded the market, the crab suppliers have reacted by providing a proof of origin label with their true-bred Dazha crabs. Yet even printed identification numbers can be forged, so that crabs from other lakes can end up in the table, masquerading as "Dazha crabs." To make matters worse, due to environmental concerns and quality control measures, Lake Yangcheng's fishing areas have been halved to 52 acres (21 ha). It comes as no surprise that both the price of the original Dazha crab and its status as a luxury foodstuff are soaring. The question of whether crabs from Lake Yangcheng really do have firmer, more flavorsome meat than those from nearby lakes can only be confidently answered by epicures in situ—but only when the osmanthus trees are giving off their sweet scent.

Dazha crabs

1 ¼ lb (600 g) Dazha crabs
2 red bell peppers, seeds and membrane removed
2 green bell peppers, seeds and membrane removed
vegetable oil, for frying
cornstarch, for dredging
1 tbsp minced ginger
1 tsp minced garlic
3 red Tuscan peppers/peperoncini
1 tsp soy sauce
1 tsp fish sauce
½ tsp salt
sesame oil
pinch of freshly ground white pepper
½ cup (125 ml) water
½ tsp cornstarch mixed with 2 tbsp water

Rinse the crabs, then cut into 4–6 pieces, but leave the pincers intact. Chop the peppers into small pieces.
Heat the oil at a high temperature, dust the crab pieces with some cornstarch and deep-fry in the oil until they turn golden. Remove them and leave to drain.
Pour off the oil until there is only about 2 tablespoons left.
Heat the oil at a high temperature, sauté the ginger, garlic, peperoncini and chopped bell peppers until it gives off a good aroma, return the crab pieces to the wok and stir-fry everything together.
Add the soy sauce, fish sauce, salt, a little sesame oil, pepper and the water and bring to a boil. Bind everything together with the cornstarch mixture and serve.

Above: With their powerful pincers, shimmering shells, hairy legs, and white underside, Dazha crabs are considered by gourmets to be the pick of the bunch.

Below: Ever since Lake Yangcheng's fishing areas were decimated, its crabs have become utter delicacies, and are particularly sought after in haute cuisine.

An idyllic land of water

Anyone who goes to China looking for the clichéd image of the Middle Kingdom common in the West is often disappointed. The "Land of Water," which lies west of Shanghai is, however, the exception. With scenery straight out of a picture book, China is at its most charming here: small towns with crooked cottages from the Ming (1368–1644) and Qing dynasties (1644–1912), canals sheltered by willows and busy with quaint boats, whose pilots wear pointed straw hats, a visual prompt for China the world over. The watery landscape on the border between southern Jiangsu and northern Zhejiang belongs to noticeably wealthy "Jiangnan" (literally "south of the river"), the region south of the Yangtze's final loop before the river gushes into the sea near Shanghai.

That this ostensibly peripheral region was able to become so rich is due not only to the fertile alluvial soil, but also to the hard work of those who lived on the once swampy land. Before the time of Christ, they were already draining large areas. At the same time they created many dikes and canals, via which good crops could now be transported quickly and cheaply to the surrounding towns.

The results were so successful, and the products so much in demand, that the Sui dynasty (581–618) ordered the existing minor canals to be connected and widened to make the "Grand Canal," so that valuable rice, along with silk, salt, tea, and other luxury goods could be brought to the imperial court at Chang'an (present-day Xi'an).

Admittedly, this could only be achieved at a great cost; thousands upon thousands of forcibly recruited workers and day laborers lost their lives on the colossal construction sites. At the beginning of the 7th century the roughly 750 mile long (1200 km) stretch to the capital city was finished, but so was the dynasty—the people had been bled dry by the gargantuan project. Yet subsequent dynasties further developed the canal, and during the Mongol reign (1279–1368) it was even extended as far as Beijing.

Today the Grand Canal, at almost 1,120 miles long (1800 km), remains the longest canal system in the world, even though it is no longer used in its entirety. It is still important for the exchange of minor goods between individual settlements in the region, but for heavier transportation, rail and road are used instead.

Most tourists, however, find that the Grand Canal still has plenty to offer. Even if they are bussed in to the "Land of Water," a boat ride on the canal remains a real attraction, and a small stretch of the canal, at the very least, usually features in the itinerary, such as trips from

Above left: Jiangnan does not have an entry in the Guinness Book of Records as the region with the most bridges, but it surely deserves a mention!

Left: The whole region is criss-crossed by little canals.

Right: Careful modernization has ensured that towns on the Grand Canal such as Tongli have retained their idyllic character.

Tongli and Zhouzhuang. The latter is the most famous town in the region, and justifiably so. Designated a UNESCO World Heritage Site in 1998, the region owes its present-day success as a tourist destination to its city fathers. Unlike in Suzhou, where whole streets have visibly undergone radical modernization, in Zhou-zhuang the architects were more scrupulous. Lovingly restored and free of modern buildings, the town, with its family houses, temples, and arched stone bridges, is the perfect place for an excursion to "old China," for both Chinese tourists and foreigners.

The small towns of Tongli, Wuzhen, and Zhujia-jiao near Shanghai are equally worthwhile and are growing in stature as tourist draws, to the point that a new tourist bus station is under construction in Shanghai itself, with the aim of making the journey to the area easier. If visitors to the "Land of Water" are returning to Shanghai, the European women usually have some kind of freshwater-pearl necklace peeping above their collars—pearls are a typical souvenir from the region. Chinese travelers carry shrink-wrapped bags filled with the local specialty, "Wansan Ti," in their luggage; a knuckle of pork marinated in dark soy sauce, it is popular far beyond Zhouzhuang, and is given when visiting friends and colleagues.

Below: The structures of buildings are sometimes several centuries old and date from the Ming and Qing dynasties.

Wansan Ti pork knuckle

1 tsp Sichuan pepper
1 tbsp vegetable oil
2 ¾ lb / 1.25 kg knuckle of pork
2 tbsp sugar
½ cup / 125 ml peanut oil
1 ½ tbsp rice wine
1 ⅔ cups / 400 ml soy sauce
1 ½ tsp salt
5 thick slices of ginger
2 tbsp chopped leek
1 tsp cornstarch mixed into 2 tsp water

Pour 1 tablespoon of hot vegetable oil over the Sichuan pepper and leave to stand, then decant the oil and keep to one side. Lay the pork in a large clay pot and fill with 1 quart (1.2 liters) boiling water. Boil for 20 minutes (so that it is half done), remove from the pot and let it drain on paper towels. Caramelize 1 teaspoon of the sugar in a pan over a low heat, stirring constantly. Spread the pork with the caramelized sugar and leave to cool.

Heat the oil in the wok until it begins to smoke, add the pork and fry it briefly, until the skin turns pink. Take out and leave to dry.

Allow the oil in the wok to cool down to warm. Add the remaining sugar and caramelize by stirring constantly. Boil 3 ¼ cups (750 ml) water, add the rice wine, soy sauce, salt, ginger and leek, then suspend the bag of herbs and spices in the water. Add the pork last of all. Simmer over low heat for 3 hours. Take out the pork and put it in a large steamer placed over the wok. Steam the pork for 1 hour, remove from the steamer and place it in the wok along with the broth. Bring to a boil, and stir in the cornstarch mixture. Once the broth has thickened, add the reserved Sichuan pepper oil. Pour the sauce over the knuckle of pork and serve.

This dish is traditionally eaten with the fingers, rather than chopsticks.

An idyllic land of water **113**

Black, red, white—Chinese rice vinegar

The first mention of it appeared in texts from the Zhou period (1066–221 B.C.). Then, in the Song period (960–1279) it was named as one of life's essential items, alongside firewood, rice, oil, soy sauce, salt, and tea—vinegar.

Whether used in marinating, cooking, seasoning, pickling, or as a dip, Chinese cuisine cannot be imagined without this acidic all-rounder; without it there would be no sweet-and-sour sauce, no hot-and-sour soup, no pickled vegetables, and no fiery bite to Sichuan cooking; vinegar offsets the piquancy of such dishes.

The Chinese developed the different types of vinegar over centuries, but the base was always the same: an alcoholic or sugary liquid, which oxidizes and ferments according to the method of production. Sometimes this liquid may consist of alcohol in the form of spirits or wine; sometimes starchy products like wheat, millet, and rice, or fruit. In the Tang period (618–907) vinegar was produced using soaked wheat in the north of the country, and using boiled rice, peaches or grapes farther south. The art of aromatizing the vinegar with peach blossom or kumquat leaves was also being practiced. Today rice vinegar has won out as the most prominent variety in China's supermarkets.

In contrast to Western varieties of vinegar, Chinese rice vinegar is quite mild, as it contains only around 3 or 4 percent acid. It is produced from fermented rice, in the form of rice wine, which is made by adding yeast to glutinous rice. This is replaced, in its turn, by acetic acid, so that it can mature to become rice vinegar.

Connoisseurs distinguish between three different types of rice vinegar: black, red, and white. Of these, white vinegar, the most acidic Chinese variety, is used mostly in cold dishes and for pickling. According to tradition, the markedly milder, slightly sweet red vinegar gets its red coloring from the addition of red yeast (*Monascus purpureus*). It is used mainly in soup, fish, and seafood for its bittersweet flavor. The dark, almost black vinegar (similar to Italian balsamic vinegar, but milder) has a special place in Chinese cuisine. The almost treacly, brown-black Zhenjiang vinegar (also known as "Chinkiang rice vinegar") is prized as the crème de la crème of China's vinegars. Contrary to popular belief, it comes not from Zhejiang Province, but rather from the city of Zhenjiang in Jiangsu Province. Chinese chefs swear by the spicily sweet, slightly smoky vinegar made from rice, which gives a special touch to all wok dishes and stews as long as it is added toward the end of cooking. It is also an essential ingredient in noodle dishes, or as a dip for

dumplings. Connoisseurs shun varieties of black vinegar from other regions or copycat products, which are likely to contain caramel or syrup alongside rice, water, and salt.

Below left: A Chinese-style "bioreactor"!

Below middle: Alcohol being converted into acetic acid.

Below right: Many Chinese recipes would be unimaginable without vinegar.

Bottom left: Vinegar maturing in wooden vats.

Bottom middle: The vats are covered to prevent too much of the flavor from escaping.

Bottom right: It is impossible to miss the array of different varieties of vinegar in any store.

Left: Who needs balsamic vinegar? In China there is a different type of vinegar for every dish.

Below: Quality control is all-important in vinegar factories.

Bottom: At the smaller factories visitors can fill their own plastic bottles with vinegar.

Black, red, white—Chinese rice vinegar **115**

Exquisite tea services—pots from Yixing

If you want top-quality teapots or teacups made of zisha clay, there's only one place to go in China: Yixing. This city on the western shore of Lake Tai is famous among tea connoisseurs well beyond China for its potteries, where the local zisha clay is elaborately hand-crafted into exquisite tea services.

The delicate teapots boast a plethora of vastly diverse shapes and hues. Many are modeled on ancient artifacts such as sacrificial vessels; the shapes of others take their cue from nature. Teapots may evoke gnarly branches, flower sepals or fruit; petals may twine around the middle of the teapot; a filigree snake may serve as the lid handle, or a dragon's head as the spout. These elegant details make the teapot a real treasure. Purists favor clean, geometric shapes and can tolerate, at most, a little calligraphy on the middle. Yet whether round or angular, playful or elegant, the perfection of every pot is evident in its balanced shape, the well-fitting lid, the smooth line between the body and the spout, and the drip-free arc of the tea when poured. The little everyday pieces also vary in color; the palette ranges from sunny yellow and brick-red to green and dark brown depending on the type of zisha clay used and the temperature at which the pot is fired.

Yet however much the Yixing pots appear to differ from one another, they have one thing in common: the material properties of the zisha clay, which is mined from dikes up to half a mile deep and specially prepared. Due to the kaolin (porcelain clay) content the material remains large-pored even after firing, without becoming moist. This allows oxygen from outside the pot to reach the tea, developing its full aroma inside. The special thing about these pots is that their porous texture soaks up the flavor of the tea, preserving and intensifying it with frequent use.

This "memory" is also an unbeatable argument for buying several pots, as a single pot should only be used for preparing one kind of tea. For this reason, when brewing a Wulong tea, say, connoisseurs use a small pot with a capacity of about 1 ¼ cups (300 ml), as this allows better infusion. For jasmine tea, however, they would use a pot with a capacity of 1–2 quarts (1–2 liters), because it only needs to be brewed once. The list of types of tea and their respec-

Far left: The magical moment in a colossal tea ceremony.

Left: Yixing pots come in many different shapes.

Below left: But they have one thing in common: they are all perfectly balanced.

Handling Yixing teapots

Anyone looking to buy a Yixing teapot should consider beforehand what kind of tea it will be used for, and "prepare" the pot accordingly. More fastidious types rinse the pot thoroughly with water before using it for the first time, and brew very strong tea in it, leaving it to stand for several hours to take effect. For the teapot to retain an even stronger flavor, it should be put in a larger pot with cold water, and heated slowly. Shortly before it boils, the teapot is filled with the chosen tea, boiled for five minutes and then removed. The pot should remain in the gently simmering water for a further 30 minutes, before the pot is removed and left to dry by itself. Teapots should never be cleaned with detergents or in the dishwasher.

tive Yixing pots is endless—over time it has become a veritable science.

Indeed, the city on the shores of Lake Tai has a long history of pottery production. The first clay pots were being produced here more than 6,000 years ago. Yet Yixing—or rather Dingshuzhen, 12 miles south of the city itself—only became famous for its reddish-brown tea services in the late Ming period. From the 16th century the practice of brewing tea—which called for a pot—replaced the earlier tradition of boiling it in water. Yet the emergence of such an exquisite product from Yixing was brought about not only by erstwhile "tea trends," but also the quality of the clay and the artistry of its inhabitants. The Yangtze Delta had long since become a rich region, home to many wealthy literati and officials, and this made the sale of artistic luxury goods particularly profitable.

Today Yixing is a town of about 260,000 people, and is still riding the wave of its reputation as China's pottery mecca. The trade in antique teapots is particularly high here, especially if they have a vintage polish. With time, through constantly being touched, the rough, sandy surface is rubbed smooth and acquires a matt yet lustrous patina. If there are rather too many "antique Yixing pots" on offer at the market, however, you can be sure that most of them are not genuine.

Bottom: Tea services from Yixing tick all the boxes for quality and beauty.

Above right: Perfect tea requires a perfect pot, essential for a rounded taste.

Right: Real Yixing pots have a seal of authenticity on their underside. This means that the cost of pieces by Yixing's masters can go into three figures.

Shanghai

上海

Katrin Schlotter

You either love it or hate it. A neutral attitude to the megalopolis of Shanghai is well nigh impossible. For some the cosmopolitan "city on the sea" is a microcosm, representing the driving force and the very future of China; for others it is simply too hectic, too shrill, too western-ized and too expensive. But one thing it does have is history.

This self-governing city has the status of a province, and is not only in a central location—roughly half way along the coast between Beijing and Hong Kong—it is also the epicenter of the booming Yangtze region, along with the neighboring provinces of Zhejiang and Jiangsu. The Shanghai administrative area extends over 2,448 square miles (6,340 sq km) and is currently home to more than 18 million inhabitants. Ten million live in the city itself, which means that around 13,000 people are crammed into one square kilometer—by way of comparison the population density in London is 5,100 per square kilometer, while in New York it is 2,050. However, compared with the Kowloon district of Hong Kong, Shanghai seems almost empty. Careful town planning and a num-ber of apartment building programs during which millions of people moved into the satellite towns, have resulted in an impressively spa-cious urban landscape. Signs that world-famous architects have been involved can be seen in almost all parts of the city. Magnificent build-ings, residential and commercial districts, museums, parks, and shop-ping malls form a kind of architectural ensemble that breathes life into the slogan of the 2010 World Expo to be held in Shanghai: "Better city, better life."

This cosmopolitan city is the industrial, commercial, and financial center of China. In constant competition with Hong Kong, this port on the Huangpu River is absolutely bursting with economic power. Since 1992, the gross domestic product (GDP) has been achieving growth rates in double figures. In 1998 it reached 200 billion US dollars. Among the strongest branches of industry are automobiles and steel, electronics and IT, airports and container ports, and the service sector, which con-tributes more than half of GDP though trade, banking, real estate, trade fairs, and logistics. More than half a million private companies, more than 20,000 branches of foreign companies, and around 40 univer-sities—including the famous Fudan and Tonji Universities founded in 1905—give the economy increased momentum.

Above: Even in this huge city there are small, secluded corners where people can have a chat and drink their tea in peace.

Facing page: Colorful mixture of styles in the People's Park. For many years the 270-foot (83-m)-high, art deco Park Hotel was the tallest building in China.

Shanghai

Above: 10 million people equals around 13,000 inhabitants per square kilometer, so the only way to build is up.

Below: Under the watchful eye of the lucky dragon...

Bottom: ...the people of Shanghai occasionally take things easy.

In matters of culture, the media, fashion, and lifestyle, Shanghai is always one step ahead of the rest of China. The inhabitants of Shanghai just love setting new trends and being seen in places like Shanghai's most popular shopping street, the Nanjing Lu. You may see them in Prada suits, jogging suits and sneakers, or flowered pajamas—especially on hot summer evenings there will be a relaxed mixture of styles. Not for nothing has Shanghai always been considered the melting pot par excellence—by rich and poor, artists and artisans, foreigners and Chinese alike. Millions of migrant workers from the poverty-stricken hinterland have made their way to Shanghai to earn some money, just like many of the ancestors of the present day inhabitants of Shanghai.

There has been a settlement here since prehistoric times, and the harbor has long been important for the region, but the city's heyday really began in 1843, when it was opened to traders from the west after the Opium Wars. Americans, Britons, and Frenchmen founded concessions—districts with their own government and jurisdiction—carried on trade (including opium) and brought western ideas to the country. Between 1900 and 1937 Shanghai blossomed into the cosmopolitan commercial center of China. No other Chinese city offered so many

opportunities. Speculators, adventurers, intellectuals, and refugees, including many Russians and Jews, came streaming into the city of dreams. Shanghai led the way in the provision of gas, water, and electricity services as well as in education and health care. Many of the newcomers were successful in sharing the wealth of the growing, but relatively small, upper class, though the majority of the population was living in poverty. Drug addiction and prostitution became widespread. In the years that followed, the city was shaken by disturbances and strikes. In 1927 these were violently suppressed by the nationalists under Chiang Kai-Shek. For the rich, the truly "golden" age of the 1920s and 1930s came to an abrupt end with the Japanese occupation in 1937, which was followed 12 years later by the communist victory. For several decades politicians took over from the entrepreneurs—and education was replaced by political indoctrination. Political reforms were not carried through until the mid-1990s, when Shanghai once again became what it had secretly always been: the city of visions.

Above left: "The Gateway to the World," "the Paris of the East," or "the Pearl of the Orient"— there are many different names for Shanghai, which now shines out again in all its former glory, especially along the Bund, the waterfront promenade.

Above right: An imposing 1,370 feet (421 m) high, the Jin Mao tower is one of the tallest buildings in the world.

Below: Shanghai's most famous tea house, the Huxinting in the Yu Garden, dates from the 18th century and is a haven of peace, despite its many customers.

Inspired—Shanghai cuisine

Even though the tradition-conscious Chinese do not allow the "young" cuisine of Shanghai to be considered as one of the eight important regional cuisines of China, it is so creative that it has been setting the standard for modern Chinese cookery since the mid-1990s. Because its people are open to new influences and ready to experiment, they are constantly creating new kinds of dishes and restaurants that send gourmets everywhere into raptures.

In Shanghai you can find examples of almost every traditional cuisine from China and the rest of the world—sometimes even under the same roof. A few high-class restaurants that compete to outdo one another in matters of design have picked out the best elements from the cuisines of the world and re-combined them into a "Shanghai fusion cuisine." Others, such as the Whampoa Club, look at traditional Shanghai dishes and interpret them in a modern way. In addition, there are the classics and delicacies of Chinese cooking. Unlike other Chinese cities, where the restaurants mostly offer the dishes of the region so that a kind of regional separatism rules, Shanghai restaurateurs pin their hopes on culinary diversity—all on the same menu. By contrast, at the hot food stalls and in the "snack streets," such as the recently restored Yunnan Lu, the Huanghe Lu, or the western part of the Wujiang Lu, they offer the rather more traditional xiaolongbao dumplings, and tofu or noodle dishes.

As Shanghai grew into a cosmopolitan city and millions of people moved in from all parts of the country, the original Shanghai or Benbang cuisine underwent a change. Over the last 200 years, new arrivals from the neighboring provinces of Zhejiang and Jiangsu enriched the existing cuisine with their exquisite recipes and refined it into the cuisine known as "Haipai," which absorbs foreign influences.

Despite the fact that the ingredients in the Yangtse delta are almost the same everywhere—mainly rice, noodles, and tofu, fresh and pickled vegetables, with fish and seafood (especially eels and crayfish) plus poultry and pork—Haipai cuisine is slightly more refined than its predecessor. Flavorings are no longer just oil, soy sauce, and sugar but also vinegar or Shaoxing rice wine. The latter is used as the basis for hongshao (red cooked) dishes. In a reddish sauce made from ginger, rice wine, soy sauce, and sugar, seasoned with a little star anise and bean paste, fish, poultry, and vegetables are transformed into delicious Shanghai-style braised dishes—with kind regards from Zhejiang, the home of "red cooking." Pork, tofu, and sea cucumber are braised with bamboo and ham. These dishes are so aromatic that they do not need spicy seasonings. Shanghai cuisine is generally harmonious, mild, and slightly sweet. And of course other cooking methods are used as well as braising and steaming.

"Drunken" crustaceans, eels, or chickens are definitely a Shanghai specialty. According to the original recipe, "drunken shrimp" were served live in rice wine. They absorbed the flavor and as soon as the alcohol had more or less anesthetized them they were eaten raw. When you bit into them, they were supposed to twitch one last time.

A less lively creature is the "drunken chicken," which is marinated in rice wine after it has been cooked and is served as a cold appetizer. Shanghai cooks also sometimes use several cooking methods at once. For instance, mandarin fish is first deep-fried and then has sauce poured over so it sizzles. The other way round, that is first boiled and then drizzled with oil, makes eel into a crispy bite.

In the autumn, Dazha crabs trigger a kind of crab mania in Shanghai. You might almost believe they were an original Shanghai dish, but they come from the Yangcheng Lake in Jiangsu (see p. 110). Recently Shanghai crab and crayfish breeders have tried to raise the species on the island of Chongming off the Shanghai coast. Although the climatic conditions here are similar to those of the Yangcheng Lake, the crabs

Right: Mass production of xiaolongbao—even in China's restaurant trade, cooking means one thing above all else: teamwork.

Below: Here a vegetable seller tries unorthodox advertising methods to peddle his wares to the husband and father or wife and mother.

have not yet reached the ideal weight of up to
1 ½ pounds (700 g). But when they are prepared
in the delicious Shanghai way—either steamed
in classic fashion or as crab sorbet—this is not
really a problem.

Choy sum with bamboo shoots

Generous 1 lb (500 g) choy sum
2 oz (50 g) bamboo shoots
5 tbsp peanut oil
1 tsp salt
1 slice of ginger, finely chopped
Shaoxing rice wine
1 tsp pea starch, mixed with 2 tsp water
1 tbsp pork dripping or lard

Wash and trim the choy sum. Blanch the bamboo
shoots briefly in boiling water, drain, and cut in
slices. Heat the oil in a wok, add the choy sum,
bamboo shoots, and ginger, salt, and fry lightly.
As soon as the vegetables are tender, bind with
the starch and water mixture, add Shaoxing rice
wine to taste, drizzle with the pork dripping,
remove from the wok and serve.

Top: The xiaolongbao in the little bamboo baskets
and their accompanying delicacies look very
appetizing.

Above: In tea houses they always serve a little
something to eat along with the jasmine tea.

Above: If spinach can make Popeye into a muscle
man, Chinese fast food can turn you into a kung–
fu fighter.

Shanghai delicacies

Freshwater shrimp

1 piece of leek (¾ inch / 2 cm long)
1 piece of ginger (¾ inch / 2 cm long)
1 tbsp coriander seeds
20 unpeeled freshwater shrimp
⅔ cup (150 ml) vegetable oil
2 tsp rice wine
½ tsp salt
1 ½ tbsp sugar
2 tsp soy sauce
1 tbsp water
1 tsp sesame oil

Chop the leek and cut the ginger in thin slices. Crush the coriander seeds. Rinse the shrimp and remove the feelers if desired. The shells will be cooked with the shrimp.
Heat ½ cup (125 ml) oil in a wok until it smokes. Add the shrimp, fry until tender, and remove immediately. Heat the remaining oil in the wok until it smokes, add the ginger, coriander and leek, and stir-fry. Add the rice wine, salt, sugar, soy sauce, and water, and cook for 5 minutes. Drizzle over the sesame oil and stir in before serving.

Bamboo shoots with pork

9 oz (250 g) (lean) pork
9 oz (250 g) bamboo shoots
¼ cup (60 ml) vegetable oil
1 thick slice of ginger, finely chopped
1 tbsp chopped scallions
3 ½ tbsp Shaoxing rice wine
2 tsp salt
1 ½ tbsp soy sauce
½ tsp freshly ground white pepper
1 ½ tbsp sugar
1–2 tsp sesame oil

Bring plenty of water to a boil in a pan. Cut the pork in slices and blanch briefly. Remove the meat and set aside. Cut the bamboo shoots in diamond-shaped pieces and blanch briefly. Remove them and drain.
Heat a wok, add a little oil, and brown the ginger and scallions lightly until they release their aroma. Add the pork and brown. Add the rice wine, salt, soy sauce, pepper, sugar, and a little water, and bring to a boil. Skim and braise for 20 minutes on low to medium heat. Add the bamboo shoots and braise with the rest. Drizzle over the sesame oil, transfer the mixture to a dish, and serve.

Shaomai dumplings with glutinous rice

3 cups (600 g) glutinous rice
5 ¼ oz (150 g) lean pork
vegetable oil for frying
7 tbsp soy sauce
1 tsp Shaoxing rice wine
1 ½ tbsp sugar
1 piece of scallion (¾ inch / 2 cm long), finely chopped
1 thick slice of ginger, finely chopped
5 ¼ oz (150 g) pork dripping or lard
4 ⅓ cups (500 g) all-purpose flour
7 tbsp vegetable stock
1 cup (250 ml) water

bring to a boil. Add the glutinous rice and stir in. As soon as the rice has absorbed the liquid, stir in the pork dripping, remove the contents of the wok from the heat, and allow the rice filling to cool.

Bring ²/₃ cup (150 ml) water to a boil. Put the flour in a bowl, pour over the boiling water, and stir until it forms a thick paste.

Add the remaining (cold) water and knead to a smooth dough. Shape the dough into a long roll and pull off small portions (about ½ oz/15 g each).

With a rolling pin, roll the pieces of dough into rounds about 3 ½ inches (9 cm) in diameter.

Place each round of dough in the palm of your left hand and put a spoonful of rice filling in the middle. With the fingers of your left hand, press the edges of the dough round the glutinous rice while pressing the surface of the rice down flat with your right hand to make a little shaomai dumpling.

Put the dumplings in a bamboo steamer, steam without the lid for 10 minutes over high heat, then remove and serve while hot.

Duck soup

1 small duck (about 1 ¾ lbs / 800 g)
1 piece of ginger (1 ½ inch / 4 cm long)
1 oz / 30 g marinated bamboo shoots (Bian Jian)
1 slice boiled ham, cut in strips
1 ½ tbsp rice wine
1 tsp salt
5 ¼ oz (150 g) dried cellophane noodles

Wash the duck thoroughly inside and out, and chop in pieces with a cleaver.

Put the duck pieces in a wok with 2 quarts (2 liters) cold water. Bring to a boil over high heat, then add the ginger, bamboo shoots, ham, rice wine, and salt and simmer for 2 ½ hours over low heat. Add the cellophane noodles, cook for 10 minutes, then remove the soup from the heat and serve.

Wash the glutinous rice and leave to swell in cold water for 4–5 hours.

Pour off the water, transfer the rice to a bamboo steamer and steam in a pan over high heat until tender. Dice the pork in small pieces.

Heat a wok, add a little oil, and brown the diced pork.

Add the soy sauce, rice wine, sugar, scallions, ginger, and stock, and

Left: Bamboo shoots with pork

Facing page below: Freshwater shrimp

Right: Duck soup

Below: Shaomai dumplings with glutinous rice

A flying visit to the past

An ultramodern airport, completely replanned residential and business districts, in which the shiny façades of luxury hotels and company headquarters reach for the sky—but tell me, where is the historical Shanghai? The answer is not far away: not in the synthetic city of Pudong, but on the opposite side, on the west bank of the Huangpu River, in Puxi.

Along the Bund, the mile-and-a-half (almost two-km)-long waterfront promenade, a row of 52 magnificent neoclassical or art deco buildings has been preserved, which still represents Shanghai's colonial past. For about a hundred years (around 1847–1945) the Americans, British, and French, not to mention the Germans, Japanese and Russians, with their banks, consulates and firms, ran their businesses from the Bund. Each building has its own fascinating story: the former British customs office, built to resemble Big Ben; the HSBC Bank, once the second largest bank building in the world; the Shanghai Club, at whose 108-feet (33-m)-long mahogany bar the colonial masters discussed the world; or the Peace Hotel. In the 1930s (when it was run under the name Cathay) it was the most cosmopolitan hotel in China, offering not only glittering cocktail parties and costume balls but also the most up-to-date cuisine of its day. Around 70 chefs worked there, preparing the finest international dishes—everything from Russian caviar, French foie gras, and Italian cheese, to classic British roast pork.

A completely different picture can be seen in the Chinese Old Town. This lies inside the ring road that was built on the foundations of the city walls, which were erected in 1553, and large parts of it have now been restored. At the time of the Ming dynasty (1368–1644), there were already half a million Chinese living in Nanshi, the southern part of the city. With Shanghai's increasing wealth the "Chinese town" was bursting at the seams, and today it is still the most densely populated quarter of Shanghai. In the shadow of the tourist sights of the old town there are winding alleys that have not yet been modernized, lined with gray, single-story stone cottages. Here washing dangles from bamboo poles alongside marinated ducks; old women sit chopping vegetables with their backs to the street; next door the neighbor is washing her hair—in the street.

Right: Where the modern age has not completely broken through, life still goes on mainly in the street.

Below: The reverse side of the Shanghai economic medal: while some people make millions in a few minutes, others have to work hard to earn a living.

In these modest residential districts running water and sewage systems can still not be taken for granted. Wherever the demolition ball has not yet struck, life continues outdoors for the most part, more or less as it did a hundred years ago.

A few streets farther on, the old town is absolutely teeming with magnificent historic buildings. Hordes of tourists jostle their way through this part of the old town, which has been restored in traditional style, along Old Street to the City God Temple, over the Nine Turn Bridge leading to the pavilion of the Hu-xinting Tea House in the Yu Garden, which was laid out in 1559. Formerly a private park, it brings together all the elements of Chinese garden art in just five acres (two hectares). It is surrounded by the Yu Yuan Bazaar, with shops full of antiques, silks, tea utensils, and pearl jewelry. This busy district, where richly decorated houses with curved roofs are as crowded together as the visitors, has a scent of joss sticks and delicious food.

While the Shanghai Lao Fandian, Lu Bo Lang, and Shanghai Dexing restaurants serve typical local delicacies such as duck soup, braised fish and shellfish, and shark fin, the Chunfeng Songyue attracts customers with its vegetarian cuisine. The Nanxiang Mantou Dian is the place to go for the most famous snacks in Shanghai, the juicy xiaolongbao dumplings. Around a hundred years ago, their creator, a Mr Wu from Nanxiang, offered to sell his soup-filled dumplings to the Huxinting Tea House. He could not have known that a restaurant chain would later spread his idea through the whole of Asia.

Above: A little chat between neighbors is good manners in the Old Town.

Below: In among the small alleys, you suddenly come upon the highly decorative and expensively renovated buildings of the Yu Yuan bazaar.

Xiaolongbao—a cultural treasure in a basket

Even the fast-living people of Shanghai keep up their traditions. And a list of a total of 83 cultural treasures also contains Shanghai's most popular snack, xiaolongbao—juicy dumplings steamed in bamboo baskets. It is hard to believe how many different things you can have in such a small pocket of dough: not only a juicy filling of chopped pork or crab meat, but also hot "broth"—a sensory experience that will wow your taste buds! Connoisseurs have extremely strict criteria for perfect xiaolongbao. The dough pocket must be almost transparent, the filling of pork, ginger, and rice wine should be smooth, and the broth full of flavor. This forms when the solid gelatin from the connective tissue in the pork is liquefied during steaming. Though the ingredients have been prepared beforehand, the next bit is improvisation—child's play for Chinese cooks. They lay a wafer-thin circle of dough on one hand, put the ingredients on top and form a delicately pleated bag, which they twist at the top and drop into the bamboo basket to steam. They do not do all this hours in advance, they only start after the order has been taken. These tasty little works of art are served with Zhenjiang vinegar and wafer-thin slices of ginger. Whether you get the best xiaolongbao in the Nanxiang Mantou Dian, the Ding Tai Feng or the Crystal Jade is a matter of debate.

But wherever you eat them, you are advised to be cautious. The broth-filled dumplings are extremely hot and tear easily. It is best to take plenty of time, pick one up by its tip with your chopsticks and lift it out of the bamboo basket. Then you dunk it in the sauce and put it on a spoon. That way you avoid dribbling broth down your chin or in your neighbor's lap.

Xiaolongbao with pork and ginger

Aspic:
9 oz (250 g) pork rind
1 piece of ginger (1 ½ inch / 4 cm long), sliced
1 piece of leek (1 ½ inch / 4 cm long), chopped
2 tsp rice wine
½ tsp white pepper

Filling:
3 ½ oz (100 g) homemade aspic (for recipe, see below)
9 oz (250 g) pork (with about ⅓ fat)
1–2 tsp finely chopped ginger
½ tsp salt
½ tsp white pepper
1 tsp rice wine
1 ½ tsp sugar
4 tbsp water

Dough:
1 ¾ cups (300 g) all-purpose flour

Aspic:
Wash the pork rind and cut in thick strips. Pour 4 cups (1 liter) water into a pan, add the pork rind, then the sliced ginger, leek, and rice wine. Bring to a boil over high heat. Skim off the froth with a skimmer. Reduce the heat and let the liquid simmer for 1 hour until it thickens, then add the pepper. Pour the mixture into a bowl and leave to cool and set.

Cut the aspic into small cubes.
Chop the pork finely and tip into a bowl. Add the ginger, salt, pepper, rice wine, sugar, aspic cubes, and water, and mix well (see facing page).

Tip the flour onto the worktop and make a well in the middle. Gradually add 7 tablespoons of water and work in slowly. Then knead the dough until it is smooth and no longer sticks to your fingers. Cover with a damp cloth and leave to rest for 30 minutes.
Sprinkle a little flour over the worktop. Knead the dough again and then shape into a roll about ¾ inch (2 cm) in diameter. Divide the roll into 16 equal pieces.
Roll out the pieces of dough into rounds about 3 inches (7–8 cm) in diameter. Lay each round on one hand and put a little filling in the middle. Fold the edges of the dough together over the filling and press together firmly.
Line a bamboo steamer with a damp cloth. Lay the dumplings on this and steam in a wok over high heat for 10 minutes.
Serve with dark vinegar.

Left: The length of the line of waiting people vouches for the quality of the xiaolongbao.

Centre: The dumplings are not prepared in advance, but freshly made after being ordered.

Below: Eating with chopsticks is an art to be learnt.

1 For the filling for the xiaolongbao, cut the pork in strips...

2 ...then dice...

3 ...and finely chop.

4 In a bowl, season with salt...

5 ...add the ginger...

6 ...and mix well with the remaining ingredients.

7 For the dough, tip the flour onto a worktop and make a well in the middle.

8 Pour water into the hollow...

9 ...slowly mix the flour and water...

10 ...and knead well...

11 ...until the dough no longer sticks to your fingers.

12 Leave the dough to rest for 30 minutes.

13 Then knead the dough thoroughly again...

14 ...and form into a thick roll.

15 Divide the dough into two equal "sausages"...

16 ...and pull each one lengthways into a thin roll.

17 Cut each roll of dough into the same number of small, equal-sized pieces...

18 ...and roll these out into rounds.

19 Spoon a portion of filling onto each with a bamboo spatula or a tablespoon...

20 Pull the edges of the dough over the filling all round and twist together in the middle.

21 Put the xiaolongbao one by one into a bamboo basket—lined with a cloth, baking parchment, or similar...

22 ...and steam over high heat.

A stroll through the present

Visitors to Shanghai can go to and fro at will between different worlds and times—between east and west, past and future—while still remaining in the here and now—just during a pleasant stroll from the Bund along the Nanjing Lu shopping street to the People's Park. Since its complete renovation in the 1990s, the waterfront promenade along the Bund, with its company headquarters, luxury shops, galleries, high-class restaurants and bars, has once again become a magnet for the rich and beautiful, as it was in the glory days of the 1920s. Since 1999, the leader of the pack among gourmet restaurants has been M on the Bund, whose delicious fusion cuisine is considered to be the gastronomic highlight of Shanghai. And that is not all: it is a perfect place for a romantic dinner in a Mediterranean atmosphere, on the terrace if the weather is fine, where you have a wonderful view over the Bund to Pudong. After that, we can recommend a drink in the Glamour Bar, which really lives up to its name. Two buildings farther along, in Three on the Bund, gourmets can look straight up from the 4th floor into the starry gourmet heaven. In his restaurants Jean Georges and Nougatine, star chef Jean Georges Vongerichten creates highly-praised French nouvelle cuisine with Asian overtones, while another star chef, David Laris, offers fusion cuisine with a focus on seafood in the elegant Laris restaurant. But at Three on the

Bund fusion cuisine is not all they serve. The revitalized Shanghai cuisine of top chef Jereme Leung, who is considered the Paul Bocuse of Asia, has marked out the Whampoa Club and made the splendid art deco restaurant into one of Shanghai's premier addresses. To counter-balance all these luxury dishes we need steaks and burgers. The New Heights offers its guests all the flair of a brasserie plus a roof terrace with a view over Pudong. In addition, in the Cupola, the former bell tower, the Three on the Bund has luxurious private rooms for two to eight persons available—above the rooftops of Shanghai.

Back on the attractively paved surface of the Bund, visitors reach the Peace Hotel and the Nanjing Lu, Shanghai's shimmering shopping street. The Nanjing Dong Lu runs from the east as far as the People's Square, where it becomes the Nanjing Xilu running westward to the prestigious Jing'an district. It was formerly known as the "Bubbling Well Road," the main artery of the International Concession. Stretching for 3 ½ miles (6 km) and now largely laid out as a

Below: Modern Shanghai restaurants look trendy and stylish, and the staff uniforms have to match this image.

Right: Fusion and international cuisine are in vogue in Shanghai. It has to appeal to Chuppies (Chinese Urban Professionals) as much as to foreign visitors.

wide pedestrian precinct, the street is lined with department stores, classy boutiques, cinemas and, of course, restaurants. It is a real shopping experience, attracting around a million visitors a day. By night, the neon signs transform the Nanjing Lu into a fascinating sea of color and light—and the focus of Shanghai life. Whether they come to stroll, dine, or play chess, the Nanjing Lu also offers the locals plenty of entertainment.

Located next to the broad People's Square, which served as the racetrack in colonial times, the People's Park is the perfect place for a rest. A few steps farther on are the Shanghai Theater and several museums, including the Shanghai Museum, the Shanghai Art Museum and the Urban Planning Center, where visitors can see the development of Shanghai presented in the form of an accurate scale model. If all these impressions have given you an appetite for genuine Shanghai snacks, in the "snack streets" you will find skewers of grilled fish or meat, deep-fried xiaolongbao, dumplings filled with chicken, stinky tofu, crabs, and much more. Just follow your nose and remember: where there are the most people waiting in line you get the best-tasting food!

Right: In the fashionable Xintiandi theater district of Shanghai, 20 years ago there were still old, mostly run-down, houses.

Below: Shanghai's magnificent shopping street, the Nanjing Lu, shows its brightest and best side mainly at night.

A passionate man—
Top chef Jereme Leung

In restaurant and travel guides, the Whampoa Clubs of top chef Jereme Leung are listed among the Shanghai restaurants that absolutely must be visited. Recently the Hong Kong-born master chef has provided additional opportunities for exquisite dining through his restaurant and consultancy company JL Concepts in Singapore, Bangkok, and elsewhere.

Since 2004, the Whampoa Club Shanghai has set new standards with its premises in Three on the Bund. From the superb location, the jade place mats that were made especially for the club, through to the fine tea service—the daring and successful combination of old and new is already evident from the aesthetic viewpoint alone. Gaudy room-dividers in lilac, pink, and yellow positioned in front of classical 1920s art deco indicate that people here no longer think along the usual lines. With a little bit of luck, guests will manage to get a table with a view of the Pudong skyline and the passing ships on the Huangpu. Meanwhile a bewildering variety of delicacies appears on the plates. Jereme Leung has unearthed and reinterpreted numerous traditional Shanghai recipes. For instance, the classic Shanghai appetizer "drunken chicken" appears not as a monumental whole on a bare plate, but cut in delicate strips draped in a cocktail glass with iced Shaoxing rice wine, as do the crab claws with cellophane noodles.

Thanks to Leung's skill, xiaolongbao dumplings and sharp-roasted cod on Chinese ginseng are also given a completely new note.

Traditional Shanghai recipes reinterpreted—it takes a second glance to reveal why this is so special. In the early 1920s, Shanghai cuisine had become so polished that the city on the Huangpu was considered the culinary center of China. At the time of the Japanese occupation, the civil war, and the victory of communism, many recipes were forgotten. The art of fine cooking came to be considered as decadent and bourgeois. Especially during the Cultural Revolution (1966–1976), many top chefs suffered political persecution, cookbooks were burnt, cookery schools were closed, and restaurants were converted into huge canteens for mass dining. Not until the 1990s did Shanghai cuisine experience a renaissance.

The fact that just one chef, who was not even originally from Shanghai, sought out these lost traditions and gave them new life is of minor importance. Jereme Leung, now one of the few high-ranking grand masters of Chinese cuisine, started work in his parents' restaurant at the age of 13. He quickly rose to be head chef and lent a special touch to the cuisine of top Asian hotels, such as the Mandarin Oriental in Malaysia and Indonesia, the Hong Kong Excelsior, and the Four Seasons in Singapore. On his many journeys through China, he went in search of the culinary roots of Chinese regional

Top right: First Shanghai (2004), then Beijing (2007): the Whampoa Clubs skillfully combine traditional and modern—in both their interior décor and their cooking.

Right: The exquisite design makes use of stunning contrasts.

Below: Jereme Leung's culinary inventions have made him famous throughout the world.

cuisine. His passion for reinvigorating the traditional cuisine with new ingredients and methods has made Jereme Leung into one of Asia's most famous chefs.

In order to discover the secrets of the fine Shanghai cuisine of the 1920s, Leung sought advice from former master chefs. Five top chefs—the youngest was 60, the oldest 72—introduced Leung to the Shanghai cuisine that was thought to have been forgotten. As Leung himself admits, he gained not only knowledge but also weight. This may perhaps be one of the reasons why his new versions of traditional dishes are not only innovative but also fresh and low in fat.

After his great success in Shanghai, the Whampoa Club Beijing opened in 2007. Almost more beautiful than the one in Shanghai, this one is in a house with a courtyard surrounded by the skyscrapers of the financial district, and combines Chinese tradition with minimalist elegance. However, when it came to redeveloping the traditional Beijing cuisine, Leung proceeded more cautiously than in Shanghai. Unlike Shanghai, which is open to all things new, especially in matters of cuisine, Beijing tastes are rather more conservative.

Left to right below: Jereme Leung's new culinary creations do not just appeal to the eye. The very sight of them can make guests feel satisfied, even before they have tasted the different flavors and discovered which ingredients have gone into the little works of art on their plates.

A glimpse of Shanghai's future

No other Chinese city has developed so rapidly into a trendsetter for the whole of China as the metropolis on the Huangpu. Only after Deng Xiaoping's policies of reform and openness achieved success in the South China Special Economic Zone did Shanghai resume a leading role in the modernization of China and become the city of the future. The Pudong and Xintiandi districts are just two of many examples.

On the eastern bank of the Huangpu, the futuristic skyline of the finance and business quarter represents both wealth and urban vision. It includes Asia's highest television tower, the Oriental Pearl Tower (1521 feet/468 m), the Shanghai World Finance Center (1599 feet/492 m), and the Jinmao Tower (1365 feet/420 m), which rise skywards but stand on a base of sand. The plan to produce the 220-square-mile (570-sq-km)-district out of the alluvial land was only drawn up in 1990. Today the area contains Pudong International Airport, the Lujiazui Financial Center, the Stock Exchange, as well as luxury hotels, restaurants and bars that rise to dizzying heights.

Even just the elevator ride to the top of the pagoda-shaped Jinmao Tower is an experience: 88 floors in just 45 seconds—what an uplifting feeling! The view from the highest viewing platform or one of the windows of the restaurant in the Grand Hyatt Shanghai, whose 555 beds occupy floors 53 to 87, would be hard to surpass. You are on at least cloud seven when you float into the Cloud Nine Bar on the 87th floor. If you want to go any higher, go to the 101-story-high Shanghai World Finance Center. The Park Hyatt Hotel with the 100 Century Avenue Restaurant on floors 91 to 93 provides competition. In the show kitchens of what used to be the world's highest restaurant, they prepare the finest Western, Chinese, and Japanese dishes. One floor up, its bars offer live jazz and art exhibitions. Ultramodern skyscrapers seem to be typical of Shanghai, but they are far from being all there is. In the restored quarter of Xintiandi on the northern edge of the Luwan district, architects have proved that old and new can be brilliantly combined. Here there once stood dilapidated Shikumen houses—also known as traditional Chinese terraced houses. Then the Hong Kong Shui On Group acquired the area. With the help of the Boston architectural practice Wood & Zapata, they had the buildings gutted and rebuilt stone by stone. It is probably not by chance that these streets did not fall victim to the demolition ball. The Chinese Communist Party was founded in one of the Shikumen houses. For political reasons, if for no other, permission could not be given to demolish a building with such an important historical heritage. The entertainment and nightlife quarter of Xintiandi, with its many street cafés, restaurants and galleries, is now seen as an example of how modern and traditional architecture can be successfully combined. One of many such examples is the T8 Restaurant and Bar, located in a 19th century Shikumen house. Here, wood, Chinese antiques, steel, and glass combine to create an atmosphere of elegance. And the cuisine is equally impressive: dishes such as caramelized salmon with green mangos and longans, tuna in a sesame crust with daikon radish, and slowly braised lamb provide pleasure for the gourmet palate.

For German visitors who are not feeling totally at home in this modern vision of China or simply feeling homesick, there is one further option, Germantown, at the city gates. Under the direction of the Frankfurt architect Albert Speer an entire residential district was built here in the German style. Other architects followed in his footsteps and built in British or Venetian style—which just goes to show that even the Chinese sometimes like the exotic!

Above: Nowhere else in China are chefs so open to new ingredients, cooking methods, and ways of presentation as in Shanghai.

Right: Visitors to the elegant piano bar in the Grand Hyatt Hotel admire the installation "Daily Fragments" by the ceramic artist Liu Jianhua.

Bottom: "Art 50" on the 50th floor of the Novotel in Pudong revolves once on its axis in an hour and a half.

Bottom right: In the Chinese mind, globalization has no negative connotations.

A Shanghai worker's day

Shanghai—the sprawling city on the Huangpu that sets the economic and cultural standards is usually associated with pictures of a "sea" of skyscrapers, the juxtaposition of traditional Chinese architecture and international style, and not least, all the aspects of cosmopolitan "savoir-vivre." But there is another Shanghai. Where a square kilometer houses around 13,000 people, the living conditions of many of Shanghai's inhabitants are reduced to the bare necessities. The Hongkou district is one such area. Although this part of the city was firmly under Japanese control at the start of the 20th century, up to 1941 more than 14,000 additional European refugees from the Nazi terror found asylum here. As a result, another "Little Vienna" grew up here within the district that was also known as "Little Tokyo."

Nowadays the low, colonial buildings are mainly occupied by workers who earn their living by their daily toil—like Dai Mengjue, 29, and his father, Dai Rencai. The two men live in an old three-story dwelling house in Dongyuhang Street. On the first floor are the kitchen and a small room containing the family altar; on the second floor are the father's bedroom and the bathroom, and the son sleeps in the room on the third floor. Dai Mengjue is employed by the Shanghai Tobacco Corporation and works alternating shifts—this week every day from 9.00 p.m. to 9.00 am.

The food stall owner knows Dai and serves him noodle soup with meat.

We collect Dai Mengjue from the factory at the end of his shift and accompany him home.

After breakfast, Dai Mengjue looks forward to his bed more than anything—at last he has a busy night's work behind him.

The room of a Shanghai bachelor: a calendar and a poster on the wall, newspapers, books, and the television in prime position.

While the son rests, his father Dai Rencai prepares their evening meal in the kitchen.

He does not really enjoy cooking, but when his son is on night shift, he makes an effort.

Dai Rencai also bears health in mind, so he makes sure they have fresh vegetables regularly.

This evening, Dai Mengjue will soon be enjoying several favorite dishes, because there is duck soup with cellophane noodles (see recipe p. 127), eggs with ham, freshwater shrimp (see recipe p. 126), and boiled alfalfa.

Dai Mengjue has slept during the day. When his father comes to wake him, he is watching television.

Once a day, Dai Rencai withdraws into the little room with the family altar to pray.

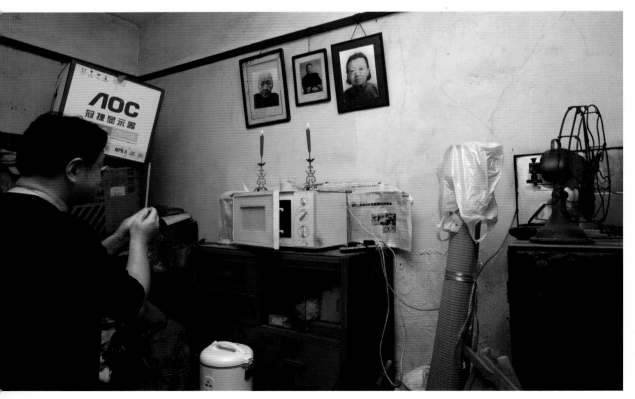

Here he remembers his parents and his dead wife. The microwave serves as a base for the altar.

Father and son begin their early evening meal with a cup of hot tea.

Over dinner, Dai Mengjue talks about his work, his colleagues, and his friends at the factory.

Dai Rencai recommends the alfalfa, but his son prefers the ham and eggs.

In the weeks when Dai Mengjue has to work night shifts, he hardly has any free time, because the tobacco factory is outside the city center, so every evening he has to travel a long way before he starts his shift, first on his new moped—on which he likes to go for a little spin along the Bund, the embankment along the Huangpu river, on his free days—and then the rest of the way by company bus.

In these weeks the lives of father and son follow clearly regulated paths. While Dai Mengjue sleeps, Dai Rencai looks after the house. He does the washing and cleaning, the repairs (and in an old house there's always something to be repaired), the cooking ... and he does the shopping every day—usually ready-meals from the nearby supermarket. But twice a week he gets fresh fish, meat, and vegetables from the market. Today he found alfalfa (*Megicago sativa*) there. Although in Europe it is mainly used as cattle fodder, it is especially rich in provitamin A and calcium, as well as minerals and proteins, and Dai Rencai prepares a spinach-like vegetable from the delicate stems of this legume. For quite a long time now, as a consequence of healthier and more ecology-conscious eating, the shoots of this easily germinated plant are also becoming more commonly seen on western dinner tables, enriching salads, crudités, and sandwiches with their nutty flavor.

After the meal, Dai Mengjue stays a little while longer to send emails...

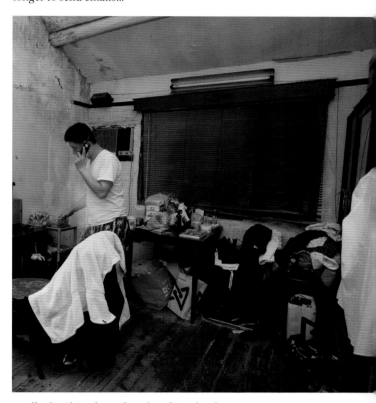

...call a few friends, make a few dates for the weekend...

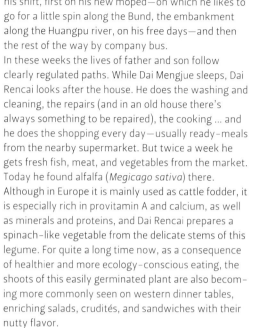

...and have a quick look on the Internet to see what films are on and listen to music at the same time.

Then it is time to set off for the tobacco factory once again.

In the dark, Dai Mengjue jumps on his moped and waves to his father. "Good night—see you in the morning!"

Anhui

安徽

Katrin Schlotter

The Central Chinese province of Anhui is one of the most beautiful regions of China, and simultaneously one of the poorest. It has become synonymous with migrant labor. Anyone who comes into contact with construction workers in Shanghai will hear the Anhui dialect spoken, almost as often as well-off families who are looking for a childminder. In 2007, the per capita income of the inhabitants of Anhui was 1,580 US dollars, about a third of that in the wealthy adjacent provinces of Zhejiang and Jiangsu. Two great rivers dominate the province—in the northern plains the Huaihe, in the southern mountains the Yangtze. So it lies within the spheres of influence of two weather systems—and it almost seems as if Anhui cannot decide whether it has a temperate climate or a subtropical climate. Changeable weather, wide variations in temperature and irregular precipitation mean the farmers have to work hard. Nevertheless, agriculture plays an important role here. But heavy industry has been promoted as well. Auto factories and steel plants are concentrated around the provincial capital, Hefei, which has 1.5 million inhabitants, and the cities of Wuhu, Anqing, and Ma'anshan. The province also has considerable reserves of coal, iron ore, and copper.

Anhui was not always poor. Up until the Qing Dynasty (1644–1912), the region surrounding the southern city of Huangshan-Shi (which was formerly well known under the name of Huizhou) was the center of the Huizhou culture. There may no longer be any prosperous merchants there today, but its picturesque villages (Hongcun and Xidi, for example), with their typical white dwellings with black, curved roofs, have been a UNESCO World Heritage Site since 2000.

But the main attraction in Anhui, which is visited by about 60 million tourists every year (mostly Chinese) is Huangshan, the "Yellow Mountains." This is one of the five most famous mountain ranges in the country. It is really a whole chain of mountains, which even foreigners recognize at first glance as an essentially Chinese landscape. The fissured cliffs and the weatherworn pine trees of the Huangshan are a recurrent motif in classical Chinese painting. Chinese couples visit the summit of the Huangshan range to bring good fortune to their marriage—if they attach a padlock to a railing there and throw away the key, their married life will be happy as long as they live. Those interested in spiritual matters visit the Jiuhuashan, one of the four holy mountains of Buddhism. It is considered as being sacred to the Boddhisatva Dicang, the patron saint of travelers.

Top above: Only a few hours by auto from Shanghai and yet a completely different world—for Anhui is very definitely a rural society.

Above: Life in the villages of Anhui is very far removed from the comfort and the well-stocked tables of the big cities. Life moves at a much slower pace here.

Facing page: The alluvial soil on the banks of the Yangtze is intensively farmed.

Hefei

Unknown but classic—the cuisine of Anhui

For many years now, typical Chinese restaurants in the West have featured dishes from Beijing, Guangdong or Sichuan on their menus. Specialties from Anhui, by contrast, are completely unknown here. Even in China, travelers rarely encounter the Anhui style of cooking, in spite of the fact that "Hui cuisine" is considered as being one of the eight great culinary traditions of China. Many people may think this is because not every tradition can preserve its fame for centuries and be exported into the wider world, but essentially, this inland province is thought of as being relatively poor. Moreover, it was not until 1667 that Anhui was actually declared to be a province in its own right. It was previously part of Jiangsu. The inhabitants of Anhui are not too happy if people lump the Anhui cuisine together with the Jiangsu style of cooking because the two share similar dishes and a common history. Their taste in food and drink essentially reflects the glittering era of the merchants of Huizhou. They were the ones who developed the trade links between the north and the south, and brought wealth to their region, following the transfer of the imperial court of the southern Song dynasty (1126–1279) to Hangzhou in the province of Zhejiang. For about 300 years, the influential merchants from the area around the Huangshan mountains made their mark on the economy, on politics, education, and culture. They also enriched the culinary tradition of Anhui.

Nowadays, specialty restaurants are reviving many classic dishes from the Hui cuisine, like whole soft-shelled turtles, stewed with ham, bamboo, garlic, ginger, and rice wine, considered as being a strengthening delicacy. And black stone frogs, which weigh in at around 8–9 ounces (250 g), have a leading role in the Anhui cuisine, being considered good for your health and strength. Other frequently used ingredients are reptiles and Bengal tigers, and indeed wild herbs, ferns, and mushrooms. The rare ingredients alone made sure that the Anhui cuisine could not spread all over the world.

But it does not rely on rare ingredients and nothing else. Bamboo, mushrooms, and ham, together with fresh and salted river fish, as well as noodles and tofu, enrich the many-sided cooking of the mountains. Farther to the north, in addition to rice, sweet potatoes, and tofu, we will usually encounter fish, crabs, poultry, beans, water chestnuts, and lotus on the menu. Particularly well known are stewed doves, Luzhou ducks, and Fuli chickens, together with the transparent silverfish, which can be 2 inches (5 cm) long. And there is no shortage of dishes associated with famous people from history. A stew containing sea cucumbers, squid, tofu, chicken, and ham is named for the reforming external affairs specialist Li Hongzhang (1823–1901). While entertaining an American delegation, he won his place in culinary history by ordering a stew made from every available ingredient.

The most popular technique among the cooks of Anhui is stewing in broth or soy sauce. Only fish and crabs are steamed. Wok dishes and stews containing bamboo, mushrooms, and wild herbs have ham added to give off a powerful, salty aroma. Partly fermented fish and stinky tofu also help to provide a distinctive taste and, together with the unusual ingredients, help to create the unmistakable character of Anhui's cuisine—and so it should be for one of the eight culinary traditions of China.

Below: Freshly-baked filled dumplings, *Mei gan cai* (pig's ears) are a favorite specialty for street snack vendors.

Below bottom: The delicacies and other ingredients used in the Hui cuisine are almost completely unknown in the West.

Right: Vegetables are very important to cooking in Anhui.

Fried smelt with egg

¾ lb (350 g) smelt (eg. rainbow smelt, whitebait…)
½ tsp salt
½ tsp freshly ground white pepper
1–2 tbsp Shaoxing rice wine
1 tbsp mixture of pureed scallions and ginger
1 small egg
1 tbsp cornstarch
breadcrumbs
4 cups (1 liter) peanut oil
1 ½ tbsp sesame oil
1–2 tbsp finely chopped scallions

Rinse the smelt and pat dry. Season to taste with salt and pepper, adding rice wine, and the pureed scallions and ginger. Leave to marinate for a short while.

Stir the egg together with the cornstarch; coat the smelt and roll in the breadcrumbs. Heat a wok to high temperature and add the peanut oil. Add the smelt carefully and deep-fry until golden yellow, then remove immediately and drain well.

Replace the oil in the wok with the sesame oil, heat up, add the scallions, and fry rapidly. Place the smelt on a serving plate and scatter over the scallions.

Huangshan snails

3 fresh green chiles
1 small scallion
1 piece ginger (2 inch / 5 cm)
4 garlic cloves
1 tbsp Shaoxing rice wine
½ tbsp soy sauce
1 tsp salt
½ tsp freshly ground white pepper
1 tsp cornstarch, mixed with 2 tsp water
¾ lb (350 g) snail meat, ready for cooking
1–2 tbsp vegetable oil

Cut the chiles into rings. Slice the scallion, ginger, and garlic.

Stir the rice wine, soy sauce, salt, white pepper, and the cornstarch and water mixture in a bowl. Bring 4 cups (1 liter) of water to a boil in a wok. Briefly blanch the snail meat, then remove using a perforated ladle and pat dry.

Above: Bamboo shoots, beansprouts, tofu, noodles, and soybeans—you don't need many ingredients to prepare tasty fast food.

Clean the wok, add the oil and heat up. Add the chiles, scallions, ginger and garlic, and fry briefly. Add the snail meat and stir in the rice wine mixture until it thickens, and serve.

The snails must not be cooked too long otherwise they become rubbery.

Teatime—and not all tea comes from Qimen

The province of Anhui is known far beyond its borders for its fine green tea—and its black *Qimen* variety is one of the ten best-known types of tea in China. In the West, it is commonly known as "Keemun tea," and tea-lovers consider it to be the acme of Chinese black teas.

Its fine-rolled, dark brown leaves, which have golden tips, release a multifaceted aroma. Depending on the variety, the bouquet can recall honey and apples, orchids, or roses. Many varieties give off rather fruity notes, with earthy and woody undertones. Others again release an aroma of cedar or pinewood and have a slightly nutty taste. *Hao Ya A*, the silvertips tea, is considered as being the best Qimen variety.

However, the multiple aromas cannot be appreciated unless the tea is correctly prepared. The amount of tea used will vary depending on the tea's quality, the size of pot, and personal taste. But in addition the water, as ever, plays a decisive part. It should be soft and/or filtered, and it should be poured over the tea boiling hot. Chinese tea-lovers prefer to pour tea out from little Yixing pots, since high-quality Qimen varieties can be re-used several times, with subtle differences each time.

First, a little water is poured on the tea for cleaning purposes and to release the aroma. The liquid is poured away. Not until the second brew is the full aroma discharged, after three to five minutes. And the color of the brew made from *Qimen* tea can vary enormously, from orange-yellow to dark red. Incidentally, this is the origin of the Chinese designation *Qimen hongcha*: red Qimen tea.

However, the true homeland of black tea is not in Anhui, but in the province of Fujian, in the Wuyi mountains. It was there that tea growers hit upon the idea of rolling up faded tealeaves, allowing them to oxidize, and finally drying them over a fire. It soon became clear that black tea kept for a long time, and so it could be transported—something had been created which could be exported to the West. An intelligent civil servant recognized the opportunity to make a profit, and in 1875 he brought the process to his own part of the country, Qimen. It was a success. Even nowadays, *Qimen*, which started its career as the main ingredient of the British royal family's "Breakfast Tea," enjoys great popularity.

Top right: You cannot have tea without cookies. The top picture shows "Kisses from Anhui cookies"—the color and shape of the cookie look like black inkstones. But cookies tasting of sesame seeds and nuts (bottom picture) are very popular as well.

Below: Flowers mingled with tealeaves release a unique aroma when the tea is poured out.

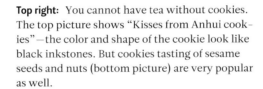

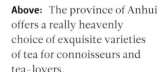

Left: One of the best-known brands from Anhui, "Monk's tea."

Below: A real work of art and best prepared in a glass pot. The green tea bead, which has osmanthus flowers in it, is placed in the container (1). Then hot water is poured over it (2). Now the tea bead slowly opens (3) and releases the treasures within, the flowers and their scent (4).

Above: The province of Anhui offers a really heavenly choice of exquisite varieties of tea for connoisseurs and tea-lovers.

1   2   3   4

1 The art of teamaking starts with choosing what type of tea you want. And here you can see what is understood by the word "teaspoon" in China.

2 Connoisseurs swear by Yixing pots from Jiangsu (see p. 116), which are not much bigger than a human hand.

3 A temperature of 167–194 °F (75–90 °C) is considered as being optimal for the first brew. This should be left to infuse for only a short time—about 20 seconds.

4 Some people think the first brew is only good for throwing away; however, others regard this as scandalous extravagance.

5 When several people take part in tea testing, the tea cups are stacked on top of each other while the tea is poured, so that the first cup stays hot.

6 The tea is drunk from small tea bowls. People say they can really see the aroma of the tea rising from them.

Left: The region around Huangshan is blessed with the best tea plantations and growing areas in the world.

Below: What coffee is to Western cultures, tea is to China—and this applies to old and young alike.

Left: In contrast to black tea, the leaves of green tea are not fermented. This has an influence on the constituents, and thus also on the taste and the preparation. The long tea leaves are placed in a glass (1) and then hot water is poured over them (2). As with all teas, the quality of the water is decisive. Moreover, if it is too hot, the tea becomes bitter, and sometimes even undrinkable. High-quality green teas can be used for several brews. However, the tea should not be left to infuse for more than 1–2 minutes. Often the first brew isn't even drunk, just thrown away (3).

1   2   3

The Huizhou mercantile culture

Without any clearly definable plan or purpose, and although lacking the necessary resources and contacts, the inhabitants of the Huangshan region succeeded in basing a culture which is still talked about today upon an accident of history—relying only upon family solidarity, the will to survive, and some clever investments.

The origins of the Huizhou mercantile culture go back to the Southern Song dynasty (1126–1279), when the imperial court fled from Kaifeng (in Henan province) to Lin'an, present-day Hangzhou, in the province of Zhejiang, and settled down there. Palaces, houses, and indeed the entire infrastructure had to be either transferred southward or constructed anew. The entire region forming the present provinces of Zhejiang, Jiangsu, Jiangxi, and Anhui profited from this. The inhabitants of Anhui, in particular, knew how to use their resources and the advantages of their location. They established their reputation by conducting negotiations between the various parts of the region. Family associations combined their possessions in order to send someone from their ranks off to foreign parts, taking with him

the hopes of the entire clan. Initially it was the construction boom that made it possible to amass the capital required for investments, through deals involving bamboo, timber, and enamelware, and through their artisan work. Soon afterward, luxury goods like tea, salt, silk, India ink, ink blocks, and paper served to increase their wealth.

Even during the Ming dynasty (1368–1644), 70 percent of the population of Huizhou were working as dealers. A few generations later, they were operating all over China and Southeast Asia as pawnbrokers. And clearly some cooks went to other areas as well, so that local specialties with rare ingredients from the mountain areas (such as soft-shelled turtles or dried bamboo shoots and mushrooms) reached the neighboring regions. According to the historical records, in the Ming and Qing periods (1644–1912), the inhabitants of the Jixi area alone owned over 600 restaurants in 14 provinces, and even in 1937 there were 130 Huizhou restaurants in Shanghai alone.

Thanks to the local people's strong family loyalties, the area surrounding the Huangshan mountains naturally flourished—and not only from an economic point of view. Merchants invested in the education of their offspring, so

Above: Though they may seem rather nondescript at first sight, the buildings in Hongcun still conceal some extremely informative architecture from the Ming and Qing eras.

Left: Artistic carvings on entrance doors speak of the glory of days gone by.

Below: Among the historical figures who came from Anhui was Li Hongzhang, one of the most powerful men in China in the late 19th century. His former residence in Hefei can be visited.

Right: Behind these rather plain facades in Hong-cun lie some richly furnished inner courtyards. The village is considered as being an incomparable example of Chinese domestic architecture.

Far right: Xidi is also one of the little villages which withstood the ravages of the cultural revolution. The bizarre street system and the cleverly devised drainage system are two remarkable features of the village's architecture.

Below: The best way to warm cold bones when it rains is with a hearty snack.

that scholars and officials from Anhui became increasingly influential politically. The extent to which they also left their mark on artisan work and architecture can still be recognized today in the picturesque locations of Tunxi, Shexian, Xidi or Hongcun.

It is almost as if time had stood still. White cottages with slate gray roofs from the Ming and Qing periods are surrounded by green fields and lakes, as in a classical landscape painting. Protected by high walls ornamented with artistic stone carvings, the houses stretch out along sparklingly clean, elaborately paved streets, which are surfaced in such a way that they are not slippery even when wet. Here and there, monuments rear up into the sky—a kind of combined memorial and gateway arch, which honors the services rendered by famous mercantile families.

But it is not just artistic temples, bridges, and monuments that bear witness to the prosperity and artisan work of the Huizhou merchants. The dwelling houses, two or three stories high, also demonstrate their builders' prudence. The rainwater was not just allowed to drain away unused, but was captured by skillful roof construction. The houses are almost all arranged around an inner courtyard, which not only provides light and air, but also gives scope for an imposing entrance. And yet, then as now, the courtyard houses appeared rather simple from outside. The lavish displays of wealth—such as wood carvings, stone carvings, and lacquered carvings—are found (where they exist at all) only within the walls.

Top: The village of Tangyue is ringed by one of the most famous collections of so-called gates of honor. These were created by order of the emperor for special services, although most of those honored in this way had to pay the construction costs themselves.

Left: Even if villages like Xidi, Hongcun or Tunxi are nowadays museum villages, everyday life still goes on as usual behind the facades.

Facing page: The hall of Zhui Mi belongs to one of the best maintained dwelling houses in Xidi.

Below: The splendor and beauty of Huizhou architecture is demonstrated only in the details of the artistically designed interiors.

Below bottom: Shexian is also one of the assortment of villages between Hangzhou and Nanchang which have retained their original character.

The Huizhou mercantile culture **153**

Delicacies from Anhui

The landscapes of the province alternate between enchanting mountains and lush green fields. The fields in the valleys and plains are full of rice, wheat, maize and corn, beans, cotton, tobacco, rapeseed, and millet, and there are fruit orchards too. Anhui is one of the most important agrarian regions of China and can thank its special climatic conditions for a number of delicacies that grow outstandingly well here.

In the area around the Huangshan mountains, the small and particularly aromatic **Huangshan kiwi fruit** (*Actinidia chinensis*) can be found. They are not only popular raw, but also cooked or dried. The Shezian region is known for both the rather crunchy **Chinese white pear** (*Pyrus bretschneideri*), which ripen wrapped in paper bags, without direct sunlight, and the sugary sweet **Santan loquats** (*Eriobotrya japonica*).

The spherical **Fudai poplar plums** (*Myrica rubra*), the white and deep red varieties of which are on sale in the markets, are also considered as a local specialty. When the slightly sour fruit, which can be up to about an inch (3 cm) long, are removed from their waxy shells, they are processed to provide juices, or sold in sugar syrup.

Without the **Xiangfei nut** (the seed of the Chinese yew nut tree, *Torreya grandis*, from the Yixian region), Anhui would lose a special delicacy. The nuts grow on trees which can be up to 500 years old (and which are also called "long life trees"), and they take about two years to ripen. Then they are shelled, roasted, and salted. Healing properties are attributed to the nuts, which are both a delicacy and a symbol. They are not just seen as snacks, but they are also thought to strengthen the lungs and stomach.

Top right: A plant with many uses: The lotus serves as an ornamental plant, and its rizomes are processed for use as a vegetable and in salads; the seeds are a favorite snack.

Bottom right: Sugar cane is another valuable crop cultivated in Anhui.

Below: Dried and sugared kiwi fruit pieces are favourite morsels—especially at teatime.

Healing powers are also attributed to the **Huizhou chrysanthemum** (*Dendranthema verstitium*). According to traditional Chinese medicine (TCM), the little white flowers (almost yellow) have an effect that is refreshing and simultaneously relaxing. They are also good for the eyesight. Fresh or dried, they are used to make green tea more aromatic.

In the remote mountainous regions, by contrast, tender bamboo shoots and ferns flourish, and wild mushrooms grow in narrow cracks in the cliffs. Even today, they are harvested, though it's hard work. Frogs, rock cod, carp, and soft-shelled turtles, which have spent their entire lives splashing about in clear mountain waters, also seem to be in their element in clear broths. Anyone who has once tasted a dish made with these specialties knows how to appreciate the quality of the Huizhou cuisine.

Above top: Dried bamboos

Above: The bean-shaped Santan loquats smell like apples, but they taste more like apricots.

Center left: The famous Xiangfei nuts take about two years to ripen.

Far left: They are sold in packs to make a popular snack.

Left: The unique, crispy tubers of water chestnuts enhance many vegetable and meat dishes.

Delicacies from Anhui   **155**

Specialties of Anhui cuisine

Tofu à la Zhu Hongwu

3 ½ oz (100 g) half and half fat and lean pork
few shrimp
2 tsp cornstarch, mixed with 4 tsp water
2 ¼ lb (1 kg) pork dripping or lard
1–2 tbsp finely chopped scallions
1 tbsp finely chopped ginger
1 tsp Shaoxing rice wine
salt
2 tbsp bouillon stock
generous 1 lb (500 g) tofu

Batter:
4 egg whites
2 tbsp cornstarch

Broth:
7 tbsp bouillon
½ tsp salt
½ tsp sugar
1 tsp rice vinegar
2 tbsp cornstarch

Finely chop the pork. Wash the shrimp, pat dry, finely chop and mix with half the cornstarch and water mixture. Heat a wok, add a little pork dripping and shake the melted fat round the wok, then pour it out. Put the scallions and ginger in the wok, together with the pork and shrimp, and stir continuously, taking care not to let the mixture form clumps. Add the Shaoxing rice wine, salt to taste, and 2 tablespoons bouillon and bind with the remaining cornstarch and water mixture. Turn out onto a plate and leave to cool.
Cut off the outer skin of the tofu on all sides and cut the block into 24 rectangular slices measuring 1 ½ x ¾ inches (4 x 2 cm). Lay the slices flat on a plate. Divide the shrimp and meat filling equally over 12 tofu slices, then cover these with the other 12 tofu slices and press together. Beat the egg white in a bowl until it becomes frothy, add the cornstarch and stir. Melt the remaining pork dripping in the wok on a high heat. Dip each tofu "sandwich" all over in the egg white, place in the wok and deep-fry until a solid crust forms, then remove using a ladle. When all 12 pieces have been cooked, heat the fat on a high heat again and deep-fry them for a second time, until they are golden yellow. Remove and allow them to drip dry. Pour away all but 2–3 teaspoons of fat from the wok. Add the bouillon to the wok, carefully add the tofu cookies and season with salt and sugar. When the broth is simmering on low heat, add the vinegar and bind the fluid with starch. Remove the wok from the stove and distribute the dish onto serving plates.

Bell pepper with meat filling

15 green mini bell peppers
1 ½ tsp cornstarch
9 oz (250 g) pork
1 slice cooked ham (or chicken if preferred)
1 egg
1 tbsp cornstarch, mixed with 2 tbsp water
8 water chestnuts
1–2 tbsp very small dried shrimp
1–2 tbsp finely chopped scallions
1 tbsp finely chopped ginger
½ tsp salt
½ tsp freshly ground white pepper
2 tsp Shaoxing rice wine
2 tsp soy sauce
3 ½ tbsp lard (rendered pork fat)
1 tsp sugar
chicken broth

Remove the stem, seeds, and membrane of the peppers; dust the inside of the peppers with starch, so that they do not explode when cooked. Finely chop the pork and ham and stir together with egg and cornstarch mixed with water. Add

the water chestnuts and shrimp. Stir in the scallions and ginger together with the salt, pepper, and rice wine, and mix well. Fill the peppers with the mixture.

Heat the lard in a wok and fry the peppers. Transfer the peppers to a bamboo steamer. Add chicken broth to the wok, cover with the steamer and steam the peppers. When the peppers are tender, pour the broth into a bowl and stir in the soy sauce, salt, sugar, and sufficient cornstarch powder to thicken. Pour the sauce over the filled peppers and serve.

Fragrant soybeans

generous 1 lb (500 g) soybeans
cloves
2 tbsp fivespice powder
2 tbsp Shaoxing rice wine
2 tbsp soy sauce
2 tbsp finely chopped licorice

Rinse the soybeans, put into a wok and cover with water. Add a few cloves and the fivespice powder, to taste. Cook for 5 minutes on high heat, then reduce the heat.

Add the rice wine and soy sauce, cover with a lid and let everything simmer until the soybeans become wrinkled and the sauce thickens. Remove the wok from the stove, add the licorice, stir everything together and serve.

Lotus with lotus seeds

5 tbsp lotus seeds
8–9 oz (250 g) lotus root
vegetable oil for frying
2 scallions, cut into pieces
1 chile, cut into rings
1 cup (250 ml) water
2 tsp salt
1 tsp sugar
$\frac{1}{2}$ tsp freshly ground white pepper
$\frac{1}{2}$ tbsp sesame oil

Rinse the lotus seeds and cook in boiling water in a wok for 20–25 minutes. Drain and set aside. Wash the lotus root and cut into $\frac{1}{4}$-inch (5-mm) slices.

Heat some oil in the wok. Briefly fry the scallion slices and the chile rings, add the lotus root slices and fry for about 8 minutes. Then add the cup of water and allow to boil. Add salt, sugar, pepper, and sesame oil, together with the lotus seeds, and stir-fry everything together. Cover and simmer over medium heat for 3–5 minutes and then serve.

Chinese drinking games

Drinking games (*jiuling*) are an old tradition in China. Many sources maintain that originally they served a higher purpose—to make sure that educated people did their drinking in a civilized manner. As when Confucian scholars of the Tang dynasty (618–907) competed to make up the most ambitious literary riddles, recite the most obscure verses from the classics without any mistakes, or compose an impromptu poem. An arbitrator made a decision if any disputes occurred as to whether someone had failed to carry out a task properly and so had to empty his glass as a penalty. People usually drank rice wine, but not infrequently they drank clear liquor instead, which was sometimes more than 50 percent alcohol. True to the Chinese toast—*Ganbei*, which calls on you to "dry the glass"—the contents of the glass had to go down in one. It was tough luck on anyone who lost more than once. As his alcohol intake increased, he had less and less chance of solving the tricky brainteasers, lost more and more frequently, and very quickly got dead drunk. In this way, what were originally highly intellectual pastimes rapidly turned into ordinary boozing sessions.

Even today, in addition to beer and wine, the most popular drink for what are usually less challenging drinking games (like the very popular "Stick, tiger, hen," known all over China) is a highly alcoholic liquor such as Maotai (54–55 percent) or Erguotou (56 percent). This game, like almost all Chinese drinking games, is played with two contestants each time—usually among friends after a meal in a restaurant or in the village bar—and almost exclusively involves men. This is how it goes. The stick hits the tiger, the tiger eats the hen, the hen eats the worm (which is not mentioned in the name of the game) and the worm nibbles the piece of wood. Both players pick up their chopsticks and tap them to each other each time in rhythm after the three keywords have been spoken in unison: stick (*bangzi*), tiger (*lao-hu*), hen (*ji*). On the fourth beat both men must simultaneously shout out

one of the four keywords. The one whose keyword is "superior" has won. And the loser has no choice but to empty his glass—down in one, it goes without saying.

Another game called "15, 20" (*shiwu, ershi*) is a little more demanding, as it calls for some quick adding-up. Two players call out one of the following numbers aloud: 0, 5, 10, 15 or 20. At the same time, each player extends both hands into the center—either balled up to form a fist (0 points) or with one finger sticking out (5 points). Whoever calls out the right answer for the sum of all the numbers shown by the four hands wins, and can enjoy watching the other man "dry his glass." Of course, the more times a contestant falls short of the right answer and has to obey the rules of the game and reach for his glass, the less likely he is to win. To quote the long-serving China correspondent of the German newspaper *Süddeutsche Zeitung*, Kai Strittmatter: "A game in which the loss of one's ability to count and the increasing consumption of liquor work together in an extremely effective way."

In Chengdu, the capital of Sichuan province, they have something of a variation: *Shuo Cai Yao Cai* (Call for riches, you'll get riches). This variation is played with one hand only, and you show either a fist (0), a thumb (1), a thumb and forefinger (2), or else ring finger, middle finger and pinkie (3). So the total will lie between one and six, and here again you have to shout the right number out aloud.

When playing such drinking games (of which there are many variants with many systems of counting), well-educated Chinese people also like to quote from the historical novel *Sanguo Yanyi* (The Story of the Three Kingdoms) and call out "The *three* invitations of Zhuge Liang" or "The *seven* arrests of Meng Huo." For traditional education is once again revered in China, and thus an old tradition is currently being revived. As in the old days, so today, people mix drinking with cultivated games—"getting drunk like gentlemen."

ELKE SPIELMANNS-ROME

Left: In all the best Chinese department stores, you'll find at least one shelf of high-proof liquors.

Top right: Maotai is the brand of Chinese liquor best known in the West, but it is far from being the only one.

Right: The Chinese for liquor is *bai jiu*, which roughly translated means "white alcoholic drink." Most liquors are based on sorghum, rice or millet.

Left: As archaeological finds have shown, alcohol has been produced in China for well over 5,000 years.

Top: The consumption of alcoholic drinks (as well as tea) at a banquet is practically compulsory in China. Beer and liquor are among the favorite forms of alcoholic beverage. And people like to play drinking games.

Right: Usually two people play against each other. The loser has to empty his glass—and "no heel taps": a rule of the game which makes for a lively evening, but is not really the best way to avoid a headache on the following day.

Above: A game for those who can do sums quickly, and in which it gets more and more difficult to concentrate the way you should: "15, 20".

Top right: "Stick, tiger, hen" corresponds to our popular game "Scissors, stone, paper"—the difference being that in the Chinese variant alcohol plays a more important role each time around.

Right: Poor loser! In the course of an evening, he may end up drinking quite a lot of alcohol. However, drinking games of this kind keep within bounds, for anyone who is completely drunk loses face—a situation that in China would quickly lead to social isolation.

Zhejiang 浙江

Katrin Schlotter

This eastern Chinese coastal province, south of the Yangtze Delta might be rather small, with an area of just under 40,000 square miles (102,000 sq km), but it has a lot to offer: venerable trading towns, monasteries on remote mountains and coasts, the best tea and silk, and exquisite cuisine. And we must not forget the other unique thing about this region: the character of its 50 million inhabitants.

Apart from its heyday in the 12th century—when the current provincial capital of Hangzhou was the seat of the imperial court and thus the epicenter of Chinese culture—life for the people here was often a struggle. Yet with the advent of reforms and policies of greater openness in the 1980s, Zhejiang blossomed once more. If you ask well-informed sources about the reason behind this renaissance, a dramatic pause is followed by the stock answer, "It's our attitude, the Zhejiang spirit: work hard, live simply, and maintain your contacts!" Their compatriots elsewhere in China regard the Zhejiangese as particularly well-connected and intrepid businesspeople.

The reforms at the beginning of the 1980s, which made private initiatives worthwhile, came in the nick of time. Ahead of all the other provinces, small businesses made up of families or whole villages pooled their resources in order to do the groundwork for state-run companies, or manufacture specific products such as plugs, socks or shoes. These small firms worked in a stimulating, newly competitive market, and the owners and the party officials profited equally from their collaboration with one another. The better the relations between them, the easier it was for the companies to get licenses, tax concessions, and loans. For the party officials, as their villages and towns grew in wealth so did their prospect of sharing in the profits and moving up in the party hierarchy. In the absence of research funds for product development, many firms seized upon the obvious alternative: to manufacture copies. Their trump cards, small production plants and a great sense of comradeship allowed them to manufacture goods much more cheaply than established competitors, even for export. Only at the beginning of the 1990s, when private enterprise was becoming more widely accepted, did these private businesses emerge from the shadows of collective farms and the like.

Today Zhejiang's more than 400,000 private enterprises generate more than 80 percent of the region's total gross domestic product (GDP), which amounted to approximately 245 billion US dollars in 2007. The

Top: Many parks and temple complexes are relics of Zhejiang's heyday during the Song dynasty (960–1279), when the provincial capital Hangzhou was the seat of the imperial court.

Above: The frenetic hustle and bustle has a long tradition even in the small villages along the Grand Canal.

Facing page: Shaoxing, one of the oldest trading towns in the province, is dotted with canals and bridges.

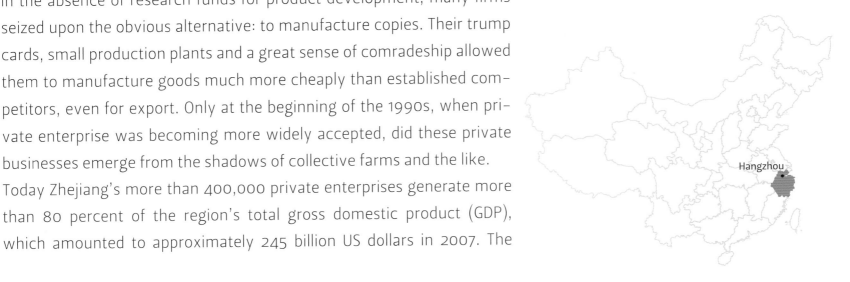

Hangzhou

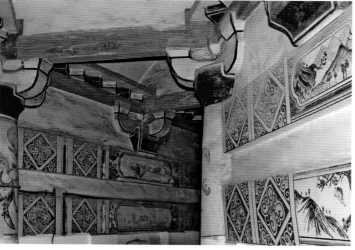

Top: Now famous as a high-powered, business-oriented region, Zhejiang was once a cradle of spirituality.

Above: This is evident today in the many well-maintained Buddhist and Taoist monasteries.

GDP per head is just under 5,000 US dollars, making this the fourth most commercially successful province in China. Alongside socks, ties, toys, household appliances and furniture, machine construction, electrical and chemical industry, and the IT sector play an important role. Service industries have settled predominantly in the north, around the provincial capital of Hangzhou, and IT, electronic and software development companies benefit from their proximity to Shanghai.

To the north, Zhejiang's fertile plains and gentle hills border onto affluent Shanghai and the province of Jiangsu; to the south, its steep mountain ranges define the boundary with Anhui, Jiangxi, and Fujian. Over 70 percent of Zhejiang is mountainous; while forest and bamboo groves sprawl over the heights, rice, corn and maize, sweet potato, cereals, rapeseed, and sugarcane thrive in the valleys, alongside tea and mulberry trees for the rearing of silkworms. The subtropical climate means that there is lots of sunshine and plenty of rain, and typhoons occur regularly. In winter the temperature can plummet to below freezing point, yet in the humid summers it can soar to over 104 °F (40 °C). Over 3,000 islands are dotted along Zhejiang's coastline, over 1,240 miles (2000 km) long. One of the most beautiful is the Zhoushan archipelago, off the shore of the harbor town of Ningbo, with its rich fishing grounds, rocky grottos, and beaches ideal for swimming. It is also home to one of China's four holy

mountains, Putuo, with its Buddhist monasteries. In the Ming era (1368–1644) several thousand monks withdrew to here in order to honor Guanyin, the goddess of mercy.

Over 165 million tourists, 4 million of them from abroad, visited Zhejiang in 2006, often making for Shaoxing, which is as famous for its canals as for its rice wine, or the riverside villages of Xitang, Nanzu or Wuzhen. Yet, for the Chinese, it is Hangzhou that is heaven on earth—undoubtedly due in no small part to its exquisite cuisine.

Above left: The area around Hangzhou is particularly prized as a tea-growing region, and is the origin of the famous dragon well tea.

Above: The island of Mount Putuo, off the coast of Zhejiang, is the home of Guanyin, China's most famous bodhisattva.

Below left: The Grand Canal, the world's longest man-made waterway, runs through the province.

Below: Zhejiang is renowned, first and foremost, as a province abundant in fish and rice. Yet many other agricultural products also thrive in its subtropical climate.

Gourmet heaven

Whether the dish is Longjing Shrimp, Dongpo's Pork, West Lake Carp, or Beggar's Chicken, the cuisine of Zhejiang, one of the eight culinary traditions of China, dazzles with its mild yet aromatic specialties.

In the 12th century it assumed royal status; at the imperial court in Hangzhou the best chefs in China conjured the most sumptuous meals out of the plentiful ingredients grown in the Yangtze Delta region. Many of these dishes are still famous today. Specialties such as Longjing Shrimp, coated with egg white before stir-frying and then cooked with fresh tealeaves, once tickled the palate of the emperor. The recipe for pork in the style of the official and poet Su Dongpo dates back 900 years, and today the pork belly still gets its exquisite flavor from slow-cooking for hours, roasting and steaming in rice wine and soy sauce. More elaborate in sourcing its ingredients but much quicker in its preparation is West Lake Carp, Hangzhou's, if not Zhejiang's, most famous dish—a grass carp is caught live, and kept for three days in fresh water without food so that it acquires its special flavor and firm flesh, reminiscent of crabmeat. It is briefly steamed or boiled and sprinkled with sweet-and-sour sauce, and has a remarkably delicate taste. Legend has it that the recipe for Beggar's Chicken, a dish that holds a special place in the hearts of the Zhejiangese, came from a resourceful beggar who wanted to grill a stolen chicken over a fire. As he didn't want the smell to give him away, he slathered the chicken in a thick layer of clay. Today salt, lotus leaves or plain old aluminum foil are used instead to retain the flavor when roasting, but the result is the same—wonderfully succulent chicken, so soft that the meat falls from the bone.

Chinese experts differentiate between the styles of "Zhe cuisine" that have emerged from the cities of Hangzhou, Ningbo, and Shaoxing, all steeped in tradition. While the former imperial city of Hangzhou favors dishes that involve simmering, braising, frying and roasting, the port city of Ningbo, which has access to the sea via its wide rivers, is known principally for its boiled fish and seafood, including oysters and turtles, and its sweet and salty snacks made from rice flour. In the interior, around the canal-streaked city of Shaoxing, the renowned eponymous rice wine plays the starring role. River fish and poultry here often get their special flavor from the Hongshao method of red cooking, which is wildly popular not only in eastern China, but throughout the Chinese-speaking world.

Red cooking involves simmering and braising fish, meat or tofu in a mixture of caramelized sugar, dark soy sauce, Shaoxing rice wine and Zhenjiang vinegar, sometimes for only 20 minutes, but often for several hours. The reddish-brown sauce is normally seasoned with ginger, fermented bean paste, and star anise, but, depending on the region, fennel seeds, black cardamom, cassia, dried tamarind or five-spice powder may also be added. Above all, the aromatic broth enhances everyday family meals, giving even simple ingredients like tofu or eggs a special flavor. It is common practice to reserve some of the Hongshao stock and use it several times—the flavor intensifies with each use!

At home, ready-made blends of spices from Asian food stores offer a tasty alternative, even if they fall short of a homemade Hongshao mixture. Under the broiler they can transform a simple pork chop into a Chinese culinary delight! Alongside meaty pleasures, vegetarian cuisine also plays a big part in Zhejiang, thanks to the Buddhists who pursued the worldly delights of

Bottom: Thanks to privatization small farmers can now make a profit from selling their products at the market.

Right: The clay crust of "Beggar's chicken" locks in the flavor of the tender meat (see recipe p. 177).

Far right: Su Dongpo (1037–1101), one of the most famous poets in ancient China, watches over countless restaurants, making sure that his eponymous pork dish (see p. 167) is prepared correctly.

cooking in their monasteries. Tender pseudo-meat dishes feature on the menu, but they are prepared with tofu to give the illusion of being genuine. Vegetarian ingredients like soybean sprouts or bamboo shoots, tofu, and mushrooms taste nothing short of heavenly when red-cooked à la Zhejiang!

Dongpo's pork

3 ¼ lb (1.5 kg) pork belly (with a thin rind)
2–3 scallions
2-inch / 5-cm piece ginger, roughly chopped
7 tbsp sugar
scant ⅔ cup (150 ml) soy sauce
generous cup (250 ml) Shaoxing rice wine

Wash the pork belly and rind thoroughly and cut into about 20 rectangular pieces, each about ½ inch (1 cm) thick.
Roughly chop the white sections only of the scallions.
Heat a wok and add ⅔ of the chopped scallions and ginger, and layer the pieces of pork over the top. Add the sugar, soy sauce, and rice wine, and sprinkle over the remaining scallions. Put the lid on the wok so that it is airtight, and turn up the heat. Cook the mixture for a few minutes over a high heat, then reduce the heat to the lowest setting and leave everything to braise for about 2 hours. Remove the lid and turn the pieces of meat, before finishing the meat over a very low

heat, with the lid on. Take the wok off the hob and skim any excess fat from the surface of the liquid.
Put the pork with its rind into two clay pots, put the lids on and seal them with special paper (*tao-huazhi*), but you can use aluminum foil instead) so that they are airtight. Place the clay pots in a bamboo steamer and steam for 30 minutes over a high heat, until the meat is very tender (alternatively you can make everything airtight and steam it in a wok). Serve immediately with soy sauce.

Su Dongpo, whose real name was Su Shi, was a poet, painter, calligrapher, and politician from the Song dynasty in the 11th century, and is one of the greatest Chinese poets. Legend has it that the dish named after him was invented when he became immersed in his work on a poem, forgetting a pot of simmering pork on the stove. After several hours of cooking it had become deliciously tender.

Above: Pickled ginseng roots are considered a pharmaceutical panacea in China.

Far left: Fish, meat, rice or tofu—there is no need to go hungry here.

Left: Rice wine is not only used in cooking. The venerable distillate is one of the oldest spirits in China.

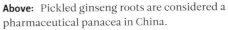

Left: Spit-roasted crabs: in the eastern regions of the province fish and seafood are offered everywhere as a snack.

Hangzhou: Chinese city of romance

The mere prospect of a journey to Hangzhou provokes immediate excitement among the Chinese: the capital of Zhejiang Province is one of the most beautiful cities in China, and is the country's wedding destination of choice. Yet the city, with a population of 2 million, is no romantic, isolated hamlet, but a wealthy coastal metropolis whose skyline bears witness to the fact that it has benefited from the Chinese reforms.

In the past, Hangzhou was one of China's most affluent cities. Even before the time of Christ it had developed into a center for silkworm cultivation and silk spinning, and it remains so today. Tea from Zhejiang Province was also popular in the most sophisticated circles. It is no coincidence that the Grand Canal—for a long time the most important transportation route between northern and southern China—ended at Hangzhou.

During the Southern Song dynasty (1126–1279) Hangzhou was the capital of China, following the flight of the imperial court from the Jurchens, invaders from northern China. At the time, Hangzhou was already one of the largest cities in the world, with a population of 1.5 million.

When the Mongols conquered China in 1279 the center of power shifted once again to the north, this time to Beijing. Yet Hangzhou remained an important city in economic terms. Given this heritage, visitors may be surprised to see that almost no buildings remain from the city's heyday; during the Taiping Rebellion (1850–1864), which rocked the whole of China, Hangzhou was all but razed to the ground. Almost all of the historical buildings, such as the magnificent Lingyin Temple complex, are reconstructions, albeit artistic ones.

Yet Hangzhou's reputation as an "earthly paradise" can be attributed to the West Lake (Xihu), at the heart of the city. Back in the 8th century a shallow creek of the Qiantang river was dammed, transforming it into a lake. Over subsequent centuries, the city fathers allowed many other landscape features to take shape: islands, pagodas, embankments, and bridges—new embellishments were always being added. Unsurprisingly, the West Lake is considered the pinnacle of the art of Chinese landscaping.

Rowing over the water at dusk, waiting in the moonlight and listening to the chirring of crickets while the lights slowly come up on the shore: this is the romantic image of China. Yet Hangzhou's West Lake makes an impression not only on lovers, but also on Chinese landscape designers; at least 36 Chinese cities have constructed a replica of the lake, which covers approximately 2 ¼ square miles (6 sq km). Only Japan has copied it more times!

The lake's most notable attraction is the "Island of Little Oceans," with its tiny ponds, tea houses, and gardens. The grand finale of a romantic walk around the lake has to be under the lights strung between the many trees on the shore, where there are small restaurants with select yet tantalizing menus. West Lake carp is always on the menu, and no self-respecting Chinese would visit Hangzhou without sampling this West Lake fish cooked in a

Right: The main attraction for all Chinese and foreign visitors to Hangzhou lies at the heart of the city: the West Lake and its shore.

Below: Classy stores offer one of the region's most famous products, dragon well tea.

Below right: With an average depth of 5 feet (1.5 m), the pleasure boats on the West Lake are more like Venetian gondolas than spacious tourist steamers.

sweet vinegar sauce, the region's most famous dish. Delicacies can be savored at the chic Louwailou Caiguan on the West Lake island of Gushan. Local dignitaries have been dining at this restaurant overlooking the lake for more than 160 years.

Tea-lovers make the most of their sojourn in Hangzhou by visiting the famous and outrageously expensive plantations of dragon well tea, or *Longjing Cha*, south of the city. With prices per kilo anything up to 590 US dollars, this top green tea certainly is not a bargain to snap up as a souvenir. In view of the price, it goes without saying that you cannot use any old water to make the tea. Experts swear by the nearby "Running Tiger Spring"; if on the way there you meet whole groups of people toting plastic bottles, they're not stranded motorists, but Chinese tea aficionados.

Top: "Above, the heavens; below, Suzhou and Hangzhou," goes a Chinese proverb.

Above: The Buddhist rock sculptures at the Lingyin monastery are on the list of national cultural treasures.

Left: The Marco Polo monument at West Lake is a reminder that the great traveler to the Orient also raved about Hangzhou. Whether he was ever really here or not remains a mystery.

A Chinese wedding

Chinese weddings, like those everywhere else in the world, are big family gatherings, with work colleagues, bosses, and friends invited along with the families of the bride and groom. A Chinese wedding party normally comprises more than a hundred guests. The celebration often takes place in a restaurant, and nowadays is informed by Western elements just as much as traditional Chinese rites and customs. These include a guest list, decoratively packaged treats for everyone, and photographs of the entire festivities, or indeed, often a video recording of the whole event. In many cases the host is a matchmaker or wedding planner; he (or she) conducts the marriage rites. Wedding presents, often money, preferably come in red parcels, since red is the color of luck and can't crop up often enough on such an occasion! Another Chinese tradition is to play some sort of prank on the newlyweds—the more pranks played on the wedding day, the happier the marriage! Yet the highlight is the wedding banquet, at which there are at least as many special dishes as there are guests. Whether in Beijing, Shanghai, Chengdu or Hangzhou, such a wedding quickly makes for the most expensive day of one's life. But Shi Peng and his bride Sun Ming Fang put this sobering thought from their minds, and want for nothing on their wedding day!

The couple writes their wish for "harmony" on the cake with chocolate-filled pastry bags.

The host conducts the ceremony, at which Sun Ming Fang wears a white wedding dress.

There is a parcel of candies for every guest, decoratively wrapped by the bridal couple.

Meanwhile the table is laid for the banquet; the array of dishes seems almost endless.

In another room those who have just arrived write their names on the guest list and present their gifts.

Before the couple takes their vows, HE puts her shoes on for HER, according to Chinese custom.

The exchanging of rings is captured on video camera, along with all the other highlights of the wedding ceremony.

While the wedding is being celebrated in the function room, it's all systems go in the kitchen.

Because everything is freshly prepared, vegetables are being washed right up to the last minute.

All the dishes are freshly prepared. The shredded chicken is put into the oven.

So many guests means lots of cabbage is required—shredded and seasoned with Zhenjiang vinegar.

Inside, the party is in full swing; outside, restaurant staff welcome arriving guests.

The bamboo containers are refilled with rice wine several times over the course of the evening.

Shi Peng and Sun Ming Fang's guests can hardly wait for the most convivial part of the celebration.

Yet before all that, the newlyweds are presented to everyone again with the bride's proud parents.

Waitresses bring wine so that the couple can toast to happiness with every single guest!

This goes on until Shi Peng and Sun Ming Fang have clinked glasses with every single guest.

Good wishes are exchanged, firstly between the bridal couple and the parents of the bride.

As custom dictates, Sun Ming Fang has changed out of her wedding dress and into a silk "Qipao."

Really good Chinese tea is also served alongside alcohol throughout the banquet!

Wedding recipes

Pineapple rice

1 ¼ cups (250 g) rice
1 pineapple
2 tbsp raisins
1 tbsp sugar
2 tbsp ground almonds

Rinse the rice and leave to soak in cold water overnight.
Cut the stalk off the pineapple, and carefully hollow out the pineapple without damaging the shell. Mix the rice with the raisins, the pineapple flesh, and the sugar, and stuff into the hollowed-out pineapple. Steam for 30 minutes. Sprinkle the finished pineapple with the ground almonds.

Jasmine-scented eggs

1 ¾ oz (50 g) jasmine leaves
6 eggs, whisked
salt and pepper
2 tbsp vegetable oil
baby leeks or scallions, sliced diagonally,
    to serve

Wash the jasmine leaves and blanch them briefly. Add to the whisked eggs and season with salt and pepper, to taste.

Heat the oil in the wok, add the eggs and scramble, stirring constantly. Sprinkle with the baby leek or scallions before serving.

Bitter melon with pork

14 oz / 400 g bitter melon
5 ½ oz / 150 g pork
1 leek, white part only
2–3 tbsp oil
1 tsp soy sauce
1 tsp rice wine
½ tsp salt

Wash the bitter melon and cut into pieces ½ inch (1 cm) thick. Cut the pork into thin strips. Finely chop the leek.
Heat the oil in a wok until it begins to smoke, then add the leek and fry for 1 minute. Add the pork, soy sauce, and rice wine, and stir in. Add the salt, followed by the bitter melon, stir-fry for 5 minutes and serve.

Right: Jasmine-scented eggs and pineapple rice

Below: Bitter melon with pork

Zucchini with pork

14 oz (400 g) zucchini
5 ½ oz (150 g) pork
2–3 tbsp vegetable oil
½ tsp finely chopped red chile
½ tsp salt
1 tsp rice wine
1 tsp soy sauce
finely chopped scallions, to serve

Wash the zucchini and cut into thin slices. Cut the pork into thin slices. Heat the oil in a wok, add the chile, and stir-fry. Add the meat, followed by the salt, rice wine and soy sauce. Stir-fry for 3 minutes until the meat is cooked through. Add the zucchini and stir-fry. Sprinkle with the chopped scallions and serve.

Below: Zucchini with pork

Silver needles and black dragons

For tea-lovers there is nothing better than ensconcing oneself in one of the peaceful tea houses on the shores of the West Lake, savoring a variety of teas, and, sip by sip, discovering the great array of flavors that the world's oldest tea culture has to offer.

Over 2 thousand years of tea cultivation in China have brought forth hundreds, if not thousands of varieties of tea. Yet whether green or black, all types of tea originate from one single original tea plant (*Camellia sinensis*). This evergreen tea bush, a species of camellia plant native to China, thrives in areas up to 8,200 feet (2500 m) in subtropical, temperate climates. The sun, rain, cloud, and soil are all as important to the flavor of the tea as the time at which it is picked and the care with which the leaves are processed. According to the degree of oxidation (also called fermentation), unfermented green tea may turn into half-fermented Oolong tea (*wulong* = black dragon) or fully fermented black tea (see p. 148). In China green tea has always been predominantly produced and drunk, especially in the eastern Fujian, Zhejiang, and Anhui Provinces. Oolong tea is produced in Fujian, Taiwan, and Guangdong, whereas black tea, for instance, is produced in Yunnan or Anhui and mostly exported. When sampling tea, it is best to start with the most

exquisite variety of all, white tea, which is produced mainly in the northeast of Fujian. White tea from the Da Bai Hao plant is named after the silvery, silky-smooth leaves, which surround its tea buds. High-end varieties like "silver needle" tea (*Baihao Yinzhen*) consist solely of unopened tea buds, while less expensive varieties like "white peony" (*Bai Mundan*) contain a maximum of two young leaf tips. The tender buds are picked individually by hand from the springtime onwards, with around 30,000 buds needed to produce one kilogram of tea. After picking they are dried by the breeze on racks, packed into large baskets, and sometimes they are briefly heated to dry them off once more. The white tea gets its mild, pure flavor from this refining process.

The production process for yellow tea is rather more lavish. After it is picked, the similarly expensive tea is first dried by heating, then repeatedly packed in paper, toweling or boxes for up to three days, and finally roasted. The most famous yellow tea is *Yunshan Yinzhen*, from Hunan.

Xihu Longjing, *Dongting Biluochun*, and *Huangshan Maofeng* are among the best Chinese green teas. Their hallmark is their fresh, floral aroma. The best quality

varieties are made of only the youngest leaves, hand-picked from the tea bushes, which sprout at the very beginning of spring. Since these young shoots are barely ³/₄ inch (2 cm) long, 70,000 to 180,000 of their tips are required to make a kilogram of tea. After plucking, the leaves are wilted for a couple of hours, and then sorted. As soon as the flavor begins to develop, the teamaker commences the roasting. For West Lake Longjing tea and Bi Luo Chun tea from Suzhou, the leaves are roasted in a cast-iron pan so that the flavor of the tea becomes more intense. In the case of Mao Feng tea from the Huangshan mountains, however, oven-roasting the leaves actually prevents the leaves from breaking. There are also various processes that lock in the flavor; Bi Luo Chun tealeaves, for instance, are rolled into small spirals, and gunpowder tea into pellets.

Teamakers process gunpowder tea in the same way as Oolong tea, a semifermented variety. After wilting, the young tealeaves are crushed together repeatedly,

Below left: This Hangzhou tea shop provides a classy tasting and shopping experience.

Below: A store clerk in a Chinese tea shop must possess a sense of smell and knowledge of tea at least as good as those of a salesperson in a Western perfumery.

Bottom: Tea flowers that open when brewed are a visual and aromatic delight.

so that their edges break up and become oxidized. When they reach the required level of fermentation (20–80 percent), they are roasted, rolled, and then dried partly over charcoal, which gives Oolong its characteristic smoky flavor alongside its sweet and fruity taste. The most famous Oolong teas are *Tie Guanyin* or the ruinously expensive *Da Hong Pao* from the Wuyi mountains, which can be steeped up to seven times, resulting in astonishing new aromas every time.

Left: A paradise for tea-lovers!

Below: Tea is fashionable as a drink at nightclubs and parties too!

Bottom: Tea has a place in China's cultural pantheon alongside the country's ancient poets and thinkers.

Zhejiang specialties

Pan-fried yellow croaker with vegetables

1 yellow croaker (generous 1 lb / 500 g); carp
   can be used as a substitute
9 oz (250 g) fatty pork
3–4 fresh shiitake mushrooms
1 oz (25 g) dried bamboo shoots
1 tbsp zha cai (pickled Chinese vegetables)
1 green bell pepper
4 cups (1 liter) peanut oil, for frying
2 scallions
1 small scallion, chopped
2-inch (5-cm) piece of ginger, chopped
2 garlic cloves, minced
1 1/2 tbsp hot chili bean paste
1 1/2 tbsp Shaoxing rice wine
2 tsp rice vinegar

2nd-stage sauce:
generous cup (250 ml) vegetable stock
1 1/2 tbsp soy sauce
1 1/2 tbsp sugar
1/2 tsp salt
1 tbsp sesame oil

Scale and clean the fish and remove the gills.
Thoroughly wash the fish, and then lay on a
chopping board. Score the fish with cuts 1/2 inch
(1 cm) apart, cutting down to the bones but not
into pieces. Cut the pork, shiitake mushrooms,
dried bamboo shoots, zha cai, and bell pepper
into 1/4-inch (5-mm) wide dice.
Heat the peanut oil in a wok over a high heat. Add
the fish and fry until it is golden brown on both
sides. When the fish is almost done, take it out
and drain in a strainer.

Leave about 7 tablespoons of oil in the wok and
reheat it to a high temperature. Stir-fry the scallion, ginger, and garlic until it gives off a good
aroma, then add the chili bean paste and stir-fry
everything until it becomes a smooth sauce.
Sauté the pork, mushrooms, bamboo shoots, and
zha cai briefly in the sauce, then add the fish. Add
the rice wine and vinegar and let everything simmer gently, uncovered.
To make the 2nd-stage sauce, add the vegetable
stock, soy sauce, sugar, and salt and bring to a
boil, and mix everything well. Simmer for 7–8
minutes over low heat.
Finally, reduce the sauce over fierce heat, then
take out the fish, place on a serving plate and
keep warm.
Return the wok to the heat, add the pieces of bell
pepper to the sauce and stir-fry briefly. Add the
sesame oil and let everything simmer until you
can see only the oily sauce, without any clear liquid. Pour the contents of the wok over the fish
and serve.

Pan-fried shrimp with green tea

9 oz (250 g) shrimp
1–2 tsp green (Longjing) or Oolong
   (Tie Guanyin) tea
1 garlic clove, chopped
1 slice of ginger, to taste, chopped
vegetable oil, for frying

Sauce:
1/2 tsp soy sauce
1 tsp Shaoxing rice wine
1 tsp sugar
1 tsp cornstarch

Rinse and devein the shrimp and cut in half. Place
the green or Oolong tea in a heat-resistant pot
with the garlic and ginger, and pour over boiling
water.
To make the sauce, mix together the soy sauce,
rice wine, sugar, and cornstarch. Heat a little oil
in a wok. Strain the tea and stir-fry the leaves
briefly with the shrimp.
As soon as the tealeaves begin to look slightly
burnt, remove the shrimp and tealeaves from the
wok using a slotted spoon.
Leave a little oil in the wok, reheat and add the
tealeaves and the shrimp once again. Stir-fry
briefly. Add the sauce, stir-fry to mix, and serve.

Air-dried pork with bamboo shoots

3 1/2 oz (100 g) spring bamboo shoots
1 red bell pepper, seeds and membrane
   removed
3 stalks garlic chives
7 oz (200 g) Chinese air-dried pork (*la rou*)
vegetable oil, for frying
salt (to taste)
sesame oil

Finely slice the bamboo shoots. Slice the red bell
pepper and the garlic chives diagonally. Blanch
the bamboo shoots briefly in boiling water, then
remove and leave to drain.
Put the meat in a pan, pour over sufficient boiling
water to cover and cook for 1–2 minutes, then
remove and cut into thin slices.
Heat the oil in a wok and stir-fry the meat until it
gives off a good aroma, then turn out onto a plate
and keep to one side.
Leave a little oil in the wok, and sauté the bamboo shoots and the bell pepper, then add the
meat and the garlic chives, and season with salt,
to taste.
Drizzle a little sesame oil over the top and serve.

Left: Pan-fried yellow croaker with vegetables

Left: Beggar's chicken

Below: Pan-fried shrimp with green tea

Bottom: Air-dried pork with bamboo shoots

Beggar's chicken

1 chicken (2 ¼ lb / 1 kg)
2 tbsp soy sauce
3 ½ tbsp Shaoxing rice wine
1 tsp salt
4 cloves
2 star anise
¼ tsp nutmeg
3 tbsp pork dripping or lard
1 whole scallion, finely chopped
4 tbsp chopped scallions (white part only)
piece of ginger (1 in / 3 cm-long), minced
⅓ cup (50 g) diced chicken meat
1 cup (100 g) diced lean pork
⅓ cup (50 g) chopped shrimp
2 tbsp diced cooked ham
3–4 shiitake mushrooms, cubed
about 14 oz (400 g) bacon in one piece
4 fresh lotus leaves, soaked
6 ½ lb (3 kg) clay
4 tbsp sesame oil

Marinate the chicken in the soy sauce, rice wine, and salt for one hour, and then remove. Crush 2 of the cloves and the 2 star anise using a pestle and mortar, and mix in the nutmeg. Rub this mixture over the chicken.

Heat a wok, add the pork dripping and allow it to melt over a medium heat.

Sear the scallion and the ginger until they give off a good aroma, then sauté the diced chicken, lean pork, shrimp, cooked ham, and the shiitake mushrooms one after the other in the wok, removing each in turn and setting to the side. Stick a clove into the meat under each of the chicken legs. Stuff the cavity of the chicken with the diced ingredients. Wrap the chicken in the slice of bacon, followed by two lotus leaves, greaseproof paper, and another two lotus leaves, and tie securely.

Pound the clay to a powder (if not already in powder form) and mix to a "dough" with water, then spread the clay in a layer about ½ inch (1.5 cm) thick on a damp dish towel. Place the trussed-up chicken in the middle of the clay, knot the four corners of the towel together and

wrap it around the chicken so that it becomes encased in the clay. Remove the towel carefully, so that the clay does not come unstuck from the chicken.

Heat the oven to a high temperature, 400 °F (200 °C). Place the clay-wrapped chicken on a baking tray covered with baking parchment, put it into the oven and bake for 40 minutes at high temperature. If the clay becomes hard and cracked, seal up the gaps with damp clay and cook for another 30 minutes at high temperature. Then reduce the heat and bake the chicken for another 90 minutes, before turning down the heat once again and cooking the chicken at a very low temperature for 90 minutes.

Take the chicken out of the oven, chip off the hard clay casing, and remove the lotus leaves and greaseproof paper. Drizzle the chicken with sesame oil and serve.

According to the legend about this recipe, a beggar who had stolen a chicken packed it in clay and hid it in some hot coals, so as not to be caught. When he later dug it up, he discovered that it tasted absolutely delicious.

Firewater et al—Chinese spirits

The range of alcoholic drinks in China is vast. Here everything from grain spirits and pomace brandies to rice, fruit and milk wines, beer, and wine are produced, not to mention consumed, with meals, especially at all kinds of parties or banquets, but also during the highly popular drinking games described in the Anhui chapter (see p. 158).

Beer is brewed predominantly in Heilongjiang Province and Qingdao, in Shandong. Chinese winemaking is also concentrated in this coastal province. The **milk wine** *airag* and the **milk schnapps** *arkhi* are Mongolian specialties, and are described in detail in the chapter on Inner Mongolia (see p. 430). Grain distillates, however, are distilled all over China, from millet or wheat in the north, sometimes with the addition of barley, and from rice in the south (south of the "noodle and rice line").

Rice wine is one of the longest-produced spirits in the Middle Kingdom, and contains relatively little alcohol (about 15 percent). The premier and best-known variety comes from Shaoxing, in eastern Zhejiang Province. It is produced primarily for the Chinese market, with only about 5 percent exported worldwide, of which half goes to Japan. The leading labels are Zhuangyuanhong, Jiafan, and Shanniang. There are more than 700 rice wine producers altogether in China. It is produced mainly in Zhejiang, Jiangsu, and in Shanghai, on the coast.

The production of rice wine is a lengthy process that sometimes stretches over several years. The longer the process and the older the wine, the more valuable and expensive the end product. Traditionally rice wine is made from glutinous rice, yeast, millet, and spring water. Shaoxing's spring water has a distinctive, rather tangy taste and adds to the unique flavor of the rice wine. The ingredients are stored in lime-washed clay pots, so that they can be left to ferment over several months or years at room temperature.

Rice wine is usually drunk hot, from small porcelain cups, among friends; sometimes it may also be sampled at room temperature, but never chilled. Yet the noble drop has a long tradition not only as a drink, but also as a special ingredient for use in cooking and marinating. When cooking, a little good rice wine is always a good fallback ingredient; if there is no rice wine available, a dry light sherry will suffice. Sake, the clear Japanese rice wine, is not always suitable as a substitute, as its taste is markedly different from that of its Chinese counterpart.

The alcohol content of Chinese brandy or **schnapps** (*baijiu*) is around 50–65 percent. Distillates from sorghum are of particularly high quality. The best and most popular varieties of Gaoliang schnapps come from the town of Maotai, in the southern Chinese province Guizhou (formerly known as Kweichou). This has led to this product being protected with designation of origin. **Maotai**, known worldwide as Mou Tai Kweichou is light yellow and about 55 percent alcohol. Heads of state are obliged to savor its unmistakable

aroma many a time on visits to China; toasts are always made with Maotai at Chinese state banquets.

Less expensive varieties of Gaoliang schnapps are ideal for marinades, including the rose-flavored schnapps **Meiguilu jui** (45 to 50 percent), a Gaoliang distilled with rose petals and sugar (available in the US as Mei Kuei Lu Chiew).

Other popular varieties of schnapps are **Xifeng Jiu** (45 to 49 percent) from Shaanxi Province, the five-grain spirit **Wuliangye** (52 percent), and **Zhuyeqing**, which is known abroad as Chu Yeh Ching Chew or as the bamboo schnapps Xinghuacun. This grain spirit owes its aromatic taste to the addition of herbs and bamboo leaves. The firewater **Erguotou**, a wheat spirit with up to 65 percent alcohol, is very popular in Beijing.

The renowned Tang-dynasty poet Li Bai (701–762), who was not averse to a good drop, wrote many poems about drinking which are still keenly cited today. Malicious rumors have it that he drowned in a lake when, in a tipsy state, he tried to embrace the reflection of the moon. Kong Yiji, the protagonist in the eponymous story by the famous Chinese writer Lu Xun (1881–1936), written in 1919, also came to a sticky end.

Born in Shaoxing and raised next to a wine tavern, as a child Lu Xun was witness to the harmful effects of drinking to excess, and in his work forcefully describes how a Confucian scholar gradually falls under the influence of rice wine, ending his days heavily indebted and a cripple. Nevertheless, this rather chilling story does not seem to have damaged the reputation of Shaoxing's much-loved drink, and the enjoyment of rice wine and other spirits continues to be an integral part of Chinese society.

ELKE SPIELMANNS-ROME

Far left: Rice wine is to Chinese cuisine as balsamic vinegar is to Mediterranean cooking.

Above left: Often likened to sherry, the different types of rice wine also vary in quality.

Left: The best—and most expensive—varieties have fine packaging to match.

Left: While European wine connoisseurs salivate at the sight of oak barrels, Chinese experts get excited at the sight of lime-washed clay pots.

Below left: The rice wine develops its unique flavor in these clay pots.

Below right: The national drink is stored on a grand scale; rice wine consumption in China is enormous.

Bottom left: Bottling and control processes are still done manually at good manufacturing plants.

Bottom middle: The pot is sealed, so that the wine can mature in peace...

Bottom right: ...before it is finally bottled in ornate carafes.

Ultimate delicacy—Jinhua ham

The black-and-white Jinhua pig has apparently thrived in the subtropical areas between the Yangtze and the southern Chinese Pearl River for thousands of years. Arguably China's most famous pig, its head and rump are jet-black, with a hefty white body in between. Yet its haunches have made a name for themselves throughout Asia; its hind legs must be toned and well-structured, with narrow ankles, so as to deveop into superb Jinhua ham after eight to ten months.

As early as the Song dynasty (960–1279), ham from the city of Jinhua, brought to the market air-dried, smoked or marinated in sugar or salt, has been a highly prized ingredient; it lends any dish, whether a simple stock or a delicacy, a strong, slightly sweet flavor. China's most famous ham tastes rather like Iberian ham, and the way in which they are made is also similar. The whole leg, including the trotter, is completely salted down up to seven times over the course of a month, at a temperature of 41–50 °F (5–10 °C), in order to prevent the formation of putrefaction bacteria. The next step is to remove the salt from the slightly dried ham. It is scrubbed and steeped in water, carved into the desired bamboo-leaf shape and branded to show proof of origin. Then the ham is dried in the sun for about a week, followed by six to eight months of ripening in a room cooled to 59 °F (15 °C) and at just under 60 percent humidity. If the enzymes have done their work, it only remains to clean the leg and rub it with oil. The longer the ham is left to ripen, the more flavorsome it is.

Above: Fish marinated with Jinhua ham

Left: Jinhua ham compares favorably with the Spanish hams Jamón Serrano and Lomo Ibérico.

Fish marinated with Jinhua ham

Marinade:
1/2 tsp salt
1/2 tsp rice wine

3 1/2 oz (100 g) fillet of freshwater fish
1 green bell pepper
3/4 oz (20 g) bamboo shoots
1 egg white, whisked
1 tbsp cornstarch
1 1/2 cups (350 ml) vegetable oil
1 tsp rice wine
1 tbsp cornstarch mixed with 2 tbsp water
1 tsp sugar
3 1/2 oz (100 g) Jinhua ham

Mix together the ingredients for the marinade. Cut the fillet of fish into thin slices spread with the marinade and leave for 10 minutes. Cut the bell pepper and bamboo shoots into strips roughly as big as the slices of fish.

Dip the marinated fish first into the whisked egg white, then coat with the dry cornstarch.

Heat 1 1/4 cups (300 ml) of the oil to high temperature in a wok and add the pieces of fish, stirring with a chopstick so that they don't stick together. Deep-fry for 3 minutes, and then remove.

Heat 2 tablespoons of the oil in the wok, add the pepper and bamboo shoots, stir-fry for half a minute, and then remove.

Heat the remaining oil in the wok. Add the fish, pepper and bamboo shoots, and stir-fry. Add the rice wine, cornstarch–water mixture, and sugar and stir-fry for 1 minute. Finally, stir-fry the ham for 1 minute and serve.

Above: The end result of intensive treating and long ripening—the genuine article comes complete with the pig's foot!

Right: The slightly sweet taste of Jinhua ham helps even the simplest dishes to reach new heights.

福建

Katrin Schlotter

Fujian

Half way between Shanghai and Hong Kong, directly opposite the island of Taiwan and covering an area of 46,872 square miles (121,400 sq km), lies the province of Fujian with its population of 36 million people.

With a gross domestic product (GDP) of around 124 billion US dollars (2007), Fujian is one of China's wealthiest provinces. Foreign trade plays an important role and Fujian's main exports include synthetics, textiles, and electronics. Despite only 10 percent of the land being suitable for farming, this subtropical province nevertheless supplies the bulk of the country's tea, citrus fruit, and bananas. Thanks to its forest hinterland, Fujian is also one of China's main producers of timber, bamboo, and paper. Over the past centuries, trade and seafaring have brought the province several periods of prosperity but on each occasion bans on maritime trade have led to economic collapse. This has led to a constant fluctuation between migration and emigration, particularly in the maritime towns of Fuzhou and Quanzhou, as well as along the coast. The hinterland, however, remained relatively unaffected by these events. Far away from the cultural centers along the coast, from which they were separated by massive, craggy mountain ranges, these upland dwellers developed individual traditions and dialects as a result of their isolation. It was not until the 1950s, when infrastructure began to be developed, that access to the coast became easier and provided this isolated region with a direct link to the outside world.

The province's coastal position was not always to its advantage, however. Since the People's Republic was founded in 1949, China has claimed the island of Taiwan as its 23rd province. Taiwan, on the other hand, considers itself an independent country. Consequently, the ensuing military clashes over the islands in the Taiwan Straits, particularly over Jinmen (Quemoy), continued to be a disincentive to investment in Fujian's economy for the next 30 years.

With the introduction of China's reform and openness policies during the early 1980s and the opening of the Taiwan Strait for cross-strait trade, trading activities began to flourish once more. The longstanding ties between Fujian and Taiwan—around 70 percent of Taiwanese come from Fujian and speak the same dialect—were also quickly revived. Investment programs and new businesses, as well as an increase in the number of Taiwanese traveling or visiting their former homes on the mainland, have lent a considerable impetus to the economy and tourist industry.

Top: Fuzhou is now a modern metropolis with very few leftover reminders of the days when it was a traditional Chinese port.

Above: Some of Fujian's inland regions have remained largely untouched by the economic upturn. Even so, the people, especially children, are still very relaxed toward foreigners.

Facing page: The Minjiang is the longest river in a province rich in water resources yet only part of it is navigable by large ships. Numerous freshwater fish and shellfish farms have been established along its banks.

Fujian **185**

Fujian cuisine— Buddha's temptation

Rich seabeds and rivers, fertile farmland, an abundance of fruit and mushrooms, herbs from the mountain regions and, not least, a large number of immigrants from other parts of China—together, these factors form the perfect basis for the incredible variety of recipes found in Fujian cuisine. Also known in China as Min cuisine, it is one of the country's eight main styles of regional cookery

Fujian chefs are particularly noted for their soup specialties, their cutting techniques, and their culinary inventiveness. A variety of ingredients—often meat and fish combined—are cut into wafer-thin slivers, delicately seasoned and combined to create an aromatic dish. Many of the recipes call for a special type of paste made from red-colored, fermented, sticky rice, which gives the dish a slightly sweet-and-sour note. Simmered gently in a delicate consommé, the ingredients develop a unique flavor.

Unsurprisingly, chefs from Fuzhou, the province's capital city, claim first place among Fujian cooks for specialties such as shark's fin or turtle soup. Their Xiamen counterparts, on the other hand, contest this accolade, citing their own peanut soup and numerous fish dishes, especially those involving oysters and lobster. Quanzhou chefs, not to be outdone, wax lyrical about their different snack specialties, and the situation is the same in Long'an, Nanping, or Sanming. The never-ending list of local specialties might well give the visitor the impression that to most Fujians, food is the most important issue in the world.

In order to appreciate the diversity of recipes and understand the rivalry, it will help to know that Fujian cuisine is usually divided into three different flavor categories: the fairly mild, slightly sweet-and-sour cuisine typical of Fuzhou; the fruitily sweet, slightly hot dishes and delicious dipping sauces of southern Fujian; and the salty, spicy cuisine found in the west of the province. Ingredients and culinary traditions still vary to this day, depending on whether it is a coastal or mountain region.

Along the 1,864 miles (3,000 km) of coastline, with its countless bays and islands, the sea yields around 200 different species of fish and over 90 varieties of shellfish. Freshwater fish are also available from rivers and fish farms, and pork and poultry are abundant. Crops such as rice, wheat, sweet potatoes, sugar cane, soybeans, peanuts, and every conceivable type of vegetable and fruit, including organically grown varieties, thrive in those fields that have not been sacrificed to industry. In the mountain regions, on the other hand, the menu traditionally includes river fish, snakes, snails, turtles, frogs, hare or goat, served with noodles, rice, bamboo, mushrooms, and herbs. In times of plenty, therefore, Fujian chefs are utterly spoilt for choice in the face of so many excellent ingredients.

The province has nevertheless experienced hunger on several occasions—as a consequence of drought, for example, or flooding caused by the Min River, both of which have in the past led to shortages of rice and vegetables. In such circumstances, sweet potatoes supplied a nutritious alternative, as they did in other areas. Dried, roasted or ground into flour, they still form an integral part of numerous dishes. Noodles, pancakes, and ravioli-style dumplings are all made from a mixture of wheat and sweet potato flour.

It is quite likely that Fujian's reputation for special expertise in cutting and slicing techniques is a throwback to poorer times, when it was crucial to use valuable ingredients sparingly. Culinary experts in Fujian maintain that ingredients are only able to develop their full flavor if cut into wafer-thin slivers or thinly sliced lengths. The fact that soup dishes are a specialty of the province may likewise be a consequence of harder times—a soup stock, fleshed out with a small amount of rice or noodles and a few other dry ingredients, would fill more mouths than a handful of rice. And the specialties? To the Western mind perhaps, one would have to be very hungry indeed to contemplate cooking and eating a swallow's nest. Alternatively, it could be argued that Chinese tastes had become so sophisticated that ordinary dishes were no longer enough to satisfy a jaded palate, a view that is certainly endorsed by Fujian chefs.

Carp steamed in red vinegar

1 carp (generous 2 lbs / approx. 1 kg)
2–3 quarts (2–3 liters) water
3 ½ tbsp soy sauce
7 tbsp rice wine
1 tsp finely chopped ginger
3 tbsp cornstarch
3 tbsp sugar
3 ½ tbsp rice vinegar

Wash the fish and cut along its backbone without actually separating the two halves of the fish. Make three to five incisions in the flesh without damaging the outer skin. Place the fish in boiling water with the skin uppermost and cook for three minutes. Remove the fish from the pan. Pour off the cooking liquid but retain 1 cup (250 ml) and return this to the saucepan. Place the fish in the liquid, add the soy sauce, rice wine, and finely chopped ginger and bring to a boil. Check the fish is cooked through, lift it onto a plate and keep warm. Dissolve the cornstarch in 2 ½ tablespoons water and add to the sauce together with the sugar and vinegar. Bring to a boil and simmer until the liquid thickens, then pour over the fish and serve.

Top: Chinese fast food: a lavish selection, perfectly cooked and clearly displayed, freshly and tastily prepared, bite-sized portions...and regular, satisfied customers.

Above left: Anyone strolling along Fuzhou's market streets will find it difficult to resist the inviting range of food on offer at the small snack bars and food stalls.

Above: A clever and efficient method of keeping individual portions warm.

Soup—good for the body as well as the soul

A few meager vegetables in a watery broth—is that what we understand by Chinese soup? At best, this warm liquid can be described as neutral in flavor, which is precisely its intended function. Whether served in small bowls between courses or at the end of a meal, its purpose is simply to neutralize flavors or provide an intake of liquid. However, Chinese chefs would agree that a "proper" soup, served as one of a sequence of courses, is something entirely different: sophisticated shark's fin, swallow's nest or snake soup, for example, can transform a menu into a festive banquet—and elevate the chef to the status of master of his art.

Apart from specialty soups of this kind, China boasts innumerable varieties of soup, each consisting of ingredients and flavors typical of the individual region—ranging from delicate vegetable broth with mushrooms and tofu to the hearty noodle soup, which is common in many parts of China and regarded as a main course. Rather more unfamiliar to the Western palate are the thick rice soups, which are a popular breakfast dish (congee) in many places, or sweet soups made from red bean paste.

If soups in China all taste "Chinese" in some way, this does not necessarily have anything to do with the way the broth is prepared. The stock is made—as with other soups—from bones, meat, or fish, and water. It is allowed to simmer for several hours and is only enriched with other flavors during the second stage of cooking. The addition of a little ginger, a dash of rice wine, and a few dried abalone to go with the meat—it is the combination of ingredients which, in conjunction with the stock, gives the soup its unique flavor. The color, texture, and contrast of a soup's ingredients also play an important role. A perfect soup might, for instance, combine delicate tofu with crisp water chestnuts and tasty bamboo shoots.

In China, soups are not regarded as simply a means of satisfying one's appetite—they are also a means of quenching one's thirst and providing comfort for the soul. However, there is one primary consideration which eclipses all others when creating a soup: namely, the beneficial medicinal effects of the ingredients. In Chinese medicine, lotus heart and rice soup, for example, is not only regarded as a beauty remedy, but is also good for strengthening the immune system. Wan Tan soup is reputed to mobilize the body's defense system and strengthen the stomach and spleen—as does corn soup, which has the added bonus of delaying the signs of old age. And last but not least: snake soup, which is supposed to increase the libido. The list could go on for ever. Anyone who is concerned about their physical wellbeing will select a soup depending on the respective season and the state of his or her health.

Chefs in Fujian have a reputation for being true soup experts. A meal here would consist of two or three different soups, and a banquet would comprise at least five or six. The dish known as "Buddha jumps over the wall" (fotiaoqiang), reputedly created in 1876 in Fuzhou's Juchunyuan restaurant, is one of Fujian's most famous specialties. To describe it simply as soup or even as a stew would probably be enough to trigger a revolution throughout the whole of Fujian. The aroma of this extravagant and expensive specialty soup is created from a combination of up to 30 highly prized Chinese ingredients, including delicacies such as abalone, sea cucumber and shark's fin. In addition, squid, chicken and duck, mushrooms, bamboo shoots as well as ham, and pigeons' eggs may also go into the making of this dish. The ingredients, which vary depending upon the recipe and are kept a closely guarded secret, are placed in rice wine with various spices, including ginger, star anise, and rock candy and brought to a boil, before being left to simmer gently. Preparation continues over the course of several days. According to legend, the aroma of the dish was so delicious that not even Buddha could resist its temptation and—despite it being a meat dish—he jumped over the walls of the monastery to sample it. The recipe on p.189 is a demonstration of its complexity.

Peanut soup with egg

7 oz (200 g) fresh peanuts, shelled
3 tbsp rock candy sugar
2 eggs

Cook the unskinned peanuts in boiling water in a saucepan or wok over a medium heat for 15 minutes. Drain, peel off the skins, and beat the eggs. Fill a saucepan or wok with 4 cups (1 liter) of water and bring to a boil. Add the peanuts and continue to cook over a low heat until they are soft. Purée the mixture in a blender until smooth, then add the rock candy sugar, allowing it to dissolve for a few minutes before adding the beaten eggs.

Below: A soup containing more than 20 ingredients deserves a fitting presentation.

Bottom: Pumpkin soup—very attractively presented in a hollowed-out pumpkin.

Left: This soup is romantically named "Half moon reflected in the river."

"Buddha jumps over the wall" soup

5 ¹⁄₂ oz (150 g) shark's fin
1 cup (250 ml) Shaoxing rice wine
3 scallions, (2 inch / 5 cm long), 2 of them
   chopped
1 piece of ginger (2 inch / 5 cm long), about
   two-thirds of it chopped
6 abalone
4 cups (1 liter) chicken stock
1 ³⁄₄ oz (50 g) fish lips (an ingredient consisting
   of the lips and other shark's skin parts)
1 chicken (about 2 ¹⁄₄ lb / 1 kg), plucked but
   not dressed
2 duck stomachs
1 ³⁄₄ oz (50 g) fish stomachs (swim bladders
   of various species of fish, sun-dried,
   then fried)
generous 8 oz (250 g) sea cucumber
5 ¹⁄₂ oz (150 g) cooked ham
generous 8 oz (250 g) winter bamboo shoots
1 ³⁄₄ oz (50 g) pork tendons
12 boiled and shelled pigeons' eggs
¹⁄₃ cup (75 ml) soy sauce
generous 1lb (500 g) pork dripping or lard
2 tsp salt
1 star anise
5 tsp powdered cassia (ordinary cinnamon
   may be used as a substitute)
1 ³⁄₄ oz (50 g) conpoy (dried scallops)
3 ¹⁄₂ oz (100 g) shiitake mushrooms
1 fresh tea leaf

Soak the shark's fins in water, add 4 tablespoons
rice wine, 1 chopped scallion and half the
chopped ginger and leave to soak for 10 minutes.
Cut the abalone crosswise and place in an
uncovered saucepan with 4 tablespoons rice
wine and 1 cup chicken stock. Chop the fish lips
into small pieces then cover them with boiling
water. Add one chopped scallion, the remaining
chopped ginger, and 4 tablespoons rice wine
and leave to draw for 10 minutes.
Cut the head and feet off the chicken.
Chop the chicken and the duck
stomachs into small pieces and
blanch for a few minutes in boiling
water. Finely chop the fish stomachs. Thinly slice the sea cucumber,
ham, and bamboo shoots. Chop the
pork tendons, break the pigeons' eggs
into a shallow dish, pour over a little soy
sauce, leave for a few minutes then drain
it off, and fry the eggs briefly in the pork
dripping.
Quickly fry the one whole scallion, the whole
piece of ginger, the chicken (cut into pieces) and
the duck stomachs, then add the soy sauce, salt, a

little rice wine, a little chicken stock, star anise, and
cassia and stir-fry. Cover and cook for 20 minutes,
then remove the ginger and the scallion.
Place the chicken, shark's fin, ham, conpoy,
abalone, shiitake mushrooms, bamboo shoots,
3 cups chicken stock, and tea leaf in a clay wine
pitcher with a 2 ¹⁄₂ quart (2.5 liter) capacity and seal
it closed. Leave the contents to stand for one hour,
then cook over a low heat for two hours (but leaving room for the steam to escape from the pitcher!)
before adding the sea cucumber, pork tendons, fish
lips, and fish stomachs and cooking for a further
hour. Finally, add the fried pigeons' eggs.

Top: Soups are relatively rare items on the menu
in European snack bars, but in southern China,
broths and bouillons are popular quick meals for
many people.

Top right: The Eight treasures soup is not quite as
time-consuming to prepare as "Buddha jumps
over the wall."

Fuzhou—a city of skyscrapers and pagodas

Skyscrapers, pagodas, and banyan trees—Fuzhou, the province's capital city, is, in every sense of the word, an up-and-coming metropolis with a population running into millions. The economic growth of the past few years is evident in all parts of the city: new highrise apartments and office buildings tower into the sky. Parks are springing up on sites that just a few years ago housed industrial plants. It is the expressed aim of the municipal authorities that Fuzhou is to become greener and to provide an even better quality of life in the future. Nevertheless, despite all the modernization programs this maritime trading port is reluctant to relinquish its old traditions.

Evidence indicates that this independently minded city on the Min river estuary was already in existence around 2,200 years ago. In the 2nd century B.C. it was the capital of the Yue kingdom and during the 10th century, it became the capital of the autonomous state of Min. Some of the city's landmarks, such as the Black and White Pagodas, the banyan trees, and several monasteries and temples, date from the Song dynasty (960–1279) when the Fuzhou was a flourishing port and up-and-coming

center of foreign trade. This period of prosperity came to an end in the 15th century, however, when the Chinese empire limited foreign trading to Guangzhou in southern China. It was not until four centuries later that China, after suffering defeat in the Opium Wars, was forced to open up all its ports—including Fuzhou—to European merchants. Trade and commerce proceeded to flourish once more. The curved archways and decorative stone carvings in the narrow streets of the Old Town still bear testimony to the lifestyle of the residents of this once affluent city in the late 1800s. An area covering almost 100 acres (40 ha) in the center of the city, known as Sanfang-Qixiang, has so far withstood the encroaching skyscrapers and is still inhabited—even if the young people have long since moved into modern apartments. Only the old residents remain and they pass much of their time, which virtually seems to stand still here, drinking tea. This is the perfect atmosphere in which to preserve the old traditions, like preparing yanpi, a local specialty made from pork, which is beaten for hours until it is paper thin and then used as an outer wrap, as with ravioli-style dumplings.

Fuzhou cuisine

Fuzhou cuisine has certainly preserved its individual identity. As in other maritime towns, fish and shellfish are high on the menu, but in Fuzhou their unique flavor comes from being prepared in a broth containing red yeast rice, a fermented sticky rice. Red yeast rice, known as *hong qu* in its dried state and *hong zao* when wet, is said to have originated in Fuzhou and has been used in China and Southeast Asia for centuries as a food preservative and food colorant and for seasoning various dishes. Whether used as a paste for spreading on pork, duck, or chicken meat, or as a seasoning for sauces and soups, this ingredient is used in numerous recipes and adds a sweet-and-sour flavor to the dish. In traditional Chinese medicine, red yeast rice is believed to regulate the digestion and improve blood circulation. Recent studies have shown that its ingredients do indeed lower cholesterol levels.

It was traditionally prepared by mixing a small amount of rice wine with cooked sticky rice, which has been fermented with the red yeast known as *Monascus purpureus*. The mixture was then poured into an urn, sealed with paper, and left to mature for 30 days. As with soy sauce, there are several different brands available at varying stages of maturity, a factor that can alter the flavor considerably. Some cooks still prefer traditional methods of preparation, but others opt for ready-made products, rice wine marc or just rice wine. Typical Fuzhou specialties, such as mussels in chicken broth, or snails, only develop their distinctive sweet-and-sour flavor thanks to the addition of red fermented rice. Fuzhou's residents' partiality

Left: The small snack bars have their food on display right at the entrance.

Below: Sweet and sour pork with litchis.

for slightly sweet dishes is also evident in other regional specialties, such as pork with litchis or taro purée. This is made from round taro corms, which are used in the same way as potatoes, but taste like water chestnuts. Pounded into a purée and mixed with eggs, lard and sugar and sprinkled with dates or fruit, taro purée provides a popular finish to a typical Fuzhou meal.

Sweet-and-sour pork with litchis

5 ½ oz (150 g) pork
Shaoxing rice wine
2 tbsp cornstarch
¼ green bell pepper
½ red bell pepper
1 small piece of Chinese radish (daikon)
6 eggs
1 tsp clear (distilled) vinegar
1 tbsp (Chinese) tomato sauce
1 tbsp sugar
½ tsp freshly ground white pepper
3 ½ tbsp vegetable oil, more if necessary
1 tbsp chopped scallions
1 tsp finely chopped garlic
1 ¾ oz (50 g) litchis, peeled
1 fresh green chile
few slices of haw fruit, to taste
salt

Thinly slice the pork and place in a marinade made from ½ teaspoon salt, sufficient rice wine to cover, and 1 teaspoon of the cornstarch. Cut the bell peppers and radish into triangles. Drain the pork and coat the slices in beaten egg, then toss in the remaining cornstarch. In a bowl combine the vinegar, tomato sauce, sugar, ¼ teaspoon salt and the white pepper into a sauce and set aside.
Heat the vegetable oil in a wok and stir-fry the pork pieces.
Remove the meat from the wok, then reheat the oil. Lightly stir-fry the scallions and the finely chopped garlic. Add the bell peppers, green chile, radish, litchis, and haw fruit and stir-fry. Add the sauce to the wok and mix together. Add the fried pork, stir-fry briefly until everything is hot, and serve at once.

Above: Pagodas are a common sight all over Fuzhou.

Center: A sharp knife is an indispensible piece of equipment in Fujian cuisine, which involves skilled cutting techniques.

Below: When the streets are clogged up with traffic, the quickest way to deliver food to the customer is on foot.

Steamed abalone with black beans

generous 1 lb (500 g) abalone, ready to cook
1 tbsp black beans, finely chopped and salted
2 tbsp corn oil
1 tsp finely chopped garlic
⅓ cup (75 ml) stock
½ tsp salt
1 tsp sugar
1 tsp Shaoxing rice wine
1 tsp light soy sauce
½ tsp freshly ground white pepper
1 tsp sesame oil
2 tsp grated ginger
1 tbsp chopped scallions
1 red chile, finely chopped
salt

Wash the abalone and pat dry, sprinkle evenly with salt. Heat 1 tablespoon corn oil in a wok and quickly fry the black beans and garlic. Remove from the wok, leave to cool slightly, then coat the abalone with the mixture. Place the abalone in an uncovered steamer and cook for 15 minutes. Remove from the steamer and keep warm. Pour the residual sauce into the wok. Add the remaining corn oil and heat, add the stock and bring to a boil. Add the salt, sugar, rice wine, soy sauce, pepper, and sesame oil and stir thoroughly. Pour the sauce over the abalone. Sprinkle with the ginger, scallions, and chile and serve.

Steamed abalone and garlic

11 oz (300 g) young abalone, prepared for cooking
3 tbsp corn oil
3 tbsp finely chopped garlic
½ tsp salt
½ tsp sugar
2 tsp light soy sauce
1 tbsp scallions, finely chopped

Wash the abalone thoroughly and dry. Heat the oil in a wok. Place the garlic in a bowl and pour the hot oil over it. Stir into a sauce with the salt and sugar. Brush the abalone with the garlic sauce and cook in an uncovered steamer for three minutes. Remove the abalone from the steamer, drizzle with soy sauce, and garnish with scallions to serve.

Sauces that tickle the Chinese palate

Chinese cuisine, in contrast to Western cookery, relies on a vast number of sauces and pastes, which are used for marinating, seasoning or dipping. Many of these have been around for centuries, partly because when food was in short supply or only seasonally available, they were useful for enlivening even the most basic dishes and giving them a distinctive and full flavor.

Soy sauce: the all-round star of the Chinese kitchen
Until well into the 1930s, every town and village had its own "sauce garden" *jiang yuan*, in other words, a shop which sold homemade sauces and preserved food items. In those days, soy sauce was made primarily from fermented soybeans that were fermented in earthenware urns or vats and allowed to mature outdoors in the sunlight. The liquid from the first fermentation was the most valuable and was reserved for use as a first-grade dipping sauce. The urn was then refilled with saltwater and the mixture was left to ferment once more. The second drawing produced

a lighter soy sauce for use in cooking. The viscous solution left in the bottom of the vat—known as "old men's extract"— was mixed with brown sugar, bottled and homogenized. It was used for coloring and flavoring hearty meat or poultry dishes.
A distinction is still made between light and dark soy sauce but most soy sauces are now chemically manufactured and contain, in addition to the fermented soybean shoots, various thickening and binding agents, spices, colorants or flavor enhancers. As an alternative to the thinner, lighter varieties, a heavier, darker version may be produced by adding flour and caramel (burned sugar), or molasses. When buying soy sauce, always check that the product is a high-quality, well-matured Chinese soy sauce, containing as few ingredients as possible. In this way, you can be sure that it will serve its original purpose of enhancing the flavors of fish, poultry, vegetables, rice or noodles rather than swamping them. You may find the following rule of thumb useful: light sauce for light meat, soups and for dipping, dark sauce for heavier meat dishes.

Fish sauce as a seasoning and salt substitute
Fish sauce—particularly popular in China's southern coastal regions—is very similar to soy sauce both in the way it is made and the manner in which it is used. This thin, light brown sauce consists of a mixture of salt and fermented small fish, which, because of their size, are unsuitable for cooking purposes. There are hundreds of different fish sauces available throughout Southeast Asia, some of which may also contain fish parts or shrimp. In this part of the world—and especially in Vietnam and Thailand—fish sauce has been used as a seasoning and a salt substitute for many centuries.

Oyster sauce: not the slightest bit fishy
What would broccoli and beef be without oyster sauce? The dish would be simply too bland. This thick sauce, which is particularly popular in southern China where it is used in wok dishes, normally consists of oyster extract, sugar, soybeans and starch. Traditionally, oysters were boiled in water, then removed and a fresh batch added to the cooking water. This process was repeated until a thick, brown oyster stock resulted. Nowadays, this lengthy procedure has been shortened by chemical production, which uses caramel or malt extract and starch. As with all ready-made products, the same rule applies: the fewer ingredients and the more expensive the product, the better the quality of the sauce.

Soy sauce

Oyster sauce

Bean sauce: black, red, and yellow

These paste-like black and yellow bean sauces are traditionally produced from fermented soybeans. Most Chinese make their own bean sauces. The salty beans are rinsed, mashed, and flavored according to individual taste with chili, ginger or garlic. The resulting paste is good for marinating fish and meat. If used in cooking, it is fried quickly in advance of the other ingredients. Once it has been prepared, the bean sauce only needs to be heated up. When served with lobster, beef with bell pepper or grilled pork chops, it will delight the most serious Cantonese food lover. Some regions also use other types of fermented beans. In Sichuan, for example, fava beans (broad beans), are used to make chili bean paste, a hot variety, as the name suggests, while azuki beans are the basic ingredient of red bean paste. The beans' slightly sweet flavor makes this paste a delicious creamy filling for ravioli-style dumplings, pancakes or other sweet dishes.

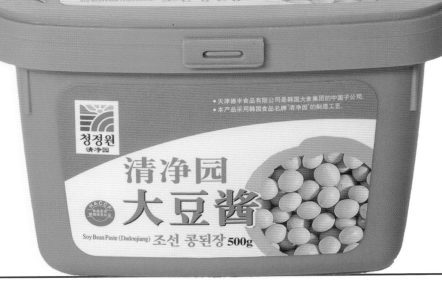

Bean sauce—available in black, red and yellow

Continued on p.194

Continued from p. 193

Hoisin sauce: an all-rounder

If you are not in the mood for cooking an elaborate meal, hoisin sauce can perform miracles and turn a few simple ingredients into a delicious Chinese treat. Whether used as a marinade or a dip, its rounded, slightly sweet, sharp and salty flavor goes well with just about anything, but makes a particularly good companion to Peking duck or broiled dishes. This reddish brown sauce, which originated in southern China, is made from fermented soybeans, sugar, vinegar, salt, chili, garlic, and sesame oil.

Chili sauce: hot and fiery

There are hundreds of chili sauces on the market, ranging from sweet, or sweet-and-sour, to devilishly hot, some with added apples, some with added plums. The degree of hotness varies considerably, but the classic chili sauce in China, particularly in Sichuan, is called *lajiao*. If preparing this sauce at home, use fresh red chile peppers, finely chopped, place them in salted water and leave to soak outdoors for a few days. Alternatively, fry the finely chopped chile peppers in oil and then use the chile-flavored oil as the hot seasoning. Both versions are ideal for marinating, seasoning, or dipping.

Plum sauce: fruity flair

Plum sauce, which is mainly used for dipping, may also be used to give pork and poultry dishes, or fried spring rolls a delicate fruity and slightly piquant flavor. Ready-made sauces consist of plums or plum extract, sugar, vinegar, and chili. It is also easy to prepare at home by puréeing dried plums with a small amount of vinegar, brown sugar, garlic, and chili paste and bringing the mixture to a boil for a few moments.

Sa cha sauce: exotic flavor from southern China

The slightly spicy flavor of sa cha sauce, which is popular in Fujian and Guangdong, is produced by a combination of chiles, roasted peanuts, dried fish and shrimp, sesame paste, and garlic with the occasional addition of mustard and five-spice powder. It is often used in cooking or as a dipping companion for hearty meat dishes.

Hoisin sauce

Chili sauce

Sa cha sauce

Sesame sauce: mild on the palate

Toasted sesame seeds, ground into a delicate, slightly oily paste, lend a wonderfully aromatic flavor to noodle dishes. This sauce, which is particularly popular in northern and western China, goes extremely well with mild chicken dishes.

Sesame sauce

Squid in ginger sauce

5 ½ oz (150 g) baby squid
3 ½ oz (100 g) Chinese chives
3–4 fresh shiitake mushrooms
1 ½ cups (350 ml) vegetable oil
½ tsp Shaoxing rice wine
clear bouillon, or stock
1 tsp soy sauce
½ tsp ginger juice
1 tbsp cornstarch, mixed with 2 tbsp water
1 tbsp chopped scallions
½ tsp sesame oil
salt

Wash the squid and place in a bowl. Wash the chives and cut into ¾-inch (2-cm) lengths. Wash and thinly slice the shiitake mushrooms.

Heat the oil in a wok. Add the squid and stir-fry for about five minutes. Drain the squid in a strainer, retaining the oil.

Return about 3 tablespoons oil to the wok. Add the rice wine, a small amount of bouillon, soy sauce and ginger juice and bring to a boil, then add the water and cornstarch mixture to thicken. As soon as the sauce has thickened, add the squid, chives, and shiitake mushrooms, season with salt and stir-fry all the ingredients for a few minutes. Place on a serving dish, garnish with the scallions and drizzle with sesame oil.

The island city of Xiamen

Although Xiamen, also known as Amoy, is one of the country's top economic centers, it also enjoys the reputation of being one of China's most relaxing cities. Where else could tourists wander at night through narrow streets to the accompaniment of chirping cicadas and gentle piano music or enjoy a dish known as "pearls of the South Sea"?

With a population of 2 million residents, the island city of Xiamen is the most economically successful city in Fujian. It was one of the first special economic zones to open up to foreign investment in 1981. Since then, numerous international firms have established bases in Xiamen. This colorful showpiece city boasting its own airport and seaport is situated on an island in the mouth of the Jiulong river within view of Taiwan. Thanks to the policy of détente, their mutual history, and shared economic interests, Taiwan, once considered a class enemy, has, since the 1980s, become a respected business partner.

Although Xiamen produces and exports a vast amount of goods for the rest of the world, it has managed to preserve a relaxed way of life. The automobile-free island of Gulangyu, covering an area of just 0.77 square miles (2 sq km) and

situated just a few minutes' drive from Xiamen city, is particularly quiet and peaceful. Apart from the sound of gently rolling breakers and the soft strains of piano music—there are more pianos on Xiamen than anywhere else in China—there are scarcely any other sounds to be heard, apart from tourist groups, marveling over the colonial-style atmosphere of past centuries. Decorative villas, reminiscent of Tuscany, and old gardens, clustered closely together, evoke a sense of historic Europe in the middle of China.

After China's defeat in the Opium Wars, Xiamen was obliged to open up its port to foreign trade. During the second half of the 19th century, Western traders settled on Gulangyu island where, despite Japanese occupation in World War II, they apparently led an extremely comfortable life. Despite the military clashes over the Taiwan Strait and despite the Cultural Revolution, these influences are still reflected in the splendor of the city's architecture.

The art of good living is demonstrated by the delicacies that issue forth from Xiamen's kitchens. Despite the large number of elegant restaurants and atmospheric bars, local gourmets opt

Left: These ladies charge only 10 Yuan (about 1 $; 1 Euro; £0.87) for a portion of *haili jian* (oyster omelette) from their kitchen.

Below: Sweet, sour, or hot sauces are the ideal accompaniment to crisp spring rolls.

Right: A visit to the temple of Nan Putuo monastery is the ideal destination for anyone visiting Xiamen and wanting to relax after too much culinary indulgence.

for regional specialties such as oysters, lobster, sea cucumber, abalone, crabs, rock lobsters, or eels. Xiamen cuisine offers every conceivable type of sea creature. Whether delicately steamed, roasted, fried, or enhanced with a sweet, slightly spicy sauce, the dish will always be prepared to perfection.

Equally delicious are the soups and snacks typical of this region: thick soups made from rice and duck meat, or from ducks' blood are the local classics. A particular regional favorite is Peanut soup with egg (see p. 188), a sweet, creamy soup made from chopped peanuts, served with dumplings or pancakes. Other light snacks include oyster omelettes, crisp spring rolls, or pancakes stuffed with peanuts and soy bean sprouts, sometimes served with plum sauce, and sometimes with hot mustard sauce. And to keep the palate stimulated, southern Fujians hold another small specialty up their sleeve: a chilled delicacy consisting of jellied sea worm, cooked in its own juices and served with a sweet and spicy sauce.

One of the best places to go to escape from this apparently shameless abundance—at least temporarily—is the Nan Putuo Buddhist temple. Spectacularly situated on the side of a mountain with views over Xiamen, Gulangyu and the sea, this temple, dating from the Tang dynasty (618–907), extends over an area of 11 ½ square miles (30 sq km) and comprises magnificent halls, statues of Buddha, pagodas, and landscaped gardens. Not only does the temple complex incorporate a monastery, but also a vegetarian restaurant that prepares food in accordance with the rules of Buddhism. The elegant names alone, such as "Pearls of the South Sea," "Silk Rain and Lonely Clouds," or "Half Moon Reflected in the River," are sufficient to inspire the visitor.

Xiamen-style squid

generous 1 lb (500 g) small squid, fresh or frozen
3 ½ tbsp vegetable oil
2 scallions, separated into green and white portions and finely chopped
1 piece of ginger (¾ in / 2 cm long), thinly sliced
4 large mixed bell peppers, cut into bite-sized chunks
salt

Blanch the fresh or defrosted squid in saltwater by boiling for two minutes, then drain.
Pour half the oil into a wok and heat until it is very hot, then quickly stir-fry the white parts of the scallions and half the ginger, stirring constantly. Add the squid, season with salt and stir-fry for a further 2–3 minutes, stirring constantly. Remove the squid from the wok and drain. Wipe out the inside of the wok and heat the remaining oil, then add the green scallions and remaining ginger. Add the chunks of bell pepper, season with salt and stir-fry for about two minutes, stirring constantly. Return the squid to the wok and stir-fry all the ingredients together for a maximum of one more minute.

Xiamen-style fried noodles

7–8 dried shiitake mushrooms
3 ½ tbsp vegetable oil
11 oz (300 g) salted wheat-flour noodles
3 ½ oz (100 g) shrimp
Shaoxing rice wine
3 oz (80 g) chicken breast (or pork)
10–12 small conpoy (dried scallops)
½ scallion, finely chopped
2 red onions, finely chopped
1 ¾ oz (50 g) carrots, cut into matchsticks
1 ¾ oz (50 g) broccoli florets
a small amount of white cabbage, or lettuce leaves, shredded
⅓ cup (50 g) cornstarch
salt, white pepper
onion oil or sesame oil

Soak the shiitake mushrooms in warm water to soften.
Heat the oil in a wok, then carefully add the noodles. Once they begin to turn golden-yellow, turn them over using chopsticks so that they become golden-yellow on all sides. Remove the noodles from the wok and drain, retaining the oil in a pitcher. Clean the wok thoroughly. Once the noodles are cool, fill the wok with water and bring to a boil. Return the noodles to the wok and cook until they have softened and lost some of their salty flavor. Remove from the wok and drain. Rinse the shrimp and remove the black intestinal vein. Cut the chicken into thin strips, place in a dish and cover in a marinade of rice wine, salt and a pinch of ground white pepper, and cornstarch for 10 minutes. Drain the shiitake mushrooms and cut into strips.

Above: Buddhist monks were obviously no strangers to the fact that food holds body and soul together and developed a sophisticated, delicious—and mainly vegetarian—cuisine in their monasteries.

Heat the conpoy in a ½ cup of water for 4 minutes in the microwave. Heat 2 tablespoons of the reserved oil in the wok, add the finely chopped scallions and red onion, and sauté for a few moments. Add the shrimp and chicken, stir a few times before adding ½ teaspoon rice wine, mushrooms, and vegetables. Stir-fry all the ingredients together until they are semicooked. Add the conpoy and water and bring to a boil. Add the noodles and cook, stirring constantly, until the noodles have absorbed the liquid. Remove the noodles from the wok and place on a serving plate making sure some of the other ingredients are visible on top of the noodles and drizzle with onion oil (or sesame oil).

Vegetarian cuisine in China

Vegetarian food, which for many years carried a stigma of poverty in China, is currently experiencing a revival in popularity. The abundance of fresh vegetables, the effect of Western influences, and the rediscovery of long forgotten culinary traditions once practiced by Buddhist or Taoist monks together provide the perfect combination for producing a wide variety of delicious dishes to delight meat-eaters and vegetarians alike.

Basket upon basket of tomatoes, bok choy, and soybean sprouts are stacked outside the entrance to the Nan Putuo temple at the foot of Wulaofeng mountain (Five Old Men's Peak) in the southeast of Xiamen, alongside tubs filled with blocks of tofu and freshly picked soybean and bamboo sprouts. Monks, laden with sacks of morel and shiitake mushrooms, push their way through the narrow entrance into the well-stocked store room, bringing fresh supplies to their restaurant, a scene which is replayed all over China, especially in and around monasteries and temples. Buddhist and Taoist monks have, since time immemorial—and for a variety of reasons—embraced a way of life that renounces the eating of meat. One of the principles of the Buddhist religion is a respect for all life, including that of animals. However, this did not necessarily mean that Buddhists were willing to resign themselves to tasteless food. Consequently—over the course of many centuries—they created a special type of cuisine that produced a near perfect imitation of meat dishes. In form and consistency the meat substitute resembles duck or pork meat yet consists of nothing more than soybean or wheat protein. A complicated procedure of kneading, coloring, drying, and molding produces a substitute ingredient which looks and tastes very much like meat. To save time and effort, it is now possible to purchase ready-made "vegetarian duck" or "vegetarian pork" from Chinese stores. Taoists also believe in the beneficial effects of vegetarian dishes. A balance between yin and yang, maintained by an appropriate diet, will insure a stable state of health, which is regarded as a prerequisite for longevity.

The current revived interest in vegetarian cuisine is not entirely motivated by religious beliefs, however: it is more a reflection of the attitude and changes in people's approach to food. Most Chinese, even nonbelievers, regard fresh and naturally produced fruit and vegetables as a basic requirement for one's good health and wellbeing. An increasing number of restaurants, particularly in major Chinese cities like Beijing, Shanghai, and Guangzhou, now offer vegetarian menus, which include both modern and Buddhist-inspired dishes.

It is no coincidence that this trend is a relatively recent phenomenon in China. Growing affluence among increasingly broad sections of the population means that the stigma once attached to vegetarian food is gradually disappearing (after a long period when a meat-free diet was regarded as uninspiring food for the poor). Nevertheless, the Chinese staple diet has, since time immemorial, consisted predominantly of carbohydrates and vegetables. Apart from noodles, sweet potatoes, rice, and vegetables, the majority of the population survived for hundreds of years on nothing else—and sometimes not even that. Hunger—the product of social injustice, political failure or natural disasters—has always been a concern in China. Only those who could afford it served meat on special occasions, such as festivals or celebrations, an occurrence so infrequent that the sense of appreciation for such a rare luxury was all the greater. Nowadays, increasing affluence means that more and more people are able to make a conscious decision regarding the type and composition of their diet. Whatever the motives for choosing vegetarian cuisine, one thing is certain: China's new vegetarian cuisine is so varied that it will banish all thoughts of meat or poverty.

Left: Fujian has a limited amount of cultivable agricultural land due to the topography of the province. Rice grown in paddy fields is the main crop and covers more than 85 percent of the total cultivable area. Other crops include sweet potatoes, wheat, sugar cane, and tea.

Iceberg lettuce with oyster sauce

1 ½ lbs (600 g) iceberg lettuce
1 tsp salt
vegetable oil

Sauce:
⅓ cup (75 ml) vegetable oil
1 tsp finely chopped garlic
2 tbsp oyster sauce
4 tsp Shaoxing rice wine
freshly ground white pepper
2 tsp sugar
2 tsp soy sauce
½ cup vegetable stock
2 tsp cornstarch, mixed with 4 tsp water
1 tsp sesame oil

Wash the lettuce and spin-dry in a lettuce spin-
ner, if possible. Fill a wok with water, add the salt
and a little oil and bring to a boil. As soon as the
liquid is boiling, blanch the lettuce for a few
moments before removing it. Spin-dry the lettuce and place in a serving bowl or small individual bowls.
To make the sauce, heat the oil in the wok and
stir-fry the garlic. Add the oyster sauce, rice
wine, a pinch of the pepper, the sugar, soy sauce,
and stock and bring to a boil, then thicken with
the water and cornstarch mixture. Drizzle in the
sesame oil, and pour the sauce over the lettuce
and serve.

Chile cabbage

14 oz (400 g) white cabbage
1 piece of ginger (1 inch / 3 cm long)
1 piece of leek (1 inch / 3 cm long)
2–3 garlic cloves
3 tbsp vegetable oil
1 tsp rice wine
1 dried chile
2 tsp soy sauce
2 tbsp coriander seeds
2 ½ tsp sugar
1 tbsp sesame oil

Wash the cabbage and cut into 1-inch (3-cm)
strips. Slice the ginger into thin strips and
finely chop the leek and garlic.

Heat the oil in a wok and stir-fry the ginger, garlic, and leek before adding the rice wine and chile.
Fry for a few moments, then add the cabbage.
Continue frying until it is cooked, stirring constantly. Stir in the soy sauce, coriander seeds,
and sugar and, lastly, stir in the sesame oil just
before serving.

Bok choy with garlic and black beans

1 ¼ lb (600 g) bok choy
1 tbsp salted black beans
1 tbsp salt
3 tbsp vegetable oil
2 tbsp oyster sauce
1 tbsp sugar
few roasted peanuts, finely chopped

Tear the bok choy into small pieces and wash
thoroughly. Using a knife, finely chop the black
beans.
Fill a saucepan with water, bring to a boil, add 1
tablespoon salt and 1 tablespoon oil and blanch
the bok choy for a few moments. (The oil helps
the bok choy retain its green color.) As soon as
the bok choy is tender, remove it, using a slotted
spoon, rinse in cold water, then drain. Heat the
remaining oil in a wok, gradually add the black
beans and fry gently. Next, add the oyster sauce
along with 1–2 cups of water and the sugar. Cook
the ingredients over a moderate heat. Arrange
the bok choy on a serving dish, pour the sauce
over the bok choy and garnish with a few finely
chopped and roasted peanuts.

The sweet fruits of Fujian

Thanks to its sunny, warm climate with lots of rain virtually everything in the subtropical province of Fujian blooms and thrives all year round. The list of cultivated produce resembles the fruit display at a delicatessen store: oranges, longans (or "dragon eyes"), litchis, dates, pomelos, bananas, pineapples, and loquats. Many of these sweet fruits have been grown in Fujian for centuries.

The first record of **oranges** in China dates back to the 4th century and during the course of history this fruit has taken on something akin to cult status. Not only is the fruit itself a symbol of good fortune, but even its name is auspicious: in Chinese, the word "orange" sounds like the word for "praying for good luck." No family celebration or Lunar New Year festival would be complete without an exchange of "good luck" oranges.

Magical powers are also attributed to **pomelos**, large, thick-skinned relatives of the grapefruit. Bathing in a bath of pomelo leaves and rind before one's wedding or the New Year festival is said to purify not only the body, but also the soul and spirit. Oranges and pomelos are widely used in Fujian cuisine—freshly squeezed, cooked in sauces, pickled, or even dried.

The **loquat** is the fruit of the evergreen Japanese medlar tree, which thrived in Fujian for centuries before finding its way to Japan. This pear-shaped orange or yellow fruit is comparable to the apple in taste. The Chinese name for it is *pipa*—exactly like the traditional Chinese (and similarly shaped) string instrument. These delicate fruits are eaten fresh or dried, and are regarded as beneficial for treating stomach complaints.

Litchis also originated in southern China and one of the earliest references to this fruit was found in 4th-century writings. Its sweet flesh, hidden beneath a pink-red rind, was apparently so coveted by Chinese emperors that they demanded litchis as a tribute.

Longans ("dragon eyes") were likewise offered as a tribute. This yellow fruit is very similar in size and shape to the round, strawberry-sized litchi. Both fruits are frequently used in soups, sweet-and-sour dishes and desserts: they can also be freshly squeezed for their juice. In northern China, longan and litchi twigs are placed underneath the bed of a newly wedded couple as a good luck charm to bless the couple with children.

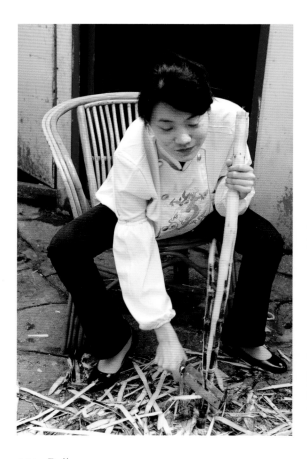

Although **bananas**, **dates** and **pineapples** are tropical fruits, they only reached China by a circuitous route. Whether date palms arrived in China from Persia by land or sea remains uncertain, but they have certainly thrived in Fujian's subtropical climate. Bananas, originally from Malaysia, and pineapples, which were brought to Macau by the Portuguese during the 17th century, prefer a tropical climate and are grown widely in Guangdong, where they feature in numerous desserts. In Fujian cuisine, on the other hand, they are mainly used for their juice.

Left: A feast for the eye: this can scarcely be dismissed as mere decoration: it is more like a sculptural work of art. Fruit or vegetable carvings are often used to decorate special dishes, particularly in restaurants or at festive banquets.

Facing page, above: To most Europeans, litchis are probably the most familiar variety of Chinese fruit. There is documentary evidence of the litchi tree being cultivated in southern China around 1000 years B.C.

Facing page, far left: Fujian is one of China's largest producers of sugar cane. Not only is sugar cane used to produce alcoholic drinks, but it is also grown for its juice, a popular drink in southern China. The sugar cane stems are first peeled...

Facing page: ...then pressed in special machines.

Artistic indulgence—fruit and vegetable decorations

Whether it be carp, tigers, dragons, phoenix, chrysanthemums, or lotus flowers—each and every one of these symbols of good luck or harmony commonly feature as decorations at festive banquets. It is amazing to think that such artistic creations can be made by hand, carved out of the firm flesh of fruit and vegetables, such as melons, carrots, radishes, taro, or pumpkins. Each individual hair, each fish scale, even the sinuous movements of a tiger can be mirrored by a skilled Chinese carving expert. The work of art he creates is the product of great skill, patience, a considerable amount of practice—and, possibly, a carrot!

The art of fruit and vegetable carving in China dates back to the Tang dynasty (618–907). Even then, banquets were elaborately decorated to inspire additional appreciation for individual dishes which, in turn,

reflected high regard for the respective guest. Decorative effects were also designed to highlight special dishes and heighten pleasure—a luxury that for centuries remained the exclusive preserve of the imperial court. For the past few years, however, the art of fruit and vegetable sculpture has been experiencing a revival: many cookery schools now include decorative carving as part of their curriculum. After all, no banquet—be it a wedding or another festive occasion—would be complete without a feast for the eyes that simultaneously promises good luck.

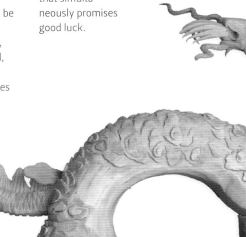

Delicacies—a source of pleasure and prestige

How does an ingredient become a delicacy? The answer is simple: it must be rare and expensive. As long as it is only the upper classes who can afford deer's penis, bear's claws or frog's legs, the enjoyment derived from such a dish is not just culinary but is also based on prestige. It is the myth that counts—and a good story has always been the best form of marketing.

Turtle, shark's fin, or bird's nest (created by a bird similar to a swift), are regarded in China as the choicest of delicacies. Whether as a dish reserved exclusively for the emperor, or a choice ingredient that was good for one's health or increased potency, or even as a symbol of longevity and strength—every Chinese delicacy has its own history, which even now elevates anyone who is lucky enough to sample something so exotic to the ranks of the powerful, the rich, the beautiful and the influential. You are what you eat, even in China. And the rarer and more expensive the delicacy, the greater the social cachet for whoever consumes it. Confronted with so much pleasure, personal wellbeing and prestige, warnings about protecting endangered species must often take second place—at least in China where the term *"dongwu"* (animals), literally translated, means "moveable object."

Rather than visiting the zoo, anyone interested in studying the turtle population of Southeast Asia should go to a Chinese specialty restaurant. No matter what regulations are in force to protect various species and regardless of existing import restrictions, the fact remains that turtles are regarded as a delicacy in China and are passionately coveted as a soup ingredient, for example. Consommé of turtle meat, chicken, mushrooms, dried longans, and red wolfberry has, for centuries, enjoyed a reputation for promoting natural strength and was frequently served at imperial banquets. The turtle also symbolizes longevity. Vast amounts of money are still paid to this day for dishes and essences extracted from the rare three-striped box turtle, which can supposedly cure cancer.

Shark's fin is also reputed to be good for boosting natural strength and they have been an integral feature of Chinese banquets since the days of the Song dynasty (960–1279). Whether the high calcium and iron content in the fins actually does turn shark's fin soup into a potency-boosting concoction, or whether this is merely a myth based on the belief that the power of the mighty shark is somehow transferred to the dish, is something that remains debatable. The

demand for sharks' fins was in any case so great that the Chinese long ago found themselves dependent upon imports from Southeast Asia. Consequently, this already rare delicacy has become even scarcer and correspondingly even more expensive and desirable. The tail and dorsal fins are usually sold in dried form. The method of preparation depends on the quality but, generally speaking, the fins are initially soaked and simmered for several days before being added to a soup containing chicken and crabs, in which they develop their unique flavor. Aficionadas of the dish search for a fin that retains its shape well; is simmered in several stages in a variety of consommés, absorbing the respective flavors from each one and then served whole. This is a dish that very few chefs have mastered to perfection.

Bird's nest soup is prepared in a similar fashion: in other words, it is enriched with crab meat or chicken and is just as time-consuming to prepare as shark's fin soup. The precious nests are built by cave swiftlets (from the *collocalini* family of swifts) and consist entirely of dried and hardened birds' saliva. They are found—if at all—in the coastal caves of Southeast Asia and are reputed to contain large quantities of protein as well as essential trace minerals absorbed from the sea and maritime air, both of which are believed to boost the body's vital energy and increase potency. Connoisseurs make a distinction between white—i.e. cleaned—nests and predominantly black nests, which still contain tiny feathers. Over the course of several days, both types are rinsed, soaked, and boiled. It is remarkable that they retain any flavor at all. In many cases, they are prized purely for their gelatinous consistency. No one raises an eyebrow at the astonishing cost of birds' nests, (even though the gathering of them is hazardous) which can command prices over 1,000 US dollars a pound for top-quality white nests.

Above left: Sea cucumbers are considered a special delicacy not only in China but also in Spain.

Above right: Chinese chefs remain unperturbed by criticism on the part of biologists or environmental protection agencies: sharks' fins are still one of the "four treasures of the sea" in Chinese cuisine.

Left: Shark's fin soup is reputed to have great healing powers.

Right: Bird's nest is one of the most expensive specialties found in Chinese cuisine.

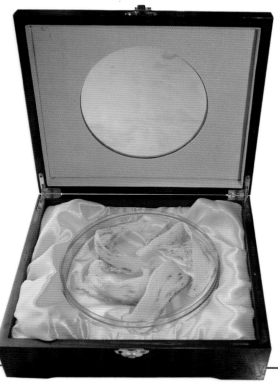

Bird's nest with rock candy sugar

1 bird's nest (9 oz / 250 g), soaked in water
9 oz (250 g) rock candy sugar

Pour 2 cups (500 ml) of water into a wok and add
the rock candy sugar. Dissolve the sugar over a
low heat, stirring constantly. Drain the resulting
syrup through a strainer lined with cheesecloth.
Place the bird's nest in a bowl and pour over $2/3$
cup (150 ml) of the syrup. Drain off the surplus
syrup from the bowl and pour it over the bird's
nest a second time. Place the bird's nest in a
bamboo steamer and steam for 5 minutes over a
high heat. Serve immediately.
Corn soup is often served as an accompaniment.

Above: If you are Chinese, no explanation is
needed for the diversity of different ingredients at
the delicatessen market.

Center left: Southern Chinese cuisine is completely ruthless when it comes to offering a range
of exotic ingredients. Needless to say, frogs also
feature among the range of delicacies.

Center right: Though unlikely to appeal to a Western palate, a Chinese gourmet would regard this
dish—a painstakingly decorated sea cucumber
soup—as a veritable feast for both the eyes and
stomach.

The hinterland—a bitter idyll

The road which leads from the coast into Fujian's hinterland passes through picturesque Chinese landscapes: the train rattles past green rice-growing terraces, meandering streams, traditional villages, and subtropical forests while warm air wafts in through the open windows. However, life in Fujian's mountain region is not quite as idyllic as it may seem at first glance. Every single yard of arable land must be wrested from the mountain slopes and turned into terraces and for most farmers, the idea of industrial aid, let alone a tractor, remains no more than a dream. Even if they had enough money for such a thing, the parcels of land are so small that there is no alternative but to cultivate them by hand. Climate conditions are equally difficult: subtropical temperatures can rise as high as 104 °F (40 °C) with a humidity factor of over 90 percent. Furthermore, there is always the risk that the hinterland may be struck by a storm during the typhoon season, which can cause flooding and considerable devastation before it abates.

Nor was this region always a peaceful place. For many centuries, poverty and hunger were the cause of constant raids. As a result, many family groups retreated to roundhouses, which were virtually impenetrable from the outside and could shelter hundreds of people within the inner courtyard. About 4,000 of these buildings, some of which extended up to 230 feet (70 m) in diameter, have survived to this day. The Hakka people, who constructed these unusual buildings, originally lived in northern China, but were gradually forced southward during the first millennium into what was regarded as the barbarian south. Although Fujian was considered part of the Chinese empire, the ruling powers rarely ventured into this subtropical mountainous region so far away from the coast. Any conflicts arising between the Hakka immigrants and the local population had, of necessity, to be resolved by the warring parties themselves. Little wonder, therefore, that the Hakka clans retreated to their "yuanlou," or roundhouses. The kitchen and living areas were generally located at ground level, food supplies were stored on the second floor and the top floor was reserved for sleeping quarters. The roundhouses were virtually windowless—only the walls facing inward were provided with windows—and protected by massive gates. However much protection the roundhouses offered, however, the hunger remained. By the end of the 19th century, the hinterland was experiencing a major emigration wave. To escape the bitter poverty, more than a million Fujians took up service as coolies and were transported on British ships to Singapore, Malaysia, and other colonies.

Nowadays, the road to a better future is not such a long one: anyone lucky enough to find a job on the coast is regarded as having succeeded. Over the next few years, the route to success is likely to be dramatically shortened: a new railroad link, over 370 miles (600 km) long, is due to be built in 2012, which will run right through the hinterland from Nanchang in Jiangxi province to Fuzhou.

Below: However picturesque it may appear, ferrying people across the numerous rivers in Fujian's hinterland is extremely tough work.

Right: Far removed from the prosperous towns along the coast, the standard of living in these rural areas is relatively poor.

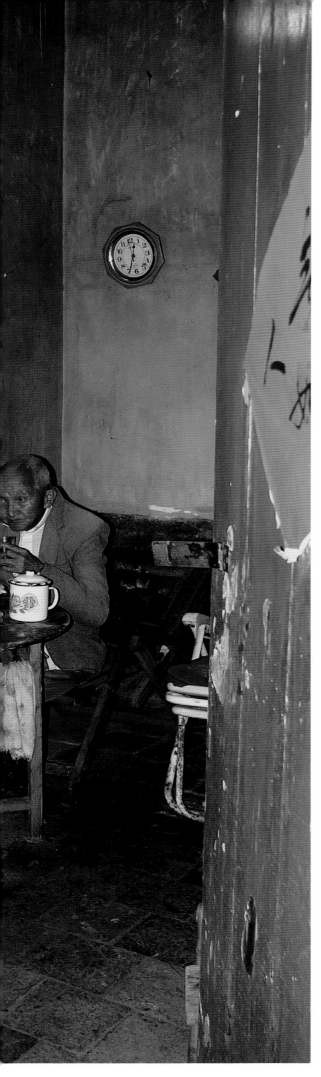

Right: A trip along the Min river, which cuts through the mountain ranges of Fujian province from northwest to southeast, will utterly delight landscape photographers and anyone with a romantic disposition.

Below: To defend themselves against attack, the Hakka people built roundhouses between two to six floors in height. Resembling a fortress on the outside, a completely different world is revealed in the inner courtyard where the community conducted its social life.

Bottom: Unfortunately, idyllic scenery does not fill empty stomachs and virtually no other Chinese province has—over the past hundred years—had to cope with the high levels of emigration experienced by Fujian.

The wild Wuyi mountains

In the far north of the hinterland, along the border with Jiangxi province, lies another distinctive feature of Fujian's landscape: the Wuyi mountains. Situated in a unique landscape of bizarre rock formations, cascading waterfalls, gloomy valleys with lush vegetation, these mountains rise to a height of 6,889 feet (2100 m) and are regarded—with justification—as one of China's most scenic regions and an embodiment of harmony with nature, as well as a source of inspiration to the spirit and soul in equal measures. Perhaps it was precisely this that led to the area becoming the cradle of neo-Confucianism, a philosophical school of thought which evolved here during the 12th century, thereby investing the Wuyishan area with cultural significance.

In 1987, large parts of the Wuyishan region were added to UNESCO's list of World Heritage Sites—not solely on account of its beautiful scenery but also because the area is home to about 500 species of vertebrates, as well as 3,000 varieties of flora, some of which are exclusive to Wuyishan. Far from China's cultural centers, this remote region also has a surprising number of historical treasures. The origins of the boat-shaped coffins suspended from steep cliffs high above the emerald green Jiuqu Xi, the Nine-Bend River, remain a mystery to this day. They are estimated to be over 2,000 years old.

The mountainous region to the west remains relatively unknown. One possible reason for this is that there is no further need for special efforts to boost international tourism: Taiwanese and Chinese now residing in other Southeast Asian countries have, after all, been flocking to this popular holiday destination of the wild and romantic Wuyi mountains—or, more precisely, the 27 square miles (70 sq km) known as the "Wuyishan-Scenic Resort" around the Jiuqu Xi river— since the 1980s. It is important in this respect not to confuse UNESCO's Wuyishan biosphere reserve, which covers 219 square miles (567 sq km), with the much smaller resort of Wuyishan. Although the visitor may well find it deliberately confusing, these two areas merely share borders with one another. The same applies to Wuyishan city, which, interestingly enough, is situated outside the actual resort of Wuyishan.

Thanks to the large numbers of visitors, what most Chinese regard as the main attraction, i.e. experiencing the sunrise from one of the mountain peaks, holds decidedly less appeal for nature lovers in search of peace and quiet. A more enticing prospect, on the other hand, is a visit to one of the tea farms, situated a little off the main tourist track. These establishments have, for centuries, been cultivating one of China's finest—and most expensive—tea products, Oolong tea. With a bit of luck, the visitor may also be able to sample some of the dishes typical of this mountain region.

Numerous species of bamboo, wild mushrooms and herbs, which are ideal for use in dishes

such as Bamboo sprouts with sausage, flourish in the region's warm, humid climate. Noodle and tofu dishes, as well as carp, frogs, snails, turtles, hare, and deer, also feature in local cuisine. Nature has, after all, provided an abundance of choice in terms of wild game and freshwater fish. The Wuyishan region is especially famous among Chinese gourmets for its snake dishes. Snake meat is similar to steamed chicken. Snake blood is even more highly prized, particularly among the male population, on account of its aphrodisiac properties.

Bamboo sprouts with sausage

generous 1 lb (500 g) bamboo shoots
1 ³/₄ oz (50 g) Chinese sausage
3–4 shiitake mushrooms, soaked in warm water
¹/₂ tsp sugar
¹/₂ tsp salt
1 ham bone, medium-sized
2 tsp cornstarch, mixed with 4 tsp water
1 tsp sesame oil

Thoroughly wash the bamboo shoots and cut into pieces as follows: holding the bamboo shoot firmly with one hand, slice off a piece diagonally, then roll it forward and slice off another piece using the same diagonal motion. Slice the sausage and the shiitake mushrooms. Bring the bamboo shoots to a boil in a pan of water, then reduce the heat to low and simmer for a further 15 minutes. Place the cooked bamboo shoots in a wok. Add the sausage, mushrooms, sugar, salt, and ham bone and stir-fry all the ingredients for a few minutes. Once the liquid in the wok has almost completely evaporated, remove the ham bone. Thicken the mixture in the wok with the cornstarch and water mixture. Sprinkle with sesame oil and serve.

Facing page, far left: An experienced tea picker can harvest up to 66 lb (30 kg) of tealeaves a day.

Facing page, above: Equipment used to harvest tea.

Facing page, below: Tea bricks are a traditional method of preserving tea. The dried tea is powdered, moistened with rice water, packed into molds, and compressed. These may be imprinted with designs and the name of the producer.

Above: Oolong tea is produced in the Wuyi mountains, which extend for 310 miles (500 km) along the border with the neighboring province of Jiangxi.

Right, above: The tea ceremony originated not in Japan, but in China.

Right, below: More than 3,000 species of fauna have been recorded in Wuyishan region.

Far right: Oolang (Black Dragon), Tie Guanyin, and Yancha are the most famous and most expensive tea varieties produced in Fujian.

Chinese mushrooms

Neither vegetable nor animal and consisting of 90 percent water, mushrooms nevertheless enjoy something approaching cult status in Chinese cuisine. Not only are shiitake, silver ear, and lion's mane mushrooms regarded as the crowning glory of vegetarian dishes but they are also widely respected for possessing singular medicinal properties. According to traditional Chinese medicine (TCM), every single one of the hundred or so different species of fungus has a beneficial effect on health—such as strengthening the immune system, helping overcome circulatory problems, or improving respiratory conditions. Shennong, a legendary ancient emperor who lived around 3000 B.C. and is credited with having introduced agriculture to China, compiled a book on medicinal plants, entitled *Shennong bencao jing*, in which he extolled the life-extending properties of the lingzhi mushroom—a theory that was actually not so far off the mark.

Clinical studies have shown that the **lingzhi** or **reishi mushroom** (*Ganoderma lucidum*), also known as the lacquered bracket mushroom, does indeed help improve the immune system and is used in Japan and China in cancer treatment, among other things. Monks have been carrying out empirical research into the beneficial effects of fungi since time immemorial. In subtropical mountain regions, mushrooms—either fresh or dried—provided them with an important food source and the fact that many of the wild mushrooms gathered were found to have a positive effect on health is reflected in the remedies and formulas which have survived to this day. Monks also developed methods of cultivating wild mushrooms. The cultivation of **straw mushrooms** (*Volvariella volvacea*), on rice straw for example, is said to have been introduced during the Tang dynasty by Buddhist monks in the Nanhua monastery in north Guangdong.

With their long, aromatic stalks and little yellow heads, **Enoki** or **golden needle mushrooms** (*Flammulina velutipes*)—known in China as *jinzhen gu* and in Japan as *enokitake* are very popular. Not only does this frost-resistant fungus grow on trees and tree stumps, but it is also grown in vast quantities in plastic bottles—it is sixth on the list of the world's most widely cultivated edible mushrooms. Enoki mushrooms are sold in bundles in Chinese stores. The roots and lower stems should be removed before cooking. Their sweetly delicate, slightly nutty flavor is best appreciated in salads and soups although they may also be served with hot-pot as a buffer to its hot spiciness.

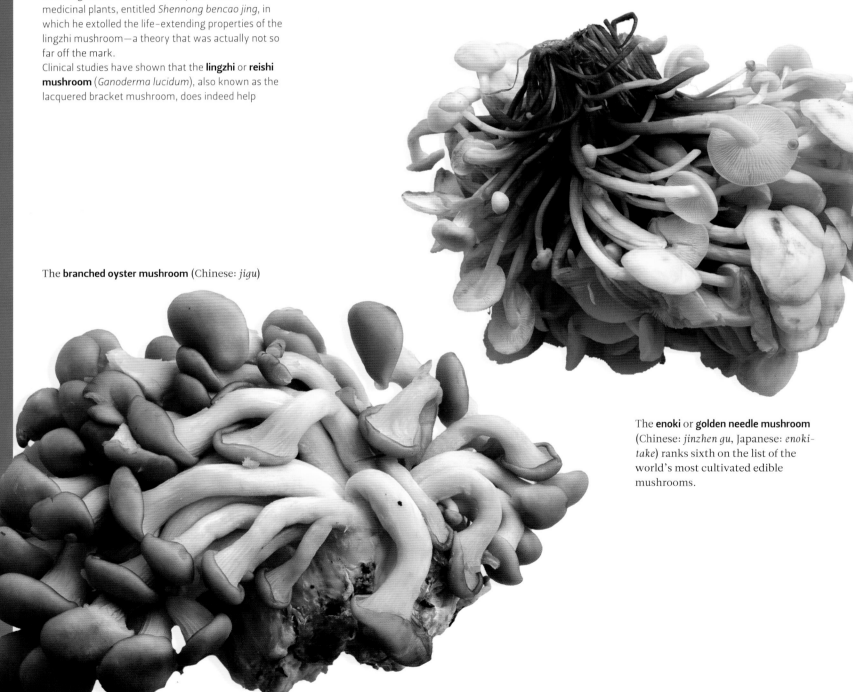

The **branched oyster mushroom** (Chinese: *jigu*)

The **enoki** or **golden needle mushroom** (Chinese: *jinzhen gu*, Japanese: *enokitake*) ranks sixth on the list of the world's most cultivated edible mushrooms.

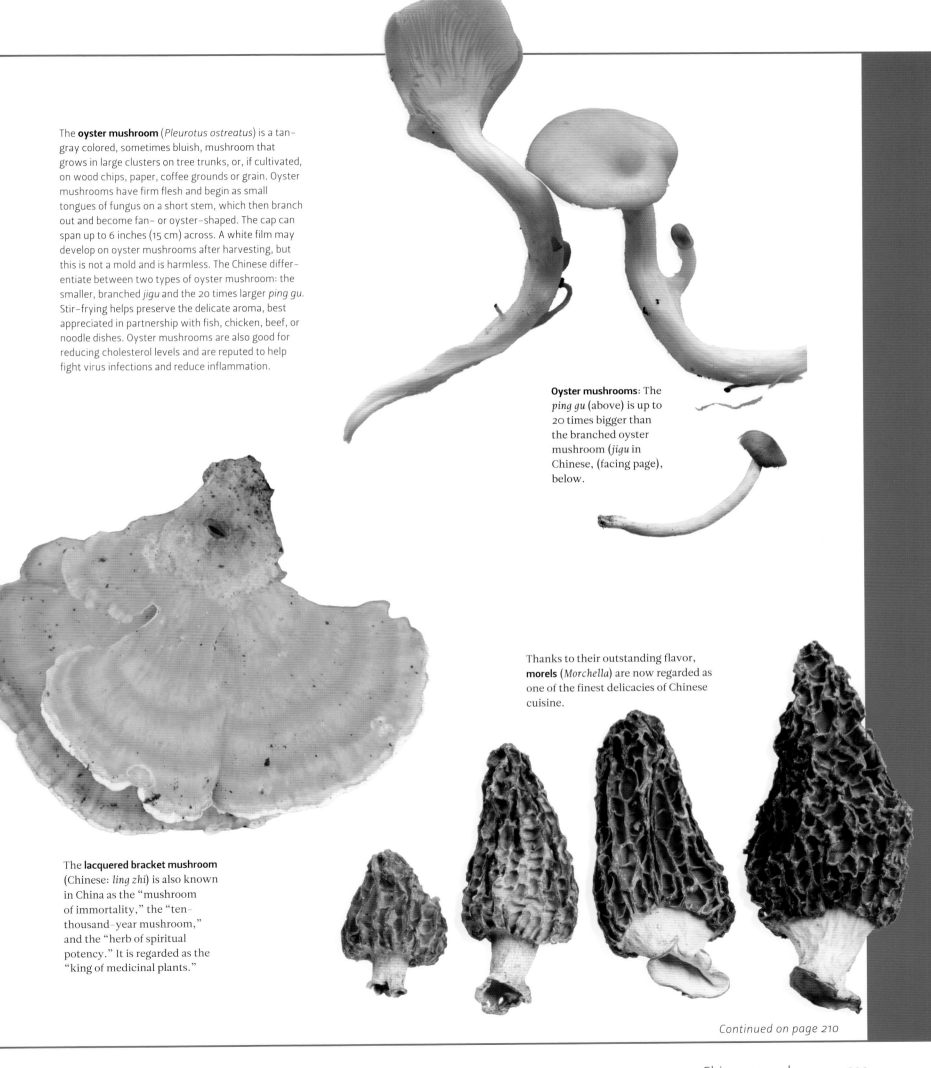

The **oyster mushroom** (*Pleurotus ostreatus*) is a tan-gray colored, sometimes bluish, mushroom that grows in large clusters on tree trunks, or, if cultivated, on wood chips, paper, coffee grounds or grain. Oyster mushrooms have firm flesh and begin as small tongues of fungus on a short stem, which then branch out and become fan- or oyster-shaped. The cap can span up to 6 inches (15 cm) across. A white film may develop on oyster mushrooms after harvesting, but this is not a mold and is harmless. The Chinese differentiate between two types of oyster mushroom: the smaller, branched *jigu* and the 20 times larger *ping gu*. Stir-frying helps preserve the delicate aroma, best appreciated in partnership with fish, chicken, beef, or noodle dishes. Oyster mushrooms are also good for reducing cholesterol levels and are reputed to help fight virus infections and reduce inflammation.

Oyster mushrooms: The *ping gu* (above) is up to 20 times bigger than the branched oyster mushroom (*jigu* in Chinese, (facing page), below.

Thanks to their outstanding flavor, **morels** (*Morchella*) are now regarded as one of the finest delicacies of Chinese cuisine.

The **lacquered bracket mushroom** (Chinese: *ling zhi*) is also known in China as the "mushroom of immortality," the "ten-thousand-year mushroom," and the "herb of spiritual potency." It is regarded as the "king of medicinal plants."

Continued on page 210

Continued from page 209

China, which produces 15 million tons of edible mushrooms annually, is responsible for 75 percent of worldwide production. While wild and medicinal mushrooms are gathered mainly from subtropical mountain regions, including the provinces of Guangxi or Yunnan, the excellent income potential has resulted in Chinese cultivators springing up like mushrooms, so-to-speak, all over the country. Fujian province is one of the main producers in this respect. The most widely cultivated mushroom is the internationally popular champignon or button mushroom followed by oyster and shiitake mushrooms.

Known in the West by its Japanese name of **shiitake** (*Lentinus edodes*, Chinese: *xianggu* or *donggu*), this mushroom is particularly popular on account of its intensive flavor and medicinal properties. The shiitake, which is native to China, grows wild on the trunks of ancient oak trees, but is known to have been cultivated here for around a thousand years. It can be bought fresh or dried, although dried shiitake have a more intense flavor. Usually available in well-stocked Chinese stores, experienced connoisseurs know that when choosing shiitake mushrooms, they should look for plump, dark-brown specimens with marbled caps.

They should be soaked for up to two hours in warm water before removing the stems and slicing the heads into strips. Shiitake mushrooms go particularly well with chicken or tofu dishes, but are also served as a nutritious delicacy with sea cucumber. As is the case with all types of mushroom, they are added to the dish last of all. Their intense flavor means that other strong seasonings can be dispensed with. Lentinan, a compound which has been isolated in shiitake, is used in China and Japan as an anticancer agent in the prevention and treatment of tumors. It is also attributed with antiviral, antibacterial, and cholesterol-lowering properties.

The rubbery, brownish-black **cloud ear mushrooms** (*Auricularia polytricha*, syn. *Hirneola polytricha*), otherwise known as Mu Err mushrooms, and the closely related Jew's ear mushroom (*Auricularia auricular-judae*) are found virtually all over the world growing on old tree trunks or, if cultivated, on appropriate growing media. This frilly mass, which, if indeed it resembles an ear at all, could only be likened to that of a prize fighter, is an important ingredient in Chinese cuisine—less on account of its taste (since it has very little flavor) than for its color, consistency, and beneficial medicinal properties. Mu Err mushrooms are

usually sold in dried form and should be soaked for half an hour before use in a large saucepan filled with hot water (they greatly increase in size when reconstituted). The stems and any dirt should be removed. The combination of color and textual contrast, not to mention a certain chewy crispness, make cloud ear mushrooms a popular ingredient in wok dishes and soups. Mu Err mushrooms have much to offer: they contain iron, potassium, phosphorus, silicon, and vitamin B1 and are believed to reduce inflammation and improve circulation.

Cloud ear mushrooms (Chinese: *Mu Err*), lack flavor but are crisp and nourishing.

The aromatic **shiitake** mushroom (Chinese: *xianggu* or *donggu*) is an integral part of Chinese cuisine.

Young ink caps (*Coprinus comatus*), or **drumstick mushrooms** as they are called in China, not only have a delicate flavor, but are also prized for their remedial and medicinal properties.

Silver ear mushrooms (*Tremella fuciformis*; Chinese: *yiner*), which grow on tropical hardwood as well as being cultivated, are particularly prized in Chinese cuisine. This attractive, almost transparent, white fungus with its slightly sweet flavor is often featured as a separate course during a banquet—either in the form of a sweet soup, usually including wolfberries, papaya, and lotus seeds, or in savory form with chicken. It is only available in dried form in the West. Silver ear mushrooms are believed to improve the immune system and effective in the treatment of depression, high blood pressure, liver and lung conditions.

The *houtou gu* or **monkey head mushroom** (*Hericium erinaceus*) is a spectacular fungus, in terms of appearance, flavor and content. It is also known in the West as hedgehog or lion's mane mushroom. This stemless, white fungus, which grows on trees and is also native to western Europe, does indeed resemble the spines of a hedgehog or a piece of coral. It can grow up to 12 inches (30 cm) in size and is also cultivated commercially. This type of mushroom is popular both in China as well as various other countries because of its culinary value as well as its medicinal properties. It has a strong aroma evocative of the woodland floor, a consistency reminiscent of seafood, and a flavor similar to that of chicken or veal—small wonder, therefore, that it is an extremely popular ingredient in vegetarian dishes. These mushrooms are rich in potassium, zinc, iron, germanium, selenium, and phosphorus and are used in traditional Chinese medicine (TCM) for the treatment of stomach disorders, respiratory problems, high cholesterol, nervous disorders, and tumors.

Some of the medicinal properties attributed to the **monkey head mushroom** (Chinese: *houtou gu*) have been scientifically proven.

The **rooting shank mushroom** (*Oudemansiella radicata*), another favorite edible mushroom, has the nickname "long life mushroom" in China (Chinese: *changs-hou gu*).

Silver ear mushrooms (Chinese: *yiner*) go well in vegetable wok dishes, or in clear soups.

Bamboo—a great all-rounder

Bamboo cane can reach almost 100 feet (30 m) in height and grow to a diameter of 8 inches (20 cm). It can break through rock formations with apparent ease and gives the impression of being as elastic a rubber. Bamboo can survive even fully-fledged typhoons without damage. It is astonishing to think that, botanically speaking, this plant belongs to the family of grasses. There are around one thousand different species of bamboo worldwide, around 500 of which are native to China. Bamboo has, since time immemorial, been one of the key natural products and construction materials that are part of Chinese everyday life, be it in the form of paper, chopsticks, building materials, medicinal plants, or as a vegetable. Thanks to the root mass which surrounds the rhizomes and, depending on species, bamboo spreads horizontally, sending out long underground tendrils—this Chinese all-rounder can find a foothold virtually anywhere. Depending on the variety, new shoots grow out of the rhizomes or from the base of the plant, which in turn grow into new bamboo plants. Given ideal climate conditions, i.e. tropical or subtropical regions, bamboo can spread into dense forests.

Among the edible species of bamboo, Moso bamboo (*Phyllostachys pubescens*) is the most sought after. Its rapid growth rate—up to 47 inches (120 cm) a day—makes it an ideal variety for cultivation. Its canes offer an ecologically viable alternative to wood and it produces more—and less bitter—shoots than other types of bamboo. With almost 20 percent of China's overall cultivable land situated in Fujian, the province is one of the main cultivation areas for Moso bamboo. As with other species of bamboo, propagation takes place largely underground via rhizomes, which grow between July and September when they sprout new buds. These then sprout into winter bamboo shoots, which are usually harvested by hand between October and February. Immediately after harvesting, these fragile winter shoots are sold fresh to local wholesalers without any further processing. They in turn distribute the produce to local markets. Greatly coveted for their tenderness, these winter bamboo shoots can command high prices as a seasonal delicacy. Spring bamboo shoots are harvested between March and May. After harvesting, they are processed for large companies in nearby factories where they are peeled, washed, boiled, and vacuum-packed. What is not sold directly to hotels and restaurants is sent for further processing in another factory, where it is processed and canned. Whichever bamboo shoots are used, they must always be boiled before eating, as raw bamboo shoots, like many other vegetables, contain a toxin similar to cyanide.

Not only do bamboo shoots—and particularly organic ones—taste good, but they are also healthy. They contain large amounts of silicic acid, which is used in traditional Chinese medicine (TCM) as a remedy in cases of depression or lack of energy. The shoots are also a good source of vitamins B1 and C, as well as other mineral compounds and trace elements. Their high water content and the fact that they are rich in protein and dietary fiber makes them a filling and nutritious option for a diet plan—provided they are prepared by a low-calorie cooking method.

In the West, food connoisseurs have to make do with canned or frozen bamboo shoots since fresh bamboo shoots, or organic bamboo sprouts are virtually unobtainable. A tasty alternative to the canned version are dried winter bamboo shoots which—after thorough washing and preferably overnight soaking—will conjure up the flavor of days long ago for, traditionally speaking, it was Chinese monks in remote mountain regions who gathered bamboo shoots from the wild forests, dried them, and used them to prepare their delicious fasting fare.

Rice noodles with bamboo and soybean shoots

1 tbsp salt
11 oz (300 g) rice noodles
9 oz (250 g) commercially prepared bamboo
8 oz (220 g) soybean shoots
4 tbsp peanut oil
5–6 tbsp soy sauce

Fill a saucepan with water and bring to a boil. Add the salt and rice noodles and stir round to prevent the noodles sticking together.

Boil the noodles for about 4 minutes (they should not be allowed to become too soft) and continue stirring. Quickly rinse the cooked noodles in cold water.

Wash the soybean shoots and bamboo, and thinly slice the bamboo. Heat the peanut oil in a skillet or wok and fry the noodles over a high heat for about 4 minutes, stirring occasionally. Add the soybean shoots and bamboo and continue frying for about another 3–4 minutes. Finally, add the soy sauce and serve.

Right: Textiles, building material, musical instruments, weapons... the list of potential uses for bamboo is virtually endless. Pandas, like all connoisseurs of good food, are primarily interested in the young bamboo shoots.

Guangdong

广东

Katrin Schlotter

Almost everyone has heard of it, —the large coastal province of Guangdong, near Hong Kong, measuring just on 69,500 square miles (180,000 sq km)—though perhaps without consciously realizing it. It is probably better known in the West as "Canton," which is used just as frequently for the provincial capital of Guangzhou as for the province of Guangdong. The province's boundaries are marked by the Nanling Mountains, some of which rise to 6,000 feet (2,000 m), and a coastline almost 2,000 miles (3,000 km) long. Between them lies a flat plain in which three rivers join together to form the mighty Pearl River (Zhu Jiang). It is difficult to imagine a more diverse landscape. And yet Guangdong has more to offer than lush banana groves or dazzlingly green rice fields. When people talk of "the workshop of the world," or "the motor for China's economy," or even of "the turbocharger for the global economy," that also refers to the province and the Pearl River delta. Many products, from T-shirts right through to computers, are manufactured or processed in Guangdong. And for some time now they have also been sold there, or are newly popular there. Moreover, Chinese cuisine (as known to the West) had its origins here, as most of the Chinese diaspora comes from Guangdong, and many of these people began their careers abroad by working as cooks. With its bustling port cities and their countless markets and businesses, its remarkable temples and its unusual culinary specialties, the province is also rightly on the travel itinerary of numerous tourists.

In the year 2007 this export-orientated province was one of the richest provinces in China, with 14.5 percent economic growth and a gross domestic product (GDP) which exceeded 419 billion US dollars. This is only partly accounted for by the profitable economic framework conditions and networks, the perfect position on the coast, the close connections with Cantonese communities abroad, and the close proximity of Hong Kong and Macau. There is also a very good infrastructure, with airports and container harbors serving international markets, together with a strong commercial tradition and an open attitude to the rest of the world. Thanks to the presence of prestigious universities, there is also a high level of education.

Guangdong is extraordinary from several points of view. Over 1,250 miles (2,000 km) from the imperial court, an independent culture developed, which was sometimes at odds with the central government. The Cantonese mentality was sometimes thought of as being too flexible, too

Top above: The most likely place to find a couple "whispering sweet nothings" to one another in the park in China is somewhere that Western influences were felt quite early—for example, in Guangdong province.

Above: Whether people are eating or working, the smallest social unit in China is the group.

Facing page: "China's economic motor"—that's what they call Guangdong. This is where the first special economic zones were set up. This is where the first skyscrapers were built.

Guangzhou •

Guangdong **217**

Top above: As in Europe, the farther south you go, the more activity there is in the evening and on into the night.

Above: When it comes to neon lights, central Guangzhou has nothing to learn from New York's Times Square.

revolutionary, and thus a threat to the harmony and unity of the Middle Kingdom. But, as befitted free spirits, they still kept their culture alive in the tropical south of China—or, in the last resort, they went abroad, taking their own music, cuisine, and language with them. Cantonese, often described as a mere dialect, is markedly different from Mandarin. With up to nine different tonalities, and with some characters that can have more than one meaning, Cantonese is a challenge, even for the Chinese. In spite of this, the Cantonese people's wanderlust has helped their language to spread far beyond the borders of the province—for instance, to Guangxi, Hong Kong, Macau, Southeast Asia, and the United States.

However in Guangdong itself, the Cantonese singsong accent, with its hard, closed sounds, mingles with other dialects from other parts of the province. For example in the east, around Chaozhou, people speak Minnan, a language originating in South Fujian. In the north, the Hakka dialect is widespread. With such a babel of tongues, people sometimes have to resort to gestures. And moreover, millions of Chinese from the poorer parts of the country pour into the rich city of Guangdong (sometimes legally, sometimes not), in the hope of obtaining well-paid work in the factories. Nobody knows exactly how many migrant workers there are. One estimate is 30 million. Officially, about 80 million people live in Guangdong, and two thirds of these are in the densely populated cities. The differences in income

between the cities and the countryside are enormous. Thus the mean annual income in Guangdong's cities in 2007 was 2,200 US dollars. In the countryside, by contrast, it was only 710 US dollars.

In the light of this big difference in incomes, it may seem hard to believe that there are any farmers left in this industrial province at all. And yet Guangdong offers fertile tropical or subtropical plains watered by its rivers, which are suitable both for fish farming and for arable and dairy farming. Rice paddies and computers—it's not a contradiction in Guangdong.

Above: Guangzhou's parks are a lush green. China's town planners are slowly realizing that the number of highrise buildings is not the only criterion to determine the quality of life in a city.

Below left: Undoubtedly an additional factor in China's economic miracle—the living craft tradition...

Below: ...alongside modern industrial production.

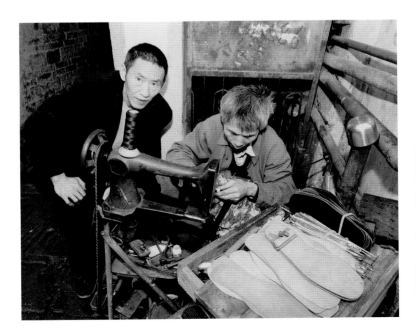

Guangdong—traditionally open to the world

The history of Guangdong goes back more than 2,000 years. The area inhabited by the Yue people was incorporated into the Chinese empire in the 3ʳᵈ century B.C. Even today, Guangdong is referred to as Yue for short. Once Emperor Qin Shi Huangdi (259–210 B.C.) had united China for the first time, from the Gobi Desert to the South China Sea, the Nanhai prefecture was established (in 214 B.C.) with its capital in Panyu (present-day Guangzhou).

When the Qin dynasty collapsed, the ex-prefect Zhao Tuo proclaimed himself Emperor Wu of Nanyue (183 B.C.). This empire stretched from the Pearl River all the way to Vietnam, even if it lasted only for a short time (203–111 B.C.). The tomb of Zhao Tuo's grandson, lavishly decorated in bronze, ceramics, and gold, was discovered by accident in 1983 in the course of construction work, and can still be visited today in the Nanyue Royal Tomb Museum in Guangzhou.

In 111 B.C., the Nanyue empire was reconquered by the Han dynasty (206 B.C.–220 A.D.). But it was only at the time of the Tang dynasty (618–907) that close ties were established with the empire. Despite continuous changes of government and various waves of immigration, seafaring and commerce were developed. Guangzhou maintained frequent contacts with Indian, Arab, and Persian traders. The Ming dynasty (1368–1644) saw the arrival of Western merchants as well. These external contacts not only led to a flourishing trade in goods, but also to cultural exchanges. The continents exchanged religions, ideas, and also technical processes. The Portuguese, who settled in Macau in 1557, established a worldwide commercial network that extended from China to Latin America.

And yet, at the behest of the imperial court, the days of openness and trade in Guangdong were

followed by a return to isolation. The aim was to protect the Chinese empire from an excess of foreign influence, from westernization, and from pirates. In 1662, in an attempt to put an end to the attacks by the pirate Zheng Chenggong (also known as Coxinga), which had been going on for 20 years, the Qing ruler of the time had the coastal strip between Shandong and Guangdong evacuated. Everything left behind was burned to the ground—a historical event that is hardly ever referred to in Chinese textbooks even nowadays. No wonder, since almost all contemporary evidence from this period vanished in the turmoil.

In the year 1757, the emperor issued a decree with far-reaching consequences. Henceforth, China's foreign trade would be channeled exclusively through Guangzhou. Foreigners

Below: In busy, busy Guangzhou, fast-food joints and snack bars provide a welcome break.

Facing page: There's scarcely anything you cannot buy in the market halls.

could settle only on the island of Shamian—the city was barred to them. They were to be subject to Chinese law, and could develop their businesses only through Chinese merchants' associations. This was also a period when Guangzhou's population was growing larger and larger, for trade was flourishing: Chinese goods such as tea, silk, cotton materials, lacquered goods or porcelain were in demand, not only in Japan, Southeast Asia, and the United States, but also in Europe. The cultivation of tea or the artisan and handicraft industries dominated what was already an exporting economy even then. Rice, on the other hand, had to be imported—a situation that often led to hunger and destitution.

At first, the Chinese profited by the port's monopoly on the empire's coast. It was the rich

Below: Touching goods and checking them over is not just allowed in China, it is something you are explicitly requested to do.

Below bottom: Those who have no market stall are happy to display their wares directly onto the street, especially if they are selling "bulk produce."

Above: Animal-lovers would certainly feel the need to speak out about this.

Left: If you have no market stall, hold your own garage sale.

Right: Guangdong's cuisine is considered as being particularly aromatic—not least because fruit and vegetables are always bought fresh.

merchants, above all, for whom tea turned into pieces of silver. But when, from 1820 onward, the British began to send in illegal imports of Bengali opium and also wanted to be paid in silver, the tables began to turn. As the demand for opium grew (it is thought that by 1830 there were already 10 million Chinese opium addicts), China went into a trade deficit. And yet Guangzhou continued to prosper, because, in spite of restrictions, neither the British dealers nor the Chinese merchants wanted to give up the lucrative source of income. When the emperor imposed the death penalty for trafficking in opium and dispatched his commissar, Lin Zexu, to Guangzhou, trouble broke out. Lin had 350 foreigners imprisoned in their offices and threw 2.8 million pounds (1.4 million kg) of opium into the sea. This resulted in two opium wars (1839–1842 and 1856–1860), both of which China lost. The merchants' associations were dissolved, reparations were paid, Hong Kong was ceded to the British, and ports were opened to foreigners, who were also granted concessions and had the right to be judged under their own laws. This was a humiliation

for an empire that was already growing weaker. In Guangzhou, the British and French administered their own concessions on the tiny island of Shamian, but soon a new rivalry developed as additional treaty ports were opened up. Shanghai began to overhaul Guangzhou as the leading center for Sino-European trade.

Moreover, a famine led to massive unrest in Guangxi and Guangdong, which culminated in the Taiping Rebellion of 1850, an uprising which cost the lives of over 20 million people. The insurgents were under the leadership of Hong Xiuquan (1813–1864), a Hakka Chinese who came from Guangdong and had been educated in a mission school, but had failed his examinations. He believed himself to be the son of God. The rebels, many of whom were Hakka, succeeded in conquering half of China. In addition to promises of religious salvation, the Taiping insurgents called for the land to be distributed fairly and for the abolition of private property, the overthrow of the "foreign domination" of the Qing rulers, and the introduction of an aesthetic lifestyle. The "Heavenly Empire of Great

Peace," which extended all the way from the south to Nanjing (now the capital of Jiangsu province), was overthrown in 1864 by Qing troops, with the support of the French and the British. From the mid 19th century onward, poverty and hunger, political turmoil, and wars provided the impetus for a wave of emigration overseas, with Fujian and Guangdong as the departure points. In the hope of a better life, the hardiest signed on as cheap labor in the silver mines of Peru, on the sugar plantations of Cuba, as golddiggers in California or construction workers building the American railroads. However, many of these did not even survive the sea voyage to the New World. By contrast, those who emigrated to Southeast Asia usually had better luck. Chinese immigrant communities of one kind or another were formed in Malaysia, Burma, and Thailand, and became successful traders. In 1926, their combined capital was estimated at 644 million US dollars. Meanwhile in the homeland the Chinese empire collapsed. In 1912, the Republic of China came into being. Communists and Nationalists battled for power, world wars shook the fragmented country, and in 1949 the communist People's Republic of China was born. Throughout all this, most of the overseas Chinese stayed away from their country of origin. It was only when the People's Republic introduced the reform and openness policy that Guangdong began to look interesting to them again. From 1979 onward, Guangdong acted as an experimental laboratory for the modernization of China. Parallel to the planned economy, the government set up capitalist enclaves for foreign investors in order to obtain foreign currency, attract know-how to the country and promote exports. Three of these four "Special Economic Zones" (SEZ) were established in the coastal province of Guangdong. And the daring experiment succeeded—thanks not least to the support of some of the Cantonese exiles.

Above: The meat stalls offer a wide selection of cuts and portions. Should the customer wish it, they can be individually shaped and prepared.

Left: Many small farmers are perfectly willing to do some backbreaking transportation work. They bring samples from the entire range of their field crops and culinary production for sale in the city markets.

Guangdong—traditionally open to the world **223**

Guangdong's refined cuisine

Deep-fried shrimp, steamed fish, chicken in lemon sauce, grilled pork, and delicate dim sum—each morsel more delicious than the last—plus a can of Coke, after weeks of deprivation. A good 25 years later, many an experienced traveler to China feels his mouth watering when he remembers the Guangzhou of the 1980s. By comparison with the frugal north of the country, wealthy and colorful Guangzhou was already overflowing with luxury and joie de vivre in the early 1980s. The reform and openness policy awakened people's vitality and business acumen. They immediately started cultivating every tiny strip of land. At last, the Cantonese were being allowed to make money again (with fruit and vegetables, for example). The city slaved away from morning to night, and the markets were overflowing with foodstuffs. International restaurants, hotels and fast-food joints competed for the visitors' favors. In Guangzhou, you could get anything you could find at home—and for many Westerners, the Guangzhou version was better. The typical Chinese taste they knew from the Chinese restaurants of Hamburg, Paris or London was something the overseas Chinese had brought with them from Guangdong. In China, Cantonese cuisine, also referred to as Yue cuisine, is considered as being one of the eight great regional culinary traditions. Even top chefs in the north admit it while gnashing their teeth. Cantonese cuisine is the best, the most varied, and the most refined in China—it has been influenced by other regions and countries and there is nothing uniform about it. It is usually divided into Guangzhou cuisine, Hakka cuisine, and Chaozhou cuisine (which includes influences from Fujian)—though the high level of internal migration and the province's good infrastructure mean the differences between the individual traditional regional cuisines are increasingly being blurred. Whether the dishes are Guangzhou style or Chaozhou style, the ingredients themselves are extremely varied, ranging from fish and seafood through meat specialties (some of which are a little unusual) to a rich choice of vegetables. And there is an equally wide variety when it comes to types of preparation. The attraction of the dishes lies in the fact that, thanks to the skills of the Cantonese cooks, the individual aromas of the ingredients can always be clearly distinguished. The deciding factor here is the freshness of the ingredients: eggplant, asparagus tips, water spinach, bok choy (Chinese leaf), choi sum (another type of Chinese leaf) and other kinds of vegetable are harvested at the right moment and transported to the markets in the early morning. Animals are not killed until the last minute. Tanks full of fish act as "menus," snakes are slaughtered at the table. By contrast, the Cantonese generally refrain from using strong spices or thick sauces. If the fish has a fiery, sharp taste, they

Left: Before the produce ends up in the consumer's wok, the vendor carries it on foot to market and only then is it sold on to the middlemen.

tend to suspect that it is no longer fresh. On the other hand, mild spices are allowed, which emphasize the inherent aroma of the dish—such as light soy, fish or oyster sauces, chicken broth, and rice wine, supplemented with ginger, garlic, and black bean paste. Meat and poultry dishes, in particular, are often served with a sweet fruit element added—for instance, duck with pineapple or beef with mango. Openness, a desire to experiment, and even a delight in taking risks—these are the Cantonese characteristics which are reflected in their cuisine. In good times, foreign ingredients and culinary traditions came to Guangdong via the old trade routes. Comfort and wealth meant that the upper class, at least, had time to enjoy life, and so the culinary arts were developed, mainly in the port cities. The ships also imported goods from overseas which stimulated new tastes—in the form, for example, of sweet potatoes, peanuts, Indian corn or tomatoes. However, the province was also repeatedly ravaged by poverty, wars, floods, and famines, so in poor regions, the struggle for survival did not simply call for well-developed techniques of cultivation, preparation, and preservation. It also meant the most unexpected animals could wind up on the menu. Many creatures that were sources of protein—such as snakes, dogs or cats—are still very popular today because they are thought to have a "strengthening effect."

Above: Fresh vegetables—the be-all and end-all of Guangzhou cuisine.

Right: In China, everyone knows that cooking does not begin in the kitchen. It starts with a trip to the market.

Sweet-and-sour pork—Cantonese-style

9 oz (250 g) pork tenderloin
2 tsp Shaoxing rice wine
1 tbsp cornstarch, mixed with 2 tbsp water
1 tbsp all-purpose flour
1 ½ tbsp soy sauce
1 ½ sugar
1 ½ tbsp rice vinegar
1 ½ water
3 ¾ cups (900 ml) vegetable oil
1 tbsp chopped scallions
1 tbsp sesame oil
salt

Cut the pork into thin pieces and put into a bowl. Add 1 teaspoon Shaoxing rice wine and a large pinch of salt, together with ⅓ of the cornstarch mixture and the flour, thoroughly mix and then set aside.
Stir the soy sauce, sugar, the remaining rice wine, the vinegar, the remaining cornstarch mixture, and 1 ½ tablespoons of water together into a sweet-and-sour sauce, and set aside.

Heat 3 ½ cups (850 ml) of the vegetable oil in a wok at medium heat (about 300 °F/ 150 °C). Add the pieces of pork, deep-fry for 1 minute and remove them. Reheat the oil (to about 300 °F/ 150 °C), deep-fry the meat for another minute, remove, and allow to drain well.
Fry the chopped scallions in the remainder of the oil, then add the meat once more.
Pour the sauce into the wok and stir-fry everything. When the sauce has thickened, drizzle sesame oil over the dish. When ready, tip the contents of the wok onto a serving platter.

Specialties from Guangdong

Pumpkin soup

1 oz (25 g) dried Chinese red dates
1 oz (25 g) cored longan fruit, peeled and
    seeded
1 oz (25 g) red beans
1 oz (25 g) lotus seeds
generous ½ cup (100 g) rice
4 oz (100 g) glutinous rice, presoaked
1 ½ tbsp sugar
1 pumpkin (about 1 ½ lb / 700 g)

Soak the dates for 20 minutes. Heat the longan
fruit, the red beans, the lotus seeds, and the
dates for 20 minutes in 2 cups (500 ml) water.
Cook the rice and the glutinous ("sticky") rice for
40 minutes on medium heat in 1 ½ quarts
(1 ½ liters) water. Add the cooked dates, longan
fruit, red beans, and lotus seeds to the rice soup,
together with their cooking water. Add the sugar
and simmer for 10 minutes on a low heat.
Cut off the top of the pumpkin and scoop out the
flesh with a spoon. Then steam the pumpkin for
20 minutes over high heat. Steam the flesh separately. Remove the pumpkin from the steamer
and pour the cooked soup into the cavity. The
cooked pumpkin flesh can be served along with
the soup.

Chinese leaf in an earthenware pot

2 ¼ lb (1 kg) fresh Chinese leaf (Brassica
    juncea) from the local Asian shop
9 oz (250 g) shoulder of pork, with fat and skin
⅓ cup (75 ml) of vegetable oil
2 tsp rice wine
2 cups (500 ml) water
1 tsp salt
½ tsp freshly ground white pepper
1 tbsp sesame oil

Wash the Chinese leaf, blanch for 1 minute in
boiling water, drain and briefly cool in cold water.
Remove and allow to drain thoroughly. Cut the
meat into thin pieces.
Heat half of the oil in a wok, add the Chinese leaf
and stir-fry for 1 minute, then remove.
Heat the remaining oil in the wok and add the
pork. Add the rice wine and stir-fry until the
meat is cooked. Remove the meat and place in a
heatproof earthenware pot. Arrange the cooked
vegetable over the meat.
Stir in the water, salt, pepper, and sesame oil, set
the earthenware pot on the stove over low heat
and allow to simmer for about 30 minutes.

Sa cha ribs

Generous 1 lb (500 g) pork ribs
2 tbsp cornstarch
2 ½ cups (600 ml) vegetable oil, for deep-frying
1 piece of ginger (about 1 inch / 3 cm), cut into thin pieces
4–5 tbsp sa cha sauce
2 tsp rice wine
2 tsp soy sauce
1 tsp sugar
1 tsp white pepper
1 tsp cornstarch, mixed with 2 tsp water
2 tsp sesame oil
1 small piece of leek, chopped, for garnish

Use a sharp meat cleaver to cut the ribs into pieces 2 inches (6 cm) long and 1 inch (3 cm) wide. Bring 1 ¾ cups (400 ml) of water to a boil, add the rib pieces and blanch for 2 minutes. Remove the ribs and refresh in cold water an drain thoroughly. Put the rib pieces in a large bowl, dust the cornstarch over them and mix well.

Heat 2 ¼ cups (550 ml) of oil in the wok until it begins to smoke, add the ribs and deep-fry until the oil is almost boiling. Remove the ribs with a ladle and allow to drain.

Add the remaining oil to the wok, add the ginger and stir-fry until an aroma is released.

Stir in the sa cha sauce, rice wine, soy sauce, sugar, the pepper, and some water. Add the deep-fried ribs to the wok, put the lid on and cook everything over medium heat for 30 minutes, checking that nothing is sticking. Remove the lid, add the cornstarch mixture and the sesame oil. Stir until the sauce thickens, then put the ribs onto a serving plate with the sauce. Garnish with chopped leek.

Deep-fried dumplings with papaya filling

Dough 1 (Su You):
⅓ cup (75 ml) vegetable oil
1 ¼ cups (150 g) all-purpose flour
1 tbsp sugar
3 ½ tbsp water

Dough 2 (Su Pi):
¾ cup (100 g) all-purpose flour
¼ cup (60 ml) vegetable oil

Filling:
7 oz (200 g) papaya
⅓ cup (75 g) sugar
2 tbsp butter
2 tbsp cornstarch
4 cups (1 liter) vegetable oil, for deep-frying

For **dough 1**, knead all ingredients in a bowl to form a dough. Cover the dough with a damp cloth or plastic wrap and leave to rest for 30 minutes.

For **dough 2**, knead the flour and oil in a bowl, cover, and again leave to rest for 30 minutes. For the **filling**, scrape out the papaya flesh with a spoon and chop. Thoroughly mix in the chopped papaya with the sugar, butter, and cornstarch. Put into a saucepan, add 3 ½ tablespoons of water, bring to a boil, and simmer until the mixture thickens. Knead dough 1 and form it into a cylinder with a diameter of about ¾ inch/2 cm. Cut the cylinder into 16 pieces of uniform size. Roll out the pieces into circles with a diameter of 2 ½ inches (6 cm). Use a cookie cutter to make neat circles.

Repeat the process for dough 2.

Place a sheet of dough 2 on top of a sheet of dough 1, knead, and roll out again.

Put a small amount of filling into the center of each circle. Twist the edges of the dough together over the filling and press firmly to seal. Fold the edges down and press together lightly. Heat the oil in a wok and add the dumplings. Deep-fry them over a medium heat until they are golden yellow, remove with a slotted spoon and drain thoroughly.

The Pearl River Delta sets the trend

"It does not matter whether the cat is black or white, as long as it catches mice." The motto of the Chinese economic reformer Deng Xiao Ping (1904–1997) was certainly music to the ears of the Cantonese—especially as in other parts of the country they are considered as being pragmatic and ready to take risks, and having good heads for business.

At the start of the 1980s, in parallel with the planned economy, the government set up capitalist enclaves in Guangdong for foreign investment, the so-called special economic zones (SEZ). This was part of the reform and openness policy. The regions around Shenzhen, Zhuhai, and Shantou appeared best suited for this, as the role models for this step forward—Hong Kong and Taiwan— were located close by, over the border. While Hong Kong was still under British rule at the time and Taiwan considered itself to be a separate country, in the eyes of the People's Republic they were both Chinese provinces. And why not take advantage of the capitalist neighbors and let them invest?

Since then, a total of nine cities and regions—including the provincial capital, Guangzhou, the political and economic hub of the experiment, and the two special economic zones Shenzhen and Zhuhai—have been brought together to form one of the most economically successful areas in the world, the Pearl River Delta. In the area where, a quarter of a century ago, rice paddies and fish ponds glittered in the sunlight between the arms of the river, Chinese and foreign companies now manufacture goods which are exported all over the world.

Auto manufacturers and parts suppliers, petrochemical firms, and electronics and IT companies—these are the three most important growth industries of Guangdong. Moreover, about 650,000 private companies have been established between Guangzhou and Shenzhen alone. They are responsible for about 40 percent of the GDP. Thanks to the good infrastructure and the high standard of living, international investors no longer just use the Pearl River Delta as the cheap workshop of the world. They now also see it as a sales market for their goods. This is particularly true for the service sector. From logistics and telecommunications, through commerce, finance, and real estate, right through to trade fairs and the leisure industry. Nowhere in China is the demand for services and products as high as it is in the Pearl River Delta. It is no wonder that the inhabitants of Guangzhou and Shenzhen are among the richest in China, and have some of the highest disposable incomes. And the region has once again become a testbed—this time for new trends and product brands for the Chinese market.

The Pearl River Delta long ago made the transition from an isolated, capitalist "foreign body" to the integrated economic motor of the whole country. From the point of view of economic policy, the region is not only linked to the Special Administrative Regions (SAR) of Hong Kong and Macau, but also, since the summer of 2004, it has links with other provinces in the interior and on the coast.

In addition to Hong Kong and Macau, the so-called Pan Pearl River Delta Region (or the "9 + 2" region) includes the provinces of Guangdong, Sichuan, Fujian, Hunan, Jiangxi, Guangxi, Yunnan, Guizhou, and Hainan. While Hong Kong and Macau live mainly by trade and by providing services, Guangdong and Fujian produce goods for export. As wage levels rise in the rich southern provinces, and as Chinese companies with their own products enter into competition with foreign investors, manufacturing companies are beginning to migrate into more distant areas (i.e. cheaper regions). With the help of the rich southern provinces, areas within the Pearl River Delta which were once predominantly agricultural are seeing their infrastructures expanded and are becoming economically integrated. This development brings another advantage with it. The jam-packed Pearl River Delta has fewer factories, the pollution levels fall a little, and hi-tech industry can move on.

And another test is under way. It looks as if the Chinese government could attain its objective and smooth out the inequalities of income without driving the manufacturing companies out to countries where wage rates are lower. And so they can build up high-quality industries of their own—plasma screens instead of plastic flowers.

Below: The waters of the Pearl River Delta flow slowly and ponderously on to the South China Sea.

Left: Behind the calm idyllic façade seethes one of the fastest expanding economic regions in China.

Right: This also includes Chaozhou, a city of 2 million people—the center and the birthplace of the Chaozhou cuisine which is highly esteemed all over the region.

Bizarre Cantonese delicatessen

What amazes people is the variety. People who are not Cantonese are genuinely shocked. Let's admit right away that one of the most prevalent prejudices regarding Cantonese cuisine is that in Guangdong people eat just everything—from ducks' tongues right through to chickens' claws. This is true, and yet it is only part of the truth. The battle between the phoenix and the tiger does not refer to a parable, but to a Cantonese specialty, a stew made from snakes and cats. Another equally sensuous description refers to "fragrant meat," but this does not mean the tasty red marinated and fried strips of pork that fill the streets of Guangzhou with their aroma. It is a dish made from dog flesh. Like any culinary tradition, the Cantonese cuisine also has its own delicacies which other cultures might find it difficult to appreciate.

Everything relating to food and delicatessen is appreciated by the more than 60,000 visitors who come to the notorious Qingping market in Guangzhou every day. On a large site, measuring about 118,000 square feet (11,000 sq m), very near the attractive "colonial age" island of Shamian, there is a world which challenges all your senses. From fresh and dried exotic vegetables through tanks full of fish right through

Left: Western visitors to Guangzhou's Qingping market may be offered some produce for sale which appears rather bizarre—here we see various kinds of tree fungi.

Right: Not only goods are exchanged in the market, but also news, gossip, and rumors.

to scorpions and locusts—what is crawling around here in the morning will be on the menu this evening. If in the past the customers had to watch lots of animals being beaten to death, so that they would have the right gamey taste, things are done more discreetly now. Since such epidemics as the respiratory disease SARS, which was thought to have been spread via the live animal markets in Guangdong, the authorities are keener on making sure that dealers adhere to the product description regulations and hygiene rules.

And also, many Cantonese have recently opened their hearts to pet animals, and instead of eating dog they would prefer some other

Above: What are described as birds' nests are the nests of swiftlets, a species of bird belonging to the swift family. The main constituent is their tough and gelatinous saliva, which contains protein.

Right: The entire market area is broken down by product. In some of the narrow alleys, you will find only meat or fish vendors—fruit and vegetable stalls are elsewhere.
Traditional Chinese medicine products are also on sale, as are spices and every cooking utensil you can think of.

Bizarre Cantonese delicatessen **231**

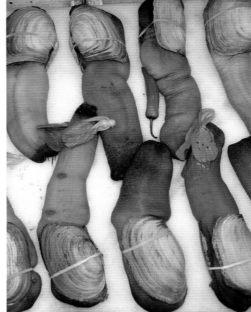

Above left: Sea worms are also on the menu on the South China coast...

Above right: ...as are all kinds of mussels. It is said of the South Chinese that they can create a dish from anything that "moves with its back to the sun."

Right: The cook is proudly showing off the specimen that he and his colleagues are about to prepare.

Below: This is the rule that applies for all meat and fish dishes in the Chinese coastal regions—as far as possible, the animal should not be killed until just before it goes into the wok.

equally sought-after delicacy such as abalone, sea cucumbers, shark's fins or snakes. All these specialties are decidedly expensive, so that you need not worry that anyone will serve you with them accidentally.

Yet it is precisely the foreign business contacts (unless they have made it known in advance that they are vegetarians) who are likely to be invited along to a typical snake banquet—an adventure in itself since, as you would expect from any good restaurant, when the snake season begins in autumn the fat cobras, pythons, and other snakes which are available for selection are lying there on display very much alive, or winding themselves round the waitress's arm. The creature's heart has scarcely stopped beating when the first course appears. As a goodwill gesture from the kitchen, or even taken directly from the living creature, snake's blood and gall juice are served, together with a shot of liquor, to male diners only—good for potency, you are jovially assured. Next up to ten different snake dishes arrive on the table—sometimes accompanied by chicken, cloudy ear mushrooms, and bamboo; sometimes in the form of a "strengthening" soup with ginger, wolfberries, and chrysanthemum flowers. Whether it is the effect of the snakemeat or the highly alcoholic liquor—for whatever reason, it is a decidedly merry banquet.

Abalone and sea cucumber (two seafood delicacies much prized in Guangzhou) are much less spectacular than a snake banquet, but are claimed as being no less effective for one's potency. Abalone costs about 150 US dollars (100 euros) for 2 ¼ lb (1 kg). In spite of their shimmering shells, which can be made into jewelry, abalone (of which there are about 60 different varieties) are small to large-sized edible sea snails: gastropod mollusks in the family Haliotidae. "Wild" sea snails, which can be up to 12 inches (30 cm) long, are very hard to find nowadays. The Chinese have seen this as an opportunity, rather than an obstacle, and now breed most of the abalone eaten in the world on 300 Chinese aquafarms. While abalone are generally available only in cans or in dried form in the West, in Guangdong you can get them both fresh and perfectly prepared. If they are cooked for the right time, abalone (which are actually tough) have a tender consistency. Served with asparagus or mushrooms, they are a real treat.

When sea cucumbers are sold in the market, they are brownish-black, stone hard, and up to 16 inches (40 cm) long. As with bird's nest soup, it takes a few days for the dried, salted, and smoked sea cucumbers to be ready for cooking, and they release their aroma only in combination with mushrooms, bamboo, ginger, and onions.

To judge by the texture of these boneless sea creatures, which belong to the echinoderm phylum of marine animals, this is another case where they have probably been elevated to their status as a delicacy due to male fantasies. The flabby sea creatures, which lie on the seabed apparently lifeless in warm coastal waters, become stiff and erect if touched.

Above top: Snakes can be prepared in various ways—they are often enjoyed in soups, but they can also be roasted or deep-fried.

Above: Snake-based preparations are also widely used in traditional Chinese medicine. They are considered as being yang dishes, which warm the blood if consumed in winter.

Journey through Guangdong

On the one hand, swarming port cities and pulsating economic centers. On the other, picturesque landscapes and remote cities still almost unknown in the West. The province of Guangdong, which has an area of about 69,500 square miles (180,000 sq km), about the size of the state of Missouri, offers some exciting contrasts between town and country and between the present and the past. Let's take a whistle-stop tour.

Each of the cities with over a million inhabitants in the Pearl River Delta—i.e. Guangzhou, Shenzhen, Dongguan, Foshan, Zhongshan, Zhuhai, Jiangmen, Huizhou and Zhaoqing—has its own character, and yet taken together they stand for prosperity and internationalism. At the center, naturally, stands the provincial capital of Guangzhou, which is over 2,000 years old, and which nowadays has about 9 million inhabitants. With the New International Baiyun Airport, the Canton Export Industries Trade Fair, the Pazhou Exhibition Center (the biggest exhibition hall in Asia) and the third biggest harbor in China, it acts as an international hub for trade, logistics, transportation, and services. But Guangzhou does not just have a pulsating economy. Above all, it pulsates with life. Modern shopping streets with innumerable restaurants and bars, a colonial era atmosphere on the island of Shamian, old temple sites and pagodas, together with extensive parks, make Guangzhou a metropolis which is quite simply a good place to live—not least thanks to the outstanding cuisine.

The Shenzhen SEZ near Hong Kong is just as versatile from the culinary point of view, and yet completely different. A city of 12 million people, which sprang straight from the drawing board, it is considered as being the center of China's hi-tech industries. Behind the glass and steel façades, world-shaking stock exchange deals and export transactions are going on. As late as the 1970s Shenzhen was a fishing port with 30,000 inhabitants. Nowadays, in addition to its international-style urban life, the rich economic metropolis can offer the entire history of China and of the world in miniature, concentrated in experience parks.

By contrast, the city of Foshan (6 million inhabitants) was already a significant economic and trading center a thousand years ago. The city is famous for ceramics, wood carvings, and paper silhouettes, and also for its historic buildings, such as the Foshan ancestral temple which dates from the Song period (960–1279), in which the traditional Yue operas are still performed today. And the Liangyuan gardens, a wondrously beautiful park dating from the year 1796, is another place where visitors can forget the passage of time. This center of culture is said to be the place where the martial art of Kung Fu was born, together with lion dancing. Foshan has just as impressive a profile in culinary terms as well—goose wing with orange peel and frogs with walnuts are just two of the local specialties.

The industrial city of Zhaoqing, about 63 miles (100 km) west of Guangzhou in the interior, also forms part of the Pearl River Delta economic region. The city, famous for its inkstones, can look back on a long history. Since the Sui era (581–618), Zhaoqing has been regarded as the political, economic, and cultural center of a mountainous region. The old city, with its pagodas and historic sites, such as the Qingyun temple from the Tang dynasty (618–907) and the city walls from the Song era bring an impressive history to life. All around

Top left: There is scarcely another region of China in which spirituality and business acumen are so closely linked as in the ambitious metropolises of South China.

Left: The dragon as the bringer of good fortune; thanks to the openness policy, Guangdong's special economic zones are among the winners in the era of globalization.

the city lies a picturesque landscape with many striking features—not just limestone mountains, lakes, caves, and hot springs, but also fertile fields. Rice, sugar cane, soya, peanuts, lotus, and bamboo grow extremely well in the tropical climate. One of the local specialties is steamed *zongzi*, pyramid-shaped sticky rice dumplings, a juicy mass of sticky rice, mung beans, pork, sausage, and mushrooms wrapped in bamboo leaves.

The Chaoshan region surrounding Chaozhou, Shantou, and Jiyang in the east has a cultural affinity with Fujian and Taiwan due to its location. Its inhabitants not only speak a variant of the Minnan dialect (which is spoken in Fujian), they have also incorporated many traditions from Fujian into their cuisine. The harbor city of Shantou, which has been one of the three Guangdong SEZ since the reform and openness policy was launched, was already a pulsating center of overseas trade in the mid 19th century under the name of Swatow. Not only did Shantou send tea and sugar cane from one continent to another, but it also sent millions of people looking for prosperity as well.

Above: An image which will probably soon belong to the past. Old parts of the city are bound to be swept away by the economic boom.

Top right: Like a defiant bulwark against commercialism, a Buddhist or Taoist temple is now surrounded by a residential area.

Right: Steel and glass palaces define the urban image today, even in relatively small cities such as Shantou.

Yum cha and dim sum

There are two things it is simply better to enjoy in Guangdong than anywhere else: yum cha and dim sum. These Cantonese terms, which can be paraphrased as "drinking tea and eating lots of tasty snacks," express the essence of the Cantonese attitude to eating: company, fun, variety, and enjoyment.

So, just as in many other countries when people have a coffee break they hand round coffee and cookies, so yum cha and dim sum go together. The yum cha tradition, which spread overseas from Guangdong via Hong Kong and Macau, can be experienced at its best in Guangzhou—not on your own, of course, but with friends or relatives. Even early in the day the restaurants (many of which are the size of a gymnasium) are filling up. You can scarcely find anywhere to sit if you have not booked. Noisy, steamy, with all sorts of scents in the air—it's almost like being at a fairground. Doors swing open, waitresses push little trolleys full of steaming baskets and little plates stacked one on top of another, and move from table to table. A quick glance, a brief nod, and you have your tea, together with the first five or six dim sum and some sauces for dipping.

A hundred different appetizers, snacks, and short-order dishes keep on rolling by. There are sweet ones, salty ones, deep-fried or steamed, solid or delicate—little dumplings filled with meat, vegetables or seafood, and rolls or tender morsels. Like the Italian antipasti or the Spanish tapas, there is no end to the variety and refinement of the dim sum—provided the chef knows his job.

A single glance at the artfully folded dumplings is enough to make one thing clear. This requires creativity, patience, and an enormous amount of skill. It is not for nothing that the creation of dim sum is considered as being an established part of a chef's training in Guangdong. The dumplings consist of a silky-smooth, almost transparent envelope made from wheat or rice flour and rolled out as thin as a breath. And in the middle of the dumplings, which are not even as big as the palm of your hand, you place a few little pieces of shrimp or a spoonful of finely chopped mixed ingredients, and then you artistically fold it into the right shape, without letting it fall apart, or allowing a naughty mushroom to escape, or letting the dumplings open up while they are being steamed in the bamboo baskets or deep-fried.

Top left: The staff here scarcely have any time for a breather.

Left: It seems an understatement to call this a restaurant. There are hundreds of people here on the hunt for dim sum. If you haven't reserved, you have little hope of grabbing a seat.

Top right: A temple of pleasure—what looks like the entrance to a concert hall or an opera house is the way into a dim sum restaurant.

Right: In spite of this assault by the masses, the guests are individually served. They can select their sauces or side dishes here.

made with radishes or fortune cookies. Those with a sweet tooth will find what they are looking for in sweet dim sum, such as yeast pastries filled with red bean paste, mango pudding, or little egg cakes. On the other hand, deep-fried dim sum are not for those who are watching the calories. The range extends from spring rolls through squid or shrimp right through to deep-fried chicken feet. There is just nothing missing—as long as you are eating in Guangdong.

And of all the varied taste experiences associated with yum cha, there is naturally one that can not be omitted—the tea. Whether it is Longjing, Pu-erh or Oolong tea, all hot teas, according to traditional Chinese medicine (TCM), are effective in aiding digestion. However, in Guangdong jasmine tea is a particular favorite to accompany dim sum.

Dim sum with meat filling

Dough:
2 ½ cups (275 g) low-gluten flour
¾ cup (125 g) rice flour
1 cup + 2 tbsp (125 g) confectioner's sugar
1 envelope dried yeast
3 ½ tbsp vegetable oil
baking powder
bicarbonate of soda

Filling:
4–5 tbsp low-gluten flour
1 tsp tapioca
1 tsp cornstarch
vegetable oil for frying
1 scallion, finely chopped
2 tbsp oyster sauce
1 tbsp rice wine
generous ½ cup (70 g) confectioner's sugar
3 tbsp tomato sauce
1 tbsp soy sauce
7 ½ oz (200 g) "Cha-Shao" pork (Cantonese-style grilled pork)

Continued on page 238

The creation of the different dim sum may certainly just be something which creates a general mood, but it takes up at least as much time and resources as baking cookies. It would scarcely occur to a Cantonese to pass up the sacred yum cha experience—in the morning after some early sporting activity, or on Sunday with the family.

The incomprehensible variety of the dim sum can be described only in approximate terms. Among the classic dumplings are *Har Gau* (filled with shrimp), or *Shaomai* (left open at the top and filled with finely chopped pork, shrimp, and black mushrooms). Another filling that tastes simply luxurious is a mixture of pork, water chestnuts, and mushrooms. Purely vegetarian dumplings (for example, with tofu and herbs) are admittedly not so widespread, but you can certainly get them.

Cha Siu Bau are especially popular little dumplings, and are a Cantonese specialty. Grilled pork marinaded in honey, hoisin sauce, and five-spice powder, wrapped in a fluffy light yeast dough. You can get them baked as well, just like the cookies

Continued from page 237

Stir the flour together with the tapioca, corn-starch and 4 tablespoons water: set aside. Heat the oil in a wok and briefly fry the scallions on high heat until an aroma is released. Add the oyster sauce, rice wine, confectioner's sugar, tomato sauce, and soy sauce and leave to simmer for a short time. Add a generous ³/₄ cup/200 ml of water and slowly stir in the tapioca mixture and boil until threads appear in the sauce. Cut pork into small pieces, pour over sauce, mix everything well and set aside.

Sift the flour and rice flour with the confectioner's sugar. Tip onto a work surface and make a hollow in the center. Place yeast, oil, ³/₄ cup/175 ml of water, baking powder and bicarbonate of soda in the hollow and work the dry ingredients in slowly from the outside to the inside. Knead until a flat, shiny dough is formed. Cover the dough with plastic wrap and allow to rest for 40 minutes. Form the dough into a cylinder and cut into 10 pieces. Roll out the pieces of dough to form cir-cles and use a tablespoon to put a portion of fill-ing on each circle.
To close the dumplings, fold the edges upward and press them together firmly to seal. Put each dumpling on a piece of thin baking parchment, place in a bamboo steamer, cover with the lid and allow the dumplings to rest for 30–40 minutes. Cover the bottom of a saucepan with water, sus-pend the bamboo steamer inside and steam the dumplings uncovered for 10–12 minutes at a high heat, then remove and serve.

Dim sum with vegetable filling

8 oz (200 g) soft tofu
4 oz (100 g) bok choy
10 dried shiitake mushrooms, soaked to soften
sesame oil
1 ³/₄ cups (200 g) gluten-free flour
2 tbsp cornstarch
²/₃ cup (150 ml) of boiling water

Cut the tofu into small pieces and press through a sieve to make a tofu porridge. Rinse the bok choy, pat dry, and cut up small.
Blanch the shiitake mushrooms for 2 minutes, remove, pat dry and cut up small.
Mix the tofu porridge, the bok choy, and the mushrooms together. Sprinkle with a little sesame oil.
Sift the flour with the cornstarch in a bowl, and slowly stir in sufficient of the ²/₃ cup/150 ml of water to achieve a pliable dough which is not sticky. Shape it into a cylinder, cut into pieces of equal size, and roll these out into circles.
Put some filling on each circle, and fold into a dumpling. Press the edges together firmly to seal. Put the dumplings on baking parchment and place in a bamboo steamer. Cover the bottom of a saucepan with water, suspend the bamboo steamer inside and steam the dumplings uncov-ered for 5–6 minutes over high heat, then serve.

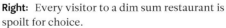

Right: Every visitor to a dim sum restaurant is spoilt for choice.

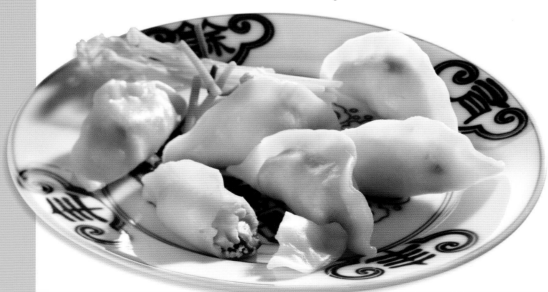

Dim sum with shrimp filling

3 ½ cups (450 g) gluten-free flour
3 tbsp cornstarch
½ tbsp salt
6 tbsp pork dripping or lard
4 ½ oz (125 g) shrimpmeat
3 ½ oz (100 g) fat pork
4 ½ oz (125 g) dried bamboo shoots, cut in
   strips
½ tbsp freshly ground white pepper
4 ½ oz (125 g) scallions, cut in strips
½ tsp sugar
2 tbsp sesame oil

Sift the flour with the cornstarch and salt and mix together with boiling water, knead to a dough and leave to rest covered for 5 minutes. Knead well again, add 5 ½ tablespoons of pork dripping and knead.

Finely chop the shrimpmeat and set aside in a bowl. Briefly pour boiling water over the fat pork, cool with cold water and finely chop. Soften the bamboo shoots in water, rinse them, add the remaining pork dripping and the white pepper and mix well.

Add the chopped shrimp, chopped pork and the scallion strips, the sugar and the sesame oil, and mix well. Put the mixture in the freezer.

Roll out the dough into circles as described on page 238. Distribute the filling evenly onto the circles and fold them over into half-moons. Press the edges together firmly to seal. Steam in a bamboo steamer for 10 minutes over high heat, then serve.

Right, top to bottom: Dim sum comes in every possible shape and color and with every possible filling. It is hard to believe, but most of the recipes for the little snacks originated in the traditional tea houses.

Aromatic jasmine tea—fit for an emperor

"Best jasmine tea—with even more jasmine flowers!" No dealer in China could hype his wares with these words. Contrary to what is assumed in the West, the quality of China's favorite aromatic beverage does not depend on the number of dried flowers it contains.

In contrast to rose petal tea or cinnamon flower tea, which are both based exclusively on dried flowers, a connoisseur will find not a single petal in high-quality jasmine tea. Fresh flowers are certainly used to give the tea its aroma. But in their dried condition they have long ago lost their scent, which is certainly intensive but extremely transient. The pretty little flowers, which are usually mixed in with high-priced teas, thus have no effect on the taste, but are primarily there for decorative purposes.

Whether in Fujian, Guangdong, Jiangxi or Guangxi, the main taste carrier used for the

jasmine aroma is unfermented tea. The tea specialists from Fujian have mainly specialized in refining the flowers used for the white and green varieties of tea. So Yin Zhen serves as the high-quality basis for jasmine tea (*molihua*), although it might also be Longjing, Biluochum or Maofeng. The general rule is this: the better the type of tea, and the more contact there is between tea and flowers, the finer the taste will be. Since the refined jasmine aroma quickly dissipates, the teamakers have been testing out the best possible ways of building it into the tea for generations. While some swear by steaming the tea over a flower bath made from jasmine, others prefer to mix tea and flowers directly—the so-called "marriage."

In high summer, when the evergreen Arabian jasmine shrub blooms (*Jasmineium sambac*), the white flowers release the majority of their

intensive scent at night. Early in the morning, when the calyxes have closed up again, the teapickers begin to harvest them carefully. Millions of flowers have to be collected to make a ¹⁄₂ lb (1 kg) of tea. In the evening, the "marriage" takes place, shortly before the flowers cool down to the point at which their calyxes open up again. Then the teamaster mixes them with the tea already harvested in the spring. About four hours later (the teamaster knows exactly when this occurs), the flowers have already released all their aroma to the tea. While for simple types of jasmine tea the aromatization process comes to an end here, for high-quality jasmine tea the actual work is only just beginning. The flowers are removed by hand or using a blower, and replaced by fresh ones. The more often this "marriage"

Left: Jasmine tea is based on green or semifermented teas.

Right: To obtain 2 ¹⁄₄ lb (1 kg) of essential oil, you need about 8 million jasmine flowers.

1 The preparation of jasmine tea is a delight to the eye as well. The phoenix dragon pearls have already been placed in a container... .

2 ...and hot water is now poured over them. The water should no longer be boiling. The optimal temperature is about 180° F (82 °C).

3 After about two minutes, the tea is poured into the drinking bowls. Jasmine flower tea can be used for several servings without any problems.

between fresh flowers and tea takes place, the more intensely scented the resulting tea will be. Up to seven stages will characterize a truly high-quality jasmine tea.

The art of making jasmine tea, passed on over many centuries, originated in the tea-growing regions of South China, around Fujian and Guangdong, where jasmine and tea have both flourished for more than a thousand years. The jasmine shrub was brought to China from Persia as early as the 3rd century (although it is a matter of some dispute when precisely jasmine tea was first created). But by the Song era (960–1279) the tempting aromatic beverage was so popular that the emperor demanded it as tribute—he is said to have been particularly fond of the "phoenix dragon pearls" (little jasmine tea beads from the imperial tea garden of Fujian near the city of Jian'ou). The popular tea, which nowadays flourishes high in the misty, mountainous regions between Fujian and Jiangxi, owes its name to the teabushes, which remind people of a dragon emerging from the water, with phoenix (the teapluckers) dancing around them.

People still enjoy the phoenix dragon pearl variety today. When the tealeaves have absorbed the jasmine aroma by being passed over a steaming flower bath, or following repeated marriages, they are artistically rolled together by hand to form small beads. About 14,000 hand-rolled beads add up to 2 1/4 lb (1 kg), and you need about 20 beads for a pot of tea. Heat the water to about 180 °F (82 °C), and let the tea brew for two minutes, and the phoenix dragon pearls will open and release their flowery aroma—just as they do in the subtropical night of South China.

Right: You should reckon on about 20 phoenix dragon pearls for one pot of tea. The fact that they are hand-rolled explains the high price of jasmine flower tea—about $80 for 1 lb (500 g).

Below: Something for the eyes to drink in! Chinese teacups, by the way, usually have a lid.

A short pilgrimage

The city of Shenzhen, in the southern part of Guang-dong province, is one of the fastest growing cities in the world. In just 30 years (1979–2008), the population of the inner city has grown from 30,000 to over 12 million. It is hard to believe that close by this "boomtown" lies a center of contemplation and meditation. It is called Hongfa Si—a Buddhist temple, situated in a picturesque setting, on a mountain in a park to the east of Shenzhen. Anyone who thinks the inhabitants of the nearby metropolis can no longer have time for religious contemplation will learn better here. The Hongfa temple, which is still not very old (it was built in 1985) is the most visited Buddhist temple the city possesses, for the people of Shenzhen believe that anyone who prays for riches here will obtain them one day.

So does the young sinologist Liu Heshi. He was originally from Tianjian—one of the four direct government cities of China, located to the southeast of Beijing—and he moved south to Shenzhen where, as the proprietor of a business dealing in Southeast Asian specialties, he purchases, for example, birds' nests, and other expensive delicatessen items. At the beginning of his second year in business, he has come to Hongfa temple to pray. For him the trip to this place of pilgrimage is also an opportunity for a refreshing walk, as the path to the temple takes him through a magnificently laid out park.

At the park entrance, Liu Heshi obtains a plan with information and descriptions of the paths.

The path, which leads up to the temple mountain, goes past a lake and through dense pine forests.

You pay to visit a temple—here it is 20 RMB (renminbi, "people's money"), about 2 to 3 dollars.

An almost endless flight of steps—the last part of the path up to the temple grounds.

Joss sticks are on offer in the entrance hall, as in other Buddhist temples.

In one of the many aisles, the abbot of the Hongfa temple is depicted on an information panel.

Many shrines offer pilgrims an opportunity to pray and to light joss sticks.

The joss sticks are free, but the temple volunteers are happy to receive donations.

The temple precincts carry the scent of countless joss sticks burning in the pans of various shrines.

As a souvenir of his visit to the temple, Liu Heshi has his photograph taken next to the bust of the abbot.

Those praying put their hands together and repeatedly make a *kowtow* (a deep bow), while softly or silently repeating a mantra.

People like souvenirs in China—these are decorated with dragons and pinned-on flowers.

Souvenirs with Buddhist symbols remind the pilgrim of the things he prayed for in the temple.

After praying, Liu Heshi treats himself to a meal in the vegetarian restaurant near the temple.

The Hongfa temple is a popular destination for visitors at the weekend—including families.

Liu Heshi is not actually eating the classic dish of Buddhist cuisine—eightfold treasure—but he has got two healthy vegetarian dishes instead: pickled tofu and vegetables.

Chinese-style Buddhism

Buddhism originated in India and arrived in China via the Silk Road in the 1st century A.D. From there it made its way to Japan and Korea. The enlightenment of the religion's founder—an Indian nobleman named Siddharta Gautama, who is thought to have lived in the 5th century B.C. and became the Buddha—laid the foundation stone for the belief system, which nowadays is mainly popular in Asia.

Siddharta came from a wealthy family, and grew up in comfortable circumstances without any worries or cares. According to legend, while traveling he encountered suffering, seeing first an old man, then a sick man, and finally a dead man, and this made a very deep impression on him. He resolved to find a way to free human beings from their suffering. So he left his family and became a monk. Through a combination of fasting and deep meditation, he finally succeeded (according to tradition) in finding the origin of all suffering and in attaining enlightenment (bodhi). From that moment onward, he dedicated himself to the task of spreading his teaching among the people. He preached the so-called four noble truths and the eightfold way—which have since become the central aspects of Buddhist teaching and of the associated way of life. The four noble truths describe attachment to material, and indeed physical things, and the desire to obtain them, as the origin of suffering. Those who recognize this process and free themselves from it can overcome suffering.

The way to do this is to follow the eightfold path, which calls, among other things, for right thinking, right speech and right behavior. It is not enough to conquer desire and to free oneself from all desires before death. Human beings undergo "reincarnation" (rebirth). But only those who have no desires left will be enlightened. And only the enlightened ones have respect for all other living things, which is essential for the obtaining of the supreme goal of the Buddhists, entry into Nirvana. Those who enter Nirvana are freed from the cycle of rebirth and are thus freed from suffering.

Buddhism spread over Central Asia to China along the Silk Road, and was affected by numerous local influences on its journey. This happened in China itself as well, where it combined with existing elements of popular beliefs, Taoism and Confucianism, which created various schools of thought. Thus it was Mahayana Buddhism (mahayana = great vessel) which aroused the most interest here, since, in contrast to Hinayana Buddhism (hinayana = small vessel, monastery Buddhism), it placed the emphasis on the perfecting of all and not of a few individuals. One reason why it was easier for this idea to gain acceptance in China was because it was traditional there for the family and society to be considered more important than the individual. Mahayana Buddhism provided a path of release (and thus a way to enter Nirvana) for all people (even the laity).

The Mahayana tradition features so-called boddhisatvas—enlightened ones who, thanks to their compassion for humanity, do not enter Nirvana but remain on Earth in order to provide support for human beings in their path to perfection. The worship in China of the boddhisatvas has close parallels with Confucian ancestor worship.

Buddhism's golden age in China came just before and during the Tang dynasty (618–907). This wave of conversions also provided the impetus for the imposing sculptures in Luoyang and Datong which demonstrate, in an impressive manner, just how strong the Buddhist influence must once have been in China. Giant Buddhas sculpted in stone, and over 10,000 Buddhist monasteries bear witness to the dynamism that Buddhism generated. It is said that there were over a hundred thousand monks in China at this time. Since the Chinese translations of Buddhist texts at the beginning of the 2nd century made by Taoists had severely distorted the Buddhist texts, even if largely unconsciously, by using Taoist terminology, the Chinese emperor sent several hundred monks to India to study the original texts and to make new translations. It was also at this time that Chan Buddhism was developed (known in the West under its Japanese name of Zen Buddhism), together with other schools of Buddhism such as Tiantai (tiantai zong) and the Pure Country School (jingtu). All these schools originated in China, and have therefore developed Chinese characteristics. In Chan Buddhism, which was very strongly influenced by Taoism, the main emphasis was laid on meditation. The Tiantai school developed into one of the most significant Mahayana schools, and is mainly based on Buddhist philosophy. The Pure Country School, on the other hand, was preferred by ordinary people, as here philosophy and meditation played a less important role.

An authentically Buddhist culture dominated China during the Tang era, which gave way to a newly revitalized Confucianism at the end of the 9th century. Only in Tibet did Buddhism continue to be a significant religion—it is also referred to as Lamaism, with the Dalai Lama as its religious leader—and there it developed many schools of its own. Since Buddhism has no sacred texts and no dogmas, it was not difficult for the Tibetans to adapt it and interweave it with the

Right: Buddha, seated and making the hand gestures symbolizing enlightenment. Enlightenment is the central goal of Buddhism.

Below: Lighting and burning joss sticks—one of the rituals which the laity also perform.

shamanistic Bön religion that had predominated there for millenia. In the neighboring provinces too, and among several ethnic minorities in China, Buddhism continues to be the most popular religion. Since the end of the Cultural Revolution (1976), Han Chinese are adopting an increasingly open attitude to the religion once more. Even the monasteries have been growing in importance in recent years. ELKE SPIELMANNS-ROME

Tofu with vegetables and mushrooms from the wok

3 ½ oz (100 g) nameka mushrooms
11 oz (300 g) solid tofu
1 tsp finely chopped green chiles
1 tsp finely chopped red chiles
3 ½ tbsp peanut oil
1 scallion, chopped
1 piece of ginger (about 1 inch / 3 cm long), chopped
2 garlic cloves, finely chopped
1 tbsp strong chili bean paste
2 tsp sugar
1 ½ tsp cornstarch
salt

Rinse the mushrooms and pat dry. Cut the tofu into cubes and finely chop the chiles. Blanch the mushrooms and the tofu and leave to drain. Heat the oil in the wok and add the scallion, ginger, and garlic. Fry together with the chile bean paste until all the aromas are released. Add the sugar and a pinch of salt, together with 2 tablespoons of water, and stir-fry. Add the mushrooms, tofu, and chiles and stir-fry. Finally, bind with the cornstarch, stir everything together well and turn out onto a plate to serve.

Left: Buddhism, which originated in India, incorporated elements from other philosophic and religious trends in China.

Right: Buddhist cuisine is based on the most important beliefs of the religion. Among other things, this means no meat can be eaten.
.

Buddhist cuisine (*zhai cai*)

The Buddhist respect for life means they are forbidden to eat meat. Buddhist cuisine has made a virtue of necessity and brought meatless cooking to perfection, creating dishes which, thanks to the skillful preparation of tofu, flour, gluten, and other ingredients, can scarcely be distinguished from meat dishes. Nowadays, these methods are also used in the preparation of ready-made products, which are internationally marketed. Thus, tofu can be prepared and spiced in such a way that its consistency resembles that of chicken or chopped meat. You can find it in the chiller cabinet in Asian stores, health food stores, and increasingly in supermarkets.

Sustainable eco-trend? Organic food from China

China has atmospheric pollution, excessive fertilization of arable land, and contaminated water. And as if that was not enough, Westerners hear more and more stories incriminating foodstuffs from China. Organic food from the Middle Kingdom—for many people, this sounds like a contradiction in terms. And yet the outlines of a new trend are becoming clear.

Since food is in shorter supply and is therefore becoming more expensive all over the world, China, with its population of over 1.3 billion people, has once more become of interest to the populations of the West. The Chinese Ministry of the Interior proudly proclaims that China, which has only 9 percent of the world's farmland, is feeding 21 percent of the world's population—i.e., feeding itself. And that's not all. A glance at Chinese export statistics shows that, as regards many agricultural products, China is the leading supplier, or is at least one of the top ten suppliers. In 2005, for example, just on half the pears produced in the world, half the apples, and half the vegetables came from the Middle Kingdom. About 900 million peasants are cultivating around 300 million acres (122 million ha) there.

As the demand for foodstuffs from China increases, the requirements for product quality grow more stringent as well. Thus the demand is increasing for foodstuffs with a clean record—both for export and in China itself. The Chinese government is satisfying this demand for methods of cultivation that do not involve harmful substances—not least for financial reasons. In the end, only foodstuffs that do not constitute a health hazard should, or could, cross China's frontiers en route to, say, Japan or America, or to the countries

of the European Union. And secondly, organically cultivated products are more profitable. Chinese customers also opt for the markedly more expensive organic products if they can afford it. They too consider them to be healthier, tastier, and better value, as they are free from residues of pesticides or antibiotics.

Once again, the statistics show how much China is investing in organic crops. While, measured in terms of the area organically cultivated all over the world, the country was in 45th position in 2000, it had moved up to second place as early as 2006, behind Australia. In 2007, China had 11 percent of the land used for organic farming worldwide.

There was initially some uncertainty as to whether the Chinese classification was comparable with that used in Europe. But, because Chinese and international

certification centers are creating uniform worldwide standards, the organic certification marks are becoming more credible. Green tea was the first certified organic product that China exported (to the Netherlands, in 1990). Since then, organic cultivation has become more extensive everywhere in the country. Most of the certified areas lie in the northwest—in Inner Mongolia, Jilin, Liaoning, and Hebei—and in the southeast—in Jiangxi, Fujian, Jiangsu, Hubei, Shandong, and Yunnan. While the organic crops from the northwest are usually beans, cereals, and plants grown for vegetable oil, in the southwest they can be tea, fruit, rice, ginger, soybeans, and vegetables. Wild herbs, bamboo, mushrooms, and honey come mainly from nature reserves—for example, the Chinese lime-blossom honey from the black bees in the Raohe nature reserve on the Sino-Russian frontier, which measures only 2,700 square miles (7,000 sq km)—

Bottom left: Manual selection guarantees best-quality sweet potatoes.

Bottom: Cucumbers and gherkins are among the types of vegetable that are extremely well suited to organic cultivation.

Right: Seeds can easily be obtained from snake cucumbers.

Center right: Organic cultivation relies heavily on manual labor, which is entirely compatible with the traditional working practices of Chinese farmers.

Bottom right: More than one-tenth of the land under organic cultivation worldwide today is being worked by the Chinese.

Above: A neat trick—greenhouses can be used for other things than growing vegetables...

Left: When it comes to organic products—whether grown in greenhouses or in the open air—China is one of the leading nations.

Below: The basic tenets of organic farming prohibit excessive fertilization and the use of pesticides. The higher the standard of living of the population, the higher the requirements laid down for satisfactory organic products. Corn and sweet potatoes are among such products in China.

something special for the European breakfast table. Another thing completely in accord with Chinese tradition is that certified organic honey or royal jelly is reputed to have medicinal powers.

Even if the Chinese organic sector is relatively young, organic methods of cultivation form part of a tradition that goes back thousands of years. They still flourish in some places in remote rural areas even today— even if this is not always to the peasants' advantage. Many of them are too poor to be able to afford expensive fertilizers or seed varieties. However, terraced fields and very ingenious irrigation systems mean even the smallest and most inaccessible spot of land can be cultivated. It can be kept fertile for a long time by alternately using it for planting crops and for pasturing "inhabitants," who leave behind their natural manure—even if the crop yields are limited. Here and there you can still see peasants in Guangdong today who bring ducks onto the wet rice fields in their boats in the morning. As a part of a complex, time-honored feeding chain, the ducks eat and fatten themselves up there—but that's not all. Other creatures (eels, for example) grow fat by eating the ducks' droppings.

Thanks to the big difference in income between those living in the towns and those on the land, many peasants migrate to the cities—a problem recognized by the Chinese government. So, to promote social stability and create a "harmonious society," it has set up an aid program for the peasants. Among other things, they are to be given support in making the change from conventional to organic methods of cultivation.

Left: It's not just the dishes that are extraordinary in the Chaozhu cuisine. Many of the ways they are prepared are rarely found elsewhere in China. One special method is to cook things slowly in big ceramic jars over a low flame.

In a class of its own—Chaozhou cuisine

It can often be almost bewildering how many different regional cuisines there are in China. And on top of that, they have so many names. Chaozhou cuisine is sometimes concealed behind the names "Chuchow cuisine," "Teochew cuisine" or "Chaoshan cuisine." It seems to be a regular source of controversy, for sometimes the Fujian people will claim this culinary tradition as their own, and sometimes the Cantonese.

The region that surrounds the commercial center of Chaozhou, with its wealth of traditions, forms part of Guangdong province. However, being far to the east, in a breathtakingly beautiful landscape, located on the Han river and surrounded by three mountains, this city of arts and crafts (and cooking) also lies near Fujian. And here the people of Chaozhou developed and preserved clear traditions of their own in the course of their history, as the inhabitants of a port city, a city of culture open to the world. Their love of detail can be seen,

for example, in the stone and wood carvings in the magnificent Kaiyuan temple, which dates from the year 738, or in the porcelain ware, embroidery, goldsmith's work, and lanterns which are still made for export today. The same tendency is also reflected in the Chaozhou cuisine. Elaborate carvings convert ordinary fruit or vegetable ingredients into a dragon, a phoenix or a bird. And the dishes are likewise combined in an equally skillful manner, so that

Tea tasting instead of wine tasting

In the region surrounding Chaozhou, Shantou, Fuzhou, and Quanzhou, and in Taiwan, a special way of drinking tea has been developed over the centuries—Gongfu tea. Whether it's elaborate or simple, this ritual is an entertaining type of tea tasting. The tea most often used is Oolong tea, which is brewed in small clay pots and served in tiny bowls. The tea utensils, which are attractively and artistically decorated, are laid out on a high-sided tray. In the more elaborate form of the Gongfu tea ceremony, the emphasis is on the taste and aroma of the individual types of tea, while the more everyday type of Gongfu gathering stresses good fellowship. A pleasantly warm summer evening, a few seats around the teatray—and look! here come the neighbors for our own little Gongfu tea party.
Drinking tea is regarded as a sociable experience. You just forget all your worries and relax. First, the bowls on the tray (which are usually reddish brown) are

prewarmed with hot water. Meanwhile the guests chat happily away about the special spring water being used, the tea, and the quality of the teapot—though they can talk shop as well. In the next stage, the host fills the pot with tea, brews up using boiling water, and, after a while, pours the tea into the drinking bowls (complete with leaves). While the first tea aroma is being drawn into the bowls, the talk may perhaps turn to more private matters. When the first bowls have been either drunk or poured away, and fresh tea has been brewed, the time has come. The host skillfully pours the tea into the bowls and passes them to the guests, using both hands. Now is the time to note the tea's color and breathe in the aroma. Finally, the tea can be appreciated in little sips. And so it goes on—more tea is brewed, more conversation, more tea-drinking—the ritual takes its course.

Above: The porcelain itself puts you in the mood for the ceremony. Everything must be in the right style, from the ceramics to the little teatable.

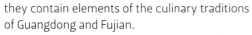

they contain elements of the culinary traditions of Guangdong and Fujian.

On the one hand soups, little fish balls and specialties recall Fujian, and on the other hand the fresh ingredients and the sweet, fruity elements are more like the Guangdong cuisine. As there is water nearby, choice fish and seafood dishes are prominent on the menu—for example shrimp, lobster, oysters, eel, bream. The last-named have that special Chaozhou taste when they are steamed in a special strong meat broth, together with plum sauce and tomatoes. Also typical of the region are cold dishes such as iced shrimp or Yu-sheng salad, made from raw fish—with radishes, carrots,

ginger, lemon leaves, peanuts, and sesame. The favorite accompaniment to the innumerable boiled and deep-fried snacks is sa cha sauce, or a dip made from chiles, roasted peanuts, dried fish and shrimps, sesame paste, and garlic. And yet it would be a mistake to think the people of Chaozhou are satisfied with tiny, lightweight delicacies. Fat goose—sometimes steamed, sometimes stewed—makes a luxurious meal. When you are faced by the variety of the Chaozhou cuisine, only one approach will help you. Try things out and drink lots of tea—preferably at a Gongfu ceremony.

Oyster omelet

7 ½ oz (200 g) oysters
4 eggs
1 tbsp cornstarch, mixed with 2 tbsp water
2 tbsp all-purpose flour
1 tsp salt
½ cup (125 ml) vegetable oil, for frying

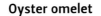

Beat together the eggs, cornstarch mix, flour, and salt and add the oysters. Heat the oil in a skillet. Pour in the batter and·fry each side for 5 minutes over medium heat.

Top left: With the help of these inserts, the dishes are cooked in portions in big ceramic pans.

Second row left: It looks spicy and it is—pickled bamboo shoots in sesame paste.

Top right: Rice noodles with chopped meatballs—one of many typical Chaozhou dishes.

Above: Because of Chaozhou's location in the Han Jiang delta, both freshwater fish and seafood are compulsory ingredients of the cuisine.

Fish and seafood from Guangdong

"If you want to eat, go to Guangdong"—so goes an old Chinese proverb. And when it comes to fish dishes, it has a lot of truth in it. But irrespective of where you are or what regional style of cooking is being used, fish is a really indispensable part of Chinese cuisine. However, fish plays an especially important role in the South China provinces of Fujian or Guangdong—firstly, thanks to their location on the South China Sea, secondly because of the great river deltas. So these regional cuisines can boast numerous dishes using both saltwater and freshwater fish.

The basic principle is this: whether you are in a market or a restaurant, the fish must be fresh. So it will be kept alive in a pool or an aquarium until shortly before it is prepared.

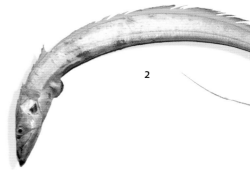

Below: All restaurants make a point of offering their guests as wide a variety of fish as possible, and keeping the fish as fresh as possible.

1 Japanese threadfin bream (Nemipterus japonicus)

2 Hairtail (Trichiurus lepturus)

3 Little yellow croaker (Pseudosciaena polyactis)

4 Red sea bream (Pagrus major)

5 Chinese silver pomfret (Pampus chinensis)

6 Rabbitfish (Siganus fuscescens)

7 Pacific mackerel (Pneumatophorus japonicus)

8 Japanese seaperch (Lateolabrax japonicus)

9 Spanish mackerel (Scomberomorus commersoni)

10 Greater amberjack (Seriola dumerili)

11 Giant scarlet shrimp (Plesiopenaeus edwardsianus)

12 Indian mackerel (Rastrelliger kanagurta)

13 Yellowtail scad (Carangidae)

14 Mangrove crab (Scylla serrata)

15 Black pomfret (Formio niger)

16 Yellow pike conger (Muraenesocidae)

17 Squid (Loliginidae)

18 Abalone (Haliotis asinina)

19 Geoduck clam (Panopea abrupta)

8

9

10

11

12

13

14

15

16

17

18

19

Substantial, tasty Hakka cuisine

They can be found overseas, in Southeast Asia or in China—the Hakka Chinese are scattered all over the world. No one knows exactly how many of them there are, but the total number of Hakka has been estimated as being 30, 60, or even 100 million. Most of them, though, call Guangdong home. In particular, the Hakka culture has survived here right up to the present day in the rural areas around the cities of Huizhou and Meizhou.

In contrast to the fresh, slightly spicy dishes of Cantonese cuisine, the traditional Hakka dishes seem decidedly solid, lush, and salty. Nourishing stews, dishes containing dried or marinated ingredients, or even stewed meat dishes reflect a past in which, in spite of adverse circumstances, the Hakka Chinese made the best of their lives—and also of the ingredients typical of their cuisine.

The Hakka are certainly a subdivision of the Han Chinese, and yet they are bound together by their own culture, which is expressed, above all, in their language and their culinary tradition. Their ancestral home was in the north, in the middle stretches of the Yellow River (the Huang), and during the millenia they spent there the Hakka were often forced to flee southward due to famines or great political upheavals. They were often very unwelcome and even today they are referred to as "guest families." They had no choice but to retreat to the inhospitable areas of Guangdong or Fujian, though they were not always safe even there. So the Hakka clans lived together in fortified structures which could accommodate hundreds of families, and joined together to combat the adverse circumstances of their lives. Not only did they have to resist attacks, but

also often had to make do with very little land to farm. While the men provided security, the women looked after the fields and cared for their families. It is no wonder that the hardworking life of the Hakka women left no time for Chinese concepts of beauty like the tradition of binding women's feet.

The Hakka managed to obtain food from even the harshest land, and they carefully preserved it with salt or vinegar for harder times. Anything which was remotely edible could be used as an ingredient. They marinated root vegetables and dried herbs or meat. And since there was no time for long and complicated techniques of cooking, they went against the Chinese tradition and prepared stews that could be reheated and used for several days. Moreover, due to the climatic differences between the north and the south, some traditional

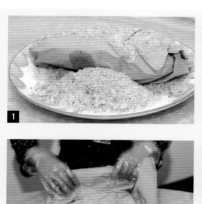

1 Before being wrapped in wax paper, the chicken is salted inside and filled with spices.

2 Wrapped in a double layer of wax paper, the chicken is laid in salt...

3 ...covered in it completely, and then carefully baked in a clay pot.

10 Place as much as possible of the ready-to-eat chicken on a plate, together with the bones.

4 After about 10 minutes, the chicken can be removed from the clay pot and unwrapped.

5 Then carefully remove the first layer of greaseproof paper...

6 ...and then the second; the meat is already beautifully cooked through.

7 Now the chicken must be released for the remaining stages of the process.

8 Then the skin is carefully removed...

9 ...and pieces of chicken meat are taken from the bones.

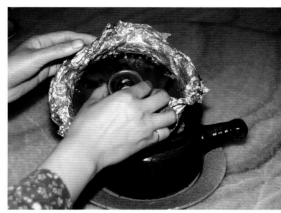

Top left: A typical Hakka menu, with a lot of dishes in relatively small portions.

Above top right: Most Hakka dishes are cooked very slowly.

Above right: Stews or soups with chicken meat are a staple of any Hakka menu.

ingredients such as, for example, all-purpose flour, were not available in the south. This is said to be the reason why the *jiaozi*, the dumplings prepared from noodle dough, developed into a dish which suited the local circumstances: tofu stuffed with chopped meat.

The Hakka cuisine can still be found in Guangdong or Fujian today, with its chopped meat dishes, chicken baked in salt, and solid dishes with pickled vegetables. But it is not confined to these areas. Eventually, during the 19th and 20th centuries, many of the Hakka migrated to Hong Kong, Taiwan, Southeast Asia, or farther afield. Though far from their old homes, they certainly still recalled their origins, but they have adapted over time. The modern Hakka cuisine uses wild herbs, fine fruit sauces or steamed dishes to add a new touch of lightness.

Chicken in salt crust

1 chicken (3 ¼ lb / 1.5 kg)
1 piece ginger (about 1 inch / 3 cm long), finely chopped
2 tbsp pork dripping or lard
1 tbsp sesame oil
1 small scallion, finely chopped
1 star anise
4 ¾ lb (2.5 kg) rock salt
2 tsp sea salt
1 tsp table salt
1 ½ tbsp vegetable oil
fresh cilantro, for garnish
2 sheets wax paper

Heat a wok over low heat. Add 1 teaspoon of sea salt, then the finely chopped ginger, and briefly fry, then remove and divide into 2 portions.
Add a little pork dripping to both portions of ginger and set aside. Stir the remaining pork dripping together with the sesame oil and the other teaspoon of sea salt to form a spicy sauce and set aside. Spread some vegetable oil over 1 sheet of wax paper and set this aside.
Rinse the chicken, pat it dry, and make a cut in each wing and in the neck, without separating any parts from the body. Rub the inside of the chicken with table salt, add one portion of ginger, the scallion, and the star anise. First wrap the chicken in the sheet of wax paper which has not been coated with oil, and then in the coated wax paper.
Heat a large wok over high heat, add the rock salt and stir-fry at a high heat until

the salt turns slightly red. Remove the salt and put ¼ of it in a clay pot. Lay the wrapped chicken on the salt in the clay pot and pack round with the remaining rock salt. Allow the chicken to bake at a low heat in the covered clay pot for 10 minutes.
Pour ⅓ cup (75 ml) of water into the clay pot, and replace the lid. Bake the chicken for a further 10 minutes, then remove and unwrap it. Pierce a leg with a sharp skewer to check that the juices run clear and therefore the meat is cooked. If not, rewrap the chicken and cook until the juices eventually run clear. Remove the skin and cut it into pieces, then take the meat from the bones and cut it, lengthwise, into pieces. Mix the meat and skin with the spicy sauce.
Using the bones as a base, arrange the meat in the center and place the skin on top of it, making it as close as possible to the shape of a chicken. Layer a serving plate with cilantro leaves and arrange the chicken on top. Dunk the pieces of meat in the remaining portion of ginger and pork dripping mixture while eating.

Substantial, tasty Hakka cuisine **253**

Beef and poultry

Beef with broccoli in oyster sauce

1 tbsp light soy sauce
1 tsp rice wine
1 tbsp cornstarch
7 ½ oz (200 g) beef
vegetable oil, for frying
2 garlic cloves, chopped
2 slices of ginger
2 dried red chiles, chopped
1 cup (100 g) broccoli florets
1 tbsp oyster sauce
salt

Stir together the light soy sauce, the rice wine and the cornstarch to make a marinade. Cut the beef into thin slices and add to the marinade until ready to cook.

Remove the beef slices from the marinade and drain, reserving the marinade. Heat the wok, add the oil and stir-fry the beef slices until they change color. Add the marinade, garlic, ginger and the chiles.

Add the broccoli and stir-fry, then add the oyster sauce and stir-fry again briefly. As soon as the broccoli is cooked, season to taste with salt and serve immediately.

Duck with ginger

½ a duck
5 ½ oz (150 g) fresh ginger, cut into matchsticks
1 tsp freshly ground white pepper
1 tsp Shaoxing rice wine
1 tsp light soy sauce
2 tsp sugar
1 tsp dark rice vinegar
vegetable oil, for frying
1 large garlic clove, chopped
green and red bell peppers, cut into strips, for
  garnish
rice wine, for garnish
salt

Stir 2 tablespoons ginger together with the pepper, rice wine, ½ teaspoon salt, soy sauce, 1 teaspoon sugar, and the rice vinegar to form a marinade. Chop the duck into small pieces with a sharp kitchen cleaver. Briefly blanch in boiling water, then place in the marinade for 15 minutes. When ready to cook, remove the duck pieces and drain.

Heat the oil in a wok, add the garlic, and the pieces of duck and stir-fry over high heat for about 5 minutes, until the fat is released from the duck meat. Add the remaining ginger and stir-fry for a little longer.

Season with the remaining sugar and salt to taste, together with more dark rice vinegar (if required). Add sufficient water to cover the duck pieces. Simmer over medium heat until almost all the liquid has evaporated. Before tipping out onto a serving platter, add rice wine, to taste, and serve garnished with the green and bell pepper strips.

Above: Duck with soy sauce

Below left: Beef with broccoli in oyster sauce

Below: Duck with ginger

Below right: Sweet-and-sour chicken

Duck with soy sauce

2 best-quality ducks (prepared, each
    weighing 3¼ lb / 1.5 kg)
⅔ cup (150 g) cooking salt
2 quarts (2 liters) master sauce (for recipe,
    see below)
8–10 cloves
2 pinches chili pepper
1 ½ oz (40 g) chopped scallions
4 thin slices of ginger
7 tbsp Shaoxing rice wine
cinnamon stick
2 star anise
fermented red rice

Rub each duck lightly inside and out with the salt,
tap to remove the excess and discard. Place both
ducks in a container and drizzle over the master
sauce and leave to absorb the flavors for 1–2
hours at room temperature. Drain off the master
sauce and set aside. Stuff each duck with 4–5
cloves, 1 pinch of chili pepper, ½ the scallions,
2 slices of ginger, 1–2 tablespoons of rice wine,
½ the cinnamon stick and 1 star anise.
Bring the reserved master sauce to a boil in a
large wok, add 1 duck and cook over high heat.
Add the remaining rice wine and cook the duck
for 40–60 minutes. As soon as the duck's wings
lift slightly, put the duck onto a plate and let it
cool for 20 minutes. Meanwhile cook the second
duck in the remaining master sauce in the wok.
Pour the sauce over the ducks and serve with
the rice.

Master sauce

1–2 tbsp star anise
1–2 tbsp licorice root
3 cinnamon sticks
1–2 tbsp orange peel
1 tbsp fennel seeds
1 tsp ground ginger
1 tbsp Sichuan pepper
10 cloves
3 quarts (3 liters) water
2 cups (500 ml) soy sauce
1 cup (250 ml) rice wine
1 ½ tbsp salt
2 cups (350 g) brown sugar
4 scallions, chopped
4 thick slices of ginger

Put all the spices into a hot wok and stir-fry
them until they release an aroma. Add the water,
the soy sauce, and the rice wine. Then stir in
the salt and the sugar. Add the scallions
and the ginger and let the sauce
thicken over medium heat.
Strain the sauce through a fine
sieve and discard the spices. The
sauce can be kept for 1–2 weeks, but
should be reheated every 4 days. If it becomes
too concentrated, add some more water.

Sweet-and-sour chicken

2 chicken legs (about 1 ¼ lb / 600 g)
½ an egg
2 tbsp cornstarch
2 cups (500 ml) vegetable oil, for deep-frying
1 piece of ginger (1 inch / 3 cm long), cut into
    fine strips
1 small scallion, cut into fine strips, for garnish

Marinade:
sesame oil, sufficient to cover the meat
1 pinch freshly ground white pepper
⅓ tsp salt

Sauce:
3 tsp rice wine
3 tbsp water
1 tbsp tomato sauce
3 tbsp sugar
1 tsp starch
¼ tsp salt

Stir the ingredients together for the marinade.
Take the meat from the bones, cut it into big
pieces and leave it to marinate for 30 minutes.
Take the chicken out of the marinade and let it
drain. Stir the half egg and the cornstarch into a
paste and mix in with the chicken.
Heat the wok, add the vegetable oil and heat on a
high flame. Add the pieces of chicken and deep-
fry until they are golden yellow. Take the meat
out of the oil.
Drain all the oil from the wok except 1 tablespoon.
Return the wok to the stove and briefly fry the
ginger over high heat until they give off an aroma.
Add all the ingredients for the sauce, stir and boil
until it thickens. Add the pieces of chicken and
stir-fry. Tip the contents of the wok onto a serving plate and garnish with the scallions.

Exotic fruit from South China

Pineapples, bananas, kiwi fruit or citrus fruits—they all flourish magnificently in the subtropical regions of China such as Guangdong, or on the island of Hainan. Exotics such as snakeskins or dragon fruit are little known in Europe. Here is an exotic fruit basket, filled with the South China fruits with the most interesting tastes:

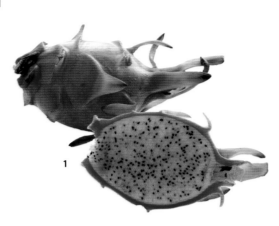

1 Dragon fruit (Hylocereus undatus)

The pink-colored dragon fruit, also known as "red papaya," is a member of the cactus family, as its bizarre exterior indicates. Central America is the country of origin of this climbing cactus, but China is one of the most important areas for growing dragon fruit. The shell of the attractive oval fruit, which grow up to 4 inches (12 cm) long, conceals white flesh with countless black seeds, which are also edible. The taste of the dragon fruit is reminiscent of kiwi fruit—and it is eaten in the same way. The fruit can be spooned out as soon as it is soft.

2 Durian (Durio zibethinus)

The yellowish-green, spiky fruit, about the size of a man's head, grows in tropical parts of Asia on trees that can be as much as 120 feet (40 m) high. As soon as it is ripe, it falls from the tree—when it can also be a nuisance. In Singapore and Hong Kong, for example, there are notices in hotels or at airports prohibiting the importation of durian fruit. The reason for this is their smell. When they are ripe, they stink like a rotting garbage heap or like very smelly cheese. The creamy flesh has a taste all its own—something like a mixture of honey, avocado, and onion. Durian fruit are very popular in South China, and also very expensive. They are usually eaten raw. To eat one, you break it open to get at the yellow flesh. However, you should not eat the fruit if you are drinking alcohol, as this can make you feel nauseous.

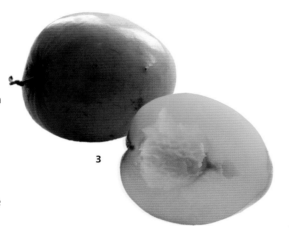

3 Guava (Psidium guajava)

The most likely place in South China to find this green fruit, about the size of an apple, surrounded by a soft, waxy rind, is in the markets of Guangdong and Hong Kong, as it is very popular in these cities. They grow in warm tropical regions on evergreen trees. When they are ripe, the yellow rind conceals a fibrous, whitish-yellow flesh containing edible seeds. The taste is reminiscent of pears, strawberries, and peaches.

4 Pomegranate (Punica granatum)

The round, reddish brown fruit (the one shown here is an example of the lighter-colored type) can be up to 4 inches (12 cm) wide, and belongs to the myrtle family. It is particularly popular in Iran (formerly Persia, where it originated), and in China. It represents longevity and fertility. Under the leathery skin, thin membranes divide the fruit into compartments, and these contain hundreds of transparent , crunchy, juicy red fruit beads, within which are seeds. It comes as no surprise that in China the pomegranate also symbolizes large families and passion.

5 Kaki (Diospyros kaki)

Persimmon, also known as kaki, have been well known in China and East Asia for about 2,000 years. The trees can grow up to 30 feet (10 m) high. Their egg-shaped fruit, which are about 2 inches (6 cm) in size, are a deep orange color when they are ripe. If they are eaten too early, the high tannin content gives them a bitter taste and makes your tongue feel rough. When they are ripe, the sweet juices flow like honey. In China, they are also popular when dried. The kaki fruit did not reach America and Europe until the mid 19th century. The fruit, a variant of the so-called Sharon fruit, which is cultivated in Israel, has a brighter color and tastes less of tannins, which gives it a milder flavor.

6 Carambole (Averrhoa carambola)

The fruit grows on evergreen trees and can be up to 4 inches (12 cm) long. When it is cut open it looks like a star—which is why it is also known as "starfruit." As soon as the green fruit turns yellow (and brownish at the edges), it is ripe. The carambola which has been known in China since the 4th century is markedly sweeter than the variant, which is native to Malaysia. People enjoy eating the fresh fruit, drinking the juice, and eating the fruit in dried form.

Kumquat (Fortunella japonia)

The orange-yellow oval fruit, which is about 1 ½ inches (4 cm) long, originates from South China. As regards the color, the peel and the taste, it resembles a bitter, tiny orange. The little trees are used as decorative plants in China, and are given as presents to bring good fortune. The fruits have an edible, sweetish peel, within which lies the orange-colored flesh, divided into segments. The bittersweet taste is extremely popular in China, and the fruit are eaten fresh, or preserved in sugar syrup or dried in salt.

Mango (Mangifera indica)

The oval fruit, which can grow up to 8 inches (20 cm) long, was brought to South China from eastern India by Buddhist monks. Today, there are over a thousand varieties worldwide. The peel and the flesh are sometimes greeny-yellow and sometimes orangey-red, and so the color is not an indication of the degree of ripeness. When purchasing them, you should pay more attention to the size and the scent. Early-ripening, low-fiber types are the best. It is best to remove the flat pit in the center, and then to cut the mango lengthwise. If you carve the interior of the fruit halves thus obtained in a diamond pattern and turn them inside out, the juicy flesh can easily be removed with a knife.

Below: China is now one of the biggest fruit producers in the world. This is obvious from any market in South China. But a large part of production is also exported abroad.

7 Papaya (Carica papaya)

The pear–shaped fruit, which can be up to 12 inches (30 cm) long, came to China from Central America in the 17th century at the latest. Their rind varies from green to an orangey red, depending how ripe they are. The flesh is yellow or reddish. The rind can not be eaten and the seeds are generally discarded. The sweet fruit, which is decidedly high in vitamin C, is particularly popular in South China, where it is consumed in soups or eaten fresh as fruit, or else the juice is drunk.

8 Salak (Sallaca zallaca)

The dark brown, pear–shaped fruit, about 3 ½ inches (9 cm) long, which grows on the salak palms (native to Southeast Asia), is also known as "snakeskin fruit," because of its rough rind, which resembles a snake's skin. It is easy to remove this. The flesh inside is smooth and beige-colored, and is divided into three segments or more. The fruit also contains seeds. It can be consumed as a fruit, and has a sweet–and–sour taste with a hint of strawberries. It is best eaten, like all other tropical fruits, in the area where it ripens, as this is the only way these exotics release their full aroma.

Hong Kong

香港

Katrin Schlotter

The view from Victoria Peak over the sea of Hong Kong's skyscrapers is quite incomparable! To dive into it and find out about the mixture of eastern and western culture in everyday life as you shop, dine, or visit the temples is at least as unique an experience. This former British colony in China's sub-tropical south is rightfully considered to be one of the most dynamic cities in China, if not the world.

The Special Administrative Region of Hong Kong, which has around 7 million inhabitants, is situated in the delta of the Pearl River and surrounded by the province of Guangdong. It covers around 425 square miles (1100 sq km) and extends southward from the peninsula of the New Territories and Kowloon (Nine Dragons) as far as the 230 plus islands, which include Hong Kong Island as well as Lantau and Lamma Islands. It is a place of striking contrasts: here pulsating commercial centers, there uninhabited bays and wild areas.

For some people, Hong Kong is the gateway to the world, for others it is the bridge into China—either way, it is a perfect place for trade. The British changed the original Cantonese name "Heunggong" (Fragrant Harbor) to Hong Kong—but that was not all they changed. As a colonial power, from the mid 19th century they transformed the barren island into a bustling trade center between China and the West, which still occupies a special place today.

Since the British colony was returned to the People's Republic of China on July 1 1997, the official description of Hong Kong is the Special Administrative Region of Hong Kong of the People's Republic of China. With the political slogan "One country, two systems," Hong Kong will also retain its largely democratic and market economy system until 2047, while the People's Republic has responsibility for foreign and defense policy. As in Macau, internal political policy is based on a constitution of its own, the Basic Law, which guarantees an independent judiciary and civil rights.

Hong Kong is considered to be the most liberal market economy in the world, both a paradise for traders and a tax haven—not just because of the hospitable climate but even more because of the mentality of its inhabitants. The legendary "can do spirit" means that in Hong Kong almost anything is possible, 24 hours a day. This is confirmed by the economic data: With a growth of 6.3 percent per year in 2007, the gross domestic product (GDP) was 203.8 billion US dollars, the per capita income around 30,000 US dollars (by way of comparison: in Greece the

Top: The other face of Hong Kong: if you leave the heart of the metropolis, you can find small fishing villages and bays, where you are completely unaware of the hurly-burly of the nearby city.

Above: In the center it is often more than just busy, well into the night. Double-decker buses are one of the favorite means of public transport.

Facing page: The city skyline: In the background, Kowloon; in the foreground, the tower blocks of the Central District, as seen from the 1790-feet (500-m)-high Victoria Peak.

Hong Kong

Top: Only a quarter of the total area of Hong Kong is built up. There are some 250 islands and islets off the city coast.

Above: There life goes on at a more relaxed pace than in the hectic city.

Above right: In Hong Kong people often enjoy life—and eating—in public places.

Below: Symbols of the financial center: On the left, the Bank of China building, and next to it on the right, the Hong Kong & Shanghai Banking Corporation (HSBC).

per capita GDP in 2007 was around 28,300 US dollars). Over 6,000 overseas firms have established branches in the commercial, service, and financial center of Asia, partly in order to benefit from the certainty of Hong Kong's legal position through the lucrative trade agreement with mainland China. In addition, Hong Kong has an excellent infrastructure; the passenger, freight and container ports are among the biggest in the world. In future, an 18-mile (30-km)-long bridge between Hong Kong and Zhuhai in the neighboring Guangdong province and Macau will enable stronger links to be forged between the formerly separate economic regions.

With 6,410 people per square kilometer, Hong Kong today is one of the most densely populated regions in the world. In Kowloon, over 43,000 people are crammed into a single square kilometer. This is hardly surprising as, despite land raising and the leveling of the jagged landscape, only about a quarter of the surface of Hong Kong can be built on. As a result, the people of Hong Kong usually live in very small apartments in tower blocks built very close together. Social life often takes place outside the home, in the open spaces between the apartment blocks and glittering façades, in restaurants, shopping malls or parks. These present a colorful picture. You see many Filipinos, Indonesians, Thais, as well as Americans and Europeans, yet 93 percent of Hong Kong's inhabitants

are Han Chinese. There are three official languages: English, Cantonese, and Mandarin.

International, rich, crowded, and hectic: but this is all just a first impression of Hong Kong. If you stay longer, you see the quieter side of the special qualities of this Chinese city. On a boat trip past the remoter islands, in the mangrove swamps of the New Territories, or in one of the many temples, time seems to stand still. If you think there is no place for tradition and nature in modern Hong Kong, you will be agreeably surprised.

Above left: For the New Year celebrations, every building is decorated and illuminated both inside and out.

Above: Every global player in finance or insurance has a company building in Hong Kong!

Below: Where space is tight, the buildings shoot upward. However, there are parks and recreational areas in between the Hong Kong skyscrapers.

A rock in the surf—the history of Hong Kong

Jagged cliffs, surrounded by shallows and sparsely populated: that was Hong Kong Island at the start of the 19th century. Compared with the ports of Guangzhou and Macau, which were then in their heyday, it was a totally insignificant place. But from 1840 this was to change abruptly and completely.

When Great Britain was conquering the world as a trading power, China was not left out. A ban on the lucrative opium trade was with an armed response. It resulted in the First Opium War (1839–1842), in which China was defeated. Under the Treaty of Nanjing, the British received Hong Kong Island, among other things—not a great achievement at first glance, but the inhospitable island possessed a large natural harbor in a strategically favorable loca-

tion on the mouth of the Pearl River at the Gateway to China. Hong Kong became an exclave under English law and construction began. By 1851 Hong Kong already had 33,000 inhabitants, 95 percent of whom were Chinese who were permitted to stay in Hong Kong for commercial purposes. After the Second Opium War (1856–1860), again won by the British, they also acquired the Kowloon Peninsula. But even that would not be enough to satisfy them. In 1898, they took a 99-year lease on the New Territories, which was a much bigger area in the north of Kowloon as far as the Shenzhen River, plus more than 230 islands. In this way they acquired not only additional living space and better defense potential, but also access to a source of drinking water and new land for supplying food.

From the middle of the 19th century, Hong Kong served as a lucrative trading station between countries overseas and the Chinese mainland. As the city grew and trade developed, ship-yards, small industries, and banks were established. By around 1900, 40 percent of all Chinese exports passed through Hong Kong to the world outside. Around the turn of the century, when the imperialist endeavors of France, Russia, and Japan in particular were putting pressure on the Chinese Empire from the outside while poverty and rebellion raged within, British Hong Kong offered asylum. The enclave was overrun by several waves of Chinese immigrants, especially after the collapse of the empire in 1911. However, the subsequent political turmoil and wars hit the population of Hong

Right: In Hong Kong you can hardly avoid culinary pleasures. People often eat outdoors, and there is little fear of infection.

Far right: The range on offer is vast. The hot-food stalls are just the thing if you are hungry for a snack between meals.

Below: The political guideline "One country, two systems" can be seen here in peaceful harmony. On the left, the Hong Kong flag with a stylized five-petaled bauhinia flower; on the right, the flag of the People's Republic of China.

Bottom right: Tasteful surroundings with an impressive view.

Kong—which had now risen to over a million—very hard.

Trade collapsed, and with it the most important source of income for the population. In addition, during the 1920s and 1930s, resentment against the imperialists led to strikes by the Chinese workers and seamen. When Japan occupied Hong Kong during World War II on December 8, 1941, the economy and food supplies broke down. Anyone who could, fled abroad or to politically neutral Macau. From then until the Japanese capitulation in August 1945, the population of Hong Kong decreased by around a million—to less than 600,000 inhabitants.

After the end of the war, hundreds of thousands streamed back into Hong Kong, which was once again under British rule. In January 1947, the enclave was home to some 1.8 million people. The numbers continued to increase, because civil war was raging on the mainland between the Nationalists and the Communists. After the Communist victory and the founding of the People's Republic of China (1949), hundreds of thousands more—including the educated and westernized upper classes and a few Western companies—sought refuge and fortune in Hong Kong. The economy blossomed again, though now trade and the port were not sufficient to sustain the constantly increasing population. Then, in the mid 1950s, the industrialization of Hong Kong began. It started with

countless small industries, producing mainly textiles, toys, and electrical goods, which were then followed by large companies.

Despite improved conditions in the labor market, a massive apartment building program, and the establishment of new schools, the start of the Cultural Revolution in China also saw protests in Hong Kong, but there was no room for communist ideology in capitalist Hong Kong. The farther the Cultural Revolution progressed, the more victims of political persecution, including intellectuals and businessmen, dared to escape. They crossed the border into Hong Kong, mostly with empty pockets, but making up for their lack of means with a wealth of ideas, courage, knowledge, and contacts, which were to prove very helpful in the future. When the reformer Deng Xiaoping (1904–1997) as leader of the People's Republic, established the special economic zones of Shenzhen, Zhuhai, and Shantou in the neighboring Guangdong province as part of his policy of openness, a structural change began in Hong Kong. From the 1980s, many Hong Kong companies had been moving their production to the cheaper Pearl River Delta, to their old homeland so to speak, and Hong Kong once again became what it had previously been: the commercial, financial and services center of Asia. And so it remains today, with one important difference: since 1997, the "little dragon" Hong Kong has been part of China.

Top left: It is not only the food that is cosmopolitan, but also the design. In Hong Kong it is not hard to find a restaurant to suit every taste and pocket.

Top to bottom: You can eat in truly British style in the relics of colonial times (here the Peninsula Hotel), while Winnie and Angela promise exquisite entertainment in the piano bar. The people of Hong Kong themselves still find traditional shops for special foods and ingredients indispensable, although here too foreign influences are very much on the agenda.

The cuisine—traditionally cosmopolitan

Roast squabs with cinnamon flowers, lobster in black bean sauce, whole sucking pig, with dim sum, Peking duck or beggar's chicken. All the variety of Chinese cooking is concentrated in the microcosm of Hong Kong. Added to this you have pasta, sushi, and tandoori—international cooking traditions that have been established here for decades. In around 8,000 licensed restaurants you can find almost every delicacy in the world, with one rarely-found exception: the original Hong Kong cuisine.

Unlike other regions of China, which developed their own culinary traditions early on, in the middle of the 19th century Hong Kong was still a blank page in the history of cooking. It was not until it became a British colony that, in the wake of the waves of immigration, culinary influences from China and abroad spilled over into the "fragrant harbor." It was started by the inhabitants of Guangdong, who were attracted

by the up-and-coming port. As cooks for the British or running snack stalls on the quay-side—they could earn more as part of the culinary diaspora than in their home province. So Guangdong cooks left their mark on Hong Kong cuisine in many ways with their traditions and their love of experiment.

Until the 1950s, while some restaurants and hotels such as the Peninsula, founded in 1928,

Left: Delicacies and unusual foods can be bought in specialist shops ...

Right: ... and on market stalls, where you do not have to search for long.

prepared the finest traditional recipes for the Hong Kong upper classes, the streets were full of hot-food stalls known as *dai pai dong*. These stalls offered simple, nourishing dishes such as rice porridge, noodles, deep fried fish balls, and tofu. The Hong Kong government awarded licenses (dai pai) to public employees who had been wounded in the war as a way of offering them new opportunities to earn money while at the same time making sure that the many immigrants were fed, as in many cases the new arrivals had no cooking facilities in their lodgings. More and more dai pai dong lined the streets so, when numbers became too great, the government restricted the licenses and concentrated the food stalls into a few stretches of road, for instance in Temple Street. As the inhabitants of Hong Kong became more prosperous, a very varied gastronomic scene began to develop in the 1960s, with noodle kitchens, poultry grills, and *cha chaan teng*—simple restaurants with formica tables, television, and neon signs, a combination of bar and meeting place. These cha chaan teng still offer numerous exciting flavors from east and west, from cheese on toast and noodle soup to *ying yeung*—a drink made of coffee, tea, and milk. As well as these places, traditional Cantonese tea houses offered dim sum and tea, restaurants served banquets for weddings and other celebrations. New impulses came from the

Above: The restaurant ship by the Kowloon shore rocks gently and pampers the guests with its culinary treats.

Right: However, it does not always have to be a big, tourist restaurant. Original Hong Kong cuisine can also be found on a smaller, more manageable scale.

Below: Jade, flowers, birds, or goldfish—Hong Kong is blessed with many markets. The most interesting for western visitors are undoubtedly the food markets, where every imaginable curiosity can be found.

Top right and center right: Even if the cuisine is not averse to western innovations, in the markets you can see the influence of Guangdong cuisine, which can make something edible out of almost anything animal or vegetable.

Bottom right: The goods for sale are hard for the uninitiated to identify. But even confirmed Hong Kongers can often only identify what is on offer by the label.

mainland, when many top cooks fled to Hong Kong during the Cultural Revolution (1966–1976) because their cooking was considered decadent in China. By contrast, in Hong Kong, imperial specialties that people had long been deprived of, such as Peking Duck, ducks' tongues, and birds' nests, were very well received. Hong Kong cuisine, which had until then been mainly influenced by the Guangdong tradition, now absorbed traditional recipes from the whole of China.

But that was not enough. The more international and also—after the Chinese adopted the policy of openness and the enclave was returned to China—the more Chinese Hong Kong became, the more glittering variety there was in the restaurant scene, with everything from international hotels with luxury restaurants to trendy bars and street food stalls. In recent years the latest sensation has been restaurants in private homes, sometimes referred to as "speakeasies," where enthusiastic cooks serve delicious food in their own living rooms. In addition, concept restaurants, which revive traditional cooking like that of the boat people or the itinerant traders, attract the pampered palates of the Hong Kong people. Street stalls, bars and top quality restaurants all want the same thing: to stand out from the crowd—just like the Hong Kong cuisine.

Left: The fish, freshly grilled while the customer looks on, costs 15 H K dollars, which converts to about 2 US dollars.

Below: Work in the Hong Kong night markets is often hard—especially on the many hot-food stalls.

Hong Kong style pork ribs

1 lb 5 oz (600 g) pork ribs
garlic
red bell pepper
ginger
black bean sauce
vegetable oil for frying
½ tbsp oyster sauce
2 tsp light soy sauce
1 tsp dark soy sauce
1 tsp corn starch
freshly ground white pepper
sesame oil

Cut the ribs in small pieces with a cleaver. Rinse, pat dry and put in a bowl.
Finely chop a little garlic, red bell pepper, and ginger. Heat vegetable oil in a wok, add a little black bean sauce, and the garlic, bell pepper, and ginger, and brown briefly until it releases its aroma.
Add the ribs and stir-fry. Add the remaining ingredients (oyster sauce, soy sauces, corn starch, white pepper, and sesame oil) and mix. Stir-fry for 10 minutes over high heat, and serve immediately.

Hong Kong restaurant quarter

Sophisticated Cantonese cuisine, international specialties or the atmosphere of the night market? An exclusive sushi bar with a view over the Hong Kong skyline or freshly-caught shellfish on the Sai Kung harbor promenade? Hong Kong cuisine is so diverse it knows no regional or culinary boundaries. Here are a few appetizing morsels from a stroll through the districts of Hong Kong—from Kowloon and Hong Kong Island to the New Territories.

Shop and be amazed: Kowloon

Nathan Road, Hong Kong's shimmering shopping street, runs through Kowloon like a main artery, northward from Tsim Sha Tsui to the districts of Yau Ma Tai and Mong Kok. In the most densely populated part of Hong Kong beats the heart of Chinese cuisine. In between the shopping malls and apartment blocks, luxury hotels and temples, museums and markets, you can experience everyday Hong Kong cooking—in noodle shops, poultry rotisseries or neon-lit cha chaan teng, in snack bars or in the night market in Temple Street. Here you can stay your hunger with wonton soup or roast goose. Just a few blocks farther on, gourmet hearts may easily skip a beat at the sight of countless high class restaurants and hotels with their latest culinary creations. For instance, in the Peninsula Hotel, the eternally rejuvenated "grande dame" of Hong Kong, connoisseurs can find luxury-class European and Asian delicacies, from French haute cuisine in the Restaurant Gaddis, Peking duck and dim sum in the Cantonese Springmoon, all the way up to the Felix on the 29th floor, which was designed by Philippe Starck. The Aqua and Hutong restaurants in the One Peking skyscraper are no less impressive. The breathtaking view of the Hong Kong skyline is (almost) enough to make the customer forget the exquisite Italian, Japanese, and northern Chinese food. Closer to the ground, but definitely not "of the soil" is the fashionable Knutsford Terrace district of Kowloon, whose cocktail bars and restaurants attract the local night owls In the Vodka Room of the Russian Balalaika Restaurant, guests—warmly wrapped in Russian parkas and fur hats—can taste over 100 different types at −68 °F (−20 °C).

Right: The Aqua is just one of many high-class restaurants in Hong Kong. Incidentally, it also has a branch on a junk, which can cater for 80 guests.

Below: Cool, hip and stylish—with excellent avant-garde cuisine and a splendid view of Hong Kong harbor from the 30th floor into the bargain.

Top: Here, in the Balalaika in the heart of the Lan Kwai Fong district they preserve memories of Russian cuisine—and Russian drinking habits.

Above middle: True to tradition the vodka here is served at –68 ˚F (–20 ˚C).

Above: At these temperatures only two things help: a fur coat outside and strong liquor inside.

Commerce and leisure on Hong Kong Island

As you take the Star Ferry, that symbol of Hong Kong tradition, across the arm of sea that lies between Kowloon and the 31-square-mile (80-sq-km)-Hong Kong Island, the imposing skyline points the way to the commercial and financial centers from Central to Causeway Bay. In the midst of the banks and business houses, between shopping malls and exhibition centers, the colonial sights, temples, parks, luxury hotels, and restaurants can easily make you forget all thoughts of work and business dealings. The trendy, internationally influenced districts of Lan Kwai Fong and Soho, with their strings of galleries, clubs, and restaurants, radiates a party atmosphere after close of business. International delicacies, drinks in the open, or Chinese tea ceremonies—no gastronomic desire is left unfulfilled. Since the early 1990s, Soho, the garish nightlife district south of Hollywood Road, has been providing galleries, restaurants and shops for entertainment in the residential and commercial area half way to Victoria Peak. On the 1,790-feet (550-m)-high peak, the visitor experiences more than just culinary flights of fancy. The ride on the Peak Tram, which has been transporting people to Hong Kong's most famous mountain top since 1888, is an experience in itself. When you arrive at the top, you have a breathtaking view of the skyscrapers, the harbor, and, with a bit of luck and good weather, you can see as far as the fishing port of Aberdeen—for example from the Mediterranean-style garden terrace of the Peak Lookout Restaurant, if you can tear your eyes away from the delicious fish platter they serve there.

In contrast to the busy north, the Happy Valley race course, hiking trails, bathing beaches, and yacht clubs give the central and southern parts of Hong Kong Island a relaxing holiday atmosphere. It is not surprising that this part attracts many nature-lovers and, of course, tourists, who visit the Ocean Park, the Stanley Market, or Aberdeen. Protected from typhoons, Aberdeen was for many years the anchorage for tens of thousands of Boat People (*dan jia*). They spent their entire lives on the sampans,

their raft-like houseboats. When the Floating City with its waterborne markets and traders fell victim to the fires in the 1980s, many of the people moved into the apartment blocks, but a few hundred families still continue to spend their lives on the sampans. Though the Boat People used to earn their living from fishing and trade, nowadays they rely mainly on harbor tours for tourists.

A meal on the restaurant ship Jumbo Floating Restaurant (part of the Jumbo Kingdom complex), which has entertained more than 30 million guests since 1976, is another attraction. In the restaurants of this enormous junk, which is firmly anchored to the land, the cooks prepare not only European and Chinese specialties but also dishes of the Boat People, which they serve during a tour by sampan. Boat People food can also be tasted in Stanley, on the southern tip of Hong Kong Island, in the Shu Zhai restaurant. This restaurant has been preserved in traditional style and surprises guests by serving Boat People-style fish and shellfish in addition to tea and dim sum. Offerings of stir-fried mussels and crabs bear witness to the simple lives of the fishermen, who lived on what they could harvest from the sea, supplementing it with fruits and vegetables that keep well, such as tomatoes, cauliflower, sweet potatoes, or melon.

Relaxation and pleasure: Lamma and Lantau Islands

Only half an hour by ferry from Hong Kong Island, Lamma Island, the car-free, third largest island in Hong Kong, is the place to enjoy nature. Hiking trails run through the green hills, past winding bays and sandy beaches, linking the little towns of Yung Shue Wan and Sok Kwu Wan. These two towns, where people still make their living partly from fishing, attract visitors with their open-air fish restaurants. And the best place to enjoy the freshly-caught fish and seafood of the region is where it was caught—by the coast. On the seafront promenade of Sok Kwu Wan there is a string of restaurants, where guests can select living fish from glass tanks, before it is prepared in the kitchen in Cantonese style. Deep-fried crabs with honey and pepper or steamed lobster with garlic taste especially good on a warm evening with a view over the harbor, perhaps in the Rainbow Restaurant.

Lantau, which at 55 square miles (142 sq km) is the biggest of Hong Kong's islands, is full of opposites. New residential areas and satellite towns contrast sharply with the old houses built on piles of the fishing village Tai-O. So do the international Chek Lap Kok Airport and the Disneyland Amusement Park. But that is only half the story, as Lantau consists mainly of wonderful nature parks and also houses the Buddhist monastery of Po Lin and the biggest

Right: Hong Kong cuisine has as many different faces as the various parts of Hong Kong. But from the culinary point of view, as well as having long been the boiling and melting point for western influences, the various regional cuisines of China have also left their traces here.

statue of the sitting Buddha in the world the 110-foot (34-m)-high Tian Tan Buddha.

Satellite towns and larder: The New Territories

A similar picture can be seen in the remainder of the New Territories, which include not only more than 230 islands but also the land to the north of Kowloon between Hong Kong and mainland China. Formerly sparsely populated, nowadays the subtropical mountain landscape is broken up along the traffic arteries by satellite towns and industrial areas. However, there is still plenty of space for nature and tradition in the remaining 270 square miles (700 sq km) or so. Countless temples, including the Temple of Ten Thousand Buddhas, walled villages of the Hakka people (originally from northern China), and an almost infinite number of nature parks transform the hinterland into a recreational

area and open air museum. In addition, agricultural land, oyster farms, aquaculture and rich fishing grounds make the New Territories the larder for Hong Kong. The harbor town of Sai Kung, for instance, set in the middle of 29 square miles (75 sq km) of natural paradise, is a top address for lovers of fine fish dishes. All along the harbor promenade, there are fish restaurants like the Tung Kee Seafood restaurant that not only display the enormous variety of fish and shellfish to be found in Hong Kong waters but also try to outdo one another in the excellence of their cuisine.

Top left to bottom left: In the whole of China, the serving of food is accompanied by a very popular form of entertainment:
Karaoke is one of Hong Kong's "favorite sports" — in private or in public. Mixing the two leisure pursuits of singing and eating is especially popular. And in Hong Kong, if you look around a bit, you are certain to find a karaoke bar where they cook delicious food and cater for all the family.

Below: Hong Kong never sleeps. Most restaurants and bars on the shopping streets are open 24 hours a day.

Alive, alive, oh!—buying fish in Hong Kong

Wherever you look, you can spot anything from croakers to groupers, from bamboo shrimp to green tiger shrimp, and crabs of all sizes alongside oysters, abalones, sea urchins, eels, and grass carp. If it lives in the sea, Hong Kong fish markets will almost certainly fulfill your desire for it. It is incredible to think that there are hundreds of fish and shellfish that are native to Hong Kong waters, not to mention those they import from all over the world.

Every afternoon the same spectacle is presented on the Sai Kung harbor promenade. Shortly before the fishermen return, housewives and chefs throng the quayside, because just below them the fishermen will soon be selling their day's catch in the floating fish market. "Hey there, Lao, have you got any Japanese icefish today? How much? As much as that? How much are you selling for, Wang?"—"Half price to you, Ma, my friend!" Exchanges like this echo across the wall. Fish that have previously been sorted by species into different colored tubs of water thrash about in the landing net. And so it goes on, to and fro, until the fish's fate is sealed. In baskets attached to long bamboo poles, goods and money change hands across the high quayside wall. People who cannot cook the fish themselves take it straight to a nearby restaurant and have it cooked there in any way they like.

In the fish market in Lei Yue Mun at the eastern entrance to Hong Kong harbor, which has been on the list of gourmet addresses since the 1960s, fish is sold in a slightly different way. Medusa fish, sea bream, big-eye, and grouper splash about in seething tanks, but sea urchins, shrimp, mantis shrimp and horseshoe crabs are also ready and waiting—fascinating for western visitors, who do not get to see 20-inch (half-meter)-long lobsters or giant squid every day. The selection of unusual sea creatures is breathtaking—and they are edible into the bargain! All you have to do is point at the creature you want and it will be weighed, killed, and, if desired, cooked in a neighboring restaurant.

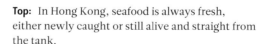

Top: In Hong Kong, seafood is always fresh, either newly caught or still alive and straight from the tank.

Above: In the markets, the goods do not have to be displayed for long before they change hands.

Above right: Even the most fearsome looking creatures are offered for sale freshly caught.

Right: A Hong Kong specialty: Anyone buying crabs in the fish market can take them straight to a nearby restaurant and have them cooked there right away.

Top: The firm, white flesh of the grouper is extremely popular in Chinese cuisine.

Above: Bargaining in markets is of paramount importance, but there is rarely any objection to the quality of the wares.

Above right: Gourmets enjoying the rich inventiveness of southern Chinese cuisine have to be thankful for the availability of every imaginable kind of fish and cooking method.

Right: You hardly ever see finer lobsters than those in Chinese fish markets.

Eating habits and opportunities

This pretty cup is actually for hot noodle soup, not tea.

The staff are up early, as the first breakfast customers will arrive around 7.00 am.

Corresponding to the international cooking traditions that have added new flavors to private and professional cooking in Hong Kong, most recently since the time of British rule, there are as many different eating habits—and opportunities. For breakfast or lunch, a snack in between, a tea or coffee break, dinner, or a late-night supper, in Hong Kong you can find the right place to assuage your hunger and satisfy your tastes, at any time of day, to suit every culinary preference—and every pocket. The following stroll through Kowloon—the center of the Special Administrative Region of Hong Kong—leads to traditional Chinese, Western, and Asian restaurants, fast-food chains, and dai pai dongs—the popular hot food stalls in Temple Street.

As many of the local people allow themselves more time for their meals at weekends, our tour also takes place on a Saturday. We start with a traditional Chinese dim sum breakfast and then try a Western breakfast buffet in a four star hotel. We are expected for lunch in a Chinese snack shop in Temple Street, a shopping street in the Mong Kok district that is popular with young people. On the way there we pass several branches of international fast food chains.

As in many places in China, self service is the norm here. It is also quickest that way.

Pensioners are often the first customers. They like to take a bit more time over their breakfast.

The orders bearing the name of the dish and the customer's table number go through to the kitchen.

Here they are serving rice porridge (congee) and spring rolls along with the filling dim sum.

No Chinese breakfast is complete without these *mantou*—hot, steamed bread rolls.

Alongside all kinds of hot dishes you can get cold accompaniments, such as tomatoes or tofu sausages.

Chinese youngsters are attracted by sweet cakes as well as German sausages.

Fresh food is highly prized, not only by the many international visitors who come to Hong Kong.

The western-style buffet of this hotel in Nathan Road is recommended by young people.

The big choice of muesli, quite normal in the Hotel Europa, looks exotic to Hong Kong locals.

The view from the breakfast room on the top floor of the hotel alone made our flying visit worthwhile!

Like young people all over the world, Hong Kong youngsters like to drop into McDonalds.

Chinese menus may look familiar from outside but are bewildering for foreigners once they get inside.

As the Chinese eat their main meal in the evening, the fast food chains are very busy at lunchtimes.

If you are overcome by hunger, you can satisfy it with a bigger hot meal.

The Chinese snack shops in Temple Street also offer midday snacks in a bag.

You can choose from countless rice dishes with vegetables, meat, or marinated tofu...

...or best of all hot Chinese—and that means tasty—noodle soup.

But suppose instead of fast food, you had a tasty *Hai Nan Ji Fan*—Hainan chicken with rice?

If you want to savor your food rather than eat in a hurry, the City Golf Club is the right place to be.

And then, because it looks so delicious, attractively garnished curried shrimp?

Our guide, Mrs Tse, enjoys both before she continues with her Saturday shopping.

But even a choice luncheon table cannot stop you from looking forward to the evening hotpot.

A lot of side-dishes are served with it and added one by one to the soups: mushrooms, beef, vegetables, tofu, and salad...and, of course, tea—preferably jasmine tea.

The classic Chinese hotpot consists of two soups: one white and mild, the other red and hot.

A fish soup hotpot: the mild one contains leeks, the hot one ginger and chili.

The night market in Temple Street: a magnet that attracts countless tourists.

At weekends in Hong Kong, you can also dine stylishly on choice dishes, though of course in a different price range from the snack shops of the shopping streets. All the same, the restaurant of the Hong Kong City Golf Club offers good value for money. After recovering our strength there, we pass the remainder of the Saturday afternoon in leisurely style—until our evening appointment with the hotpot. It is worth taking sufficient time and conversational material, because eating hotpot is not for sad souls or those who want to be alone. Nor is the following late-evening visit to the night market, which transforms Temple Street into a brightly lit avenue for strolling and eating. At the end of the street—close to the Wong Tai Sin, the most famous temple in Kowloon—we find one of the best dai pai dongs in the city, where hardly anyone can resist the freshly-made oyster omelet.

Before the night passes its high point, we get back to where we started from, and in Nathan Road we find an exquisite spot, the Yagura Japanese Restaurant. Here, over the midnight sushi—and the recollections of the many and varied tastes we have enjoyed, the laughing, chatting faces and the warmth of our encounters with the people of Hong Kong—a sneaking desire for peace and quiet sets in. And what could this be, other than a kind of midnight Hong Kong blues?

Seafood is especially popular—crabs, crayfish, shrimp, oysters, sea cucumbers etc.

I wonder if we will find this dai pai dong near the Wong Tai Sin Temple again next time?

In the dai pai dong, we encounter locals waiting for delicious oyster omelets.

However, those who do not care for oysters may fancy freshly grilled fish.

It is not just the interior that is Japanese, so is the menu—and also the way the wide range of sushi dishes is presented.

The elegant Yagura Japanese Restaurant invites us to relax after the hustle and bustle of Hong Kong.

Just before midnight, we join this young Hong Konger eating sushi.

Guests can take away the elegantly wrapped chopsticks as a souvenir.

The night market in Temple Street

Clattering and rattling, posts and trestles, wire netting and huge pink and blue striped plastic awnings—you might almost think they are setting up for an open-air concert, running parallel to the Nathan Road shopping street through the center of Kowloon. But it isn't quite the same, because here they are getting ready for the night market in Temple Street.

Every evening, the traders divide up whole street areas between the Tin Hau Temple, from which Temple Street gets its name, and Jordan Street, to set up their stalls for the famous Hong Kong night market. Well protected against possible rain showers by the awnings, the unholy chaos of poles, boards, and fabrics is transformed in an instant into real treasure chests for all kinds of interesting things. Silk ties, purses, masses of electrical goods, watches, and slippers—every corner of the stalls is crammed with goods of every imaginable kind and origin. One stall after another, for around 650 yards

(600 m) on both sides of the street, transforming Temple Street—in the mornings a relatively quiet street of shops—into one of the most exciting shopping streets in the world, complete with trading and haggling.

Fortune tellers also set up their booths, with boards showing the facial features or the lines on hands advertising the arts they will soon be displaying. The thousand-year-old art of drawing inferences about a person's character, past, and future from the features and proportions of their faces is extremely popular in Hong Kong. Information such as "love troubles: not surprising with that hairline," "Long earlobes: long well-being," or "with a red cell phone business will be better," brings a sense of direction into a confused life—and all for just a few H K dollars, simple and practical. Predictions in English, French, or Japanese cost correspondingly more. If you are not satisfied with the forecast, you go to the next soothsayer: maybe the signs of the zodiac will say something more positive.

A couple of blocks farther on, the snack stalls owners are setting up for business. While assistants arrange colorful plastic stools around

the folding tables, the cooks are already at work. Prepared ingredients are arranged, woks heated, many ingredients fried in readiness—after all, the night market lasts from 6 o'clock in the evening until far into the night. The customers, tourists or locals, will be longing for all kinds of snacks in the coming hours. Shopping and eating, preferably at the same time, are among the Hong Kongers' favorite pursuits.

A little bit later, the scents of all kinds of different foods waft over the crowded night market. Just as in the old days, the dai pai dong serve all kinds of snacks, from deep-fried squid and pork rind to fish balls and stinky tofu, which can be recognized at a distance by its sharp, cheesy smell. Two steps farther and your nose is filled with the scent of grilled pork skewers, followed immediately by spicy shrimp or oyster omelets with cilantro.

If you do not like to eat as you walk along, you can sit at one of the little tables, elbow to elbow with your neighbor, order a bowl of noodle soup, steamed snails, or a rice pot. This dish consists of rice and all kinds of meat,

Above: A real paradise for bargain hunters and brand name pirates: the night market in Temple Street.

Right: No-one needs to go without here. Between the market stalls the food supply situation is excellent.

Facing page, top: The perfect combination, not only for tourists: Hong Kongers too like the combination of shopping and eating.

Facing page, bottom: Close together: Social differences hardly matter. Everyone is equal when eating.

which is braised for about 20 minutes so the rice at the outer edge of the bowl is crispy. With it, there is Tsingtao beer from the bottle. Of course there are sweet things available as well: stalls with freshly squeezed fruit juices, deep-fried cakes and cookies, or a coffee shop at the next corner.

Easy and uncomplicated, noisy and fun, here you get close to the everyday Hong Kong. Families with children, colleagues, friends, and tourists saunter along until well past midnight. Every minute brings some new discovery— with a bit of luck you may even come across a couple of performers belting out Cantonese opera arias to the night sky.

Giving luck a helping hand

Long noodles for birthdays, fish for New Year celebrations: In China people set great store by symbolic foods. Long noodles represent a long life—that is something even non-Chinese can understand. But why do they eat fish at New Year? In many cases the answer can be found in the Chinese language. For instance, the sentence "There is fish every year" *Nian nian you yu* has a second meaning, as the Chinese word for fish *yu* sounds exactly like the word for abundance. So in China they like to wish each other "Every year there is abundance." A river carp is particularly auspicious, because its name *liyu* sounds identical to the word for business advantage. In China the carp is also a symbol for tenacity and perseverance. People say it is like the spawning salmon leaping to surmount the rapids of the upper reaches of the Yellow River (Huang)—upstream!

Another food that is a must at New Year is *jiaozi*, dumplings whose shape symbolizes gold bars. They are eaten on the eve of the Chinese New Year with just the closest family members in order to keep the money in the family.

For the Lantern Festival—in Chinese, *Yuanxiao Jie*, and also at the end of the New Year festivities—they eat glutinous rice balls with a sweet filling, which have the same name. In the south they are also known as *tangyuan* little soup balls. These little globes symbolize family harmony and completeness. The round moon cookies, sweet or savory morsels which are given as presents for the Moon Festival, also stand for family solidarity.

In addition, many kinds of fruit are endowed with symbolic meaning in China. For instance, the word for apple, *ping*, sounds like the word for peace and security and is therefore a favorite present for guests to bring with them. If you are visiting someone who is ill, you must absolutely not bring an apple with you, because the similarity of its sound to the word for illness, *bing*, is considered to be a bad omen.

You have to be equally careful about eating and giving pears, at least when it is a question of sharing pears. In particular, you should never share pears with partners or even future marriage partners: that is because in Chinese sharing pears, *fen li*, sounds exactly like getting divorced. Not a good omen for a future married couple! However, if you have accidentally eaten pears together, the best thing to do is to eat a few lotus seeds, *he*, afterward. Their name sounds like the word for harmony, so according to folk tradition they guarantee a stable marriage without turmoil.

Traditionally the desire for children is supported by placing a pomegranate in the bed of the newly married couple. The many seeds of the pomegranate, *shi liu*, symbolize many children. Dates, *zaozi*, are particular favorites in this connection. In Chinese their name sounds like the word for "early son," so dates symbolize the desire to bear a son soon.

Peaches, *tao*, are relatively harmless in their symbolic meaning; like noodles, they stand for a long life. This goes back to a legend that has grown up around the eight Taoist immortals, *Ba Xian*. According to this legend, in the garden of the Queen Mother Xi Wangmu in the Western Paradise, there stands a peach tree, whose fruits confer the gift of immortality. This tree bears fruit only once every 3,000 years, and then Xi Wangmu invites all the immortals to a banquet of life-giving energy.

In China, symbolic qualities are also ascribed to numbers and colors. For instance, if you are inviting people to a meal, you must ensure that there is an even number of people at the table. An odd number augurs badly. The numbers six, *liu*, and eight, *ba*, have particularly positive connotations; they stand for success and prosperity. For the Chinese, the unlucky number is four, *si*, because it is pronounced like the word for death. In the south of China this also applies to the number ten, *shi*, as there it is pronounced "si," unlike the standard pronunciation in the north of the country. Whereas people in western countries often avoid the 13th floor in hotels, the 4th and 10th floors are extremely unpopular with the Chinese.

Red, *hong*, is the color of good luck in China, while white, *bai*, is the color of death. If you want to impress as a host, you should choose red table decorations. Guests also bring gifts wrapped in red paper, whereas white paper is taboo. The color yellow, *huang*, was formerly the prerogative of the Chinese emperors; however, in more recent times it has come to stand for pornography, so its symbolism is ambiguous.

ELKE SPIELMANNS-ROME

Right: A fish stands for riches and prosperity. That is one of the reasons why it must be part of the New Year meal.

Above: Peaches symbolize long life. Taoist mythology even regards them as a symbol of immortality.

Top: This kind of citron is known as a "Buddha's hand" and symbolizes long life.

Above: The kaki fruit is also known as the persimmon, Sharon fruit, or Chinese plum and is a symbol of stability.

Right: The symbolism of the pomegranate is self-evident: its many seeds symbolize abundance and consequently many children.

Below: While in the context of Western Christian and biblical culture the apple is a symbol of knowledge and seduction, in China it stands for peace and harmony.

Belief in the gods in modern Hong Kong

There are as many different religious convictions in Hong Kong as there are different groups of people. Wherever you look, almost everywhere in busy Hong Kong you can see signs of religious practices. In fact, for the majority of the population, the colorful mixture of Buddhism, Taoism, and ancestor worship is a fixed part of everyday life.

In the home or in the little electrical goods store, there are small domestic shrines, usually lit by red candles for good fortune and prosperity, where the ancestors, spirits, or gods are kept happy with gifts in the form of fruit or joss sticks. Almost all cell phones have lucky charms dangling from them, little jade Buddhas, Chinese characters promising prosperity, or little dolls meaning you will be blessed with many children. Automobile license plates should also take account of good omens, as only if you have the right numbers, for instance an eight, will you be safe in traffic—in contrast to the number four, which sounds the same as the character for death.

How important the gods are for the people of Hong Kong can be seen very clearly in the well attended temples, located in the middle of residential areas, along the coast, or on the mountain tops. There are around 400 Buddhist monasteries and 300 Taoist temples in Hong Kong—some ancient, others newly built. They usually house several gods under one roof, sometimes Buddhist and Taoist together. Which of these gods are considered to be helpful depends on the situation of the individual who is seeking advice, and if they are not sure, it can never be wrong to have twofold spiritual support.

The goddess Tin Hao—responsible for the welfare and protection of seafarers—is accorded particular importance in the traditional fishing harbor of Hong Kong. More than 20 temples, mostly close to the coast, are dedicated to her. Equally highly revered is Bodhisattva Guanyin, a Buddhist goddess of mercy, who refrained from entering Nirvana in order instead to help mortals on their way there. The Taoist saint Wong Tai Sin not only promises to heal the sick but is also an important contact for all questions about the future, which may even include the results of horse races. Countless fortune tellers also help with this. The opulent Wong Tai Sin Temple in Kowloon, which can be recognized from afar by clouds of smoke from burning joss sticks, is currently being restored at a cost of 1.8 million US dollars. In future this should allow not only more gods but also more silence and order inside. But can an LED installation showing the Chinese zodiac according to the time of year ever replace the masses of firecrackers and incense?

Equally impressive is the bronze Tian Tan Buddha on the Island of Lantau, at 110 feet (34 m) high and weighing 280 short tons (250 tonnes) the world's biggest statue of the seated, meditating Buddha. Its facial expression and attitude personify virtue and wisdom, symbolize peace and honesty, and promise benevolence and salvation. It watches not only over humankind but also over the Po Lin monastery situated 268 steps below it. The temple complex dates back to three monks who sought enlightenment in the remote mountains of Lantau at the beginning of the last century. However, the statue itself was only produced in the 1990s, in Nanjing on the mainland. Today the magnificent complex consists of several halls, pagodas, and gardens, and also offers a highly-rated monastery restaurant—vegetarian, of course.

Almost 13,500 statues of Buddha—each one unique—smile at the visitors to the 20-acre (8-ha)-Temple of the Ten Thousand Buddhas, in Shatin in the New Territories. This splendid complex was founded by the monk Yuet Kai and is on two levels. On the lower level is the main temple, built in 1957 and containing around 12,000 small statues of Buddha (dedicated to Bodhisattva Guanyin). If you climb up more than 400 steps, lined with life-size golden statues of Buddha, you reach more temple buildings. In this complex people worship not only the embalmed, gold-clad body of its founder but also the deceased members of their own families. Despite all its modernity, belief in the gods and ancestor worship still play an important role in Hong Kong.

Left: Buddhas, Bodhisattvas, saints—in the Temple of the Ten Thousand Buddhas everyone is guaranteed to find a saint to protect them.

Bottom left: Ancestor worship, as celebrated within the family circle, plays a big part in daily life.

Below: The Taoist Man Mo temple is one of the oldest in Hong Kong. Countless incense spirals hang from its roof. Their smoke is said to carry the prayers of the faithful to the gods.

Above: The Chinese like to give their prayers added emphasis by lighting enormous numbers of joss sticks.

Left: In Hong Kong, people are not very discriminating about religion. In the Temple of the Ten Thousand Buddhas, Taoist sculptures are found alongside statues of Buddha.

Below: Every home has a shrine, where the ancestors are worshiped.

Belief in the gods in modern Hong Kong **285**

Spring Festival and Moon Festival

In the Chinese community, great symbolic power has always been attributed to the moon. This is mainly due to the fact that the peasants' lunisolar calendar is based on it, according to which the first new moon after the winter solstice—between January 21 and February 21—marks the turn of the year. That is when the Chinese New Year Festival is celebrated. Since the introduction of the Gregorian calendar it has been known as the Spring Festival, *chunjie*, to distinguish it from the western New Year on January 1st, which is also celebrated in China in these times of globalization. However, the traditional Chinese Spring Festival still holds prime place in the Chinese festival calendar.

Continued on page 288

Right: The ideal Spring Festival gift—for yourself and others. Flowers symbolize a happy start to the New Year, and the color red stands for good luck.

Below: Mythical beasts, a kind of cross between a dragon and a lion, decorate the table between the New Year cookies and the glutinous rice balls.

Left: No shopping alley or chain store would be brave enough not to put up proper New Year decorations.

Top: Passers-by and potential customers are courted by dragons outside the stores.

Above: During the New Year Festivities, it is traditional to remember your ancestors. Food brought for them should put them in a good mood on the other side.

Below: What the ancestors do not eat there, can always be polished off by the family and descendants afterward.

Continued from page 286

In the People's Republic there are three official public holidays, which can be extended by a skillful shifting of working hours in many companies to make a whole week's holiday. Like the Christian Christmas, the Spring Festival is first and foremost a family festival, and around the time of the festivities, the trains, buses, and planes in China are full to bursting because everyone is going home to their family. This is particularly true of the migrant workers: peasants who spend the year working on the building sites of the rich coastal towns and hand over a considerable portion of their year's wages to their families in the country at New Year. They are greeted by banners with good wishes, which are traditionally hung over and to the sides of the entrance. On New Year's Eve, they exchange news and then eat delicious home made jiaozi dumplings in familiar circles. The exceptionally long and noisy firework displays serve to drive away evil spirits and are an absolute must. It has to be a bit expensive, and in consequence food prices in China go through the roof each time the annual festival comes round.

New Year cakes, *niangoa*, are little balls of glutinous rice, a traditional dish usually served with a filling of fruit or vegetables. Resourceful businessmen sell them as a luxury product with fine ham and shark fins. During the time of celebration and feasting, the Chinese also remember the ancestors and the gods. On the first day of the New Year, many families go the temple or the family grave, to make an offering to the ancestors. Everything they need on the other side is presented in paper form and burnt: clothes, furniture, automobiles and cell phones. Choice foods are also laid by the graves. What the ancestors do not eat, the family eats later.

The Spring Festival is celebrated extensively all over China. Those who like to do so with plenty of color and noise go to Hong Kong. The many tower blocks with their festive illuminations create a breathtaking background, and for 5 days, Hong Kong becomes the arena for numerous cultural and traditional activities, which attract thousands of extra visitors to the city every year. One of the highlights is the nightly New Year parade that wends its way through the harbor area with colorful costumes and loud music. Traditionally, the festivities finish with the Lantern Festival at the first full moon of the year. In the town of Harbin in the north-eastern province of Heilongjiang they celebrate the festival in a unique way. Every year they hold an Ice Lantern banquet (see p. 456) with ice sculptures illuminated in different colors.

In the second half of the year, the moon again gives occasion for a great Chinese festival: on the 15th day of the 8th lunar month—that is in the middle of autumn, *zhongqiujie*, around mid-September to early October—they celebrate the brightest and clearest full moon of the year. Originally this festival marked the end of harvest time; however, this meaning has been lost in the cities of modern China. Today the Moon Festival is seen as a reason to invite family and friends to an exclusive, festive banquet. Before they start to eat, they drink to a "happy Moon Festival." And one thing is essential: moon cake, *yuebing*, which comes with many different types of fillings, both sweet and savory. But people have long since stopped baking them themselves. Instead, the supermarkets sell a wide variety.

ELKE SPIELMANNS-ROME

Above right: Corporate identity is no help: At traditional Chinese festivals decorations run riot.

Right: The big shop with the moon cakes: usually people buy them ready-made rather than bake them themselves.

Left: In Hong Kong (and in other parts of China) they let off fireworks twice for New Year. They indulge in this pleasure—incidentally a Chinese invention—both on New Year's Eve (December 31) and then again a few weeks later (usually in February), when the rockets are set off again.

Below left: Traditionally the New Year festival is an opportunity to get together with all the family. The Hong Kong restaurant industry is geared up for this.

Below: New Year wishes are written on slips of red paper.

Unusual restaurants in private homes

A residential or business complex, an inconspicuous entrance. No restaurant sign, no information, just a doorbell. "We've come to the wrong place," is often people's first thought in the exciting hunt for Hong Kong's unofficial temples of fine food. If the door opens, they have got it right. This is where connoisseurs dine—and culinary surprises await them.

There are a 100-or-so *sifang cai* restaurants in Hong Kong, which are indeed restaurants but are not like official restaurants. In English, they are sometimes referred to as "speakeasies" or simply "private restaurants," but the Hong Kong name can be translated as "private kitchen." It is a bit like eating in a private club; keen cooks—including former managers, artists and housewives—serve their specialties as a daily or weekly menu within their own four walls. The basic idea is amazingly simple: you reserve in advance and eat whatever is put on the table. It could be Sichuan, Shanghai or French cuisine. What *sifang cai* offer is largely determined by the origins and preferences of the owners.

So the inviting Yellow Door is famous for its delicious Sichuan and Shanghai menus and its selection of wines. The guests of the Club Qing believe they have been transported back into the past, as they enjoy imperial banquets and tea ceremonies. The Xi Yan, which is always booked up months in advance, has achieved cult status with menus that combine traditional Chinese cooking and nouvelle cuisine. In Mum Chau's, Da Ping Ho, or Mr Li's Shanghai Private Kitchen it is all about Chinese regional delicacies, whereas customers of the Le Blanc and the Magnolia feel as if they are actually in France or New Orleans. The variety of dishes served in these private restaurants could hardly be greater.

Word about how well these chefs cook—for the sheer love of it, how hospitable they are, and how attractive the atmosphere is travels quickly through Hong Kong. The addresses of new *sifang cai* spread like wildfire. When it comes down to it, personal recommendation is always the best advertisement. The neat thing is that, if you do not have an official restaurant address, you do not need a license. How could you prove that an artist is running a restaurant, when all he is doing is displaying his creations privately and offering something to eat at the same time. However, if the authorities find out about a "private kitchen" through internet forums or city magazines, a few conditions will be imposed if it is to continue in business. All the same, these are not as strict as those for regular restaurants. No more than 24 customers at once can visit the "club," takeouts are banned, and the opening times must not exceed three and a half hours.

The idea of restaurants in private homes caught on in Hong Kong at the end of the 1990s, when rents shot up and the economy weakened. In order to reduce the high costs of running a restaurant, many hosts retreated to the upper floor of a residential and business block. The SARS virus, which also restricted public life in Hong Kong in 2003, had another impact. For fear of infection, people preferred to sit down in a *sifang cai* rather than make an appearance in the crowded, fashionable eating places.

Nowadays, the attraction of private restaurants lies in their individuality and exclusivity. This kind of glimpse into the cook's private life with all its preferences and idiosyncrasies, and the cozy atmosphere are things that no high class restaurant can offer. What is more, if you have to book your table several weeks in advance or if you are only allowed to come in the company of a regular patron, the VIP status is considerably enhanced along with the anticipation of enjoying the meal.

Right: Individual and exclusive: Anyone dining in a "private kitchen" will certainly get more preferential treatment than in a large restaurant.

Below: Unobtrusive and without any large neon signs: The best "private kitchens" are in the center of Hong Kong's residential areas.

Above: "You eat what is on the table" is the watch-word here. And as it should be with Chinese menus, there is usually plenty of it. However, a mixture of different, often non-Chinese cooking styles is entirely possible, dependent on the preferences of the person running the *sifang cai.*

Below: Even if the regulations applying to private restaurants are less strict, the standards are the same, because word of mouth is always the best advertisement, so no restaurant owner wants to be the subject of criticism.

Roast pigeons

Two small pigeons (each 7 oz / 200 g)
2 tsp salt
1 piece of leek (2 inch / 5 cm long)
1 piece of ginger (1 ½–2 inch / 4–5 cm long)
4 star anise
1 stick cinnamon
½ tsp fennel seeds
4 cups (1 liter) vegetable oil

Maltose sauce:
1 tbsp maltose
¾ cup (200 ml) water
2–3 tsp powdered water chestnuts
2 tsp rice vinegar

Wash the pigeons and cut off the feet, if neces-sary. Mix together the ingredients for the maltose sauce. Bring 4 cups (1 liter) water to a boil with the salt, leek, ginger, star anise, cinnamon stick, and fennel seeds, and simmer for 30 minutes. Then add the pigeons and cook for 10 minutes. Remove the pigeons and then pour over the maltose sauce.
Hang the pigeons for 4–6 hours.
Heat the oil in a wok at medium heat (up to about 340 °F/170 °C). Suspend the pigeons over the wok on long skewers and spoon the oil over them until they are golden brown. Then cut each pigeon into six pieces and arrange on a plate.

Macau 澳门

Katrin Schlotter

Situated in China's subtropical south, just 40 miles (65 km) away from Hong Kong, is Macau, a special administrative zone in the People's Republic of China. One might think that with 525,000 inhabitants compressed into an area of about 11 square miles (29 sq km), it scarcely merits a mention. Yet Macau has one very special attraction to offer: while keeping its mixture of East–West cultural heritage alive, it is also regarded as *the* gambling El Dorado of the future. This special administrative zone is comprised of the Macau peninsula, including the city of the same name, together with the islands of Taipa and Coloane, which are linked by Cotai. Since it was returned to the People's Republic in 1999, it has operated under the policy of "one land, two systems." Macau consequently enjoys a status similar to that of Hong Kong. Whereas Macau's foreign policy and national security is the responsibility of the People's Republic, its economic and social system will remain unchanged until 2049, as will the gambling industry. Macau is the only enclave anywhere in China where gambling is legal and it has experienced a dramatic upturn in its fortunes since the gambling industry was liberalized at the beginning of 2002. To encourage growth, a massive improvement had to be made in the infrastructure. A strip of land, known as the "Cotai Strip," was reclaimed to link the islands of Coloane and Taipa, new bridges were built and more frontier crossings were set up along the border with the Chinese mainland. China gradually eased the restrictions on individual Chinese citizens from the mainland wishing to visit Macau. Faster ferry links were established connecting Macau with the Pearl River delta and new direct flights were introduced to neighboring Asian countries and the rest of the world. At the same time, Chinese and foreign casino managers, including big Las Vegas names such as Sands and Wynn, began building luxury casino resorts and these entrepreneurs are continuing to invest. Their efforts have already borne fruit—growing numbers of tourists have vindicated the billions of dollars' worth of investment. The government is also profiting from this development since any gambling prizes are heavily taxed...Macau's economy is booming!

Macau's inhabitants, 95 percent of whom are Chinese from the provinces of Guangdong and Fujian, are quite laid back about Macau's transformation from a sleepy port to a buzzing hot spot of gambling and different cultures. Despite all these changes and the fast and furious pace of life in Macau, there is always time to enjoy a delicious meal of *African chicken*, two or three glasses of *vinho verde*, a coffee with the finest cream and, naturally, a chat with the neighbors.

Top: Macau's oldest and most beautiful temple dates from 1488. The temple is dedicated to the goddess A-Ma, guardian of fishermen, who continues to watch over the bay named in her honor "A-Ma Gao."

Above: As so often happens in modern China's urban centers, the old districts of Macau have been surrounded by skyscrapers.

Facing page: The imposing stone façade of St. Paul's Cathedral in the heart of the Old Town and the grand stairway leading up to it are reminders of Macau's Portuguese past.

Macau

Macau's past—turbulent times

Macau's last great golden age as a trading center was 400 years ago. During the Age of Discovery, the Portuguese, who were then Europe's greatest maritime and colonial power, landed in the Pearl River delta in the mid 16th century during their search for a suitable trading base between Portugal, India, and Japan. Fortune favored them in two respects: not only did they survive the perilous journey and attacks by pirates, who infested the South China Seas, but in 1557 they were also the first and only Europeans to be granted—following unsuccessful negotiations with the authorities on the Chinese mainland further north—permission to settle here, around a bay that was protected by the goddess of seafarers and fishermen, A–Ma. This bay, called A–Ma–Gao in Cantonese, was then named Macau by the Portuguese.

With China's consent, the Portuguese assumed the lucrative role of sole, legal agent for all trading activities between China and Japan, which included silk, porcelain, tea, and spices. As a result, Macau quickly grew into Asia's most important commercial center. Since a spiritual leader was clearly needed to complete the community, Macau's first Catholic bishop was appointed in 1576. The town continued to flourish as a trading center for almost a hundred years before the Dutch and the British gained the upper hand in the worldwide struggle for colonial supremacy. After China ceded Hong Kong to the British in 1842, the Portuguese were obliged to adopt a different market strategy. With commercial business now being relentlessly hijacked by neighboring Hong Kong, the Portuguese hit upon gambling as a means of filling their coffers and gaming was consequently legalized in 1847. By the time Portugal's supremacy over Macau was recognized by China in 1887 in the "Treaty on Friendship and Commerce," the enclave had long since become dependent on its revenues from gambling. Even Macau's industrialization during the 20th century did not fundamentally alter this situation in any way.

During World War II, Macau—unlike Hong Kong—was spared Japanese occupation and provided asylum to many refugees. It subsequently found itself once again facing a set of new circumstances. In 1951, Portugal declared Macau an overseas province. In 1976, however, in the aftermath of the "Carnation Revolution" (1974), Macau was awarded the status of a territory under Portuguese administration but with its own constitution. It was not until Portugal relinquished its territorial sovereignty over Macau that China resumed diplomatic relations with Portugal in 1979. Negotiations between Portugal and China on Macau's future began in 1986 and a decision was reached the following year to grant Macau the status of a special administrative region of the People's Republic with effect from December 20, 1999. Since then, Macau has operated under the policy of "one land, two systems," which could more accurately be expressed as "one land, two systems—and a large number of cultures."

Left: A–Ma temple, built in the 14th century in honor of the goddess of seafarers, is one of Macau's oldest buildings and is listed as a UNESCO World Heritage Site. Its pavilions, prayer niches and altars are dedicated to the Taoist patroness of seafarers, A–Ma, as well as to the Buddhist goddess of mercy, Kun Iam.

Below left: High humidity is a typical feature of Macau's subtropical climate. When temperatures begin to rise in April, people are grateful for every breath of air they can catch from the balcony.

Below right: Although Macau's shopping streets are very busy, the city is reputed to be quieter and more relaxed than neighboring Hong Kong.

Left: Since the Old Town was added to UNESCO's list of World Heritage Sites, the administration has been at pains to preserve the legacy of the city's old buildings.

Below: The Old Town is best explored on foot. The Largo do Senado (Senate Square) is an ideal starting-point for a tour of the town.

Bottom: The area around Largo do Senado bears testimony to the days when Macau was a hub of East-West cultural exchange.

Macau's culinary heritage

Coconut, saffron, and rosemary do not sound like typical ingredients of Chinese food any more than *achar*, *balichang*, or *limao de Timor*. Yet connoisseurs of Chinese cuisine will prick up their ears at the mention of these ingredients, chutneys, and spicy pastes. Macanese cuisine—one of the world's oldest examples of fusion cuisine—is a successful blend of southern Chinese and Portuguese cuisines, delicately seasoned with spices from all over the world, making it a unique culinary experience in its own right.

Like so many things, Macanese culinary traditions have their roots in the days of Portuguese colonialism. When Portuguese sailors and merchants landed in Macau in the mid 16th century, they brought with them not only their own recipes and ingredients, such as olive oil, wine,

and sweetmeats, but also a vast number of ingredients from the colonies. Spices, such as chili, nutmeg, cloves, and curcuma, found their way to Macau via the Portuguese trade routes between Africa, America, and Southeast Asia. Once here, they encountered the fresh cuisine of Guangdong. Since then, these newfound culinary delicacies have bubbled away in Macanese cooking pots and evolved into an altogether unique style of culinary tradition, as illustrated for example in the recipe for African Chicken, a dish said to have been brought to Macau by African slaves.

Many preparation methods—such as marinating and braising—have, like spices, merged in a fusion of East-West cooking techniques, producing many delicious crisp and tender culinary delights.

Seafood, particularly crayfish and giant shrimp, likewise takes on a distinctive—and somewhat addictive—flavor, when prepared in the Macanese style: a paste made from chili, ginger, garlic, scallions, and cilantro is rubbed under the scales along the back of giant shrimp. These are then fried on both sides until they turn red in color. A dash of rice wine sprinkled over the shrimp finishes off the dish to perfection.

Small fish and crabs combined with bay leaves, garlic, black peppercorns, and wine are processed into a paste, *balichang*, used for flavoring sauces or it can also be served with meat dishes.

This diversity of flavors is reflected in the range of food offered on menus. Cha-Gordo, for example, a traditional Macanese feast of little dishes, involves tables laden with pickles and chutneys (vegetables and fruits conserved in vinegar or lime juice), dumplings stuffed with ground beef, fried fish cakes, cheese on toast, or vegetable pasties. Main courses will include elegant fish and chicken dishes, as well as substantial stews, such as *minchi*, a classic dish of fried ground meat, prepared with mushrooms, potatoes or pumpkin, or rice noodle dishes such as *lacassa*.

Left: There is space even in the tiniest kitchen—even if none of these ladies is likely to be awarded any coveted Michelin Guide stars, which six Macau restaurants now boast.

Right: Were it not for the Chinese lettering, this sign could easily be in Lisbon or Porto.

Below: Even though most of Macau's nightlife is centered upon its hotels and casinos, the streets are rarely quiet or deserted.

To finish a meal, Macanese cuisine offers a virtually endless variety of sweet dishes and cakes, which, along with a coffee or a glass of port, may provide the crowning moment to a delicious culinary experience in this food lovers' paradise.

The world of casinos

In Macau, wherever you look, good food is a priority. There are restaurants in every corner of the city catering for every taste and to suit every wallet. Food stalls, Chinese bars, cosy Portuguese or Macanese taverns, as well as Japanese, Korean, and even Western-style eateries abound, not to mention any number of cafés and bars. The appetite for different types of food is insatiable and the more Macau develops as a mecca of gambling and tourism, the more colorful is its gastronomic scene, ranging from noodle bars to haute cuisine. The casinos and theme parks, in particular, offer a whole range of new culinary experiences to their clientele, most of whom come from mainland China.

For many people—whether it be rural farmers intent on a personal flutter, or possibly trying their luck on behalf of the whole village, or managers from China's new middle classes—a visit to Macau not only means having fun at the casinos, but also getting a glimpse of a completely different world—namely of a Europe situated just the other side of the Chinese border. Since Chinese people only have short holidays and any time spent in Macau therefore will inevitably be limited, a theme park has been created adjacent to the Old Town, now listed as a world heritage site. At the "Fisherman's Wharf" complex, which is open 24 hours a day, visitors can marvel over themed areas which recreate sights and scenes from ancient times and from other continents before indulging in a session of international shopping and dining. To the European mind it may seem a little bizarre to sit down to a meal of Macanese food in surroundings which artificially mimic the ambience of old colonial days when the original Old Town is only a stone's throw away, but the Chinese tend to be more pragmatic in this respect. Their policy is to cram as many experiences as possible into the minimum amount of time.

When they are not actually involved in chancing their luck at the gaming tables, visitors to the luxury casinos have the opportunity to sample various international cuisines without even having to leave the casino. Leading the way in this respect was Dr. Stanley Ho, a Macau casino baron, who opened the Rebouchon de Galera restaurant, an establishment specializing in French gourmet cuisine and boasting an outstanding wine menu, in his highly traditional Casino Lisboa, thereby adding a classic European-style menu to what had, until then, been predominantly Chinese-style cuisine.

Various other glittering Las Vegas-style gambling palaces, such as Sands Macao and Wynn Macau, followed suit. In addition to their casino facilities, these also include five-star hotels, shopping malls packed with numerous international designer stores, and restaurants to suit every pocket, all under one roof. However, many of the top restaurants, smoking lounges, and bars remain the preserve of the "high rollers," in other words, the professional gamblers who enjoy special VIP service—from a helicopter shuttle service, private rooms, to six-course meals, individually prepared in one's suite, there is no wish that cannot be fulfilled.

Even the vast majority of ordinary players can sample delicacies from all over the world. Buffets offer a range of Macanese, southern Chinese, or even Western cuisine, as well as Korean and Japanese dishes, often prepared and cooked—in

Left: Around 20 million people visit Macau's casinos each year.

Right: Twenty-four hours a day, seven days a week—and no limit on the stakes!

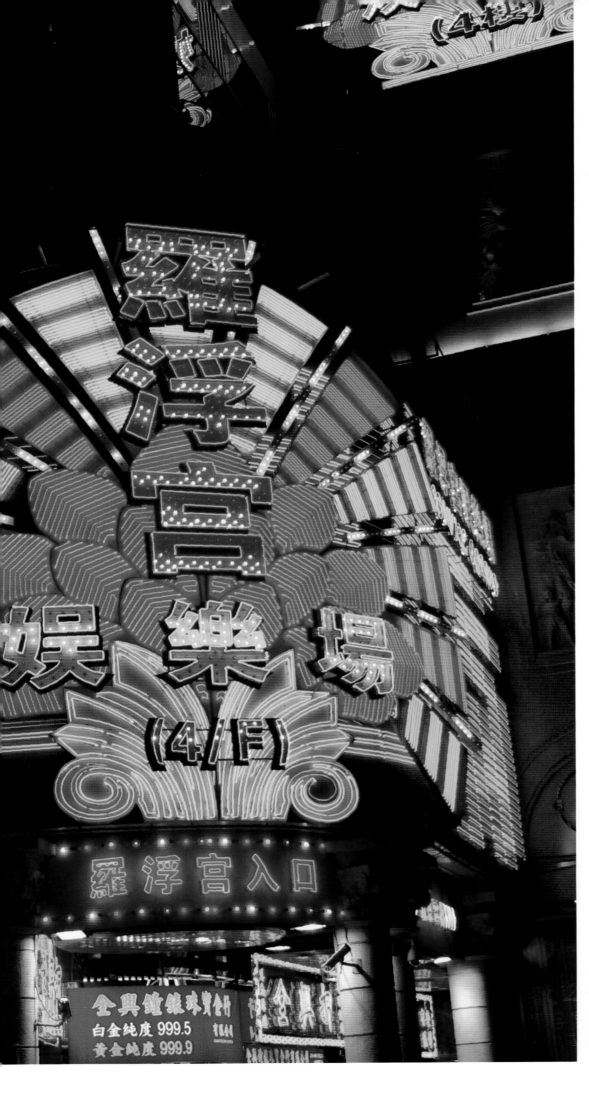

keeping with recent trends in restaurant dining—right in front of the customer.

And there is one further trend that is beginning to emerge—casinos that feature "worlds of experience." Since summer 2007, the Archangel Gabriel has been watching over a really top-class casino resort on the newly reclaimed Cotai land strip, known as the Venetian Macao Casino Resort. Costing around 5 billion US dollars, it is currently the world's largest casino complex and was built by the US Las Vegas Sands Corporation. Modeled on Venice, it comprises nearly 30 restaurants between the Grand Canal, St. Mark's Square, and the Rialto Bridge. Instead of noble Italian pasta, however, one is more likely to find a wide choice of international culinary delights, ranging from Chinese specialties, such as shark's fin soup and abalone, to sushi, freshly flown in from Japan, and US-reared beef. There are also snack bars offering fast food, or even "halal food," prepared according to Muslim food preparation laws. This is, after all, a place where every wish can come true.

Below: Tycoon Stephen Alan Wynn is just one of many entrepreneurs who have invested in Macau's billion-dollar, luxury hotel resorts and casinos.

A stroll through the market hall

The route to Macau's most famous market hall, known as "Red Market," passes birds chirruping in small aviaries, stalls selling exotic fruit and subtropical flowers and is, in itself, a feast for the senses. Drawn by the shouts of rival traders selling their wares, housewives and chefs intent on their shopping mission push past fish-sellers with their heavy crates and enter the red-brick building, which was built in 1936 and is now a listed building. The market is the first port-of-call for all food lovers.

Inside the building amid the hustle and bustle, people jostle for prime position in order to view the produce and haggle over the price. Wherever the crowds are thickest, there is bound to be some specialty on sale. A crowd of people is gathering between the stalls of deep red sausages and silver stockfish—what might be on sale there? Perhaps exactly the right sort of small fish and miniature crabs to make *balichang*, or Macanese shrimp paste. Surrounded by all these spices and conserves, the hundreds of different varieties of fruit and vegetables, the clucking hens, and other livestock, one gains a very real sense of Macau's culinary traditions.

Eels writhe in tubs of bubbling water, while, next to them, crabs struggle to escape from their baskets. Fish and shellfish are left alive until a customer materializes. One well-aimed blow, a few final moments of convulsive twitching with gills gasping—this is not a sight for those of a sensitive disposition, whose only experience of dead animals is limited to prepackaged meat bought from supermarket shelves. The Chinese are concerned first and foremost with a product's freshness. Given the subtropical climate and the long transport routes, this is a top priority when shopping for food.

Fresh goods are delivered to the Red Market twice a day, usually from the neighboring regions across the border. For several centuries, nearly all food items, except for fish, have been imported from the province of Guangdong which is just next door. The reason for this is clear: when the Portuguese leased the Macau peninsula in the 16th century, there was no room in this small area for any arable or livestock farming. They were far more concerned with promoting commerce, and building summer residences and churches. Macau's last remaining acres of arable land disappeared as its population grew. Macau largely depended—as indeed it still does to this day—on China for its food supplies. From a culinary point of view, this is an advantage since it combines the freshness of Cantonese produce with the sophistication of Macanese cuisine: a perfect marriage.

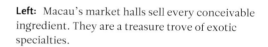

Macau chicken

Marinade:
3 ½ tbsp dry white wine
1 tsp salt
½ tsp black pepper
2–3 bay leaves, chopped
2–3 pinches of powdered saffron

1 chicken, (about 2 ¼ lb / 1 kg), cut into 6–8 pieces
olive oil, for frying
1 onion, roughly chopped
1 garlic clove, roughly chopped
1 tsp red curry paste
1 tomato, roughly diced
4–5 firm potatoes, parboiled for 15 minutes, then peeled and quartered
⅔ cup (150 ml) coconut milk, well beaten
3 ½ tbsp milk
salt

2 hardcooked eggs, shelled and cut into quarters
8–10 thin slices of chorizo sausage, or air-dried ham may be used instead
2 tsp shredded coconut
4 black olives
freshly ground pepper

Left: Macau's market halls sell every conceivable ingredient. They are a treasure trove of exotic specialties.

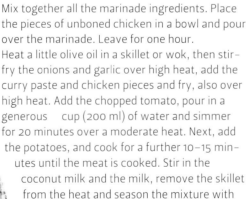

Mix together all the marinade ingredients. Place the pieces of unboned chicken in a bowl and pour over the marinade. Leave for one hour.
Heat a little olive oil in a skillet or wok, then stir-fry the onions and garlic over high heat, add the curry paste and chicken pieces and fry, also over high heat. Add the chopped tomato, pour in a generous   cup (200 ml) of water and simmer for 20 minutes over a moderate heat. Next, add the potatoes, and cook for a further 10–15 minutes until the meat is cooked. Stir in the coconut milk and the milk, remove the skillet from the heat and season the mixture with salt to taste.
Arrange the dish with the egg, sliced sausage, shredded coconut and olives, sprinkle with freshly ground pepper and cook under the broiler for a few minutes until the coconut begins to turn brown.

Top left: The choice of meat is overwhelming. In addition to poultry, beef, pork, and game, you will find types of meat which are unobtainable in Europe.

Top right: The same is true of fish and seafood. The choice is endless. Fish is one of the few locally available food resources which also means transportation distances are short, an important consideration in subtropical temperatures.

Above left: Product freshness is a top priority for shoppers in the market halls. Customers may, if they wish, have the meat prepared according to their individual requirements.

Above center: 55 RMB (around 8 US dollars/£4.84/Euros 5.4)—the top price for a whole duck.

Above right: Food stalls selling snacks can be found in every market hall in Macau. It is, after all, a well-known fact that food shopping makes you feel hungry.

Hot favorites—sweet and spicy sausages

Bright bundles of shiny red sausages, sorted according to thickness, length, and age, can be seen dangling from market stalls or souvenir shops virtually all over Macau. *Lap Cheung*, as they are called in Cantonese, which along with the dried meat and mushrooms, and not forgetting the sweet cookies (see p. 310), are one of Macau's specialties. Sausages, especially the ones found in Cantonese cuisine, can be made from any number of different ingredients but despite all the clichés, they do not contain dog or monkey meat. These thin, shiny red sausages are produced from pork while the almost black varieties contain duck, goose, or pork liver. Depending on the particular variety, the seasoning can include soy sauce, rice wine, sugar, paprika, pepper, cinnamon, anise, fennel, or ginger.

In times of poverty, Chinese sausages were regarded as a cheap alternative to meat, which was only served, if at all, on special occasions. A few slices of sausage, mixed with rice or vegetables would give a warm dish a meaty flavour as well as making it seem that much more nutritious. Regardless of whether they are fiery hot sausages from western China, or sweet and slightly spicy ones from southern China, sausages still form an important part of everyday Chinese fare. Unlike Western types of sausage, which are boiled, salted, or smoked, Chinese sausages are air-dried—always a risky business in a warm, humid climate, which is why Lap Cheung are traditionally made in winter, in other words when the air is dry and cool. The uncooked sausages only keep well if they are dried at temperatures between 59 °F and 71 °F (15–22 °C) and after fermentation has produced a specific pH-value which prevents the growth of

harmful bacteria. The Chinese use sugar instead of salt as a preservative. This accounts for their sweetish flavour, which can be something of a problem to the Western palate.

There are two traditional types of sausage in Macau and the reason for this is that while the Chinese and Macanese are partial to their *Lap Cheung*, the Portuguese, naturally enough, have always preferred their own chouriço sausage (also known in Europe by its Spanish name "chorizo"), which was imported from their homeland. This firm, air-dried, or lightly smoked sausage made from pork and fat has a distinctly salty flavour and is seasoned with garlic, paprika, and chili. The different varieties—some also contain cumin, thyme, or oregano—are thinly sliced and served cold, as a starter. Fried chouriço may be added to a variety of Portuguese dishes, such as Caldo verde, to give them a distinctive flavor.

Caldo verde

1 tbsp salt
1 tsp white pepper
6 medium-sized potatoes, peeled and quartered
⅔ cup (150 ml) olive oil, for frying
6 garlic cloves, crushed
1 onion, finely diced
3 ½ oz (100 g) chorizo sausage, or Debreczin, or air-dried ham, thinly sliced
1 bunch of spinach, bok choy, or Chinese cabbage, finely chopped

Heat 2 ½ quarts (2.5 liters) water, add the salt and pepper and bring to a boil. Add the potatoes and boil until cooked. Drain (but save the water), transfer the potatoes to a bowl and mash well, then return the mashed potato to the water. Heat most of the olive oil in a wok or skillet and stir-fry the garlic until lightly browned. Add the diced onion and stir-fry until almost transparent, then add the sliced sausage or ham and fry until the onions are transparent and the sausage is cooked.

Mix the ingredients from the wok with the mashed potato mixture in the saucepan and stir well. Bring to a boil, then add the green vegetables and cook for about 5 minutes. Serve hot in individual bowls and drizzle a little olive oil over each portion.

Left: The star attraction here is the sausage—or rather the sausages, for there are two main types of this popular delicacy: sweet and spicy, or wholesome and salty.

Left: The bundles of sausages seen hanging in Macau's butchers' stores are a good advertisement for the quality of goods on display. Sausages have long since shed their reputation for being merely a cheap alternative to meat. They now have an accepted role—as an appetizer, for example—in various types of southern Chinese cuisine.

Below: Macanese sausage—made in the traditional European fashion—is similar to Spanish chorizo or Portuguese chouriço. It is a firm, spicy, coarse sausage made from pork, which derives its deep-red coloring from paprika and chili.

Portugal in a wok

Galinha a Cafreal
African chicken

1 chicken, (about 2 ¼ lb / 1 kg)
7 tbsp butter, melted
8–10 garlic cloves, finely chopped
2 fresh red chiles finely chopped
2 fresh green chiles, finely chopped
1 tsp salt
2–3 bay leaves, finely chopped
3 ½ tbsp chicken stock
⅔ cup (150 ml) coconut milk

Position the chicken on a chopping board in such a way that the backbone can be separated using a large kitchen knife (without actually cutting right through the chicken!).
Turn the chicken over and make an incision in the breastbone. Using a board or similar object, press the chicken flat and place it in a suitable casserole dish.
Finely chop 6–8 garlic cloves and mix with half the butter, the chiles, salt, and bay leaves, thinning the mixture, if necessary, with a little stock. Spread this marinade over the chicken, cover, and leave in a cool place for 10–12 hours. When ready to cook, finely chop the remaining garlic cloves and add with the remaining butter to the coconut milk and stock and whisk gently until it begins to froth.
Place the marinated chicken in a roasting pan, skin side upward, and roast for about 1 hour in the oven at 300–320 °F (150–160 °C), basting regularly with the butter and coconut milk marinade so that the skin becomes brown and crisp.
To serve, remove the chicken from the oven, stir the sauce well and pour over the chicken.

Shrimp curry

3 ½ tbsp butter
1 small onion, finely diced
2 garlic cloves, finely chopped
1 fresh chile, finely chopped
1 ½ tsp curry powder
5 tbsp cornstarch
1 ⅔ cups (400 ml) chicken stock
2 bay leaves
14 oz (400 g) shrimp
⅓ cup (75 ml) coconut milk
1 tsp salt
1 pinch white pepper

To serve:
8 quails' eggs, hardcooked
4 ½ oz (125 g) shrimp, peeled and blanched

Melt the butter in a wok but do not overheat. Add the onions, garlic, and chile and stir-fry lightly before adding the curry powder and cornstarch, stirring constantly. Pour in the chicken stock and continue stirring. Add the bay leaves and slowly bring the curry to a boil.
Reduce the heat and stir in the shrimp. Reduce the heat and simmer for a few minutes. Continue stirring carefully, pour in the coconut milk, bring to a boil and season with salt and pepper.
Remove the bay leaves, if preferred.
The curry should be served hot, garnished with the shrimp and quails' eggs.

Baked perch with mussels in tomato sauce

1 river perch (about 2 ¼ lb / 1 kg), gutted and descaled
⅔ cup / 150 ml dry white wine
juice of 1 lemon
1 tsp salt
3 ½ tbsp olive oil
1 red and 1 green bell pepper, seeds and pith removed, roughly chopped
1 onion, sliced into thick rings
4 garlic cloves, crushed
2 tomatoes, thinly sliced
⅓ cup (75 ml) fish stock
3 ½ tbsp tomato paste
2 bay leaves
7 oz (200 g) mussels, without shells

Using a sharp knife, make a few shallow incisions in the skin of the fish.
Mix 3 ½ tablespoons of the white wine with the lemon juice and salt and pour over the fish. Leave to marinate for 20 minutes, then fry in a wok for 5 minutes on each side in 1 tablespoon of olive oil. Remove and set aside.

Pour the remaining olive oil into a large wok and heat gently. Stir-fry the bell peppers, onions, and garlic for about 5 minutes. Add the sliced tomato, the remaining wine, and the fish stock, then stir in the tomato paste and bay leaves and bring the mixture to a boil. Reduce the heat, cover with a lid and simmer for about 25 minutes. Finally, add the mussels and continue stirring.

Preheat the oven to 355 °F /180 °C (or 320 °F/ 160 °C if using a fan oven). Place the fish in a large ovenproof dish, pour over the tomato and mussel sauce and bake for 8–10 minutes.

Coloane—back to nature and tradition

This is Macau's quieter, southerly island and is situated just a short taxi ride from the city center. Once the home of farmers and fishermen, the arrival of Portuguese traders in the 16th century turned Coloane into a veritable pirates' nest—the last attack on richly laden Portuguese vessels was as recent as a hundred years ago.

Despite being directly connected to the neighboring island of Taipa—and despite its deep-water harbors, leisure parks and golf courses—Coloane's forest-clad hills and network of walking trails offer an atmosphere of peace and quiet and its narrow village streets still exude an air of nostalgia. During the daytime, life centers on the small businesses and workshops, but in the evening the focus switches to the village square. Next to the cream and white Chapel of St. Francis Xavier—and along the neoclassical arcades—are numerous traditional restaurants fronting the old square. On balmy subtropical evenings, up to a hundred people could be dining here, seemingly part of one big family celebration. Exotic scents waft across the square, the spicy aromas of shellfish, ginger, and garlic. Baked scallops, fish soup, mountains of bright red shrimp, fried sardines, and fish specialties fresh from the coast are on the menu here, prepared simply but perfectly according to old family recipes. Nowhere else in Macau will you find such an authentic blend of ingredients, aromas, and atmosphere and a sense of having been transported back to colonial times.

After dining, it is worth taking time to look at the chapel. Sent to Lisbon as a papal envoy, Francis Xavier was the first Jesuit missionary to set off for India in 1541 to bring the Roman Catholic faith to "heathens" all over Asia. He died not far from Macau, never having managed to reach China. His guiding conviction that the only way to spread the Christian faith was to link it to local rituals and customs has remained alive and, sure enough, inside the little chapel built in 1928, red Chinese lanterns hang alongside images of the Virgin Mary and Jesus, both depicted with rosy, Chinese features. And the Holy Ghost seems to float above the crucifix on the sky-blue wall, in contrast to how it is usually portrayed in Christian churches: above Christ on the Cross.

Over the course of history, there have been repeated periods of vigorous debate within the Church as to whether—and if so, to what extent—local religious influences should be allowed to be absorbed into Christian beliefs. Nonetheless, Christianity has managed to survive several centuries since the diocese in Macau was founded in 1576 and religious freedom has continued to be upheld there even after it was handed back to China. Today, about 7 percent of the population are members of the Roman Catholic faith and 2 percent of the population are Protestants.

The main religion among the Macanese, however, is still the original Chinese religious philosophy that combines elements of Buddhism, Taoism and Confucianism. As is demonstrated time and time again in Macau, diversity is what really matters.

Giant shrimp à la Macau

8 fresh red chiles, finely chopped
4–5 scallions, finely chopped
4 garlic cloves, finely chopped
paprika, mild and sweet variety
3 ½ tbsp dry white wine
8 giant shrimp, washed, but not peeled
3 ½ tbsp olive oil, for frying
2–3 bay leaves, finely chopped
1 tbsp clarified butter

Combine the chiles, scallions, garlic, a pinch of paprika, and wine to make a marinade. Place the giant shrimp in a bowl and pour over the marinade. Leave to stand in a cool place for about one hour.

Remove the shrimp from the marinade and stir-fry quickly in hot olive oil for 4–5 minutes until they turn red on the outside. Remove the shrimp from the oil and keep warm.

Pour the marinade through a fine strainer and retain the liquid. Mix the vegetables from the marinade with the bay leaves and fry in the butter for a few moments over a high heat. Add the liquid from the marinade, mix the ingredients together and bring to a boil. Pour the resulting sauce over the hot shrimp and serve immediately.

Above: Coloane is a quiet, picturesque place, situated on Macau's southern island, with a population of just over 3,000 people. Nonetheless, it is packed with inviting restaurants on every corner.

Above: Only 7 percent of Macanese are Roman Catholics. Almost every chapel contains relics from the days when Roman Catholic priests came to China to convert "heathens."

Macau's sweet desserts

One of the classic desserts on the menu in China is a plate of fresh orange segments. Although this dish is undoubtedly a healthier, more sensible, and perfectly reasonable option, this must nonetheless come as something of a disappointment to anyone with a sweet tooth. The enticing array of sweets and desserts typical of Macau could not be more different, however.

The aroma of cream, eggs, caramel, and a suggestion of cinnamon and lemon rises from warm egg custard tarts, evoking for many of us perhaps a nostalgic memory of innocent childhood. Once the delicate layer of caramel has been breached, these little delicacies melt on the tongue—until it encounters the puff pastry shell, a crisp finale. Small wonder, therefore, that these *pasteis de nata* have become a Macau specialty. However, it was a British pharmacist, Andrew Stow, the proprietor of "Lord Stow's Bakery" in Coloane, who created his own version of this Portuguese confectionery and produced a tart so delicious that its fame has spread far beyond the territorial confines of Macau. This is possible due in part to the fact that the tarts combine key elements of

Chinese cuisine: sweet and sour, sweet and bitter, soft and crisp.

Nowhere else in China is there such a diversity of cakes, puddings, or cookies as in Macau. The recipes for desserts such as *papos de anjos*, *barrigas de freiras*, and *toucinho do céu* were originally created by nuns in Portuguese convents. It is remarkable to think they were invented purely to use up leftovers. Since the nuns used huge quantities of egg white to starch their habits, they were always left with a large amount of egg yolk—the perfect basis for truly heavenly confectionery and desserts.

Like so much else, the dessert recipes, which were first introduced to Macau by the Portuguese, have—over the centuries—acquired various Chinese characteristics. The addition of a caramel topping with cinnamon, for example, has given the egg tart an authentic—in other words, Chinese—flavor in just the same way that cream pudding has evolved into coconut pudding.

Macau's sweet temptations never fail to leave the visitor with one thing: a delighted smile and lasting memories.

Left: Cookies, confectionery, and other sweet delicacies—Macau is definitely the Chinese paradise for anyone with a sweet tooth.

Below: Traditional moon cakes are a Chinese specialty, which are eaten and presented as gifts to celebrate the lunar festival. They usually contain egg yolk in the center, surrounded by sweet or sometimes savory paste.

Coconut pudding

1 ¼ cups (300 ml) milk
½ cup (100 g sugar)
large piece of unwaxed lemon
   peel
2 tbsp cornmeal
½ cup (120 ml) coconut milk
4 egg yolks, lightly beaten

Stir the sugar into the milk,
add the lemon peel and
bring the milk slowly to a
boil. Leave to cool, removing the lemon peel.
Stir the cornmeal into the
coconut milk, add the egg yolks
and beat the ingredients together
until frothy, then pour the mixture into
the milk and bring slowly to a boil over a low
heat, stirring constantly until the pudding thickens and turns creamy.
Divide the dessert into four small bowls and leave
to cool before serving.

Below: Portuguese *pasteis de nata:* creamy egg
tarts, topped with caramel, on a base of crisp
puff pastry, and exuding an aroma of cinnamon
and lemon.

Below left and bottom: It is difficult to say whether
this mouth-watering confectionery is Portuguese
or Chinese in origin but they are all, without
exception, delicious and sweet.

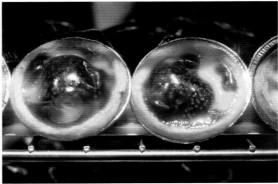

Festivals—dragon dances and Easter eggs

The Macanese festival season, which keeps the town busy all year long, begins on New Year's Eve with the loud banging and whizzing of exploding fireworks. In Macau, with its background of Chinese and Portuguese influences, traditional Chinese festivals—which are dictated by the lunar calendar—alternate with Christian festivals. There are about 20 official public holidays in Macau, not counting the many international events—such as Formula 3 racing—and the Macau Grand Prix motorbike racing. Here is a brief summary of the different festivals:

Chinese New Year Festival

Whereas New Year celebrations in the West are mainly just about having fun, the activities surrounding this all-important Chinese family festival, known as *chunjie* (more on this subject in the chapter on Hong Kong, p. 286) are geared toward making sure of happiness and wellbeing throughout the coming year. Disputes are set aside, debts paid off, the gods pacified, and the apartment cleaned. There is one distinctive feature about the Chinese New Year in Macau, however: namely, that local civil servants are not allowed to enter the gambling casinos—except on the first three days of the new lunar year, which falls between the end of January and the middle of February.

Easter and Christmas

Processions, pilgrimages, and nativity plays—the Christian community has introduced its own traditions and festivals into Macanese everyday life, including the kind of elaborate decorations and lavish meals one would experience in Portugal. Easter is celebrated with chocolate eggs and egg tarts, while Christmas is the peak season for cookies and cakes, even among the non-Christian population.

Qing Ming and Feast of the Hungry Ghosts

The Qing Ming Festival at the beginning of April is traditionally a time for remembering one's ancestors. In contrast to western traditions, a visit to the cemetery is a jolly occasion for the Chinese. Ancestors are supposed to be contented "on the other side" and, in order to dissuade them from any notion of returning to this world and making mischief as bad spirits, their families decorate their graves with flowers, burn paper money and other essential items, such as cell phones or cars, in paper form. Steamed chicken, crispy duck, and fruits are brought to the grave—in Macau the food is accompanied by three small glasses of wine. The communal family picnic at the grave is supposed to bring good luck—both in the here and now, as well as in the afterlife. To cater for restless spirits, who have no relatives to care for them, the Feast of Hungry Ghosts is held in August on the streets and celebrated with Chinese firecrackers, opera performances, and delicious food.

Buddha, Tam Kung, and the Drunken Dragon

Three festivals— Buddha's birthday, Tam Kung, and the Festival of the Drunken Dragon—are held on the same day in May—on the eighth day of the fourth lunar month. While Buddha's birthday is celebrated with recitations and cleansing rituals, Tam Kung, the Taoist weather god, is honored by gong-beating, Chinese firecrackers, and Chinese opera, the intention being to drive away bad spirits, which might cause inclement weather. The Festival of the Drunken Dragon is another noisy occasion when young Macanese wearing dragon costumes dance their way in a colorful and inebriated procession through the old city center.

Right: The participants in the Festival of the Drunken Dragon dance and drink their way from Kuan Tai Temple near Senate Square to the harbor as an expression of— undoubtedly well deserved—gratitude to this mythical creature for fertility and good fortune.

Right and below right: The New Year celebrations on the first day of the Chinese lunar year (usually in February) are traditionally celebrated with elaborate meals, fireworks, and dragon dancing.

Right: Eggs at Easter and delicious moon cakes during the autumn moon festival—both excuses to indulge oneself in Macau.

Below right: Dragons are regarded in China not only as protectors and bringers of good luck but also as symbols of male potency.

This spectacular festival is based on a legend and is intended as an expression of thanks to the dragon for fertility and wellbeing.

The moon festival

The romantic moon festival, celebrated on the 15th day of the eighth month (end of September), is traditionally celebrated outdoors in the park or on Coloane beach with family and friends. This is the night to marvel at the full moon, which on this night is particularly beautiful and round—even in places across the sea—while thinking of loved ones far away. This festival has particular significance in Macau as many of its residents have migrated here and live far away from their families. Moon cakes, which people give each other during the moon festival, are supposed to provide comfort in the face of separation. About the size of the palm of your hand and around two inches (5 cm) deep, these sweet or salty cakes come in any number of delicious varieties. The cake usually contains an egg yolk at its center, which is enveloped by a sweet bean paste, by nuts, dates, sesame or coconut. On the outside, the cakes are decorated—like so many things in Macau—with good luck symbols: better to be safe than sorry.

Yunnan

云南

Elke Spielmanns-Rome

Time seems to pass more slowly in Yunnan, a singularly beautiful region bordering on Vietnam, Laos, and Myanmar (Burma). The land "south of the clouds" is blessed with a rich biodiversity of flora and fauna, outclassing all the other Chinese provinces. Flowers alone are practically mass products here, especially roses and orchids; in the provincial capital, Kunming, wedding limousines are always decorated with a veritable avalanche of petals. In 1999 Yunnan came to worldwide attention as the host of the International Horticultural Expo. Yunnan has a greater diversity of plants than almost any other region on earth, and its epithet, "the Kingdom of Plants," is no mere boast: over 18,000 plant species—about 60 percent of China's flora—are native to this province.

Yunnan, which covers an area about two-thirds the size of France, stretches across the far southwest of China and offers many areas where nature has been left to its own devices, from snow-covered mountains to valleys with tropical or subtropical vegetation. The province is traversed by great rivers like the Yangtze and the Mekong, and has stunning lakeland scenery. Yunnan is also China's most prolific mushroom-growing area. The province is rich in resources, particularly coal, crude oil, natural gas, metals, and nonmetals. The chief source of income is the tobacco industry, but Yunnan is also China's most important producer of flowers, nuts, and coffee, and the region's pu-erh tea is exported all over the world. Yet Yunnan contributes to less than 1 percent of China's foreign trade. About 80 percent of the population makes its living from farming, and purchasing power is very low as a result; Yunnan is one of the country's poorest provinces.

A southwestern outpost

Far away from the dynastic powerbases, Yunnan was long governed by independent kings. The kingdom of Dian (c. 600 B.C.–A.D. 100) lay near the present-day provincial capital of Kunming; discoveries of bronze and jewelry attest to its sophisticated culture, markedly different from that of central China. When the power and influence of the Qin (221–206 B.C.) and Han dynasties (206 B.C.–220 A.D.) spread to this region, Dian became a tributary state of the Han kingdom.

In the 7th century the Bai people established the Kingdom of Nanzhao in western Yunnan, and made Dali their first capital, with Kunming their second city. Although the Bai initially formed an alliance with the Chinese Tang dynasty (618–907) against the Tibetans, they ended up

Top: Yunnan's rice terraces are among the most spectacular man-made landscapes in southwestern China.

Above: Far from the hustle and bustle of the big cities, life in Yunnan takes a leisurely pace, set by the rhythms of farming.

Facing page: Tiger Leaping Gorge, northwest of the city of Lijiang, is both a miracle of nature and an exhilarating sight. It is one of the deepest ravines in the world.

Yunnan **317**

Above: Visitors can see bizarre rock formations at the Shilin stone forest, southeast of Kunming.

Above right: The stone sculptures in the karst landscape are up to 100 feet (30 m) high. They were scoured out of the rock over time, or created by erosion.

defeating the Chinese troops stationed in the region and controlling the trade routes to Myanmar (Burma) and India. When the Kingdom of Nanzhao fell in the 10th century, the Kingdom of Dali arose in its place, only to be overrun by the Mongols in the 13th century; Yunnan was subsequently absorbed as a province of the great Mongolian Yuan empire (1271–1368) and remained a hard-to-reach border bastion, with scattered military strongholds and a population made up of many different tribes. The Chinese empire saw Yunnan as a kind of "outpost" in the far southwest, and being sent there meant the end of an official's career, and life in the Diaspora. Later, however, many a disgraced official wished never to leave the heavenly province.

Yunnan was remote and the emperor far away. Predictably, mounting rebellions began to jeopardize the central authority. Following the founding of the Manchurian Qing dynasty in the north in 1644, Chinese unity still remained to be achieved. Three generals succeeded in conquering southern and southwestern China at the end of the 1650s, and subsequently appointed themselves rulers of the captured territories. Yunnan and Guizhou provinces were controlled by General Wu Sangui (1612–1678), who created a new dynasty and crowned himself emperor. In 1681 Kangxi, the Qing emperor, succeeded in bringing the southern areas of the province under his scepter after intense fighting.

About 200 years later it was the turn of the Muslim Hui people to rebel against the Qing regime in Yunnan. The large number of Hui in the province dates back to the time when Muslim traders and craftsmen followed on the heels of the Mongol incursion into the area. The high property taxes and extra duties that the Qing emperor imposed upon the poor province brought the long-simmering conflicts between the Chinese and Muslim populations to boiling point in 1855. Public riots resulted in the Chinese undertaking a wide-ranging offensive against the Muslims, who responded by occupying Kunming (albeit for a brief period only) and capturing the city of Dali. Here the leader Du Wenxiu established the "Pacified Southern Kingdom" and named himself "Sultan Suleiman." The Qing troops only succeeded in recapturing Dali in 1873.

From the end of the 19th century onward, western powers also attempted to gain a foothold in Yunnan. The French came from Indochina, and the British entered the Chinese border province by way of Myanmar. Around the turn of the century several towns in Yunnan were opened up for foreign trade, and in 1910 the French completed the railroad from Hanoi to Kunming.

When Japan began its unstoppable advance during the Second Sino-Japanese War (1937–1945), the nationalists (Kuomintang) shifted their capital from Nanjing to the west, to the city of Chongqing (then part of

Above: The Yangtze, China's longest river, wends its way sluggishly through the landscape. Along with the Mekong, the Red river, and the Salween, it is one of the four great rivers that flow through the province.

Below: Rice, maize, and wheat are the three principal cereals cultivated in Yunnan. The climate and the richness of the soil promise good harvests in the many large valleys hemmed in by mountains.

Top: In many places, rice paddies must be cultivated without the use of machines.

Above (middle): Almost all villages hold a weekly market.

Above: If no machines or draft animals are available, the fruits of daily labor must be transported on foot.

Sichuan Province). One of the greatest feats of their leader, Chiang Kai-shek (1887–1975), was making the neighboring Yunnan part of his base in order to ensure its safety. The autocrat of the province, a member of the Yi tribe, declared himself willing to collaborate with Chiang. Yet his refusal to implement the strict censorship demanded by the nationalists meant that Kunming developed into a center of free thought, where university lecturers and students who had fled from other parts of the country were able to teach and study. In the first two years of the war alone, over 60,000 refugees settled in Yunnan—presenting challenges for a province which up to that point had been home to only about 150,000 people.

When the Japanese banned shipping on the Yangtze, Chongqing's only means of access to the sea, and the military equipment and gasoline supplied by the Americans, was via the legendary Burma Road, constructed in 1938. When the Burmese (as it was known then) end of the route fell into Japanese hands in 1942, the Americans continued to provide supplies by air, a more dangerous method. The construction of the Burma Road, over 700 miles (1150 km) long, by 160,000 ill-equipped men, women and children, within the space of a year, was an international sensation. The magnitude of the project invites comparisons with the building of the Great Wall.

A province of minorities

Like other border regions of China, the southwest is distinguished by the sheer diversity of the tribes living here. They make up half of Yunnan's population (alongside Han Chinese). It is home to 25 of more than 50 Chinese national minorities, among them the Bai, Dai, Hani, Hui, Jingpo, Lahu, Lisu, Miao, Naxi, Wa, Yao, Yi, Zhuang, and Tibetans. They enjoy a limited level of autonomy and certain special rights. In spite of modernization and intermingling with the Han population, so far the minorities have largely been able to keep their own identity.

The Mosuo tribe, which lives in the magical landscape around Lake Lugu, in northern Yunnan, is also famous throughout China. They are the only people on earth to live as a matriarchy. Young Mosuo couples do not marry, but live apart during the daytime, with their respective mothers, but sleep together in the woman's parental home, where their children are also brought up. The children belong exclusively to the woman, but are supported by the man for the duration of the relationship. There is no formal marriage ceremony or setting up house together, and if a couple no longer gets on, they separate, and are free to form new relationships. Only women can inherit.

This "women's realm" also sparks particular interest among tourists, who visit Yunnan all year round. Since China was opened up (in the late 1980s), the region's economy has been strengthened, initially by international visitors, but more recently by domestic tourism—unfortunately often at the cost of the environment. Large tourist industry corporations primarily organize group tours, and are in the hands of enterprising Han Chinese. This means that up until now members of local minorities in Yunnan have barely seen the fruits of economic development. Often they are the victims of tourism, rather than its beneficiaries.

Above: Yunnan is home to members of around 25 different national minorities. Despite intermixing with the Han Chinese, they have maintained their distinctive cultural characteristics to this day.

Left: One of Yunnan's regional specialties is its fruit and vegetable markets, which are far less frenetic than their city counterparts.

Yunnan's culinary diversity

The diversity of Yunnan's population and the isolation of many areas have fostered and preserved different local cooking traditions. Of more than 20 native ethnic groups, the culinary styles of the Bai and Dai, the Yi and the Naxi are particular stars in the province's culinary firmament. The cold and mountainous north is primarily home to the Bai, who keep goats and cows, and are especially renowned for their cheese.

The Naxi were originally peasants, but nowadays are to be found mostly in the city of Lijiang, in northern Yunnan, at the foot of Yulong Shan (Jade Dragon Snow Mountain). They love hearty but spicy food. One of their specialties is steamed blood sausage, made from rice, fresh pig's blood, and pork intestines. The Dai live in the southeast, in the Xishuangbanna district. Traditionally they cultivate wild rice and often cook their dishes inside bamboo cane; a typical specialty is rice cooked this way. Black rice served inside a pineapple (*boluo fan*) is a fruity complement to the otherwise savory Dai fare. In Jinghong, the district capital, fresh tropical fruits such as persimmons, coconuts, papayas, and bananas can be bought all year round.

The Yi mainly live in small mountain villages, and subsist on arable farming and raising livestock. Their specialties have also made their mark on Yunnanese cuisine, featuring hearty dishes such as pork meatballs, steamed potatoes with spicy puffed rice, and sweet rice pancakes. Yunnan's real culinary highlight, *qi guoji*, is chicken in a ceramic pot, simmered with ginger and scallions for several hours. In many areas, medicinal plants such as ginseng are added to the dish.

One thing that unites Yunnan's multifarious culinary traditions, formed by such diverse regional and cultural influences, is its penchant for mushrooms. Yunnan is China's top mushroom-growing area, and mushrooms are sold by the thousand in mushroom markets in the province's villages and towns. Mushroom collectors usually keep their wares in small baskets, arranged on the ground: colorful boletus, pale silvery ceps, and dried truffles sit alongside sacks full of freshly dried morels. Wild mushrooms grow predominantly in the mountainous regions and are harvested in July and October; cultivated mushrooms are in season all year round. The shaggy ink cap or lawyer's wig mushroom (*Coprinus comatus*, chin, *jitui gu*) is especially popular in regional cuisine. It is generally blanched before frying, perhaps with green chile. The shiitake mushroom (*Lentinus edodes*, chin. *xianggu*), also known by its Japanese name in these parts, grows in Yunnan and is popularly used as an ingredient in Chicken in a ceramic pot, as is the mushroom that we know as the caterpillar fungus (*Cordyceps sinensis*). The caterpillar fungus is also used in traditional Chinese medicine (TCM), and has a long history as a delicacy in luxury restaurants in the rich cities on the coast, which has then driven their price up to staggering heights.

One Yunnanese delicacy whose fame has spread beyond the borders of China is ham from the city of Xuanwei. Along with Jinhua ham from Zhejiang Province, it is one of China's most exquisite varieties of ham. Many Europeans claim that Xuanwei ham tastes similar to Spanish Serrano ham, but the Yunnanese are adamant that Yunnan ham (*yuntui*)—as the local specialty is also known—is unique, and the best in the world. The method by which it is produced follows a long tradition, with the end result an air-dried, cured ham with a thin rind, tender meat, and a sensational flavor. It is usually served cold and eaten with bread. Dried meat is also popular among the Yunnanese—a partiality that they share with the nomads on the steppe lands of Inner Mongolia. One of the province's specialties is dried yak meat, deep-fried and spiced with chile and ginger.

In southwestern Yunnan, dishes are heavily influenced by the cuisine of Myanmar. Coconut and palm sugar, which are unknown in other local cuisines, are wildly popular here.

Far left: Fresh vegetables are on offer at every market stall in Yunnan.

Left: Members of national minorities here often dress in very colorful clothing.

Chicken cooked in a banana leaf

1 chicken (about 2 ¼ lb / 1 kg)
1 scallion, cut into pieces (each about
   1 inch / 3 cm long)
1 tbsp coriander seeds
½ tsp chili powder
2 tsp Sichuan pepper
1 tsp salt
1 large banana leaf, for wrapping

Place the chicken on a chopping board and beat it flatter with the blunt edge of a cleaver. Stuff it with the scallion, coriander seeds, chili powder, Sichuan pepper, and salt, and leave to stand for 30 minutes. Wrap the banana leaf around it and steam over high heat for 1 hour.

Deep-fried beef

generous 1 lb (500 g) topside beef, in one
   piece
2 scallions
1 piece of ginger (2 ½ inch / 6 cm long)
a few dried red whole chiles
1 tbsp sesame seeds
1 ½ tbsp salt
1 tbsp sesame oil
1 ½ tbsp sugar
1 tbsp rice wine
2 cups (500 ml) soybean oil
2 tsp Sichuan pepper
3 ¼ cups (750 ml) beef stock
1 ½ tbsp soy sauce
1 tsp chili oil

Cut the meat in half. Chop the scallions into pieces. Slice the ginger. Soak the dried chiles to soften in water, then seed and cut into pieces ½ inch (1 cm) long. Toast the sesame seeds in a dry wok.

Mix the meat with the scallions, ginger, salt, sesame oil, sugar, and rice wine, and marinate for 1 hour. Then cook over high heat in a bamboo steamer until the meat is completely tender. Remove the meat and set aside to cool. Remove the scallions and ginger and set aside. Cut the meat into strips 1 ½ inches (4 cm) long and ½ inch (1 cm) wide.

Heat the soybean oil in a wok, add the meat strips and fry, then remove with a slotted spoon. Pour off most of the oil, leaving ⅓ cup (75 ml) in the wok.

Reheat the oil and add the Sichuan pepper. As soon as it begins to stick to the bottom of the pan, remove it with a slotted spoon and discard. Once the oil has cooled off a bit, add the chiles and fry until they become a dark violet color. Then return the scallions and ginger to the wok and fry briefly. Add the beef stock, soy sauce, and meat. Reduce the sauce over medium heat, adding the chili oil and the toasted sesame seeds at the end. Remove the chiles, scallions, and ginger before serving.

Top left: Not just for tourists: Tibetan restaurants are the scene of much singing and dancing.

Top: The history of the Miao people is said to date back 4000 years.

Above: Vegetables pickled and marinated in alcohol are a feature of many Yunnanese dishes.

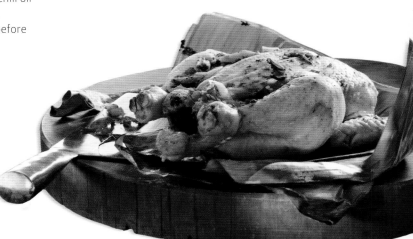

Silken smooth—rice noodles

Rice noodles are on a par with Xuanwei ham, wild mushrooms, and pu-erh tea as one of Yunnan's most famous delicacies. Like everywhere in Southeast Asia and southern China, rice noodles have been established fare for centuries (after all, more rice is grown here than wheat), but in Yunnan they have a special place of honor, exemplified by the famous dish Crossing-bridge noodles.

As is so often the case with Chinese specialties, there is a legend associated with this dish. During the Qing era (1644–1912) a man was studying for the imperial examination, which for about 1300 years (606–1905) decided the intake of state bureaucrats, and thus determined a candidate's social advancement. In order to study, he cloistered himself on Nanhu Island, near the town of Mengzi.

His wife brought him his favorite meal every day (a rice noodle dish, of course), but it would get cold while she was walking up the long footpath. One day she prepared an invigorating chicken stock, and was astonished to notice that an oily film had formed on the surface, keeping the stock underneath piping hot. This gave her the idea of adding the rice noodles and wafer-thin slices of meat, fish, and vegetables to the hot stock just before the bridge that led to the island. Her husband passed the exam thanks to the crossing-bridge noodles, and Yunnan got its signature dish, which has long since been extremely popular not only here, but also in places like Shanghai and Beijing.

In the restaurants of today it is cooked in a similar way to a fondue. Thin strips of chicken or pork are placed on a turntable alongside uncooked quail eggs, bean sprouts, mushrooms, cilantro, and scallions. Then comes a bowl full of rice noodles and the piping hot stock, which does not let off any steam due to the oily film on the top. Chicken and duck simmered with pork bones for hours, then seasoned with sesame and chili oil, give this stock its strong flavor, which allows the various ingredients to develop their aromas. The eggs and slices of raw meat and fish are added to the stock first of all, and briefly stirred; then follow the vegetable strips, which are quick to cook; and finally, the rice noodles. The ingredients only take a few minutes to cook, and taste sublime! Caution is advised, however; due to the layer of oil, the very pieces that the westerner goes to such trouble to fish out of the stock with his chopsticks will still be extremely hot.

When perfectly prepared, Yunnan rice noodles (*mixian*) are long, white, silky smooth, and yet with a little bite. You need a certain amount of experience to make your own rice noodles. Traditionally they are produced from whole grains of rice, which are soaked and reduced to a delicate, silky paste by water, before being poured in thin layers into molds and steamed, or as a firmer "dough" pressed into the desired shape. An easier alternative—though nowhere near as delicious as fresh Mixian rice noodles from Yunnan—is to buy dried rice noodles from an Asian supermarket. Since these have already been cooked, the first step is to steep them in a large pot full of boiling hot water until they begin to separate from one another (10–30 minutes, depending on the type and thickness of the rice noodles). They should be boiled for only a few more minutes after this, or else they will become sludgy.

KATRIN SCHLOTTER

Crossing-bridge noodles

½ plump chicken (approx. 1 ¾ lb / 750 g)
½ full grown duck (approx. 1 ¾ lb / 750 g)
3 long pork bones (marrowbones), for stock
1 ¾ oz (50 g) chicken breast
1 ¾ oz (50 g) pork tenderloin
1 ¾ oz (50 g) snakehead fish (or squid)
1 sheet of bean curd skin
1 ¼ oz (35 g) Chinese garlic chives
1 scallion, white part only, chopped
freshly chopped cilantro leaves
14 oz (400 g) rice noodles
½ tsp salt
pinch of ground white pepper
1 ½ tsp sesame oil
3 tbsp pork dripping (or chicken/duck dripping or schmaltz)
2 tbsp chile-infused sesame oil
finely grated ginger

Clean the chicken, duck, and the stock bones. Place them in a wok with 2 quarts (2 liters) of water and leave to simmer over low heat for about 3 hours. Strain, retaining the stock, strip off the chicken and duck meat, and discard the bones. Set aside the stock and the meat. Cut the chicken breast and pork tenderloin into wafer-thin slices and place on a plate. Slice the snakehead fish in the same way, and immerse briefly in boiling water, before removing and placing on a plate. Soak the bean curd skin and cut into slices. Add these to boiling water for 2 minutes, then rinse and set aside. Wash the garlic chives, cook briefly in boiling water, chop into pieces and set aside. Cook the rice noodles and set aside. Place the cooked chicken and duck meat in a large bowl, bring the stock to a boil in a pan and pour over the meat. Add the salt, pepper, sesame oil, dripping, and the chile-infused sesame oil. Make sure that the contents of the bowl remain hot (reheat briefly, if necessary). Place the bowl with the soup on the table, then pick up slices of the uncooked chicken, pork, and fish one by one with chopsticks and move them back and forth in the stock until they are cooked. Finally, add the garlic chives, bean curd skin, scallions, cilantro, and ginger to the soup, followed by the rice noodles. The slices of meat and fish can be dipped into sauces according to taste. The stock should be drunk once all the food has been eaten.

Left and below left: Unsurprisingly, homemade rice noodles taste better than the processed variety.

Below: The ingredients for the dish "Crossing-bridge noodles"; the stock is drunk at the end, once everything has been eaten.

Pu-erh tea

This distinctive tea, named after the town of Pu-erh in southern Yunnan, is not to everyone's taste. Although fans of young pu-erh tea rave about its fruity, refreshing taste, with notes of bamboo and lotus leaves, others describe it as musty, smelling of old socks, or "earthy," at best; it's hard to credit that they're talking about the same tea. The reason for these conflicting opinions is that pu-erh tea comes in various different grades of quality and maturity, and may be sold in several forms—loose, in bricks, in slices, or compressed into bamboo stems.

Green, raw pu-erh tea, which is processed in its unfermented state, is seen as fundamentally distinct from the black, fermented variety. Unlike other types of tea, if it is treated and stored carefully, pu-erh (particularly the green sort) develops special nuances of flavor, according to its age. These can range from grassy or fruity to woody and earthy. This makes mature pu-erh tea not only a luxury foodstuff for gourmets, but also a coveted investment and a collector's item.

This status is due to a coincidence: pu-erh tea, which was apparently popular a good 1,700 years ago, was offered as a tribute for the imperial court even in early times. After being picked, the remarkably long-leaved tea, grown on tea plantations on land over 6,560 feet (2000 m) above sea level near the town of Xishuang-banna, was brought to the prefecture of Pu'er. It was then processed, and from there embarked on a month-long journey north by horse, or, in later times, by boat. Over the course of the journey the taste of the tea matured.

Unlike other types of tea, which are made up of the fresh buds and leaves of young tea bushes, according to connoisseurs only the large, fully-grown leaves of old Qingmao tea trees from Yunnan should be used to make pu-erh tea. These are picked by hand (removing any broken leaves), roasted in large iron pans, and sometimes rolled. They must then be dried in the sun, sorted once again, steamed, and finally compressed into shape, so that they can be left to mature for the next few decades (!) in a dry place, finally becoming the sought-after, mature green pu-erh tea.

In commercial production, however, there is no time to wait decades for a tea. To solve this, in the mid-1970s tea producers developed processes that let the tea mature within a few months. So-called black pu-erh tea is made by crushing the tealeaves together, sprinkling with water and turning them over (allowing the microbes to go about the business of maturation), before the tea is dried once again, processed and stored. This method lends the black tea its woody, earthy aroma, which the green variety only develops after years.

Yet pu-erh tea has become famous in the West not only for its nuanced flavor, but also its alleged medicinal benefits; as early as the imperial age it was rumored to help with indigestion and weight problems. This image endures to this day: it is said to lower cholesterol, stimulate the burning of fat, and improve the complexion. It comes as no surprise, then, that pu-erh is marketed as a rejuvenating and slimming tea.

KATRIN SCHLOTTER

Left: Pu-erh tea has been around for approximately 2,000 years; it is still dried in the open air.

Below left: Since then, however, the methods of production have changed.

Below: Pu-erh tea must still be picked by hand, and it is priced according to weight.

Top: The Qingmao tea tree, whose leaves are used to make pu-erh tea, is bigger than the conventional tea bush.

Above (middle): The region's internationally famous, top-quality products make it a natural attraction.

Above: Skilled tea-pickers can manage a daily harvest of up to 65 lb (30 kg).

Right: Yunnan's specialty tea is sold in aptly designed canisters.

A land of lakes and parks

Yunnan's biggest lake is Lake Dian, southwest of the provincial capital, Kunming, but the prize for the most beautiful scenery goes to Lake Er, north of the city of Dali. It is hard to imagine a landscape more beautiful than this: Lake Er in the east, surrounded by lush fields; to the west the Cangshan Mountain, with its snow-capped peaks and green valleys. Dali (same name as the city), the autonomous district of the Bai people, not only has an abundant supply of food, but is also a great place to relax.

You can hardly fail to notice the Bai people's penchant for "their" color (bai = white) when in Dali: men wear white shirts, and the houses in the old town are also white, as is Dali marble, which is mined in the region. The city's main attractions, the statues of Buddha in the temple pagoda, are likewise made of white marble. They are a testament to the religious life of the Bai, who are mostly Buddhists; nevertheless, Taoist temples and Christian churches are also represented in Dali.

Every year, tourists from elsewhere in China and all over the world make their way to Dali and the 25-mile (40-km)-long Lake Er, almost 6,560 feet (2000 m) above sea level. The lake is most famous for the cormorant fishermen who ply its waters in their small boats. The cormorants are trained to catch fish from a young age. Before they go fishing, the fisherman ties a loop around the bird's neck, so that it cannot swallow its catch. Only when the cormorants have caught enough fish for the day are they allowed to help themselves, and gulp down the little fishes with relish, without the snare around their necks. Technical advancements in fishing have meant that this once-widespread method has been supplanted by modern boats, and nowadays the cormorant fishermen only go out on Lake Er for the sake of tourists. They can be seen from the shore, or visitors can hire a boat themselves, in order to watch the spectacle at close range, or simply to

enjoy the landscape and the view of the many Bai villages that lie around the shores of the lake. Sadly, this idyll, like so many unspoiled areas in China, is being threatened by increasing pollution.

Another oasis of calm is the scenic Cuihu Park, in the northwest part of Kunming, which provides relaxation in equal measure. This little park covers about 3/4 square mile (2 sq km) and has a lake, dubbed "Jade Lake" on account of its soft green waters. The park is Kunming's green lung, and the scenic, verdant shores of the lake shore are the perfect place to unwind, for locals and tourists alike. Those interested in ornithology can also strike it rich here: red-beaked seagulls have been coming from Siberia to winter here since the mid-1980s, and can be observed from the small island in the middle of the lake. In the late 17th century a pavilion was built here, named The Pavilion of the Green Waves (Biyi Ting) for the color of the lake, which is fed by nine springs. It is best to come first thing in the morning if you want to enjoy the lake in peace. At this hour, lots of the city's residents gather under the willow trees on the shore to practice tai chi or fan dances. Things liven up in the afternoons, when countless visitors descend upon the gardens around the lake to watch games of mahjong. The air is filled with the clacking of the pieces, the clinking of teacups, and a multitude of gossiping voices. Evenings are more tranquil; the lake belongs to

Left: Anyone seeking calm and natural surroundings will feel at home in Yunnan's mountain areas.

Below left: The Jade Lake in Cuihu Park lies in the northwest of the provincial capital, Kunming.

Below: Mornings are the best time for enjoying the glorious tranquility of romantic gardens, in the very center of the metropolis.

Bottom: A panoramic view of Dali, which is mainly home to the Bai people, a national minority.

lovers, who delight in the romantic atmosphere, especially on summer nights when the moon is reflected in the Jade Lake.

Shaggy ink caps with green chiles

7 oz (200 g) shaggy ink cap (lawyer's wig)
   mushrooms
2 fresh green chiles
4 tbsp vegetable oil
1–2 tbsp finely chopped scallions
1 piece of ginger (1 inch / 3 cm long), sliced
2 garlic cloves, sliced
salt (to taste)
1 tsp cornstarch
a little sesame oil, to serve

Slice the shaggy ink caps and the green chiles, and blanch briefly in boiling water.
Put the oil in a wok, and add the scallions, ginger, and garlic, and sauté. Add the shaggy ink caps and the chiles, and sauté. Season to taste and bind together with the cornstarch. Remove from the stove, drizzle with a little sesame oil, and serve at once.

Kunming's eternal springtime

Every climate zone may be represented in China, from bitter winters in the far north to tropical summers in the south, but certain provinces within the country are remarkable for featuring several different climes. Yunnan has its varying altitude to thank for this: mountainous, ice- and snow-covered regions on the borders with Tibet and Sichuan; a tropical climate near Myanmar (Burma) and Laos, in the far south; and temperate areas on the fertile plateaus of the heartland. Here—almost 6,560 feet (2000 m) above sea level—lies the provincial capital, Kunming. Its epithet, "city of the eternal springtime" is wholly justified; Kunming enjoys a wonderfully agreeable climate, with the mercury steady at 75 °F (24 °C) almost all year round.

Today Kunming is a modern provincial capital with wide, palm-lined streets, high-rise glass and steel office buildings, shopping centers, and large housing complexes. The old Kunming, with its traditional two-storied wooden houses, narrow alleys, and colorful markets, is largely a thing of the past, but one part of the old town which is still standing has been preserved as a historic site.

There is, however, a palpable sense of remoteness from the megacities in eastern China. Kunming's people and natural surroundings make it something quite different. With 3 million people living in the downtown area, it is the capital of the province, which is home to almost half of China's ethnic minorities. These are all represented in the provincial capital too, making up almost 10 percent of the city's residents. Yunnan's topography means that it is blessed with an abundance of flora unequaled in China, revealed in the city's markets, where a vast array of fruit, vegetables, not to mention flowers, is sold all year round. It's no wonder that Kunming was chosen as the host of the International Horticulture Expo in 1999!

The town lies in an area steeped in history. Lake Dian, over 25 miles (40 km) long, stretches away to the south. The kingdom of Dian was founded on its shores in the 1st millennium B.C. The sophisticated culture of this civilization is evident in its fabulous bronze artifacts depicting scenes from nature and social activities, and distinctive jade and turquoise jewelry. The Dian kingdom became a tributary state of the Chinese Han dynasty in about 100 B.C.

Nowadays Lake Dian, with historic temples and a new theme park along its shores, makes a favorite excursion for people from Kunming. The old buildings on the craggy western shore promise a unique trip back in time through the history of Yunnan: temples dating back over 900 years to the era of the Bai kingdom, Nanzhao, which stretched from here to Dali, in the west; a building from the Yuan period (1271–1368), when Yunnan was absorbed into the Mongol kingdom; and the grave of the Yunnanese composer Nie Er (1912–1935), whose "March of the Volunteers" became the national anthem of the People's Republic in 1949. In spite of all this, the purification of the 115-square-mile (300-sq-km)-lake, which has become heavily polluted by domestic sewage and industrial effluent, presents a serious challenge for the future.

Yet Kunming's true landmark is the "stone forest" southeast of the city, within Lunan Autonomous County, home to the Sani minority. Spread over a total area of 640 acres (260 ha), these bizarre stone formations were formed over 270 million years ago. It is thought that there was once a sea here, and that giant limestone deposits built up on the sea floor.

Left: It is not immediately obvious that Kunming, home to 3 million people, is a "green" city.

Right: Part of the old town is now preserved as a site of historic interest.

After the area silted up, rainfall washed out the limestone deposits, resulting in unique rock formations. Visitors can wander along the narrow paths and steep stairways through the dense forest of rocks, which owe their names to the Chinese love of allusions and abundance of legends. You only need to step off the well-worn paths to let your imagination run wild in an otherworldly landscape of jagged gray rocks and bare ocher and orange earth.

Chicken in a ceramic pot

1 chicken (2 ¼ lb / 1 kg)
1 scallion, cut into pieces
1 piece of ginger (2 ½ inch / 6 cm) long, cut into thick slices
3–4 shiitake mushrooms (average size)
1 tsp white pepper
2 tsp rice wine

Clean the chicken and cut into pieces with a kitchen cleaver, and place the meat and bones in a ceramic pot. Add a little cold water and the scallion, ginger, and shiitake mushrooms, and steam the chicken for 4–5 hours. Remove the scallion and ginger, season with the remaining ingredients and serve immediately.
Tip: For a clean taste, no traces of blood should remain on the chicken. To make sure that the chicken is clean, blanch in boiling water before steaming.

Top right: Having your pork and eating it: amateur chefs will hardly be able to believe their eyes in Kunming's meat markets.

Above right (middle): Pieces of meat are cut to order on the market stall.

Right: With spring-like temperatures all year round, Kunming is simply made for strolling.

The Yi and the Bai

The Yi people encompass a number of different tribes (including the Nuosu, Nisu, Nasu, Sani, Ashe, Lalu, and Luoluo), but they have been officially grouped together under the Chinese name *Yi shaoshu minzu* since the 1950s. Today a total of around 8 million Yi live in the People's Republic, most of them in Yunnan Province, where they make up the biggest ethnic minority.

They speak six different dialects, which are so disparate that it is impossible for one Yi group to understand another. Instead, they use standard Chinese as a common language, as it is spoken by all Yi, or at least it is by the younger generation.

The Yi have settled predominantly in the mountainous areas of Yunnan, Sichuan, Guizhou, and Guangxi provinces. They live in small villages and earn their living from arable farming, raising livestock, hunting and fishing. Their staple foods include potatoes, oats, and buckwheat, and they flavor their dishes mainly with locally grown black cardamom (*caoguo*).

In earlier times, the Yi lived in a caste society. At the top of the hierarchy, with less than 10 percent of the population, was the group commonly known as the Black Yi, aristocrats who owned about 80 percent of the land. The White Yi (about half of the population) were obliged to work in the landowners' fields for a set period of time. Farther down the ladder were the Aija and the Xiaxa, who were kept as slaves and had no rights. This social system was only abolished by the Communist government in 1958. The nationalization of property and the establishment of people's communes in this area were aimed partly at suppressing the traditional structure of society. Nevertheless, the clan system is rooted in the Yi mindset to this

very day. The effects of this are by no means all negative, however; the solidarity of family clans provides strong social stability in times of great change.

The Yi religion is based on animistic and shamanistic beliefs, according to which their mythological ancestry gives them a particular affinity with animals and plants. Even today, the village shaman—called the Bimo—has a distinguished social status; he is the principal keeper of traditions, and also the healer and sacrificer, with the authority to celebrate both weddings and funerals. In earlier times, the Bimo was often the only person in the village who could read and write Yi script. In fact, little has changed in this respect, as today the children learn only the Chinese language and script at school.

Every year the Yi, young and old alike, celebrate the New Year (also called the Torch Festival), which takes place in summer, on the 24th

Above right: Yunnan's mountain-dwellers lead an utterly different life to the Han Chinese.

Right: While the younger generation of Yi have taken to modern life wholeheartedly, the older Yi are still deeply rooted in their traditions.

Far right: Yi village communities are normally made up of 20–30 families.

Left: Life in the mountain areas centers around farming; as farmers and livestock breeders, the Yi have a close connection with nature.

Bottom left: The Yi people's penchant for lacquer paintings and carvings can be seen in the design of their front doors.

Below: The women wear bright costumes, bringing a splash of color to the drabness of much Chinese life.

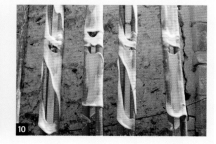

Above: Flames blaze away on the stove, day in, day out, often in cramped living areas.

Right: The younger generation of Bai is already attempting to bridge the gap between traditional headscarves and modern blue jeans.

1 When making Rushan cheese, fresh cow's milk is first heated in a wok.

2 Homemade vinegar activates the souring process. Stirring...

3 ...separates the curdled nuggets of cheese and whey. They are drained through a strainer.

4 The nuggets of cheese are stirred together again in the wok...

5 ...and then kneaded together by hand to form a smooth mass.

6 The still-warm cheese can now be stretched by hand.

7 Next, one end of the cheese is wrapped tightly around a long bamboo rod to dry...

8 ...and stretched once more. Another bamboo rod...

9 ...makes the structure into a kind of frame,...

10 ...around which the cheese is rolled, and stood to dry in the open air.

day of the sixth month. The annual feast day customs include singing and dancing, along with tournaments such as tug-of-war and dragon boat races. As the name of the festival suggests, bonfires and torches are lit everywhere on this day in order to drive evil spirits and vermin away from the fields. The Yi are not ones to pass up an opportunity for a full-blown banquet, either; the traditional dishes are always accompanied by homemade potato fries. The peeled potatoes are cut into thin slices and then deep-fried in a wok, before being seasoned with salt and chili powder.

Bai cheese

The autonomous region of Dali lies in scenic western Yunnan, on the shores of Lake Er and at the foot of the Cangshan Mountain, nearly

Left: For the Bai, cooking and eating only take place within one's own community.

Below left: Life is hard in Yunnan's mountain villages; the industrial revolution has not yet really reached these areas.

Pork meatballs

14 oz (400 g) ground pork
1 piece of ginger (1 ½ inch / 4 cm long), finely chopped
2 garlic cloves, finely chopped
1 tsp salt
2 tsp rice wine
1 tsp white vinegar
1 tsp sugar
1 tbsp sesame oil
1 cup (250 ml) vegetable oil
1 piece of baby leek, finely chopped, to serve

Mix the ground pork, ginger, garlic, salt, rice wine, white vinegar, sugar, and sesame oil together, and form the mixture into small meatballs. Heat the oil in a wok and fry the meatballs. Remove, and place in a large heatproof bowl. Add 7 tablespoons of water and steam the dumplings over high heat for 20 minutes. Remove and sprinkle with the baby leek.

always wreathed in clouds. Eighty percent of the Bai mountain people live here; other members of this ethnic minority live in the provinces of Guizhou and Hunan.

The lake's mild climate is particularly favorable for growing rice, winter wheat, beans, rapeseed, millet, and sugarcane. As a result, most Bai live from farming, although some also work as cormorant fishermen, albeit mostly now as a tourist attraction. The surrounding forests offer a rich supply of game and wild herbs, which can also be used for medicinal purposes. The Bai also make money from raising livestock, principally goats and sheep. Yet these are also a source of milk for cheese-making. Among the Han Chinese, the taste for milk products is rather uncommon, and the production and consumption of goat's milk (rubing) and cow's milk cheese (rushan) is an idiosyncrasy of the Bai, who consider both to be real delicacies.

Rubing cheese is a treat popularly served to guests on special occasions. Its appearance and taste are quite similar to mozzarella (Italian buffalo cheese), and it is normally sliced and sautéed in a little oil, before being seasoned with a pinch of salt or sugar. Alternatively, it may be deep-fried after being coated with egg and cornstarch.

Rushan cheese, on the other hand, is sold in small, rectangular sheets that look a bit like filo (or phyllo) pastry. These are cut into small cubes and deep-fried in hot oil, rising to the top like doughnuts. Deep-fried rushan is crispy yet light, and melts in the mouth. It is mainly served at banquets and other festive meals.

The Bai, who today put on popular folklore shows for tourists, once ruled over their own kingdom. From the 7th to the 13th century the Bai Kingdom—Nanzhou, later Dali—controlled southwest China and even parts of Vietnam, Myanmar, and Laos, before Kublai Khan swept into the south and brought the Bai lands under his dominion.

The tea ceremony *Sandaocha* ("three-course tea") is said to date back to the kingdom's heyday, with the Bai performing it to welcome grand state guests as early as the Tang era (618–907). Today the Bai still use this ceremony to greet special guests. A bitter tea is served first, followed by a sweet tea with brown sugar, which has a little rushan cheese in it. The third-course tea is made of ginger, honey, cinnamon, and pepper, and has a remarkably spicy, lingering flavor. As for the meaning of the tea ceremony, the bitter taste of the first tea is meant to make the guest reflect on his bad deeds, the second tea evokes memories of good times, and the third tea is intended to inspire contemplation of one's own behavior. Today the ceremony is often performed for tourists and accompanied by singing and dancing Bai girls, who are famous all over China for their music and voices.

The Yi and the Bai **333**

Coffee and tobacco

In economic terms, coffee and tobacco are currently among Yunnan's most important agricultural products. The South American plant, which was introduced to China at the end of the 19th century, and has been cultivated in the southwestern province since 1905, thrives in the optimal conditions provided by the subtropical climate and the soil of the mountainous areas, particularly for the cultivation of slightly bitter, mild highland coffee (Arabica).

Coffee in China: careering ahead

Yunnan's coffee has a United Nations project to thank for the rapid transformation of this exotic plant into a significant economic force. In the 1990s the UN promoted coffee cultivation as an alternative to growing opium poppies across China, Vietnam, Laos, and Myanmar. It was a resounding success. Within ten years, the area for coffee cultivation had to be extended from 9,800 to 64,250 acres (4000 to 26,000 ha). Today, over 80 percent of Chinese coffee is grown in Yunnan—mostly to be exported to Europe and America.

Until a few years ago, the coffee was mostly used to produce instant coffee due to the lack of experience in cultivating and processing the fruits (coffee berries), and the subsequently poor quality of the beans. Yet the coffee growers have learnt a lot since then, and have greatly improved the quality of their beans. They have also set themselves the ambitious goal of stimulating the Chinese market once again, and are banking on their country developing a coffee-drinking culture of its own. Although China is the most populous country in the world, it currently accounts for only one percent of coffee consumption worldwide. Tea is still the beverage of choice here. Yet globalization has long had China in its grip; the younger generation and Chinese people returning home from abroad are increasingly turning to coffee, which is seen as chic and a sign of sophistication. International coffee-shop chains (such as Starbucks) have also appeared in the large cities, with branches penetrating even places like the Forbidden City in Beijing. They have part-ownership of specific coffee plantations, and are relying on the low world market price to make coffee affordable for the Chinese. Coffee is still too expensive for those on an average wage, so only the highest earners frequent modern cafés, along with foreigners who cannot bear to go without their favorite drink when abroad.

Left: Previously fit to be sold only as instant coffee, today Yunnan's coffee is important to the economy.

Bottom left: Knowledgeable waiting staff are on hand in Chinese cafés to advise customers new to coffee.

Below: In the space of only ten years, Yunnan's coffee-growing areas have increased sixfold.

Right: In many places, coffee is already being celebrated in the same way as tea-drinking.

Tobacco—much-loved, gorgeously packaged

Deep gorges, the Great Wall, dragons, and goldfish: the fabulous excesses of Chinese cigarette packaging make it a far cry from its European and American equivalents. Most depict the breathtaking Chinese landscape, which— like the country's technical achievements—are intended to elicit a sense of patriotism, prompting the urge to buy. Dragons and goldfish bring good luck; the fact that smoking is unhealthy is often completely forgotten as money changes hands.

China has the largest number of smokers in the world, 350 million, of which two thirds are men. Although the People's Republic is also the world's biggest tobacco producer, at 38 percent, this has virtually no impact on the world market, as the crops are almost all grown to satisfy the domestic demand.
Tobacco arrived in China in the 17th century, after having been brought to Europe from America. From Europe, like so many other goods, it was exported by merchants and missionaries along the Silk Road to China and Japan. This variety of the nightshade plant has been cultivated in Yunnan ever since, especially the Maryland and Virginia species. The country's largest tobacco-growing areas and processing plants can be found in the southern province, although it is also grown in 11 other provinces (including Henan, Guizhou, and Sichuan).

Virginia tobacco grows almost everywhere, and is easy to bring under cultivation. It has a sweet, fruity aroma, and is an essential component of many tobacco blends. Yunnan is also famous for its bamboo water pipes, 3 feet (1 m) long and up to 4 inches (10 cm) in diameter. These pipes are a favorite prop for old men sitting by the side of the road, listening to the gentle gurgle of the pipe as they smoke.
The imperial court of the Qing dynasty (1644–1912), however, favored snuff over cigarettes; in a way, the small, elaborately decorated snuffboxes of yesteryear, once highly fashionable, can be considered the forerunners of today's artistically designed cigarette cartons. Jasmine, mint, or other Chinese herbs were often mixed into the snuff. Like the native peoples of South America, many Chinese believed in the curative properties of tobacco; snuff was said to alleviate headaches and improve digestion.
Yet this fallacy is now a thing of the past; China has long had an agreement with the World Health Organization (WHO) to combat tobacco addiction, and widespread campaigns provide stern warnings about the health dangers of smoking.

Top: Unhealthy? Regardless, tobacco is used in traditional Chinese medicine.

Above (middle): The lion's share of Chinese tobacco is produced for the domestic market.

Above: The tobacco harvest, as with tea, is mostly carried out by female pickers.

Left: Almost 40 percent of the world's tobacco is produced in China.

Specialties of Yunnan

Rice pancakes

1 ⅓ cups (200 g) rice flour
2 tbsp sugar
a little sesame oil, for brushing
vegetable oil, for frying

Mix the rice flour with the sugar and just enough water to knead into a dough. Divide the dough into pieces.
Press the pieces into round, palm-sized pancakes, and roll out. Brush the pancakes with sesame oil. Heat the vegetable oil in a wok and fry the pancakes on both sides.

Duck with pineapple

5 ½ oz (150 g) fresh pineapple (or a 1-inch / 3-cm slice per person)
2 fresh whole red chiles
1 piece of ginger (4 inch / 10 cm long)
1 ½ tsp salt
4 tbsp sugar
1 ½ tbsp light rice vinegar
7 oz (200 g) duck meat
2 tsp egg white
1 tbsp cornstarch
1 cup (250 g) pork dripping or lard, more if necessary
garlic paste
1–2 tbsp minced scallions
2 tsp rice wine
1 tbsp sesame oil

Sauce:
1 tbsp stock, thickened with 1 tsp cornstarch
a little sesame oil
½ tsp sugar
1 tsp cornstarch mixed with 2 tsp water

Cut the pineapple into 1-inch- (3-cm)-thick slices. Roughly chop the chiles, peel the ginger and cut into thin slices. Season the chiles and ginger with the salt and set aside for 30 minutes, then rinse and pat dry. Mix the sugar and the rice vinegar in a bowl. Add the slices of ginger and a

size. Whisk the egg in a bowl, gradually adding the cornstarch. Use the mixture to brush the stuffed eggplant all over, sealing the opening. Heat the oil in a wok, add the eggplant pieces and fry until they are golden-brown. Remove the stuffed eggplant and open slightly to check that the pork is cooked through. It should be crispy on the outside, and the cooked pork savory and tender on the inside.

Celery with sour pickled vegetables

11 oz (300 g) celery stalks
7 oz (200 g) sour pickled vegetables (*Suan Cai*)
1 piece of leek (2 inch / 5 cm long), chopped
3 tbsp vegetable oil
salt

Cut the celery and the sour vegetables into
³/₄-inch (2-cm)-wide pieces.
Heat the oil in a wok and stir-fry the leek, add the celery and stir-fry to soften. Add the sour vegetables, stir-fry to heat through, and season to taste with salt before serving.

third of the chiles and marinate for about an hour, then remove with a slotted spoon. Cut the duck meat into thin slices. Mix the egg white and the cornstarch, and use to coat the duck.
To make the sauce, blend the stock thickened with cornstarch, sesame oil, sugar, and corn-starch-water mixture and set aside.
Place the pork dripping in a wok and warm over medium heat. Add the slices of ginger and fry, then remove with a slotted spoon and set aside. Add the garlic paste, scallions, and the rest of the chopped chiles and sauté until the mixture gives off a good aroma. Add the slices of ginger and the slices of duck. In a separate pan, bring the rice wine to a boil, add the sauce and stir to thicken, then add the pineapple. Add the sesame oil at the end of cooking, stir everything together once more, and serve immediately.

Stuffed eggplants

¹/₂ cup (100 g) ground lean pork
1 tsp soy sauce
1 tsp salt
1 tsp sesame oil
1–2 tbsp scallions, finely chopped
1 tbsp ginger, finely chopped
1 large eggplant, (about 7 oz / 200g)
1 egg
¹/₃ cup (50 g) corn- or potato starch
1–2 tsp vegetable oil

Mix the ground pork with the soy sauce, salt, sesame oil, scallions, and ginger.
Peel the eggplant and make two or three cuts from the middle to the stalk, without cutting all the way through. Carefully scoop some of the flesh out to make a hollow, and stuff the filling into this space.
Cut the stuffed eggplant into four pieces of equal

Lijiang—one city, two worlds

"Women hold up half the sky." With these words, Mao Zedong promoted equality for women, pointing the way to the work brigades that would construct a socialist society. Yet this image seems an understatement for the Naxi people, who live in the border lands between Yunnan and Sichuan provinces, and also Tibet. Here, the women carry the heavens on their shoulders, not to mention their clothing: the white roan and black cotton of their cloaks symbolize day and night, and the seam where the dark cloth meets the light leather is adorned with seven round embellishments, the "seven stars." The message is clear: the firmament rests on the shoulders of the Naxi women. In Lijiang, it is the women who carry out most of the work. Unsurprisingly, the city's most bustling, crowded thoroughfare is called "Women's Street."

The city of Lijiang lies at the heart of the Naxi region, in a valley at an altitude of 8,530 feet (2600 m). The 18,370-foot (5600-m)-high, snow-capped Jade Dragon Snow Mountain towers on the northern horizon. Lijiang has two parts. The first, a Chinese district with countless government and administrative buildings, residential blocks for the Han Chinese, and the facelessness that characterizes so many modernized country towns, fuses with the other part, the Old Town, home to the Naxi and their traditional wooden houses with ornate interiors, market squares and small shops selling colorful goods, to form a polished whole. The

Left: Lijiang's Old Town has been a UNESCO World Heritage Site since 1997.

Right: The Naxi, an ethnic minority, make up about 20 percent of Lijiang's population. They have maintained their traditional culture to the present day.

Left: Lijiang, "the city beside the beautiful river," lies on a plateau at an altitude of 8,530 feet (2600 m), on the southeastern spur of the Himalayas.

Right: The traditional heritage is not only kept alive for the sake of tourists; the Naxi preserve their culture, which includes shamans.

older part of the town is criss-crossed by narrow cobbled alleys and innumerable canals. In many places visitors will see three water basins standing beside one another: the first is fed by a spring and used only for drinking water; this flows into the next basin, which is used for washing vegetables, and from there into the third basin, for washing clothes.

In 1996 large parts of the town were destroyed by a heavy earthquake, yet the Naxi's traditional wooden houses suffered far less damage than the new concrete edifices. In the following year, the Old Town of Lijiang was designated a UNESCO World Heritage Site.

One downside of the town's heightened status as a World Heritage Site, and the financial wherewithal that has poured in from abroad ever since, has been the hordes of tourists, mainly from elsewhere in China, who do nothing to support the community that has grown up in the town. When visiting the Naxi part of town, it is common practice for the group travelers to patronize Chinese hotels on the outskirts, and only visit the Old Town clustered together on sightseeing walks, behind the gaudy flag of their tour guide. The two worlds glide past one another, without ever coming into contact.

In scholarly terms, the Austrian-American botanist Joseph Rock (1884–1962) was one outsider who really got under the skin of Lijiang. Between 1922 and 1949 he lived in a neighboring village and explored northwestern Yunnan and Sichuan on extensive expeditions, on which he collected a vast number of plants, birds, and mammals, eventually sending them to the West. Fearing the threat from other cultures, he devoted especial attention to his study of the Naxi way of life.

The Naxi people, who currently number about 300,000, are descended from the Tibetan Qiang tribe. They once lived in family groups, organized along matrilineal lines, as the Mosuo at Lake Lugu do today in their "Women's Kingdom." Yet the principle lingers on in Lijiang: here the women wear the trousers. They do the heavy work, and if a street needs to be repaved, or a house built, the work is almost always done by female hands.

The Naxi people's cultural heritage includes a thousand-year-old literary language, a system of pictographs passed down over centuries by the shamans (called *Dongba*). The shamans were responsible for contact between the Naxi and the outside world. Today they still recite from the traditional script at religious ceremonies, and they perform rituals and participate in festivities, although these are often laid on for tourists.

Top: Farming plays an important role in the area around Lijiang.

Above (middle): Almost a third of the town was destroyed by an earthquake in 1996, yet many of the traditional buildings were unscathed, while modern high-rises collapsed.

Above: Tourists to the town are mostly Han Chinese. Highlights of a trip to Lijiang include a dance with members of the national minority.

Xishuangbanna—home of the Dai

The largely mountainous Xishuangbanna Autonomous District lies on the borderland with Myanmar (Burma) and Laos, alongside the Lancang river (which becomes the Mekong in Vietnam). This area in southern Yunnan has a damp, tropical climate that is perfect for rice growing, which forms the livelihood of the Dai people, among others. The Dai, a Thai people, lost their independence in the Ming era (1368–1644). They call their district Sipsong-panna, or "12 rice fields." The name also dates from the time when the area was annexed by the Chinese empire; at one point, the local regent appointed by the Ming emperor reduced the number of administrative units to 12, so as to make tax collection easier in the previously fragmented region.

Xishuangbanna is famous for its primeval forest, which is completely native in the remotest areas, and is today protected as a nature park. More than 5,000 types of plants, some only discovered in the last few years, can be found here, including countless rhododendron and primrose species, forsythias, azaleas and anemones. It is also a habitat for endangered animals, including elephants, hunted for their ivory tusks and because they can destroy farmers' harvests. Others are monkeys, leopards, water buffalo, and peacocks, which the Dai see as a symbol of peace and good fortune. Xishuangbanna's most spectacular event is the annual Water-Splashing Festival, which attracts thousands of Dai and many tourists to the Lancang river region. The Dai hold this lively festival to mark the New Year, which, according to their calendar, normally occurs in mid-April. On this day everyone walks around

with bowls of water, liberally dousing one another, so that by evening there is not a single dry shirt left.

This custom, originally a ritual, serves to wash away the old year and welcome in the new. Those splashing the water also symbolize the hoped-for rain, which will make sure there is a good harvest—and a full larder—in the coming year. Of course, having fun is all part of the festival, and it is particularly popular among young single men and women from the villages, as well as a welcome opportunity to look for a suitable partner.

Other highlights of the Dai New Year Festival include the dragon boat race, which is held on the Lancang river, and the various dances performed to traditional music by the Dai women

Left: Boat races are a long-established feature of the Dai Water-Splashing Festival.

Bottom left: Dai women are distinguished by their coiled hair and sarongs.

Below: Blessed with an optimal climate, tropical fruits like mango and pineapple also thrive in Xishuangbanna.

Chicken and rice in bamboo cane

1 ½ cups (250 g) rice
5 tbsp unsalted soy paste
salt (to taste)
1 tbsp sugar
3 tbsp vegetable oil
1 dried red chile
generous cup (150 g) peas
3 ½ oz (100 g) chicken
5 ½ oz (150 g) bamboo tips
3 ½ oz (100 g) Cantonese-style sausage
2 large silver morels
4 bamboo shoots
1 bamboo cane, halved lengthwise

Leave the rice to soak in water for a minimum of 4 hours. Bring to a boil and add the soy paste, salt, sugar, oil, chile, peas, and chicken, and cook for at least 30 minutes. Chop the bamboo tips and the sausage roughly, finely chop the silver morels, and slice the bamboo shoots.
Put the cooked rice in a bowl with the meat and the chopped ingredients, and mix well.
Stuff the mixture into one half of the bamboo cane and press down on it lightly. Cover with the second half of the bamboo cane and tie both halves together tightly with string. Steam over low to medium heat for 2 hours, then remove, cut away the string, lift off the upper half of the bamboo and serve immediately.

in their colorful sarongs, especially the peacock dance, which is said to bring luck. The dances are based on traditional religious rites from pre-Buddhist times (the Dai took up Buddhism between the 6th and 8th centuries).
Dai food centers around rice, which thrives abundantly in this area, and is painstakingly cultivated by hand on picturesque rice terraces to this very day. One popular method of cooking rice is to soak it, then season to taste with salt, soy paste, red chiles, and a little sugar, before cooking it in a 8-inch (20-cm)-long bamboo cane, cut lengthwise and sealed with a banana leaf. The soft, delicious rice is eaten with chopsticks straight from the cane. You can bulk or spice up the dish by adding chicken, pieces of sausage, mushrooms or chiles (see recipe). This traditional dish is usually served to guests.

Top: Two-storied bamboo buildings are typical Dai dwellings; the first floor is a storeroom or the place where livestock is kept, and the living quarters are on the second floor.

Above left: The highpoint of the Dai year: the Water Festival is celebrated not only with traditional dancing and performances...

Above: ...but also with traditional music.

Hunan

湖南

Katrin Schlotter

Almost unknown in the West, the province of Hunan, where some 68 million inhabitants live in an area of just 81,850 square miles (212,000 sq km), has great significance for the Chinese. It is the home province of Mao Zedong, whose term as Chairman of the Chinese Communist Party from 1935 to 1976 determined the fate of the country. However, this province in southeast central China is also known for its wild, romantic landscape and for a red hot spicy cuisine.

To the north of the provincial capital of Changsha, the fertile alluvial plains are crossed by rivers and lakes that flow into Lake Dongting, the second biggest lake in China. The province gets its name from this lake: Hunan means "to the south of the lake." Extending across the northwest are the Wuling mountains, with the mysterious Zhangjiajie National Park, where strange, age-old quartz sandstone pinnacles tower above misty gorges. Also in that area is the Autonomous Prefecture of Xiangxi, the home of the Tuja and Miao peoples. The ancient city of Fenghuang gives the impression of having been forgotten by time. Its streets, which run along the river banks, are lined with houses with curved roofs, built on stilts. In the southwest you also feel as if you had been transported to another world, the peasant Hunan of the olden days. Bamboo forests, rice terraces, and villages nestle into the mountain landscape. In the interior, around 60 miles (100 km) to the south of Changsha, the 72 peaks of the Hengshan mountain range have, since time immemorial, drawn pilgrims from the whole of China and held them in thrall. In this mountainous, legend-shrouded landscape there are a number of monasteries, including the Nanyue Temple, founded in 725—one of the most beautiful and, with a total area of around 25 acres (10 ha), one of the biggest Buddhist and Taoist temples south of the Yangtze.

Subtropical Hunan becomes roasting hot in summer and is known as the granary of China. The rice fields of Hunan yield two abundant harvests a year, making the province the most important producer of rice in China, as well as one of China's leading provinces for the production of tea, citrus fruits, canola, tobacco, fish, and pork. Hunan is also rich in minerals such as antimony, tungsten, lead, and zinc. Apart from the processing of these metals, the economy is based chiefly on the chemical, automobile, steel, and engineering industries. Textiles, paper, firework cases, and ceramics are particularly important for the export trade. Wealth is concentrated in the golden triangle between Zhuzhou, Xiangtang, and Changsha. Progress is reflected in an agreeable lifestyle—and, of course, in eating habits.

Top: The sandstone pillars of the Wulung mountains, rising to a height of up to 650 feet (200 m), are a UNESCO World Heritage Site.

Above: The future of the province is sitting in the beautifully decorated baby carrier of a peasant woman from the mountains.

Facing page: The times when operas were still called "The Conquest of Tiger Mountain" or "The Red Women's Battalion" are past. Nowadays, classical works are being staged again.

Changsha

It doesn't get any hotter—Hunan cuisine

If you think Sichuan cuisine is hot, you have never tried Hunan. It is so fiery that it even takes their Sichuan neighbors' breath away—so it is not surprising that the so-called Xiang cuisine is not so very well known in the Western world.

As one of the eight great traditions of Chinese cuisine, it has a history going back some 2,000 years, as can be seen from grave finds from Mawangdui, near Changsha. It seems that even then the Hunan diet was diverse, rich, and oily. Of more than 3,000 burial objects, a good two thirds were intended to stay the hunger of Lady Dai, who died in 160 BC. After all, the wife of the nobleman Dai (or Li Cang), who is reputed to have loved good food when she was alive, should also enjoy such delicacies as sparrows' eggs, wine, and lotus after death. So she also needed her favorite dishes, clay figures as symbolic servants, and the finest lacquer ware. Over the course of time, regional cooking traditions also developed. On the alluvial plains around the Dongting Lake, rice, lotus, turtles, and crayfish played an important part. In the rural southeast they had pork and poultry on the menu as well as vegetables, while in the mountains their diet was mainly composed of bamboo, wild mushrooms, and game. Even back then, food was mostly steamed or braised for hours, fried, or roasted—and given a strong flavor by the liberal use of ginger, onions, garlic, and pepper. In addition they added fermented soybean paste, pickled vegetables, and especially smoked ingredients such as ham, fish, and poultry. From the 17th century on, the very substantial dishes were given an extra kick: chili seasoning. Brought by the Portuguese

explorers, chile peppers traveled from South America as far as Hunan in the Chinese hinterland, where they encountered not only fertile soil but also the Hunan people's predilection for spicy foods. Today there are around 4,000 dishes in Hunan cuisine—and, however varied they may be, they are all distinguished by one thing: their sharp, spicy, slightly sour flavor.

The sharpness is just unbelievable: it brings tears to your eyes, mists up your glasses from the inside, and has the sweat streaming from every pore, even the hollows behind your knees! Unlike Sichuan sharpness, which has a refreshing, almost numbing effect because of the use of Sichuan pepper, Hunan sharpness is pure and overwhelming. The reason is that they use the exceptionally fiery seeds and stems of the chile as well—and often raw, into the bargain. Chiles are more or less a vegetable accompaniment to Hunan dishes such as Dong'an chicken, stinky tofu, and even eels. While the people of Sichuan make their omnipresent chili oil (lajiao) by pouring hot oil over dried, ground chili, Hunan cooks use freshly chopped, salted and slightly fermented chiles for their dou jiao sauce. With steamed fish head, fermented stinky tofu, or smoked ham—dou jiao sauce is a must with Hunan's favorite dishes.

According to traditional Chinese medicine, this stimulating sharpness is believed to drive the moisture out of the body during the hot summer months, but the people of Hunan cannot

do without it in winter either and like to gather round the hotpot. Every imaginable ingredient is slowly cooked in a mass of chiles; for slightly less hot-headed spirits, a milder soup simmers in the other half of the hotpot, just as it does in Sichuan.

Boiled rice eel

10 oz (300 g) rice eel
5 fresh green chiles
3 ½ oz (100 g) dried bamboo shoots
3–4 shiitake mushrooms
2–3 perilla leaves
1 egg white
salt
1 ¼ lbs (500 g) pork dripping or lard
1 ½ tbsp Shaoxing rice wine
½ tsp light rice vinegar
2 tsp cornstarch mixed with 4 tsp water
1 ½ tbsp meat stock
freshly ground Sichuan pepper
1 tbsp sesame oil
freshly chopped cilantro for garnish

Place the eel on a chopping board, make a cut in the skin and, holding the flesh in place with the knife, pull away the skin. Plunge the eel flesh briefly in boiling water, remove the bones, and cut the flesh into strips 2 inches (5 cm) long and ⅛ inch (3 mm) thick. Wash the chiles and cut in thin strips along with the bamboo shoots and a few shiitake mushrooms. Then finely chop the perilla leaves.

In a bowl, beat the egg white to a foam and stir in about 2 pinches of salt. Add the strips of eel and mix well.

Heat a wok over medium heat, add all but 4 tablespoons of the pork dripping and let it melt. Add the strips of eel and fry for about 30 seconds,

Left: Here, rice noodles are being dried by the roadside.

Right: Hunan is home to one of the eight great regional cuisines of China, so the province has a tradition of restaurants with high standards.

stirring all the time with chopsticks. Remove the eel and drain in a colander.

Melt the remaining pork schmaltz in the wok and heat fiercely. Add the bamboo shoots, shiitake mushrooms, and a little salt and stir-fry briefly. Then add the eel and the rice wine and continue stir frying. One at a time, add the rice vinegar, perilla leaves, cornstarch mixture, and stock and stir together to make a sauce. Give the wok a quick shake and tip the contents onto a plate. Season with Sichuan pepper, to taste, and drizzle with sesame oil. Garnish the edge of the plate with cilantro and serve immediately.

Top left: No Hunan restaurant can manage without the many hands of the hardworking kitchen staff.

Top right: Here too, freshness is of paramount importance.

Above: Equal rights prevail, at least when it comes to food preparation. Both women...

Middle right: ...and men wash, trim, peel, and chop the many fresh ingredients.

Bottom right: The selection in the night markets of Changsha will satisfy any customer.

Wealthy Changsha

With its residential blocks and skyscrapers, its Westernized shopping streets and narrow, typically Chinese alleys with little food stores and markets, Changsha resembles many other large Chinese cities. Yet because of the cult of Chairman Mao, there is still a whiff of communism blowing through today's "socialist market economy," which takes care of welfare here in the cultural, economic, and political center of Hunan.

The administrative region, which covers around 4,650 square miles (12,000 sq km), is home to over 6 million inhabitants, around half of whom live in Changsha. Changsha stands on the banks of the Xiangjiang River, a 540-mile (870-km)-long lifeline running northward through Hunan to the Dongting Lake and into the mighty Yangtze River. Early on in its existence, Changsha became important as an inland port and trading center for rice. Nowadays the highway, rail, and flight connections are so good that you forget that the province is situated in the interior of the country. Largely because of the good infrastructure, national and international companies have set up branches here and a lot of foreign investment has flowed into the city. Changsha has now become one of the 20 wealthiest cities in China.

Of course it was not always like that. Changsha has been destroyed several times by fires and wars, but here and there you can still find impressive traces of the past. In primeval times, Hunan was settled by the Miao and Yao peoples. During the Spring and Autumn Period (722–481 B.C.) it was part of the kingdom of Chu, and under the Qin dynasty (221–206 B.C.) the migration of Han Chinese to the area brought it into the sphere of written Chinese history. The name Changsha dates from this time. From the grave finds of Mawangdui, discovered in Changsha in 1972, we can see how prosperous the rulers already were at the time of the early western Han dynasty (209 B.C.–9 A.D.). Among the archaeological treasures to be seen in the Hunan Provincial Museum, the perfectly preserved mummy of Lady Dai and 3,000 luxurious burial offerings still appear absolutely sensational. During the Song Period (960–1279), Changsha flourished as an educational center. At the Yuelu Academy, founded in 976 and one of the four oldest and most important educational institutions of ancient

China, the teachings of Confucius were studied and disseminated. The splendid building, which has been brilliantly restored, stands overlooking the Xiang River on the eastern slope of the Yuelu Hill, in the middle of a 14-square-mile (36-sq-km) landscaped park, attracting many visitors, especially in summer.

Changsha has made a name for itself not only as an educational center, but also in connection with the rice trade. The wisdom of the old proverb still holds true: "If the harvests are good in Huguang (which then covered the modern provinces of Hunan and Hubei), the whole kingdom will flourish." But in the commercial, financial, and industrial center that is Changsha, they have long since been selling high-tech goods as well as rice.

The wealth of the provincial capital is also to be seen in Hunan's number one leisure activity: dining. Luxury hotels and restaurants offer international and regional delicacies, while in the countless snack bars and night markets, the tables groan under the weight of the snacks. Whether you want Maren crispy duck, pickled stinky tofu, fiery Kouwei shrimp, or dumplings, in Changsha almost every culinary desire can be fulfilled, except perhaps for a bucket of rice to alleviate the sharpness!

Dong'an chicken

1 chicken
1 piece of ginger (2 ¼ inch / 6 cm long)
5 dried red chiles
1 scallion
3 ½ oz (100 g) pork dripping or lard
3 ½ tbsp light rice vinegar
1 ½ tbsp Shaoxing rice wine
freshly ground Sichuan pepper
7 tbsp stock
2 tsp cornstarch mixed with 4 tsp water
1 tsp sesame oil for serving

Put the chicken in a pan of water, cover, and boil for 8–10 minutes until ¾ cooked. Remove from the pan, remove all the bones, and cut the meat from the breast and drumsticks in thick strips 2 inches (5 cm) long and ½ inch (1 cm) wide. Cut the ginger in thin strips. Finely chop the chiles. Slice the white parts of the scallion. Heat a wok over high heat and melt the pork dripping in it. Add the chicken strips, ginger strips and chiles and brown until the aroma is released and the schmaltz turns red. Add the vinegar, rice wine, ground Sichuan pepper, to taste, and the stock. Bring to a boil over high heat, then simmer over low heat until the liquid has almost completely evaporated (about 2 hours). Add the chopped scallion, bind with the cornstarch mixture, and stir-fry briefly over high heat. Drizzle with sesame oil, transfer the contents of the wok to a dish and serve immediately.

Above: The bridge over the Xiangjiang in Changsha is 4,062 feet (1250 m) long.

Facing page: During the second Sino-Japanese war (1937–1945), large parts of the provincial capital were destroyed and not rebuilt until after 1949.

Left: Today Changsha is a pulsating metropolis …

Bottom left: …whose older inhabitants have succeeded in understanding how to withdraw from hectic city life.

Shaoshan—in memoriam Mao

Chairman Mao is no longer of any great importance for the political business of the day, but all the same Western tourists in China often encounter him swaying gently to and fro in the form of a talisman hanging from the rear-view mirror of a taxi. However this has little to do with reverence for the person of Mao Zedong (1893–1976). Mao was indisputably powerful, and people believe that such a potent personality must still have great influence from the other side of the grave. He keeps away evil spirits as well as traffic accidents. Even this small insight shows how important Mao Zedong once was in China, if he has to pay for it posthumously by scaring off spirits. However, the Mao personality cult has left particularly impressive traces on Shaoshan in the heart of Hunan. If Mao had not existed, Shaoshan, with its 100,000 inhabitants, would probably have remained a humble, unknown, small town—at first sight picturesque—in a region that is agricultural through and through.

This is where Mao Zedong was born in 1893, the son of a prosperous farmer, so he in fact belonged to the very class that he would later demonize as "bourgeois." As a young man he was full of enthusiasm for Western ideas and involved in the anti-Manchu movement, which had taken up the cause of the overthrow of the Qing dynasty. After his schooldays in Changsha, Mao left the province in 1918 and found employment in Beijing as an assistant librarian. In 1922 he joined the Chinese Communist Youth League and at the end of the 1920s he returned with a crowd of supporters to the mountains of Jiangxi Province, where he founded the Soviet Republic of Jiangxi (1931–1934). But it was only in 1935 that he was able to get his ideology accepted in the Party. He built the revolution not on the working class (which hardly existed in China) but on the peasants, who were living in poverty and without rights everywhere in the country. On October 1, 1949 Mao finally proclaimed the People's Republic of China and became Head of State.

But Shaoshan's finest hour did not arrive until a year later. In the 1960s, when Mao saw his power disappearing because of internal party strife, he proclaimed the "Great Proletarian Cultural Revolution" (1966–76), allowed himself to be worshiped almost like a god, and had his opponents prosecuted as class enemies under the cloak of social revolution. Shaoshan suddenly became almost a place of pilgrimage. Millions of Red Guards came to Hunan from all over the country to visit Mao's birthplace. They even built a special railroad from Changsha to the remote town. Nowadays, curious tourists walk through Shaoshan and the Mao's Family Restaurant chain serves Mao's favorite dishes. Mao is still admired, especially in country areas, probably because—among other things—he was the first Chinese leader to look after the interests of the peasants, but also because, for the Chinese, a critical argument with Mao would also necessitate casting a critical eye over their own youthful actions. Many of those now in their sixties were involved in the Cultural Revolution as Red Guards. The Chinese Communist Party's official position is expressed in the formula "70/30," 70 percent good, 30 percent bad. Many Chinese secretly turn this evaluation round the other way.

Shaoshan and its worship of Mao make many Western visitors feel it is at best bizarre. The only thing Chinese and Westerners agree on concerns Mao's favorite dish—red-cooked belly of pork—it tastes fantastically good!

Top right: The house where Mao Zedong was born is a remarkable attraction—and will probably remain so for some considerable time.

Right: Even if his name hardly plays a part in everyday politics any more, the historical significance of the Great Chairman is carved in stone in the truest sense of the word.

Red-cooked belly of pork
(Mao Zedong's favorite dish)

1 lb 10 oz (750 g) belly of pork
1 star anise
2 cinnamon sticks
1 piece of fresh ginger (1 ¼ inch / 3 cm long),
   chopped
sugar candy
½ tsp dark soy sauce
½ tsp red sugar syrup
Shaoxing rice wine
vegetable oil for frying
1 tbsp salted black beans
1 piece of scallion (1 ¾ inch / 4 cm long),
   chopped
3 g dried chiles
4 cups (1 liter) meat stock
1 tsp salt
½ tsp juice from pickled fermented tofu
2 garlic cloves, chopped
freshly chopped scallion to garnish

Top: Here the great Chairman rested in bed...

Above: ...and here they cooked for him.

Left: In Mao's lifetime there was already a real
trade in devotional objects connected with him.

Middle left: Nowadays you no longer find the so-
called "little red book" among them. Its contents
would hardly be compatible with current state
doctrine.

Below left: "The Great Helmsman" as Mao was
once known, is now so depoliticized that he only
appears as a trashy souvenir.

Blanch the pork in boiling water, take it out, rinse,
and drain. Cut in 2-inch (5-cm) cubes. Put these
in a heatproof dish with the star anise, cinnamon
sticks, ginger, sugar candy, soy sauce, sugar
syrup, and a little rice wine. Put the dish in a
bamboo steamer until the meat is almost completely tender. Set the flavorings aside after
steaming to be used again. Heat the oil in a wok,
add the meat and fry over low heat until golden
brown. Remove and drain.
Reheat the oil in the wok, and one by one fry the
salted black beans, scallion, ginger, cinnamon
sticks, and chiles in it until they release their aromas. Add the meat, pour over the meat stock,
flavor with the salt and the juice from the fermented tofu, and continue simmering for 1 hour.
When the meat is really tender, add the garlic and
stir-fry briefly. Sprinkle with freshly chopped
scallion before serving.

Born of need—pickled vegetables

The winters in the north of China are hard and long. In earlier times it was almost impossible to get fresh vegetables in the local markets at this time of year, so the housewives usually stock up with vegetables in summer and autumn. They preserve them with the aid of vinegar, salt, and various spices in order to lay in reserves of vitamins for the winter. The original, simple way of preserving things has, over the centuries, developed into a culinary art. The fact that pickled vegetables retain their color helps to promote their popularity, as, along with taste, aroma and consistency, a balanced combination of colors in food is one of the standard criteria for a successful Chinese dish. Nowadays pickled vegetables *paocai* can be found in countless varieties and types of flavor—and are a must in every Chinese household and restaurant.

In Beijing and the northern provinces of Heilongjiang and Inner Mongolia in particular, a fat earthenware pot is part of the basic equipment of every household. In it they usually keep Chinese leaves, but also root vegetables such as radishes and carrots, or cucumbers. In Yunnan, Guizhou, and Tibet, you also see pots of this kind standing in front of the houses in every village. There the custom is to stand the pots in the sun for two to four days immediately after pickling the vegetables, probably in order to speed up the fermentation process. Then the pots are stored, as is usual elsewhere, in a cool place.

In the north, the recipe for pickling is very simple. The vegetables are placed in the pot in layers, each of which is liberally sprinkled with salt. Cooling the pickled Chinese leaves turns the sugar contained in the leaves into acetic acid, which kills off the bacteria and preserves the cabbage. Pickled cabbage is crisp and tastes sour and salty. It sharpens the appetite and aids digestion. It is similar to sauerkraut and is popular with Chinese tourists in Germany, who do not otherwise get on very well with German food. Pickled cabbage is also excellent for filling jiaozi, the popular dumplings, and as an ingredient in a Heilongjiang stew *suancai dun fentiao* and for hotpot (fire pot).

The method of preparation in South China differs from that in the north, where the vegetables are only salted and no liquid is added. In other regions, a liquor made of various ingredients is usual. In the province of Sichuan, for example, the vegetables, usually Chinese leaves and radishes, are pickled in brine with a shot of rice wine or schnapps and a refined mixture of spices made up of chiles, flower pepper, ginger, star anise, and cinnamon.
The vegetables preserved in this way are taken out of the earthenware pot in portions as needed, and it is topped up with fresh vegetables, plus salt and a little wine, so that the brine retains its consistency. From time to time a pinch of sugar and some extra spice is added to the brine, so it will always be the same, as they say in Sichuan. There too they like to use pickled vegetables in cooking, and even more as accompaniments to their breakfast rice soup, or before or after meals as a kind of palate-cleanser, or simply as a snack in between.

A new variation, which is gaining in popularity, is known as "water shower." Cucumber, celery, or bell peppers are briefly plunged in water containing just a splash of the traditional spiced brine. After this treatment, the vegetables retain their consistency, and have a lighter, less intense taste than if pickled in the traditional way.

However, not everyone in China makes their own pickles. After all, you have long been able to buy these delicacies in every supermarket. One of the best known brands from Beijing is "Liu Bi Ju." This family business can look back over more than 400 years of traditional vegetable pickling. The imperial court was once a regular customer of theirs. One of this quality brand's best known products is Jiang Baogua, a combination of sugar melon, vegetables of various kinds, and a spicy paste that was already popular at the time of the Ming Dynasty (1368–1644). Today these pickled vegetables, prepared according to traditional recipes, are exported to as far away as America and Europe.

ELKE SPIELMANNS-ROME

1 These are the ingredients: In the background, Chinese leaves, carrots, and radishes. In the front pepper, sugar, and pickled chiles are at the ready—and the indispensable vinegar and schnapps.

2 The cabbage, radishes, and carrots are roughly chopped in large pieces. With a Chinese kitchen knife large quantities of vegetables can be chopped quickly and easily.

Left: Paojiang—pickled ginger—is one of the classic Chinese pickles.

Mixed pickles Sichuan style

3 ½ oz (100 g) carrots
3 ½ oz (100 g) white cabbage
3 ½ oz (100 g) white radish (daikon)
1 oz (30 g) salt
2 tsp Sichuan pepper
⅛ cup (30 g) sugar crystals
2 tbsp white vinegar
1 ¾ oz (50 g) green pickled mung beans (chili beans)
2 tbsp clear wheat schnapps

Wash the carrots and white radish, peel, and cut in rough pieces. Cut the white cabbage in big pieces.

Half fill the earthenware pot with water and add the salt, Sichuan pepper, sugar crystals, white vinegar, mung beans and schnapps. Add the carrots, cabbage, and white radish.

Cover and leave the vegetables to marinate in the pot for three days.

Then remove the vegetables from the pot and cut in thin slices. Mix with chili oil before serving.

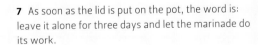

3 Then the pot is filled with vinegar. A mild rice vinegar is best. Sherry vinegar is not really to be recommended.

6 ...and finally the carrot. However the order is by no means crucial.

4 Next the prepared vegetables are put into the pot. First the radish...

7 As soon as the lid is put on the pot, the word is: leave it alone for three days and let the marinade do its work.

5 ...then the white cabbage...

8 Then the vegetables can be taken out of the pot, sliced, and mixed with chili oil. Mixed pickles look decorative if served in a glass carafe.

Hunan specialties

Rice crust with pork tenderloin and vegetables

3 ½ oz (100 g) pork tenderloin
1 ¾ oz (50 g) soaked shiitake mushrooms
1 ¾ oz (50 g) dried bamboo shoots
6 oz (175 g) rice crust (see below)
vegetable oil for frying

Spicy sauce:
½ tsp salt
1 tsp soy sauce
1 tsp sugar
1 tsp Shaoxing rice wine

Mix together the ingredients for the spicy sauce. Cut the pork tenderloin in slices and mix with the spicy sauce. Briefly blanch the shiitake mushrooms and bamboo shoots and set aside.

Break the rice crust into rectangular pieces. Heat the oil in a wok and fry the rice crust until golden brown, then remove and transfer to a plate. Drizzle with a little of the hot oil.
Stir fry the slices of pork. When the meat is tender, add the shiitake mushrooms and bamboo shoots, stir-fry briefly, then pour the contents of the wok over the rice crust and serve immediately.

Rice crust

Soak rice in hot water, then bring to a boil and cook until tender. Line a baking sheet with parchment and spread with a thin layer of the cooked rice. Put in the oven to dry out at low heat (about 140 °F/60 °C). If a lot of steam is given off, keep the door slightly open by jamming a wooden spoon in it.

Stinky tofu, fried with fresh red chile and chili oil

3 blocks of fresh silk tofu
2 ½ quarts (2.5 liters) stock
canola oil for frying

Stock:
Generous 1 lb (500 g) fresh bamboo shoots
10 shiitake mushrooms
3 ½ oz (100 g) eel (with bones)
3 ½ oz (100 g) salted black beans from
   Liuyang (or black bean paste)

Spicy sauce:
4 tbsp chili oil
1 tbsp sesame oil
3–4 tbsp soy sauce
⅔ cup (150 ml) chicken stock

Put the ingredients for the stock in a large saucepan with 2–3 quarts (2–3 liters) water, boil, allow to cool, pass through a strainer, and reserve the stock.
Marinate the tofu in the stock (for the time, see Tip below). Remove the tofu, rinse briefly in clear water, and drain. Mix together the chili oil, sesame oil, soy sauce, and chicken stock to make a spicy sauce.
Heat the canola oil in a wok over medium heat, add the marinated tofu blocks and fry over low heat for about 5 minutes, until the outer skin is crisp and the inside is still soft. Then take them out with a draining spoon and lay them on a plate. With chopsticks, bore a hole in each of the tofu blocks. Give the spicy sauce a good stir and pour into the holes before serving.

How long the tofu should draw in the stock depends on the time of year. In spring and autumn it is 3–5 hours, in summer 1–2 hours, and in winter 6–10 hours.

Left: Rice crust with pork tenderloin and vegetables

Facing page: Tomatoes with eggs

Facing page, main picture: Giant shrimp with chile

Tomatoes with eggs

eggs
3 tomatoes
3 ½ tbsp oil
1–2 tbsp freshly chopped scallion
1 tsp salt
1 tbsp sugar

Beat the eggs in a bowl. Dice the tomatoes. Heat three-quarters of the oil in a wok, add the scallion, stir-fry, add the tomatoes and cook until it forms a sauce. Add the salt and sugar and stir in. Add the beaten eggs and stir-fry for 1 minute. Serve immediately.

Giant shrimp with chile

enerous 1 lb (500 g) unpeeled giant shrimp
4 tbsp vegetable oil
dried red chiles, to taste
1–2 tsp Sichuan pepper
1 garlic clove, finely chopped
1 thick slice ginger, chopped
1 star anise
1 cinnamon stick
½ tsp salt
1 tsp soy sauce
1 tsp Shaoxing rice wine

Wash the giant shrimp thoroughly, brush if necessary, and drain.
Heat the oil in a wok, add the shrimp, fry briefly until the shells turn red, then remove them from the wok.
Put the dried chiles and Sichuan pepper into the wok and stir-fry until they release their aroma.

Briefly fry the garlic and ginger over medium heat until the aroma is released.
Put the shrimp, star anise and cinnamon stick in the wok, add a little water, and stir-fry over high heat. After 1 minute, add the salt, soy sauce, and rice wine, and simmer briefly.
As soon as the wok gives off the intense aromas of the star anise and cinnamon, add a little more water.
Simmer for about 30 minutes more until the liquid has evaporated, then take out and serve immediately.

Rice buying made easy

Almost all Chinese meals consist mainly of rice, so in China the word for boiled rice *fan* has become a synonym for all kinds of things to eat. "Chi fan le ma"— Have you eaten rice yet?—is a common greeting, and includes other basic foods. So, rice. But what kind of rice? One glance at the selection on the yards of shelving in an Asian store and the Western gourmet is overcome by doubt. Jasmine rice? Or would basmati rice be better? Broken rice or whole grain? And can sushi rice also be used?

Basically—despite the existence of many varieties throughout the world—the rice question is very easily solved. Chinese rice is typically long-grain, polished, that is white, and sticky. While brown, partly polished rice is considered particularly healthy in the West and white rice is served with a trace of guilty conscience, in China there is no doubt about it. Brown rice, which has had the husk removed but still contains the bran and the germ, is seen as food for the poor and is not fit for guests—not least because it not only tastes different but also because it is not very sticky, an essential quality when using chopsticks. Even light, grainy, parboiled rice is not perfectly suited to Chinese dishes.

The classic kind of rice that is particularly suitable for Chinese dishes is **fragrant** or **jasmine rice**. Its name comes from its characteristic aroma. It is distinguished by its fine flavor and sticking properties. Depending on quality, it is also obtainable on the market as broken rice, i.e. with broken grains. Whether it originates from China or Thailand is unimportant compared with its flavor. By contrast, **basmati rice** is an Indian variety, whose flavor certainly goes well with Chinese food, but it is not quite so easy to manage with chopsticks as fragrant rice. The sticky, slightly sweet Japanese **round corn rice**, also known as sushi rice (although it is not used for sushi), is not considered authentic in China, but it does provide an alternative. **Glutinous rice** is eaten throughout Southeast Asia. Thanks to its high starch content, it sticks to the fingers like glue—and it has to, because people here often eat with their right hand. In China, glutinous rice is mainly used for *zongzi*, rice dumplings wrapped in bamboo leaves.

Right: Even if machines—however primitive they may be—make the work in the rice fields easier, water buffalo (which can be seen in the background) are still used in large numbers.

1 The preparation of *zongzi* is not so very hard. The most important thing is: it has to be glutinous rice!

3 —and any aids can be used, including the corner of the table when pulling tight or teeth for holding one end of the thread.

2 A steady hand is needed for stuffing bamboo leaves. Then they are skillfully tied, one after the other ...

4 Apart from rice, bean broth, egg (boiled or fried), and dates can also be used for the filling.

Preparing long grain rice is child's play—especially if you own a rice cooker, which you can now buy in almost any Asian store. Reckon on about half a cup per person. If you do not have a rice cooker to hand, wash the rice in cold water as many times as necessary until the water remains clear, and put it on to boil with no salt and double the amount of water (i.e. two cups of water to one cup of rice). As soon as the water boils, reduce the heat to the lowest setting and leave the rice to swell for about 15 minutes with the lid on.

Incidentally, it can occasionally happen that you do not get any rice in good restaurants in China. This is not due to forgetfulness on the part of the staff, but simply because rice is considered to be an accompaniment to fill you up. A good host therefore offers so many delicious things to eat that the "cheap" accompaniment is no longer deemed necessary. That is a shame, actually.

Left, top to bottom: The rice harvest requires teamwork. After it is cut, the rice is first threshed and dried. The husks, which make up around 20 percent of the original weight, are removed in a mill, leaving the rice grains with just a thin, brownish silvery skin.
Part of the further processing in the rice mill is grading. The most important quality for each grade is the proportion of broken rice. The maximum proportion of broken rice permitted in top quality types such as these is 5 percent.

Above: China is far and away the biggest rice producer in the world. The vast majority is harvested without mechanical aid.

Lotus and water chestnuts

Thousands of rivers and lakes run through the province of Hunan. The four biggest rivers—Xiangjiang, Zishui, Yanjiang, and Lishui—flow into the Dongting Lake in the north, which is the second largest freshwater lake in China. As well as providing drinking water it also serves as an equalizing reservoir for the Yangtze. In times when water is plentiful, the mighty floods make the lake, which usually has an area of around 3,590 sq yards (3000 sq m), swell and spread to six times its normal size. The constantly changing waters produce a great variety of flora and fauna, including the colorful lotus flowers, which are more than just very pretty to look at.

The incomparably beautiful pink lotus blossoms rise up out of a sea of circular, dark green leaves that drift on the water. Apart from the great symbolic value attributed to the lotus, which is a sign of purity in Buddhism and Hinduism, its culinary versatility must not be undervalued. Among the edible parts of the Indian **lotus** (*Nelumbo nucifera*), one of the most surprising is the unprepossessing root (rhizome), which looks a bit like a string of plump sausages. If you peel it and cut straight through it, you get a beautifully patterned hollow container that is perfect for holding a filling of ground meat or rice. But you do not have to fill lotus roots; with their mild, slightly sweet taste and crisp bite, you can also use them in salads, soups, marinated or preserved in a sweet syrup.

Lotus seeds are eaten fresh or dried as a fruit, or they can be preserved, sugared, or puréed as a dessert.

Fish, meat, rice, or vegetables wrapped in a lotus leaf and steamed acquire a delicious flavor.

Lotus root with glutinous rice

Generous 1 lb (500 g) lotus root
Generous 1 lb (500 g) glutinous rice
1 ½ tbsp sugar
2 tsp honey

Wash the lotus root thoroughly and trim. Cut off (but do not discard) the ends so that the air holes in the roots become visible.
Wash the glutinous rice, and leave to swell in hot water for 1 hour. Then fill the holes in the lotus root with rice and close them with the ends of the roots.
Put the rice-filled roots in a steamer. Add water and bring to a boil over high heat.
Steam the lotus roots for 1 hour over low heat, remove from the pan and leave to cool. Then cut in thick slices and arrange on a plate.
Leave a little water in the pan. Dissolve the sugar in it and bring to a boil. Skim, and simmer over low heat until the syrup thickens. Add the honey, stir and leave the mixture to cool. Pour the syrup over the stuffed lotus roots before serving.

The **water chestnut** (*Eleocharis dulcis*) thrives in the wetland areas around the Dongting Lake, especially in rice paddies. The stems of this water plant, a member of the sorrel family, may grow to over 39 inches (1 m) high, rather like the European papyrus. However, the part that is of interest to gourmets grows below the surface of the water. In spring small gray-brown to dark brown knobs, which look a little like chestnuts, form on the roots (rhizomes). They are ready to harvest when the visible part of the plant begins to wilt. Apart from water, the knobs, which are a favorite throughout Asia, contain mainly starch, so they can also be used for sweet dishes. Their slightly sweet flavor is most often used to complement vegetable and meat dishes, but is also found in soups and salads. The special thing about them is their consistency. Whether they are fresh, cooked, or from a can, they retain their unique, crisp bite. Attempts to cultivate water chestnuts outside China, Japan, the Philippines, and India have so far mostly failed. This apparently undemanding plant needs not only water and plenty of sun but also a precise day/night rhythm that only occurs close to the equator in order to form the knobs. If you come across water chestnuts in Asian food stores, you should snap them up—these delicacies are very easy to prepare.

Sweet-and-sour water chestnuts

7 oz (200 g) water chestnuts
2 ½ cups (600 ml) vegetable oil for frying
4 tsp soy sauce
2 tsp rice wine
4 tsp vinegar
4 tsp sugar
salt
1 tsp cornstarch mixed with 2 tsp water

Batter coating:
½ tbsp cornstarch
1 ½ tbsp all-purpose flour
1 egg
4 tsp water

For the coating, mix the ingredients well in a bowl to make a batter. Coat the water chestnuts one at a time with the batter.
Heat the oil fiercely in a wok, but not so much that it smokes. Add the water chestnuts one at a time. Fry for 3–4 minutes over moderate heat. Scoop them out with a large draining spoon and drain.
Pour off the oil, except for 4 tablespoons. Stir in the soy sauce, rice wine, vinegar, sugar, and a pinch of salt. Then add the cornstarch mixture and simmer gently, stirring continuously, until the mixture thickens. Add the water chestnuts and serve immediately.

Facing page, bottom left: Here the holes in the lotus root have already been filled with glutinous rice and will then be steamed in the closed bamboo steamer.

Facing page: Because of its waxy coating, the upper surface of the leaves of the Indian lotus is virtually water and dirt proof. This "lotus effect" makes the plant a symbol of purity in China.

Above right: Chinese water chestnuts (here fried in batter) are not related to the European sweet or horse chestnuts.

The versatile egg

Almost one in two of the world's eggs is laid by Chinese hens—more than 430,000 billion per year in total. But China does not only produce the most eggs, but is also the world leading consumer of eggs, with an annual consumption of 345 hens' eggs per capita (compared with 178 in England). It is impossible to imagine Chinese cuisine without chicken, duck, quail, and goose eggs—and of course thousand-year eggs.

You don't just see them, you can smell them too—**tea eggs** are popular everywhere. Almost everywhere, even in the tiniest supermarket, there are tea eggs simmering and sending out scented clouds of egg, anise, tea, and cinnamon. Basically, a tea egg is nothing more than a hardcooked egg that is given a gentle knock after boiling to produce tiny cracks through which the spicy aroma of black tea, soy sauce, and spices can permeate. When peeled, tea eggs reveal a marbled pattern and an unusual flavor.

As in Europe and America, **scrambled egg** is also considered a simple and tasty dish. However, the Chinese version is not quite as simple as the Western one. The beaten eggs are usually given a good shot of oil and a little rice wine. Merely sprinkled with chives, or topped with thin strips of shiitake mushroom and soy sprouts, shrimp, crab meat, ham, or fresh tomatoes, eggs can be transformed into a special treat.

Egg dumplings are reminiscent of omelets with delicious fillings. Regional boundaries are the only thing that limits the variety of fillings. First, in a pan, you make an omelet about the size of the palm of your hand, and as soon as it has begun to set, put a couple of tablespoons of ham, oysters, or seafood in the middle. Then you fold all the sides of the omelet to the middle. A shot of hot oil over all the seams and it is ready—a favorite snack, not only at night markets.

Savory **egg puddings** consist of broth and eggs, which are steamed on their own or with mushrooms, ham, or crabs—a mild but very tasty kind of soufflé that melts in the mouth. The province of Macau is famous for sweet versions of this pudding made with eggs and coconut milk.

Right: An abundance of eggs: Tea eggs, and the delicacy known as thousand-year eggs are just a small part of what Chinese cooks can make of chicken, duck, quail, or goose eggs.

Below: Caution hot! Thousand-year-eggs with chiles in soy sauce.

Below right: Thousand-year-old eggs will keep for months because of fermentation.

However varied the recipes for **thousand-year-eggs** may be, the one thing they are not is a thousand years old. It is more a question of a method of preservation that lasts for months. First raw hens' or ducks' eggs are pickled in brine, then—depending on region and tradition—they are surrounded with coals, chalk, ashes, mud, or rice straw and stored in an airtight place. During this procedure the white is transformed into a gelatinous mass, while the yolk gets a consistency rather like soft cheese. After 45 days at the earliest, the eggs are ready to be eaten. As a rule, people no longer produce their own thousand-year-eggs; instead they are sold in markets or supermarkets. They are considered a delicacy in China and, perhaps accompanied by pickled ginger, used as a tasty appetizer or a little extra on the menu.

The ancient process of fermentation that makes eggs keep was also used for the much-prized **turtle eggs**. In China these particularly nutritious eggs are still thought to be an aphrodisiac.

Salted duck eggs, with their rich, bright yellow yolks, are considered indispensable in Chinese cuisine. They are either pickled raw and unpeeled in salt solution for 20–40 days or first put in brine for about 10 days, and then in a paste of salted mud or charcoal and then wrapped in rice straw. These very salty duck eggs must then be cooked for 10 minutes before they are used as an accompaniment or as a filling for moon cakes that will bring good luck.

Thousand-year-eggs, which at first glance look more like grave finds than edible duck eggs, are prepared in a similar way. While Westerners have problems with the sight of the jelly-like, greenish-black egg white and the greenish-yellow yolk, many Chinese love the unmistakable taste that reminds you of old cheese.

Right: Tea eggs simmer for about an hour at quite a low temperature, as they take up the aromas of the spiced tea.

Sichuan

四川

Elke Spielmanns-Rome

Sichuan has always been one of China's most heavily populated provinces. Situated in the heart of the country with a population of around 90 million, it is the China's largest province and has often played a key role in the country's politics. Events in Sichuan triggered the 1911 revolution, which toppled the emperor and led to the birth of the Republic of China. Chinese nationalists retreated to Sichuan when the Japanese occupied eastern China during the Sino-Japanese war, and Sichuan was also the first province to introduce agrarian reform, a policy which signaled the beginning of China's modernization.

Sichuan ("Four Rivers") is situated in southwestern China and runs from east to west, spanning a distance of more than 600 miles (1,000 km). Located in the eastern part of the province is China's fertile "Red Basin," a rich grain-producing area, which produces up to three harvests a year and is consequently densely populated. In contrast, Sichuan's mountainous western region—thanks to its limited accessibility—is home to just 10 percent of the province's population, many of them Tibetans. Sichuan is bordered to the west by the steeply rising Tibetan mountains and in the same way that these snow-covered peaks extend across the province's borders and down into the Sichuan Basin, Tibetan culture has crossed the borders into western Sichuan in a similar manner.

At the same time as the Shang civilization (16–11 B.C.) was flourishing in the lowland plains of northern China, as far as the middle reaches of the Yangtze river, a parallel ancient civilization, known as the Shu culture, was evolving in Sichuan. Its unusual masks and bronze figures are still intriguing archaeologists to this day. During the 3rd century B.C., Sichuan was the headquarters of the Qin, who would eventually unite China for the first time. In agricultural terms, the land was already quite well developed by this time. From the time of the Han dynasty (206 B.C.–220 A.D.), a river control project safeguarded the irrigation of the entire area surrounding Chengdu and turned the region into one of China's most productive cultivated areas. During the period of the Three Kingdoms (221–280 A.D.), Sichuan, or the Kingdom of Shu, as it was known at the time, was an independent state. Even after China's unification in the 6th century, the kingdom retained a large degree of autonomy.

During the 20th century, Shu played an important part in the fall of the Chinese empire. Here, as in other parts of China, the railroads had been built with a large amount of private capital. In 1911, the imperial Qing government announced plans to nationalize the railroad projects, at the same

Top: Due to a combination of technological, ecological and social reasons, the Three Gorges Dam on the Yangtze has always been a highly controversial construction project.

Above: Chongqing is situated at the confluence of the Yangtze and Jialing rivers. The extent of this municipality's administrative boundaries and its 32-million strong population make it the largest city in the world.

Facing page: The subtropical, forested slopes of Sichuan are home to the giant panda, which eats 22–44 lb (10–20 kg) of bamboo each day.

Chengdu• •Chongqing

Sichuan **365**

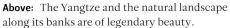

Above: The Yangtze and the natural landscape along its banks are of legendary beauty.

Above right: The huge Three Gorges Dam project required the resettlement of nearly 2 million people. Within just a few years, whole new towns had been built from scratch along its shores.

Below: Sichuan cuisine is hot stuff. Chiles are almost regarded as part of the staple diet.

time signing an agreement accepting foreign capital investment. When it was discovered how low the indemnity paid to local investors in Sichuan was going to be, massive protests broke out and investors joined forces with revolutionaries. In a bid to bring the railroad protests under control, the Qing government moved army units into Sichuan from the neighboring province of Hubei. The revolutionary forces took advantage of the resulting power vacuum to capture Hubei's provincial capital of Wuhan. In the wake of this success, many provinces followed suit and declared their independence. Eventually a Republic was declared, ending thousands of years of Chinese imperial rule.

Soon afterwards, Sichuan fell into a state of anarchy. Marauding bands of robbers and plundering soldiers roamed the countryside and the atmosphere of uncertainty in rural areas led to poor harvests, and consequently to rising prices in the towns. Sichuan became an independent self-administration district, which only cooperated with Beijing on foreign policy matters. The real power was in the hands of so-called warlords, who divided up the province among themselves, and by 1924, the province had fragmented into 20 small military territories. Nor did the province's government, formed in 1928, prove capable of abolishing the warlords' territorial system. The population suffered considerably until well into the 1930s as a result of clashes between the armies of rival warlords.

When the Sino–Japanese war erupted in 1937/38 the national government moved the capital and its seat of government to Chongqing. The Japanese air force began carrying out raids on the city in the spring of 1939 and continued bombing it for several years. During the hungry years following Mao's "Great Leap Forward," Sichuan suffered considerably. Up to 10 percent of the population is said to have perished. In the mid 1970s, Zhao Ziyang, the provincial governor and party secretary of Sichuan, introduced a number of rural reforms in order to encourage a sense of individual responsibility and stimulate initiative on the part of the peasants. Thanks to these reforms, Sichuan became an important agricultural province once more. Zhao Ziyang, who later became Premier of the People's Republic, fell out of favor with the Party in 1989, however, on account of his reformist political beliefs and humanistic attitude.

In 1997, the eastern part of the province was merged with the major cities of Wanxian and Fuling to become a municipality under direct government administration. This amalgamation created an administrative district which, with a population of around 32 million people, makes it the largest "city" in the world.

Above: A thick layer of smog hangs over Chongqing in winter.

Below: Sichuan's "Red Basin" is an extremely fertile and agriculturally important lowland region.

Some like it hot—Sichuan cuisine

Sichuan cuisine is one of the country's eight main schools of regional cuisine and is representative of western China. Sichuan is best known for its hot dishes and its inhabitants like their food well seasoned, sometimes so hot that it numbs the taste buds. Extravagant use of chili and Sichuan pepper, it is argued, stimulates the palate, something many Central Europeans find difficult to emulate. The Sichuan people are also firmly convinced that hot, spicy dishes will help reduce dampness in the body and, given the province's high humidity in summer, this is indeed a pleasant notion!

Sichuan dishes tend to be simple compared with Peking Imperial Palace cuisine and as a result cannot compete in terms of extravagance. This is partly due to the isolated situation of the province, which is surrounded by

high mountains. Neither tropical fruits nor seafood were ever available here and the predominantly rural cuisine consisted mainly of meat dishes. While other regions of China place great store upon bringing out the flavor of individual ingredients, Sichuan dishes are noted for their diversity of spices and sauces. Nonetheless, the main consideration here, as everywhere else in China, is to achieve the perfect combination of flavor, color, shape, and aroma in the different dishes.

The most important ingredients in Sichuan recipes are Sichuan pepper, fresh chiles, which are part of almost every dish, and other commonly used spices, such as star anise, ginger, coriander, fennel, and garlic. Over the course of time, dishes from other regions have been absorbed into Sichuan cuisine and—by the

simple addition of chiles or Sichuan pepper—have been easily adapted to suit local tastes.

In the culinary world, Sichuan is also famed for its large number of different cooking methods, of which there are apparently more than fifty. These range from deep-frying, *gan zha*, and steaming, *zheng*, to an explosive type of quick frying, whereby the ingredients are stir-fried quickly in very hot oil over a high heat. Twice-cooked pork is another specialty of Sichuan cuisine: the pork is first boiled, then quickly stir-fried.

One of the most popular and best-known dishes is Hot chicken chunks with peanuts, a specialty that has also gained popularity outside China. A restaurant in Bonn, Germany, serves this spicy, hot dish under the name of "Chicken burnt at the stake."

Facing page, far left: When the spice and vegetable market opens its doors in the early morning, a fair amount of muscle power is required in order to set up the stalls.

Facing page: Getting through the narrow passages between the stalls can be quite difficult.

Above: Perhaps not quite as elegant as Peking cuisine and not as sophisticated as southern Chinese food...

Below: ...no other type of regional cuisine can compete with Sichuan dishes in terms of spicy hotness.

The province's most famous dish is still *mapo doufu*, a tofu dish named after a pock-marked, *ma*, old lady, *po*, who created it. She was the chef at a restaurant in Chengdu and cooked a delicious tofu dish, prepared from a mixture of tofu and ground pork, and seasoned with a mouth-numbing combination of Sichuan pepper and chili. The dish's reputation quickly spread beyond the confines of the city to become one of China's most popular dishes of all time.

Dishes with *yuxiang*, seasoning—(literally: fish fragrance)—are also very popular in Sichuan. Yuxiang pork can be eaten with impunity even by people who dislike fish. It has a distinctly spicy flavor without being in the least fishy! The seasoning consists of a salty, hot, and slightly sweet-and-sour combination of spices, including chili, garlic, ginger, scallions, soy sauce, and vinegar. Apparently, this delicious seasoning was originally only used for fish dishes, hence the name "fish fragrance."

Another well-known Sichuan specialty, which is popular not just in China, but throughout the world, is *(huoguo)*, or hotpot. The best version of this dish can be found in Chongqing.

The best place to go to sample traditional Sichuan dishes is Jinli Street in Chengdu, the

province's capital city. Here you will find numerous little stalls offering local specialties, some of them prepared in unusual ways. Pigs' kidneys, cut into small pieces, for example, are dropped into a pot containing hot oil, where they virtually explode, *bao*, or a mixture of rice and vegetables are cooked inside—and eventually eaten from—a piece of bamboo. Sugar blowers also provide an interesting spectacle. Taking a lump of maltose (malt sugar), they blow air through a straw into the sugary mass, skillfully shaping it into a variety of artistic figures. The choice is yours: from pigs to pandas, virtually anything is possible. Chinese people usually choose the animal that represents the sign under which they were born in the Chinese animal zodiac.

Hot tofu—mapo doufu

7 oz (200 g) tofu
1–2 tbsp fermented soybeans
1–2 tbsp hot chili bean paste
1/3 cup (75 ml) vegetable oil
3 1/2 oz (100 g) ground beef
1 piece of ginger (1 inch / 3 cm long), chopped
chili powder

2/3 cup (150 ml) meat or vegetable stock
2 tsp soy sauce
3 garlic cloves, freshly chopped
1 tsp sugar
salt
1/2 tsp cornstarch, mixed with 1 tsp water
crushed Sichuan pepper, to garnish

Cut the tofu into 3/4-inch (2-cm) cubes and blanch quickly in lightly salted boiling water. Remove from the water with a skimmer and place in fresh cold water. Chop up the fermented beans and stir the hot chili bean paste. Heat the wok, pour in the oil and fry the ground beef until it is crumbly.

Next, add the chili bean paste and fry with the meat. Add the fermented beans, ginger, and chili powder and stir-fry all the ingredients until the meat has absorbed the color of the paste. Pour in the stock and bring to a boil.

Add the tofu to the wok and simmer for 3 minutes.

Add the soy sauce, garlic, and sugar and season with salt, to taste. Thicken the contents of the wok with the cornstarch mixture and tip onto a serving dish, garnishing it with the crushed Sichuan pepper.

Above: Vegetables and spices are staple ingredients of Sichuan cuisine.

"Fish fragrant" pork

11 oz (300 g) pork tenderloin
10 dark Mu Err mushrooms
7 oz (200 g) bamboo shoots
1 ½ tbsp cornstarch mixed with 3 tbsp water
1 tbsp scallions, finely chopped
1 tbsp soy sauce
2 tbsp dark rice vinegar
1 tbsp rice wine
1 tbsp sugar
½ tsp salt
½ tsp sesame oil
3 tbsp water
vegetable oil, for frying
1 tbsp freshly chopped ginger
1 tbsp finely chopped garlic
1 tbsp chili powder

Cut the pork fillet into thin strips. Soak the Mu Err mushrooms in warm water, then wash thoroughly and cut the mushrooms and bamboo shoots into strips.

Place the pork in a bowl, mix in half the cornstarch and water mixture and allow to stand for 5 minutes. Place the scallions in a bowl, add the soy sauce, vinegar, rice wine, sugar, salt, sesame oil, water, and the remaining cornstarch mixture, mix thoroughly and set aside.

Heat the vegetable oil in a wok. Add the strips of pork and stir-fry until they are slightly cooked on the outside. Then push the meat to one side of the pan with a spatula. Add the garlic, ginger and chili powder to the center of the wok and fry until the aromas begin to be released, then mix these ingredients with the meat.

Add the bamboo shoots and Mu Err mushrooms, stir-fry all the ingredients for 2 minutes and finally pour over the sauce mixture. Stir-fry for a further 20 seconds until the sauce has thickened slightly, and then tip the mixture onto a plate to serve.

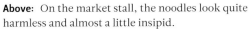

Above: On the market stall, the noodles look quite harmless and almost a little insipid.

Left: But with the right spices, even an innocent pot of noodles can turn into an explosive experience.

The curative powers of spices

The continent of China spans several climatic zones. This is reflected in the correspondingly large range of spices found in the individual regional cuisines. Evidence from ancient times suggests that Sichuan pepper, cinnamon, and other spices were already being used to flavor dishes in the 3rd century B.C. Thanks to the Silk Road and other trade routes, China's natural abundance of flora was further supplemented by importing foreign plants, such as the chile.

Some of the classic spices in Chinese cuisine include garlic, scallions, and ginger, while Chinese chives, coriander, Sichuan pepper, fresh chiles and chili powder, and star anise are also standard ingredients. The Chinese have always attached great importance to healthy eating which is why a large number of theories based on traditional Chinese medicine (TCM) regarding the beneficial effects of various spices and foods have been absorbed into everyday life.

Garlic (*Allium sativum*) is an extremely old cultivated plant, which was originally grown in China for its medicinal properties. It has been used for thousands of years as a remedy for conditions such as high blood pressure and indigestion problems. In addition to valuable trace minerals (potassium, phosphorus, iron, and iodine), garlic also contains various vitamins and some essential, sulfur-containing oils. Because of its antibacterial properties, it is often eaten raw in northern China to prevent colds. It loses some of its efficacy once it is cooked. In Shandong cuisine, it is frequently combined with ginger and scallions, while Sichuan chefs also add chili or Sichuan pepper to the mix. China is by far the world's largest producer of garlic, accounting for almost two thirds of the world's total output.

Scallions (*Allium fistulosum*) are an essential ingredient in Chinese cuisine. Only the lower white portion of the onion is used in cooking while the upper green portion is thinly sliced into mildly aromatic rings and sprinkled over food as a garnish just before serving—a feast not only for the palate but for the eyes as well. According to TCM, eating the raw white bulb will prevent the loss of yang energy and counteract any problems caused by cold weather, such as feverish colds or shivering fits.

The **shallot** (*Allium ascalonium*) is another member of the onion family that is commonly found in many regional Chinese dishes. It has a reddish tinge and a delicate onion flavor, which makes it ideal for eating raw. Shallots are often combined with ginger in Chinese cooking—to temper the intensive flavor of fish, for example.

Ginger (*Zingiber officinale*) is one of China's oldest spices, a fact also documented in the "Dialogues" of Confucius (551–479 B.C.). It is the root of the ginger plant that is used for culinary purposes. When cut open, it releases a pleasant, aromatic fragrance. The fibrous tuber (with or without the peel) can either be

grated using a special wooden grater, or chopped into small pieces with a knife. Raw ginger has a very strong flavor and is mainly used in marinades or dipping sauces. It is often paired with fish or seafood dishes, such as Squid in ginger sauce (from Fujian province) or Shrimp with ginger (from Shandong). Thanks to its medicinal properties, ginger occupies an important place in TCM: a freshly brewed ginger infusion will warm the body from within, help ease the symptoms of colds and reduce fever. It is also believed to stimulate the heart and circulatory system and improve the flow of blood.

Chinese **chives** (*Allium tuberosum*) are very similar to Western chives, but the flavor is more like that of garlic (hence the alternative name of garlic chives). In Chinese cuisine, chives are mainly used in combination with scallions, or served with dipping sauces. They can also be sprinkled over a dish just before serving. They are reputed to strengthen yang and are also sometimes jokingly referred to as "Viagra leeks" on account of their alleged aphrodisiac properties.

Chili (*Capsicum chinense*)—whether in the form of a paste, dried or fresh chiles—is the main ingredient used in Chinese cuisine to give food a fiery, hot flavor. It is consumed in large quantities, particularly in the western provinces of Sichuan and Hunan. If a dish is not quite hot enough, people here will nibble on a raw chile pepper on the side. This member of the capsicum family originated in South America, where it has been cultivated for over 7,000 years. The plant was brought

back to Europe by Christopher Columbus toward the end of the 15th century, along with potatoes and tomatoes and from here they ultimately found their way to China. Since they were easy to cultivate, they spread rapidly to become the main spice used in western China's regional cuisine. Meanwhile, a huge variety of different colored chiles with varying degrees of intensity are now grown in China and a selection of red, green, orange, yellow, and even violet-colored chile peppers can be bought from the markets. The color has no bearing whatsoever on the intensity of the "heat"—the hot flavor is mainly concentrated in the seeds. Those who prefer their food a little milder should therefore be sure to scrape the seeds from the inside of the chiles, once they have been cut open lengthwise. Chiles may also be used to make chili oil, which is ideal for flavoring various types of food and dipping sauces. Chili oil is easily made by chopping up one or more chile peppers and pouring very hot oil over them. Once cooled, the oil, which should now be an appetizing shade of red, is bottled and can be stored in the refrigerator for several weeks. Making chili sauce, however, is a much more time-consuming procedure. By far the easier option is to visit a Chinese store, where you will undoubtedly find a large selection of ready-made chili sauces that are such an important part of Sichuan cuisine. Chili is also used in TCM to provide the body with inner warmth, especially on cold winter days.

Continued on page 374

Above: The aromas which assail the nostrils on a visit to a spice market are almost indescribable.

Left: Spices, which are only used in tiny amounts in Western cuisine, are on sale here by the sack-load.

Right: Top-quality hot seasoning: chiles—either dried...

Below: ...or pickled.

The curative powers of spices **373**

Continued from page 373

Cilantro (*Coriandrum sativum*) bears a resemblance to parsley, which is why it is sometimes known as Chinese parsley. The Chinese use both the leaves and seeds of this plant. Cilantro leaves have a distinctive lemony aroma and pungent, bitter flavor (which is not to everyone's taste). Fresh cilantro is not normally cooked in the dish itself—instead its leaves are sprinkled over the finished dish as a garnish, as in the case of Lanzhou Lamian (from Gansu province), for example. The dried, ground seeds (coriander) of the plant are used in Yunnan to flavor poultry dishes—Chicken cooked in banana leaf, for example. According to TCM, cilantro is good for stimulating digestion and easing stomach pain.

Sichuan pepper (*Zanthoxylum piperitum*) (literally "flower pepper" in Chinese) is one of the best-known ingredients in Chinese cooking. It is produced from the fruit of the pepper tree. When eaten, it creates a tingly numbness in the mouth which is why it is also known in China as *mala*, meaning numbingly hot. This type of pepper is widely used in Sichuan cuisine, but it has gradually also found its way into various other regional cuisines. What is true of all spices is particularly true of Sichuan pepper: once ground, the reddish-brown kernels quickly lose their aroma which is why it is advisable to grind the peppercorns just before use. If they are gently roasted beforehand, they will not only develop an even more intensive aroma, but will also be easier to grind. According to TCM, Sichuan pepper has a beneficial effect on stomach complaints.

Fennel (*Foeniculum vulgare*) is a well-known ingredient of Chinese cuisine and is also used for medicinal purposes as a pain reliever. Strictly speaking, it is the plant's dried, ground seeds that are used for seasoning. In most cases, however, ground fennel seeds are combined with ground Sichuan pepper, star anise, cloves, and cinnamon to create what is known as **five-spice powder**, which is used, for example, in the preparation of Fried bream (from Heilongjiang province). This spice is also readily available in the West.

Star anise (*Illicium verum*) derives its name from its distinctive shape: eight-pointed star-shaped pods containing the seeds of the fruit. Its aroma is similar to that of fennel, which is why it is also known in China as "eight-pronged fennel." The dried pods may be added whole to the cooking pot, or else ground before use. Star anise is used in China to flavor hearty meat and fish dishes and is one of the traditional ingredients of five-spice powder. It is used in Heilongjiang province to season fish stew. In Chinese TCM it is attributed with antibacterial properties and used to treat inflammation.

Cinnamon (*Cinnamomum cassia*) has a sweetish, woody—and, at the same time, slightly bitter—flavor and is mainly used in Chinese cuisine as an ingredient in braised dishes, for example, Braised donkey meat

(from Gansu province). The quills of cinnamon bark are added whole to the dish but are not eaten. Chinese cinnamon (also known as cassia) is stronger in flavor than Ceylonese cinnamon (*Cinnamomum zeylanicum*). Since cassia contains courmarin, which in high concentrations can be hazardous to health, it should only be consumed in small amounts. Ground cinnamon is one of the traditional ingredients of five-spice powder. Cassia is used in TCM as an antispasmodic.

Cloves (*Syzygium aromaticum*), which in their ground form are also known as clove pepper, have a slightly hot, bitter, woody flavor, which can sometimes be overwhelmingly strong. If they are cooked whole, it is essential to remove them from the dish before eating. Their main use in Chinese cuisine is as an ingredient in five-spice powder. Cloves, which are rich in essential oils, are used in TCM primarily for their antibacterial properties. They are also useful as an antispasmodic in the treatment of bronchial disorders and stomach pain.

The seeds of black **cardamom** (*Elettaria cardamomum*) are extremely popular in China on account of their cool, astringent aroma. In Yunnan province, in particular, the ground seeds are often used in meat dishes. According to TCM, cardamom improves concentration and stimulates circulation. Because of its strong flavor, it should only be used in small amounts (a pinch at a time) for cooking purposes.

Glutamate (glutamic acid), though a common ingredient in Chinese cuisine, tends to be avoided in Europe as it can cause nausea, headaches, and numbness and is also suspected of causing brain damage if consumed in large quantities. Glutamate is a flavor enhancer and appetite stimulator. It was originally produced from pod fruit, marine algae, and wheat but is industrially manufactured nowadays by fermenting microorganisms.

Facing page, above: Star anise is an essential ingredient of five-spice powder.

Facing page, below: Sichuan pepper (flower pepper) is not really a hot spice as such. Instead, it produces a kind of tingling sensation which after a few seconds has an almost numbing effect on the tongue and mouth. It is not related to (black) pepper, but comes from a plant belonging to the rue family which is widespread in Sichuan province.

Above: Ground cinnamon is also a traditional ingredient in five-spice powder. Depending on the recipe, the whole cinnamon stick may be added to the dish during cooking, but should not be eaten.

Below: They look hot and taste hot: famous chile peppers, freshly prepared.

Chengdu—city of brocade

Chengdu, the capital city of Sichuan province, has always been a fairly remote and affluent town. Surrounded by fertile land, it has always boasted a thriving handicraft industry and has been a hub of commerce. Valuable silk brocade has been produced here since the days of the Eastern Han dynasty (25–220 A.D.) when it was transported by caravan along ancient trade routes as far as Central Asia. It is this costly fabric which earned Chengdu its nickname of Jincheng, meaning "city of brocade," a name still used to this day.

Centuries earlier, one of the province's governors resolved to develop the Sichuan Basin into one of China's most productive regions. River water was channeled through a system of canals, designed both to irrigate the surrounding areas and also put an end to frequent devastating episodes of flooding. The Dujiangyan irrigation system (37 miles/60 km from Chengdu), created 2,300 years ago, is an example of an extremely sophisticated water control project, which modern-day China has successfully developed to increase the irrigated area.

During the era of the Three Kingdoms (221–280), Chengdu, at that time a significant center of trade and crafts, was proclaimed capital of the Shu Kingdom. Centuries later, during the Song dynasty (960–1279), the first paper money was printed here. Chengdu, which means literally the "perfect metropolis," surrounded itself with a moat and a city wall with gates at all four points of the compass. The removal of the last sections of the defense fortifications in the 1960s marked the end of the old town's structure and signaled the start of extensive building work. Nowadays the city accommodates over 4 million inhabitants. Chengdu was once the capital of a "Great Western Kingdom"—if only for two years. Zhang Xianzhong (1606–1647), one of the rebel leaders who overthrew the Ming dynasty (1368–1644), had fled to Sichuan from the armed forces of the Qing rulers (1644–1912) and made the well-fortified-city of Chengdu his capital. He set up an administration and equipped his "kingdom" with a powerful army, but was defeated soon afterward as a result of overambitious foreign policy goals and cruelty toward his own people. Not only did he try to capture southern and eastern China, but he also had designs on Mongolia, Korea, the Philippines, and Vietnam. He imposed severe penalties and killed large numbers of his own officials and soldiers. By the time he was overpowered in 1646, Chengdu lay in ruins.

Despite Chengdu's status as provincial capital and seat of regional government, its location in the middle of the province made it less easily accessible than Chongqing to the south, which is situated on the upper part of the Yangtze. In 1890, when the Western powers were preparing to divide up China among themselves, Chongqing was opened to foreign trade with the West—but not Chengdu, which was also denied foreign consulates. Thanks to a combination of skillful Western diplomacy and Chinese flexibility, a brisk exchange was nevertheless conducted through the province governor.

Despite its turbulent history, particularly during the rule of the warlords in the early 20th century when towns in Sichuan were plundered and their populations suffered hardship and hunger, Chengdu has always retained its relaxed atmosphere. The city is noted for its tea houses, for not only has tea been grown and traded here since time immemorial, but Sichuan people are also passionately fond of drinking this beverage. The tea houses used to be social meeting-places, venues for exchanging news, and a stage for storytellers, whose tales were the predecessors of classic Chinese novels. Today, although tea houses have declined in number, they remain a focal point for elderly citizens and anyone who has time for a game of cards, mah jong, or Chinese chess—or who simply wishes to sit and watch as the tealeaves

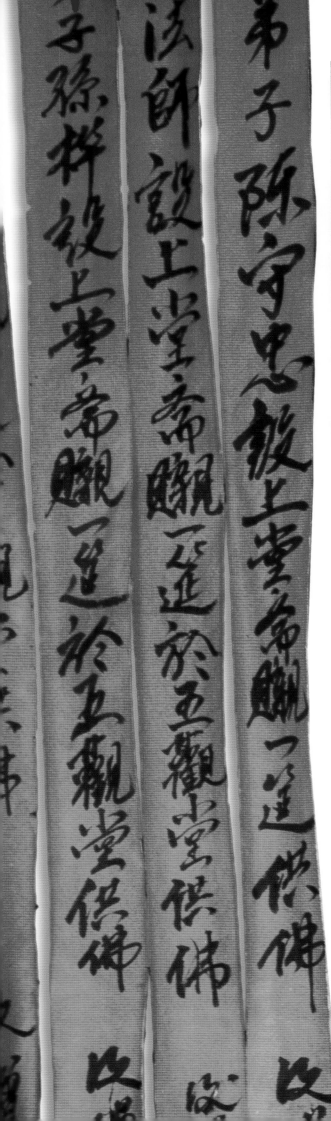

Far left: Sichuan brocade is a popular souvenir for tourists to take home. Decorated with calligraphy, it makes a perfect keepsake.

Left: The days when one's choice was restricted to two or three types of cabbages are long gone.

Above: The Chengdu branch of Tong Ren Tang, a Beijing pharmaceutical company, is over 250 years old.

slowly sink to the bottom after hot water has been poured over them.

Sichuan-style rabbit

11 oz (300 g) rabbit meat
7 tbsp soy sauce
1 egg white
1 tbsp cornstarch
vegetable oil, for frying
1 tbsp Sichuan pepper
2 garlic cloves, sliced
1–2 tbsp finely chopped ginger
3–4 dried chiles
3–4 tbsp roughly chopped scallions

Sauce:
2 tbsp soy sauce
1 tbsp rice wine
1 tsp rice vinegar
1 tbsp sugar
1 tsp cornstarch, mixed with 2 tsp water

Chop the rabbit into chunks and place in a bowl. Mix the soy sauce, egg white, and cornstarch and pour over the meat. Leave to marinate for about 10 minutes. Meanwhile, combine the sauce ingredients and then drain the meat. Pour some oil into a hot wok and stir-fry the meat for a few minutes before removing. Reheat the oil until it begins to bubble. Add the

Sichuan pepper, sliced garlic, and chopped ginger and stir-fry gently. As soon as the ingredients begin to release their aromas, remove from the wok using a slotted spoon or skimmer. Crumble the chiles, add to the wok along with the chopped scallions and stir-fry for a few moments. Return the rabbit meat to the wok and stir-fry for about 30 seconds over a high heat. Pour in the sauce, then drizzle over a little sesame oil and continue cooking for a few more minutes before serving.

Chengdu—city of brocade **377**

Tea houses—a mirror of society

Tea houses *chaguan* are extremely popular institutions throughout China. Here—over a civilized cup of tea—people can enjoy a chat, read the newspaper—or even emails nowadays—exchange information, talk business, play Chinese chess, or be entertained by storytellers, acrobats, or local opera companies, or even lose money in a game of mah jong. In the past, tea houses were used as meeting-places by people from all sections of society. The writer Lao She (1899–1966) described them as a "microcosm of society." He chose the background of a Peking tea house for his drama, *The Tea House*, published in the late 1950s, as a way of mirroring society and highlighting the changes taking place in modern China. In 1988, a tea house was named after him in his hometown of Beijing (described more fully in the chapter on Beijing).

China's tea house traditions date back over a thousand years to the Tang dynasty (618–907), experiencing their heyday during the Song period (960–1279). During the more recent past, they have experienced rather mixed fortunes: nearly all tea houses were closed down during the Cultural Revolution (1966–1976) at the behest of Mao, who wanted to destroy everything which embodied the old, traditional China. It was not until the 1990s that tea houses began to open up again all over the country. Meanwhile, ancient China seems to be facing an even deadlier "enemy" in the shape of the economic boom. Over the past few years entire districts have been razed to the ground in many towns to make way for new skyscrapers. Many historical buildings, including a large number of tea houses, have fallen victim to this wave of modernization.

Chengdu is renowned for its strong tea house culture. A popular saying in the city, which usually has a layer of cloud overhead, is: "People rarely see blue sky overhead, but there is always a tea house within sight." This saying permits us a glimpse of one particular characteristic shared by the residents of Chengdu—not only do they have a special fondness for the pleasant tea house culture, but they also have a reputation throughout China for being talkative and pleasure-seeking. Chengu people, on the other hand, are proud of their way of life and counter with a saying of their own: "If someone from Beijing finds himself with five hours of free time, he will spend it looking for a job in order to earn even more money. Chengdu people, on the other hand, would spend the first two hours shopping, cooking, and eating so that they could spend the remaining three hours in a tea house."

Chengdu's healthy tea house culture has evolved partly due to its topographical position. Situated in a valley basin—in the middle of a province which is, in turn, surrounded by mountain ranges—the city remained completely isolated from the outside world for many centuries. Without modern means of communication,

people were barely able to discuss the country's political and economic situation. The tea house consequently provided a meeting-place for exchanging news. Many Chengdu residents would take their breakfast in a tea house in order to catch up with the latest gossip early in the day—or even spread some of their own. Sichuan tea houses were once well-known for their tasteful façades and elegant tea services. A typical tea house would be equipped with teapots made of purple copper, pewter saucers, and lidded drinking bowls made of elegant Jingdezhen porcelain.

Apart from the big tea houses, which have seating for several hundred customers, Chengdu also boasts many smaller establishments providing no more than a handful of tables. These traditional, very simple tea houses are mainly situated in the narrow streets of the Old Town. Open air establishments, *litian chaguan*, can be found along the banks of the river and in public parks. The larger tea houses also host performances by the Sichuan opera, or other artists, including acrobats, shadow puppeteers, or magicians.

Tuo tea—a high-yield variety of compressed, brick tea—is extremely popular in Sichuan, although green and white teas, jasmine tea *molihua*, and "eight treasures" tea, *babaocha*, are also standard varieties served in tea houses. The customer is usually given a handleless cup with a lid, containing a layer of tealeaves in the bottom. Hot water can be poured over the tealeaves as often as the customer wishes. The waiter will demonstrate impressive skill in pouring the water into the cups in a high arc, but the guest can, if he so desires, serve himself, in which case he is presented with a thermos flask of hot water, which is refilled as often as necessary. The tea is accompanied by cookies or other snacks, such as steamed or fried ravioli-style dumplings containing delicious fillings.

The tea houses of Hangzhou, the capital of Zhejiang province, serve mainly dragon tea *(longjing cha)*, which is grown in the nearby West Lake region. It is reputedly the best tea China has to offer and is particularly flavorsome when prepared with water from Hangzhou's famous Hupao spring.

Tea houses that hosted traditional Chinese storytelling performances were known as "Shu tea houses" where the storytellers, usually old men, recounted tales from well-known novels, especially favorite episodes from stories such as "The Three Kingdoms," or "The Robbers of Liangshan Moor," which remain to this day set-pieces performed by the Peking Opera. Each day a new chapter would be related so that the telling of a whole story could often last over a period of several months. The paying audience would visit the tea house every day to catch the next installment—a tradition which has been revived in recent times.

Steamed dumplings

7 tbsp (50 g) confectioner's sugar
11 oz (300 g) glutinous (sticky) rice flour
water
vegetable oil, for greasing
2/3 cup (100 g) peanut flour

Mix 2 tablespoons of sugar with the rice flour, add a little water and form into a dough.
Using a paper towel, rub the surface of a heatproof dish with vegetable oil. Place the dough onto the dish and stand this in a saucepan containing water. Heat the water and steam the dough for 15 minutes. Remove the dish from the pan and allow to cool.
Stir the peanut flour around a nonstick skillet over a low heat for 5 minutes until the aroma begins to be noticeable. Then tip it onto a plate and mix with the remaining sugar.
Cut the cooled dough into pieces with scissors and toss them in the peanut flour. Arrange on a plate to serve.

Left: Tea houses are a microcosm of society, as well as a place to relax and exchange news. Little notice is taken here of any differences in social status.

Below left: Spirituality plays a key role in the ceremony of serving— as well as drinking— tea. Every aspect of the tea ceremony symbolizes unity and harmony, two factors which lie at the heart of Buddhism.

Below: Sichuan's tea houses often serve steamed dumplings as an accompaniment to the tea.

Porcelain from Jingdezhen

Many extremely fine pieces of porcelain, which were "as white as jade, as shiny as a mirror, as thin as paper, and rang as true as church bells" have come from Jingdezhen, the capital of Chinese porcelain, in the province of Jiangxi. European aristocrats had developed a particular liking for the blue and white style of Chinese porcelain during the Ming dynasty (1368–1644). European craftsmen had been striving to copy and reproduce this precious commodity since the 15th century, but it was not until 1709 that their efforts were rewarded with success when Johann Friedrich Böttger, a German alchemist at the Dresden court of King August the Strong, Elector of Saxony, finally discovered the secret of manufacturing porcelain in Europe.

Chongqing—the largest city in the world

Chongqing, or town of "double happiness," is the largest inland port on the upper reaches of the Yangtze. The historic heart of the city—albeit an almost exclusively modern development—is situated on a hilly promontory bordered to the south, by the Yangtze, and to the north, by the Jialing river. Even the river-banks are now crammed with modern sky-scrapers and are connected to the downtown area by cable car. In former times, these shores were lined with elegant villas, providing wealthy Chinese and foreigners with a highly desirable cool summer retreat. During the hot season, Chongqing lives up to its nickname as one of China's "furnace cities." Nonetheless, hotpot (see p. 388) is one of the city's classic favorite dishes, and one which Chongqing people continue to enjoy even in scorching temperatures. On some days, it almost seems as if the entire population of Chongqing has congregated in the streets and alleyways to eat hotpot.

Chongqing was formerly part of Sichuan province, but in 1997—along with Shanghai, Beijing, and Tianjin and their surrounding areas—it was declared a municipality under direct government administration (with a current population of more than 32 million inhabitants). Not only did this contribute to the region's growth as an industrial and commercial center, but it also helped stimulate the development of the poorer provinces in the west of the country. Since then, Chongqing's economy has flourished more rapidly than ever. The city now accounts for 25 percent of the whole of Sichuan province's economic power. If you take an evening river cruise and half close your eyes against the dazzling lights of the city, you could almost imagine yourself in Hong Kong. Chongqing's city fathers are working hard to turn this fantasy into reality. Particularly helpful in this respect is another huge project downstream on the Yangtze, namely, the gigantic—and somewhat controversial—Three Gorges Dam that supplies Chongqing, Sichuan province, and eastern China with cheap electricity for its economic growth. Its 26 turbines can, in theory, produce up to 84 gigawatt hours of electricity per day. The construction of the dam has also resulted in deep water for shipping on the Yangtze. However, the project is surrounded by controversy, mainly because of fears concerning its environmental impact on the region and the potential risk of it becoming a military target. It also lies in a recognized earthquake zone.

As recently as a hundred years ago, the upper Yangtze with all its potential and the province of Sichuan as a whole were not easily accessible. Before the construction of the railroad, this "gold and grain store" in the heart of China could only be reached from the east by traveling upstream along the Yangtze. Furthermore, the Yangtze gorges downstream from Chongqing were a further obstacle and could only be navigated by junks. When the river was running low in winter, mail from Shanghai to Chongqing could sometimes be in transit for three months.

Foreign steamships found it impossible to negotiate the rapids and it was not until 1900 that a British commercial steamer and two river gunboats succeeded in getting through for the first time. By the early 1920s, the upper section of the Yangtze was navigable to steamers for eight months of the year.

In 1890, Chongqing was opened up as a treaty port by the British for trade with the West. This inland port, situated at an important junction of trade routes, was the first—and for many years the only—place in the province open to foreign trade. However, the hilly terrain was a considerable handicap to commerce and most of the porterage was done by coolies (*ku li*, in Chinese, meaning "hard labor"). Even now, the city still relies upon countless porters to unload the ships' cargoes and transport them up and down the narrow streets and steep lanes. They can also be seen helping well-to-do women carry their shopping bags home from the supermarket or clothes store. An elevator helps people negotiate the different levels between the lower and upper parts of town. Chongqing, unlike most other Chinese cities, is unsuitable for bicycles.

In 1937, after the outbreak of the Sino-Japanese War, the national government (Guomindang) moved the capital city and seat of government to Chongqing and as a result became the target of heavy Japanese air attacks after 1939.

Left: Compared with a boomtown like Shanghai, Chongqing led a shadowy existence for many decades. All this changed dramatically at the start of the new millennium.

Right: Heavy loads are still transported around this hilly city on foot—by porters, shown here relaxing during a break.

Hot chicken chunks with peanuts

generous 1 lb (500 g) chicken breasts
½ tsp salt
2 egg whites
freshly ground white pepper
1 tbsp cornstarch
7 oz (200 g) peanuts, freshly shelled
4 cups (1 liter) vegetable oil
3 small dried chiles
1 tbsp chopped scallions
4 thin slices of ginger
1 small garlic clove, sliced
1 tbsp rice wine
1–2 tbsp clear stock
½ tsp sugar
1 tbsp soy sauce
rice vinegar
1 tsp cornstarch, mixed with 2 tsp water
1 tbsp chili oil

Cut the chicken breasts into chunks and place in a bowl. Add the salt, egg whites, a pinch of pepper, and cornstarch and mix thoroughly. Blanch the peanuts in boiling water before removing the skins. Heat the wok and pour in the oil. Stir-fry the peanuts until they are the color of egg yolk, then remove and set aside.

Reheat the oil and fry the chiles until they turn dark brown. Pour off all but 3 ½ tablespoons of the oil from the hot wok. Add the scallions, ginger, and garlic and fry for a few minutes. Add the chicken chunks, rice wine, stock, sugar, soy sauce, a few drops of rice vinegar, and cornstarch mixture and shake around in the wok until the chicken is cooked through. Add the peanuts, season with chili oil and mix well. Serve at once.

Top: "The city on a hill where nobody rides a bicycle" is how the Chinese describe Chongqing—quite a wise idea given the racing traffic.

Left: The town planners of Chongqing know full well that there is sometimes no room for sensibilities when it comes to building enormous, new apartment blocks.

Soybeans—an all-round source of protein

The basic raw material from which so many different products, including soy sauce, soybean sprouts, and tofu, are created has one overriding characteristic: it is bitter and hard to digest. Nevertheless, the soybean (*Glycine maxima*) plays an important role in China as a key source of oil and protein. It is no surprise, therefore, that the cultivated soybean plant is considered native to northeastern China where its wild predecessor, glycine soya, also originated.

The Chinese have been cultivating the soybean plant for at least 3,000 years, originally, admittedly, only for use as a fertilizer. Under the Zhou dynasty (1066–221 B.C.) soy was considered one of the "five sacred harvest crops" along with rice, millet, wheat, and barley and by the 4th century B.C., cultivation had spread farther south. Over the centuries, the Chinese learned how to produce and use soy milk and invented tofu. They also discovered ways of using soybeans in fermented form as a paste, or sauce (see also the chapter on Fujian). The West did not discover soybeans as a crop until much later, in the 18th century, and only came to appreciate its value as a source of plant oil after World War II. Until then, it had not been possible to cultivate or acclimatize this short-day plant—i.e. one which needs short days, in other words, a subtropical climate, in order to flower.

This useful plant is a member of the legume family and varies in habit depending on whether it is a variety with limited or unlimited growth. Some varieties have a bushy, branching habit and can grow more than 3 feet (1 m) high, or else trail over 6 feet (2 m) in length. Small clusters of white or purple flowers, about a ¼ inch (5 mm) across, are borne in the axil of the leaf, which, after about three months, produce pods of seeds ¾–4 inches (2–10 cm) across. The pods vary in color from straw-colored to dark gray and contain up to five green, yellowish-brown, or black-violet seeds, the soybeans. The plant withers and loses its leaves before the beans are ripe.

This "miracle bean" ranks in third place after rice and wheat on the list of Chinese staple foods. The reason for this is obvious: no other plant has such a high protein content—between 30 and 50 percent—and therefore provides a useful alternative to meat. For many centuries, meat remained the preserve of the upper classes. The majority of Chinese could only afford it—if at all—on special occasions, and Buddhists renounced it altogether for religious reasons. Soybean products still account for an important part of the Chinese population's protein intake, but only in the form of processed products. Since hydrolyzed soy protein, i.e. which has been broken down into digestible form by water, heat, or other catalyzers, contains all the essential amino acids needed by the body, it is ideal for use—in the form of tofu, for example—to replace meat and fish. Soybeans also contain 15–20 percent oil, are rich in vitamins A and B, calcium, iron, and other minerals, yet low in calories and cholesterol. Nowadays, soy is even valued medically as a miracle drug because of all the components and phytochemicals it contains.

Soybean production has meanwhile become an economically significant industry. No other agricultural product can produce such a high protein yield per area as the soybean. The primary cultivation areas include the United States, Brazil, and Argentina, where mainly genetically modified varieties are grown in vast monocultures. Advocates of this method of cultivation commend the high yields and resistance to pesticides, while critics warn against unforeseeable dangers to man and nature. Exporting countries mainly sell soybeans as animal feed but soy is often present as an additive in a number of industrial products, such as fabric softeners, cosmetics, as well as being a source of biofuel. Soy is an ingredient in a variety of foods, for example, as a binding agent in breakfast cereals, in buttery spreads, sauces, or in sausages, and ice cream. Around 20,000 to 30,000 foodstuffs are now believed to contain soy components.

Whereas soy products have only enjoyed increasing popularity in the West since the early 1980s, the Chinese have had time to perfect the art of soybean processing over several thousands of years. In addition to tofu, soy sauce, and soy pastes, soybean shoots are likewise an integral part of Chinese cuisine—and are so easy to grow. Just leave a few soaked, yellow soybeans to germinate in a warm, dark place for a few days on damp cotton wool, during which time a crop of fresh, aromatic, and extremely nutritious shoots of soybean seedlings will have sprouted. These will be bigger and nuttier than the mung bean sprouts usually marketed in the West under the name of "soybean sprouts." Nowadays, fresh soybean sprouts are stocked by an increasing number of organic food stores, as well as Asian stores. Their vitamin content and nutritional value, as well as their high levels of valuable acids and minerals, are greatly increased by germination and are easier to digest. The Chinese, however, rarely eat these whitish-yellow shoots in their raw state, but fry them with garlic, ginger, and scallions in a wok, add them to hotpot or use them as a filling in spring rolls—often fried in soy oil.

Soybean sprout salad

11 oz (300 g) soybean sprouts
1 red bell pepper, seeded and pith removed
1 tbsp sesame oil
1 tbsp heavy rice vinegar (chencu) from
   Shanxi province
1/2 tbsp chili oil
1/2 tbsp finely chopped garlic
2 tbsp light soy sauce
sugar
1 scallion, chopped
1 tbsp roasted white sesame seeds,
   for garnishing

Pick over and wash the soybean sprouts, then drain. Cut the red bell pepper into thin strips. Mix the sesame oil and rice vinegar with the chili oil, garlic, light soy sauce and a pinch of sugar. Bring some water to a boil in a wok and add the soybean sprouts and bell pepper. Blanch for 2–3 minutes, then turn off the heat and add the scallion for a few moments before removing again almost immediately. Remove the wok from the hob and rinse the soybean sprouts and bell pepper in cold water. Drain and place in a bowl and stir in the sauce. Sprinkle with the sesame seeds just before serving.

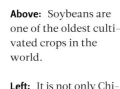

Above: Soybeans are one of the oldest cultivated crops in the world.

Left: It is not only Chinese producers and consumers who depend on the soybean crop. Soy is an important agricultural commodity which, because of fluctuations in world market prices, can throw an entire economy into a loss or profit situation.

More than half of all edible vegetable oils worldwide are derived from soybeans. The oil is extracted and what is left over is processed into soy flour, soybean meal, or animal feed. Whereas soy oil in the West is generally a "hidden" ingredient in salad dressings, or margarine, for example, the Chinese use it for frying, because of its high boiling point. The neutral flavor of this versatile yellow soy oil is a further advantage, making it perfect for salads and raw food, as well as for broiling, braising, and roasting. What is more, soy oil has a high level of unsaturated fatty acids, such as Omega 3 and Omega 6, and is therefore classed as healthy—just like the most famous Chinese soy product of all: tofu. KATRIN SCHLOTTER

Tofu—not a question of flavor

Whether the tofu in question is flower tofu, soft silken tofu, or stinky tofu, virtually no other product is capable of being processed into such a variety of textures and nuances of flavor. The different versions of tofu range from creamily sweet and silkily mild, to crisp and spicy. If prepared properly, tofu— a very versatile commodity which is particularly prized among vegetarians—is anything but insipid.

The production of tofu from soybeans was an early Chinese invention that dates back to the 2nd century B.C. However, *doufu*, as it is called in China, is far more widely known by its Japanese name of "tofu" despite the fact that it only arrived in Japan along with Buddhism during the Tang dynasty (618—907). It is also known in the West as bean curd since it resembles curd both in appearance and in the way it is made. There is one important difference, however: tofu's high levels of protein are derived not from milk, but from soybeans.

Pickled, boiled, or steamed, finely ground into a powder, filtered, pressed, or treated with coagulants, the soybean mutates into an ingredient that packs a powerful punch. In any of its variations—be it liquid, dried, frozen, or fermented form—tofu contains an easily digestible form of protein and unsaturated fatty acids. Depending on the type of coagulant used, it may also contain high levels of minerals, such as potassium, magnesium, and calcium, and B vitamins as well as phytochemicals. Tofu is cholesterol-free and low in calories and is regarded worldwide as an extremely healthy and cheap alternative to fish and meat.

What it lacks, however, is a meaty flavour. Tofu aficionados vehemently refute the suggestion that tofu is completely without flavor. The quality of the beans, the purity of the water, the care with which the tofu is prepared, and even the utensils used in the process of making and storing tofu, are all said to influence its delicate, slightly "beany" flavor. As far as most Western consumers are concerned, in appearance, consistency, and flavor, tofu most resembles mozzarella (Italian buffalo cheese)—except that it is far more versatile. Although changes in its texture are governed by its water content, this quick-change artist only gets fully into its stride when it comes into contact with the flavors of other ingredients. In Buddhist dishes, for example, bamboo- or mushroom-based recipes, the tofu has a mild flavor, yet becomes hot and spicy as an ingredient in "mapo doufu," a typical Sichuan dish. Tofu is used to supplement meat in soups, wok dishes, or hotpots, but this all-round player can also be eaten plain with a simple accompaniment of ginger, chile, and scallions. Meanwhile, the

pungent, cheesy smell of fermented tofu, sold as a snack at night markets, is enough to take the visitor's breath away!

It is remarkable to think that so many different tofu products can be produced from what is ultimately just a combination of water and beans. To make **soy milk**, the beans are soaked overnight, ground with water, then boiled, and strained. This procedure simultaneously eliminates the mixture's fibrous components and bean smell. What remains is a liquid which is similar to and as nutritious as milk. Be it in Beijing, Shanghai, or Hong Kong, soy milk—whether sweet or savory, served hot or cold—is a traditional breakfast snack. Soy milk may be flavored with sugar, or ginger syrup, or eaten as a delicately creamy dessert with mango, coconut, or papaya.

As with ordinary milk, boiling soy milk produces a thin, elastic film of skin on the surface, the consistency of which makes it very popular. The larger the saucepan, the more **tofu skin** is produced. This is carefully lifted off and laid on a bamboo tray, then hung up to dry, before being pressed, or rolled up. It is eventually used as a wrap for other food, or to imitate meat in soups and hotpots.

Tofu is produced from soy milk by adding coagulants to the hot liquid. The traditional coagulant used in China is calcium sulphate (gypsum), which has the additional benefit of increasing the calcium content. In Japan, a substance called "nigari," which consists primarily of magnesium chloride, is extracted from seawater and used as a coagulant. Depending on the desired texture, certain acid or enzyme coagulants may be used together with mineral salts to produce tofu. As with cheesemaking, the milk separates into a solid mass of soybean curds and liquid whey. The curds are strained, or placed in perforated molds and pressed to produce a block of fresh tofu. This soft, creamy-white tofu has relatively little flavor but it can be cooked in a variety of ways (steamed, fried, or braised) and its fine consistency enables it to absorb other flavors extremely efficiently.

Tofu comes in a number of varieties, depending on the amount of water extracted from the tofu curds and on the extent to which it is pressed. Once the milk has been coagulated, usually by the addition of nigari, **silken tofu** is placed in bowls and heated. Its high moisture content gives it a silky, soft texture, similar to yogurt. It can be made firmer for stir-frying in wok dishes by blanching, or by frying it over an extremely high heat, but it is mainly used in soups or eaten as a dessert. **Tofu flowers** can be served both as a savory or sweet dish. In northern China, soft "tofu" is accompanied by soy sauce, while in western China it is served devilishly hot with chili. The southern Chinese prefer it sweet with ginger or coconut. These soft varieties of tofu do not keep for too long and need

Above left: The larger the saucepan used to boil the soy milk, the larger the film of rubbery skin that can be lifted off.

Left: Tofu can be made at home, but it is a process that most people find too time-consuming. It is easier to buy tofu from the market.

Above: Pressing the tofu into blocks requires great skill. Regardless of which method is used, tofu is available in a number of varieties and consistencies.

Right: You will find every conceivable type of tofu on sale at the food markets.

careful handling, whereas pressed varieties with a low moisture content are as robust as meat and can be baked, braised, or fried in the same way. **Fried tofu**, which can be bought ready-made and plastic-wrapped in Chinese stores, is crisp on the outside and has a soft consistency on the inside. It tastes best freshly cooked at a night market where you will probably also find fried **stinky tofu** on sale—you just need to follow your nose! This is made by placing tofu in a marinade of vegetables, crabs, or wine and leaving microorganisms to do their work. Once the delicate tofu has fermented into a pungent, cheesy tofu it is fried in the open air—with good reason—and eaten with an accompaniment of pickled cabbage, vinegar, chile, and garlic. And by the way, it tastes delicious!

KATRIN SCHLOTTER

Fried tofu

7 oz (200 g) firm tofu
vegetable oil, for frying
salt
chili powder
cardamom powder

Cut the tofu into ½-inch (1-cm) slices and fry. Season with a pinch each of salt, chili powder, and cardamom powder to serve.

China's world cultural heritage

In 1985, the People's Republic of China signed the UNESCO "International Agreement on the Protection of World Cultural and Natural Heritage." As a result, important buildings such as the Great Wall and Imperial Palaces built by former dynasties (see Beijing chapter), as well as panda reserves and the Peking Man excavation site in a cave in Zhoukoudian, about 25 miles (40 km) away from Beijing, were added to the list of protected world heritage sites. In the meantime, 37 Chinese sites have been added to UNESCO's world heritage list: 7 natural monuments, 26 cultural monuments and 4 sites are deemed worthy of protection on both counts. (The following list is arranged according to category and province, and the year it was added to the list appears in brackets.) A further 89 sites have been nominated, but not yet added to the list.

Natural monuments

Hunan
  Wulingyuan National Park (1992)
Jiangxi
  Sanqing Shan National Park (2008)
Sichuan
  Huanlong National Park (famous for its limestone terraces) (1992)
  Jiuzhaigou Valley National Park (1992)
  Giant panda reserves (2006)
Yunnan, Guizhou and Guangxi
  Karst landscape in southern China (2007)
Yunnan
  Protected areas within the "Three Parallel Rivers National Park" (2003)

Cultural and natural monuments

Anhui
  Huang Shan mountain landscape (1990)
Fujian
  Wuyi Mountains (1999)
Shandong
  Tai Shan mountain region (1987)
Sichuan
  Emei Shan mountain landscape and the Great Buddha of Leshan (1996)

Cultural monuments

Anhui
  Xidi and Hongcun villages (2000)
Beijing
  Peking Man excavation site in Zhoukoudian (1987)
  Great Wall (1987)
  Temple of Heaven and imperial sacrificial altar (1998)
  Imperial Gardens, Summer Palace, Yiheyuan, near Beijing (1998)
Beijing and Liaoning
  Imperial Palaces of the Ming and Qing dynasties in Beijing (Forbidden City) and Shenyang (1987, extended 2004)
Fujian
  Tulou clay roundhouses (2008)
Gansu
  Mogao caves (1987)
Guangdong
  Diaolou towers and villages in Kaiping (2007)
Hebei
  Summer residence and temple at Chengde (1994)
Henan
  Longmen caves at Luoyang (2000)
  Ruins of the historic capital of Yin Xu, near Anyang (2006)
Hubei
  Taoist sacred sites in the Wudang Shan mountains (1994)
Hubei, Hebei, Jiangsu, Liaoning and Beijing
  Imperial burial sites of the Ming and Qing dynasties (2000, extended 2003 and 2004)
Jiangsu
  Classical gardens of Suzhou (1997)
Jiangxi
  Lushan National Park (1996)
Jilin and Liaoning and People's Republic of Korea
  Ruins and tombs of the ancient kingdom of Koguryo (2004)
Macau
  Historic center (2005)
Shaanxi
  Qin Shi Huang's mausoleum and Terracotta Army, near Xi'an (1987)
Shandong
  Temple of Confucius, cemetery and Kong family mansion in Qufu (1994)
Shanxi
  Pinyao old town (1997)
  Yungang caves near Datong (2001)

Sichuan und Chongqing
  Dazu rock carvings near Chongqing (1999)
  Qincheng mountains and Dujiangyan irrigation system (2000)
Tibet
  Historic Potala Palace complex in Lhasa, consisting of Potala Palace, Jokhang Temple, and Norbulingka Palace (1994, extended in 2000 and 2001)
Yunnan
  Lijiang old town (1997)

Since the early 1990s, the Chinese government has intensified its efforts to preserve national monuments. There are now around 400,000 protected buildings throughout the country and there are plans to have these registered on a new national data bank by 2015. These efforts are aimed at not only protecting architectural monuments in their historic settings, but also at preserving the structure of ancient towns and villages—such as the old towns of Kashgar and Lijiang in Yunnan province—in order to safeguard their unique building styles and traditional cultures for the future.

Above: Fengdu is a perfect example of how cultural heritage and economic factors can come into conflict with one another. Most of the town was flooded in 2007 as part of the Three Gorges Dam project and its inhabitants moved to newly built developments on the river. The temple complex dating from the Han dynasty (206 B.C.–220 A.D.) remains above the new water level. Fengdu was once known as the "ghost city" for it was supposed to be here that the king of the underworld resided.

Left: The temple and pavilions in this complex contain a large number of statues depicting Taoist or Buddhist deities.

Below left: Tanzi, the king of hell, and other demons demonstrate what hell is like.

Picture sequence, top right: Rich in color and detail, these painted scenes of hell decorate the walls and ceilings.

Right: The Taoist and Buddhist temple buildings remain a popular tourist attraction after much of Fengdu was submerged.

China's world cultural heritage **387**

Hotpot—ranging from slightly spicy to fiery-hot

There are many stories surrounding the origins of Chinese *huoguo*, known as "hotpot" in Chinese restaurants in the West. According to one legend, it was used in ancient China for sacrificial or ritualistic purposes. Other sources maintain that it was introduced into China by the Mongols while yet others claim that it originated in Chongqing, where impoverished port workers would cook leftover food and organ meat in tin cans—in spicy, hot broth and over an open fire. The many different theories as to its origins are matched by the large number of local and regional versions of this popular dish, but one thing is for sure, however, and that is that the hottest hotpots come from Sichuan!

The basic recipe is simple: boil some animal bones to make a stock and season it with salt and pepper. Add garlic, star anise, ginger, fennel, cardamom, chili, and soy sauce to the stock to taste. Meat, fish, seafood, dumplings, mushrooms, or vegetables, all make ideal ingredients. Various types of organ meat, such as duck's blood, chicken giblets are also very popular components of this Chinese hotpot. The imagination can be allowed full rein when assembling the ingredients for a hotpot. Vinegar, soy sauce, and sesame paste are served as dipping sauces. A marinade made from vinegar, soy sauce, rice wine, garlic, ginger, and sesame seeds is another classic seasoning and dipping sauce. Chinese stores in the West sell a large selection of ready-made sauces.

Sichuan hotpot originated in the Chongqing region, but its fame has spread far beyond the province's borders. This local variation is prepared in a pot comprising two compartments. One section contains a mild, light meat stock, flavored with ginger and scallions, *bai tanglu*, and the other section contains a hot, red broth, *hong tanglu*, which is seasoned with chiles, Sichuan pepper, bean paste, and other hot seasonings. When it comes to dunking, one is spoilt for choice. However, during winter months, the light broth is supposed to be very good for the health as it contains antibacterial properties; while in summer, the red broth takes preference as it is supposed to drive heat and moisture out of the body. Organ meat is undoubtedly one of the hotpot ingredients most favored by the Sichuanese—regardless of whether it is cooked in the mild- or hot-flavored broth and regardless of the season.

Along China's coast, and in Hong Kong, for example, the most popular ingredients are probably seafood and fish. In northern China, particularly in Beijing, the most common hotpot is the Mongolian version, which typically contains a generous amount of lamb and dates back to the Yuan dynasty (1271–1368) when Mongols ruled the Chinese empire from Beijing and their culinary traditions were incorporated into local cuisine. It goes without saying that there is also a vegetarian version of hotpot. Tofu is especially good as a meat substitute, along with various vegetable and mushroom ingredients.

As with most meals in China, hotpot is a dish that tends to be eaten in company with others. A pot filled with stock is placed in the center of a table over a heat source, rather like a fondue, which is why this dish is sometimes known as "Chinese fondue." The diners seated around the table dunk a selection of vegetables, meat, noodles, or even pieces of organ meat into the boiling liquid. Once cooked, the morsels of food are fished out of the broth using chopsticks or miniature scoops and eaten—but not before they are dipped into one of a large number of little bowls containing spicy seasonings and sauces. Not only does this flavor the food, but at the same time cools it down to a manageable eating temperature. In the West one can buy special cooking pots, known as "Mongolian fire pots" with a heat source underneath. The best (and unfortunately, also the most expensive) ones are made of copper since this is such a good conductor of heat.

Nowadays, there are Chinese hotpot restaurants all over Europe. They have special tables, specifically designed for the preparation of this delicious and sociable dish. A metal pot, sometimes divided up the middle into two sections—one side for hot, and the other for mild broth—is placed in a cavity in the center of the table and heated by a gas burner underneath. In China, every hotpot restaurant boasts its own secret recipe. Many of them can become positively addictive—an effect possibly due to the addition of opium which (rumor has it) was found in the hotpot dishes of some Chengdu and Shanghai restaurants.

Left: A hotpot meal is usually an occasion for dining in a large group so it is important to provide sufficient food for dunking.

Right: A hotpot normally includes two types of broth: one which is mild in flavor, and one which is hot and spicy.

Facing page, bottom: Note the yin and yang shape of this hotpot cooking pot!

Left: Known in the West as a "Mongolian fire pot," the broth is heated at the table.

Bottom left: A cavity in the table makes sure that everyone can comfortably reach the pot in the center.

Bottom center: Gas burners within the cavity keep the contents of the cooking pot at the correct temperature throughout the meal.

Below: The food is dunked in the pot in the same way as a fondue: novice chopstick users will have a great deal of fun in the process!

Hotpot—ranging from slightly spicy to fiery-hot **389**

Gansu

甘肃

Elke Spielmanns-Rome

Gansu province in northwest China at the western end of the Great Wall is known as the "gateway to the West." Chinese peasant farmers and nomads have lived alongside each other here since time immemorial and the brisk trade between them became the basis for the first global trading network in human history: the Silk Road.

Surrounded by mighty mountain ranges—the Longshan and Qinglin mountains to the south and the Qilian mountains to the West—Gansu formed a natural buffer against the Turkic peoples in the west. To the north is the Taklimakan (place of no return), the largest and driest sandy desert in the world. The only fertile arable land is in the southern part of the province in what is known as the Hexi Corridor along the banks of the Yellow River (Huang). China's second longest river owes its name to loess suspended in the water and carried along by the flow. This fertile, yellow sediment is washed out of the ground on the Loess Plateau in the east of the province. Its extensive grasslands make Gansu one of China's biggest cattle producers.

This region is the cradle of Chinese civilization. Archaeological finds have found evidence of early rural civilizations dating back approximately 5,000 years. Their rapid cultural development and expansion quickly absorbed all the early cultures along the Huang river as far as the China Sea. The kingdom of Qin Shi Huangdi—the great warrior, who first united China and, after the founding of the Qin dynasty (221–206 B.C.), became the first Chinese emperor—was likewise situated in the south of what is now Gansu province. Around a hundred years later, Emperor Han Wudi (141–87 B.C.) dispatched the first expeditions to the West. Their most valuable commodity—silk—was transported as far as the Roman Empire. For a long time, the Hexi Corridor remained the only traversable caravan route between China and Central Asia. This route stretched more than 621 miles (1000 km) along a 44-mile (70-km)-wide plateau on the northern edge of the Qilian mountains from Lanzhou, now the province's capital city, to the Jade pass on the northern border with Xinjiang.

By the end of the 14th century, silk, jade, paper, and porcelain were being transported to Europe along the Silk Road, while cotton, glass, and wool were making the return journey into China. This route was also a main artery for the spread of technical expertise as well as religious beliefs. Buddhism, for example, which originated in India, first gained a foothold in the fortified oasis towns along the Hexi Corridor before spreading across the entire empire, finally experiencing its heyday in China under

Top: Numerous reservoirs have been built to try and keep the Huang under control but the lakes have quickly become silted up with loess and mud.

Above: A Buddhist monastery along the ancient Silk Road was an important place, both for trade activities and the spread of religion.

Facing page: Wherever it flows, the Yellow River has a considerable influence on the landscape—whether because of its history of flooding, or simply on account of its beauty.

Lanzhou

Above left: The Mogao caves, located just over 15 miles (25 km) south of Dunhuang, were discovered in the early 20th century and systematically explored during subsequent decades. In 1987 they were awarded the status of a UNESCO World Heritage Site.

Above right: The site comprises around 1,000 caves, carved out of sandstone cliffs by Buddhist monks between the 4th and 12th century and decorated with wall paintings, sculptures, and statues of Buddha.

Below: Nearly 500 of the caves are accessible to the public and have become a popular tourist attraction.

the Tang dynasty (618–907). Gansu has many religious sites and buildings which bear testimony to the arrival of Buddhism in China where it became integrated with the indigenous Chinese philosophical system known as Taoism and evolved into a new religion known as Chan Buddhism (known in the West by its Japanese name of Zen Buddhism). The Mogao caves, or "caves of the 1000 Buddhas" to the southeast of the oasis town of Dunhuang, are frequently described as a "treasure trove of eastern art" and were added to UNESCO'S list of World Heritage Sites in 1987. Hewn out of a mile-long (1.6-km-long) stretch of sandstone cliffs are hundreds of temple caves, stacked five floors high, containing 484,375 square feet (45,000 sq m) of Buddhist wall paintings (dating from the 4th to 12th century) and countless statues representing Buddha in a wide variety of styles and dating from different periods of history. Equally impressive are the monumental sculptures found in Bingling Temple, to the south of the capital of Lanzhou. Carved into the steep cliff face and visible for many miles is the giant 92-feet (28-m)-high Maitreya Buddha sculpture.

Another "interloper" from Central Asia is Islam. Muslims began arriving in China in the 7th century and became integrated in the population by marriage to Han Chinese women. It was not long before they were being registered by the Chinese authorities as a separate ethnic group known

as "Hui." "Hui" communities have since settled in all parts of China, but they are mostly concentrated in the autonomous region of Ningxia, as well as in the eastern part of Gansu.

Only about 1.2 million of Gansu's 26 million inhabitants are followers of Islam. These also include the Bonan, an ethnic group with Mongolian origins. Other ethnic minorities in Gansu include Tibetans, Mongols, Kazakhs, Tu, and the Yugur ("yellow Uighurs")—one of the smallest recognized minority groups in China numbering fewer than 14,000.

Gansu's significance and affluence dwindled when the flow of trade along the Silk Road began to dwindle during the 14th century. By the time the province was incorporated into the People's Republic in 1949, poverty in Gansu had reached legendary proportions. It was not until the 1960s that a program of industrialization got underway based on mining and the extraction of various mineral resources (coal, oil, nickel, iron ore) and the construction of hydroelectric plants along the shores of the Yellow River. Gansu's capital, Lanzhou, has meanwhile become known as China's petrochemical center. Air pollution in the city is among the worst anywhere in the country. Yet even now, two thirds of the population still live in small, rural village communities, earning a meager living from cultivating fruit and rearing pigs.

Top left: The "Flying Horse" is the name given by archaeologists to this bronze sculpture, discovered in a tomb dating from the later Han dynasty (25–220 A.D.). A larger-than-life replica is on display in Lanzhou, Gansu's capital city.

Top right: Cheap, fast-food snacks can be bought to eat or drink from the many small food stands in Lanzhou.

Above: Gansu is the center of the Hui ethnic group, a term often used in China to refer to Muslims in general.

Below: A short boat trip on the Huang is a must for every visitor to China.

Noodles, beef, and lamb—Gansu cuisine

Gansu is a long way from the center of power and China's new super cities. The economic boom taking place along China's east coast has not yet reached this region, yet this sparsely populated, rural province, one of the poorest in the country, nevertheless boasts several outstanding delicacies of its own. Gansu cuisine—an extremely popular cuisine, which is referred to in China as, *qingzhen*, pure and wholesome—is strongly influenced by the culinary traditions of the Hui, a Muslim ethnic minority group. This is hardly surprising considering that more than one million Hui (at least 10 percent of China's entire Hui population) live in Gansu. Muslim Hui restaurants can be found throughout China. However, Hui cuisine should not be confused with Huangshan cuisine from Anhui, which instead is often referred to as "Hui cuisine" for short!

Muslim restaurateurs in Lanzhou, Gansu's capital city, specialize in a beef noodle dish known as *niuroumian*. The city now boasts more than 1,200 beef noodle restaurants and food stalls. This dish, known in Lanzhou as *Lanzhou lamian*, consists of hand-pulled noodles served in a hearty beef soup. Another distinctive feature of this specialty, in addition to the hand-pulled noodles, is the unusual ingredient of desert grass ash, which is added to the water used to make the noodle dough. The popularity of Lanzhou lamian is not confined to its native city: a well known restaurant chain by the name of Malan Beef Noodles (Malan Lamian) now has over 400 outlets all over China and even has branches in the United States, France, and Singapore.

Homemade noodles are common throughout Gansu. Whether as an ingredient in a Hui-style lamb broth, or served cold, in a refreshingly tangy brine dish with vegetables, noodles are an integral part of every meal. *Dunhuang rangpizi*, a cold noodle dish, is especially popular among local residents during the summer months. Despite their somewhat slippery texture, the addition of bean sprouts, steamed gluten, chili and other spices makes them remarkably tasty. Other homemade noodle specialties include Saozi noodles served with a delicious sauce made from *saozi* (finely chopped pork) and other ingredients, as well as homemade noodles with tofu.

In addition to noodles, Gansu cuisine also includes beef, lamb, and all types of poultry. In accordance with the teachings of the Koran, the Hui only eat "clean" meat (*halal* in Arabic), which has been slaughtered by a Muslim priest (*ahong* in Chinese) and their religion prohibits them from eating "unclean" meat—from a pig, horse, or donkey, for example. Nevertheless, these types of meat are thoroughly enjoyed by the rest of Gansu's non-Muslim population. As in other rural Chinese provinces, meat is only eaten to mark special occasions. This is particularly true of Gansu, which is an extremely poor province.

Kebap Dunhuang, which consists of thin slices of lamb in flat bread, is a specialty typical of the ancient oasis town of Dunhuang but it is also widely known beyond the confines of the province. Food stalls selling freshly baked flat bread, with or without fillings, can be found on every street corner in Dunhuang and other towns in Gansu.

This oasis town, once a stopping-point on the Silk Road, also boasts other distinctive specialties, including camel's hooves, *tuozhang*, and camel's hump *youbao tuofeng*. Nowadays, however, the camel is considered such a valuable asset and reliable means of transport that it is rarely found as an ingredient in the cooking pot. Although tourists are unlikely to encounter such exotic specialties, they should not miss the opportunity to sample Dunhuang fruit. Locally grown melons, water melons, not to mention pears and peaches, are incredibly sweet and have a wonderful flavor—and there is no comparison with the fruit, which is picked before it is ready and left to ripen during its long journey to Western supermarkets.

Far left: Kebab stands abound in Dunhuang. The headgear worn by the stallholders signals their Muslim origins.

Above left: If you are in the mood for something sweet, try some Lanzhou nut bread.

Below left: Every food stall throughout Gansu will have noodles on the menu.

Bailan honeydew melons, which are cultivated in the vicinity of Lanzhou, have a particularly interesting background as they are reputed to have American "ancestry." According to Chinese sources, Henry A. Wallace (Franklin D. Roosevelt's Vice-President) is supposed to have brought some melon seeds with him during a visit to China in the 1940s and presented them to Gansu farmers. This type of melon is sometimes still referred to in Gansu as a "Wallace melon." One other melon, the so-called Mapi Zui melon, has an even more interesting history and is said to have evolved from the famous Hami melons of Xinjiang.

There is also a legend surrounding the Dongguo pear, another local fruit. Apparently, this dish, which is boiled and served hot, was created during the Tang dynasty (618–907) by Minister Wei Zheng, whose mother was refusing to take the bitter medicine prescribed for her bad cough. Her son therefore decided to cook the medicinal herbs in sweet pear juice and his mother, who loved pears, drank the juice and quickly recovered. Many Chinese still swear by the medicinal properties of pear compôte, prepared in combination with various ingredients, for the treatment and relief of coughs.

sharp skewer to see that the juices run clear. Remove the chicken from the pan, pat dry with paper towels and leave to cool.

Meanwhile, fry the garlic and ginger in the cooking oil or chicken dripping in a wok or skillet over a medium heat. Add the breadcrumbs and sweat the ingredients until they turn into a thick golden-brown mass. Take care not to let the garlic burn, or it will taste bitter.

Pour the oil into a wok or deep-fat fryer, heat to a high temperature and fry the cooled whole chicken until it is crisp and brown.

Arrange the fried whole chicken (in China it would be served with the head) on a large platter, sprinkle generously with the golden-brown breadcrumb mixture and garnish with fresh cilantro.

This dish is typical of Dunhuang, an oasis town on the Silk Road.

Cold celery noodles

This dish is eaten cold in summer. It is made with the water leftover from the cooked noodles, which has been left to stand for several days.

1 ¼–1 ½ lb (600–700 g) homemade wheat-flour noodles, cut into ¾-inch (2-cm) strips (see p. 403)
3–4 sticks of celery, cut into ¾–1-inch (2–3-cm) lengths
2 ½–3 quarts (2.5–3) liters water

To serve:
2 green and two red chiles, to taste, thinly sliced in rings
2 bunches of fresh cilantro

Place the noodles and celery in the water, bring to a boil and cook for 2–3 minutes. Remove the noodles and retain for use elsewhere. Allow the noodle water and celery to cool, cover and leave to stand for 2–3 days. The water will begin to ferment slightly and taste of celery. Divide the cold noodle water into individual bowls, add freshly cooked noodles, and serve sprinkled with the sliced chiles and fresh cilantro.

Dunhuang-style desert chicken

Broth:
2–2 ½ quarts (2–2.5 liters) water
2 bay leaves
1–2 pieces of cassia bark (¾–1 inch / 2–3 cm long) (alternatively, a cinnamon stick may be used)
2–3 dried chiles, to taste
½ tsp ground ginger
2 cloves
ground cumin
1 tsp soy sauce
½ tsp salt

1 whole chicken, blanched (about 2 lb 10 oz / 1.2 kg, with head, if desired, but innards removed)
2–3 garlic cloves, finely chopped
1 piece of ginger (1 ½–2 inch / 4–5 cm long), grated
9 oz (250 g) breadcrumbs
7 tbsp cooking oil, or about 3 ½ oz chicken dripping or schmaltz
about 2 quarts (2 liters oil), for frying
fresh cilantro, to garnish

Make the broth with the ingredients listed, bring to a boil and simmer gently for 50–60 minutes. Add the blanched chicken, bring to a boil, then simmer gently for about one hour. Check with a

Above: Despite this being a desert region, there is a remarkably wide choice of fruit in the markets around Dunhuang.

Right: Many parts of Gansu have so far been spared the blessing—or the curse—of motorized transport. Most work is still carried out manually here with the fetching and carrying done by bicycle.

Noodles, beef, and lamb—Gansu cuisine **397**

The Hui—Chinese Muslims

China has a population of around 20 million Muslims, not all of whom belong to the Turkic peoples in the western provinces. On the contrary, they are mostly Chinese and can be found in every town throughout the country, often working in commerce or the restaurant industry. They can be distinguished by the white caps worn by the men, and the headscarves worn by the women, as well as the fact that they have the surname "Ma" (derived from the first syllable of the name Muhammad). The Hui, who number 9 million people, are China's third largest minority group. Unlike the other 40 minorities in the country, the Hui are bound together not by ethnic origins, but by their religious allegiance to Islam—and it is this that distinguishes them from the Han Chinese (with whom they are ethnically grouped). The first Muslims came from Central Asia and the Middle East, but constant intermarrying with the Han Chinese meant that outward differences soon disappeared.

Chinese Muslims have extremely diverse origins dating back to the 7th century when Arab and Persian traders began settling on the coast of China, where they were welcomed as "foreign guests" and permitted to stay. Toward the end of the Tang dynasty (618–907), Muslim soldiers from Central Asia also supported the imperial army in its clashes with nomadic tribes. When the conflict was over, the soldiers settled in the western border regions of the Chinese empire in what are now the provinces of Gansu and Ningxia. The majority of Muslims, however, arrived in China during the Yuan dynasty (1271–1368), during which time the Mongolian rulers employed them as administrative officials and stationed an army of around 4 million Muslim soldiers in the country. Even today, there are whispered references to the fact that the emperor who vanquished the Mongols and founded the Chinese Ming dynasty (1368–1644), Hongwu, was himself of Muslim descent. He granted them religious, political, and economic freedom on condition that the men married Chinese women, dressed in a conventionally Chinese fashion and only spoke Chinese. Consequently, the Hui now have no language or ethnicity of their own, but since they practice their own religion and live largely in separate communities, they have been able to preserve their own culture to some extent.

Following numerous attempts to free themselves from the rule of the Chinese imperial court, most of the Dungan—as the Hui were known in China up to the beginning of the 20th century (and still are in Turkestan)—were resettled in the impoverished regions of Gansu and Ningxia. Their separate nationality was not recognized until the 1930s and Ningxia, an autonomous region founded in 1958 in the southwest of Gansu, is still home to a sixth of the total Hui population. Unlike the Uighurs, a similarly large Muslim population group in Xinjiang, the Hui, despite their religion, are not regarded by the Chinese government as foreigners or even separatists. This is because they are Chinese, who have even integrated Confucianist beliefs into their own religion. The name "Hui" has meanwhile become synonymous in modern Chinese with Islam (Huijiao) in general.

Nowadays, the Hui tend to be mainly farmers in rural areas, or tradesmen or merchants in the towns. They are reputed to be particularly hardworking and intelligent which is why they are much in demand as skilled workers. Muslim cuisine is also becoming increasingly popular in China. Since the Hui are prohibited from eating pork, their diet mainly revolves around mutton and lamb, beef, and noodles. Most of their cooking methods are based on Peking cuisine. Lamb kebab is now a popular dish all over China and the world famous *Niuroumian* (noodles with lamb or beef in a hearty soupy broth), is a Hui dish that was originally created during the Tang dynasty.

Below: Muslims prefer to eat in company. In the words of Muhammad "Allah says: Eat together, and not separately, for the blessing is associated with the company."

Dunhuang-style kebab with flat bread

2 ¼ lb (1 kg) lamb (shoulder or breast), cut
  into fine strips
7 tbsp sunflower oil
chili powder
salt
ground ginger
cumin or shashlik seasoning
4 small flat breads (4–5 inch / 10–12 cm in
  diameter)

Spear the meat on long, thin skewers, about
14–16 inches (35–40 cm) long, leaving a space in
between and alternating lean and fatty pieces,
where possible. Holding the skewers together at
one end like a bouquet of flowers, lay them
briefly on a very hot barbecue (in China this dish
is always cooked over glowing coals), turning
them over the heat. After 30 to 40 seconds,
brush the meat quickly with oil then sprinkle
several generous pinches of each spice liberally
over the meat. Continue to grill the meat over the
fire, turning all the time. Repeat this procedure
once or twice more. Never leave the meat on the
grill for more than 30–40 seconds at a time.
Spear each flat bread, using two skewers for
each one, and toast the bread over the fire for 30
to 40 seconds on each side. Remove from the
heat, brush with oil, sprinkle with each of the
spices, to taste, and toast until suitably crisp.
Alternatively, cut the bread into ¾- to 1-inch
(2–3 cm) strips and toast these individually on
skewers.
In northern Chinese cuisine, kebabs are not made
with molded minced lamb, but consist of finely
sliced strips of meat with a relatively high fat
content.

Hui-style homemade noodles in lamb broth
Niuroumian

generous 1–1 ¼ lb (500–600 g) lamb (with fat
  and bones)
3 ½ tbsp cooking oil
2 cups (500 ml) hot water or hot lamb stock
1 tsp salt
½ tsp Sichuan pepper
11–14 oz (300–400 g) choy sum (Chinese
  cabbage, but Swiss chard, or leaf spinach
  may be used), washed and finely shredded
1–1 ¼ lb (500–600 g) homemade wheat-flour
  noodles, cut into ¾-inch (2-cm)-wide
  strips (see p. 403)
1 tbsp soy sauce

For the garnish:
2 green and 2 red chiles, sliced into thin rings
1 bunch of fresh cilantro

Bone the lamb and cut the meat into small pieces.
Pour the oil into the wok and stir-fry the lamb
over a high heat. After 4–5 minutes, slowly add

the water or lamb stock and simmer for 50–60
minutes, stirring occasionally. Season with salt
and Sichuan pepper. Meanwhile, blanch the choy
sum (Chinese cabbage), drain and add to the wok.
Remove the wok from the heat.
Cook the noodles in boiling water (see page 402
for recipe).
Divide the noodles into individual bowls, drizzle
over the soy sauce, then pour over the meat and
vegetables. Serve garnished with the chile rings
and fresh cilantro.

Above left: Homemade noodles are an essential
part of Muslim cuisine in Gansu. This picture
shows a length of noodle dough being cut into
wide sections.

Above center: When making *niuroumian*, the lamb
is quickly stir-fried with the vegetables in a wok
over a high heat.

Above right: Hui men and women normally eat
separately—unless it is a special family
celebration.

Noodles—a national treasure

In China, noodles are an integral part of a traditional birthday meal, their long strands symbolizing a long life. On an occasion of this kind, therefore, they are served uncut in a broth and topped with a spicy sauce. Generally speaking, however, noodles are considered fairly commonplace fare in China and, unlike *jiaozi*, (dumplings), did not feature in imperial cuisine. There is a kind of Chinese proverb, *xiehouyu*, in Beijing that says in effect: "A prince who eats noodles is taking second best." This would be used to describe a situation in which someone, even a prince, was obliged to make do with second best.

Nonetheless, there are some extremely mouthwatering noodle dishes in China, the main one being Lanzhou noodles. Originally a specialty of Lanzhou, the capital of Gansu province, *Lanzhou lamian* is now available throughout China as well as abroad. The handmade noodles, *lamian* are made by stretching the dough as long as possible using both hands, then transferring both ends to one hand, taking the new "end" into the other hand and stretching again, swinging the dough over and over like a skipping rope. This process is repeated until the noodles reach the correct diameter and length. It is a procedure that requires great dexterity and practice and is always fascinating to watch. Once cooked, the noodles are served in a large bowl of hearty beef broth. The addition of red chili oil and green cilantro gives the clear soup with its colorless noodles a very appetizing flavor. Beef noodles are generally a breakfast dish in Lanzhou, or are eaten for lunch at the latest. People usually stop on their way to work at one of the small food stalls—mainly run by Muslim Hui Chinese—which specialize in making *Lanzhou lamian*. A bowl of beef noodles will normally cost less than three Yuan RMB (Chinese currency *renminbi*), currently about 50 US cents. The composition of ingredients in the broth will vary from one food stall to another since each naturally has its own carefully guarded, secret recipe. Since May 2007, the art of making this beef noodle dish has even been added to the list of Lanzhou's protected cultural treasures! People still like to speculate as to whether Marco Polo (1254–1324) took Chinese noodles back to Italy with him or whether he introduced Italian spaghetti into China. Although it is impossible to know for certain whether this Italian merchant's son really did visit the Imperial Palace in Beijing or not, evidence has meanwhile come to light proving that the Chinese were indeed making noodles long before Marco Polo's travels along the Silk Road. Recent excavations not far from the Yellow River unearthed some 4,000-year-old noodles. The village of Lajia in northwest China was struck (like Pompeii) by a natural disaster when it was hit by floods in the wake of an earthquake and buried under an avalanche of mud. When the settlement was excavated in autumn 2005, archaeologists found some very well preserved noodles beneath an overturned clay pot. They were 20 inches (50 cm) long and one inch (3 cm) in diameter and appear to have been made from foxtail and broomcorn millet.

Nowadays, most Chinese noodles are made from wheat flour, although egg, rice, and cellophane, or glass, noodles are also very popular and can now be purchased in the West.

Egg noodles

Chinese instant egg noodles, known as "mie," can be bought in Asian food stores and in most Western supermarkets. Nowadays, they are one of the most familiar ingredients in Chinese cooking. Mie noodles consist mainly of wheat flour and eggs, often goose or duck eggs. Sometimes, ground seaweed, or shrimps are added to the noodle mixture. The noodles do not need cooking; it is enough to pour hot water over them and let them sit for a few minutes.

Instant noodle soup

Chinese tourist groups have gained a reputation for preferring to eat in Chinese restaurants when on holiday abroad. European food is simply too exotic for the average Chinese and the idea of a cold meal for breakfast, or late in the evening, is simply inconceivable. For this reason, Chinese tourists always carry a few packets of instant noodle soup in their baggage so that they can, in an emergency, pour hot water over the noodles and take the edge off their hunger. Instant soups of this kind are readily available in the West in a variety of flavors and are just as tasty and healthy as ready-made Chinese products.

Cellophane noodles

Cellophane noodles are made from mung bean starch and water and sold in dried form in compact bundles. These colorless noodles should not be boiled, but simply softened in hot water, which also gives them their glassy quality. If crisp noodles are preferred, they should be fried quickly in hot oil. Cellophane noodles have no flavor of their own and can therefore be used in many different ways: for example, in soups, such as sauerkraut broth, *suancai dun fentiao*, from Heilongjiang, or as a cold ingredient in salads. One particularly appetizing dish involving cellophane noodles is called "ants on the tree" *(mayi shang shu)*, a specialty from Sichuan province, in which they are served with a spicy sauce containing ground meat. The name alludes to the appearance of the dish— the little pieces of ground meat sticking to the noodles resemble ants climbing up a tree.

Left: The Jiayuguan fortress at the western end of the Great Wall has been on China's list of World Heritage Sites since 1961.

Right: A wide variety of accompanying dishes complement China's delicious noodle dishes.

Rice noodles

As their name suggests, rice noodles are made from rice flour. Like cellophane noodles, they merely need softening in hot water. They turn white in color and taste faintly of rice. One particularly famous and popular recipe known as Crossing-bridge noodles, *guojiao mixian*, is a specialty of Yunnan province. Are you curious to know how the dish gets its name? Just look in the chapter on Yunnan province!

Ants on the tree

11 oz (300 g) cellophane noodles
11 oz (300 g) ground pork
2 tbsp rice wine
2 tbsp soy sauce
2 tsp sesame oil
corn oil
2 tbsp chopped ginger
4 garlic cloves, finely chopped
1 cup (250 ml) clear stock, or water
$\frac{1}{2}$ tsp Sichuan pepper, ground
2 tsp salt
2 tsp sugar
4 scallions, finely chopped, to garnish

Soak the noodles for about 10 minutes in hot water, then drain. Mix the meat with the rice wine, soy sauce, and sesame oil. Heat a little corn oil in a wok over a high heat and fry the ginger and garlic, then add the meat. Cook over a moderate heat for several minutes.

Stir the Sichuan pepper, salt, and sugar into the stock or water and pour over the meat mixture. Fold in the noodles and bring the mixture to a boil. Reduce the heat and simmer gently until the liquid has completely evaporated.

Garnish with the chopped scallions to serve.

Below: Making *Lanzhou lamian* may look like child's play, but it is far from easy.

Center: The handmade noodles are cooked in a hearty broth. Every restaurant has its own special recipe.

Lanzhou lamian

Homemade wheat-flour noodles

Basic recipe:

4 ½ lb (2 kg) (best quality) all-purpose wheat flour
2–3 quarts (2–3 liters) water (with Penghui ash, if possible)
4–5 quarts (4–5 liters) water, for cooking the noodles
cooking oil

The recipe suggests a recommended minimum amount of 4 ½ lb (2 kg) of flour since these noodles are normally served at large gatherings (of 8–10 people).
Preparations begin 24 hours before the actual dish is cooked, when 2–3 quarts (2–3 liters) of water are poured into a large container, to which 2–3 tablespoons of Penghui are added. "Peng" is the name of a desert grass in Gansu and "hui" means ash. The solution is mixed thoroughly and left to stand overnight, by which time the water will have cleared as the ash sinks to the bottom.

Lanzhou lamian with clear beef broth

Noodles:
see basic recipe above and p. 403

Broth:
2–3 quarts (2–3 liters) of beef broth, homemade or from cubes or granules
⅔ cup (150 ml) soy sauce
⅔ cup (150 ml) red rice vinegar
3 ½ tbsp chili oil
6–8 scallions
2 bunches of fresh cilantro
generous 1 lb (500 g) lean beef, boiled and thinly sliced
6–8 eggs, hard-cooked, marinated in soy sauce, finely chopped

To make the noodles, mix the cold Penghui water with the flour and knead into a dough. Leave to stand at room temperature for at least 30 minutes. Knead the dough thoroughly once more and tear into pieces measuring about 12 inches (30 cm) long and 1–1 ½ inches (3–4 cm) wide. Knead each piece well, then shape into rolls (6–8 pieces) and place on a board. Prepare the ingredients for the broth in small bowls.
Bring the water to a boil. Lightly moisten the board and your hands with a little cooking oil and, using both hands, pull each section of dough apart. Bring the two ends of the strand of dough together, then pull this double strand apart again to the desired length, (see p. 400). By repeating this process over and over again, you can end up with 32–64 thin strands from a single piece of dough. Tear off the two thick ends, which you are holding in your right and left hands, place the noodles in the water and boil for a few minutes until they float to the surface. Quickly remove from the water.
Divide the hot noodles into individual bowls, pour over the beef broth, then add a small amount of each different ingredient, as required. The noodles should be eaten immediately using chopsticks, as they will stick together when cold.

Dunhuang-style saozi noodles

3 ½ tbsp cooking oil
7 oz (200 g) lean pork, thinly sliced
2 garlic cloves, chopped
1 piece of fresh ginger (1 inch / 2.5 cm long), grated
4–5 scallions, separated into white and green parts, finely chopped

4 carrots, finely chopped
4 medium-sized tomatoes, finely chopped
2–3 black morel mushrooms, soaked, blanched, finely chopped
1 tsp five-spice powder (more, if required)
½ tsp chili powder (to taste)
1 tbsp soy sauce
4 cups (1 liter) vegetable stock
about 3 ½ tbsp red rice vinegar
2 ¼ lb (1 kg) homemade noodles
5 ½ oz (150 g) tofu, finely chopped

1 bunch of fresh cilantro, to garnish

Heat the oil in a wok or skillet and stir-fry the meat for 1–2 minutes over a high heat. Add the garlic, ginger, the white parts of the scallion, carrots, tomatoes, mushrooms, and spices and stir-fry for 2–3 minutes, then flavor with soy sauce. Pour in a little stock and simmer all the ingredients for 4–5 minutes. Pour in more broth, if needed, and season the mixture with vinegar (the dish is supposed to taste slightly acidic). Stir in the tofu.
Place the prepared noodles in boiling, unsalted water and cook for 2 minutes. The noodles should not go soft but remain al dente.
Divide the noodles into individual soup bowls and pour some broth into each before adding the meat mixture. Garnish with a generous amount of cilantro and green scallion to serve.

The word "saozi," roughly translated, means "chopped small," and refers to the sauce that is poured over the noodles.

The term "lamian" consists of two words: "la," meaning "to pull," and "mian," meaning "noodles." This type of noodle dish is eaten for breakfast or lunch in specialty noodle restaurants, or made at home to celebrate special occasions with large numbers of guests.
The noodles for this beef noodle dish are individually prepared for each guest. Depending on personal taste, you can ask for thin "spaghetti-type" noodles, *xi de*; narrow ones, *er xi*; or wide, *kuan de*, ribbon noodles. "You are what you eat" is a saying that seems to be especially true in the case of Lanzhou residents: broad-shouldered men who do hard, physical work tend to prefer the broad noodles, while women usually opt for the daintier varieties.

1 The flour is mixed into a dough using the Penghui water, prepared the day before, then left to stand at room temperature for about 30 minutes.

2 The dough is then thoroughly kneaded: noodle-making is definitely a job that has to be done by hand.

3 The dough is now rolled out on a lightly floured surface and sprinkled with a little flour.

4 Using a narrow rolling pin, the dough is rolled up into one long length.

5 The dough is folded over several times. The two ends are then brought together, and then, holding the ends in one hand, and the middle of the strand of dough in the other, the dough is pulled apart. This process is repeated numerous times.

6 Depending on individual preference, the dough is cut into thin spaghetti-like noodles or wider ribbons.

7 This picture shows thin strands of noodles being held aloft...

8 ...and here it is "raining" much wider noodles.

9 There are noodles to suit every taste and every recipe.

The Chinese farming calendar

The Gregorian calendar was first introduced when the Chinese Republic was founded in 1912 and was officially adopted throughout China on January 1, 1929. In addition to this Western calendar, (xili), which is based on the solar year, the traditional Chinese farmer's calendar, (nongli), still plays a major part in everyday life. It is the basis for all traditional festivals. Important events, such as weddings or the opening of buildings, etc., are not simply organized for an arbitrary day—the date has to be worked out by an expert astrologer to make sure that it is auspicious.

The farmer's calendar—a lunisolar calendar—is a combination of the lunar and solar calendars. It is based on the phases of the moon, but at the same time incorporates elements of the solar calendar. There is evidence to suggest that this traditional calendar has existed for more than 4,600 years and it is said to have been introduced in 2637 B.C. by the legendary Yellow Emperor (Huangdi). The calendar follows a 60-year cycle and since 1984 we have been in the 78th cycle, which will end in 2044.

During this 60-year cycle, each year is named by a heavenly stem and an earthly branch. The ten heavenly stems are named after the five elements of wood, fire, earth, metal, and water—each in combination with yin or yang. The twelve earthly branches are represented by the twelve animal signs of the Chinese zodiac. These are also known by name in the West: 1. rat, shu; 2. buffalo/ox, niu; 3. tiger, hu; 4. hare, tu; 5. dragon, long; 6. snake, she; 7. horse, ma; 8. sheep or goat, yang; 9. monkey, hou; 10. rooster, ji; 11. dog, gou; 12. pig, zhu. Under this system, the year 2009 is associated with the celestial stem of "yin earth" and the earthly branch of the "ox."

According to one legend, Buddha, before he left the earth, invited all the animals to a farewell gathering, but only 12 accepted his invitation. Buddha thanked his guests with a very special gift: in future, every living being would be given at birth the character of one of these 12 animals and would live under this sign for the rest of his life. The animal sign "burns itself into the heart at birth," as the Chinese say. The sequence of animal signs follows the order in which the animals arrived at the gathering. The clever rat, which had hitched a ride on the head of the patient buffalo, jumped toward Buddha when the latter arrived and was consequently the first animal Buddha laid eyes upon—ahead of the buffalo and the other animals.

The lunisolar calendar

A lunar month spans 29.53 days and represents the time that passes between two full moons, in other words, the time it takes for the moon to orbit the earth. The lunar year has 12 months, and a distinction is made between the so-called "little months" with 29 days, and the "large months" with 30 days. Accordingly, a lunar year lasts 354 days, which is 11 days fewer than a solar year with 365 days. As the years pass, therefore, the lunar year diverges farther and farther from the solar year—and also from the seasons. In order to keep the solar and lunar calendars aligned with each other, leap days and leap months were introduced. Years which include leap months are particularly popular in China—both for weddings and births, as an extra long year is regarded as the best kind of good omen for a long (married) life.

In rural Chinese communities, the division of the solar year into 24 periods, jieqi, is also of great significance. These periods are based on the position of the sun, reflect the changes in nature and, consequently, help farmers make decisions about their work. The table below lists the Chinese names for the individual periods, their English equivalent, and the date when each period begins according to the Gregorian calendar.

1. **Lichun** (beginning of spring, February 4 or 5)
2. **Yushui** (rainwater, February 18, 19, or 20)
3. **Qingzhi** (awakening of insects, March 5 or 6)
4. **Chunfen** (vernal equinox, when day and night are equal, March 20 or 21)
5. **Qingming** (pure and bright, April 4 or 5)
6. **Guyu** (grain rains, April 19, 20, or 21)
7. **Lixia** (beginning of summer, May 6 or 7)
8. **Xiaoman** (grain ripening, May 20, 21, or 22)
9. **Mangzhong** (grain in ear, June 5, 6, or 7)
10. **Xiazhi** (summer solstice, June 21 or 22)
11. **Xiaoshu** (minor heat, July 6, 7, or 8)
12. **Dashu** (major heat, July 22, 23, or 24)
13. **Liqiu** (beginning of autumn, August 8 or 9)
14. **Chushu** (end of heat, August 22, 23, or 24)
15. **Bailu** (white dew, September 7, 8, or 9)
16. **Qiufen** (autumnal equinox, day and night of equal length, September 22 or 23)
17. **Hanlu** (cold dew, October 8 or 9)
18. **Shuangjiang** (fall of frost, October 23 or 24)
19. **Lidong** (start of winter, November 7 or 8)

Left: The agricultural cultivation depends very much on the geological conditions in the province. Terraced farming is a common sight in Gansu.

Below: Farm work is still often done by hard manual labor. Machinery is the exception rather than the rule.

20. **Xiaoxue** (minor snowfall, November 22 or 23)
21. **Daxue** (major snowfall, December 6, 7, or 8)
22. **Dongzhi** (winter solstice, December 21, 22, or 23)
23. **Xiahan** (minor cold, January 5, 6, or 7)
24. **Dahan** (major cold, January 20 or 21)

These periods revolve around the solar year and have variable dates in the lunar calendar. In 2008, for example, the Chinese New Year and the first day of the first lunar calendar month fell on February 7. Lichun, the start of spring according to the 24 solar terms was on February 4, which was the 28th day of the 12th month of the lunar calendar.

Chinese traditional festivals likewise conform to the various events and requirements of the farming year. The most important annual festival, the Chinese New Year, which is known as *chunjie*, spring festival, is celebrated in winter on the first day of the first lunar calendar month when work in the fields has come to a halt. Once the crops have been sown in spring, it is time for *qingmingjie*, or Ancestors' Day, a festival which is celebrated at the beginning of the 5th solar term of Qingming on April 4 or 5. After the first harvest, it is time to celebrate the Dragon Boat Festival held on the 5th day of the 5th lunar month, and after the last harvest of the year, the Moon Festival is ushered in on the 15th day of the 8th month. Finally, *chongyang* on the 9th day of the 9th month signals the start of winter. Nine is a yang number, hence the name *chongyang*, meaning "double yang."

Cold donkey meat with pumpkin and chili oil

Broth:
2 quarts (2 liters) water
2 bay leaves
1–2 pieces of cassia bark, ¾–1 inch (2–3 cm) in length (a cinnamon stick may be used instead)
2–3 dried chiles, or to taste
½ tsp ground ginger
2 cloves
ground cumin
1 tsp soy sauce
½ tsp salt
½ tsp confectioner's sugar

2 ¼ lb (1 kg) lean donkey meat in one piece (beef may be used instead)

To serve:
scallions or cilantro
pinch of cumin
chili sauce
chili oil
1 bowl of salt and finely chopped chiles
pickled sweet-and-sour pumpkin chunks

Make the broth, using all the ingredients except for the confectioner's sugar, bring to a boil, reduce the heat and simmer gently for 50–60 minutes. Add the sugar, cook for a few more minutes, then add the meat and simmer gently for about one hour (the beef may need a shorter cooking time, so check it first before the finishing time).
Remove the meat from the saucepan and set aside to cool.
Cut the meat into thin slices, garnish with scallions or fresh cilantro, and sprinkle with a little cumin. Serve with chili sauce, chili oil, the salt and chile mixture, and the sweet-and-sour pumpkin.
This specialty is typical of Dunhuang, an oasis town on the Silk Road.

Above left: Some of these cultivated terraces are centuries old. This type of farming makes sound ecological sense as it prevents soil erosion caused by fast-flowing rainwater.

Below left: The main agricultural activities in Gansu center on arable farming, but in the small villages most farmers also keep a herd of sheep, or goats.

新疆

Xinjiang

Elke Spielmanns-Rome

The Autonomous Region of Xinjiang (formerly known as Sinkiang) lies in the far northwest corner of China. Covering an area of 640,929 square miles (1.66 million sq km), this region occupies 17 percent of the country's territory and is the largest administrative zone in the People's Republic of China. Surrounded by gigantic mountain ranges—the Altai Mountains to the north and the Kunlun and Pamir Mountains to the south—and traversed by the Taklimakan the driest sandy desert in the world, this harsh and barren region is China's "Wild West." The Taklimakan, or "place of no return" as it is known, is situated in the Turpan depression and covers about 22 percent of the total area of Xinjiang. The Turpan depression, which is traversed in the west by the Tarim, China's longest river, extends from the Jiayu Pass in Gansu to the Pamir Mountains in the west.

The province is home to a population of just 19 million people (1.5 percent of the country's overall population), around half of whom belong to the Uighur ethnic group (*Weiwu'er*). This group enjoys regional autonomy, in other words substantial ethnic and religious freedom, as well as significant involvement in local administration. The Han Chinese also account for 38 percent of the population, in addition to other Turkic peoples, such as Kazachs, Kirghiz, Uzbeks, Tartars, Manchurians, and Mongols. A natural boundary exists between the Siberian nomadic steppes in the north and the Muslim urban oasis culture in the south in the shape of the Tianshan ("celestial mountains") range. Reaching heights of between 9,842 and 16,500 feet (3,000–5,000 m), it runs from Gansu province in the east to the Altai mountains in the west. Xinjiang (which means "new frontier area") has only been part of China since the end of the 19th century. Prior to this time, it was mostly ruled by Muslim Turkic peoples which is why people still refer, even today, to East Turkistan, or Chinese Turkistan (as opposed to West Turkistan/Turkistan, the region between the Caspian Sea and the Gobi Desert). Xinjiang's culture is still predominantly Muslim in character even though the region is now inhabited by a large number of Han Chinese.

History of the Uighurs

The Uighurs are thought to be direct descendants of the Huns and not related to the original Turkic tribes of the region. In former times, these nomadic cattle herders traveled the vast steppes of Mongolia and established the Uighur Khaganate (745–840), which stretched from Lake Baikal in the north to Gansu in the east and India in the southwest.

Top: China's "Wild West" is a unique area with some spectacular scenery, including the "Flaming Mountains" to the north of the Turpan Basin...

Above: ...and Heavenly Lake, which mirrors the snow-covered peaks of the Trans-Himalayas in its turquoise waters.

Facing page: Clearly visible from afar, the 144-foot (44-m)-high minaret of the Sugongta or Emin Mosque on the outskirts of Turpan marks the town as a religious center.

Ürümqi

Above: Ürümqi is the political, economic, and cultural center of Xinjiang province. In the midst of rapidly growing modern urban developments is the Old Town with its southern mosque, a popular attraction.

Below right: The Turpan oasis owes its fertility to an artificial irrigation system with a network of canals stretching over a total distance of 1,243 miles (2,000 km).

Their rule over nine nomadic peoples is reflected in the Mongolian name *Uighur*, meaning "confederation of nine tribes."

The Uighurs, who are descended from an advanced early civilization, have a language which belongs to the Turkic group of the Altaic language family and a script which was later adopted by Genghis Khan as a basis for the Mongolian language. The Uighurs also developed an extensive knowledge of medicine, which they combined with traditional Chinese medicine (TCM) and elements of Western medicine. Uighur medicine, which can be traced back 2,700 years, is a natural medicine, based on the remedial properties of herbs, animals, minerals, and fruits.

The Uighur Khaganate was eventually overrun in the 9th century by Kirghiz armies and the former occupiers fled to the Tarim Basin in southern Xinjiang where they settled in oasis towns along the Silk Road and established the Qoco, or Kocho, kingdom (850–1209, *Gaochang*). Since it proved impossible to rear livestock in this dry region, the Uighurs settled down and, after constructing irrigation canals, turned their attention to fruit-growing and commerce. Trading activities with Turkic peoples in the west brought them into contact with Islam for the first time. Most Uighurs were originally followers of Shamanism and other "natural" religions, but by the 14th century nearly all of them had converted to the Muslim faith. They also incorporated Arabic into their script and adopted the Muslim educational system, with the result that by the Middle Ages Kashgar, an early trading center, boasted as many as 18 universities.

With the exception of the period under Mongol rule (1271–1368), the Uighurs lived largely independently until the middle of the 19th century. However, when China, Russia, and Great Britain all began vying for

Why "Turpan" is called "Tulufan" in Chinese

The Chinese language consists not of letters, but of syllables, which is why foreign names have to be adapted into Chinese, for example, by phonetically imitating the word. "Turpan," for example, becomes the three-syllable word "Tu-lu-fan." Alternatively, the actual meaning of a Western name can be translated into Chinese: German footballer Bastian Schweinsteiger ("Schweini"), for instance, is known and loved in China as "Xhiao Zhu" (meaning "little pig").

superiority in Central Asia, East Turkestan became the focus of the colonial powers' wrangling. After heavy fighting, which ended in the suppression of the Uighur Turpan rebellion (1862–1878), the Qing emperor declared the region of Xinjiang a protectorate, whereupon many Uighurs fled to the neighboring countries of West Turkestan, Kazakhstan, Kirghizstan, Uzbekistan, and Turkmenistan. In 1955, in recognition of its predominantly Uighur population, the province was proclaimed the Uighur Autonomous Region of the People's Republic of China. However, this autonomy is being increasingly restricted by the central government in Beijing. At the same time, Uighur aspirations to proper independence sometimes spill over into acts of violence.

The Muslim way of life has changed very little to this day. The Uighurs continue to live as farmers or merchants in flat constructions of wood and clay, producing all they need in family-run businesses. Uighur men can be distinguished by their wide coats, knee-high boots, and square fur caps while the women wear satin dresses and brightly embroidered shoes and caps, under which their hair is usually wound into long braids.

Above: Trading has taken place along the length of the Silk Road since time immemorial. Nowadays, it is mainly agricultural produce that is sold at the markets.

Below: Muslim Uighurs can be recognized by their black caps, decorated with white embroidery. Older men are also likely to have well-groomed beards.

Top: Thanks to its position and fertility, Turpan has always been one of the most important stopping points along the Silk Road. Of particular note are the distinctive clay buildings, some of which are centuries old.

Above center: The prayer room inside the Sugongta, or Emin, Mosque in Turpan is delightful in its symmetry.

Above: Uighur women can be distinguished from Han Chinese by their clothing.

Above right: Flat bread, kebabs, and dumplings filled with mutton can be bought from every good food stall in Xinjiang.

Trade centers along the Silk Road

The growing popularity of the Silk Road as a major trade route during course of the Han dynasty (206 B.C.–220 A.D.) led to the development of numerous oasis towns, such as Kashgar, Turpan, and Ürümqi, as centers of commerce.

Caravans transporting their precious cargoes from China to the West would negotiate the Jade Pass and finally reach the Turpan Depression in the east of the province, the second lowest point on the earth's surface after the Dead Sea. Thanks to a sophisticated irrigation system, this area, sometimes known as one of China's "furnaces" on account of temperatures reaching 122 °F (50 °C), is noted for the cultivation of the famous Hami melons (see p. 416), and seedless Turpan grapes, or raisins. The depression, which extends a total of 1,864 miles (3,000 km), is fed by a system of underground channels. It is the site of the ruins of the ancient fortress cities of Yarkhoto (*Jiaohe*) and Kharakhoja (*Gaochang*) that offered a refuge to travelers 2,000 years ago. The "flaming mountains" of Turpan (*Huoyanshan*) with their red-colored slopes are the setting for an episode of the Chinese classic novel, *Journey to the West*, a dramatization of which is performed by the Peking Opera. The center of the region is the oasis town of Turpan. Its most famous structure is the 144-foot (44-m)-high minaret of the Emin Mosque. To the northeast of the town are the Caves of Bezelik, which bear testimony to the influence of Buddhism in the region. Buddhist monks carved out hermit caves in the rocky cliffs and the site eventually grew into a monastery complex. From Turpan, the caravans traveled along the northern edge of the Tarim Basin, past the oasis towns of Korla, Kuqa, and Aksu to the major markets of Kashgar, a bazaar town which used to mark the western end of the Silk Road and is now the westernmost town in the People's Republic.

Another route to Kashgar led from Dunhuang in Gansu province along the southern edge of the Tarim Basin, passing through the oasis towns of Miran, Niya, Yarkand, and Hotien (formerly Yotland). The latter is best known for its jade. This precious gemstone, which in China is regarded as the embodiment of beauty and symbolizes good fortune, is panned from the region's numerous wild mountain streams.

To the northwest of the town of Kuqa are China's oldest Buddhist caves, the towering Thousand Buddha Caves (*Qianfodong*) of Kyzyl, which contain wall paintings dating from the 3rd to the 8th century. Sadly, many of the paintings became casualties of excessive zeal: some of the pictures were damaged by European archaeologists in the heat of their explorations, and some images were destroyed by Muslim fanatics.

The capital of the Autonomous Region of Xinjiang is the oasis town of Ürümqi ("beautiful pasture"), a modern industrial city inhabited mainly by Han Chinese. It is situated on the southern edge of the Dzungarian Basin on the northern slopes of the Tianshan. The city was not given its Mongolian name until 1954. Before then, it was known by its Chinese name of Dihua. Situated at an altitude of 6,562 feet (2000 m) to the east of the town is the picturesque Heavenly Lake, which local people refer to as the "emerald among the pines" thanks to the turquoise color of its water. The 80-hour Ürümqi–Lanzhou–Guangzhou rail link is the longest in China.

Top: Pork is something of a rarity in the predominantly Muslim province of Xinjiang. One is more likely to find beef and lamb on sale at the markets here.

Above: More dairy products are sold in Xinjiang than elsewhere in China.

Below: The Han Chinese and other ethnic minorities, such as the Uighurs, do not always coexist in harmony. The Uighurs feel themselves pushed to the fringes of society and the outskirts of the towns. Many Han Chinese regard the ethnic groups as backward and often dismiss their customs and rituals as anachronistic.

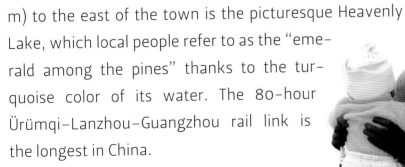

Asian with a touch of Chinese

Kashgar, Xinjiang's largest and China's westernmost city, is closer to Mecca than Beijing—not just geographically but also in culinary terms. Similarly, the Uighurs' long association with the Han Chinese has inevitably had an influence upon their culinary customs. Xinjiang people eat with chopsticks and enjoy a diet that includes not only Asian flat bread, pilau, and kebabs, but also northern Chinese noodle dishes and dumplings. Uighur cuisine also has much in common with the culinary traditions of the Muslim Hui, most of whom live in the province of Gansu and in the Autonomous Region of Ningxia—lamb kebabs, for example, and the hand-pulled Laghman noodles (lamian, as they are called in Lanzhou, the capital of Gansu). In Xinjiang, Laghman noodles are usually prepared with tomatoes, red and green bell peppers, onions, and lamb. Uighur noodles are a variation of this dish.

Tea and bread are served at every Uighur meal. In contrast to the rest of the Chinese heartland, the people of Xinjiang drink black rather than green tea without the addition of sugar or milk. Bread in Xinjiang is flat bread, known as nan. This is a very versatile type of bread, which can be used as a plate, or as a practical wrap for kebabs, juicy dumplings, and suchlike. Food stalls selling nan bread can be found not only on every street corner, but on every bend of the province's rural roads. The bread comes in all shapes and sizes with a wide variety of fillings. Some are as big as wagon wheels, while others are no bigger than the palm of your hand. Some bread is glazed and some is green thanks to the addition of chives. Some types of bread are sprinkled with onions, sesame, or other kinds of seeds while others may be topped with sugar and chopped nuts. The flat bread is baked in charcoal ovens, similar to Indian tandoor-style ovens. To prevent the dough filling with air and puffing up, the surface of the circle of dough, apart from a narrow rim, is "stamped" before baking with a "bread stamp" studded with nails, made from bundles of quills from chicken feathers. In our part of the world, the same effect can usually be achieved using a fork, although it has to be said that the patterns stamped on the bread in Xinjiang are certainly more decorative.

Bread is also an essential part of Uighur wedding rituals. The Imam invites the bride and bridegroom to dunk a portion of bread in saltwater before dividing it and eating it as a symbol of mutual faithfulness to each other. Bread is sacred to the Uighurs and none is ever thrown away. Stale, hard bread can be dipped in tea and every last crumb eaten.

Left: Running a food stall is usually a family affair.

Center left: Ürümqi's food stalls harbor some real experts in spinning flat breads.

Below left: Really delicious—barbecued mutton kebabs...

Below: ...sold ready to cook at the meat stalls.

Left: Preparations for a Uighur-style celebration banquet: a whole half lamb is brushed with a spicy, strongly curry-flavored paste.

Below: Waiting for the lamb to cook on the spit requires a fair amount of patience, not to mention a proper and liberally stirred mixture of spices.

Bottom: One thing you will certainly need for this dish is an extremely large, earthenware pot or oven, which will be able to accommodate the whole skewered lamb.

Fruits from Xinjiang's oases

Vegetables, grain, and fruit are cultivated in Xinjiang's oases. The province is known primarily as a producer of seedless Turpan grapes and the estimated 50 varieties of raisins produced from them, as well as of sweet Hami melons (see below). The fruit is mainly grown in the Turpan oasis, which is fed by a highly efficient irrigation system, developed by the Persians over 2,000 years ago. This so-called Karez system (*karez* in Uighur means "channel") is an underground network of channels which carries spring and melt water from the mountains 6 miles (10 km) away into the oasis. The area experiences dramatic fluctuations in temperature ranging from up to 122 °F (50 °C) in summer to bitter cold winter temperatures of lower than minus 20 °C (minus 4 °F). Since the Muslim Uighurs do not drink alcohol, Turpan grapes are mostly turned into raisins and are dried by storing in well-aired clay huts for about 30 days. Depending on the character and variety of the grape, the resulting raisins can be yellow, light green, bottle green, amber, or brown and also vary in flavor.

Above right: A mere glimpse of the amazing selection of dried fruit at the Turpan fruit market is enough to whet the appetite.

Right: A 2,000-year-old system of irrigation channels supplies the oases around Turpan with water from the Tianshan mountains 25 miles (40 km) away.

Hami melons

Melon is a classic Chinese dessert. Cut into bite-sized pieces, it is absolutely delicious, especially if the fruit comes from Hami.
Hami melons are oval-shaped honeydew melons (*Cucumis melo*). Yellow or greenish in color, with a rather mottled skin and salmon-colored flesh, it derives its name from a Muslim king named Hami, who sent melons to the imperial court as a tribute. Emperor Kangxi of the Qing dynasty (ruled 1661–1722) was an exceedingly cultured monarch with a weakness for everything his country had to offer in the way of culinary diversity. Only the very best would suffice as far as he was concerned and his preferred fruit were melons from the far west of his empire, which he prized for their aromatic sweetness and firm flesh.

Hami melons originally come from the Shanshan district, east of Turpan. Nowadays, they are mainly cultivated in the Hami oasis (Uighur: Kumul). In an attempt to maximize the yield and enable them to be cultivated in the wealthy eastern provinces of China, more than 180 different varieties have been cultivated. The "Golden Dragon" variety is one of the most successful cultivars produced since the mid 1990s, not only in China, but also in the United States.

third of the harvest is exported, including to the United States and Europe. To protect its trademark name, China has registered its geographic place of origin as part of the name "fragrant pears from Korla," in the same way that Lübeck has trademarked its marzipan. Korla pears are found in the West under their English name of "fragrant pear"—sold singly and individually wrapped in silk paper and available between September and April.

Turpan rice with raisins
Serves 8

7 tbsp sunflower oil
2–3 onions, finely chopped
10 carrots, cut into matchsticks
salt and pepper
1 3/4 lbs (800 g) short-grain rice
14 oz (400 g) Turpan raisins, or, alternatively, fine, light-colored raisins
8 small flat breads (nan), alternatively, Turkish flat bread sprinkled with sesame seeds and salt
8 ready-made dim sum, filled with pumpkin purée

Heat the oil in the wok until very hot, then stir-fry the onions for about 1 minute. Add the carrots, salt and pepper, to taste, and stir-fry for a further 8–10 minutes.

Meanwhile, rinse the rice three times in cold water before placing in a pan and covering with about one and a half times the same amount of cold water.

Add the rice and water to the vegetables in the wok and simmer gently over a low heat for 10 minutes, stirring occasionally.

Using a chopstick, poke 10–12 finger-sized holes through the rice down to the bottom of the wok. Cook the mixture for a further 10–15 minutes, until the water has evaporated.

Sprinkle the raisins over the rice, lay the flat bread, salted side down, on top of the rice and allow to stand for 10 minutes. Just before serving remove the bread, give the rice a good stir, tip it onto a large platter or a shallow bowl and serve garnished with the dim sum.

Serve the flat bread as an accompaniment.

Below: Turpan market with its array of nuts, raisins, and other dried fruit.

Raisins can turn a simple dish of vegetables and rice into appetizing Turpan rice. Other fruits, such as dates and apricots, are also dried for winter use. Uighurs love to nibble dried fruits with their tea or as a snack between meals, often as part of a varied assortment of raisins, almonds, dates, and hazelnuts. The local wines, some of which are produced with Russian, and some with French cooperation, are dessert and liqueur wines. Xinjiang's specialties also include pears from Korla (*Kuerle*, situated about 120 miles/ 200 km southwest of Ürümqi). Korla pears belong to the species of Ussuri pears (*Pyrus ussuriensis*) that have been cultivated in China for thousands of years and are characterized by a long stem and spindle-shaped fruit. The surface of the fruit is also coated with an exceptionally thick layer of natural wax. The flesh is crisp and juicy and is sweet to taste with a delicate aroma of pear, much like the Japanese pear (*Nashi*). Around 100,000 tons of pears are produced over an area of 111,197 acres (45,000 ha) in and around Korla. About a

The Silk Road

The name "Silk Road" covers an interconnected network of trade routes which were developed in the early days of the Chinese empire and traversed the Eurasian continent from the Pacific coast to the eastern shores of the Mediterranean. At that time, silk was by far the most valuable and sought after trade commodity among merchants. A German geographer, Freiherr von Richthofen (1833–1905), was the first person to coin the term "silk routes" toward the end of the 19th century. It was not until much later that the name began to take hold . Meanwhile, it has become such a familiar term that it has been incorporated into many other languages, including Chinese, *sichou zhi lu*.

Development and history of the Silk Road

No one knows for sure exactly when the Silk Road was first created. However, early descriptions of the trade route can be found in the *shiji*, the first universal history of China, dating from the 1st century B.C. According to this work, the passage to Central Asia was discovered by the Chinese General Zhang Qian during an expedition to the western territories in 139 B.C. A more likely scenario, however, is that the expansion of the Persian empire as far as the Pamir mountains in West Turkestan meant that for the first time a fixed, direct link to Europe existed, crossing through the two empires of China and Persia (now Iran). It was also around this time that the name "China" was coined, derived from the Indian expression for "land of silk" (cina). The fall of the Han dynasty (220 A.D.) and the disintegration of the empire halted the flow of trade along the Silk Road for a time and it was not until the reunification of the empire under the Tang dynasty (618–907) that caravans began to travel eastward again and oasis towns such as Kashgar and the imperial town of Chang'an (now called Xi'an) began to flourish as cosmopolitan cities. The Silk Road reached its heyday during the days of Mongol rule (1271–1368) when virtually the entire Eurasian continent was united under the so-called Pax Mongolica. This was a time when one could encounter Mongolian envoys in Bordeaux, French laborers in Karakorum, Venetian merchants in Peking, or Arab officials anywhere in China. The decline of the Mongol empire and Vasco da Gama's discovery of a sea route to India (in the late 15th century) led to the Silk Road falling into disuse.

Routes from East to West

Traditionally, Xi'an in Shaanxi province is believed to mark the eastern end of the Silk Road while Alexandria, or Antalya (formerly Antiochia) on the Mediterranean lies at its western end, extending an overall distance of around 5,282 miles (8,500 km). Various branch routes in the eastern section also connected to the ports of Guangzhou (Canton) and Quanzhou (Zaitan) on the Yellow Sea and even extended as far as Japan. A caravan traveling from oasis to oasis through scorching deserts, across vast steppe landscapes, and over snow-covered mountain passes would take between 8 to 12 months to complete the journey. The goods were usually traded in the major bazaar towns en route and transported in relays by a series of local merchants. The Silk Road can be roughly divided into three sections: The first section ran from Xi'an on the Yellow

Left: The Thousand Buddha Caves of Kyzil are one of China's earliest Buddhist cave complexes.

Above: A young Uighur boy shyly observes the foreign photographer.

Below: Nowadays, a camel ride along the ancient Silk Road is a popular tourist attraction.

River (Huang) along the Hexi Corridor, a narrow line of oases in Gansu province, and over the Jade Pass to Turpan. From there, it was necessary to circum-navigate the world's driest desert, the Taklimakan in the center of the Tarim Basin (south Xinjiang), in order to reach Kashgar. The caravan guides had a choice at this point either to take the dry, but shorter southern route or the more sheltered northern route by way of the southern slopes of the Tianshan mountains. From Kashgar, the second section led to Merv in what is now Turkmenistan. Having arrived here, travelers then had to choose between heading northward over the Tian-shan mountains and through Tashkent to Samarkand, or westward over the Pamir mountains. Some, espe-cially the Buddhist monks, turned south from Kashgar and eventually reached Gandhara in India via Lhasa and Karakorum. The last section led from Merv along the ancient salt caravan routes to various Mediterranean or Black Sea ports.

Trade and cultural exchange
China has been producing silk for more than 3,000 years and by the beginning of the 2nd century was exporting it as far as the Roman Empire along the Silk Road. This fabric—"as light as clouds and as trans-parent as ice"—soon became a highly desirable luxury item among the Romans. Meanwhile, it had become a crime punishable by death under Chinese law to smug-gle silkworms or their eggs out of the country. Never-theless, in the year 555, someone succeeded in doing just that and a few silkworm eggs were presented to the Byzantine emperor, marking the start of silk pro-duction outside China. All European silkworms origi-nate from those smuggled eggs.

Silk was not China's only major export in ancient times: jade, porcelain, ceramics, and bronze weapons, as well as the knowledge of how to make paper, the spinning wheel, and gunpowder have all had major influences upon European development. Conversely, European treasures, such as gold, gemstones, ivory, glass, coral, and wool returned to China along the network of silk routes. Many spices and herbs, which are now an essential part of European cuisine, first found their way to the West along the Silk Road. Peaches, oranges, mandarins, almonds, apricots, and rhubarb all came from China, as did spices, such as ginger, nutmeg, cin-namon, saffron, sandalwood, myrrh, and cloves. In turn, cucumbers, carrots, pomegranates, nuts, and pepper were introduced into Chinese cuisine.

The Silk Road was not just a route for conveying trade goods, however, but also for spreading ideas and reli-gious beliefs from one cultural region to another. So it was that Buddhism reached China around 100 A.D., gaining a foothold initially in the oasis towns and later merging with the traditional ancient Chinese religion of Taoism and developing into Chan Buddhism (known in the West by its Japanese name of Zen). Islam followed by the same route during the 8th century and is a reli-gion still practiced by the Uighurs in Xinjiang and the Hui ethnic minority group in Gansu and Ningxia.

Spiced grilled lamb

2–3 large onions, chopped
about a generous 1 lb (500 g) lamb, suitable for barbecue grilling
salt
ground cumin
chili powder

Soften the onions in water for 15–20 minutes, then marinate the lamb in the onions and water so that it absorbs the onion flavor. Dry the meat with paper towels before rubbing with the spices, then grill over hot coals.

Above: There are occasional reminders of the sumptuous fabrics that were once traded here.

Center right: The women of the ethnic minorities wear colorful costumes, regardless of whether they are Uighurs, Kirgiz, or Mongol women.

Continued on page 420

Continued from page 419

Kashgar—an oasis town on the Silk Road

Kashgar (Uighur: Kaxgar, Chinese: Kashi) lies at the foot of the Celestial Mountains (Tianshan) to the west of Taklimakan in the middle of China's largest oasis. Although it is situated 2,485 miles (4,000 km) by air from Beijing, China's westernmost city is situated in the same time zone as its capital city to the east. In 1949, China's five time zones, which were based on geographical considerations, were placed under a unified time zone. As a consequence, the hour and time of day in China's western territories are not always coordinated (see panel on p. 421). But the Uighurs, who make up almost 80 percent of Kashgar's population, live in a world and time of their own anyway. Wandering through the winding narrow streets of the Old Town, one could believe oneself transported back to the Middle Ages. The place is a hive of bustling activity, where blacksmiths, potters, barbers, and dentists set up their stalls and offer their services on the street, alongside snack bars and bakers' stalls. Fabrics, haberdashery, and food items are also on sale at the bazaar in the Old Town, as well as every conceivable kind of spice, including saffron, green cardamom and rose petals from Persia and Central Asia, and Sichuan pepper, star anise, Chinese cardamom, and fennel from China. In late summer and autumn, the markets are crammed with a huge selection of fresh fruit, shimmering in an array of different colors and smelling delicious and including pomegranates, pears, figs, water melons, honeydew melons, jujubes, to name just a few. In the tea houses you will encounter Uighurs with their Turkish looks and typical headdress—a small round skullcap known as a "doppa." The main language here is Uighur since Chinese is not very common, especially among older-generation Uighurs. Known as Shule in the days of the Han dynasty (206 B.C.–220 A.D.), Kashgar has always been a melting pot for different cultures and even Marco Polo was fascinated by the commercial energy he encountered in the town during his visit in 1275. The town now has a population of about 340,000. Uighurs on horseback riding down the middle of the highway are as much a part of the scene as veiled Uighur women and short-skirted Chinese girls. However, this is more an indication of coexistence rather than integration among the difference races. The Uighurs remain determined to hang onto their traditions while the Han Chinese tend to regard this attitude as "backward." As a rule Uighurs do not eat pork (a meat considered "unclean" by Islam), whereas Han Chinese rarely eat lamb. Uighurs like their own type of mountain water ice cream, which they mix with yogurt, honey, and nuts, whereas most Chinese prefer soft ice cream dispensed from modern ice cream machines.

The main center for Muslims in China is the Id Kah Mosque, which is also one of Kashgar's landmarks. It was built in 1442 and on festival days more than 10,000 Muslims flock here from the whole of the adjoining area. Since they cannot all be accommodated inside the mosque, many of them pray in the area surrounding the building, where the older members of Kashgar's Uighur population generally congregate on normal days.

Top: The weekly Sunday market in Kashgar has been held for centuries, yet has lost none of its fascination, either for locals or tourists alike.

Above: In addition to the food stalls, the fabric and carpet dealers are also well worth a visit.

Right: Important sites, such as the Thousand Buddha Caves, highlight the importance of the Silk Road not only for bringing trade goods into China, but also for introducing new ideas and religions.

There is, however, another side to Kashgar, namely that of an up-and-coming metropolis with a rapidly growing Chinese district, which does not, it has to be said, have all that much to offer—apart from a faceless, modern shopping center of the sort one might find in any other Chinese city. Located a little to the east of the town on the banks of the Tuman is the Sunday market, which is famed far and wide. Even the trip to the bazaar on a Sunday morning can be fraught with adventure with the access roads packed with donkey-drawn carts, horses, and livestock and any thought of overtaking is out of the question. With up to 60,000 visitors, it is thought to be the biggest market in Asia, if not the world. The Sunday market is divided into different sections, one of which specializes in domestic livestock, for example, such as sheep, camels, yaks, cattle, and horses, while another comprises grain, flour, spices, fruit, and vegetables. Carpets, silk, leather goods, furniture, fabrics, instruments, and other items are grouped together in yet another section. The town is famous for its artistic woven and embroidered carpets, which are produced by family-run businesses. You can even have your hair cut or your beard shaved at one of the market stands while bakeries, tea houses, and food stalls cater for visitors' physical comfort. One of the market's attractions is the spectacle of the shearing of fat-tailed sheep, a popular breed in Central Asia.

Chinese time zones

Time zones were first set up and officially introduced in China in 1912 under the Republic of China. The country was initially divided into five time zones, with Greenwich Mean Time (GMT) as the basis of reference: Kunlun (GMT + 5.5 hours), Xinjiang–Tibet (GMT + 6), Gansu–Sichuan (GMT + 7), Zhongyuan standard time (GMT + 8), and Changbai (GMT + 8.5). The Chinese CP abolished this arrangement in 1949 and introduced a unified time zone for the whole of the People's Republic, ignoring the fact that the country spans four world time zones. Meanwhile, Universal Time Coordinated (UTC) was introduced as a measure of actual world time and has replaced GMT. UTC + 1 hour is roughly the same as Central European Time (CET). Accordingly, Beijing, the capital of China, lies in the UTC + 8 time zone, thereby designating the Chinese time zone. It also covers Taipei and the Republic of China on Taiwan, despite ongoing debate within the island's government on the possibility of introducing a time zone of its own as a means of distancing itself from the People's Republic. Hong Kong and Macau also operate under the same Chinese time zone. However, a distinction is still made in many places—albeit in name only—between "Beijing time" (otherwise known as Chinese standard time), "Taiwan time," "Hong Kong time," and "Macau time."

Below: A giant, 59-feet (18-m)-high statue of Mao Zedong, his hand raised in greeting, still stands in Kashgar's Square of the People even though the Communist revolution has been something of a mixed blessing to the people who live in China's extreme west.

Inner Mongolia 内蒙古

Elke Spielmanns-Rome

The region known as Inner Mongolia (also called Southern Mongolia, which is what the Mongols themselves prefer) stretches across northern China in the shape of a sickle along the eastern and southeastern borders of Outer Mongolia. In the west, the Gobi Desert makes human life impossible, while the plateau in the east is characterized by endless steppes and dense forests. The dominant feature in the northeast is the Hinggan Mountains; adjacent to the western foothills of these mountains is the Hulun–Buir Plateau, with its lush pasturelands. The predominantly continental climate leads to long, harsh winters, which demands unusual levels of endurance and toughness from the human beings and animals living here.

With an area of about 425,000 square miles (1.1 million sq km), Inner Mongolia makes up a good 12 percent of the whole area of China. And yet only 23 million people live here—just 1.8 percent of the total population of the People's Republic of China. And the vast majority of the inhabitants do not belong to the minority nationality known as Mongols—quite the contrary. About 4 million Mongols share the steppes with Han Chinese (the majority of the population), but also with 47 other ethnic minorities such as the Daguren, the Ewenken, the Orochen, and the Hui (Chinese Muslims), and even Koreans. "Someone who's born in the dung smoke of a livestock–herder's yurt, and knows how to rise above it—that's a Mongol." So goes a traditional folk song from the steppe. Although they have been forced to settle down and live as a minority in their own country, the Mongols have so far managed to preserve their cultural identity in the face of Chinese modernization measures. In addition to the shared language, the Mongols' Chakhar dialect, and their history, which goes way back, this identity takes pride in their traditional cuisine. As livestock herders, the Mongols have always, and still do, live mainly on meat and dairy products, whereas the rural Chinese prefer cereals and vegetables. It is certainly true that Mongolian hotpot has recently become popular all over China, but the favorite beverage of the people of the steppes—*airag*, a type of wine made from naturally fermented mare's milk—like their popular dish, *shaomai*, a pie filled with lamb and onions, is rarely found outside Mongolia.

Even if in the past the two peoples' ways of living could not have been more different, their histories have been interwoven since time immemorial. The warlike horsemen from the north have long been feared in the Middle Kingdom; even the Great Wall could not prevent recurrent

Above: Hohhot, the lively capital of Inner Mongolia, is a metropolis with 2.5 million inhabitants in which, as always, the bicycle remains the most important mode of transport.

Facing page: Reddish brown becomes the predominant color as you move out of the steppes and approach the mountainous areas of Inner Mongolia.

Hohhot

Inner Mongolia **425**

Above top: Enormous distances make it difficult to create a modern infrastructure covering the entire area. However, grinding poverty is not evident, even in the really small villages of Inner Mongolia.

Above: The five-pagoda temple in Hohhot. Five small pagodas rise from a square base (the "diamond throne"). The Buddhist temple was erected in the 1730s.

attacks by the "barbarians" on the Chinese farming settlements. However, as long as the Mongols ("the invincible ones") were organized only in loose clans, they posed no serious threat to the Chinese empire. This situation changed when the great warlord Temujin (1165–1227), better known in the West as Genghis Khan, united the Mongol hordes at the end of the 12th century and brought a huge part of what was then the known world into the Greater Mongolian empire through an unparalleled series of victories. At one time, this realm extended from the Caspian Sea in the west all the way to the Sea of Japan in the east. The empire soon collapsed. But China remained firmly under Mongol control. Kublai Khan, a grandson of Genghis Khan, founded the Chinese Yuan dynasty in 1271, which was to reign for nearly a century. He was the first emperor of China to make Beijing the capital of the country. In his day, the city was called Cambaluc, "the city of the great khan," which Marco Polo described in shimmering colors—the Mongolian influence can still be seen in Beijing today. The great traffic arteries such as the Dongdan Road or the Xisi Road were created as long ago as the 14th century.

In the mid 17th century, the southern part of Mongolia became a protectorate of the newly established Qing dynasty (1644–1912) and from then onward it remained a part of the Chinese empire under the name of Inner Mongolia ("inner" because it was nearer to Beijing than the northern part of Mongolia). As increased numbers of Chinese peasants settled there, a basic change took place in the life of the Mongols. More and more grazing land was taken for farming, and the government compelled the nomads to settle down in permanent villages to make the administrative system more efficient. When the Chinese empire came to an end in 1911, Outer Mongolia made a successful bid for independence. The southern part of the region remained under Chinese control, and on May 1, 1947 it became the "Autonomous Region of Inner Mongolia" (Nei Menggu Zizhiqu).

As in Tibet, Guangxi, Ningxia, and Xinjiang, Inner Mongolia, being an autonomous region, grants its various ethnic groups a very large measure of freedom (which includes religious freedom) within the People's Republic. True, the area is under the authority of the government in Beijing, but the local administration (and thus a large part of the decision-making power) is in the hands of the Mongols. The capital, Hohhot (in Mongolian, *Xöxxot*: the blue city), forms the economic hub of the region, together with the cities of Baotou and Ordos (or Mu Us).While Hohhot has recently

established itself as the center of the Chinese dairy products industry, the region around Ordos is rich in natural resources. It provides the coal and natural gas that are used as raw materials by the heavy industry in Baotou. Another basic element in the Mongolian economy is the wool industry (and in particular the trade in cashmere products).

And yet the globalization movement has also reached Inner Mongolia. For some years now, China's bleak north, with its wide-open spaces and its fast-developing economy, has been the ideal location for visionary architectural projects. Thus the Mongolian industrialist and patron of the arts, Cai Jiang, in association with the internationally famous Chinese artist, Ai Weiwei, was able to obtain the help of several leading architectural practices with worldwide reputations for his ambitious urban development project in Ordos. As the center-piece of the planned Ordos Cultural Creative Industry Park (OCCIP), a new suburb will be built here over the next few years, with a hundred futuristic individual blocks of flats and cultural buildings. A hundred architects from all over the world (four of them from Germany), referred to collectively as "the Ordos 100," are busy transforming the city into an international center. Since August 2007, the works of modern Western and Asian artists can be seen side-by-side in the Ordos Art Museum, which has already been completed.

Above left: The classical Indian style, with its life-size figures, is also reflected inside the five-pagoda temple.

Above right: A friendly reception committee greets guests even before they go through the restaurant doors.

Below: Maybe we shouldn't judge the way people approach transportation in China's big cities by Western safety standards.

Yogurt and hotpot—nomad nourishment

The Mongols were originally a nomadic people. They pitched their yurts (a type of tent) wherever they found good pasture and water for their sheep, goats, yaks and camels. Hard living conditions, heavy physical work and cold winters explain why the Mongol diet relied heavily on animal fat. So dairy products feature heavily in the traditional Mongol cuisine. A distinction is made between meat ("red food," *hong cai*) and dairy products or "white food," *bai cai*. Red food is mainly eaten in winter, and white in the warm seasons.

In addition to cream, kefir, and hard cheese, white food also includes dried curd cheese and salted milky tea, which the Mongols like to convert into a nourishing soup by adding meat or dumplings. In summer, the Mongols' favorite form of refreshment is yak's milk yogurt with fresh berries. Homemade yogurt or kefir is briefly stirred or whipped into a cream just before serving, and is accompanied by a generous portion of chilled berries. But alcoholic drinks can also be obtained using milk as a basis, the most popular being the national beverage *airag* (also known as kumis), a wine which is made from fermented mare's milk—a vital "improvement," as untreated mare's milk is difficult for people to digest. In winter (but not only then!) people like a glass of something stronger, the milk-based liquor known as *arkhi*. Mongols are traditionally reputed to have

a very good head for drink, and at their traditional festivals, such as the Nadaam, they like to "sink quite a few." To provide a foundation for the alcohol, or even to "neutralize" it, a nutritious bantan soup is served (nomad-style lamb stew).

Red food—here predominantly lamb—is usually boiled or made into tasty dumplings. *Buuz* are particularly popular—steamed dumplings. They are usually filled with lamb and folded into various shapes: round, flower-shaped, or even like a half-moon. When traveling, and in winter, the Mongols are fond of *borts*—a kind of powdered meat stock. In order to preserve the meat, they first dry it, then grind it up, and, if necessary, boil it up with hot water before consuming it.

A typical winter meal is Mongolian hotpot, in which the meat is prepared in a pot with broth on the hearth in the center of the yurt. People sit round the source of warmth and are equally glad of the food and the company. Chinese cuisine has adapted this form of preparation. The local variants of Peking and Chengdue cuisine are particularly well known, though hotpot (a term now used internationally for the Mongolian dish) can now be found in Chinese restaurants all over the world as well. Hotpot restaurants have special tables with a compartment that covers a gas-powered or electric heater. To make hotpot with beef, cabbage,

and noodles, some pieces of meat are put into the pot with beef broth and some cabbage and noodles are added. Each guest is given a little slotted spoon with which to fish the cooked ingredients out of the broth.

Another typical Mongolian dish is *horhog*—lamb cooked with hot stones. On festive occasions such as the Naadam feast, or at family celebrations, a whole lamb or sheep is slaughtered and consumed (except for the organ meats). The cooking method combines compressed air and hot stones. First, some smooth river stones about the size of your hand are placed in the oven to heat up. As soon as they are red-hot, some of them are removed using tongs and transferred to a high-sided pot filled with water, which is shaped like an oversized milk churn. The water at the bottom of the pot starts to vaporize immediately, and more stones are added one by one, together with the meat. Once the pot has been filled, then, like a pressure cooker, it is shut tightly, but with a little air vent, and put on the fire. After about an hour, the meat is cooked.

The traditional Mongol way of life and their traditional cuisine can still be found in Inner Mongolia today, even if more and more Mongols have been compelled to settle down in the 60 years since the People's Republic was established. This has made a huge difference to their way of life and eating habits. Nowadays the former nomads cultivate vegetables and cereals or run livestock farms. Some have found work in the cities. So a lot of millet is eaten in the rural areas today—for example, in the form of millet gruel, to which they add strong pickles and other spices. Millet is also used to accompany dishes as a replacement for rice. Nowadays cereals have replaced the "white food" of the nomads—sometimes in combination with vegetables. The Chinese brought new dishes into Inner Mongolia—mainly fruit and vegetables, but also pork. A traditional Chinese noodle dish is prepared with pork, scallions, and ginger in this province, and served with yellow bean sauce. Previously Mongolian cuisine included only a few fruit and vegetables which grew wild, such as scallions, lilies, and apples, as well as herbs such as thyme and lavender. Today there is a much more extensive choice. But fresh vegetables are not in widespread use, due to the shortness of the summer. Apart from pickled cabbage and dried mushrooms, which are softened in water before being prepared, people mainly eat root vegetables such as potatoes, carrots, beets, and radishes.

Top right and center right: The harsh climate and the adverse living conditions (especially in winter) have made Mongolian horses into hardy animals which can survive long periods without fodder or water. They can cover immense distances in a day, and they fend for themselves in half-wild herds.

Right: Hospitality is a concept with which the nomads are very familiar. True, it is rare to find an "open door," as nowadays most yurts have a fixed door, rather than a simple felt curtain.

Mongolian hotpot with beef and cabbage

about 9 oz (250 g) thoroughly washed beef, chilled (to aid slicing)
about 9 oz (250 g) lean beef, chilled
generous 1 lb (500 g) Chinese cabbage

Broth:
1 thin leek or 3–4 scallions
about 2 ½ quarts (2.5–3) liters hot beef broth
8–10 garlic cloves
3–4 dried dates
3–4 dried lang-gao fruit
12–15 dried goji berries
6 pieces of ginger (each 1 ½ inch / 4 cm long), thinly sliced
ginseng root, (4 inch / 10 cm long), fresh or dried
1 tsp dark soy sauce
1 tsp salt
9 oz (250 g) broad rice noodles

Cut the meat into wafer-thin pieces. Wash the Chinese cabbage leaves and cut into strips. Clean the leek or scallions and cut into 1–1 ½-inch (3–4-cm-long) pieces. Pour the hot beef broth into a deep pan and put on the stove. Add all the ingredients to the broth except the meat, the noodles, and the cabbage and bring to a boil. When the broth has been simmering for a while, each diner takes a little slotted spoon, uses it to put small pieces of meat, cabbage, and noodles into the piping hot broth and then, after 1–2 minutes, fishes them out cooked and puts them in their bowl, together with some of the broth.

Milk—the nomad's rice

Milk is as highly valued by the nomads of China's northern steppes as rice is by the Han Chinese. "White food," as dairy products are known, forms a part of every meal, in the form of cheese, yogurt or curd cheese, or as a drink. And the livestock herders use the milk of all five of their "mules" here: horses, sheep, goats, yaks, and camels. During the warm summer months, the herders' diet consists almost exclusively of fresh dairy products. In winter, along with the meat they need, they include dried curd cheese or hard cheese in their diet.

Milk drinks

The national drink of the Mongols is *airag*, a wine made from fermented mare's milk, which is consumed in great quantities—even by very small children. The carbonated beverage has a low alcohol content of 2 percent maximum and has a refreshing, slightly sour taste. To make it, fresh mare's milk is strained and suspended in a bag made of oxhide near the entrance to the yurt. As time goes by, each inhabitant stirs the mass around a few times with a wooden pestle, so that it is permeated with oxygen and the fermentation process is stimulated. The taste of the airag can vary, depending on the horses' pasture and the method of preparation, and

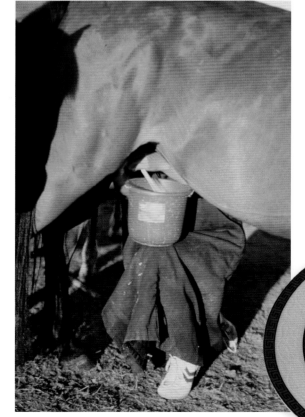

connoisseurs can detect fine distinctions here—just like wine connoisseurs in France.

When a loud cry of "*Eruul mendiin toloo*" ("Good health") is heard from the yurt, then it probably means the *arkhi* is going round. The women distill a kind of liquor from kefir or airag, which the men enjoy undiluted. "Down in one" is the unbreakable rule. True, it is very light, with an alcohol content of 10 percent. The product of the first distillation is the best and has a cheese flavor. The product of the third and final distillation tastes more rancid and sometimes upsets sensitive digestive systems. The mash left over from the distillation is used to make *aaruul*—dried curd cheese.

Milky tea, *sgtai tse*, is almost as popular as airag, and guests are always given some to warm them up when they enter the yurt. It consists of hot tea, which has been mixed with a dash of fresh milk, yogurt or thickened cream, *orom*, or a pinch of salt. Mongolian milky tea should not be confused with the popular Taiwanese pearl milk tea, which it is said was not invented until the 1980s. This consists of green or black tea, which is mixed with honey and condensed milk or milk powder and enjoyed hot or cold. The drink is named after the little balls of tapioca or potato starch, which are added as the final touch and are sucked up through a thick straw. As a lot of bubbles are generated when the drink is being prepared in something like a cocktail shaker, pearl milk tea is also known as "bubble tea" abroad.

Tarag, Mongolian kefir, is obtained from the milk of yaks, goats or sheep, and has many uses. It can be used neat as a substitute for rennet in cheesemaking, or else processed further to make milk schnapps and butterfat.

Yellow oil, *shar tos* or *huangyou*, is the name for the viscous liquid made from this mash, bulked out with cream, which is usually served in glasses. Like airag, tarag also contains carbon dioxide, together with a small amount of alcohol.

Milk-based foods

On the steppes, cheese is mainly made from the milk of yaks, sheep or goats. However, it does not usually have a strong taste of its own as the nomads, wandering over long distances as they do, have no chance to store large cheeses and let them mature. Nevertheless, cheese will keep almost indefinitely in dried or deep-fried form.

If you look round any store in Hohhot, the capital of Inner Mongolia, you will notice small white pieces of curd cheese on the shelves, packaged in little squares. This is nothing like tofu, the soybean-based curd cheese of the Han Chinese; but instead it is *aaruul*. To make this dried white cheese, yak milk is allowed to become sour, and the solid constituents are removed with a cloth. The mass is then pressed into flat squares between two boards and cut into pieces, which are laid out to dry on the roof of the yurt. Aaruul is so hard that the nomads usually suck it as they ride along.

The little golden yellow nuggets which many Mongols carry with them in bags, and which they like to eat sweetened with honey, are also hard to recognize as cheese at first glance. *Eesgii*, a thickened cheese mass, has all the whey removed from it during preparation. The resulting "crumbs" are then roasted so that

Right: Whether they are obtained from mares, camels, yaks, goats or sheep, dairy products form the basis of the nomads' nourishment during the warm summer months.

Left: Mare's milk is almost always fermented to make airag, which can also be enjoyed by people who are lactose-intolerant—and that includes most Chinese.

they will last longer. People like to stir the hard cheese together with boiled cream, flour, and fruits, and serve the mixture up as a nourishing milky porridge.

In addition to the ever-present *byaslag*, a hard cheese made from goat's milk or yak's milk, which is dried in long strips, the nomads in Tibet also make a milder and softer variant known as *haloumi*.

By contrast, dairy products play scarcely any role in traditional Chinese cuisine. One reason for this is that about 90 percent of the Han Chinese are lactose-intolerant. Another reason is that the scarce cultivable land (just on 8 percent of the world's farmland is in China) is almost exclusively used for arable farming, so that there are no wide-open meadowlands here. So calcium is sourced from soy milk, tofu, green vegetables like spinach, broccoli, and curly kale, plus sesame seeds and nuts.

Yak yogurt with fresh berries

9 oz (250 g) fresh or frozen strawberries or cranberries

sugar (to taste)

4 cups (1 liter) fresh thick yogurt made, ideally, from yak's milk (or milk from goats, sheep or mares)

Allow frozen berries to defrost slowly, sort them carefully and rinse thoroughly. Sprinkle over sugar, to taste. Stir the fresh yogurt, or beat it until it becomes creamy, and divide it among small dessert bowls. Scatter with a generous portion of berries and serve.

Below: What looks like tofu is actually aaruul—dried white cheese made from yak's milk.

Life in the yurt

"Where is your yurt pitched?" That's how people ask you where you come from in Inner Mongolia. Even if many Mongols have recently exchanged their life as nomads for a settled existence, the traditional circular tent of the steppe dwellers still remains their favorite form of dwelling. Even the mausoleum of the great Gengis Khan consists of three octagonal buildings resembling yurts, which are arranged in the shape of an eagle. The yurt, Mongolian *ger*, consists of a latticework frame with a felt overlay, and provides a dwelling for a Mongolian family the whole year round. They sleep here, work here, socialize here, eat here—and cook here, for there is a hearth in the center of the yurt. During the short, hot summer it is pleasantly cool in the tent. In winter, sheep or horse dung is used for heating. A second yurt is often added as a storage room. The yurt, which does not weigh much and can be erected in a few hours, is ideal for the herdsmen following the livestock herds as they roam around.

The Mongols traditionally migrate twice a year. Early in the year, they head off to the lush meadowlands on the Hulun-Buir Plateau in the west, and in October they return to their winter quarters in the sheltered valleys. Not just the dwelling, but also the traditional Mongolian robe, the *del*, has also been adapted for the hard life of the steppes. The cross-buttoned robe, which resembles a tunic, is fastened by a colorfully embroidered scarf and is worn over wide trousers, together with soft riding boots. Men also wear the *durban talt magai*—the "four-sided hat." Women, on the other hand, let their hair grow long and weave it round their head several times to form a plait. The horse is at the center of the nomadic life, and a proverb says that a Mongol is born on its back. In addition, cows or yaks, sheep, goats, and camels are also bred. In recent times, the Mongolian winter has grown so increasingly harsh that entire herds have frozen or starved to death. Many families who have lost the basis for their livelihood have no choice but to move into a town and earn a pittance in the mines or the steelworks.

The Mongols' close ties with nature are also demonstrated by their religious ceremonies. Most of them are believers in lamaism, the Tibetan form of Buddhism. But shamanism, together with the worship of the "eternal blue sky" and its spirits, the *tengri*, are still living traditions today. Thus shamanic dances also take place at important Buddhist ceremonies in the biggest temple in the country, the Ihedo temple in Hohhot. Here the men dance in colorful costumes, wearing animal masks, and with stag's antlers on their heads, to drive off evil spirits and to ask Heaven to grant them a good harvest.

Since it is rare to meet any "neighbors" on the wide steppe, the Mongols use the traditional festivals to exchange news and do deals—and also to find their life-partners. The biggest and liveliest of these festivals is the *Naadam* ("games and entertainment"). For almost eight centuries, it has been held every year in July to commemorate Gengis Khan's great victories, and Marco Polo himself is said to have taken part in the competitions, after a cup of salty tea and some tasty lamb pies. Many families slaughter a lamb or a sheep to celebrate the festival. The animal is roasted whole, or else a substantial bantan soup is prepared for the weary competitors.

The centerpiece of the festival is a tournament involving the "three manly disciplines"—horseriding, archery, and wrestling—that put the three skills a man needs to the test. The Mongolian wrestlers in their red and blue fighting costumes—which consist of short, tight trousers, a waistcoat fitting tight around the shoulders, and big boots—are famous for their strength all over Asia. Whoever emerges as the victor from the ninth and last round of this trial of strength is given the honorable title of *arslan*, the lion.

Bows and arrows have been national symbols for Mongolia since time immemorial. It is said of the great Khan Munkh (1208–1258) that he sent a large bow and two ritual arrows to Louis IX of France to remind him of the superiority of the Mongols. Even the awestruck Chinese chroniclers of the Tang dynasty wrote: "The inhabitants of the steppe can kill a running hare at full gallop with one shaft, hanging sideways from their horses."

At the Naadam festival felt balls the size of a fist are placed on the ground at a distance of about 225 feet (75 m). The competitors have to hit as many balls as they possibly can. The competitors' aim is considered to be so accurate that the judges, who sing a hymn of praise for each

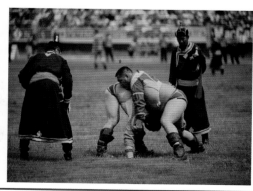

competitor who scores a hit, stand right next to the targets.

In contrast, when the horse racing begins, all that counts is the speed and endurance of the animals. Ridden by boys aged between five and ten, the tough, gaily decorated steppe ponies have to cover anything up to 19 miles (30 km) at the gallop. It quite often happens that an animal drops dead with exhaustion following this torment.

Even today, victory in the tournament means a man will be famous all over the country for the rest of his life. Though every year there are more and more young women who show that they can also perform more than adequately with the bow and arrow or on horseback. The Naadam festival has recently developed into a colorful annual market, with singing and dancing, theater, and extensive market areas.

Traditional Chinese noodles with pork

1 ½–2 tsp salt
generous 1 lb (500 g) instant noodles made from wheat flour
7 tbsp peanut oil or corn oil
generous 1 lb (500 g) pork belly, cut into small dice
2 pieces ginger (2 inch / 5 cm long), cut into thin strips
8–10 scallions, cut into thin rings
4 tbsp oyster sauce
salt
yellow bean sauce, for serving

For the noodles, fill a big pan with 3 quarts (3–3.5 liters) of water, bring to a boil, add 1 teaspoon of the salt and add the noodles. Boil for 4–5 minutes until they are al dente, then drain into a colander.

Heat about half the oil in a wok and stir-fry the meat for about 3–4 minutes (or slightly longer, depending on the wok or the stove), stirring continuously.

Salt the meat, remove it from the wok and set aside.

Drain the oil, clean the wok and heat a little fresh oil. Stir-fry the ginger rapidly for 30 seconds and add the scallions. Stir-fry the scallions, adding salt to taste, for about 1 ½ minutes. Remove the ginger and scallions from the wok and leave to drain. Clean the wok again and heat the remaining oil. Add the noodles, stir in the oyster sauce. Add the meat and the scallions with the ginger and stir-fry everything together for about 3–4 minutes. Serve hot with yellow bean sauce.

Buuz
Lamb dumplings

Dough:
4 cups (500 g) all-purpose flour
about 1 cup (250 ml) cold water
salt

Filling:
14 oz (400 g), lamb shoulder or breast, roughly minced (or beef)
1 large onion, finely chopped
1–2 garlic cloves, finely chopped
salt and pepper
½ tsp caraway seed
5–6 tbsp cold water

For the dough, knead the flour with a pinch of salt and sufficient water to achieve a pliable, but nonsticky dough.

Leave the dough, covered, to rest for about 30 minutes, then knead it again and shape into thickish, long "noodles." Cut off pieces ¾–1 inch (2–3 cm) thick from the "noodles," sprinkle with salt, dust both sides with flour, and roll out into circles somewhat thicker in the center than at the edges. (To achieve this, hold the dough circle in one hand and using a thin rolling pin held diagonally in the other hand, roll only the edges, using short strokes while constantly turning the dough circle.)

For the filling, thoroughly mix the ingredients, adding just suf-

ficient of the water to bind it all together. If the meat is rather lean, it is recommended that you add a little more water, so that the buuz do not become too dry inside. Put a heaped teaspoon of the filling in the center of each circle. Raise the 2 edges facing each other and press firmly together in the center. Repeat with the other facing edges. This creates a dumpling with four small holes, which should be big enough for steam to get out, but not big enough for any meat juice to escape. Grease the insert of a large steamer and fill with one layer of buuz. Leave a little space between the dumplings, to stop them sticking to each other when they are cooking. Fill the steamer pan with water to below the insert, the water must not reach the buuz. Bring the water to a boil, place the insert with the buuz in the pan, close the pan lid tightly and steam the dumplings for about 20 minutes on a low to medium heat. Do not open the pan while this is going on! Then take the pan off the stove. Remove the lid and fan the buuz, so that they acquire a shiny, appetizing surface and do not stick to each other. Serve hot.

The five mules of the nomadic life

Livestock herding is the main basis for the life of the nomads of the broad steppe in the provinces of Xinjiang, Inner Mongolia, Gansu, and Tibet. Breeding and tending the five "mules"—the horse, yak, sheep, goat, and camel—shape the everyday lives of the people. Not only do the great herds provide the basis for feeding a family, but—in the form of skins and felts—they also provide the material for clothing and tents. Normally, animals are slaughtered only at one specific time of year—at the start of winter, since the animals have then reached their maximum weight, and preserving the meat poses no problems at temperatures of -18 °F/-30 °C. Horses, yaks and camels are then used as riding animals and beasts of burden.

In Inner Mongolia, the horse, *ma*, has a special significance. Riding comes as naturally as running to a Mongol, and this skill, handed down in the culture and learned from childhood, once made them into dreaded conquerors. "The eyes of the steppe," as the tough little Mongol horses are affectionately known, are thus one of the oldest breeds of domesticated horse in the world. Their assistance in looking after and rounding up the herds is indispensable to the nomads, but their meat and, in particular, the drinks made from fermented mare's milk frequently appear on the menu. The long hair of their manes is used in the manufacture of the traditional two-string "horse's head fiddle." In

Chinese astrology, the horse is the seventh sign of the zodiac and simultaneously symbolizes loyalty and a free spirit.

The yak, *mao niu*, also known as the grunting ox, is a high-mountain bovine which, with its long thick coat and its small snout, is perfectly adapted to life in high, cold areas. Yak herds are kept by nomads in Tibet and in the northern part of Inner Mongolia. As it is a beast of burden and is used for haulage, the yak seldom ends its days in the stewpan, though its fatty milk is among the main sources of energy for people. Moreover, yak butter is used as suncream or body lotion. The coat, up to 13 inches (40 cm) long, is woven into large panels to form the fabric of Tibetan nomads' tents, which are heated with dried yak dung. The sheep is the animal with the most uses on the Mongolian steppe. Its wool forms the basis for the Chinese woolen industry, its milk is turned into nutritious cheese, and its meat is extremely popular. Traditional dishes are *buuz* (steamed dumplings with lamb or mutton), *horhog* (lamb cooked with hot stones), and *borc shorhoc*, the Mongolian barbecue. The eighth house of the astrological zodiac is occupied by the sheep, standing for filial piety, with a lamb shown kneeling and being suckled by its mother.

Goats are also referred to as "mountain sheep" in China. So they are known by the same Chinese word as the sheep, *yong*. In northern regions it is mainly Kashmir sheep that are

bred, and their fluffy undercoat is woven into extremely fine cashmere wool. When the animals shed their winter coat at the beginning of spring, the nomads comb out the soft undercoat and sell the untreated cashmere wool to the woolen mills in the towns, where it is cleaned and spun. China recently became the biggest producer and exporter of high-quality fabrics in the world.

Even so, most of the cultivated land in China's heartland is still reserved for arable farming. The Han Chinese have also been keeping livestock for more than 3,000 years. The five domestic animals—dog, sheep or goat, ox, hen, and pig—play an important role in traditional Chinese nutritional lore. Even in the *Medicinal Canon of the Yellow Emperor*, a classical text dealing with traditional Chinese medicine dating from the 5th century B.C. (and which is still consulted today), we read: "The five types of cereal form the basis for nourishment, the five fruits, the five domestic animals, and the five types of vegetable serve as supplements."

The most important source of meat for the Han Chinese is the pig, *zhu*. Its importance in the lives of rural folk can be gauged by the fact that the Chinese character for "house" or "home" represents a pig under a roof. Nowadays China is the biggest producer of pork in the world, with a market share of 40 percent, and the figure is rapidly increasing. Yet you will look in vain for big pig-breeding farms. Most peasants,

Left: A favorite after a night of serious drinking— bantan soup.

Right: The Mongolian version of a pressure cooker. Excess steam escapes thanks to a simple trick.

as they always have, see the rearing and slaughtering of animals as a source of additional income. The pig occupies the final house of the Chinese zodiac, and stands for manly strength.

Oxen and water buffalo provide indispensable assistance at harvest time, especially on the flooded rice paddies in south China, where they are used to pull plows. Even today, many farmers refuse to eat beef—they feel they owe too much to the animals to do that. Nevertheless, in many places beef dishes—such as beef noodles in tasty broth, which is also known in the West—have a permanent place on the menu. Low-lactose buffalo milk is also becoming increasingly popular, for it causes far fewer problems for Chinese stomachs than cow's milk. The buffalo was often classically depicted as being ridden by a young boy, in order to emphasise the placidity of the beast. The ox symbolizes the spring and is the second sign of the Chinese zodiac.

Horhog
Lamb cooked with hot stones

General comment on this typical nomad dish: As they live in extended families, it is not normal for horhog to be prepared for 4–6 people. On festive occasions, such as at the Naadam or at family festivals, an entire lamb or sheep is slaughtered, and almost all of it is then consumed. The preparation combines pressure and heat, as in a pressure cooker. Those few nomads still living in Inner Mongolia use the following method:

1 lamb (6–10 months old), freshly slaughtered, gutted, cut into large but handy-size sections, with the bones, but without the organ meats and the head
3 ¼ lb (1.5 kg) potatoes, roughly diced
1 ¾ lb (750 g) carrots, roughly chopped
1 ¾ lb (750 g) small turnips or rutabaga (swede), roughly diced
3 large onions, halved
4–5 whole garlic cloves (if desired)
3–4 tbsp salt
1 tsp freshly ground pepper
mixed wild herbs from mountains or steppe (e.g., thyme, basil, lovage, savory), dried or fresh
1 ½ quarts (1.5 liters) cold water

Traditionally, the nomads prepared this dish in a sewn-together lambskin. Nowadays, they use a 10-gallon (40-liter) milk churn with a cliplock which is not completely closed up (a piece of wood is inserted), so that the excess steam can escape. About 40–50 smooth, medium-size river pebbles are also heated on an open charcoal fire. The glowing hot stones are taken out of the heat using fire tongs and then tapped to remove the charcoal residue. The milk churn is filled with enough stones to cover the bottom and then put into the fire. A generous portion of meat is rapidly placed on the first layer of stones, along with a portion of the other ingredients and the spices. Then a second layer of stones is added, and the process is repeated until the milk churn contains all the meat. Last of all comes a layer of hot stones onto which the water is poured. Then the churn is closed in such a way that some steam can still escape.

The churn is left in the fire for about 2–2 ½ hours, while the meat gently simmers away on its own. The churn is briefly and vigorously shaken every 40–50 minutes. When the cooking period is over, the churn is taken off the fire, thoroughly shaken again and opened—carefully, as a very great deal of hot steam will escape. When the stones have been removed with the fire tongs, the meat is ready to eat.

Horhog
For 4–6 people

lb (2.5 kg) lamb with bones (ribs, shoulder, neck, back, leg, as desired)
generous 1 lb (500 g) potatoes, diced
9 oz (250 g) carrots, diced
9 oz (250 g) small turnips or rutabaga (swede), diced
1 large onion, finely chopped
1–2 garlic cloves
½ tsp salt, or slightly more if needed
freshly ground pepper
fresh or dried herbs such as thyme, basil, lovage, savory
2 cups (500 ml) cold water

Heat some river pebbles (obtainable from builder's merchants) in the baking oven at maximum temperature and arrange them in layers in a pressure cooker with a capacity of about 2 gallons (6–7 liters), until the bottom is covered. Add a layer of meat and a portion of the other ingredients, season with salt and pepper, cover with a second layer of stones, again put meat and vegetables on top, and so on. Finish with a layer of stones and the water. Close the pan and let the contents simmer on a low heat for 30–35 minutes (cooking times may vary from one cooker to another). Before opening the cooker, carefully shake the contents inside. Remove the lid carefully, take out the stones and serve the horhog hot. The nomads traditionally often consume meat without any accompaniment, so the dish can also be prepared without vegetables.

Bantan—nomad-style soup

3 ½ tbsp cooking oil
1 onion, fine chopped
11–14 oz (300–400 g) shoulder of lamb or mutton (or, beef), very finely chopped
½ tsp salt
freshly ground pepper
1 ½ quarts (1.5 liters) cold water
1 ⅓ cups (150 g) all-purpose flour

Heat the oil in a pan, then fry the onion. After 1–2 minutes, add the meat and stir-fry well. Season with pepper and salt. Slowly add the water and cook everything through for 10 minutes. Meanwhile, mix the flour with 3–4 tablespoons water and crumble into pieces. Add these to the soup while it is cooking and cook for 5 minutes on medium heat while stirring continuously. The "bantan noodles" should not stick to the bottom of the pan, much less burn. Season to taste and serve hot.

This soup is very frequently served when the guests have "tied one on"!

Genghis Khan—tyrant and peacemaker

Even 800 years after his death, people in most parts of the world are still fascinated by the phenomenon that was Genghis Khan. Even today, historians still mount exhibitions and publish books in which they try to gain a clearer understanding of the greatest conqueror of all time, and to separate fact from fiction in the stories handed down. This process is now making it clear that the image of the gruesome tyrant must be combined with that of the far-seeing ruler of a cosmopolitan empire.

Even today, the name of Genghis Khan (Mongolian, Cinggis, reigned 1206–1227) stands for gruesome conquering hordes and unquenchable bloodlust in Europe. In his own homeland, by contrast, the great military commander is seen more as a national hero or a cultural icon. He is practically worshiped as a god. His portrait is stamped on the Mongolian 10,000 törög gold coin. The memory of his victories is kept alive in national festivals such as the Naadam. Many Mongols hope that their great historical leader will return to this world like a Messiah and unite all the nations under Heaven.

Countless legends have sprung up around the man reputed to be the greatest military commander of all time (the *Washington Post* named him "the man of the millenium"), and even contemporary Mongolian biographies such as *The Secret History of the Yuan Dynasty* are rather short on facts. What is certain is that even his rise to the position of ruler of the people of the Asian plains was characterized by struggle, for the young Temujin ("sharp steel" or "blacksmith"), as Genghis Khan was named at birth, had several close brushes with death. In 1174 his father, Yisugei, the patriarch of the Mongols, was murdered. Temujin, who was nine years old at the time, was expelled from his clan, together with his mother and siblings. They faced a daily battle against starvation on the harsh steppe. Later, Temujin became a vassal of Ong Khan and was made his heir.

His celebrated victories over the Tartars, as well as his daring and charisma, impressed his compatriots, so that in 1206, at the age of 40, Temujin was named as the "oceanic ruler" (the literal translation of Genghis Khan) at a gathering of the clans. For the first time in history, all the nomad tribes were now united under the white banner as Mongols, and they set out to conquer the world.

Initially, Genghis Khan used all the might of his army to attack the hated Tartars in the west who had killed his father. Peace negotiations with the Chinese Jin dynasty broke down through Chinese treachery and so, in 1215, he took his revenge by destroying their capital Dadu (the modern Beijing). And more treachery impelled the great khan to move farther westward, where he gave the Sultan of Choresmia a good whipping, destroying Samarkand, and Bukhara. The Mongol empire now extended from the Aral Sea in the west all the way to the Yellow Sea in the east.

For the present, this was as far as the Mongol empire was to expand. For, according to the "Secret History": "In the year of the pig (1227), Genghis Khan ascended to Heaven." How he died remains a riddle to this day. Perhaps he fell from his horse and broke his leg, and the consequences of this injury led to his death (according to one version of the story). Another tale has it that he died a natural death at the age of 62. His grave has never been found to this day for, according to Mongol custom, he was buried in a shallow grave in the steppe, "so that grass and trees grew over the place." Nevertheless, a mausoleum has been erected in Ejin Horo, southwest of Hohhot, in which the ruler himself, and also his principal wife who was named Börte and two of his concubines, are venerated like deities.

Left: The Mongols were not just barbarian conquerors—an effective administration, the promotion of trade, and religious tolerance formed the basis of the so-called Pax Mongolica. Tribute is paid to Genghis Khan in the mausoleum building near the little town of Dongsheng.

Right: Not on horseback—he doesn't have a bow and arrow either. A Mongolian official watches over the Genghis Khan museum.

Genghis Khan's heirs, most of all his son Ögodei and his grandson Kublai, continued the patriarch's work, and extended the empire in the west to the very banks of the Danube. However, what halted the forward march of the Mongols into Europe was not really the courage of the Polish soldiers, as is often stated, but rather the sudden death of Ögodei Khan.

To settle the succession, a new khan had to be chosen, which meant that all the commanders had to attend a gathering in the heartland of the clans. So they all turned around and headed east. In 1279, the dead khan's nephew, Kublai Khan, finally succeeded in overthrowing the entire Chinese empire. He established the Chinese Yuan dynasty (1271–1368) and decreed that Genghis Khan should be worshiped as the supreme ancestor of the emperor. This is also the time from which our first descriptions of the Middle Kingdom date. Marco Polo is said to have spent 17 years at the court of Kublai Khan—though historians are still unsure to this day whether Marco Polo actually visited China at all, or whether he based his accounts on the tales of other travelers instead.

For a long time, the Europeans fostered the image of Genghis Khan as a bloodthirsty tyrant—for anyone who stood in his way was mercilessly wiped out. And yet even his contemporary, the Dominican monk Julianus, considered that the Mongols did not wage war in any worse manner than other nations. They were just better at it, and more successful conquerors. As well as completely revolutionizing the art of war and introducing the Mongolian alphabet, the great leader of the hordes also succeeded in establishing the Jassa, a binding code of laws. This not only prohibited torture and plunder in the lands of nations which had submitted voluntarily, as well as guaranteeing religious freedom to subject peoples. It also laid the foundations for the development of a worldwide trading network, which has gone into history as the "Pax Mongolica." For the first time, caravans could now carry their valuable wares along the Silk Road all the way to Canton (now Guangzhou) on the Yellow Sea without fear of attacks. This brought undreamt of riches to the Mongol royal house. Moreover, a lively exchange of scientific knowledge developed between East and West, which gave the Europeans access to civilizing achievements such as paper and the compass (but also to gunpowder). It was also by this route that buckwheat arrived in Europe, where it was originally known as Tartary buckwheat.

Above top: Wild speculation goes on about the grave of Genghis Khan to this day. But what is certain is that the Genghis Khan mausoleum is not where he is buried. It contains only an empty sarcophagus.

Top right: Near the city of Baotou, a metropolis of 2 million people, you can still marvel at the remains of the Great Wall.

Center right: This must be how the Mongols waged their campaigns too. The military commanders and their horsemen were undoubtedly also accompanied by teams of oxen acting as draft animals as well.

Bottom right: When Genghis Khan died, his empire covered nearly 8 million square miles (almost 20 million sq km), and was twice as big as modern China. There are inevitably monuments to commanders like him—and not just in China.

Heilongjiang 黑龙江

Elke Spielmanns-Rome

The province of Heilongjiang lies in what was once Manchuria, in the far northeast of China, on the border with Russia and Inner Mongolia. It is named after the Heilongjiang river, or "Black Dragon River," known as the Amur in the United States. Originally a land of steppes and forests populated by hunters, nomadic herdsmen, and fishermen, Heilongjiang was first settled by the Tungusic Jurchens, the ancestors of the Manchurians. They founded the Jin dynasty (1115–1234) in the city of Huining (present-day Acheng, now part of Harbin), and sought to rule over the whole of China. Jin, the "golden dynasty," is said to be named after the gold-bearing sand in the area around Huining. For strategic reasons the capital soon shifted farther south, to the city of Yanjing, which is now Beijing. This was the very first time in Chinese history that Beijing served as the capital. This led to the absorption of the Jurchens, whose unique customs, traditions, and language faded into obscurity within the imperial court. Yet the new rulers were ill-fated, as they did not succeed in completely overthrowing the Song dynasty (960–1279), but only in pushing it farther south. The latter stages of this era are thus also known as the "Southern Song dynasty" (1126–1279). The Mongolian ruler Genghis Khan had also committed his troops to conquering China. Seven years after his death in 1234, the Jin dynasty finally came to an end; the Jurchens were no match for attacks by the descendents of Genghis from the north, along with natural disasters, and campaigns by Chinese from the south to recapture territory. The Manchus, as the Jurchen tribe came to be known after 1635, only succeeded in recapturing the imperial capital Beijing in 1644. Here they founded the last Chinese imperial dynasty, the Qing (1644–1912), coming full circle with Puyi, the last emperor of this dynasty, and a Manchurian. He was forced to return to the land of his forefathers; from 1935 to 1945 the Japanese installed him as the "puppet emperor" of Manchukuo, Japanese-occupied Manchuria. Today this area is divided into three provinces: Heilongjiang, Liaoning, and Jilin. The former Imperial Palace is in Liaoning, and houses the local provincial museum.

Above: The Russian Orthodox Saint Sophia Cathedral in Harbin, built between 1923 and 1932, is a testament to the great influence exerted by Russia on Manchuria at the beginning of the 20th century.

Facing page: During Harbin's Ice Festival, public buildings, highrise blocks, and parks throughout the city center are brilliantly illuminated.

Harbin

Top: A pedestrian area in Harbin.

Above: Hot sweet potatoes are a welcome way to warm up when the temperature plummets to −22 ˚F (−30 ˚C).

Above right: Even the wide River Songhua completely freezes over in winter.

Below: The spoils of a good day's hunting at the entrance to a restaurant.

Harbin—the provincial capital

Harbin was founded by the Russians at the end of the 19ᵗʰ century as a station on the Chinese Eastern Railway. Today it acts as a rail and road hub for the whole of the northeast. Both the Russians and the Japanese recognized the strategic importance and the wealth of resources offered by Manchuria at the end of the 19ᵗʰ century, and fought for supremacy in the region. After the October Revolution in 1917, hundreds of thousands of people from the neighboring country sought refuge in Harbin. Subsequent generations of Russians played a significant part in the city's recovery, and the Russian influence on Harbin's architecture and cuisine continues to be all-pervasive today. It is this Russian flair that has led to Harbin being called "the St Petersburg of the Orient." Following the occupation of the city by Japanese troops in 1932, after Japan's surrender at the end of World War II the city passed to the Soviet Union, who nevertheless returned it to Chinese authority. After the founding of the People's Republic (1949), large numbers of people from the south of China were resettled in Harbin, and the city became a center of heavy industry. Ever since economic reforms were introduced in the early 1990s, Harbin and Heilongjiang Province have formed a bridge for trade with Russia.

The Trans-Siberian Railroad

The "Trans-Sib," as the Trans-Siberian Railroad is affectionately known, is, in these technology-saturated times, a byword for adventure and freedom. Today the classic route goes from Moscow, cutting diagonally across Siberia, to the Pacific harbor of Vladivostok. During the course of its 5,755-mile (9259-km) route, which makes it the longest railroad line in the world, it crosses seven time zones. Train no. 4 reaches Beijing after a mere 4,737 miles (7622 km), along the "Trans-Mongolian" branch line. Alternatively, train no. 20 arrives in Harbin after an almost 5,600-mile (9000-km) journey along the "Trans-Manchurian" route.

Founded by the Russians as the "Chinese Eastern Railway" at the end of the 19th century, the Trans-Manchurian originally formed part of the main line to the Pacific. After the Russo-Japanese War (1904–1905) the Chinese Eastern Railway came under Japanese control. Russia then built a new line, the present-day route, which runs within Russian territory for its entire length. After World War II, Manchuria, and with it the Chinese Eastern Railway, passed to Russia once again, and was restored to the People's Republic in the early 1950s.

Above: With over 3 million people living in the city center, and a total population of almost 10 million, the provincial capital Harbin is also the largest city in Heilongjiang.

Below: Transportation by donkey and cart may not be as speedy as traveling by motorized vehicles, but it is far more reliable in cold weather.

Top: Alongside cereal growing, Heilongjiang is one of China's foremost provinces for cattle raising.

Above: Making up only 3 percent of Heilongjiang's population, the Manchurians have dwindled to a tiny ethnic minority.

The Siberian cold

Winters in Heilongjiang are extremely long and cold: only 90 to 120 days of the year are without frost. The lowest temperature on record is –62.1 °F (–52.3 °C), on a day in February 1969. Summers are short and decidedly wet; this is the rainiest season of the year.

To guard against the cold, people in Heilongjiang tend to build massive houses and sleep on heated platforms made out of bricks, which serve as places to sit during the daytime. As a further measure against the cold, they eat lots of fatty meat and drink hard liquor. This has earned those from northeast China, and particularly Harbin, a reputation throughout the rest of the country for their ability to hold their drink, an attribute they like to show off at lavish "meat feasts" in winter. The locally brewed Harbin beer is often drunk with meals, but never on its own. China's first brewery was founded in Harbin by a Russian in 1900, three years before the internationally famous Tsingtao Brewery was established by Germans in Qingdao (Shandong Province). Today Heilongjiang is China's biggest consumer of beer, and the cool nectar flows freely at the Summer beer festival, which has been an annual occurrence since 2001.

At the beginning of the year the bone-jangling cold also allows a wildly popular tourist attraction to take shape: Harbin is the setting for the annual Ice-Lantern Festival, at which Chinese and foreign visitors can marvel at ice sculptures colorfully lit up from the inside. Another tourist draw is the ice swimmers, who repeatedly jump, loudly cheered on by the excited crowds, from an ice block into a small pool where the thick ice on top of the Songhua river has been broken through.

The water temperature is just above 32 °F (0 °C)—pleasantly warm in comparison to the temperature of the air, which is well below freezing point. Those who cannot muster up the courage to take part can content themselves with ice-skating.

Covering an area of 175,300 square miles (454,000 sq km), Heilongjiang is larger than California. The province, almost half of which is covered by forest, is home to some 38 million people, or about 2.8 percent of the Chinese population. Alongside significant mineral resources, the province is notable for its rich fishing grounds and diverse flora and fauna. The rare Siberian tiger has been bred in a game reserve south of Harbin since the 1990s. A wildlife sanctuary for the endangered "mountain spirit," as the

locals call the elusive big cat, has been set up in the neighboring province of Jilin, and is one of seven designated UNESCO biosphere reserves. The sale of tiger products is now forbidden in China, but the black market is booming: tiger skeletons change hands for up to 60,000 US dollars, while a tiger penis, said to increase virility, is sold for about half this amount.

Heilongjiang's chief crops include corn and fodder corn, wheat, millet, soybeans and potatoes. Soybeans grow particularly well here, and the province leads the market in both quality and yield. Northeast China is also the top producer of sugar beet and linseed. The forests are ideal for pheasant, deer, and other game hunting, foraging for tasty mushrooms, including the monkey head mushroom, and obtaining antlers and musk, both prized ingredients in Chinese medicine.

Top left: Heilongjiang's vast crop-growing areas make it the bread-basket of China.

Top: The province's cities, longstanding centers of heavy industry, lie amidst almost 50 million acres (20 million ha) of forest.

Above: A traveling—or rather cycling—salesman, specializing in candied fruit on sticks.

Below: There are only around 300 Siberian tigers left in the wild, and only about 200 in zoos all over the world.

The cuisine of Heilongjiang

The hearty staples of Longjiang cuisine (as Heilongjiang's culinary tradition is also known) include noodles and dumplings (*jiaozi*) with various different fillings, such as pork, venison with mushrooms, and Chinese cabbage. Simple crudités are also popular, including lettuce leaves, slices of green bell pepper, and cucumber dipped in soy sauce.

The rivers Amur (Heilongjiang in Chinese), Sungari (Songhuajiang), and Ussurij (Wusulijiang) are abundant with fish, and local specialties include fried or poached freshwater fish, such as trout, grass carp (also known as the white amur), freshwater bream, and sturgeon. Fish "à la Heilongjiang"—fried white amur cooked with rice noodles and pancakes—brings together healthy yet delicious fish and nourishing noodles.

Other specialties come from the province's vast forests: bear paws, deer and elk muzzles, venison, monkey head mushrooms, and fern

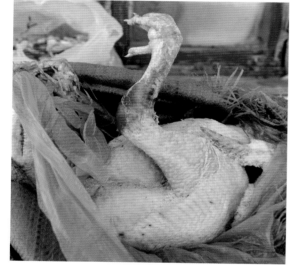

tips are all ingredients that feature in the Flying Dragon banquet (see p. 454). The custom of holding this banquet first emerged during the Manchurian Qing dynasty, when it was served to celebrate special occasions, such as the birthdays of high-ranking officials or members of the imperial family. Like all Chinese banquets, it consists of an even number of courses, to bring good luck.

The name of the banquet itself is also auspicious, as the dragon stands for power and success in China. It is easy to try out the recipe for Marinated venison kebabs and Flying dragon soup (chicken stock with monkey head mushrooms) at home; these mushrooms are also known as lion's mane, bearded hedgehog or pom pom mushrooms in the United States (see p. 211). They have an aroma of coconut, limes or other citrus fruits, and a taste that resembles chicken or veal. Not only are monkey head mushrooms tasty, but traditional Chinese medicine also credits them with healing properties; they are said to strengthen the immune system, lower cholesterol levels, and alleviate stomach pains.

Heilongjiang's history has meant that Russian influences have found their way into the traditionally Manchurian cuisine. These influences are most obvious in Harbin. The present-day provincial capital was founded by the Russians as a railroad hub at the end of the 19th century. Local cuisine is famous for its lieba bread; the Chinese word *lieba* derives from the Russian word for bread, *khleb*. Harbin sausages also taste more like Eastern European sausages than the Chinese variety. Another legacy of the Russians is Harbin beer, popular throughout China, which comes from the oldest Chinese

brewery, established in Harbin in 1900 by Russian Jews.

The long, hard winters mean that the harvest season is short, and preserved, mostly pickled foods are the order of the day. Chinese sauerkraut is especially popular, with every household making large quantities from the ubiquitous Chinese cabbage. Supplies can be stored in large clay pots for a whole year. In winter the sauerkraut is cooked up with pork belly, various kinds of sausage, and cellophane noodles to make a stew. No self-respecting meat feast is without this dish. Cold appetizers such as cooked pig's tails and ears, knuckle of pork, and sausages are also served on such occasions, followed by a warm stew of meaty pork bones, pork belly, liver, and tripe, accompanied by corn, potatoes, and sweet potatoes.

Fish dishes also feature on the menu alongside pork. In cities such as Harbin, these "meat feasts" are usually held in restaurants, and normally take the form of a convivial, often boozy meal among friends. Unsweetened wheat tea is drunk alongside Harbin beer and vodka to aid digestion of the copious dishes.

Popular snacks consist of hot sweet potatoes and cooked river snails, which can be bought from food stands all over the province.

Above left, far left, and left: The produce on sale in winter at Heilongjiang's markets includes not only fish and seafood, but also poultry, which is somewhat under-represented in the province's larders.

White amur fish stew "à la Heilongjiang"

1 white amur (approx. 3 ¼ lb / 1.5 kg), scaled,
  gutted, and filleted into 2 fillets, all bones
  removed
2–3 tbsp cornstarch
2–3 tsp light soy sauce
8–10 scallions, cut into pieces 2–2 ½ inch
  (5–6 cm) long
3–4 dried chiles
4 slices of ginger, approx. ⅙ inch (3–4 mm)
  thick
2 garlic cloves
½ tsp confectioner's sugar
7 tbsp red rice vinegar
6–8 Sichuan peppercorns
2 star anise
about 2 cups (500 ml) water
3 ⅓ tbsp cooking oil, for frying
about 7 oz (200 g) ribbon noodles
salt
5–6 wonton skins or 4–5 small, baked
  pancakes made with all-purpose flour

Coat the pieces of fish fillet with the cornstarch,
skin side only, using a fine sifter, if you have one,
and season lightly. Turn over the pieces of fish
and season the undersides lightly, then sprinkle
over a teaspoon of soy sauce, and marinate for
10–15 minutes.
Meanwhile, put half the scallions in a bowl and
add the remaining ingredients. Stir, add 3 ½–7
tablespoons water, as required, cover the bowl
and set aside.
Heat the oil in a large skillet or wok (more oil if

needed). Fry the fish, skin side only, with the
remaining scallions. Remove the fish and the
scallions, pour off the oil, and return the fish and
scallions to the skillet or wok. Pour the prepared
spice and vinegar mixture over the fish and bring
everything to a boil briefly. Turn down the heat
and cover the skillet or wok. Leave the mixture
to simmer so that the broth is gradually reduced.
Add enough water so that the fish is fully covered,
then bring back to a boil, reduce the heat and
simmer gently for another 40–45 minutes (the
cooking time depends on the size of the fish).
Finally, cut the ribbon noodles into pieces, and
the wonton skins or pancakes into narrow strips
(½–¾ inches/1–2 cm wide, 2 ½–3 inches/
6–8 cm long), add to the wok and boil everything
together briefly. Reduce the heat and leave
the dish to simmer for another
5–7 minutes.

Top left: Corn is one of the most important cereal
crops in the province.

Top: Candied fruits on skewers are a very popular
treat in Heilongjiang.

Above: There is a very vast array of produce on
sale from country stalls; you are as likely to find
pig's heads as fruit and vegetables.

The cuisine of Heilongjiang **447**

Meat feast

Winters in Heilongjiang are cold and hard, but more than anything, they are long. During this drawn out cold spell, people in rural areas mostly stay in their own homes, and social contact freezes over, too. The meat feast has thus become an important part of community and family life; it is a welcome excuse to get together for a hearty meal. Freshwater fish is often served as a counterpoint to the heavy pork. To aid digestion of the rich meal, people start by drinking unsweetened wheat tea. Once this is inside them, they move on to the popular Harbin beer, and toast every course with a shot of vodka, a custom that is upheld even in the modern cities. Meat platters are also standard fare in restaurants serving local cuisine in Harbin. The meat feast season begins at the end of February and lasts well into March. Preparations begin at least one month beforehand, when the sauerkraut is made.

Ingredients for a classic Harbin-style meat feast

Cold appetizers:
4 cooked pig's tails
2 cooked pig's ears
4 cooked, halved knuckles of pork or pig's feet
approx. 1 ½ tbsp salt
2 garlic cloves
2–3 shallots
1 piece of ginger (1 inch / 3 cm long)
1 tsp five-spice powder
1 coarse Chinese sausage per person, cut into ½-inch (1-cm)-thick slices (Polish sausages can be used instead)

Cook the cleaned and boiled pig's tails, ears, and feet for 2–3 hours (depending on their size) in sufficient water (2 ½–3 quarts/2.5–3 liters), over low heat, with the salt, garlic cloves, shallots, ginger, and five-spice. Remove the meat with a slotted spoon, and reserve the meat stock for the hotpot (see right). Leave the meat to cool. Cut the pig's ears into ½-inch (1-cm)-wide strips. Arrange the meat appetizers on different plates or serve on a meat platter, accompanied by a plate of cooked sausage.

The warm entrée: a hotpot

4 cups (1 liter) meat stock (made when preparing the cold appetizers; see recipe left)
generous 1 lb (500 g) fresh, mature pork belly
1 piece of blood sausage in its natural casing, about 4 inch (10 cm) thick
2 ¼ lb (1 kg) Chinese sauerkraut (see below)
1 tsp salt
sugar
5 ½ oz (150 g) cellophane noodles, steeped
1 Chinese sausage, cut into ¾–1-inch (2–3-cm)-thick slices

Pour the meat stock into a casserole dish and heat through. Cut the pork belly into ½-inch (1–1.5-cm)-thick slices. Cut the unpeeled blood sausage into 4 slices. Boil the sauerkraut and pork belly in the meat stock for 1 hour, then season to taste with salt and a pinch or two of sugar. Add the slices of blood sausage and the slices of Chinese sausage, and simmer for 20 minutes. Add the cellophane noodles about 5 minutes before serving. Heat the contents of the hotpot while it is being eaten so that it continues to simmer gently.

Chinese sauerkraut
(a store cupboard staple)

1 large pot, nonmetallic, ideally made of earthenware and glazed on the inside, with a capacity of 2 ½–4 gallons (10–15 liters)
10–15 heads of Chinese cabbage, cleaned, washed and cut into strips ¾–1 inch (2–3 cm) long (shredded white cabbage can be used as an alternative)
approx. 2 ¼ lb (1 kg) salt

Left: The basic ingredients of a hearty meat feast: pig's feet...

Below left: ...and parts of the pig's head.

Below: Fried freshwater bream with vegetables and herbs

Layer the strips of cabbage 3–4 inches (8–10 cm) deep in the pot, press down on them lightly, and sprinkle over a layer of salt. Repeat this process until all the cabbage is used up.

The pot should not be filled right to the brim—there should be about 4–6 inches (10–15 cm) space at the top. Pour tepid water over the cabbage. Put the lid on the pot and make sure that it is completely airtight by weighting it down with a stone or another heavy object.

The sauerkraut will be ready after about 30 days. It can then be taken out, as required, and used after rinsing with cold water. Sauerkraut is at its best when cooked.

Fried freshwater bream with vegetables and herbs

1 whole bream, approx. 1 ¾ lb (800 g), scaled, and gills removed, rinsed, and patted dry
½ tsp salt
3 scallions, cut into thin strips 3–4 inch (8–10 cm) long
1 piece of ginger, cut into thin strips 3–4 inch (8–10 cm) long,
3 ½ tbsp corn oil, for frying
½ tsp spice mixture, made of Sichuan pepper, ginger, cloves, fennel, star anise, and cinnamon
2 carrots, cut into long matchsticks
2 garlic cloves, crushed

To serve:
1 fresh red chile, seeded and finely chopped
1 fresh green chile, seeded and finely chopped
2–3 sprigs of fresh cilantro, finely chopped (parsley can be used instead)

Lightly salt the inside of the fish, then tuck in about 3–4 strips each of scallion and ginger. With a sharp knife, score the fish crosswise with a series of slits about 1 inch (2–3 cm) apart and ¼ inch (3–5 mm) deep. Brush the fish with a little oil and sprinkle the spice mixture liberally over the surface, rubbing into the slits. Heat the remaining oil in a griddle pan or skillet, and sear each side for about 8–10 minutes.

Add the remaining scallions and ginger, the carrots, and the garlic in the final 3 minutes of cooking and fry briefly, or stir-fry separately.

Before serving, garnish the fish with the fried vegetables and sprinkle with the chiles and cilantro.

In Harbin this dish is served with boiled potatoes, sweet potatoes, and corn.
This dish is popularly served at meat feasts as a complement or counterpoint to the heavy pork.

Above: The main course hotpot

Below: Chinese sauerkraut

The way to harmony: yin and yang

In the West people say that "food and drink hold body and soul together." The Chinese go even further, believing that nourishment is the key to both spiritual and physical wellbeing. Unlike Western theories about nutrition, which are based on nutrients and ingredients, in China foods are classified by their effect on the whole human organism.

The Chinese distinguish between the energy dynamic of different foods—between "hot" foods like chili, which stimulate the *qi* energy flow, and "cold" foods, such as cucumbers, which have a calming effect. The qi flows through the body in channels, known as meridians. Every meridian has a corresponding organ; the 12 standard meridians include the lung, liver, stomach, heart, and kidney meridians.

This concept, deeply rooted in the Chinese psyche, is based on the duality that lies at the heart of Chinese philosophy: yin and yang. The first reference to these two concepts appears in *Yi Jing*, (Book of Changes), written in about 700 B.C. Yin represents the feminine and passive element, the moon and darkness, while yang stands for masculinity, activeness, the sun, and the light. The world-famous yin and yang symbol, in which both elements circle around one another, each one complementing and enhancing the other, symbolizes the constantly changing balance between the yin and yang. Neither one is good nor bad; the most important thing is to strive for equilibrium between the two forces.

This idea of a balance constantly in flux gave rise to the holistic approach embodied by traditional Chinese medicine (TCM), which places the emphasis on a well-balanced diet. According to the principles of TCM, "therapy through nutrition should be tried in the first instance, and medication should only be prescribed if a particular diet is seen to have no effect."

Here "well-balanced" refers to the proper proportion of "cooling" yin foods and "warming" yang dishes. Cooling foods are often low in calories and pale in color; examples include crab, celery, buckwheat, frogs' legs, green tea, oranges, cucumbers, or bean curd.

High-calorie and spicy food is considered "warming," given its ability to stimulate or even irritate the system. Examples include dried fruits, fennel, leeks, spices, apricots, ginger, sugar, wine, tea, and chili. Fish and meat are also yang foods. The properties of the various foods can change when cooked: roasting and pan-frying mean that the food is seen as "warm," while salting or pickling mean that food becomes "cool." There is some dispute as to whether dog meat is cool or warm. In China this "warming" meat is eaten predominantly in winter, as a *pot-au-feu*, say, but in Korea it is eaten in summer to combat the heat. Another factor in Chinese dietetics is the teaching of the Five Elements, which emerged in the 5th century B.C. and took root in Taoist philosophy. The central element in this system is the earth, which lies at the center of the cosmos. The other elements are wood, fire, metal, and water, which take the form of trees, volcanoes, ore, and springs on earth.

The elements are matched to different times of the year, colors and flavors, as follows:

Water stands for winter, and it gives life.
Color: black; Taste: salty.
Wood represents the springtime, and symbolizes the beginning of life.
Color: green; Taste: sour.
Fire stands for summer and the flourishing of life.
Color: red; Taste: bitter.
Metal stands for the autumn, and symbolizes the transience of life.
Color: white; Taste: spicy.
Earth represents the central balance of the elements, and stands for the life principle itself.
Color: yellow; Taste: sweet.

If the earth is the macrocosm, these principles apply equally to the microcosm of the body. Everything that a person consumes has its own particular effect on the bodily organs. Like yin and yang, the five elements also seek to attain balance through particular combinations of foods. Courses of a meal should be balanced in terms of both their color and the energy that they impart. Different tastes are also linked with specific organs: sweet with the spleen; sour with the liver; spicy with the lungs; bitter with the heart; and salty with the kidneys.

If a person consumes too much or too little of one taste, the corresponding organism can malfunction. For instance, the lungs, linked to the metal element, are particularly susceptible to external influences in the autumn, which is also associated with the metal element. At this time of year people should avoid spicy foods, since these stimulate the lung meridian. Over-heated lungs can be detrimental to the liver, which is crucial to a person's mood. This means that the condition referred to as liver qi stagnation can soon lead to depression. As a precautionary measure, traditional Chinese medicine recommends taking "lung moisteners," foods which build up the "lung/heart qi," including pears, figs, chicken, bananas, honey, cucumbers, potatoes, radishes, walnuts, grapes, and eggs. Given the crossover between nutritional advice and medicine, it comes as no surprise that the first Chinese recipe books doubled as pharmacopeias.

Continued on page 452

Left: In Chinese cuisine all foods, whether rice, ginger, lotus seeds, or litchis, are chosen for their health and philosophical properties, as well as their taste.

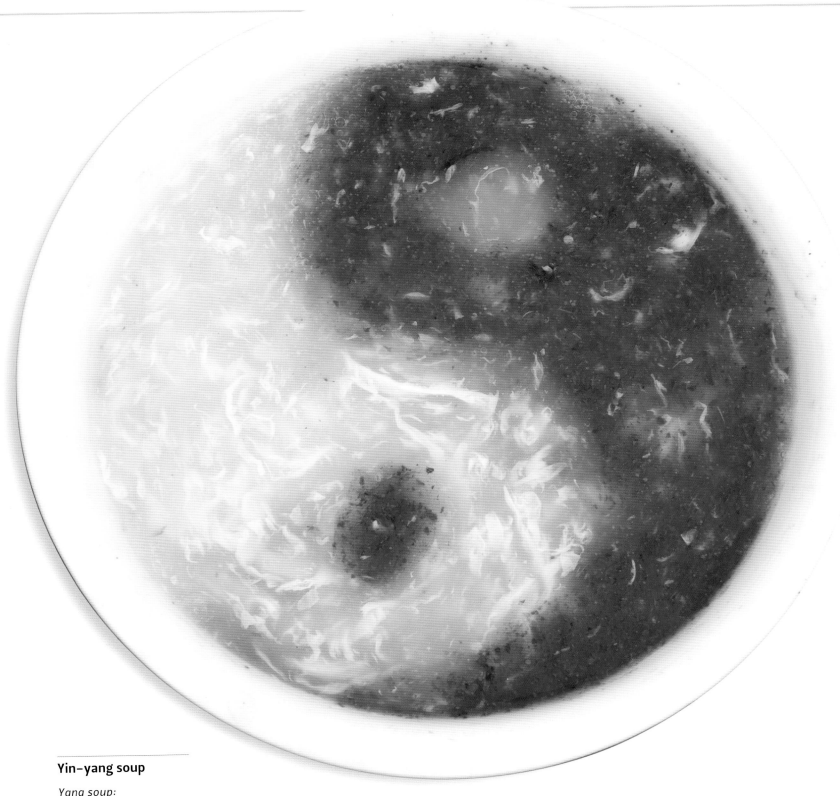

Yin–yang soup

Yang soup:
generous 1 lb / 500 g spinach
salt (to taste)
4 tsp cornstarch
½ tsp sesame oil

Yin soup:
1 ¾ oz / 50 g crabmeat
1 ¾ oz / 50 g squid, cut into rings
3 eggs
salt
4 tsp cornstarch
½ tsp sesame oil

To make the Yang Soup, wash the spinach and cook it in 4 cups/1 liter of water. Pour into a blender with the cooking water and purée. Return the spinach soup to the pot and bring back to a boil. Season to taste. Mix the cornstarch with 2 ½ tablespoons cold water and pour into the soup. Bring to a boil and stir until thickened. Stir in the sesame oil.

To make the Yin Soup, wash the crabmeat and squid and cook briefly in 4 cups (1 liter) of water. Whisk the eggs and add slowly to the boiling soup, stirring constantly, so that the eggs curdle and become strands. Season with salt. Mix the cornstarch with 2 ½ tablespoons cold water and pour into the soup. Bring the mixture back to a boil and stir until thickened. Stir in the sesame oil. To serve, pour the Yin Soup into one side of a large tureen, then carefully pour the Yang Soup into the other side in such a way that it forms the yin–yang symbol.

Continued from page 450

The Chinese like to say that they'll eat anything with four legs, apart from the table. As food was often scarce in the People's Republic, this was once a sad reality in the bitter struggle for survival. Ever since, what was once a necessity is now seen as a virtue, and the bill of fare often features all kinds of animals which are considered inedible in the West, despite the benefits of certain such dishes. One such very rare delicacy is Hashima (also called Hasma or Harsmar), the ovaries of the snow frog, native to China's Jilin Province. Hashima, which is also known as frog oil or frog fat, is a cooling yin dish, and it improves the qi flow to the kidneys and "moistens" the lungs.
It is also said to have a rejuvenating effect, tightening facial pores and combating nocturnal hot flushes. Dried hashima can be bought in tea and herbal shops, and is used to make a popular and very tasty dessert with papaya.

Crystal snow jelly with papaya

1 oz (30 g) dried "frog oil" (available in
   Chinese tea and herbal stores)
1 oz (30 g) dried Mu Err mushrooms (if "frog
   oil" is not available, use double this
   amount)
5 tbsp sugar
1/2 papaya, seeded

Soak the frog oil in tepid water for about 3 hours, until it is 3 or 4 times its original size. If necessary, change the water once or twice. Strain and leave to dry off.
Soak the mushrooms in tepid water for 1 hour, then leave to dry before cutting into small, bite-sized pieces, cutting out any membranes.
Add the mushrooms and frog oil to 2 cups (500 ml) of boiling water, and bring back to a boil briefly. Add the sugar, stir in carefully and leave the mixture to simmer for 30 minutes, until the liquid has thickened to a syrup. Meanwhile, stew the half papaya in a deep pot for 15 minutes, or wrap in aluminum foil and bake in the oven at 300 °F (150 °C). Leave to cool a little, and then spoon out the flesh. Finally, strain the mushrooms and the frog oil, leave to drain thoroughly and cool. Spoon the mixture into the lukewarm, hollowed out papaya and serve with the papaya flesh, as a dessert.

Above and facing page, right: Dried Mu Err mushrooms are carefully selected.

Facing page, far right: Even for Chinese gourmets, this exquisite dessert is a rare treat, so this restaurant board explains the history and benefits of "frog oil."

The Flying Dragon Banquet

The flying dragon banquet was first held in the era of the Manchurian Qing dynasty (1644–1912). The 16-course meal was served on special occasions, such as the birthdays of high-ranking officials or members of the imperial family. Today several restaurants in the provincial capital, Harbin, offer the banquet.

Flying dragon soup

4 dried monkey head mushrooms (or 8 large button mushrooms)
4 cups (1 liter) chicken stock
2–3 chiles
Pheasant breast and legs, deboned and cut into strips ¼ inch (5 mm) thick

Soak the dried monkey head mushrooms for 5–6 hours in cold water, changing the water several times. Wash the mushrooms and cut into thin strips.
Pierce the chiles, heat with the chicken stock, and boil for a few minutes. Remove the chiles. Add the mushrooms to the stock and simmer for 3–4 minutes. Add the pheasant meat, bring to a boil, and cook for 3–4 minutes.
Serve the soup in your most ornate tureen or bowl; this is the pièce de résistance of the Flying Dragon Banquet.

Marinated venison kebabs with roasted chiles, on a bed of onions

14 oz (400 g) saddle of venison, untied
3 tbsp dark soy sauce
3 tbsp cranberry juice
1 tbsp red rice vinegar
5 tbsp sesame oil
3 dried chiles
2 garlic cloves, finely chopped
1 piece of ginger (¾ inch / 2 cm long), grated
2 ½ tbsp sesame seeds
3 large Spanish onions, halved and cut into thick rings
5–6 scallions, cut into pieces 1 inch (3 cm) long
small wooden kebab skewers

Cut the meat into dice about ¾ inch (2 cm) thick. Mix the soy sauce, almost all of the cranberry juice, the vinegar, and one tablespoon of the sesame oil together thoroughly, stir in the meat, and marinate uncovered for 2–3 hours.
Spear two or three cubes of meat on every skewer, until all the meat is used up. Heat two tablespoons of sesame oil in a wok. Briefly sauté the chiles with the garlic and ginger, add the venison kebabs and sear everything for about 3–4 minutes, making sure that nothing sticks to the bottom of the wok. Deglaze the wok with a little cranberry juice. Add the sesame seeds to the wok and toast.
Meanwhile, sauté the Spanish onions and scallions with the remaining oil in another pan until they are crisp, yet still pale.
To serve, lay a "bed" of onions on a preheated plate or in a baking dish, then arrange the kebabs and the chiles on top. The chiles and onions are not eaten.

The venison kebabs are just one part of the multicourse Flying Dragon Banquet, so no side-dishes are required.

Above: The Flying Dragon Banquet, consisting of:

1 Roast duck (cold)
2 Cooked sausage (three different varieties, cold)
3 Bear meat (cold roast)
4 Fern tips with pork (cold)
5 Thin strips of asparagus with jellyfish (cold)
6 Braised green lettuce
7 Flying dragon soup with mushrooms and pheasant (see recipe, p. 454)
8 Venison kebabs (see recipe, p. 454)
9 Broiled nightingale with deep-fried, dried chiles, on fried cellophane noodles, on a bed of potato straws and deep-fried parsley
10 Braised "monkey head mushrooms" with cherry tomatoes, braised mini Chinese cabbages, baby corn, and glazed with a thick, clear chili sauce
11 Cooked bear paws with broccoli and crab, garnished with carrots carved in the shape of butterflies
12 Braised Chinese cabbage with soy sauce, oil, and fish sauce
13 Cooked moose muzzle with deep-fried chiles, green bell peppers, and carrots
14 Wok-fried celery with morels, scallions, and gingko seeds
15 Poached grass carp, a freshwater fish, in soy sauce, garnished with tomato slices and cucumber, and sprinkled with steamed carrots and scallions
16 Crystal snow jelly with papaya (see recipe, p. 452)

Lantern festivals—lighting up the New Year

The Chinese lantern festival (*yuanxiao jie*) welcomes the first full moon of the New Year. It is the grand finale to the period of festivities that marks the Chinese New Year, which begins on the night of the second new moon after the winter solstice, between 21st January and 21st February. On this night, the Chinese celebrate with ornate, multicolored lanterns that shine out all over the country. The lanterns are fashioned out of lacquered wood, mother-of-pearl, parchment, paper, and horn.

Common motifs include zodiac symbols, plants, and mythical creatures, but scenes from classic novels, legends, and stories also make an appearance. Some carry a riddle, and the person who solves it can take the lantern home as a trophy. This custom, which dates as far back as the Song era (960–1279), is popular to this very day, but a small fee is often charged for making a guess.

The custom of hanging lanterns up in temples and public buildings on the day before the first full moon dates back to the Han dynasty (206 B.C.–221 A.D.). Tradition has it that Emperor Wendi instituted the lantern festival on his ascension to the throne. According to another legend, the Han Emperor Ming was responsible for decreeing that lanterns should be lit to honor Buddha, so as to encourage the expansion of Buddhism, which had spread from India. Despite these

tales, the first full moon of the year had been celebrated long before this time; China's rural societies once made sacrifices to nature deities, so as to keep their wrath at bay and pray for a good harvest in the coming year.

Today children carry their very own, often handmade, lanterns proudly through the streets. In the past "running pony lanterns" were very popular. These consisted of two layers, with silhouettes of horses and other shapes stuck onto the inner layer. When the candle was lit, this inner layer spun around, giving the illusion that the horses were running.

These days Mickey Mouse and Friends lanterns are much in vogue, and public lantern displays reflect current issues and trends. As might be expected, in 2008 lanterns everywhere bore the symbol of the Olympic Games. The displays in Zigong, Sichuan Province, are notably spectacular—the town has been dubbed "lantern city of the south"—and in Heilongjiang in the north, where Harbin draws visitors from all over the world to its annual Ice Festival. Harbin's Ice Lantern Festival has developed from a tradition that originated in the Qing era (1644–1912). Back then the lanterns were very simple: water was

poured into a bucket and left outside until the water froze. Then a hole was chiseled in the block of ice, and a candle inserted into the hole. Today, however, the ice sculptures are real works of art, and the raw material comes from the Sungari river, delivered in blocks. Harbin's Zhaolin Park is the setting for world-famous structures from the Great Wall to cathedrals, pyramids, and palaces—all made of ice! Yet the ice sculptors also draw inspiration from nature; the display is embellished with ice gardens, flowers, waterfalls, lions, tigers, and dragons. Multicolored lights are enclosed in the sculptures, making the park a veritable wonderland after dark. One of the main attractions is the "ice restaurant," where tables, chairs, walls, and doors are made of ice, and there is room for 100 guests. You can order a hotpot to warm up.

Taiwan follows a different custom: in a small mountain village called Pingxi, near the capital Taipei, thousands of people gather at the end of the annual lantern festival to release huge sky lanterns into the night air, making sure to write their secret wishes on them first.

Other highlights of the Chinese lantern festival include dance performances and firework displays. Dragon and lion dances are particularly popular. The dragon dance dates back to the Song era (960–1279). The dragon, made of multicolored material, is divided into between 9 and 24 6 ½-foot (2-m) sections, and is carried by up to 100 people. The lion dance is over a thousand years old and combines elements of martial arts and dance. It is supposed to bring peace and harmony, and drive away evil.

On the evening of the lantern festival people gather together with their families and eat *yuanxiao*, sweet stuffed rice balls. Yuanxiao means "first night," and refers to both the feast itself, and the dish that is also called *tangyuan*, or "round dumplings in soup," in the south. The dumplings symbolize harmony and togetherness within the family.

Local versions of these dumplings are made in different regions of China; in the south they tend to be small, with a hearty filling, while in northern China they are larger and always sweet. Yuanxiao may be boiled, steamed or fried. Rice dumplings are becoming like the Chinese equivalent of Easter eggs; they have long been sold outside the lantern festival period. Today the traditional filling—a sweet bean paste—comes in many different guises, including sugar, Chinese hawthorn, dates, pineapple or strawberry paste, sesame, walnuts, rose petals, and even coconut milk, meat, or chocolate.

Left: The Lantern Festival and Ice Festival are the highlights of Harbin's calendar.

Below left: The lofty sculptures are replicas of famous Chinese or international buildings.

Below: The sculptures are most enchanting in the dark, when they are lit up both inside and out. Harbin's Ice and Snow Festival ranks alongside Sapporo, Oslo, and Québec as one of the top four such events in the world.

Top: The awe-inspiring ice replicas can also be admired at night.

Above (middle): The sculptures are wrought using power saws and more delicate tools.

Above: The festival first took place in 1963, and has since become a tourist highlight.

Right: When the temperature falls below freezing, scarves and hot soup provide warmth inside and out.

Jiaozi—homemade stuffed dumplings

Vegetarian dumplings

For the dough:
2 cups (300 g) all-purpose flour
²/₃ cup (120 ml) water

½ head of Chinese cabbage, thoroughly
    washed, cut into small pieces
2 tbsp salt
4 hard-cooked eggs, chopped
2 scallions
4 stalks of Chinese chives
½ fresh red chile, seeded and finely chopped
1 tbsp light soy sauce
2 tbsp peanut oil
3 tbsp chicken stock
salt

Dipping sauce:
½ cup (125 ml) red rice vinegar

Put the flour in a bowl and gradually add the
water, stirring constantly, until it becomes a
smooth dough. Cover and leave to stand for
30–40 minutes. Meanwhile, season the cabbage,
mix thoroughly and press down on it firmly.
Leave it to stand for 15–20 minutes, then pour
away any brine.
Add the hard-cooked eggs, scallions, chives, and
chile to the cabbage, mix thoroughly, and then
pour over the soy sauce, peanut oil, and chicken
stock, and mix once again. If the mixture is too

wet, pour off some of the liquid. Season to taste.
Knead the dough well and shape into rolls
approximately 1 inch (3 cm) thick.
Cut about 24 even-sized pieces out of each roll.
Roll each piece into a thin circle using a rolling pin,
and place 2 teaspoons of the filling in the middle
of each. Lift the edges of the circle up and pinch
carefully together with the thumb and index finger, so that the dumpling is firmly sealed.
Fill a large pot (6 ½-pint/3-liter capacity) with
1 ½ quarts (1.5 liters) water, bring to a boil and
carefully slide in the dumplings. Stir frequently,
ideally with chopsticks, to ensure that the
do not stick together. As soon as the water
begins to boil again, add 1 cup (250 ml) of cold
water, bring to a boil once more, and then top up
with another 2 cups (500 ml) of cold water, and
bring to a boil again. Take the pot from the stove,
and leave the jiaozi to stand for another 1–2 minutes. Remove them from the water with a slotted
spoon, and serve in small bowls, about six per
person. The custom is to spoon up the stock after
eating the dumplings.

Game meat and mushroom dumplings

To make the dough:
See the instructions for Vegetarian Dumplings

¾ oz (20 g) dried ceps or 3 oz (80 g) fresh
    ceps
1 ½ cups (300 g) ground moose meat (ground
    venison can be used as a substitute)
½ cup (100 g) ground pork
1 egg
2–3 scallions, cut into small rings
small bunch of Chinese chives, finely chopped
1 tsp freshly grated ginger
2 ½ tbsp cranberry juice (or red grape juice)
1 tsp dark soy sauce
½ tsp salt
1 tsp chili oil
pinch of black pepper

Dipping sauce:
½ cup (125 ml) red rice vinegar mixed with
    3 tsp freshly grated ginger

If using dried ceps, soak them in tepid water for
40–50 minutes, changing the water two or three
times. Strain the ceps. Cut the mushrooms into
small dice.
Put the ground meat in a large bowl and mix in
the egg. Add the mushrooms, scallions, chives,
ginger, and all the other ingredients, and mix
thoroughly, adding more seasoning if necessary.
Roll out the prepared dough, and follow the same
steps as for the Vegetarian Dumplings.
Serve the vinegar and ginger in four little bowls
as a dipping sauce.

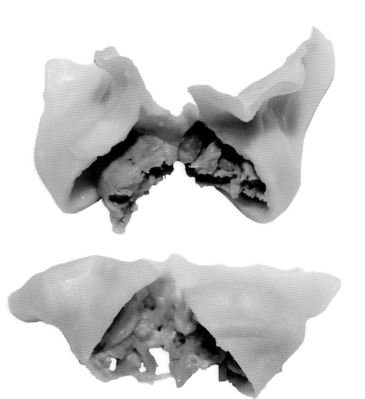

Pork and herb dumplings

To make the dough:
See the instructions for Vegetarian Dumplings

2 ½ cups (500 g) ground pork
2–3 scallions, cut into small rings
piece of ginger (¹/₅ inch / ½ cm long), grated
1 garlic clove, finely chopped
½ tsp salt
½ tsp chili sauce
1 tsp red rice vinegar
1 tsp light soy sauce
1 tbsp peanut oil

Dipping sauce:
½ cup (125 ml) red rice vinegar

Make the dough, following the instructions for Vegetarian Dumplings.
Mix the ground pork with the sliced scallions, and add the ginger, garlic, salt, chili sauce, vinegar, soy sauce, and peanut oil. Mix everything together thoroughly, leave aside to allow the flavors to develop, and season to taste.
The filling mixture must be easy to shape by hand. Roll out the prepared dough and follow the same steps as for the Vegetarian Dumplings.
Serve the red rice vinegar in four little bowls as a dipping sauce.

Sweet pancakes with red bean paste

2 tbsp corn oil, for frying
4 tbsp all-purpose flour
1 egg, lightly whisked
4 tbsp milk
4 tbsp red bean paste
about 4 cups (1 liter) deep-frying oil
2 tsp confectioner's sugar

Heat the corn oil in a skillet. Put the flour, egg, and milk into a bowl and beat to a smooth batter. Pour half of the mixture into the skillet, and fry on one side only for 2 minutes, to make a pancake.
Place the pancake on a plate, with the fried side upward. Make another pancake, and remove and place on a plate, as before.
Put 2 tablespoons of bean paste in the middle of each pancake, then roll up the pancake from the edges and seal with a little egg white.
Meanwhile, heat the deep-frying oil to high temperature (about 355 °F/180 °C) in a wok, and deep-fry the rolled pancakes for 3–4 minutes, turning carefully. Remove from the wok, reheat the oil to 355 °F (180 °C), and briefly fry the pancakes again, so that they become crispy. Remove them from the wok, drain them on paper towels, and dust with confectioner's sugar. Cut into four portions and serve hot.

Above left: In professional jiaozi restaurants there is a strict division of tasks, just as in European kitchens.

Top: It is important not to put too much filling into the dumplings, or else they will burst open in the pot.

Above: The trick is to prevent the dumplings from sticking together in the pot.

Jiaozi—homemade stuffed dumplings **459**

Cereal crops

When humans first began to grow crops over 10,000 years ago, trading-in their nomadic existence to settle on the land, and becoming farmers rather than hunters and gatherers, various cultures developed based around the cultivation of different cereals—corn in America, sorghum in Africa, wheat in the Roman Empire, barley and rye in northern Europe, and rice in Asia. The stereotype of the Chinese as rice-eaters persists to this very day, but it is less commonly known that wheat is the staple food for more than two thirds of the Chinese population. For a long time, the climate in northern China prevented rice growing, so cereals such as wheat, soy, and millet were traditionally the most important foods. North of the Yangtze, the so-called "rice-noodle line," people mainly eat noodles, dumplings, steamed buns, and they also make bread from millet, wheat and sesame (*shaobing*).

Today, China is the world's biggest producer of cereals, but it is facing a huge challenge: although it has over 8 percent of the world's arable land, it must produce enough to feed 20 percent of the world's population. With China's newfound economic prosperity, living habits are becoming more sophisticated. In the boom cities on the coast this has gone hand in hand with a rocketing level of meat consumption. In rural areas, however, most people still have a largely vegetarian diet. Eggs, fish, and meat are only served on special occasions.

Millet

Millet (Latin: *Panicum miliaceum*, Chinese: *xiaomi*) is the longest-cultivated cereal crop in China. During the earliest phases of civilization in northern China, its subspecies were the only kind of cereal in use. According to one of the Five Chinese Classics written between the 6th and the 10th centuries B.C., the *Shi Jing*, (Book of Songs), back in the mists of time Hou Ji, the "prince of crops," a demigod and the forebear of the Zhou dynasty (1122–249 B.C.), instructed the people to grow millet. Recent archaeological excavations have unearthed evidence that millet noodles were produced 4,000 years ago, and verified that millet was first cultivated in Manchuria. Grains of proso- and foxtail millet, which could date back to 7000 or 8000 B.C., have been found in southern Manchuria and the Yellow river drainage basin. Millet is also the base ingredient for kaoliang liquor, which was once hugely popular in China. Allusions to debauched, kaoliang-induced revelry can be found in the *Shujing*, (Book of History), compiled in the 6th century B.C. Today two northeastern regions, Manchuria and, notably, Inner Mongolia, produce the largest variety of millet species in the world. The cereal crop has a short growing season, and does not make deep roots in the soil, so intensive, deep tillage is not necessary. Millet has always been popular with nomads for this reason, and it is the staple food, alongside buckwheat, for the present-day nomadic Kirghiz and Mongols.

Wheat

Wheat (*xiaomai*) was being imported into the Middle Kingdom as early as 5,000 years ago, but it only came to be cultivated there much later. Today China is the world's largest producer of wheat—Henan, Shandong, and Hebei provinces provide more that 50 percent of the total yield—but it also consumes the most wheat (a type of grass, Latin: *Poaceae*, genus *Tritium L.*). Wheat flour is the base ingredient for bread, noodles, dumplings, and steamed buns. Homemade noodles with vegetables, eaten cold, are a specialty of Gansu province. Shanghai is famous for its *xiaolongbao*, dumplings filled with meat and broth. *Jiaozi*, dumplings boiled in water, are popular all over northern China, as are *guotie* ("potstickers"), which are pan-fried dumplings.

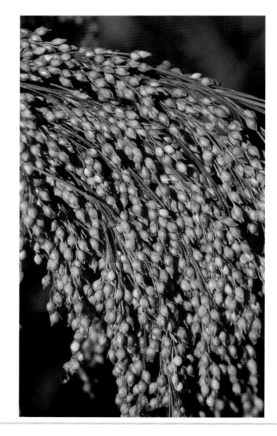

Above left and left: The days when taking in the harvest served as an ideological and political lesson are a distant memory. Today China's crops are harvested using efficient, industrial machinery.

Right: After rice and corn, wheat is the third most commonly produced crop on earth. China is far and away the biggest wheat producer— ahead of even India and the United States.

There are many different fillings: ground meat with scallions, Chinese cabbage with boiled eggs, venison with mushrooms, and many more. In Inner Mongolia steamed dumplings are called *buuz*, and are usually filled with cooked lamb. One of Heilongjiang Province's specialties is wheat flour pancakes with red bean paste.

Barley

The cultivation of barley (Latin: *Hordeum vulgare*, Chinese: *damai*) began 10,000 years ago in the "Fertile Crescent," an area incorporating the eastern coastal belt of the Mediterranean (southwest Turkey, Lebanon, Israel, and Syria) and the western parts of Jordan, Iraq, and Iran. Barley arrived in China a mere 3,000 years ago. Like wheat, it can be processed to make flour, but it is not much used in Chinese cuisine. Yet the beer breweries established by Europeans in China are a different matter: here barley is an indispensible base ingredient. It is also used to make high-proof drinks such as the millet liquor *kaoliang*.

Corn

Corn (Latin: *Zea mays*, Chinese: *yumi*) is thought to originate from Mexico, and was cultivated by the native Indians back in prehistoric times. Corn arrived in China on Portuguese ships from Brazil. The earliest reference to a corn plant is an illustration found in a mid-16th century botany guide. Today corn soup is a popular dish in Fujian Province, served as bird's nest soup. Corn is also widely used as fodder in mass livestock farming. Today more than a third of the worldwide crop harvest goes to feed animals; in developed countries this proportion rises to more than two thirds. The production of 2 1/4 pounds (1 kg) of beef "costs" about 15 1/2 pounds (7 kg) of fodder corn.

Buckwheat

Strictly speaking, buckwheat (Latin: *Fagopyrum esculentum*, Chinese: *qiao-mai*) is not a cereal crop, but it is commonly referred to as such. Genghis Khan's army of horsemen brought it to Central Europe in the 13th century, and it was often called Tartar buckwheat in the West for this reason.

Above left: Most corn is used as animal fodder.

Above right: Barley is not generally used in Chinese cuisine, except to make alcoholic drinks.

Right: Buckwheat originates from Central Asia.

Below: Today much of the harvesting in China is carried out by machines, but individual workers are still in demand.

Cabbage: northern China's darling

Chinese cabbage, Peking cabbage, Tianjin cabbage, bok choy, pak choi, white cabbage, mustard greens, or plain old "bai cai," with white stalks —there almost seem to be more names for Chinese cabbage than there are actual varieties. Yet this comes as no surprise when we learn that the different types of cabbage may have Chinese or Cantonese names, according to the region in which they are grown; on being introduced to the West, these names have, in their turn, been adjusted according to the local vernacular. In botanical terms, the various types of Chinese cabbage are classified as cruciferous plants, like Brussels sprouts, cauliflower, and white cabbage, and all are rich in vitamins.

Archaeologists working on excavations in Cishan, Henan Province, have discovered that Chinese cabbage was being cultivated as early as 6000 B.C. Today it is still the most important vegetable in northern Chinese cooking. Whether pickled, steamed or quickly stir-fried, the different varieties of cabbage promise a treat that is not only healthy, but also crisp and colorful.

The frost-proof **Chinese cabbage** (*Brassica rapa, subsp. pekinensis*) is one of the most important vegetables north of the Yangtze, and also Beijing's cabbage of choice. The light-green and yellow leaves, slightly crinkly around the edges, form a firm, cylindrical, 12–20-inch (30–50-cm)-long head, but unlike other types of cabbage it has no stalk. The delicate taste of Chinese cabbage is used to enhance simple dishes, dumplings or soups, but it is shown off to its best advantage in briefly stir-fried wok dishes. Traditionally, pickled cabbage is also a Chinese store cupboard staple, particularly in winter. Its high vitamin C and mineral content makes it especially healthy and, unlike other varieties of cabbage, it rarely causes bloating.

Pak choi, or bok choy (Chinese mustard greens; *Brassica rapa, subsp. chinensis*), also belongs to the botanical Brassica rapa family, which grows perennially in its native habitat of Guangdong and Hong Kong. Of the 15 different varieties, around nine were being cultivated as early as the 7th century. The rich green leaves and white leafstalks form rose-like heads, between 12–20 inches (30–50 cm) high. With a slightly nutty and bitter flavor, pak choi tastes more like fresh spinach than normal cabbage, and has a markedly crisp bite. It does not need any dressing except for a little oyster sauce and garlic, and its color and texture make it a popular accompaniment to meat and fish dishes. The so-called baby- or Shanghai pak choi is noticeably smaller, and tenderer as a result.

With its long, light-green stalks, tender leaves and yellow flowers, **Chinese flowering cabbage** (*Brassica rapa parachinensis*; Cantonese: choi sum) is prized as a culinary treat in the south of the country. Whether added to soup, stir-fried with lemon juice, chiles, and garlic, or with beef or crab, with its delicate flavor, tender choi sum is the favorite of the pak choi family. The plant, which grows to around 8 inches (20 cm), thrives all year round in a mild climate, and the red-leafed variety can withstand even frost.

Visually speaking, **Chinese kale** (*Brassica oleracea var. alboglabra*) bears little resemblance to its Western counterpart. Flat, blue-green leaves and creamy-white flower heads grow around the thick green stalks. The frost-resistant leafy vegetable, which is harvested by hand, grows to a whopping 12–18 inches (30–45 cm) high within 65 days and has a very high vitamin and calcium content. Depending on its age, the taste of Chinese kale ranges from sweet to slightly bitter, and it is served either on its own, stir-fried with ginger and garlic, or with beef and fish.

Woody or withered parts are removed from all types of Chinese cabbage before cooking. In order to preserve the color and texture when stir-frying, the stalks or flower heads are fried before the tender leaves.

KATRIN SCHLOTTER

Cabbage with sesame oil

7 oz (200 g) Chinese cabbage hearts
piece of carrot (1 ½ inch / 4 cm long)
1 ½ oz (40 g) cellophane noodles
½ tsp salt
1 tsp sugar

To serve:
2 tbsp dried crab
2 tbsp toasted white sesame seeds
1 ½ tbsp fresh cilantro leaves, finely chopped
2–3 tbsp sesame oil

Blanch the cabbage hearts, the carrot, and the cellophane noodles in boiling water. Drain and cut the ingredients into small pieces. Mix everything together, season with the salt, and add the sugar and a few drops of sesame oil.

To serve, sprinkle with the dried crab, the white sesame seeds, and the cilantro. Warm the sesame oil and drizzle over the dish.

Left: White cabbage (*Brassica oleracea var. capitata*)

Facing page: Chinese cabbage (*Brassica rapa subsp. pekinensis*)

Left: Chinese kale (*Brassica oleracea var. alboglabra*)

Right: Bok choy (also pak choi *Brassica rapa subsp. chinensis*)

Below: Chinese flowering cabbage (choi sum, *Brassica rapa parachinensis*)

Cabbage: northern China's darling **463**

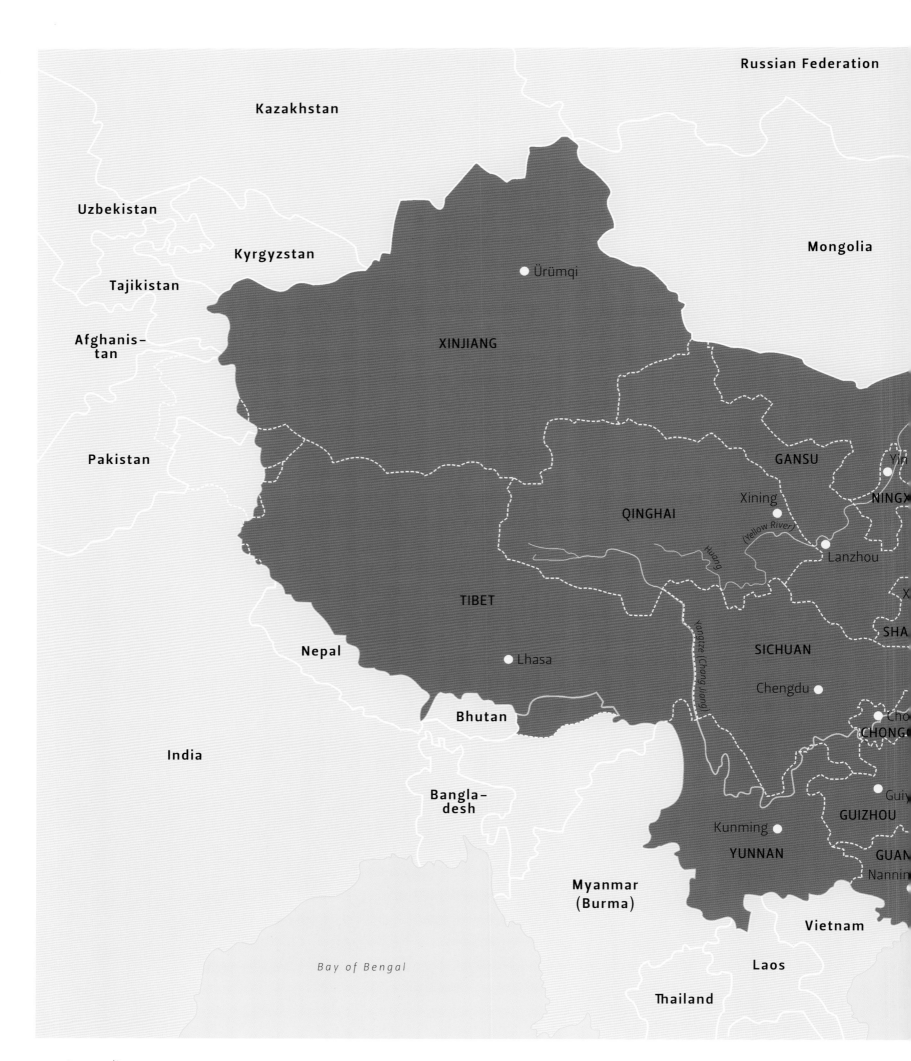

Russian Federation

HEILONGJIANG

● Harbin

JILIN

○ Changchun

INNER MONGOLIA

Shenyang ●
LIAONING

North
Korea

Sea of

Japan

Japan

...ot

BEIJING

● Beijing

TIANJIN

Taiyuan

HEBEI

● Tianjin

South
Korea

○ Shijiazhuang

...HANXI

SHANDONG

Jinan ●

Huanghe (Yellow River)

Yellow Sea

○ Zhengzhou

HENAN

JIANGSU

ANHUI

Nanjing
○

SHANGHAI

...EI

● Hefei

Yangtze (Chang Jiang)

○ Shanghai

Wuhan ●

Hangzhou

East China

...gsha

Nanchang ●

ZHEJIANG

Sea

JIANGXI

PACIFIC

...AN

Fuzhou ○

OCEAN

FUJIAN

○ Taipei

GUANGDONG

TAIWAN

Guangzhou

○ HONG KONG

MACAU

...ikou

South China

NAN

Sea

Philippines

0   300 miles/500 km

Glossary

Babaocha "Eight treasures tea," usually a green tea blend of eight different medicinal herbs, according to region. Available in any Chinese tea house.

Baihao Yinzhen "Silver needle tea," premium white tea, made only from unopened tea buds. About 30,000 buds are required to make 2 ¼ pounds (1 kilo) of tea.

Bai jiu Chinese schnapps or brandy, with an alcohol content of 50–65 percent, often based on Kaoliang schnapps, from the town of Maotai, in the southern province of Guizhou. Sold internationally as "Mou Tai Kweichou."

Balichang A Macanese specialty: shrimp paste made from tiny fish and crabs.

Bangzi laohu ji "Stick, tiger, hen": one of the most popular drinking games, and played all over China (→ *Jiuling*), this is similar to our own rock–paper–scissors, except that *Bangzi laohu ji* is played only by men, and accompanied by copious alcohol.

Baozi Stuffed steamed buns; the sweet variety often contain yellow bean- or black sesame paste, while the savory ones hold a mixture of broiled pork and/or vegetables.

Cha chaan teng Hong Kong street eateries with Formica tables, televisions, and neon tubing. In the 1960s these acted as cafeterias, bars, and social meeting places. Today they still serve up cheese on toast, noodle soup, and much more.

Cha siu bau A Cantonese specialty: yeast dumplings with grilled pork marinated in honey, hoisin sauce, and five-spice powder.

Chaguan The Chinese tea house, a microcosm of society and, once again, an institution. This is the place to savor tea (perhaps accompanied by → *Dim sum*), chat, peruse newspapers (and, these days, emails), and play Chinese chess or Mahjong. Storytellers, acrobats, and local opera singers also perform in tea houses. The largest one, seating several hundred, is in Chengdu, the capital of Sichuan. Most open-air tea houses (*litian chaguan*) are to be found on riverbanks and in public parks.

Chi fan le ma? "Have you already eaten rice?"—a Chinese greeting.

Chun Qiu The "Annals of Spring and Autumn," one of the Five Classics → *Wu Jing*.

Chunjie Spring Festival: Chinese New Year festival lasting for several days, celebrated after the first new moon after the winter solstice (between January 21 and February 21), and culminating in the Lantern Festival, → *Yuanxiao Jie*.

Da Bai Hao White tea; the most exquisite tea of them all is predominantly cultivated in northeastern Fujian. One of the top varieties is → *Baihao Yinzhen*, "Silver Needle tea."

Da Hong Pao A tea from the Wuyi Mountains (on the border between Fujian and Jiangxi) and the base for one of the most famous and expensive varieties of Oolong tea, → *Wulong*. It can be brewed up to seven times.

Dai pai dong Open-air food stalls in Hong Kong (especially on Temple Street) selling substantial snacks, including rice congee, noodles, deep-fried balls of fish, and tofu.

Dim sum A Cantonese specialty: a simply astounding array of artfully folded dumplings, rolls, or appetizers, consisting of soft pastry cases made of wheat or rice flour, with a meat, vegetable, seafood or tofu filling that may come sweet, savory, deep-fried, steamed, or in huge portions. *Dim sum* are served with tea, but also on special occasions, as a family meal on Sundays, or with friends → *Yum cha*.

Dunhuang rangpizi Slightly slippery pea-flour noodles from Gansu, served cold in summer with bean sprouts, chiles, and other spices.

Ganbei! "Empty your glass!": Chinese toast, particularly popular in → *Jiuling* drinking games and when challenging others to "down" drinks.

Hao Ya A Silver tips tea, the top variety of → *Qimen*.

Har gau A dim sum classic with crabmeat.

Hongshao "Red-cooking": a Zhejiang method of cooking fish, chicken, or vegetables by braising them in a sauce made of ginger, sugar, star anise, bean paste, and soy sauce, vinegar, or Shaoxing rice wine. This red sauce can also transform pork or tofu into mouth-watering stews.

Huangshan Maofeng One of China's best green teas, made from only the youngest hand-picked shoots, which sprout at the very beginning of spring. Mao Feng tea, from the Huangshan mountains, is roasted in an oven to prevent the tender leaves from splitting.

Huoguo A Chinese (and Mongolian) hotpot; for the basic recipe, a stock made by boiling meat bones is seasoned with salt, pepper, and—according to taste—garlic, star anise, ginger, fennel, cardamom, chiles, and soy sauce. Meat, fish, seafood, pasta, mushrooms, and vegetables are perfect for this dish, but organ meats are also used—there are no holds barred when assembling the ingredients. The spiciest version comes from Sichuan and is cooked in a pot with two tiers: one holds a mild, pale chicken stock seasoned with ginger and scallions; the other a spicy, red stock flavored with chiles, Sichuan pepper, bean paste, and other ingredients to turn up the heat.

Jiaozi Round, half-moon-shaped dumplings, known as "Chinese ravioli" in the West. Depending on the region, season, and family tradition, the pastry casing may consist of wheat, corn or rice flour, and be stuffed with ground meat, fish, seafood or vegetables.

Jing Essence: one of the "three treasures" produced by the forces of → *Yin and Yang*, present in every creature and object.

Jinhua A famous ham from Zhejiang, named after the Jinhua pig, which is much prized throughout Asia. The ham is sold air-dried or smoked, and marinated in sugar or salt.

Jiuling Drinking game: an age-old Chinese tradition, still played in countless versions today, almost always by men. At one time, Tang-era (618–907) Confucian scholars would vie with one another to conjure up difficult literary riddles, recite unfamiliar verses from the classics without making any mistakes, or compose poems on the spot. Anyone who failed at the task had to empty his cup of rice wine (or schnapps) as a punishment.

Kuaizi Pair of chopsticks used in China not only for eating, but also (in longer versions) for cooking and preparing dishes.

Lamian Long, hand-drawn noodles (*la*: to draw; *main*: noodles)—a specialty of the Hui (a

Muslim ethic group in Gansu). In the desert city of Lanzhou, the noodle dough is mixed with different varieties of desert grass. *Lanzhou lamian* are served in a strong beef broth, and offered for breakfast or lunch all over China. One restaurant chain that specializes in *Lanzhou lamian* also has branches in Singapore, the United States, and France.

Lap cheung Glossy red (Cantonese) sausages, dangling in plump bundles on the walls or from the roofs of Macau's market stalls or souvenir shops, sorted according to thickness, length, and maturity. The production process requires cold, dry air, so there are always homemade *lap cheung* in winter.

Li Ji The Book of Rites, one of the Five Classics → *Wu Jing*.

Mantou Steamed buns, substantial Chinese staples made from water, yeast, and flour, sold everywhere from street corners to restaurants and university cafeterias; in Beijing they are particularly popular for breakfast.

Mixian A rice noodle specialty from Yunnan, traditionally made from whole grains of rice, which are soaked and then ground to a wet paste with water, before being steamed in thin layers or, as a firmer dough, pressed into the required shape. *Mixian* are long, white, and silken smooth, yet with a bite. They are mostly sold fresh, rarely dried, and are an essential ingredient in Yunnan's most famous dish, *Guoqiao mixian* ("Crossing-bridge" rice noodles).

Molihua Jasmine tea: a special Chinese tea based on an unfermented green tea (e.g. *Yin Zhen*, *Longjing*, *Biluochun* or *Mao Feng*), predominantly produced in Fujian, Guangdong, Jiangxi, and Guangxi. China's most popular scented tea is given its aroma by the fresh petals of the Arabian jasmine shrub *Jasminum sambac* in a process called "mating." The fragrant palate-pleaser was popular as far back as the Song dynasty (960–1279).

Nian gao Traditional Chinese New Year cake: small balls of glutinous rice, usually filled with fruit or vegetables.

Niuroumian Beef noodles, a Muslim specialty from Gansu.

Paocai Pickled vegetables of nearly every possible variety and taste. With the help of vinegar, salt, and spices, this specialty, originally from Hunan, allowed the summer vegetable harvest—and its reserve of vitamins—to be stored over winter. Over the centuries,

however, it developed into a real culinary gem in many areas, and today no kitchen or restaurant is without it.

Qi Life force: one of the "three treasures" produced by the forces of → *Yin and Yang*, present in every creature and object.

Qimen One of the most famous varieties of tea in China, known in the West as Keemun tea, and the main ingredient in English Breakfast tea. Tea connoisseurs consider the finely rolled, dark brown leaves with golden tips as the jewel in the crown of Chinese black tea. Depending on the variety, its complex aromas are reminiscent of honey, apple, orchids or rose petals, and they occasionally let off a scent of cedar or pine wood, or reveal a slightly nutty taste. *Qimen hongcha*: red tea from Qimen.

Rubing Special goat's cheese made by the Bai (mountain people living in Yunnan) which both looks and tastes similar to mozzarella. Slices of it are fried in oil, seasoned with a pinch of salt or sugar, or breaded and deep-fried.

Rushan Special cheese made from cow's milk by the Bai (mountain people living in Yunnan). Thin, rectangular sheets which bear some resemblance to filo (phyllo) pastry are cut into small dice and deep-fried, bobbing to the surface like doughnuts. Deep-fried rushan is crispy and melts in the mouth.

Saozi Noodle specialty from Gansu: homemade noodles with a delicious sauce made from finely diced pork and other ingredients.

Shang Shu The Book of History, one of the Five Classics → *Wu Jing*.

Shaomai Steamed dumplings, open at the top; the wafer-thin pouches usually contain shrimp or crabmeat. The miniature stuffed masterpieces add to the boundless array of *dim sum*, along with → *Shuijiao* or → *Wontons*.

Shen Spiritual energy: one of the "three treasures" produced by the forces of → *Yin and Yang*, present in every creature and object.

Shi Jing The Book of Songs, one of the Five Classics → *Wu Jing*.

Shuijiao Steamed dumplings: the classic type of → *Jiaozi* consist of a thin dumpling case and a mixture of ground pork, cabbage, ginger, and scallions, or chopped duck, lamb, shrimp or pork with diced mushrooms, seasoned with soy sauce and pepper, or, depending on the region, with rice wine and sesame oil. *Shuijiao*

are particularly popular in northern China, and are eaten at any time of the day.

Tao "Way" or "insight": the guiding principle of the cosmos. According to Taoist philosophy, Tao is the creative principle behind all things, yet it also dwells within them, and is itself an eternal and immutable natural force of change. The forces → *Yin and Yang* come from this oneness, and their interplay determines every single thing in the cosmos. The highest ideal of Taoism is cosmic harmony. To this end, everyone should live in accordance with the laws of nature, the Tao.

Wonton Rich dumplings from southern China, with dough made of wheat- and corn flour, water, and egg, encasing a great variety of possible fillings: marinated vegetables with cilantro, crab, fish or chicken, or even sea cucumbers. Smaller wontons are added to soups, deep-fried or steamed in bamboo baskets.

Wu Jing The "Five Classics": reference works which were either compiled by Confucius himself or by his students. The contents were held up as a model for Chinese society from the second century B.C., particularly with regard to law and government, but also for education, literature, and religion. Anyone who wished to enter into the civil service was obliged to study the Five Classics.

Wulong "Black dragon": semifermented Oolong tea, predominantly cultivated in Fujian, Guangdong, and Taiwan.

Wu wei "Without action:" the central principle of Taoism means not struggling against nature or natural circumstances, remaining modest in all things and never acting in an exaggerated way—otherwise, the forces of → *Yin and Yang* become unbalanced. Appreciation of nature and an emphasis on harmony within society remain important elements in Chinese culture to this very day.

Xiaolongbao A specialty from Shanghai which has even made it onto the list of Chinese cultural treasures: steamed, succulent dumplings filled with pork or crabmeat and hot broth.

Xiju Longjing "Dragon tea": one of the best green teas in China, alongside *Dongting Biluochun* and → *Huangshan Maofeng*, this is made only from young, hand-picked shoots. The *Biluochun* variety from Suzhou and *Longjing* from the West Lake have a more intense aroma, as the leaves are roasted in a cast-iron pan. In the tea houses of Hangzhou, in Zhejiang,

Longjing is prepared with water from the famous Hupao Spring (Running Tiger Spring).

Yi Jing   The "Book of Changes" (also *Zhou Yi*), one of the Five Classics → *Wu Jing*.

Yin and Yang   According to Taoism, universal forces that people should strive to keep in balance through their way of living, including their diet. *Yin*, the shadow principle, stands for the femininity, passivity, and darkness, and is strengthened with "cooling" foods (e.g. green tea and cucumbers); *yang*, the sun principle, stands for masculinity, activeness, and light, and is augmented with "warming" foods (e.g. sugar and ginger). There can only be harmony when the two forces are in a state of equilibrium. *Yin and Yang* produce the three treasures, → *Jing*, → *Qi*, and → *Shen*.

Ying Yeung   Drink made from coffee, tea, and milk.

Youtiao   Golden-brown, deep-fried, salted dough sticks; almost 8- inches (20-cm) long, these energy boosters, eaten with warm, sugared soy milk, are a typical Beijing breakfast to go.

Yuanxiao Jie   Lantern Festival marking the end of the Chinese New Year festivities → *Chunjie*

Yuanxiao   Sweet, stuffed rice dumplings (also called *Tangyuan*, "soup dumplings," in the south), eaten on the evening of the Lantern Festival

Yuebing   A cake traditionally served at → *Zhongqiujie*, the Moon Festival, with countless different sweet and savory fillings. Today these moon cakes are rarely baked at home, but rather sold in the supermarket.

Yum cha   A convivial dim sum meal enjoyed among friends or family, in large restaurants.

Yunshan Yinzhen   Hunan's most famous yellow tea. Yellow tea (*huang cha*) is somewhere between green and Oolong tea, with a complex production process: young shoots are heat-dried after plucking, then repeatedly packed in paper, toweling or boxes for up to three days, and finally lightly roasted (like green tea, but not fermented).

Yuntui   famous Yunnan ham from the city of Xuanwei; this air-dried, cured ham, with a thin rind, tender meat, and an exquisite taste is served cold and eaten with bread.

Zhai cai   Buddhist, meat-free dishes. Today the recipes are also used to produce internationally marketed products which can be seen in the refrigerated sections of Asian food stores and, increasingly, in organic supermarkets in the West.

Zhongqiujie   Traditional Chinese Moon Festival which takes place on the 15th day of the eighth lunar month (mid-September to beginning of October), and originally marked the end of the harvest season. → *Yuebing*, moon cakes, are given as gifts all over the country.

Zongzi   Pyramid-shaped glutinous rice dumplings from Zhaoqing, consisting of a succulent mass of rice, mung beans, pork, sausage, and mushrooms, wrapped in bamboo leaves.

Bibliography

Alford, Jeffery and Naomi Duguid: Beyond the Great Wall. Artisan, New York 2008

Allan, Silvia and Bryan Allan: Mozzarella of the East. Ethnorêma, Bolzano 2005

Anderson, E. N.: The Food of China. Yale University Press, New Haven CT 1988

China Business Handbook 2007. Alain Charles Publ., London 2007

Cotterell, Yong Yap: Wok Magic. Weidenfeld & Nicolson, London 1987

Di, Xianghua: A Food-lover's Journey Around China. Foreign Language Press, Beijing 2007

Dunlop, Fuchsia: Land of plenty. W.W. Norton & Co. New York / London 2001. Also, Shark's Fin and Sichuan Pepper. A Sweet-sour Memoir of Eating in China. W.W. Norton & Co. New York, London 2008

Farquhar, Judith: Appetites. Food and Sex in postsocialist China. Duke University Press, Durham / London 2002

Fung, Yu-lan: A short history of Chinese Philosophy. The Free Press, New York / Toronto / London / Sydney 1984

Gernet, Jacques: A History of Chinese Civilization. Cambridge University Press, Cambridge 1996

Gong, Wen: Lifestyle in China. China Intercontinental Press, Beijing 2007

Grobe-Hagel, Karl: Hinter der großen Mauer. Religionen und Nationalitäten in China. Eichborn, Frankfurt am Main 1991

Hom, Ken: Vegetable & Pasta-Book. BBC Books, London 1987

Hong Kong 2007. Hong Kong SAR 10th Anniversary Special Edition. Hong Kong Government, Hong Kong 2007

Hu, Shiu-ying: Food plants of China. Chinese University Press, Hong Kong 2005

Hsiung, Deh-Ta: The Chinese Kitchen. St Martin's Press, New York 2002

Hsiung, Deh-Ta and Nina Simonds: China kulinarisch entdecken. h.f.ullmann, Königswinter 2007; **also** A little taste of China. Murdoch Books, London 2003

Hsiung, Deh-Ta and Sallie Morris: The Chinese and Asian Cookbook. Barnes & Noble, New York 2001

Jiangsu News Agency: Panoramic China. Jiangsu Water Town Journeys. Foreign Language Press, Beijing 2006

Lo, Kenneth: The Complete Encyclopedia of Chinese Cooking. Hamlyn, Twickenham 1987

Newman, Jacqueline M.: Food culture in China. Greenwood Press, Westport CT 2004

Pan, Ling: In Search of Old Shanghai. Joint Publ. Co. Ltd., Hong Kong, 10th edition 1999

Pao, Basil: China. Unterwegs in allen Provinzen. Frederking & Thaler, Munich 2007

Schumann, Hans-Wolfgang: Buddhismus. Diedrichs Gelbe Reihe, Munich 1998

Seitz, Konrad: China. Eine Weltmacht kehrt zurück. BTV, Berlin, 3rd edition 2004

Simoons, Frederick J.: Food in China. A cultural and historical inquiry. CRC Press, Boca Raton 1991

Spence, Jonathan D.: The Search for Modern China. W.W. Norton & Co, New York 2001

Sterling, Richard and Elisabeth Chong: Lonely Planet World Food Hong Kong. Lonely Planet, Melbourne 2001

Sterckx, Roel (ed.): Of Tripod and Palate. Palgrave Macmillan, New York 2005

Tong, Liu: Chinese tea. China Intercontinental Press, Beijing 2005

Wang, Ling: Tea and Chinese Culture. Long River Press, San Francisco, 2005

Wang, Xiao Hui and Cornelia Schinharl: Küchen der Welt — China. Gräfe und Unzer, Munich. 1999

Zhang, Zongliang: Panoramic China. Anhui: Mount Huangshan and the Hui Culture. Foreign Language Press, Beijing 2006

Zihua, Liu and Uli Franz: Die echte chinesische Küche. Gräfe und Unzer, Munich 2001

More recommended reading about China

Sinclair, Kevin: Culture Shock! China. Graphic Arts Center Publishing Company, Portland, 1991

China. Lonely Planet, Melbourne 2009

China. Polyglott (Apa Guide), Munich 2006

Fülling, Andrea and Oliver Fülling: Chinas Norden — die Seidenstraße. Reise Know-How, Bielefeld 1999

Guter, Josef: China und seine Provinzen. Komet, Cologne 2005

Harper, Damian: Best of Shanghai. Lonely Planet, Melbourne 2006

Harper, Damian and David Eimer: Beijing. Lonely Planet, Melbourne, 7th rev. ed. 2007

Häring, Volker and Francoise Hauser: Handbuch China. Trescher, Berlin 2005; Flusskreuzfahrten auf dem Yangzi. Trescher, Berlin 2006; Peking und Shanghai. Trescher, Berlin 2008

Hauser, Francoise (ed.): Reise nach China. Kulturkompass fürs Handgepäck. Unionsverlag, Zurich 2009

Hornfeck, Sabine and Xiaolong Qiu: Shanghai. Mondkuchen und Pflaumenregen. Sanssouci im Carl Hanser, Munich 2007

Kausch, Anke: China. Die klassische Reise — Kaiser- und Gartenstädte, Heilige Berge und Boomtowns. DuMont, Cologne, 2nd edition 2000

Kuan, Yu-Chien & Häring-Kuan, Petra: Der China-Knigge. Eine Gebrauchsanweisung für das Land der Mitte. Fischer, Frankfurt am Main 2006

Leffmann, David (et al.): China. Stefan Loose Travel Handbücher, Berlin 2006

Meniconzi, Alessandra: Hidden China. h.f.ullmann, Königswinter 2008

Quinn, Eilis: Best of Beijing. Lonely Planet, Melbourne 2006

Scheck, Frank Rainer (ed.): Volksrepublik China. Kunstreisen durch das Reich der Mitte. DuMont, Cologne 1987

Schmidt-Glintzer, Helwig: Geschichte der chinesischen Literatur. Primus, Darmstadt 1990

Staiger, Brunhild & Friedrich, Stefan & Schütte, Hans-Wilm: Das große China-Lexikon. Primus, Darmstadt 2008

Strittmatter, Kai: Gebrauchsanweisung für China. Piper, Munich 2004

The Charm of Beijing: Beijing Local Delicacies. China Pictorial Publ., Beijing 2006

The Charm of Beijing: Enjoy Tea in Beijing. China Pictorial Publ., Beijing 2006

Winchester, Simon: The River at the Center of the World. A Journey up the Yangtze and Back in Chinese Time. Picador, New York 2004

Magazines

Geo Spezial: China. 1987, 1994 & 2003

Geo Spezial: Die Seidenstraße. 2007

Merian: China. Peking und der Norden. 1981

Acknowledgements

This massive project came into being in a country where traveling is not always easy, and where good contacts are often essential to open doors. For this reason the publisher and the team wish to express their particular thanks to all the people and institutions who offered their support and cooperation, and also all those not known by name or not individually mentioned here.

The author Katrin Schlotter wishes to thank her family and all the friends who supported and inspired her during the writing of this book. Special thanks are due to Françoise Hauser, in Frankfurt am Main, for her help and their wonderful journeys together through China.

The publisher and the author Elke Spielmanns-Rome wish to express particular thanks to Silvia Kettelhut and Rebekka Freitag for their collaboration on sections about Chinese history and culture.

The photographer Gregor M. Schmid and the tour guide Bernd Klaube would like to give special thanks to Mr. Felly Chung, aka. Cowboy, Executive Chef at the Hong Kong Gold Coast Hotel, for his boundless, ever-obliging and unhesitating generosity when arranging countless dishes and contacts, and the tour guide Shi Hong Jian, aka. Larry, from Nanjing, for his down-to-earth tour leading.

The photographer Lisa Fransz would particularly like to thank her father, Uli Fransz, her colleagues, who were always on stand-by during the project, and Anita (Yuan) Ho, without whom many photos would not have been taken.

The publisher, the photographer Lisa Fransz, and the tour guide Yuan Ho wish to thank the following people and institutions:

Beijing
Sun Ming Fang and Shi Peng
Mrs. Wang Pei
Gold Barn Restaurant for cutting equipment and cooking methods
In & Out Lijiang Theme Restaurant for the wedding
Fang Shan Restaurant
Wu-Mart Supermarket
University of International Business and Economics
He Tang Yue Se Restaurant
Tong Ren Tang Drugstore
Quan Ju De Restaurant
Wang Ma Zi Knife Store
Changping District Agricultural and Ecological Park
Ten Fu's Tea Shop
Guangdong
Liu Heshi, Shenzhen
Xin Mei Yuan Restaurant
Yu Mi Zhi Xiang Restaurant
Hong Kong
Mrs. Min, Mrs. Tse, Jovy, and Mr. Leung
Eaton Hotel, particularly Mr. Vincent Nicot
The Metro Buffet Restaurant and Grill at the Eaton Hotel
Yagura Japanese Restaurant
Nice Capital Restaurant
Aqua Roma Restaurant
City Golf Club, particularly Mrs. Audrey Pong and Mrs. Vicky Tse
Thai Mary Restaurant at the City Golf Club
Balalaika Russian Restaurant and Vodka Bar
Shandong
Chen Yanliang, Ji Yujun, and Chen Daxu
Hai Dao Yu Cun Restaurant
Shanghai
Dai Mengjue and Dai Rencai
Sichuan
Mr. He Tao
Bayi Army Cooking School
Yunnan
Mr. Shu Tan
Yunnan Xuanwei Rongsheng Ham Co., Ltd.
Zhejiang
Shi Peng and Sun Ming Fang, Hangzhou
Shaoxing Xinzhou Haiwan Hotel, particularly the cooking team
Zhejiang Xinzhou Tourism Ltd. Corp.
Jindu Jinhua Ham Store

The publisher and the author Katrin Schlotter wish to thank the following people and institutions:

Jeff Chan, Impact Asia, Hong Kong
Dieter Jacobs, DJPR, Frankfurt am Main
Hong Kong Trade Development Council, Hong Kong and Frankfurt
Tina Kanagaratnam, AsiaMedia, Shanghai
Jereme Leung and his team from the Whampoa Club in Beijing and Shanghai, for providing information, culinary treats and warm hospitality
Daniela Mangold, Mikulla Goldmann PR, Munich
Elsa Wong, Wang Workshop Group, Hong Kong
Steven Kai Wong and his team from the Hong Kong Economic and Trade Office, Hong Kong, Brussels, and Berlin
Macau Tourist Information Office, Wiesbaden, noble kommunikation GmbH, Neu-Isenburg, and Rosemarie Wank-Nolasco Lamas of the Macau Government Tourist Office in Lisbon

The publisher, the photographer Gregor M. Schmid and the trip leader Bernd Klaube wish to thank the following people and institutions:

Beijing:
Special thanks are due to CTS, first and foremost, for their assistance
Mrs. Liu Yuanyuan, Sales Manager of the German Dept., European Department, CTS
Mrs. Maria Zhu Jie, Director of German Dept., European Department, CTS
Mr. Wang Bo, Sales Manager of German Dept., European Department, CTS
Mr. Zhang Wenquan, General Manager, European Department, CTS
Mrs. Lai Jiong, lecturer at Renmin University, Beijing, German Faculty
Mrs. May Guo, Sales Manager, Whampoa Club
Mr. Yap Poh Weng, Executive Chef, Whampoa Club
Mr. Yap Jia Wen, Restaurant Director, Whampoa Club
The staff of Wu Zhao Ming tea store, on the "tea street"
The staff of the Lao She Tea House
The staff of Tijumen Restaurant
The owner of the Fu Family Tea House on Houhai
The Li Shanlin family of the Family Restaurant in Wutong San Shan
The star chef, Jin, of Green T. House Living
The staff of the Noodle restaurant, Shanshuijian
The staff of the Quan Ju De duck Restaurant ("where all the virtues meet"), and
Mr. Shi Ning, the restaurant's business manager
The staff of the Ho Ji noodle restaurant

Hong Kong:
Mrs. Lamey Chang, Director of PR, The Peninsula, Hong Kong
Mrs. Teresa Yip, Assistant Outlet Manager, The Landmark Mandarin Oriental
Mr. Andy Cheng, Lobby Chef, The Peninsula, Hong Kong
Mr. Guillaume Harel, Restaurant Manager of the Landmark Mandarin Oriental, Hong Kong
Mr. Chan Wing Hung, Business Manager of Restaurant Enterprises Limited, Aberdeen
The staff of the Jumbo Kingdom, Dragon Court Restaurant, Aberdeen
The staff of the Café Causette at the Mandarin Oriental, Hong Kong
The staff of L'Atelier de Joël Robuchon, The Landmark, Hong Kong Central
The staff of Hoi Lung Sea Food, Mabel Lau, Lei Yue Mun, Hong Kong Kowloon

Other towns and regions:
Mr. Andreas V. Koch, Resident Manager, Shangri-La Hotel, Baotou
Mr. Ma and Ma's Family Restaurant, Dunhuang
Mr. and Mrs. Liu, Lanzhou
Mr. Xu Ning, Manager of European Dept., CITS, Lanzhou
Mr. Hu Ying, Vice Manager, JSCTS, Nanjing
Mr. Gu and Mr. Li Jun Wang, Translator, Shanghai, CITS
Mrs. Stella Yao, Personal Assistant, Whampoa Club, the Bund, Shanghai
Mr. Chris NG, General Manager, Whampoa Club, the Bund, Shanghai
Mr. Li Hui Qiang, Manager of the German Department, XOC, Ürümqi
Mr. Tony Zhang, Assistant Manager, Jinyuan Jinling Plaza, Xuzhou
The Head Chef of the Moon Shadow Restaurant at Lake Tai, Wuxi

The staff of the Landscape Hotel, Dali Old Town
The staff of the Glamor Hotel, Suzhou
The staff of the Château Changyu-Castel, Yantai Changyu Tourism Co., Ltd.
The staff of the Yuxiangge Noodle Restaurant, Lanzhou
The staff of the Hue Feng Len Restaurant, Harbin
The staff of the Donkey Meat and Sallow Noodle Restaurant, Dunhuang
Mrs. Cindy Zhao, tour guide, CITS, Huangshan City
Mrs. Ding, tour guide in Qingdao
Mrs. Jang, tour guide in Dali
Mrs. Lei, tour guide in Dunhuang
Mrs. Liping, tour guide in Nanjing
Mrs. Liu, tour guide in Nanchang
Mrs. Liu, tour guide in Hangzhou
Mrs. Mao, tour guide in Jinan and Jantai
Mrs. Wu, tour guide in Jinghong
Mr. Chang, tour guide in Harbin
Mr. David, tour guide in Xiamen
Mr. Gu Ming and Bob, tour guides in Baotou and Hohhot
Mr. Hu, tour guide in Changsha
Mr. Hu, tour guide in Suzhou
Mr. Joe (Jiang Xio Ming), tour guide in Wujishan
Mr. Li, tour guide in Guilin and Jangshou
Mr. Liang, tour guide in Nanning and Beihai
Mr. Li, tour guide in Ürümqi and Turpan
Mr. Yin, tour guide in Lijiang
Mr. Zhou, tour guide in Kunming

Index of recipes (by type of dish)

Index of recipes (A–Z)

Page numbers in bold indicate illustrations

Subject index

Picture and text credits